# GROC's CANDID GU[...]
## THE
# IONIAN
## ISLANDS

Including
## CORFU, PAXOS, LEFKAS,
## CEPHALONIA, ITHACA & ZAKYNTHOS

with excursion details to
## ANTIPAXOS & MEGANISSI

As well as
## ATHENS CITY
## &
## GREEK MAINLAND PORTS
## & WESTERN COAST RESORTS

For the package & villa, holidaymaker,
backpacker & independent traveller
whether journeying by air, car, coach, ferry-boat or train.

by
# Geoffrey O'Connell

Published by
**Ashford**
1 Church Road
Shedfield
Hampshire
SO3 2HW

D1078249

Text ©Geoffrey O'Connell, 1989
Maps and illustrations © Geoffrey O'Connell &
Ashford
Printed in Great Britain

First Published 1983
Second Edition 1986
Reprint 1988
Third Edition 1989

British Library Cataloguing in Publication Data

O'Connell, Geoffrey
Groc's Candid Guide to Corfu - 3rd edition
(The Candid Guides)
1.  Greece Corfu - visitors' guides
I.  Title  II.Series
914 95 5

ISBN 1—85253—151—7

**Errors and omissions**
Whilst great care has been taken in the compilation of this book, it is
regretted that neither author nor publisher can accept responsibility
for the use, or consequences of the use of the information and
opinions expressed herein, nor for any inaccuracies or mishaps arising
from the work. Due to the basis for gathering information for inclusion
in the book, details may well change from year to year.

**Disclaimer**
The author has no connection with any business, establishment or firm
listed herein and no warranty, guarantee or endorsement is implied or
given in their respect.
That a business, establishment or firm is not listed or detailed does not
imply any criticism. The impressions, opinions and viewpoints
expressed in this publication are highly individualistic and readers
must make their own judgements on all matters presented herein.

**By the same author:**
**BOAT BOOKS**
The Boat Owner's Maintenance Book
The Boatbuilding Book

**LOCAL HISTORY**
Secretive Southwick – Domesday to D-Day
Southwick – The D-Day Village that went to War

**HUMOUR**
Divorce without Remorse

**Forthcoming Books**
GROC's Candid Guide to:
    Turkey, Mainland & Islands.

# CONTENTS

**CORFU** including: **Corfu,** capital, port & airport.
The island topography including ROUTE ONE: Alikes, Kontokali, Gouvia, Tsavros, Dassia, Ipsos & Pyrgi, Ag Markos, (& on to the Korakiana), Strinilas, Barbati, Glyfa, Nisaki, Kendroma, Gimari, Kalami, Kouloura, Ag Stefanos, Avlaki Beach, Kassiopi, Profitis Ilias, Ag Spiridon, Amiros Beach, Roda, Karoussades, Astrakeri, Ag Andreas Beach. ROUTE TWO: Sidari, the islands of Mathraki, Othoni & Erikoussa, Peroulades, Avliotes, Ag Stefanos, Arilias Beach, Afionas, Afionas Beach, Ag Athanasios, Ag Georgios, Makrades, Krini, Castle of Angelo Kastro, Lakones. ROUTE THREE: Paleokastritsa, Liapades, Liapades Beach, Ermones Beach, Afionas Beach, Vatos. ROUTE FOUR: Ag Ioannis, Pelekas, Glifada Beach, Pelekas Beach, Sinarades, Ag Gordis Beach. ROUTE FIVE: Kato Garouna, Kato Pavliani, Pentali, Ag Matheos Beach, Korission Lagoon, Gardiki, Ag Matheos, Linia, Issos Beach, Argirades, Ag Georgios, Kouspades, Boukari Point, Notos, Petreti, Perivolion, Kalivoiotes Beach, Maltas Beach/St Babara, Alikes, Kanoula Beach, Potami, Bouka Beach, Kavos, Messonghi & Mirangi Bay, Spilio, Moraitika, Benitses, Achilleion Palace, Perama.

Artwork:Jonathan Duval & Geoffrey O'Connell
Plans & maps:Graham Bishop & Geoffrey O'Connell
Typeset:Disc preparation by Willowbridge Publishers

Output:Unwin Bros.
Tables & Headings
Typeset:County Productions

# ILLUSTRATIONS

Please do not forget that prices are given as a guide only and relate to the year in which the book is written. In recent years not only lodging and 'troughing' costs, but also transport charges, particularly ferry-boat fees, have escalated dramatically. The increased value of most other currencies to the Greek drachmae has compensated, to some extent, for apparently inexorably rising prices.

In an effort to keep readers as up-to-date as possible regarding these and other matters, I have introduced **GROC's GREEK ISLAND HOTLINE**. See elsewhere for details.

The series is entering its seventh year of publication and I would appreciate continuing to hear from readers who have any additions or corrections to bring to my attention. As in the past, all correspondence (except that addressed to 'Dear fifth' or similar endearments) will be answered.

I hope readers can excuse errors that creep (well gallop actually) into the welter of detailed information included in the body text. In order to keep the volumes as up-to-date as possible, the period from inception to publication is kept down to some six months which does result in the occasional slip up......

Geoffrey O'Connell's highly personalised style of writing encompasses books on yacht building and maintenance, humour, travel as well as a magnum opus concerning the history of Southwick village, where he and fellow traveller and wife, Rosemary, live in a Georgian house on a centuries-old Hampshire estate.

They regard themselves as geriatric, if very knowledgeable backpackers whilst ferry-boating about the Greek islands gathering information for the next guidebook.

**One of the CANDID GUIDE Series**

# GROC's Candid Guides
## introduce to readers

# Suretravel '89

A comprehensive holiday insurance plan that 'gives cover that many other policies do not reach', to travellers anywhere in the world. In addition to the more usual cover offered, the **SURETRAVEL HOLIDAY PLAN** includes (where medically necessary): 24 hour World Wide Medical Emergency Service including, where appropriate, repatriation by air ambulance.

Additionally, personal accident, medical and emergency expenses EVEN while hiring a bicycle, scooter or car.

An example premium, in 1989, for a 10-17 day holiday in Greece is £13.50 per person.

*Note: All offers & terms are subject to the Insurance Certificate Cover*

For an application form please complete the cut out below and send to:
Willowbridge Publishing, Bridge House, Southwick Village, Nr Fareham, Hants. PO17 6DZ

Mr/Mrs/Miss.................................................................Age...............................

of..........................................................................................................................

............................................................................................................................

request a **SURETRAVEL** application form.

Date of commencement of holiday...............................Duration ...................................

Signature...........................................................................Date...............................

# The Candid Guides
## unique
# 'GROC's Greek Island Hotline'

Available to readers of the guides, this service enables a respondent to receive a bang up-to-the-minute update, to supplement the extensive information contained in a particular Candid Guide.

To obtain this paraphrased computer print-out, covering the Introductory Chapters, Athens, Piraeus & the Mainland Ports as well as any named islands, up to twenty five in number, all that is necessary is to:-

Complete the form below, enclosing a payment of £1.50 (to include postage), and send to:-

Willowbridge Publishing, Bridge House, Southwick Village, Nr.Fareham, Hants. PO17 6DZ

**Note: The information will be of no use to anyone who does not possess the relevant, most up to date GROC's Candid Greek Island Guide. We are unable to dispatch the Hotline without details of the guide AND which edition.**

Planned departure dates ...............................................

...............................................

Mr/Mrs/Miss ................................................................

of..............................................................................

..............................................................................

I possess:                                    I require:

**GROC's Greek Island Guides**    Edition    **GROC's Greek Island Hotline**

to: ....................................    ...................... to:..............................

.........................................    ......................    ..............................

.........................................    ......................    ..............................

.........................................    ......................    ..............................

.........................................    ......................    ..............................

and enclose a fee of £1.50. Signature.................................Date .......................

I appreciate that the 'Hotline' may not be dispatched for up to 7-10 days from receipt of this application.

# INTRODUCTION

This volume is the third edition of Corfu and the Ionian islands, one of six in the very popular and proven series of GROC's Candid Guides to the Greek Islands. The rationale, the *raison d'etre* behind their production is to treat each island grouping on an individual and comprehensive basis, rather than attempt overall coverage of the 100 or so islands usually described in one volume. This obviates attempting to do justice to, say, Paxos in amongst an aggregation of many other, often disparate islands.

Due to the vast distances involved very few, if any, vacationers can possibly visit more than a number of islands in a particular group, even if spending as much as four weeks in Greece.

It is important for package and villa holiday-makers to have an unbiased and relevant description of their planned holiday surroundings rather than the usual extravagant hyperbole of the glossy sales brochure. It is vital for backpackers and ferry-boat travellers to have, on arrival, detailed and accurate information at their finger tips. With these differing requirements in mind factual, 'straight-from-the-shoulder' location reports have been combined with detailed plans of the major port, town and or city of each island in the group, as well as topographical island maps.

Amongst the guides generally available are earnest tomes dealing with Ancient and Modern Greece, a number of thumbnail travel booklets and some worthy, if often out-of-date books. Unfortunately they rarely assuage the various travellers' differing requirements. These might include speedy and accurate identification of one's position on arrival; the situation of accommodation as well as the whereabouts of a bank, the postal services and tourist offices. Additional requisites probably embrace a swift and easy to read resumé of the settlement's main locations, cafe-bars, tavernas and restaurants; detailed local bus and ferry-boat timetables, as well as a full island narrative. Once the traveller has settled in, then and only then, can he or she feel at ease, making their own finds and discoveries.

I have chosen to omit lengthy accounts of the relevant, fabulous Greek mythology and history. These aspects of Greece are, for the serious student, very ably related by authors far more erudite than myself. Moreover, most islands have a semi-official tourist guide translated into English, and for that matter, French, German and Scandinavian. They are usually well worth the 300 to 500 drachmae (drs) they cost, are extremely informative in 'matters archaeological' and are quite well produced, if rather out of date, with excellent colour photographs. Admittedly the English translation might seem a little quaint (try to read Greek, let alone translate it) and the maps are often unreliable, but cartography is not a strong Hellenic suit!

Each **Candid Guide** is finally researched as close to the publication date as is possible. On the other hand, in an effort to facilitate production of this volume, as early as possible in the forthcoming year, it has been found necessary to omit any information that requires waiting until the springtime of the year of publication. These details, often available as late as March, April or even May, and which include up to date air, ferry-boat and train fares, are 'punched' into the **Hotline**, for details of which read on. Naturally, any new ideas are incorporated but, in the main, the guides follow a now well proven formula. Part One deals with the preliminaries and describes the different aspects of travelling and enjoying to the full the unforgettable experience of a Greek islands sojourn. Part Two details a full and thoroughly redrafted account of Athens City, still the hub for Greek island travel, and the relevant mainland ports for connections to the island group in question. Part Three introduces the island chain, followed by a detailed description of each island, the layout being designed to facilitate quick and easy reference.

The exchange rate has fluctuated quite violently in recent years and at the time of writing the final draft of this guide, the rate to the English pound (£) was hovering about 260drs. Unfortunately prices are subject to fluctuation, usually upward with annual increases varying between 10-20%. Happily the drachma tends to devalue by approximately the same amount.

Recommendations and personalities are almost always based on personal observation and experience, occasionally emphasised by the discerning comments of readers or colleagues. They may well change from year to year and be subject to different interpretation by others.

The series incorporates a number of innovative ideas and unique services which have evolved over the years and include:

**The Decal:** Since 1985 some of the accommodation and eating places recommended in the guides display a specially produced decal to help readers identify the particular establishment. The decals are dated so a reader can identify the relevancy of the recommendation. The current issue is the third (1989-91). Previous ones have been 1984-85 & 1986-88.

**GROC's Greek Island Hotline:** An absolutely unique service available to readers of the Candid Guides. Application enables purchasers of the guides to obtain a summary detailing all pertinent, relevant comments and information that have become available since the publication of the particular guide – in effect, an up-to-date update. The Hotline is constantly being revised and incorporates bang up-to-the-moment intelligence. A payment of £1.50 (incl. postage) enables a respondent to receive the paraphrased computer print-out in respect of the Introductory Chapters, Athens, Piraeus & the Mainland Ports as well as any named islands, up to twenty five in number. An interested reader only has to complete the form, or write a letter, requesting the Hotline, enclose the fee and post to Willowbridge Enterprises, Bridge House, Southwick Village, Nr Fareham, Hants PO17 6DZ. Tel (0705) 375570.

**Travel Insurance:** A comprehensive holiday insurance plan that 'gives cover that many other policies do not reach....' See elsewhere for details.

The author (and publisher) are very interested in considering ways and means of improving the guides and adding to the backup facilities, so are delighted to hear from readers with their suggestions.

Enjoy yourselves and 'Ya Sou' (welcome).
*Geoffrey O'Connell* 1989

## ACKNOWLEDGMENTS

Every year the list of those to be formally thanked grows and this edition shows no diminution in their number which has forced the original brief entry from the inside front cover to an inside page.

Apart from those numerous friends and confidants we meet on passage, there are the many correspondents who are kind enough to contact me with useful information, all of who, in the main, remain unnamed.

Rosemary who accompanies me, adding her often unwanted, uninformed comments and asides (and who I occasionally threaten not to take next time), requires especial thanks for unrelieved, unstinting (well almost unstinting) support, despite being dragged from this or that sun kissed beach.

Although receiving reward, other than in heaven, some of those who assisted me in the production of this edition require specific acknowledgement for effort far beyond the siren call of vulgar remuneration! These worthies include Graham Bishop, who drew the maps and plans, and Viv Hitié, who controls the word processor.

Lastly, and as always, I must admonish Richard Joseph for ever encouraging and cajoling me to take up the pen – surely the sword is more fun?

*The cover picture of Logos harbour is produced by kind permission of GREEK ISLAND PHOTOS, Willowbridge Enterprises, Bletchley, Milton Keynes, Bucks.*

# PART ONE

# 1 Packing, Insurance, Medical Matters, Climatic Conditions, Conversion Tables & a Starter Course in Greek

*Leisure nourishes the body and the mind is also fed thereby; on the other hand, immoderate labour exhausts both. Ovid*

Vacationing anywhere on an organised tour allows a certain amount of latitude regarding the amount of luggage packed, as this method of holiday does not preclude taking fairly substantial suitcases. On the other hand, ferry-boating and backpacking restricts the amount a traveller is able to carry and the means of conveyance. This latter group usually utilise backpacks and or roll-bags, both of which are more suitable than suitcases for this mode of travel. The choice between the two does not only depend on which is the more commodious. At the height of season it can be advantageous to be distinguishable from the hordes of other backpackers and the selection of roll-bags may help disassociation from the more hippy of 'genus rucksacker'. If roll-bags are chosen they should include shoulder straps. These alleviate the discomfort experienced whilst searching out accommodation on hot afternoons with arms just stretching and stretching and stretching.

In the highly populous, oversubscribed months of July and August, it is advisable for independent travellers to pack a thin foam bedroll and a lightweight sleeping bag, just in case a room cannot be located on the occasional night.

Unless camping, I do not think a sweater is necessary between the months of May and September. A desert jacket or lightweight anorak is a better proposition and a stout pair of sandals or training shoes are obligatory, especially if very much walking is contemplated. Leave out the evening suit and cocktail dresses, the Greeks are very informal. Instead take loose-fitting, casual clothes and do not forget sunglasses and a floppy hat. Those holiday-makers staying in one place and not too bothered about weight and encumbrances might consider packing a parasol or beach umbrella and an inflatable sun-bed. It will save a lot of money in daily rental charges paid over to the beach entrepreneurs.

Should there be any doubt about the electric supply (and you shave) include a pack of disposable razors. Ladies might consider acquiring one of the small, gas cylinder, portable hair-curlers prior to departure. Take along a couple of toilet rolls. They are useful for tasks other than that with which they are usually associated, including mopping up spilt liquid, wiping off plates, and blowing one's nose. It might be an idea to include a container of washing powder, a few clothes pegs, some string for a washing line and a number of wire hangers. We have found the best clothes washing medium is a liquid biological detergent, one including a brightener and safe stain removal agents. Recommended is *Ariel Rapide.*

Those visitors contemplating wide ranging travel should consider packing a few plastic, sealed-lid, liquid containers, a plate and a cup, as well as a knife and fork, condiments, an all-purpose cutting/slicing/carving knife as well as a combination bottle and tin opener. These all facilitate economical dining whilst on the move as food and drink, when available on ferry-boats and trains, can be comparatively expensive. Camping requires these elementary items to be augmented with simple cooking equipment.

Mosquito coils can be bought in Greece and a Japanese container is now available in England which holds the coil, stopping it from breaking and controlling the rate of burn. The best device to repel these noxious insects is a small, two prong, electric heater on which a wafer thin tablet is placed and almost every room has a suitable electric point.

They can be purchased locally for some 1000drs and come complete with a pack of the capsules. One trade name is *Doker Mat*. The odourless vapour given off certainly sorts out the mosquitoes and is (hopefully) harmless to humans. Mark you, we did hear of a tourist who purchased one and swore by its efficacy, not even aware it was necessary to place a tablet in the holder...

Whilst discussing items that plug in, why not pack an electric coil thus allowing the brew up of a morning 'cuppa'. Tea addicts can use a slice of lemon instead of milk. Those who like their drinks sweet can utilise those (often unwanted) packets of sugar that accompany most orders for a coffee or a spoonful of the honey that will be to hand for the morning yoghurt – won't it?

Consider packing a pair of tweezers, some plasters, calamine lotion, after-sun and insect cream, as well as a bottle of aspirin in addition to any pharmaceuticals usually required. It is worth noting that shampoo and toothpaste cost about the same but sun-tan oil, which was inexpensive, has now doubled in price and should be 'imported'. Including a small phial of disinfectant has merit, but it is best not to leave the liquid in the original glass bottle. Should it break, the disinfectant and glass, especially if mingled with clothing, can prove not only messy but will leave a distinctive and lingering odour. Kaolin and morphine is a very reliable 'tummy settler' but another excellent remedy, easily obtainable in Greece and that I have always found efficacious, is *Ercefurly forte 200*. Recent correspondence, from a knowledgable reader, suggests packing *Arret* or *Imodium* capsules, instead of kaolin and morphine. Soluable *Dioralyte* will help replace lost fluid and salts (as well as being helpful to the hung over!). Greek chemists dispense medicines and prescriptions that only a doctor would be able to mete out in many other Western European countries, so prior to summoning a medico, try the local pharmacy.

**Insurance & medical matters** While touching upon medical matters, a national of an EEC country should extend their state's National Health cover. United Kingdom residents can contact the local *Department of Health and Social Security* requesting form number *E111 UK*. When completed, and returned, this results in a *Certificate of Entitlement to Benefits in Kind during a stay in a Member State*. Well, that's super! In short, it entitles a person to medical treatment in other EEC countries. Even with this arranged, it is prudent to also seriously consider selecting a comprehensive holiday insurance policy. This should not only cover loss of baggage and money, but personal accident and medical expenses in addition to cancellation of the holiday and personal liability. Check the exclusion clauses carefully. It is no good an insured person imagining he or she is covered for 'this or that', only to discover the company has craftily excluded claims under a particular section. Should a reader intend to hire a scooter ensure this form of 'activity' is not debarred, as is often the case. Rather than rely on the minimal standard insurance cover offered by many tour companies, it is best to approach a specialist broker. For instance, bearing in mind the rather rudimentary treatment offered by the average Greek island hospital, it is almost obligatory to include the option of *Fly-Home Medicare* cover in any policy. A couple of homilies might graphically reinforce the argument. Firstly the Greek hospital system expects the patient's family to minister and feed the inmate 'out-of-hours'. This can result in holiday companions having to camp in the ward for the duration of any internment. Perhaps more thought-provoking is the homespun belief that a patient is best left the first night to survive, if it is God's will, and to pass on if not! After a number of years hearing of the unfortunate experiences of friends and readers, who failed to act on the advice given herein, as well as the inordinate difficulties I experienced in arranging cover for myself, I was prompted to offer readers an all embracing travel insurance scheme. Details are to be found elsewhere in the guide. **DON'T DELAY, ACT NOW**.

Most rooms do not have rubbish containers so why not include some plastic bin liners, which are also very useful for packing food as well as storing dirty washing. A universal sink plug is almost a necessity. Many Greek sinks do not have one but, as the water usually drains away very slowly, this could be considered an academic point.

Take along a pack of cards, and enough paperback reading to while away sunbathing sojourns and long journeys. Playing cards are subject to a government tax, which makes their price exorbitant, and imported books are very expensive. Happily, some shops, tour offices and lodgings operate a book-swap scheme.

Many flights, bus, ferry-boat or train journeys are scheduled for early morning departure, so a small, battery-operated alarm clock may well obviate sleepless, fretful nights prior to the dawn. A small, hand or wrist compass can be an enormous help orientating in towns and if room and weight allow, a torch is a useful addition to the inventory.

Readers must not forget their passport which is absolutely essential to (1) enter Greece, (2) book into most accommodation, as well as campsites, (3) change money and (4) hire a scooter or car.

In the larger, more popular, tourist orientated resorts *Diners* and *American Express (Amex)* credit cards are accepted, as increasingly are *Access Mastercards*. Personal cheques, up to 25000drs in value, may be changed when accompanied by a Eurocheque bank card. Americans can use an *Amex* credit card at their overseas offices to change personal cheques up to $1000. They may also, by prior arrangement, have cable transfers made to overseas banks, allowing 24hrs from the moment their home bank receives specific instructions.

It is wise to record and keep separate the numbers of credit cards, travellers's cheques and airline tickets in case they should be mislaid or stolen. Incidentally, this is a piece of advice I always give but rarely, if ever, carry out myself. Visitors are now allowed to import 25000drs of Greek currency (in notes). Any further cash required must be in the form of traveller's cheques and or foreign currency. Originally the allowance was only 1500drs, then 3000drs followed by 6000drs (in 1988), a readjustment forced on the authorities by the continual decline in the value of the Greek drachma. Despite these more realistic figures, it may be necessary to change currency soon after arrival. This can prove to be a problem at weekends or if the banks are on strike, a not uncommon occurrence during the summer months. *See* **Banks, Chapter Seven** for further details in respect of banks and money.

Imported spirits are comparatively expensive (except on some of the duty free Dodecanese islands) but the official spirits allowance into Greece is up to one and a half litres of alcohol. So confirmed whisky or gin drinkers, who are partial to an evening sundowner, should acquire a bottle or two before arrival. Cigars are difficult to buy on the islands, so it may well be advantageous to take along the 75 allowed. On the other hand, cigarettes are so inexpensive that it hardly seems worthwhile 'importing' them. Note the above applies to fellow members of the EEC. Allowances for travellers from other countries are 1 litre of alcohol and 50 cigars. Camera buffs should take all the film required, as it is more costly in Greece than in most Western European countries.

Officially, the Greek islands enjoy some 3000 hours of sunshine per year, out of an approximate, possible 4250 hours. The prevailing summer wind is the northerly *Meltemi*, which can blow very strongly, day in and day out during July and August, added to which these months are usually painfully dry and very hot 24 hours a day. The sea in April is perhaps a little cool for swimming, but the last two weeks of May and June are marvellous months, as are September and October.

**The best time of year to holiday** The following indicates that probably the best months to vacation are May, June, September and October, July and August being too hot. Certainly, the most tourist crowded months, when accommodation is at a premium, are July, August and the first two weeks of September. Taking everything into account, it does not need an Einstein to work the matter out.

For the statistically minded:

**The monthly average temperatures in the Ionian are:**

| | Jan | Feb | Mar | Apr | May | June | July | Aug | Sept | Oct | Nov | Dec |
|---|---|---|---|---|---|---|---|---|---|---|---|---|
| Average air | C°10 | 10 | 12 | 15 | 19 | 24 | 27 | 26 | 23 | 19 | 15 | 12 |
| temperatures | F°50 | 50 | 54 | 59 | 66 | 75 | 81 | 79 | 73 | 66 | 59 | 54 |
| Sea surface | C°16 | 15 | 15 | 17 | 21 | 24 | 26 | 27 | 26 | 22 | 19 | 17 |
| temperatures (at | F°61 | 59 | 59 | 63 | 70 | 75 | 79 | 80 | 79 | 72 | 66 | 63 |
| 1400hrs) | | | | | | | | | | | | |
| Average days of rain* | 14 | 12 | 7 | 4 | 3 | 1 | – | 1 | 2 | 5 | 8 | 14 |

* Mind you there is quite a difference between the various islands. For instance Corfu has, on average, 100 rainy days
in the year compared to Cephalonia's 90 days and the 105 days of Zakynthos.

# Conversion tables & equivalent

| Units | Approximate conversion | Equivalent |
|---|---|---|
| Miles to kilometres | Divide by 5, multiply by 8 | 5 miles = 8km |
| Kilometres to miles | Divide by 8, multiply by 5 | |
| Feet to metres | Divide by 10, multiply by 3 | 10 ft = 3m |
| Metres to feet | Divide by 3, multiply by 10 | |
| Inches to centimetres | Divide by 2, multiply by 5 | 1 inch = 2.5 cm |
| Centimetres to inches | Divide by 5, multiply by 2 | |
| Fahrenheit to centigrade | Deduct 32, divide by 9 and multiply by 5 | 77°F = 25°C |
| Centrigrade to fahrenheit | Divide by 5, multiply by 9 and add 32 | |
| Gallons to litres | Divide by 2, multiply by 9 | 2 gal = 9 litres |
| Litres to gallons | Divide by 9, multiply by 2 | |

Note: 1 pint = 0.6 of a litre and 1 litre = 1.8 pints

| | | |
|---|---|---|
| Pounds (weight) to kilos | Divide by 11, multiply by 5 | 5 k = 11 lb |
| Kilos to pounds | Divide by 5, multiply by 11 | |

Note: 16 oz = 1 lb; 1000g = 1 kg and 100g = 3.5 oz

**Tyre pressures**
Pounds per square inch to kilometres per square centimetre

| lb/sq.in | kg/cm | lb/sq.in | kg/cm |
|---|---|---|---|
| 10 | 0.7 | 26 | 1.8 |
| 15 | 1.1 | 28 | 2.0 |
| 20 | 1.4 | 30 | 2.1 |
| 24 | 1.7 | 40 | 2.8 |

The Greeks use the metric system but most 'unreasonably' sell liquid (i.e. wine, spirits and beer) by weight. Take my word for it, a 640g bottle of wine is approximately 0.7 of a litre or 1.1 pints. Proprietary wines such as *Demestica* are sold in bottles holding as much as 950g, which is 1000ml or 1¾ pints.

Electric points in the larger towns, smarter hotels and holiday resorts are 220 volts AC and power most American or British appliance. A few older buildings, in out-of-the-way places, might still have 110 DC supply. Remote pensions may not have any electricity, other than that supplied by a generator and even then the rooms might not be wired into the system. More correctly they may well be wired but not connected!

Greek time is 2 hours ahead of GMT and British Summer Time (and 7 hours ahead of United States Eastern Time). That is except for a short period when the Greek clocks are corrected for their winter at the end of September, some weeks ahead of the United Kingdom alteration.

**Basics & essentials of the language** These notes and subsequent **Useful Greek** at the relevant chapter endings are not, nor could be, intended to substitute for a formal phrase book or three. Accent marks have been omitted.

Whilst in the United Kingdom it is worth noting that the *British Broadcasting Co.* (Marylebone High St, London WIM 4AA) has produced an excellent book, *Greek Language and People*, accompanied by a cassette and record.

For the less committed, a very useful, pocket-sized phrase book that I always have to hand is *The Greek Travelmate* (Richard Drew Publishing, Glasgow) costing £1.99. Richard Drew, the publisher, recounts a most amusing, if at the time disastrous, sequence of events in respect of the launch of this booklet. It appears the public relations chaps had come up with the splendid idea of sending each and every travel writer a preview copy of the book, complete with an airline tray of the usual food and drink served mid-flight. This was duly delivered at breakfast time but, unlike Bob Newhart's record of the *HMS Codfish's* shelling of Miami Beach, this was not a 'slow newsday'. No, this was the day that Argentina chose to invade the Falklands, which dramatic event drove many stories off the pages for good, including the phrase book launch!

## The Alphabet

| Capitals | Lower case | Sounds like |
|---|---|---|
| A | α | Alpha |
| B | β | Veeta |
| Γ | γ | Ghama |
| Δ | δ | Dhelta |
| E | ε | Epsilon |
| Z | ζ | Zeeta |
| H | η | Eeta |
| Θ | θ | Theeta |
| I | ι | Yiota |
| K | κ | Kapa |
| Λ | λ | Lamtha |
| M | μ | Mee |
| N | ν | Nee |
| Ξ | ξ | Ksee |
| O | ο | Omikron |
| Π | π | Pee |
| P | ρ | Roh |
| Σ | σ | Sighma |
| T | τ | Taf |
| Y | υ | Eepsilon |
| Φ | φ | Fee |
| X | χ | Chi |
| Ψ | ψ | Psi |
| Ω | ω | Omegha |

## Groupings

| | |
|---|---|
| αι | 'e' as in let |
| αυ | 'av/af' as in have/haff |
| ει/οι | 'ee' as in seen |
| ευ | 'ev/ef' as in ever/effort |
| ου | 'oo' as in toot |
| γγ | 'ng' as in ring |
| γκ | At the beginning of a word 'g' as in go |

| | | |
|---|---|---|
| γχ | 'nks' as in rinks | |
| μπ | 'b' as in beer | |
| ντ | At the beginning of a word 'd' as in deer | |
| | In the middle of a word 'nd' as in send | |
| τζ | 'ds' as in deeds | |

## Useful Greek

| English | Greek | Sounds like |
|---|---|---|
| Hello/goodbye | Γειά σου | Yia soo (informal singular said with a smile) |
| Good morning/day | Καλημέρα | Kalimera |
| Good afternoon/evening | Καλησπέρα | Kalispera (formal) |
| Good night | Καληνύχτα | Kalinikta |
| See you later | Θα σε δω αργοτερα | Tha se tho argotera |
| See you tomorrow | Θα σε δω αύριο | Tha se tho avrio |
| Yes | Ναι | Ne (accompanied by a downwards and sideways nod of the head) |
| No | Οχι | Ochi (accompanied by an upward movement of the head, heávenwards & with a closing of the eyes) |
| Please | Παρακαλώ | Parakalo |
| Thank you | (Σαζ) Ευχαριστώ | (sas) Efkaristo |
| No, thanks | Οχι ζυχαριστώ | Ochi, efkaristo |
| Thank you very much | Ευχαριστώ πολύ | Efkaristo poli |
| *After which the reply may well be:-* | | |
| Thank you (& please) | Παρακαλώ | Parakalo |
| Do you speak English? | Μιλάτε Αγγλικά | Milahteh anglikah |
| How do you say.... | Πως λενε... | Pos lene... |
| ...in Greek? | ...στα Ελληνικά | ...sta Ellinika |
| What is this called? | Πως το λένε | Pos to lene |
| I do not understand | Δεν καταλαβαίνω | Then katahlavehno |
| Could you speak more slowly (slower?) | Μπορειτε να μιλάτε πιο αργά | Boreete na meelate peeo seegha (arga) |
| Could you write it down? | Μπορειτε να μου το γράψετε | Boreete na moo to grapsete |

## Numbers

| One | Ενα | enna |
|---|---|---|
| Two | Δύο | thio |
| Three | Τρία | triah |
| Four | Τέσσερα | tessehra |
| Five | Πέντε | pendhe |
| Six | Εξι | exhee |
| Seven | Επτά | eptah |
| Eight | Οκτώ | ockto |
| Nine | Εννέα | ennea |
| Ten | Δέκα | thecca |
| Eleven | Εντεκα | endekha |
| Twelve | Δώδεκα | thodhehka |
| Thirteen | Δεκατρία | thehka triah |
| Fourteen | Δεκατέσσερα | thehka tessehra |
| Fifteen | Δεκαπέντε | thehka pendhe |
| Sixteen | Δεκαέξι | thekaexhee |
| Seventeen | Δεκαεπτά | thehkaeptah |
| Eighteen | Δεκαοκτώ | thehkaockto |
| Nineteen | Δεκαεννέα | thehkaennea |
| Twenty | Εικοσι | eeckossee |

| Twenty-one | Εικοσι ένα | eeckcossee enna |
| Twenty-two | Εικοσι δύο | eeckcossee thio |
| Thirty | Τριάντα | treeandah |
| Forty | Σαράντα | sarandah |
| Fifty | Πενήντα | penindah |
| Sixty | Εξήντα | exhindah |
| Seventy | Εβδομήντα | evthomeendah |
| Eighty | Ογδόντα | ogthondah |
| Ninety | Ενενήτα | eneneendah |
| One hundred | Εκατό | eckato |
| One hundred and one | Εκατόν ένα | eckaton enna |
| Two hundred | Διακόσια | theeakossia |
| One thousand | Χίλια | kheelia |
| Two thousand | Δύο χιλιάδες | thio kheeliathes |

*'Perhaps the keel is hogged'.*

*Akrotiri Beach, Lixourion Peninsula, Cephalonia.*

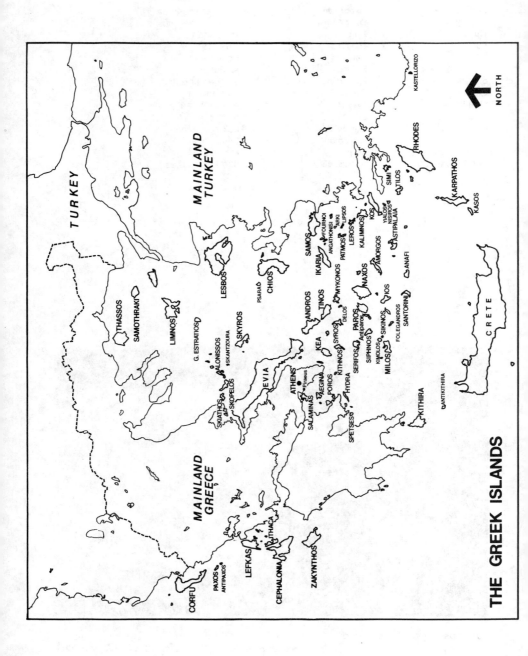

THE GREEK ISLANDS

# 2 Getting to & from the Ionian Islands & Athens

*If all the year were playing holidays, to sport would be as tedious as work. William Shakespeare*

To start this chapter off, first a word of warning. Whatever form of travel is utilised, travellers must not pack money or travellers cheques in luggage that is to be stowed away, out of sight. Some years ago, almost unbelievably, we met a young lady who, at the last moment and prior to checking-in at the airport, had stuffed some drachmae notes in a zipped side pocket of one of her suitcases. On arrival in Greece, surprise, surprise, she was minus the money.

## BY AIR
## From the United Kingdom

**Scheduled flights** The choice of airline access to the Ionian Islands rests between direct flight to Corfu or via Athens East (international) airport, from whence it is necessary to transfer, by bus, to Athens West (domestic) airport to fly Olympic Airways to mainland Preveza (for Lefkas) or the islands of Cephalonia, Corfu or Zakynthos. From Corfu it is possible to take a domestic flight to Cephalonia, Preveza or Zakynthos. Note both Olympic Airways international and domestic flights use the West airport.

*Heathrow to Athens* (3¼hrs): daily, non-stop, via *British Airways, Olympic* and others.
*East Midlands to Athens* (8hrs): Mon-Sat, via Amsterdam with *Olympic.*
*Edinburgh to Athens* (7hrs): Tues, Thurs, Fri & Sat, via Amsterdam with *Olympic.*
*Southampton to Athens* (8hrs): Mon-Sat, via Amsterdam with *Olympic.*

Scheduled air fare options include: 1st class return, economy, excursion, APEX (Advanced Purchase Excursion Fare), PEX (instant purchase, and the cheapest scheduled fare) and Eurobudget.

**Charter flights & package tours** Some package tour operators keep a number of seats available on each flight for, what is in effect, a charter flight. A nominal charge is made for accommodation (which need not be taken up, but read on...), the cost of which is included in the return air fare. These seats are substantially cheaper than scheduled APEX fares and are known as 'Charter Cheapies'. Apart from the relatively low price, the normal two week holiday period can be extended by a further week or weeks for a small surcharge. There are a variety of United Kingdom departure airports including Birmingham, Bristol, East Midlands, Gatwick, Luton, Manchester and Newcastle. But, as one correspondent has pointed out, the frequency of charter flights tails off dramatically between October and March, as does the choice of airport departure points. Do not forget this when contemplating an out-of-season holiday.

An increasing tide of near penniless British youngsters taking a charter flight to Athens and causing various problems, prompted the Greek authorities to announce their intention, from 1988, to carefully monitor charter flight arrivals. Those who did not have irrefutable proof of authorised accommodation, as well as enough money to survive, would be repatriated immediately, at the carriers expense. In the consequent muddle of internecine squabbling between the charter companies and the Greeks, the authorities agreed to relax the originally stringent threat, but only for 1988. Certainly independent travellers should have sufficient money to convince the authorities that they are sufficiently well heeled as not to become a problem during any planned stay.

To ascertain what is on offer, scan the travel section of the Sunday papers as well as the weekly magazine *Time Out* and, possibly, *Private Eye*. There are many, varied packaged holidays available from the large tour operators whilst some of the smaller, more personal companies offer a bewildering array of multi-centre, fly-drive, budget-bed, self-catering and personally tailored holidays, in addition to the usual hotel accommodation.

Exceptionally reasonable charter flights, with the necessary accommodation vouchers, are available from *Owners Abroad Ltd*, Ilford, who also have offices in Birmingham, Glasgow and Manchester. Examples of their fares and destinations in 1988 include:

Two week return fares: Gatwick to Athens from £88.75 (Economy Season) to £117.75 (High Season); Gatwick to Corfu from £85.75 (Economy Season) to £113.75 (High Season); Gatwick to Zakynthos from £95.75 (Economy Season) to £123.75 (High Season) and Gatwick to Preveza (for Lefkas) from £103.75 (Economy Season) to £132.75 (High Season).

The fares for three weeks are those above plus £25, for four weeks plus £30 and for five or six weeks, an additional 50 per cent is charged. Note that the total number of weeks allowed in Greece for travellers who arrive and depart by charter flights is six, not twelve weeks. Their rates for 1988 were subject to inexcusable surcharges and airport taxes totalling £14.95 per head. Inexcusable! Well I consider compulsory, irreducible surcharges should be consolidated in the quoted fares to allow fair prices comparisons.

Perhaps the least expensive flights available are obtainable from *Courier Flights*. These scheduled seats started off at about £65 return to Athens for the 1988 low season period. BUT passengers can only take a maximum of 10kg of hand luggage, one holdall measuring no more than 1ft x 2ft – no other baggage. Other restrictions result in only one passenger being able to travel at a time and for a minimum period of ten or fourteen days. The *cognoscenti* confirm that these seats are booked well ahead.

Amongst companies offering interesting and slightly off-beat holidays are the *Aegina Club Ltd* and *Greek Islands Club*. *Aegina* offer a wide range of tours, three different locations in up to three weeks and, additionally, will tailor a programme to fit in with client's requirements. *Greek Islands Club* also offer dinghy sailing, speed sailing and windsurfing holidays through an associated company, *Greek Islands Sailing Club*. More conventional inclusions, many in smaller, more personal hotels, pensions and tavernas than those used by the larger tour companies, are available from *Cricketers Holidays, Islands Unlimited, Something Special* and *Timsway Holidays*. The luxury end of the market is nobly catered for by *The Best of Greece*. Also *See* **Travel Agents, A To Z, Athens, Chapter Nine**.

**Students** Young people lucky enough to be under 26 years of age (oh to be 26 again) should consider contacting *STA Travel* who market a number of inexpensive charter flights (for adults as well). Students of any age or scholars under 22 years of age (whatever mode of travel is planned) should obtain an *International Student Identity Card (ISIC)*. This ensures discounts are available whenever they are applicable, not only in respect of travel but also for entry to museums, archaeological sites and some forms of entertainment.

If under 26 years of age, but not a student, it may be worthwhile applying for membership of *The Federation of International Youth Travel Organization (FIYTO)*, which guarantees discounts from some ferry and tour operators.

**From the United States of America** Scheduled Olympic flights include departures from:
Atlanta (via John F Kennedy (JFK) airport, New York (NY): daily
Baltimore (via JFK): daily
Boston (via JFK): daily
Chicago (Via JFK): daily
Dallas (via JFK): daily
Denver (via JFK): daily
Detroit (via JFK): daily
Houston (via JFK): daily

Los Angeles (via JFK): daily
Miami (via JFK): daily, 15 hours
Minneapolis (via JFK): daily
New York (JFK:) daily direct, approx. 10½ hours
Norfolk (via JFK): daily
Philadelphia (via JFK:) daily, about 11 hours
San Diego (via JFK): daily
San Francisco (via JFK): daily, approx. 14½ hours
Seattle (via London): daily
Tampa (via JFK): daily
Washington DC (via JFK): daily

Note that flights via New York's John F Kennedy airport involve a change of plane from, or to, a domestic American airline.

USA domestic airlines also run a number of flights to Greece and the choice of air fares is bewildering. These include economy, first class return, super APEX, APEX GIT, excursion, ABC, OTC, ITC, and others, wherein part package costs are incorporated.

**Charter/stand-by flights & secondary airlines** As in the United Kingdom, scanning the Sunday national papers' travel section, including the *New York Times*, discloses various companies offering package tours and charter flights. Another way to make the journey is to take a stand-by flight to London and then fly, train or bus on to Greece. Alternatively, there are a number of inexpensive, secondary airline companies offering flights to London, and the major Western European capitals.

Useful agencies, especially for students, include *Let's Go Travel Services*.

**From Canada** Scheduled Olympic flights include departures from:
Calgary (via JFK or La Guardia, NY): Mon, Tues, Thurs & Fri.
Edmonton (via Toronto, Amsterdam or London): daily
Montreal: twice weekly direct
  or (via Amsterdam, JFK or La Guardia, NY): daily
Toronto (via Montreal): twice weekly
  or (via Amsterdam, JFK or La Guardia, NY): daily
Vancouver (via Amsterdam): daily
Winnipeg (via Toronto & Montreal): Wed & Sat only.

As for the USA, not only do the above flights involve a change of airline but there is a choice of domestic and package flights as well as a wide range of differing fares.

Student agencies include *Canadian Universities Travel Service*.

**From Australia** There are Australian airline scheduled flights to Athens from Adelaide (via Melbourne), Brisbane (via Sydney), Melbourne and Sydney. Flights via Melbourne and Sydney involve a change of plane from, or to, a domestic airline. Regular as well as excursion fares and affinity groups.

**From New Zealand** There are no scheduled flights.
Various connections are available as well as regular and affinity fares.

**From South Africa** Scheduled Olympic flights include departures from:
Cape Town (via Johannesburg): Fri & Sun only.
Johannesburg: direct, Thurs, Fri & Sun.

Flights via Johannesburg involve a change of plane from, or to, a domestic airline. South African airline flights from Johannesburg to Athens are available as regular, excursion or affinity fares.

**From Ireland** Scheduled Olympic flights from:
Dublin (via London): daily, which involves a change of airline to *Aer Lingus*.

Note that when flying from Ireland, Australia, New Zealand, South Africa, Canada and the USA there are sometimes advantages in travelling to London, or other European capitals, on stopover and taking inexpensive connection flights to Greece.

## From Scandinavia

include:

**Denmark** Scheduled Olympic flights from:
Copenhagen: daily

**Sweden** Scheduled Olympic flights from:
Stockholm (via Copenhagen or Vienna): Tues, Wed, Thurs, Fri & Sat.

**Norway** Scheduled Olympic flights from:
Oslo (via Frankfurt or Copenhagen): daily.

All the Scandinavian countries have a large choice of domestic and package flights with a selection of offerings. Contact *SAS Airlines* for *Olympic Airways* details.

## AIRPORTS

**United Kingdom** Do not forget if intending to stay in Greece longer than two weeks, the long-stay car parking fees tend to mount up – and will the battery last for a 3 or 4 week layover. Incidentally, garage charges at Gatwick are about £32.00 for two weeks, £42.00 for three weeks and £52.00 for four weeks. The difficulty is that most charter flights leave and arrive at rather unsociable hours, so friends and family may not be too keen to act as a taxi service.

**Athens** Hellinikon airport is split into two parts, West (Olympic domestic and international flights) and East (foreign airlines). Coaches make the connection between the two airports. Olympic Airways buses travel to Athens centre as do city buses.

**Western (or domestic) airport**: City buses pull up alongside the terminal building. Across the road is a pleasant cafe/restaurant where the service becomes fairly chaotic when packed out. To the left of the cafe (*Facing*) is a newspaper kiosk and further on, across a side road, a Post Office is hidden in the depths of the first building.

**Eastern airport** Outwardly quite smart but can, in reality, become an expensive, very cramped and uncomfortable location if there are long delays. Let's not beat about the 'airport', the place becomes a hell-hole. Suspended flights occur when, for instance, air traffic controllers strike elsewhere in Europe. So remember to have enough money and some food left for an enforced stay. Flight departures are consistently overdue and food and drink in the airport are costly, with a plastic cup of coffee costing about 120drs. Furthermore, there are simply no facilities to accommodate a lengthy occupation by a plane load of passengers. The bench seats are very soon fully occupied – after which the floor of the concourse becomes covered with heaps of dejected travellers sleeping and slumped for as long as it takes the aircraft to depart. You have been warned.

## BY TRAIN

### From the United Kingdom & European countries (Illustration 1).

Recommended only for train buffs and masochists, but one of the alternative routes to be considered when a visitor intends to stay in Greece in excess of 6 weeks. The quickest journey of the three, major scheduled overland routes takes about 60 hours, and the 1988 second-class return fare cost in the region of £266. Tickets are valid for two months. One advantage of rail is that travellers may break the journey along the route (a little difficult on an airline flight), and another is that it is possible to travel out on one route and back by an alternative track (if you will excuse the pun). It is important to take along basic provisions, toilet paper and to wear old clothes.

A fairly recent return to the 'day of the train' reinforced my general opinion and introductory remarks in respect of this particular method of travel, bringing sharply back into focus the disadvantages and difficulties. The list of drawbacks should be enough to deter any but the most determined.

Try not to have a query involving use of the overseas information desk at *Victoria Station* as the facility is undermanned and the wait to get to a counter averages ¼hr. The staff are very willing but it is of interest that they overcome the intricacies of the official

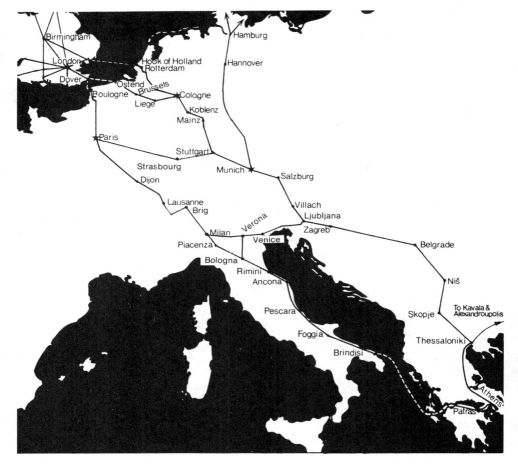

## Illustration 1 Rail Routes

British Rail European timetable ('it's all Greek to me guvnor') by overtly referring to the (infinitely) more manageable *Thomas Cook* publication.

The channel crossing is often on craft that would not be pressed into service even if war was declared on the Isle of Wight; the sea journey is too short for any cabins to be available; the duty free goods on offer are very limited and there are inordinate delays between train, boat and train.

The French trains that ply between the coast and Paris are of an excellent standard. On the other hand changing trains at the 'black hole' of *Gare du Nord* sharply focuses travellers' attention on a whole subculture of human beings who exist in and around a number of European railway stations. My favourite example of this little known branch of the human race is the 'bag-shuffler' – usually a middle-aged lady. The genus is initially recognisable by the multitudinous paper and plastic bags festooned about their person. Once at rest the contents are constantly and interminably shuffled from one bag to another and then back again, the ritual being accompanied by low mutterings. French railway stations, which are heated to a temperature relating to gentle simmer on a domestic cooker, have perfected a waiting room seating arrangement that precludes any but a drunk contortionist stretching out for a nap. In common with most other railway stations, food and drink are expensive and credit cards impossible to use, even at the swanky station restaurants. The railway station's toilet facilities are minuscule and men are charged for other than the use of a urinal and washbasin. Ladies have to pay about 2 Francs (F), a private closet costs 6F and a shower 12F. Potential users must not imagine they will be able to sneak in for a crafty stand-up wash using a basin – the toilets are intently watched over by attendants who would only require knitting needles to irresistibly remind one of the women who sat at the foot of the guillotine.

The Metro connection between the railway stations of *Gare du Nord* and *Gare de Lyon* is not straightforward and involves a walk. The *Gare de Lyon* springs a minor trap for the unwary in that the inter-continental trains depart from platforms reached after a long walk along the far left platforms (*Facing the trains*). Don't some of the French trains now resemble children's rocket drawings?

Although it may appear to be an optional extra, it is obligatory to purchase a couchette ticket for the train journey. This is a Catch 22 situation brought about by the rule that only couchette ticket holders have the right to a seat! Yes, well, not so optional! It is also necessary to pack food and drink, at least for the French part of the journey, as usually there are no refreshment services. In Italy most trains are met, at the various station stops, by trolley pushing vendors of (rather expensive) sustenance.

*Venice Station*, signed *Stazione St Lucia*, is most conveniently sited bang-on the edge of the Grand Canal waterfront with shops and restaurants to the left. Some of the cake shops sell slabs of pizza pie for about 1000 lira (L), which furnishes good stand-by nourishment. The scheduled stopover here will have to be adjusted for any (inevitable) delay in arrival. Venice (on the outward journey) is the watershed where Greek, and the occasional Yugoslavian, carriages are coupled up, after which passengers can be guaranteed to encounter a number of nasties. The replacement compartments are seedier and dirtier than their French and Italian counterparts and the lavatories vary between bad to unspeakable. Faults include toilets that won't flush (sometimes appearing to mysteriously fill up), Greek style toilet paper (which apart from other deficiencies lacks body and – please excuse the indelicacy – through which fingers break), no toilet paper at all (which is worst?), no soap dispenser, a lack of coat hooks, water taps that 'don't' – and all very grimy.

From Venice the term 'Express' should be ignored as the train's progress becomes slower and slower and slower with long, unscheduled stops and quite inordinate delays at the Yugoslavian frontiers. During the Yugoslavian part of the journey it is necessary for passengers to lock themselves into their compartment as some of the locals have an annoying habit of entering and determinedly looting tourists' luggage. There have even been 'totally unsubstantiated rumours', in the last year or two, of callow fellows spraying an aerosol knockout gas through the keyholes, breaking in and at leisure relieving passengers of their belongings. I must stress I have not actually met victims and the story may be apocryphal. It is inadvisable to leave the train at *Belgrade* for a stopover as the accommodation available to tourists is extremely expensive, costing in the region of £80 plus for a double room, per night. Additionally, it is almost impossible to renegotiate a couchette for the remainder of the onward journey. There are trolley attendants at the major Yugoslavian railway stations but the innards of the rolls proffered are of an 'interesting' nature, resembling 'biltong' or 'hardtack' burgers. Certainly when poked by the enthusiastic vendors I'm sure their fingers buckle. Another item of 'nutriment' on offer are large, but rather old cheese curd pies. A railway employee wanders the length of the train, twice a day, with a very large aluminium teapot ostensibly containing coffee. Nobody is interested in payment with Yugoslavian dinars, but American dollars, English pounds sterling or German marks almost cause a purr of satisfaction. Travellers lucky

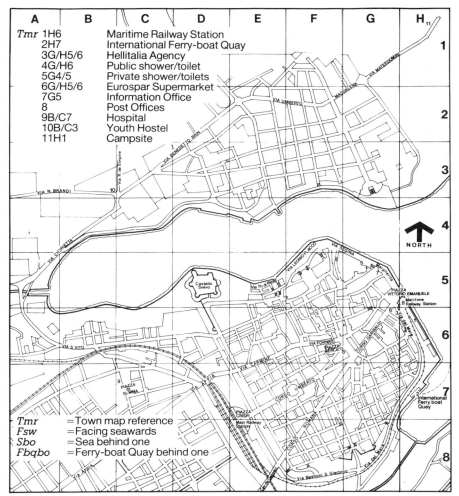

| | A | B | | C | D | E | F | G | H |
|---|---|---|---|---|---|---|---|---|---|
| *Tmr* | 1H6 | | | Maritime Railway Station | | | | | |
| | 2H7 | | | International Ferry-boat Quay | | | | | |
| | 3G/H5/6 | | | Hellitalia Agency | | | | | |
| | 4G/H6 | | | Public shower/toilet | | | | | |
| | 5G4/5 | | | Private shower/toilets | | | | | |
| | 6G/H5/6 | | | Eurospar Supermarket | | | | | |
| | 7G5 | | | Information Office | | | | | |
| | 8 | | | Post Offices | | | | | |
| | 9B/C7 | | | Hospital | | | | | |
| | 10B/C3 | | | Youth Hostel | | | | | |
| | 11H1 | | | Campsite | | | | | |

*Tmr* = Town map reference
*Fsw* = Facing seawards
*Sbo* = Sea behind one
*Fbqbo* = Ferry-boat Quay behind one

## Illustration 2 Brindisi

enough to have the services of a Greek attendant may well find he keeps a cache of alcoholic drinks for sale. An aside is that Yugoslavians are obsessed by wheel-tapping and at all and every stop (almost at 'the drop of a sleeper') appear and perform. Much of the journey beyond Belgrade is on a single line track and should, for instance, a cow break into a trot the animal might well overtake the train. At the frontier, passengers may well be reminded of the drawbacks experienced behind the Iron Curtain as they will probably be subjected to rigorous, lengthy baggage and document checks by a 'swamp' of officials, whose numbers include stern faced, unsmiling, gun-toting police.

In stark contrast the friendly Greek frontier town of *Idomeni* is a tonic. Even late at night the station's bank is open, as is the taverna/snackbar with a scattering of tables on the platform and a buzz of brightly lit noise and activity.

To avoid the Yugoslavian experience a very pleasant alternative is to opt for the railway route that travels the length of Italy to:
**BRINDISI PORT** (Illustration 2). Here international ferry-boats can be caught to the

mainland Greek ports of Igoumenitsa or Patras, from either of which buses make the connection with Athens, whilst Patras offers the possibility of another train journey on to Athens.

Despite the many thousands and thousands of tourists that pass through Brindisi every day, day in and day out, during the summer season, the town is in no way prepared for the influx. There is a total lack of public facilities to handle the disparate personal needs of the travellers. For instance, the station lavatory is locked 'out of hours', it being necessary to locate the other shower/toilet blocks available. Furthermore there is only a small public square on which the hordes have to flop out and while away the interminable hours whilst waiting for this or that ferry-boat or train.

Brindisi contains several traps for the unwary. For instance, the *Maritime Railway Station* (*Tmr* 1H6) and the quay (*Tmr* 2H7) for the Italy-Greek boats are some 200m apart, which on a hot day... The railway station has no formal ticket office or barrier. It is only necessary to dismount, turn left along the platform, left again, beside the concrete wall supporting the first floor concourse (which stretches over and above the platforms), across the railway lines and left again down the sterile dockland street, romantically named Via del Mare, to the ferry-boat complex. The road, hemmed in by a prefabricated wall on the right, curves parallel to the seawall on the left, from which it is separated by a high chain link fence, a number of railway lines and tarmacadam quay. But, before leaving the station, stop, for all the ticket offices and necessary officials are situated in the referred to upper storey buildings or in the 'Main Street', Corso Garibaldi. It is necessary to purchase a boarding pass from the Port office, on the first floor. Do not forget, as it is enough to try the patience of an angel (let alone a saint) to have to trudge all the way back to the Railway station in order to get the necessary bit of cardboard. I know from personal experience. Lastly, but not least, when booking rail tickets ask for *Brindisi Maritime*, as the town railway station is a kilometre or so inland. Another irritant is the advisability to 'clock in' at least 2 to 3 hours before a boat's departure, otherwise a traveller may be 'scratched from the fixture list' and have to rebook and pay again!

My favourite tour agency office, *Hellitalia* (*Tmr* 3G/H5/6 - tel 0831 222988), is across the road from the station, alongside a bank on the corner formed by the streets of Corso Garibaldi and Via del Mare. The staff, headed by Signor Fortunato Lorenzo, are very helpful and most informative. An attitude at odds with some of their business competitors in the High St who display Italian intransigence - rather different from Grecociliousness - the Italians are suaver! An example was the office where the man, when he deigned to serve us, advised without any apology "No the listed ferry-boat wouldn't be running later in the year, despite the printed timetable, so we couldn't take advantage of a return booking discount and no, he didn't accept American Express, despite the sticker advertising that he did".

Diagonally across the bottom of this end of the 'Main St' is the small, tree edged square, Piazza Vittorio Emanuele. As it is well endowed with park benches, it has become an unofficial waiting room with travellers and backpackers occupying all the available seating. as well as most of the flagstones. Fortunately, set in the trunk of a tree, on the quay side of the square, is a drinking water fountain. There is another beyond the *Trattoria Al Gabiano*, on Via Regina Margherita.

Lavatorial demands are satiated by one corporation and one private enterprise shower and lavatory facilities. The rather shabby, 'local authorities' unit is situated on Via del Mare (*Tmr* 4G/H6). The charges are L300 for the use of a toilet, L1500 for a chap to shower and, inexplicably, L2000 for a female to douche. The other, more wholesome but more expensive edifice (*Tmr* 5G4/5) is at No 11, beyond the imposing flight of steps along Via Regina Margherita. The owner is resident and a shower costs L2000.

Unfortunately the only laundry/dry cleaners are of the 24 hour variety. There is one on Via Regina Margherita.

Most of the town's cafe-bars, restaurants, change and ticket offices are ranged along Via Corso Garibaldi, the High St. On the left (*Station behind one*) of this road, prior to the side-street of Via de Flagila, is a very useful supermarket, the *Eurospar* (*Tmr* 6G/H5/6). Apart from the full range of provisions, there is a bread counter on the left of the entrance hall, thus doing away with the necessity of going into the store proper.

There is an Information office (*Tmr* 7G5) on Via Regina Margherita, a Post Office (*Tmr* 8G/H5/6) set in the north end of the Maritime Railway Station, the main Post Office (*Tmr* 8F/G6) adjacent to Piazza Mercato and a Hospital (*Tmr* 9B/C7) alongside Piazza di Summa.

**Youth Hostel** (*Tmr* 10B/C3) 2 Via Nicola Brandi                    Tel (0831) 413100
*Directions*: Unfortunately the Youth Hostel is some 5½km from the Maritime Railway Station, around the bay to the north. On the other hand, it is only 4km from the main Railway station, from whence Buses Nos 3, 4 & 5 pass the hostel.

The cost of bed and breakfast is L8500.

The Campsite (*Tmr* 11HI) is even more of a trudge, being further to the east.

Those who haven't dozed off may well note that the matter of a boarding pass and port taxes has been mentioned elsewhere. These are not, repeat not, included in the ferry-boat ticket prices and, as they can cost as much as L7000 per person, must be allowed for in any monetary calculations, especially when funds are low. *See* **By Ferry-Boat** for the relevant details of the sea crossing.

Travellers under 26 years of age can take advantage of *British Rail's Inter-Rail Pass* by applying to *London Student Travel, Eurotrain* or by going to a London mainline railway station. Americans and Canadians may obtain a *Eurorail Pass* prior to reaching Europe. Another option is the *Transalpino Ticket* available from the London office of the firm of the same name. All these offers hold out a substantial discount on standard train and ferry fares, but are subject to various terms and conditions. Student outfits offering cut-price train, coach and airline flights include *London Student Travel (& Eurotrain)*.

Certainly it must be borne in mind that the Greek railway system is not extensive and, unless travelling around other European countries, a concessionary pass might not represent much of a saving. On the other hand discounts in respect of the Greek railways extends to travel on some of the State Railway buses (OSE).

Examples of the various tickets, costs and conditions in 1988 were as follows:-

| | | | |
|---|---|---|---|
| **Inter-Rail ticket** | Under 26 years of age, valid one month for use in 21 countries (and also allows half fare travel in the UK on *Sealink* and *B & I* ships, as well as *P & O* ferries, via Southampton and Le Havre). | £139 | |
| **Transalpino ticket** | Under 26, valid for two months and allows stopover en route to the destination. | Single | Return |
| | London to Athens via Brindisi or Yugoslavia      from | £107.35 | £188.40 |

Other ticket options include B.I.G.E., Eurotrain and 'Athens Circle'.

**Timetables & routes** This section caused me as much work as whole chapters on other subjects. *British Rail*, whose timetable I have the greatest difficulty deciphering, and *Thomas Cook*, whose timetable I can understand, were both helpful.

Example routes include:
(1) London (Victoria Station), Dover (Western Docks), (jetfoil), Ostend, Brussels, Liege, Aachen, Cologne (change train, ¾hr delay), Mainz, Mannheim, Ulm, Munich (change train ¾hr delay) Salzburg, Jesenice, Ljubljana, Zagreb, Belgrade (Beograd), Skopje, Gevgelija, Idomeni, Thessaloniki to Athens.

An example of the journey is as follows:
Departure: 1300hrs, afternoon sea crossing, evening on the train, late night change of train at Cologne, night on the train, morning change of train at Munich, all day and night on the train arriving Athens very late, some 2½ days later at approx 2315hrs.

(2) London (Charing Cross/Waterloo East stations), Dover Hoverport, (hovercraft), Boulogne, Paris (du Nord), change train (and station) to Paris (de Lyon), Strasbourg, Munich, Salzburg, Ljubljana, Zagreb, Belgrade (change train 1½hrs delay), Thessaloniki to Athens.
An example:
Departure: 0955hrs and arrive 2½ days later at 2315hrs.
Second class single fare from £147 and return from £271.30.

(3) London (Victoria), Folkestone Harbour, (ferry-boat), Calais, Paris (du Nord), change train (and station) to Paris (de Lyon), Venice, Ljubljana, Zagreb, Belgrade, Thessaloniki to Athens.
An example:
Departure: 1415hrs and arrive 2¼ days later at 0840hrs.
Second class single fare from £135.20 and return from £266.

(4) London (Liverpool St), Harwich (Parkeston Quay), (ferry-boat), Hook of Holland, Rotterdam, Eindhoven, Venlo, Cologne (change train), Mainz, Mannheim, Stuttgart, Ulm, Munich, Salzburg, Jesenice, Ljubljana, Zagreb, Belgrade, Nis, Skopje, Gevgelija, Idomeni, Thessaloniki to Athens.
An example:
Departure: 1940hrs, night ferry crossing, change train at Cologne between 1048 and 1330hrs, first and second nights on the train and arrive Athens, middle of the day, at 1440hrs.

An alternative is to take the more pleasurable train journey through Italy and make a ferry-boat connection to Greece as follows:
(5) London (Victoria), Folkestone Harbour, Calais, Boulogne, Amiens, Paris (du Nord), change train and station to Paris (de Lyon), Dijon, Vallorbe, Lausanne, Brig, Domodossala, Milan (Central), Bologna, Rimini, Ancona, Pescara, Bari to Brindisi.
    (5a) Brindisi to Patras sea crossing.
    (5b) Patras to Athens.
An example:
Departure: 0958hrs, day ferry crossing, change of train at Paris to the Parthenon Express, one night on the train and arrive at Brindisi at 1850hrs. Embark on the ferry-boat departing at 2000hrs, night on the ferry-boat and disembark at 1300hrs the next day. Take the coach to Athens arriving at 1600hrs.
    The second class single fare costs from £163.30. and the return from £324.10.

Note it is possible to disembark at Ancona and take a ferry-boat, but the sailing time is about double that of the Brindisi sailing. *See* **By Ferry-boat**.

On all these services children benefit from reduced fares, depending on their age. Couchettes and sleepers are usually available at extra cost and Jetfoil sea crossings are subject to a surcharge.

Details of fares and timetables are available from *British Rail Europe* or *The Hellenic State Railways (OSE)*. One of the most cogent, helpful and informative firms through whom to book rail travel must be *London Student Travel/Eurotrain*. It is well worth contacting *Thomas Cook Ltd*, who have a very useful range of literature and timetables available from their Publications Department.

## From the Continent & Scandinavia to Athens Link up with one of the aforementioned main lines by using the appropriate connections sketched in Illustration 1.

Departure terminals from Scandinavia include Helsinki (Finland); Oslo (Norway); Gothenburg, Malmo and Stockholm (Sweden); Fredrikshavn and Copenhagen (Denmark).

**The above are only a guide and up-to-date details must be checked with the relevant offices prior to actually booking.**

**BY COACH** This means of travel is for the more hardy voyager and or young. If the description of the train journey has caused apprehension, the tales of passengers of the less luxurious coach companies should strike terror into the reader. Common 'faults' include lack of 'wash and brush up' stops, the presence of smugglers, prolonged border customs investigations (to unearth the smugglers), last minute changes of route and vehicle breakdowns. All this is on top of the forced intimacy with a number of widely disparate companions, some of whom may be wildly drunk, in cramped, uncomfortable surroundings.

For details of the scheduled *Euroway Supabus* apply c/o Victoria Coach Station or to the *National Express Company*. In 1988 a single fare cost from £79 and a return ticket from £137, via Italy, or £140 via Germany. This through service takes 4 days plus, with no overnight layovers but short stops at Cologne, Frankfurt and Munich, where there is a change of coach. Fares include ferry costs but exclude refreshments. Arrival and departure in Athens is at either the Peloponissos Railway Station or 44 Karageorgis Servias St, Syntagma Sq. This company offers a special one month return fare of £127.

The timetable is as follows:

Departure from Bay 20, Victoria Coach Station, London: Fri & Sat at 2030hrs, arriving at 1100hrs, 4½ days later.
*Return journey*
Departure from Filellinon St, Syntagma Sq, Athens: Wed & Fri at 1300hrs, arriving London at 0800hrs, 4 days later.

*Eurolines Intercars (Uniroute)* operate a coach service that shuttles between Athens and Paris on a three day journey. The buses depart twice a week on Wednesday and Saturday, at 1030hrs, for a cost of about 13,000drs, but note that baggage costs an extra 200drs. The French end of the connection is close by the *Metro Station Porte Vincennes* and the Athens terminus is alongside the *Stathmos Larissis Railway Station*. These air conditioned buses are comfortable but do not possess a toilet. The 'leg-stretching' stops are absolutely vital, not only for passengers to relieve themselves but in order to purchase victuals. To help make the journey acceptable passengers should consider packing enough food and drink to tide them over the trip. It is a problem that the standard of the 'way-station' toilets and snackbars varies from absolutely awful to luxurious. And do not forget that the use of the lavatories is usually charged for in Greece, Italy and Yugoslavia.

There are sufficient stops in Greece at, for instance, Livadia, Larissa and Thessaloniki, as well as at the frontier. The border crossing can take up to some 2¾hrs. The Yugoslavian part of the route passes through Belgrade and at about two-thirds distance there is a lunchtime motorway halt. At this sumptuous establishment (surprise, surprise) Amex credit cards are accepted and the lavatories are free – a welcome contrast to the previous, 'mind boggling' Yugoslavian stop, where even the Greeks blanch at the sight of the toilets! The bus and driver change at Trieste, which is probably necessary after the rigours of the Yugoslavian roads.

Use of the lavatories in the Trieste bus station has to be paid for and they are very smelly and there is the possibility of encountering a lecherous attendant 'masterminding' the ladies toilet. One of the two Italian stops is at a luxurious motorway complex. It is worth noting that all purchases at Italian motorway cafe-bars and restaurants have to be paid for first. A ticket is issued which is then exchanged for the purchaser's requirements. This 'house rule' even applies to buying a cup of coffee.

The route between Italy and France, over the Alps, takes a tediously long time on winding, narrow mountain roads with an early morning change of driver in France. It may well be necessary to 'encourage' the driver on this section to make an unscheduled halt in order to save burst bladders. The bus makes three Paris drop-offs, at about midday, three days after leaving Athens.

The best disembarkation point depends on a traveller's plans. Devotees of the Le Havre channel crossing must make for the *Gare St Lazare Railway Station*. The Metro, with one change, costs about 5 francs (F) per person and the coach's time of arrival allows passengers to catch an afternoon Paris to Le Havre train. This departs on the three hour journey at 1630hrs and the tickets cost some 100 F each. No information in respect of cross-Channel ferries is available at the Paris railway station, despite the presence of a number of tourist information desks.

Incidentally, the walk from the *Le Havre Railway Terminus* to the cross-Channel embarkation point is a long haul but there are reasonably priced taxis between the two points.

The superb restaurant *Le Southampton*, conveniently across the street from the Ferry-boat Quay, may well compensate for the discomfort of the trudge round, especially as they accept payment by *Amex*.

'Express' coach companies include *Consolas Travel*. This well-established company runs daily buses during the summer months, except Sunday, and single fares start at about £59, with a return ticket costing from £99. Other services are run by various 'pirate' bus companies. The journey time is about the same and prices, which may be slightly cheaper, also do not include meals. The cheaper the fare, the higher the chance of vehicle breakdowns and or the driver going 'walkabout'. On a number of islands, travel agents signs still refer to the *Magic Bus*, or as a fellow traveller so aptly put it – the 'Tragic Bus', but the company that ran this renowned and infamous service perished some years ago. Imitators appear to perpetuate the name.

In the United Kingdom it is advisable to obtain a copy of the weekly magazine *Time Out*, wherein the various coach companies advertise. For return trips from Athens, check shop windows in Omonia Sq, the American Express office in Syntagma Sq, or the Students Union in Filellinon St, just off Syntagma Sq. Also *See* **Travel Agents, A To Z, Athens, Chapter Nine**.

**BY CAR** (Illustration 3) Motoring to Greece is usually only a worthwhile alternative method of travel if there are at least two adults who are planning to stay for longer than three weeks, as the journey from England is about 1900 miles and takes approximately 50hrs non-stop driving.

Vehicle owners should ensure that spares are likely to be plentiful. An instance will illuminate. Recently I drove to Greece in a Mazda camping van and the propshaft went on the 'blink'. It transpired there was only one propshaft in the whole of Greece – well that was the story. Spare parts are incredibly expensive and our replacement finally cost, with carriage and bits and pieces, 36,000drs. The ½hr labour required to fit the wretched thing was charged at about £18 an hour. At the time the total worked out at approximately £194 which seemed a bit steep, even when compared to English prices. This cautionary tale prompts me to remind owners to take out one of the vehicle travel insurance schemes. The *AA* offers an excellent *5 Star Service Travel Pack* and other motoring organisations have their own schemes. At the time of making the decision, the insurance premium might seem a trifle expensive. Conversely, when faced with possibly massive inroads into available currency, the knowledge that a pack of credit vouchers is available, with which to effect payment for repairs, is very reassuring. The motoring organisations will prepare routes from their extensive resources. Certainly the *AA* offers this service but individual route plans now take 2-3 weeks to compile.

One of the shortest routes from the United Kingdom is via a car-ferry to Ostend (Belgium), on to Munich, Salzburg (Germany), Klagenfurt (Austria) and Ljubljana (Yugoslavia). There the Autoput E94 is taken to Zagreb, Belgrade (Beograd) and Nis on the E5, where the E27 and E55 are used, via Skopje, to the frontier town of Gevgelija/Evzonoi. Major rebuilding works can cause lengthy delays on the road between Zagreb and Nis.

For those who wish to drive across France, there are a number of ferry-boat ports from which to choose, including Le Havre, Cherbourg and St Malo, where the *Brittany* ferry terminal building contains some excellent shower and toilet facilities. Whichever port is used, for those who wish to stop a night in France, I am prepared to divulge the location of an excellent hotel I have stayed at three or four times over the last ten years. The ivy clad *Hotel de France*, (Tel 43444016) overlooks the main square of La Chatre sur Le Loir. Being in the area of Le Mans it is rightly very popular with the racing teams during the race weekend. The village, usually 'mapped' as La Chatre, is about midway between Tours and Le Mans on the D29. In 1988 double room prices cost from 100F, continental breakfast 18F, whilst evening meals in the restaurant, a gourmets delight, a gastronomic

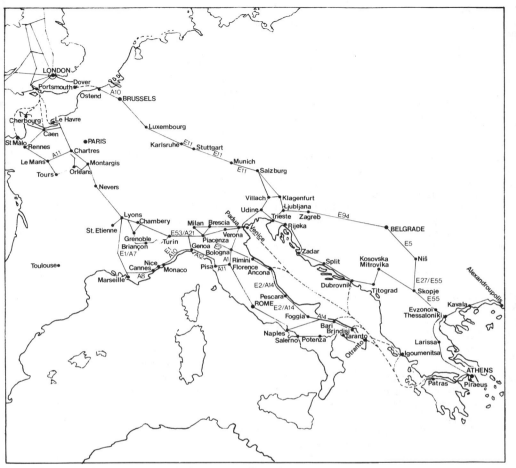

# Illustration 3  Car Routes & Ferry-boat Connections

That was an unqualified recommendation, now for a 'health warning'. Motorists who don't wish to pass away with frustrated fury should resist routing anywhere near St Etienne. My experience is that once on this city's motorway ring road system, it is impossible to get off. I'm sure there are drivers who are still careening round and round and round... A bottle of wine to any reader who can guide me out of the nightmare of the encircling road.

Travellers who choose to skirt Switzerland will have to cross over into Italy, usually angling down through Lyon and heading in the general direction of Turin. One of the loveliest Franco-Italian frontier crossings is effected by driving through Grenoble to Briancon for the Alpine pass of Col de Montgenevre. Across the border lies Turin (Torino), which bypass, and proceed to Piacenza, Brescia, Verona, Padua (Padova), Venice and cut up to Trieste. I say bypass because the ordinary Italian roads are just 'neat aggravation' and the sprawling towns and cities are almost impossible to drive through without a lot of problems and exhausting delays. Although motorways involve constant toll fees they are much quicker and less wearing on the nerves. Note that Italian petrol stations have a 'nasty habit' of closing for a midday siesta between 1200 and 1500hrs. *See* **By Coach** for hints in respect of Italian motorway cafes and restaurants.

Possibly the most consistently picturesque drive down Italy is that using the incredibly engineered, audaciously Alpine tunnelled toll road that hugs the Mediterranean coastline. This route can provide a check list of famous resorts. Proceed to Cannes and then via Nice, Monaco, and San Remo to Genoa and La Spezia. It is possible to detour to Pisa, Florence (Firenze) and Siena or simply continue on along the coast, but this magnificent, often breathtaking motorway terminates at Livorno. This route enables the Tuscany region to be driven through, probably the only area of Southern Italy not defaced by indiscriminate factory building and urban sprawl, and on to Rome (Roma). Beyond the Italian capital, it is possible to continue on past Naples – drivers should ensure that it is past Naples – to cut across the toe of Italy via Salerno, Potenza and Taranto on to Brindisi Port. Note the insistence 'on past Naples', as this city is infamous for its modern-day highwaymen. A dubious honour indeed, but reports include motorists being waved down for flat tyres or simulated road accidents and then being systematically robbed. You have been warned!

I do not wish to be seen knocking the country but, whilst on the subject, it behoves me to warn travellers to be extra careful in respect of personal belongings in the larger Italian towns. Despite the presence of an awesome number of police, most of whom are armed, pickpockets and robbers are very much at large. The police appear to be more interested in enforcing the traffic laws than catching thieves, but that may just be an impression.

An alternative route through Italy is via Turin, Milan, Bergamo, Brescia, Verona and on to Trieste which leads around the southern edge of a few of the lakes, in the area of Brescia. Excursions to Padua and Venice are obvious possibilities. From Trieste the most scenic (and winding) route is to travel the Yugoslavian Adriatic coast road via Rijeka, Zadar and Split to Dubrovnik. This latter, lovely medieval inner city is well worth a visit. At Petrovac the pain starts as the road swings up to Titograd, around to Kosovska Mitrovika, Pristina, Skopje and down to the Greek border at Gevgelija. The stretch from Skopje to the frontier can be rather unnerving due to the vast plains crossed and countless Muslims, endlessly trekking backwards and forwards. Signposting in Yugoslavia is usually very bad; always obtain petrol when the opportunity occurs and lastly, but not least, city lights are often turned off during the hours of darkness (sounds a bit Irish to me!), making night driving in built-up areas extremely hazardous. To save the journey on from Petrovac, it is possible, at the height of the season, to catch a ferry from Dubrovnik to Igoumenitsa or Patras on the Greek mainland. (*See* **By Ferry-boat**)

Detailed road reports are available from the *Automobile Association*, but I would like to stress that in the Yugoslavian mountains, especially after heavy rain, landslips can (no will!) result in parts of the road disappearing, as well as the surface being littered with rocks. There you go! Also note that the very large intercontinental lorries may prove even more of a hazard, the drivers appearing to regard the middle of the sometimes narrow roads as their own territory.

The main road through Greece to Athens, via Pirgos, Larissa and Lamia, is wide and good but the speed of lorries and their trailer units can prove disquieting. Vehicles being overtaken are expected to move right over and tuck well into the wide, hard shoulders. From Evzonoi to Athens, via Thessaloniki, is 340 miles (550km) and some of the major autoroute is now a toll road. Drivers approaching Athens via the Corinth Canal should use the Toll road as the old route is murderously slow, especially in bad weather.

To sum up, my favourite choice of route used to be crossing the Channel to Le Havre to drive through France, which holds few perils for the traveller, via Evreux, Chartres,

Pithiviers, Montargis, Clamecy, Nevers, Lyon and Chambery to the Italian border at Modane. Here the fainthearted can take the tunnel whilst the adventurous wind their way over the Col du Mont Cenis. That was until I 'discovered' the Briancon route.

In Italy, rather than face the rigours of the Yugoslavian experience, it is worth considering cutting down the not-all-that attractive Adriatic seaboard to one of the international ferry-boat ports of Ancona, Bari, or Brindisi. Boats connect to Corfu, as well as Igoumenitsa and Patras on the Greek mainland (*See* **By Ferry-boat & By Train**).

## General Vehicle & Personal Requirements
Documents required for travel in any European country used to include an *International Driving Licence*, and a *Carnet de Passages en Douanes* (both issued by the AA and valid for one year) but these are not now necessary in many countries including France, Italy, Switzerland, Germany, Greece and Yugoslavia. Drivers must have their United Kingdom driving licence and one document not to be forgotten is the *Green Insurance Card*. It is recommended to take the vehicle's registration documents, as proof of ownership, and the conveyance must bear a nationality sticker of the approved pattern and design. If a car owner carries out all the strictures each country demands, everything should be in order!

Particular countries' requirements include:

**France** Every year the French police carry out purges of motorists, and exceeding speed limits may well result in stiff, on the spot, fines. Headlights must be treated to allow for both right hand lane driving and the necessity to have yellow headlamp glass.

**Italy** All cars entering Italy must possess both right and left hand external driving mirrors. Drivers' licences have to be accompanied by an Italian translation, which is obtainable from one of the motoring organisations.

To help counter the disproportionately expensive price of petrol, tourists may apply to the relevant Italian Tourist Office for a package of concessionary petrol coupons and motorway vouchers. These go some way to offsetting the Hobson's choice in respect of the motorways, vis-a-vis the ordinary roads, and the resultant toll fees, which can mount up to about £50 for a north to south journey. Import allowances are as for Greece.

**Switzerland** Motorists should remember that the authorities require the vehicle and all the necessary documents to be absolutely correct (they would). The authorities have a nasty habit of stopping vehicles some distance beyond the frontier posts in order to make thorough checks.

**Yugoslavia** A valid passport is the only personal document required for citizens of, for example, Denmark, West Germany, Finland, Great Britain and Northern Ireland, Republic of Southern Ireland, Holland and Sweden. Americans and Canadians must have a visa and all formalities should be checked with the relevant Yugoslavian Tourist Office.

It is compulsory to carry a warning triangle, a first aid kit and a set of replacement vehicle light bulbs. The use of spotlights is prohibited and drivers planning to travel during the winter should check the special regulations governing the use of studded tyres.

Visiting motorists do not now have to buy petrol coupons in order to obtain fuel. But it is still advantageous to purchase them as they are the most cost effective method of buying petrol. The coupons are available at the frontier. Carefully calculate the number required for the journey and pay for them in foreign currency. Not only is the exchange rate allowed very advantageous, compared to that if the coupons are paid for in Yugoslavian dinars, but their acquisition allows for 10% more fuel. Petrol stations are often far apart, closed or have run out of fuel, so fill up when possible.

Photographers are only allowed to import five rolls of film; drinkers a bottle of wine and a quarter litre of spirits and smokers 200 cigarettes or 50 cigars. Each person may bring in unlimited foreign currency but only 15000 Yugoslavian dinars.

Fines are issued on the spot and the officer collecting one should issue an official receipt. To obtain help, in the case of accident or breakdown, dial 987 and the *SPI* will come to a driver's assistance.

**Greece** It is compulsory to carry a first aid kit, a fire extinguisher and a warning triangle in a vehicle. Failure to comply may result in a fine. It is forbidden to carry petrol in cans. In Athens the police are empowered to confiscate and detain the number plates of illegally parked vehicles. The use of undipped headlights in towns is strictly prohibited.

Customs allow the importation of 200 cigarettes or 50 cigars, 1 litre of spirits or 2 litres of wine. Visitors from the EEC may import 300 cigarettes or 75 cigars, 1½ litres of spirits or 4 litres of wine.

## Speed Limits
*See* table below - all are standard legal limits which may be varied by signs.

|  | Built-up areas | Outside built-up areas | Dual Carriageways | Motorways |
|---|---|---|---|---|
| **France** | 37mph (60kph) | 56mph (90kph) | 68mph (110kph) | 81mph (130kph) |
| **Greece** | 31mph (50kph) | 49mph (80kph) | 62mph (100kph) | 62mph (100kph) |
| **Yugoslavia** | 37mph (60kph) | 49mph (80kph) | 62mph (100kph) | 74mph (120kph) |

**BY FERRY-BOAT** (Illustration 3) . Some of the descriptive matter in this chapter, under the heading **By Train**, is relevant as it refers to both inter-country and ferry-boat travel, especially that relating to Brindisi Port and the international ferry-boats.

The ferry-boats on this run generally divide neatly into two. The expensive, but rather shambolic Greek ferries and the expensive, but luxurious and well-appointed Italian ferries. The Greek boats are really nothing more than an inter-island ferries of 'middling' quality, with the 'threat' of a cabaret and casino. They can be in appalling condition and the reception staff are often rude. The trappings of the Italian boats may well include a sea-water swimming pool, a ladies' hairdresser and beauty salon, a number of restaurants, a self-service cafeteria, a coffee bar and a disco. Food and drink on the craft of both countries is simply expensive. Examples include a coffee costing 165drs, a beer 150drs, *petit dejeuner* for two, of coffee and cake, 600drs and dinner 1500-2500drs a head. On the Greek craft the gourmet standards are average and the service poor whilst the Italian service and offerings are excellent, all at about the same price. Moral, try not to eat on board. Fares, in 1988, ranged from about 5500drs for deck class and 8500drs for a simple berth to 16000drs for a two berth cabin with en suite bathroom. Travellers should not rely on the purser to carry out normal currency exchange transactions and must remember that, apart from the cost of a ticket, there is the embarkation/boarding pass fee to pay.

Due to the popularity of Brindisi (Illustration 2 – *See* **Brindisi Port**, **By Train**, this Chapter), height of the season travellers must be prepared for crowds, lengthy delays and the usual ferry-boat scrum (scrum not scum). That is why the knowledgeable head for the other departure ports, more especially Ancona. Motorists should note that the signposting from the Ancona autoroute mysteriously runs out, failing to indicate the turn off to the Ferry-boat Quay – it is the south exit. But once alongside, all the formalities for purchasing a ticket and currency exchange are conveniently to hand in the concourse of an adjacent, very large, square, Victorian, 'neo something' building.

Those making the return journey from Greece to Italy must take great care when purchasing the ferry-boat tickets, especially at Igoumenitsa (Greek mainland). The competition is hot and tickets may well be sold below the published price. If so, and a traveller is amongst the 'lucky ones', it is best not to 'count the drachmae' until on board. The port officials carefully check tickets and if they find any that have been sold at a discount then they are confiscated and the purchaser is made to buy replacements at the full price. Ouch!

Passengers must steal themselves for the monumentally crass methods employed by the Italian officials to marshall the passengers prior to disembarking at the Italian ports. The resultant delays and queues that stretch throughout the length of the boat's corridors appear to be quite unnecessary and can turn normally meek and mild people into raging psychopaths.

## Sample Ferry-boat Services from Italy & Yugoslavia

**From Italy:**

| | | | | |
|---|---|---|---|---|
| *Brindisi to Patras:*<br>(& vice versa) | (April-Oct) daily | | Companies include:-<br>Fragline,5a Rethymnou St,10682<br>Athens.Tel(010301)8214171/8221285.<br>CF Eolos & Ouranos | |
| | | | Seven Islands Lines,22 Perikleous St,<br>Syntagma Sq,10562 Athens.<br>Tel(010301)3232756<br>CF Ionis & Ionian Glory | |
| | | | HML,28 Amalias Ave,Athens.<br>Tel(010310)3236333.<br>CF Egnatia,Poseidcnia,<br>Corinthia & Lydia. | |
| | | | Agapitos Lines,99 Kolokotroni St,185<br>35 Piraeus.Tel(010301)4136246.<br>CF Corfu Diamond & Sea. | |

| | | | Low Season | High Season |
|---|---|---|---|---|
| Sample ferry-boat fees<br>To Patras:- | | | | |
| per person: | deck | from | 4/5000drs | 7000drs |
| | aircraft seats | | 6000drs | 8000drs |
| | 2/4 berth cabin<br>c/w washbasin | | 7500drs | 11000drs |
| | 2 berth cabin<br>c/w bathroom | | 13/15000drs | 19/2000drs |
| cars (over 4¼m)<br>Voyage duration: 20hrs. | | | 5500drs | 10500drs |

| | | | | |
|---|---|---|---|---|
| *Brindisi to Igoumenitsa:*<br>*& Patras:*(& vice versa) | (April-Oct) daily | | Companies include:-<br>Fragline.(*See* above) | |
| | | | Nausimar,9 Filellinon St,185 36 Piraeus.<br>Tel(010301)4524290<br>CF Hellenic Spirit | |
| | | | Agapitos Lines, (*See* above) | |
| | | | HML. (*See* above) | |
| | | | Seven Islands Lines.(*See* above) | |

| | | | Low Season | High Season |
|---|---|---|---|---|
| Sample ferry-boat fees<br>To Igoumenitsa:- | | | | |
| per person: | deck | from | 4/5000drs | 7000drs |
| | aircraft seats | | 5500drs | 7500drs |
| | 2/4 cabin<br>c/w washbasin | | 6/7000drs | 10500drs |
| | 2 berth cabin<br>c/w bathroom | | 12/14000drs | 19000drs |
| cars (over 4¼m)<br>Voyage duration: 11½hrs. | | | 5000drs | 9500drs |

| | | | |
|---|---|---|---|
| *Ancona to Patras:*<br>(& vice versa) | (April-Oct) | Mon,<br>Wed,Fri &<br>& Sat. | Karageorgis Lines,26-28 Akti-Kondyli,<br>Piraeus.Tel(010301)4110461/4173001.<br>CF Mediterranean Sea & Sky |

| Sample ferry-boat fees To Patras:- per person: | | | Low season | High season |
|---|---|---|---|---|
| | deck | from | 5500drs | 7000drs |
| | aircraft seats | | - | - |
| | 2/4 berth cabin c/w washbasin | | 10500drs | 13000drs |
| | 2 berth cabin c/w bathroom | | 16000drs | 19000drs |
| cars (over 4¼m) | | | 12000drs | 15000drs |
| Voyage duration: 35hrs | | | | |

| *Ancona to Igoumenitsa & Patras* (& vice versa) | (May-June) | Wed & Sat | Companies include:- Minoan Lines,2 Leoforos Vasileos, |
|---|---|---|---|
| | (June-Oct) | Wed,Thurs Sat & Sun | Konstantinou,Athens.Tel(010301) 7512356. |
| | (May-Sept) | Wed & Sat | CF El Greco & Fedra |
| | (July-Aug) | additionally Sun, Thurs & Fri. | |
| | (April-May & Oct) | Mon,Tues & Thurs. | Marlines,38 Akti Possidonos,185 31 Piraeus.Tel(010301)4110777 |
| | (June-Sept) | Mon,Thurs & Sat. | CF Princess M, Countess M & Queen M |
| | (July-Aug) | Mon,Tues, Thurs & Sat. | |
| | | | Strintzis Lines,26 Akkti Possidonis, 185 31 Piraeus.Tel(010301)4129815. CF Ionian Sun, Star & Galaxy |

| Sample ferry-boat fees To Igoumenitsa:- per person: | | | Low season | High season |
|---|---|---|---|---|
| | deck | from | 5500drs | 7000drs |
| | aircraft seats | | 6500drs | 8500drs |
| | 2/4 cabin c/w washbasin | | 8500drs | 10500drs |
| | 2 berth cabin c/w bathroom | | 16000drs | 19500drs |
| cars (over 4¼m) | | | 12000drs | 15000drs |
| Voyage duration: 24hrs. | | | | |

| *Bari to Igoumenitsa & Patras:* (& vice versa) | (mid-April) | Wed & Fri | Ventouris Ferries,91 Pireos Kithiron |
|---|---|---|---|
| | (May) | Fri & Sun. | Sts,18541 Piraeus.Tel(010301) 4181001 |
| | (June & Oct) | Wed,Fri & Sun. | CF Grecia Express, |
| | (July-Sept) | daily | Patra & Athens Express |

| Sample ferry-boat fees To Igoumenitsa:- per person: | | | Low season | High season |
|---|---|---|---|---|
| | deck | from | 3500drs | 4500drs |
| | aircraft seats | | 4200drs | 6000drs |
| | 2/4 cabin c/w washbasin | | 8500drs | 13500drs |
| | 2 berth cabin c/w bathroom | | 11500drs | 15500drs |
| cars (over 4¼m) | | | 4500drs | 10000drs |
| Voyage duration: 13hrs. | | | | |

| Sample ferry-boat fees To Patras:- per person: | | | Low season | High season |
|---|---|---|---|---|
| | deck | from | 4500drs | 5500drs |
| | aircraft seats | | 5000drs | 6500drs |
| | 2/4 cabin c/w washbasin | | 9000drs | 15300drs |
| | 2 berth cabin c/w bathroom | | 12200drs | 17500drs |
| cars (over 4¼m) | | | 4500drs | 11500drs |
| Voyage duration: 20½hrs. | | | | |

**From Yugoslavia**

| | | | |
|---|---|---|---|
| *Dubrovnik to Igoumenitsa:* (& vice versa) Voyage duration: 20hrs. | (July-Aug) | Mon,Tues & Thurs. | Jadrolinija Line,c/o Hermes en Greece 3 Iassonos St,185 37 Piraeus Tel(010301)4520244. |
| *Rijeka to Igoumenitsa:* Voyage duration: 43hrs. | (July-Aug) | Mon,Wed & Sun | Jadrolinija Line (*See* above) |
| *Split to Igoumenitsa:* Voyage duration: 29hrs | (July-Aug) | Tues,Thurs & Sat | Jadrolinija Line (*See* above) |
| *Zadar to Igoumenitsa:* Voyage duration: 36hrs. | (July-Aug) | Tues. | Jadrolinija Line (*See* above) |

Ferries that dock at Igoumenitsa can connect with Athens by scheduled bus services and those that dock at Patras connect with Athens by both scheduled bus and train services.

The Greek mainland ports of Igoumenitsa and Patras are detailed in **GROC's Candid Guide to Corfu, The Ionian Islands, West Coast Ports & Athens.**

**Note the above services are severely curtailed outside the summer months, many ceasing altogether.**

Travellers that dock at Igoumenitsa can connect with Athens by scheduled bus services, whilst those disembarking at Patras may journey to Athens by either scheduled bus or train services.

Do not forget that the availability of ferry-boat sailings must be continually checked, as must airline, bus and train timetables. This is especially necessary during the months of October through to the beginning of May when the services are usually severely curtailed. So be warned.

## USEFUL NAMES & ADDRESSES
**The Automobile Association**, Fanum House, Basingstoke, Hants. RG21 2EA. — Tel (0256) 20123
**AA Routes** — Tel (0256) 20123
**The Greek National Tourist Organisation**, 195-197 Regent St, London WIR 8DL. — Tel (01) 734 5997
**The Italian State Tourist Office**, 1 Princess St, London W1R 8AY. — Tel (01) 408 1254
**The Yugoslavian National Tourist Office**, 143 Regent St, London WIR 8AE. — Tel (01) 734 5243
**British Rail International**, PO Box 303, London SW1 1JY. — Tel (01) 834 2345 *(Author's note – keep ringing)*
**The Hellenic State Railways (OSE)**, 1-3 Karolou St, Athens, Greece. — Tel (010301) 01 5222 491
**Thomas Cook Ltd**, Publications Dept, PO Box 36, Thorpewood, Peterborough PE3 6SB. — Tel (0733) 63200

## Other useful names & addresses mentioned in the text include:
**Time Out**, Southampton St, London WC2E 7HD. — Tel (01) 836 4411
**Courier Flights/Inflight Courier**, 45 Church St, Weybridge, Surrey KT13 8DG. — Tel (0932) 857455/56
**Owners Abroad Ltd**, Valentines House, Ilford Hill, Ilford, Essex IG1 2DG. — Tel (01) 514 8844
**Olympic Airways**, 164 Piccadilly, London W1V 9DE. — Tel (01) 846 9080
**Aegina Club Ltd**, 25A Hills Rd, Cambridge CB2 1NW. — Tel (0223) 63256
**The Best of Greece (Travel) Ltd**, Rock House, Boughton Monchelsea, Maidstone, Kent ME17 4LY. — Tel (0622) 46678
**Greek Islands Club**, 66 High St, Walton-on-Thames, Surrey KT12 1BU. — Tel (0932) 220416
**Cricketers Holidays**, 4 The White House, Beacon Rd, Crowborough, East Sussex TN6 1AB — Tel (08926) 64242
**Islands Unlimited**, Bignor, Nr Pulborough, West Sussex RH20 1QD — Tel (07987) 308
**Something Special Travel Ltd**, 13 Maidenhead St, Hertford, Herts SG14 1AN — Tel (0992) 552231
**Timsway Holidays**, Penn Place, Rickmansworth, Herts. WD3 IRE. — Tel (02404) 5541
**STA Travel**, 38 Store St, London WC1E 7BZ. — Tel (01) 580 7733
**Transalpino**, 214 Shaftesbury Ave, London WC2H 8EB. — Tel (01) 379 6735
**London Student Travel**, (Tel (01) 730 3402/4473) & **Eurotrain**, Tel (01) 730 6525), both at 52 Grosvenor Gdns, London SW1N 0AG.
**Euroways Supabus**, c/o Victoria Coach Station, London, SW1. — Tel (01) 730 3466
or c/o National Express Co.
The Greek address is: 1 Karolou St, Athens. — Tel (010301) 5240 519/6

**Eurolines Intercars (Uniroute)**, 102 Cours de Vincennes, 75012 Paris (Metro Porte Vincennes)
**National Express Co**, Westwood Garage, Margate Rd, Ramsgate CT12 6SL.    Tel (0843) 581333
or
**Victoria Coach Station**, 164 Buckingham Palace Road, London, SW1.    Tel (01) 730 0202
**Consolas Travel**, 29-31 Euston Rd, London NW1.    Tel (01) 833 4021/2026
The Greek address is: 100 Eolou St, Athens.    Tel (010301) 3219 228

*Amongst others the agencies and offices listed above have, over the years and in varying degrees, been helpful in the preparation of the guides. I would like to extend my sincere thanks to all those concerned. Some have proved more helpful than others!*

## Olympic Airways overseas office addresses are as follows:
America: 647 Fifth Ave, New York, NY 10022.    Tel (0101 212)
    (Reservations) 838 3600
    (Ticket Office) 735 0290
Canada: 1200 McGill College Ave, Suite 1250, Montreal, Quebec H3B 4G7.    Tel (0101 418) 878 9691
    80 Bloor St West, Suite 502 Toronto ONT M5S 2VI.    Tel (0101 416) 920 2452
Australia: 44 Pitt St, 1st Floor, Sydney, NSW 2000.    Tel (01061 2) 251 2044
South Africa: Bank of Athens Buildings, 116 Marshall St, Johannesburg.    Tel (010127 11) 836 5951
Denmark: 4 Jernbanegade DK 1608, Copenhagen.    Tel (010451) 126-100
Sweden: 44 Birger Jarlsgatan, 11429 Stockholm.    Tel (010468) 113-800

## More useful overseas names & addresses include:
**Let's Go Travel Services**, Harvard Student Agencies, Thayer Hall B, Harvard University, Cambridge,
    MA02138 USA    Tel 617 495 9649
**Canadian Universities Travel Service**, 187 College St, Toronto ONT M5T IP7 Canada.    Tel 417 979 2406
**Automobile Association & Touring Club of Greece (ELPA)**, 2 Messogion Street, Athens.    Tel (010301) 7791 615

*'The local ferry'.*

*Fiscardon, Cephalonia.*

'Looks phallic to me'.
      A memorial in honour of the toiling peasants of Ithaca, close to Exogi.

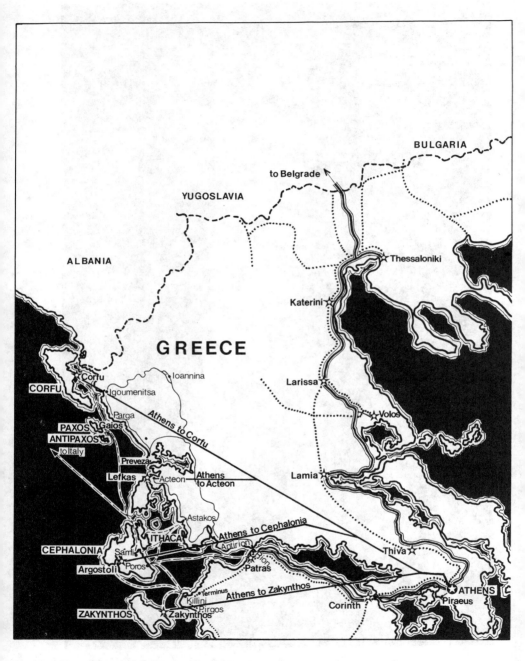

**Illustration 4 Air, Ferry, Rail & Road Routes to the
Ionian Islands**

# 3 Travel between Athens & the Ionian Islands

*I see land. I see the end of my labour. Diogenes*

The Greek islands are very thick on the water, numbering between 1000 and 3000, depending upon which authority you wish to believe. Approximately 100 are inhabited of which some 8 are located in the Ionian islands that I have chosen to agglomerate in the group. (Illustration 14).

In the past, the only way of setting foot on an island was to make for the relevant port and board a ferry-boat. Over the years a specialised and efficient system of water-borne travel developed.

Apart from the advent of international air flights direct to the larger island of Corfu, the creation of a number of smaller airfields, to accommodate domestic flights, has made it possible to fly to Athens and take a flight to the islands of Cephalonia, Lefkas (actually Preveza on the adjacent mainland) and Zakynthos. Illustration 4 details the various travel connections between the mainland and the Ionian islands.

**ARRIVAL BY AIR** It can prove difficult to obtain a seat for domestic flights on the spot, especially at the height of the tourist season,as Greeks now utilise the services extensively. It may be preferable to forward book, through a local Olympic office, prior to arrival. Ferry-boat travel was always much cheaper than flying, but for a few years this differential all but disappeared. In fact, in some cases flying was even cheaper than a 3rd class ferry-boat ticket and certainly less expensive than a 2nd class fare. Savage price hikes in air fares, between 1986-88, restored the ferries economic advantage. The uplift is such as to restore the old differentials, ferry-boat travel now being at least 50% cheaper than flying.

Travellers arriving in Athens, other than by aircraft, and wanting a domestic flight from the West airport, can catch one of the Olympic coaches or city buses to the airport. These depart from the Olympic terminal and offices (96-100 Leoforos Sygrou) and Syntagma Square – day and night at a cost of 100-150drs, depending on the hour, compared to the 450-600drs charged by a taxi (*See* **Arrival By Air, Athens, Chapter Nine**). Approximately an hour must be allowed between catching the airline bus and the relevant plane check-in time.

Many travellers do not wish to stop over in Athens. If this is the case, and arriving other than on an Olympic flight, it is possible to travel from the East to the domestic, West, airport using the connecting bus service.

The staff of Olympic, the Greek airline, are usually very helpful and their English good, although occasionally it is possible to fall foul of that sporadic Greek characteristic, intransigence.

It is worth considering utilising internal flights on one leg of a journey, especially if Athens is the point of arrival or departure. The possible extra cost of the flight, over and above the overland and ferry fares, must be balanced against the time element. For instance, Athens to Corfu island occupies 10½ hours on the ferry-boat from Patras to Corfu, plus the 4hr train journey. This compares to the Athens-Corfu flight time of about 50mins. One other advantage of domestic air travel is that the fares can be paid for by the use of *American Express, Diners* or *Access Mastercard*, possibly saving precious drachmae, especially towards the end of a holiday. On the other hand, the cost of domestic flights has been steeply increased over the last couple of years (as have ferry-boat fares).

**Ionian Island Airports** Corfu, Cephalonia and Zakynthos are at the smarter end of the Greek island airports, bearing little resemblance to some of their 'country cousins' on the remoter islands. Preveza was, until recently, a military airport but the shackles have been allowed to loosen.

**Please refer to the relevant island chapters for details of airline timetables.**

**ARRIVAL BY BUS** *See* **Athens (Chapter Nine), Greek Mainland Ports & Western Coast Resorts (Chapter Ten)**, as well as the relevant island descriptions, for details of daily scheduled bus services to the mainland ports that connect by ferry-boat to the various Ionian islands.

**ARRIVAL BY FERRY** In the following comments I am calling on many years experience of travelling third and tourist class on any number of ferry- boats.

In general, where sleeping arrangements are available, they will prove satisfactory if certain basic rules are followed. First claim a bunk by depositing luggage on the chosen berth, it will be quite safe as long as money and passports are removed. The position of a berth is important. Despite the labelling 'Men' and 'Women', a berth can usually be selected in either sleeping area. Try to choose one adjacent to stern deck doors to ensure some ventilation - due to the usual location of the third and tourist class accommodation beneath decks, it can get very hot and stuffy. A last tip is to lay a towel over plastic bunk covering to alleviate what otherwise would prove to be a sticky, uncomfortable night. Some ferries only have aircraft type, fold back seats in the 3rd/tourist class. Travellers should attempt, where possible, to find a lounge in which the television is muted and Gipsy children are noticeable, by their absence.

The third class lavatories are often in an unsightly condition even prior to a craft's departure. To help enjoy reasonable surroundings and have the use of a shower, quietly proceed into the next class and use their facilities (but don't tell everybody). Both the toilets and the showers suffer from the usual deficiencies listed under **Greek Bathrooms, Chapter Four**, so be prepared.

Important points to take into account when ferry-boating include the following:

1.  The ferries are owned by individual steamship companies and an employee of one line will be unable, or unwilling, to give enquirers information in respect of another company's timetable. Incidentally, this individual ownership results in a wide disparity in quality of service and general comfort between different ferry-boats.

2.  The distances and voyage times are quite often lengthy and tiring. Additionally the duration of the overall passage sometimes (no always) results in the timetable going awry, with delays in scheduled departure times at islands well into a ferry's voyage.

3.  There are usually four basic fare classes: first, second, tourist and third/deck class. The published fares on scheduled ferries are government controlled and the third/deck class option represents good value. Purchasers must ensure that they state the fare class required as failure to do so may well result in a more expensive, tourist ticket being bought instead of the cheaper, deck class. Apart from the aforementioned four categories, there may well be a variety of first and second-class sleeping accommodation, including private and shared cabins.

There are a number of 'Express' ferries and tourist trip boats, usually plying a particular island-to-island journey, on which charges are considerably higher.

4.  Food and drink on the ferries used to be comparatively expensive, but price rises on the land have not been mirrored at sea. On the other hand the service on the older boats is often discourteous and inefficient, so it still may be advantageous to pack provisions for a long voyage.

Wholesome and inexpensive ferry-boat picnic food includes: tomatoes, cucumber, bread, salami, ham, *Sunfix* orange juice and a bottle of wine (or two!). Take some bottled water. Greek chocolate (especially with nuts) is very good but does not keep well in the ambient daytime temperatures.

5.  The state of the toilets and the lack of basic supplies makes it mandatory that one

or two lavatory rolls are packed, easily to hand as it were. The usual lack of washroom facilities commends the stowage of a pack of 'wipes'. Quite frankly, on some occasions it will be necessary to stand on the rim of the toilet bowl as the only way of using the facility. Sorry!

6.   Tickets should be purchased from a ticket agency prior to a voyage, as they can cost more when bought on board. Ticket agency offices vary from 'the plush' to boxed-in back stairs. Clients who have checked the scheduled prices should not go wrong. On the other hand they must be sure their price list is up-to-date as fare increases over recent years have been very large. For instance the cost of a 3rd class Patras to Corfu ticket increased from 1205drs to 1862drs between April 1985 and July 1988.

7.   At the height of the season, the upper deck seats are extremely hot during the day and uncomfortably chilly at night. It is advisable to stake a claim to a seat as early as possible because the ferries are usually very crowded during the summer months. Voyagers who intend to lay out a sleeping bag and sleep the night away on the deck would do well to remember to occupy a seat, not the deck itself, which is more often than not sluiced down in the night hours.

8.   Travellers should ensure they have a good fat book and a pack of cards to while away the longer sea voyages. Despite the awesome beauty of the islands and the azure blue sea, there are often long, unbroken periods of Mediterranean passage to endure, interrupted only by the occasional passing ship and the dramatic activity and ructions that take place during a port call.

9.   Travellers sensitive to discordancy, and who find disagreeable a cacophony, a clamour of sound, may well find unacceptable the usual raucous mix experienced in the average 3rd class lounge. This is auditory assault often embodies two televisions (tuned to different programmes, the picture constantly flickering, suffering a snowstorm or horizontally high jumping in a series of stills) overlaid by the wail of Greco-Turkish music piped over the ship's tannoy system. Best to fly!

One delight is to keep a weather eye open and hope to observe a shoal of dolphins diving and leaping in the ship's wake. Their presence is often made discernible by the loud slapping noise they make when re-entering the water.

Ferry-boaters must take care when checking the connections, schedules and timetables as they can, no do, change during the year, especially outside the summer months from May through to September, as well as from one year to another. So be warned.

Do not forget, when the information is at it's most confusing, the Port police are totally reliable, but often a little short on English. Their offices are almost always on, or adjacent to the quayside.

Please refer to **Greek Mainland Ports..., Chapter Ten** and individual island chapters for full details of ferry-boat timetables.

## CRUISE SHIPS
Fly/cruise packages on offer are based on seven days, or multiples thereof and are, in the main, rather up-market. They call in at selected islands for a part or full day, with excursions where applicable.

Other holiday-makers should note that the large influx of this 'genus' of fun loving tourist can have quite an impact on an island, and the *cognoscenti* normally vacate the particular port of call for that day.

## GREEK ISLAND PLACE NAMES
This is probably the appropriate place to introduce the forever baffling problem which helps to bedevil the traveller – Greek place names. For instance, the island of Santorini may well be designated Thira. The reason for the apparently haphazard nomenclature lies in the long and complicated territorial owner-ship of Greece and its islands, more especially the latter. The base root may be Greek, Latin, Turkish or Venetian. Additionally the Greek language has three forms – Demotic (spoken), Katharevousa (literary) and Kathomiloumeni (compromise), of which Demotic

and Katharevousa have each been the official linguistic style. Even as recently as 1967-74 the *Colonels* made Katharevousa, once again, the authorised form, but Demotic is now the approved language. Help!

Street names can be equally confusing and I have plumped for my personal choice sometimes stating the alternatives, but where this is not possible, well, there you go! I mean how can Athens' main square, Syntagma, also be spelt Syntagina, Sintagma or Syntagmatos? Street names are also subject to some uncertainty as the common noun Odhos (street) is often omitted, whilst Leoforos (avenue) and Plateia (square) are usually kept in the name. The prefix Saint or St is variously written as Agios, Ayios, Ag or Ai.

Hotel and pension titles often give rise to some frustration where a Guide has listed the Roman scripted appellation. To the uninitiated (most of us?), *Hotel* Αυλη does not at first, second or third sight look like *Avli*, does it?

Due to scholastic, critical comments I must defend my habit of mixing Roman and Greek script when referring to establishment and street names. For example, I may write the Greek ΑΚΤΗ ΕΘΝΙΚΗΣ ΑΝΤΙΣΤΑΣΗΣ, which translates to the Roman *Akti Ethnikis Antistasis*. My only defence is that 99.9% of readers transmit that which they see to the brain without being able to make the mental gymnastics necessary to substitute the different letters. This is markedly so in respect of those letters that have no easy or direct equivalent. Will my more erudite friends excuse the rest of us dyslexic Grecophiles!

A *Nome* approximates to a small English county, a number of which make up a province such as the Peloponnese or Thessaly.

At this stage, without apologies, I introduce my own definition to help identify an unspoilt Greek town as follows: *where the town's rubbish is still collected by donkey, with wooden panniers slung across its back, slowly clip-clopping up a stepped hillside street, the driver, not even in sight but probably languishing in a stray taverna!*

| Map nomenclature | Greek | Translation |
|---|---|---|
| Agios/Ag/Ayios/Aghios | Άγιος/Άγια | Saint |
| Akra/Akrotiri | Ακρωτήρι | Cape/headland |
| Amoudia | | Beach |
| Ano | Άνω | Upper |
| Archeologikos (horos) | Αρχαιολογικός χώρος | Ancient (site) |
| Cherssonissos | | Peninsula |
| Chora/Horo/Horio/khorio | Χωριό | Village |
| Kato | Κάτω | Lower |
| Kiladi | | Valley |
| Klimaka | | Scale |
| Kolpos | Κόλπος | Gulf |
| Leoforos | Λεωφόρος | Avenue |
| Limni | Λίμνη | Lake/marsh |
| Limani | Λιμάνι | Harbour |
| Lofos | | Hill |
| Moni/Monastiri | Μοναστήρι | Monastery |
| Naos | Ναός | Temple |
| Nea/Neos | Νέο | New |
| Nissos/Nissi | Νήσος | Island |
| Odhos/Odos | Δρόμος | Street |
| Ormos | Όρμος | Bay |
| Oros | Όρος | Mountain |
| Palios/Palaios | Παλιός | Old |
| Paralia | | Seashore/beach |
| Pediada | | Plain |
| Pelagos | | Sea |
| Pharos | | Lighthouse |
| Pigi | | Spring |

| Plateia | Πλατεία | Square |
|---|---|---|
| Potami | Ποτάμι | River |
| Prokimea | | Quay |
| Spilia | Σπηλιά | Cave |
| Steno | | Straight |
| Thalassa | | Sea |
| Vuno | Βουνό | Mountain |

## Useful Greek

| English | Greek | Sounds like |
|---|---|---|
| Where is... | Που ειναι | Poo eene... |
| ...the Olympic Airways office | τα γραφεία της Ολυμπιακής | ...ta grafia tis Olimbiakis |
| ...the railway station | ο σιδηροδρομικός σταθμός | ...sidheerothrom kos stathmos |
| ...the bus station | ο σταθμοζ των λεωφορειων | ...stathmos ton leoforion |
| ...the boat | το πλοιο | ...to plio |
| ...the nearest underground station | ο πλησιέστερος σταθμός του ηλεκτρικοο | ...o pleessiesteh'os stathmos too eelektrikoo |
| ...the ticket office | το εκδοτήριο των εισιτηρίων | ...to eckdhoterio ton eessitirion |
| ...the nearest travel agency | το πλησιέστερο πρακτορείο ταξιδιων | ...to pleessiteh'ro praktorion taxidion |
| I'd like to reserve... | Θελω να κρατησω | Thelo na kratiso |
| ...seat/seats on the | θέση για | ...thessee/thessis ghia |
| ...to | για | ...ghia |
| ...plane | αεροπλανο | ...aeroplano |
| ...train | τραινο | ...treno |
| ...bus | λεωφορειο | ...leoforio |
| ...ferry-boat | πλοιο | ...plio |
| When does it leave/arrive | Ποτε φευγει/φθανει | Poteh fehvghi/fthanee |
| Is there... | Υπαρχει | Eeparhee... |
| ...from here to | απ εδωστο | ...Apetho sto |
| ...to | στον | ...ston |
| Where do we get off | Που κατεβαινομε | Poo katevenomhe |
| I want to go to | Θέλω να πάω στους ... | Thelo na pao stoos... |
| I want to get off at | Θελω να κατεβω στο | Thelo na katevo sto... |
| Will you tell me when to get off | Θα μου πείτε πού να κατέβω; | Thah moo peete poo nah kahtevo |
| I want to go to... | Θέλω να πάω στους ... | Thelo na pao stoos |
| Stop here | Σταμάτα εδώ. | Stamata etho |
| How much is it | Ποσο ειναι | Posso eene |
| How much does it cost | Πόσο κάνει η μεταφορά | Posso kani i metafora |
| ...to | στο | ...sto |
| Do we call at | Θα σταματήσουμε στην ...; | Tha stamatissome stin |

## Signs often seen affixed to posts & doors

| Greek | English |
|---|---|
| ΑΦΙΞΙΣ | ARRIVAL |
| ΑΝΑΧΩΡΗΣΙΣ | DEPARTURE |
| ΣΤΑΣΙΣ | BUS STOP |
| ΕΙΣΟΔΟΣ | ENTRANCE |
| ΕΞΟΔΟΣ | EXIT |
| ΚΕΝΤΡΟ | CENTRE (as in town centre) |
| ΕΙΣΟΔΟΣ ΕΛΕΥΘΕΡΑ | FREE ADMISSION |
| ΑΠΑΓΟΡΕΥΕΤΑΙ Η ΕΙΣΟΔΟΣ | NO ENTRANCE |
| ΕΙΣΙΤΗΡΙΑ | TICKET |
| ΠΡΟΣ ΤΑΣ ΑΠΟΒΑΘΡΑΣ | TO THE PLATFORMS |

| | |
|---|---|
| **ΤΗΛΕΦΩΝΟΝ** | TELEPHONE |
| **ΑΝΔΡΩΝ** | GENTLEMEN |
| **ΓΥΝΑΙΚΩΝ** | LADIES |
| **ΑΠΑΓΟΡΕΥΕΤΑΙ ΤΟ ΚΑΠΝΙΣΜΑ** | NO SMOKING |
| ΤΑΜΕΙΟΝ | CASH DESK |
| ΤΟΥΑΛΕΤΕΣ | TOILETS |
| ΑΝΟΙΚΤΟΝ | OPEN |
| ΚΛΕΙΣΤΟΝ | CLOSED |
| ΩΘΗΣΑΤΕ | PUSH |
| ΣΥΡΑΤΕ | PULL |

*'That's a big screw! The remains of an olive press'.*

*In the hills by Makratika, Paxos.*

# 4 Island Accommodation

*How doth man by care oppressed, find in an inn a place of rest. Combe*

Package villa and tour organised holiday-makers will have accommodation arranged prior to arrival in Greece. In contrast, the most important matter to the independent traveller is undoubtedly the procurement of lodgings, especially the first overnight stay on a new island or at an untried location.

The choice and standard of accommodation is bewildering, ranging from extremely simple **Rooms**, in private houses (usually clean but with basic bathroom facilities), to luxury class, almost indecently plush hotels able to hold their own with the most modern counterpart, almost anywhere else in the world. The deciding factor must be the budget and a person's sensibilities. My comments in respect of standards reflect comparisons with Western European establishments. Those referring to prices are usually in relation to other Greek options, as the cost is averagely in excess of half that of the United Kingdom equivalents.

Travellers stepping off an island ferry-boat are usually a wisp in a swarming throng made up of Greeks, tourists and backpackers engulfed by a quayside mass of Greeks, tourists and backpackers struggling to get aboard the same craft. Visitors may well be approached by men, women and youngsters offering accommodation. It is a matter of taking pot-luck there and then, or searching around the town to make a more measured selection. The later in the day, the more advisable it is to take an offer, unseen. But it is obligatory to establish the price, if the rooms are with or without a shower, is the water hot and how far away they are located. It can prove unnerving to be 'picked up' and then commence on an ever-lengthening trudge through the back streets of a strange place, especially as Greek ideas of distance are rather optimistic.

Any accommodation usually requires a traveller's passport to be relinquished. As a passport is also required to change money and to hire a car, or a scooter, it is a good idea, if married or travelling with friends, to have separate documents. Then, if necessary, one passport can be left with the landlord and another kept for other purposes, as required.

Official sources and many guidebooks lay much emphasis on the role of the Tourist police in finding accommodation, but this cannot be relied upon as the offices may well be closed on arrival. Moreover changes in the structure of the various police forces, over the last few years, has resulted in the once separate and independent Tourist police being integrated with the Town police. I for one regard this as a very retrograde step. Such a pity that the Greeks, innovators of this excellent service, should now abandon the scheme, more especially in the light of the ever increasing number of tourists. Perhaps, having achieved their goal of ensuring Greece as a number one holiday spot, the authorities are going to allow the tour guides and couriers (that go 'hand in sand' with the ever increasing number of package tourists) to take over the Tourist police role in an *ex officio* capacity? Preposterous! I hope so.

A fruitful source of accommodation leads are tavernas, which more often than not result in an introduction to a **Room** or pension owner. Failing that, they usually send out for someone.

**BEDROOMS** Greek bedrooms tend to be airy, whitewashed and sparsely furnished. The beds are often hard, as are the small pillows, and unyielding mattresses may well be laid directly on to bed-boards, not springs.

It is advisable to inspect bedroom walls for the evidence of blood-red splats. These indicate flattened, but once gorged, mosquitoes and result from a previous occupant's night-time vigil. Well designed rooms usually have a top-opening window screened off with gauze so that they can be left ajar without fear of incursions by winged, creepy-crawlies. Where no gauze is in evidence, it is best to keep the windows tightly closed at night, however alien this may be. Those not in possession of a proprietary insect repellent may well have to reconcile themselves to a sleepless night. Tell-tale buzzing echoing in the ears indicates one has already been bitten. It is comparable to being attacked by Lilliputian Stuka night-fighters.

Hanging points are noticeable by their absence. Often there will be no wardrobe. If one is *in situ*, there is unlikely to be any hangers, not even the steel-wire type, and the cupboard doors may be missing. A rather idiosyncratic feature is that clothes hooks, when present, are often very inadequate, being more suitable for hanging coffee mugs by the handles.

Even more maligned and even more misunderstood than Greek food is:

**THE GREEK BATHROOM** I use the descriptive word bathroom, rather than refer simply to the toilets, because the total facility requires some elucidation. The following will not apply to Luxury, Class A or B hotels – well, it should not!

The plumbing is quite often totally inadequate. Instead of the separate wastes of the bath, shower and sink being plumbed into progressively larger soil pipes, thus achieving a 'venturi' effect, they are usually joined into a similar diameter tube to that of the individual pipes. This inevitably causes considerable back pressure with inescapable consequences. If this were not sufficient to cause a building inspector (who?) nightmares, where 'Mama' owns a washing machine it is invariably piped into the same network. That is why the drain grill, cunningly located at the highest point of the bathroom floor, often foams. The toilet waste is almost always insufficient in size and even normal, let alone excessive, use of toilet paper results in dreadful things happening, not only to the bathroom, but probably to a number of bathrooms in the building, street and possibly the village. If this were not enough... the header tank rarely delivers sufficient 'flush'. It has to be pointed out that Greeks have had, for many years, to be economic in the use of water and some islands ration it, turning off the supply for a number of hours per day, in the height of the summer. (*See* **Drinking Water, Chapter Six**).

Common faults are to find the lavatory without a seat; flooded to a depth of some inches; the bathroom light not working; no toilet roll; door locks not fitted as well as dirty WC pans and or any combination of the above. Furthermore, the wash basin may well be without a drain plug. Amongst other reasons, the lack of a plug is to stop flooding if a sink tap is accidently left turned on, when the mains water is switched off, and not turned off when the water supply is resumed!

The most common type of en suite bathroom is an all purpose lavatory and shower room. Beware! Years of research reveals that the shower head is usually positioned in such a way as to not only wash down the occupant but to drench the (amazingly) absorbent toilet roll as well as the bathers clothes, towel and footwear. Incidentally, the drain point is usually located so as to ensure that the bathroom is kept awash to a depth of between 1″ and 3″ ... and the resultant pool invariably lies where a toilet sitter's feet fall – if you read my meaning.

It is not unusual for there to be no hot water, even if a heating system is in evidence. Government energy conservation methods, the comparatively high cost of electricity and the use of moderately sized solar heating panels all contribute to this state of affairs. Where solar panels are the means of heating the water, remember to beat the rush and shower as early as possible, for the water soon loses its heat. Why not share with a friend? If hot water is available, but it is not heated by solar energy, then it will be necessary to locate the relevant electric switch. This is usually a 4 way position, ceramic knob hidden away behind a translucent panel door. On the other hand... To be fair to owners of accommodation, it is standard practice to charge for the use of hot water showers so it pays the landlord to have the switch out of sight and reach. Room charges may well be increased by as much as 100drs per day, per head, for the use of a shower, but this ought to be detailed on the Government controlled price list that should be displayed, and is usually suspended on the back of the bedroom door.

One stipulation on water-short islands that really offends the West European (and North American?) sense of delicacy, is the oft present, hardly legible sign requesting guests to put their 'paper' in the wastebin supplied, and not down the pan! I must own up to not always obeying this dictum and have had to make a hurried departure from a number of islands, let alone a pension or village, when the consequences of my profligate use of toilet paper have become apparent.

**THE BEACH** Some backpacking youngsters utilise the shore for their night's accommodation. In fact all island hoppers must be prepared to consider the beach as a stand-by, at the more crowded locations, during the months of July and August. I have only had to spend two or three nights on the beach in the nine or ten years of island excursions but admit to not venturing forth during the height of season months of late July, August and early September. On the other hand, the weather could not be more ideal for sleeping under the stars, the officials are generally not too fussed and may well direct travellers to a suitable spot. But beware of mosquitoes and tar.

**CAMPING** In direct contrast to *ad hoc* sleeping on the beach, camping, except at approved sites, is strictly forbidden. The law is not always rigorously applied. The restriction comes about from a wish to improve general hygiene, to prohibit and discourage abuse of private property and as a precaution against forest fires. The NTOG operate most of the licensed sites, some of which are spectacularly located, but there are some authorised, privately run camping grounds, which are also price controlled. A *Carnet-Camping International*, although not normally requested, affords campers worldwide, third-party liability cover, may result in a discount and is available to United Kingdom residents from the AA and other, similar organisations.

If moved on by an official for sleeping on the beach or illegally camping, it is advisable not to argue and go quietly. The Greek police have fairly wide, autonomous powers and it is preferable not to upset them unnecessarily.

As a guide, overnight campsite fees in 1988 were charged as follows:
Adults per person 450-550drs; children $\frac{1}{2}$ adult rate; tent hire 600-700drs and motor caravans 800-900drs.

**YOUTH HOSTELS (ΞΕΝΩΝΑΣ ΝΕΩΝ)** Establishments in Athens include the *YMCA (XAN)* and *YWCA (XEN)* as well as the *YHA*, which also has one or three outposts on the islands. This latter appellation more often than not is applied to ethnic, privately owned pensions catering for young travellers. They are habitually rather down-at-heel and tend to be operated in a somewhat Spartan, slovenly manner.

It is preferable to have YHA membership, taking the Association's card along. Approximate prices per night at the YMCA and YWCA are 900drs and in a Youth Hostel 400-450drs.

**ROOMS** The story goes that as soon as a tourist steps off the ferry, he (or she) is surrounded by women crying *Rooms (Dhomatio)*, and whoops, within minutes the traveller is ensconced in some wonderful Greek family's private home.

History may well have been like that, and in truth the ferries are still met at almost every island, the inhabitants offering not only rooms but pensions and lower category hotels. *Rooms* are the cheapest accommodation and are generally very clean, sometimes including the option of breakfast which is ordinarily charged extra. Prices reflect an island's popularity and the season, but the average 1988 mid-season cost was 1500-2500drs for a double room, depending upon the classification. Government approved and categorised rooms are subject to an official tariff, and are slightly more expensive than freelance householders.

At the more tourist popular island resorts an unwelcome phenomena has reared 'his' ugly head. This is the long stay, enterprising layabout who rents a large double or triple bedroom, for the summer season, from a hapless, unsuspecting owner of accommodation. The 'entrepreneur', a species to be avoided, then daily sublets out the room, cramming in some five or six unfortunates a night.

Apart from a prospect being approached leaving the ferry, the Tourist police would, in the past, advise about available accommodation but this role is being drastically reduced in their amalgamation with the Town police. The Tourist police offices were signed, if at all, 'ΤΟΥΡΙΣΤΙΚΗ ΑΣΤΥΝΟΜΙΑ'. Householders display the sign 'ΕΝΟΙΚΙΑΖΟΝΤΑΙ ΔΩΜΑΤΙΑ' or simply 'ΔΩΜΑΤΙΑ', when they have a room to rent.

**PENSIONS ('PANSION, ΠΑΝΣΙΟΝ')** This category of lodging was a natural progression from *Rooms* and now represents the most often found and reasonably priced accommodation on offer.

The older type of pension is rather reminiscent of those large, Victorian English houses, that have been divided up into bed-sits. In the main though they have been purpose built, usually during the Colonels' regime (1967-74) when government grants were freely available for the construction of tourist quarters. The owner more often than not lives in the basement and acts as concierge. The rooms are functional and generally the guests on each level share a bathroom and shower and (a rather nice touch when provided) a communal refrigerator in which visitors can store their various provisions and drinks. Mid-season charges for 1988 varied between 2000 and 2500drs for a double room.

Sometimes a breakfast of coffee, bread and jam, perhaps butter and a boiled egg, is available at a cost of about 150drs and represents fair value compared with the cost of a cafe breakfast.

**TAVERNAS (ΤΑΒΕΡΝΑ)** Tavernas are, first and foremost, eating places. Some tavernas, especially those situated by, or near, beaches, also have accommodation available. The drawback is that the more popular the taverna, the less likely guests are to get a full night's sleep, but the more involved they will be with the taverna's social life, which often continues into the small hours. Charges are similar to those of a Pension.

**HOTELS (ΞΕΝΟΔΟΧΕΙΟΝ)** Shades of difference and interpretation can be given to the nomenclature by variations of the bland, descriptive noun hotel. For instance ΞΕΝΟΔΟΧΕΙΟΝ ΥΠΝΟΥ indicates a hotel that does not serve meals and ΠΑΝΔΟΧΕΙΟΝ a low grade hotel.

Many independent travellers would not consider hotels as a first choice. The high classification ones are more expensive than pensions and the lower grade hotels often cost the same, but may well be rather seedy and less desirable than the equivalent class pension. Greek hotels are classified L (Luxury), A, B, C, D and E and the prices charged within these categories (except L) are controlled by the authorities.

It is unfortunately almost impossible to neatly pigeon-hole and differentiate between hotels and their charges as each individual category is subject to fairly wide standards, and charges are dependent on a multitude of possible percentage supplements and reductions as detailed below:

Shower extra (C, D and E hotels); number of days stayed less than three, plus 10 per cent; air conditioning extra (A and B hotels); out of season deductions (enquire); high season extra (ie months of July, August and the first half of September, plus 20 per cent; single occupancy of a double room, about 80 per cent of the double room rate. The higher classification hotels may well insist on guests taking demi-pension terms, especially in high season.

The following table must be treated as a guide only and is based on 1988 prices:

| Class | Comments | Guideline, mid-season double-bedroom price |
|---|---|---|
| L | All amenities, a very high standard and price. Probably at least one meal in addition to breakfast will have to be purchased. Very clean. En suite bathrooms with very hot water | -- |
| A | High standard and price. Most rooms have en suite shower or bath. Guests may well have to accept demi-pension terms. Clean. Hot water. | 6000-8500 |
| B | Good standard. Many rooms have en suite shower or bath. Clean. Hot water. | 4000-6000 |
| C | May be an older hotel but many new, purpose built, package tourist hotels plump for this category. If of the ancient variety, will exhibit faded elegance, shared bathrooms. Cleanish. Possibly hot water | 2000-4000 |
| D | Older, more faded. Shared bathroom, which may well be 'interesting'. A shower, if available will be an 'experience', and the water cold. | 1500-2500 |
| E | Old, very faded and of dubious cleanliness. The whole stay will be an 'experience'. Only (very) cold water. | 1200-1500 |

The prices indicated include government taxes, service and room occupancy until noon.

Where in the text reference is made to 'official rates', these are the prices listed in the *Guide to the Greek Hotels*. Generally prices detailed throughout this guide are those applicable to 1988.

**THE XENIAS** Originally government owned and promoted to ensure the availability of high standard accommodation at important tourist centres, but now often managed by private enterprise.

**FLATS & HOUSES** During the summer months this type of accommodation, referred to by travel agents and package tour operators as villas, is best booked prior to arriving in Greece. Not only will pre-booking be easier but, surprisingly, works out cheaper than flying out and snooping around.

The winter is a different matter, but probably not within the scope of most of our readers.

**Further useful names & addresses**
The Youth Hostel Association, 14 Southampton St, London WC2E 7HY.        Tel. 01 836 8541

## Useful Greek

| English | Greek | Sounds like |
|---|---|---|
| I want... | Θελω | Thelo... |
| ...a single room | ενα μονο δωματιο | ...enna mono dhomatio |
| ...a double room | ενα διπλο δωματιο | ...enna thiplo dhomatio |
| ...with a shower | **με ντους.** | ...me doosh |
| We would like a room for... | Θα θελαμε ενα δωματιο για | Tha thelame ena dhomatio ghia... |
| two/three days/a week/ until | **δυο/τρεις μέρες/μια** εβδομαδα/μεχρι | thio/trees meres/meea evthomatha/mekhri |
| Can you advise of another... | Ξερετε κανενα αλλο... | Xerete kanena alo... |
| house with rooms | **σπίτι με δωμάτιο** | speeti meh dhomatio |
| pension | πανσιον | panseeon |
| inn | πανδοχειο | panthokheeo |
| hotel | **ξενοδοχείο** | ksencdhokheeo |
| youth hostel | **ξενώνα νέων;** | xenonas neon |
| How much is the room for a night? | Ποσο κανει το δωματιο για τη νυχτα | Poso kanee dho dhomatio ghia ti neektah |

| | | |
|---|---|---|
| That is too expensive | Ειναι πολυ ακριβα | Eene polee akriva |
| Have you anything cheaper? | Δεν εχετε αλλο πιο φθηνο | Dhen ekhete ahlo pio ftheeno |
| Is there... | Υπαρχει | Eeparkhee |
| a shower | ενα ντουζ | doosh |
| a refrigerator | ενα ψυγειο | psiyeeo |
| Where is the shower? | Που ειναι το ντουζ | Poo eene dho doosh |
| I have to leave... | Πρεπει να φυγω | Prepee na feegho... |
| today | σημερα | simera |
| tomorrow | αυριο | avrio |
| very early | **πολύ νωρίς.** | polee noris |
| Thank you for a | Ευχαριστω για την | Efkareesto ghia tin |
| nice time | **συμπαθητική ώρα** * | simpathitiki ora |

*This is the exact translation, which would never be used, however, in Greek. An expression meaning rather: 'thanks for the fun' is:

| | |
|---|---|
| Ευχαριστω για την | Efkaristo ghia |
| διασκεδαση | tin thiaskethasi |

*'Having a chat and a bit of a knit'.*
*An olive grove close to Ag Apostoli Church, Paxos.*

# 5 Travelling around an Island

*A man is happier for life from having once made an agreeable tour. Anon*

A few introductory remarks may well be apposite in respect of holiday-makers' possessions and women in Greece. The matter is discussed elsewhere but it is not out of place to reiterate one or two points (Rosemary calls it 'carrying on').

**PERSONAL POSSESSIONS** Do not leave airline tickets, money, travellers' cheques and or passports behind at the accommodation. A man can quite easily acquire a wrist-strap handbag in which to conveniently carry these items. The danger does not, even today, lie with the Greeks, but with fellow tourists, down-and-outs and professional thieves 'working a territory'.

**WOMEN** There has been, in recent years, a downward slide towards the 'percentage ploy'. Young Greek men, in the more popular tourist areas, have succumbed to the prospects offered by sexually liberated, overseas women holiday-makers, especially those openly courting sun, sand and sex. Greek girls are still subject to rigorous parental control, so it is not surprising that the local lads turn their attentions to other, possibly more fruitful, pastures. Greeks who indulge in this pastime are derogatorily referred to as *Kamaki* – 'spearers of game', after the traditional fishing trident. It's up to you girls, there is no menace, only opportunities!

Now back to the main theme of the chapter, but, prior to expanding on the subject, a few words will not go amiss in respect of:

**BEACHES** A surprisingly large number of island beaches are polluted, in varying degrees, mainly by seaborne plastic and some tar. Incidentally, olive oil is an excellent medium with which to remove this black menace which sticks to towels, clothes and shoes better than the proverbial .... to a blanket.

Lack of anything but a small rise and fall of tide removes the danger of swimmers being swept out to sea but, on windy days, the tug of the sea's undertow might prove dangerous to a weak swimmer.

Jellyfish and sea urchins can occasionally be a problem in a particular bay, jellyfish increasingly so. One of my Mediterranean correspondents advises me that cures for the jellyfish sting include ammonia, urine (ugh) and a paste of meat tenderiser (it takes all sorts I suppose).

The biggest headache (literally) to a tourist is the sun, or more accurately, the heat of the sun. To give an example of the extremely high temperatures sometimes experienced, in Athens a few years ago birds were actually falling out of the trees, and they were the feathered variety! Every year dozens of tourists are carted off, suffering from acute sunburn. A little often (sun that is) must be the watchword. Generally the islands benefit from the relief of the prevailing summer wind, the *Meltemi*.

Nudism was once severely punished by puritanical authorities. Nowadays, as long as tourists, who wish to sunbathe topless, bottomless or both, utilise those beaches allocated for the purpose, there will be no trouble. These may be official or simply a relatively remote area where the proverbial blind eye is turned. Over the years, as Greek families have increasingly appreciated the delights of the beach, the 'home-grown' young women have increasingly gone topless. In the same spirit of 'permissive' adventure, more and more middle-aged Greek ladies have taken to the sea, often in all enveloping black costumes and straw hats. Some, to preserve their modesty, appear to swim in everyday clothes.

Despite the utterly reasonable condemnation of modern day advances in technology by us geriatrics, one amazing, welcome leap forward for all travelling and beach bound mankind is the *Walk-Master* personal stereo-casettes. No more the strident, tinny beat of the transistor (or more commonly the 'ghetto-blaster'), now simply the jigging silence of headphone enveloped, transfixed faces. Splendid!

It may well be that a reader is a devoted sun worshipper and spends every available minute on the beach, patio or terrace, if so there is no need to read any further. On the other hand when a holiday-maker's daytime interests range beyond conversion of the sun's rays into painful, peeling flesh, and there is a wish to travel around a particular island, then the question of *modus operandi* must be given some thought.

First, purchase an island map and one of the colourful and extremely informative tourist guides available on the larger islands. After which consider the alternative methods of travel and appraise their value.

*Clyde Surveys Ltd* produce an excellent map of the Ionian, now marketed by *Bartholomews*.

**ROADS** The main roads of most islands are passable but asphalted country lanes often degenerate alarmingly, becoming nothing more than heavily rutted and cratered tracks. Generally much road building and reconstruction is under way. Beware, as not all roads, indicated as being in existence by imaginative map makers, are anything more than, at the best, donkey tracks or may simply be non-existent. Evidence of broken lines, marking a road, must be interpreted as meaning that any highway present will certainly not be paved.

**ON FOOT** Owing to the hilly terrain of the islands and the daytime heat encountered, readers might have had enough walking without 'looking for trouble'. A quick burst down to the local beach, taverna. shop or restaurant, and the resultant one hundred or so steps back up again, may well go a long way to satiating any desire to go 'walkies'. If needs be, walking is often the only way to negotiate the more rugged donkey tracks and the minimum footwear is a solid pair of sandals or 'trainers'. Plan not to walk during the midday hours, to wear a hat, to take along sufficient clothes to at least cover up, should the sun prove too hot, and pack a bottle of drinking water.

**HITCHING** The comparative paucity of privately owned cars makes hitch-hiking an unsatisfactory mode of travel. On the other hand, if striking out to get to, or return from a particular village, most Greek drivers stop when thumbed down. It may well be a lift in the back of a Japanese pick-up truck, possibly sharing the space with some chickens, a goat or sheep or all three!

**DONKEY** Although once a universal 'transportation module', the donkey is only available for hire,nowadays,on a specific journey basis in particular locations. A personal prejudice is to consider donkey rides part of the unacceptable face of tourism, added to which it tends to be exorbitantly expensive.

**BUSES** Buses (and taxis) are the universal method of travel in Greece, so the services are widespread if, naturally enough, a little Greek in operation. Generally they run approximately on time and the fares are, on the whole, extremely reasonable. Passengers must expect to share the available space with fairly bulky loads and, occasionally, livestock.

The trick is to first find the square on which the buses 'terminus'. Then locate the bus office where the tickets are pre-purchased and on the walls or windows of which might be displayed timetables and the fares structure. The real fun starts if the bus is not only 'sardine packed', but fares are collected by a conductor who has to somehow make his way through, round and over the passengers. Be available well prior to scheduled departure times as buses have a 'nasty habit' of departing early. Try to ensure any luggage is placed in the correct storage compartment for the particular destination, otherwise it may go missing.

Buses are often crowded, especially when a journey coincides with a ferry-boat disgorging its passengers. The timetables are more often than not scheduled so that a bus or buses await a ferry-boat's arrival, except perhaps very early or late arriving craft. A bus rarely leaves a potential client standing, they just encourage everyone aboard.

Do not fail to observe the decorations festooned around and enveloping the driver. Often these displays resemble a shrine which, taking account of the way some of the drivers propel their bus, is perhaps not so out of place. Finally, do have change available as coins are always in short supply. It is helpful to know that local buses may be labelled TOPIKO (TOΠIXO).

A critic took me to task for not stressing that the summer bus schedules listed throughout the text of the Guides are subject to severe curtailment, if not total termination, during the winter months from October through to May. So, smacked hand Geoffrey, and readers please note.

**TAXIS** As indicated, taxis are the 'other' mode of island travel, are usually readily available and can be remarkably modern and plush. On the other hand...

Ports and towns nearly always have a main square on which the taxis rank, but, come the time of a ferry-boat's arrival, they also queue on the quayside. Fares are governed by the local authorities and, at the main rank, are often displayed giving examples of the cost to various destinations. Charges are reasonable by European standards, but it is essential to establish the cost, prior to hiring.

It may come as a shock for a 'fare' to have his or her halting, pidgin Greek answered in 'pure' Australian or American. But this is not surprising when one considers that many island Greeks have spent their youth on merchant ships or emigrated to the New World for ten to fifteen years. On their return home, with the future relatively financially secure, many take to taxi driving to supplement their income (and possibly to keep out of the little woman's way?).

**BICYCLE, SCOOTER & CAR HIRE** On a general note, it is very sad to notice the increasing incidence of *No Parking* and *Free Parking* signs at the very popular resorts. Oh dear!

On the whole, bicycles are very hard work and poor value in relation to, say, the cost of hiring a scooter – an option endorsed when the mountainous nature of most islands, and the midday heat, is taken into consideration. The once popular Italian machines are progressively being replaced by the ubiquitous, semi-automatic Japanese motorcycles. Although the latter do away with the necessity to fight the gears and clutch, they are not entirely suited to transporting two heavyweights. I once had the frightening experience, when climbing a steep mountainside track, of the bike jumping out of gear, depositing my passenger and I on the ground, leaving the scooter whirling found like a crazed mechanical Catherine wheel.

It is amazing how easy it is to get a good tan while scootering. The moderate wind draws the sun's heat, the air is laden with the smell of wild sage and oleanders and with the sun on one's back... marvellous!

Very rarely is a deposit requested when hiring a bike or motorbike but a passport is required. Always shop around to check out various companies' charges. Generally the nearer to a port, town or city centre a hirer is, the more expensive the machines will be. Take a close look over the chosen mode of transport prior to parting with any money, as the maintenance of any mechanical unit in Greece is usually poor to non-existent. Bicycles and scooters, a few years old, will be 'pretty clapped out'. A client must check the brakes, they will be needed, and should not be fobbed off without making sure there is a spare wheel.

Increasingly, the owners of two wheeled vehicles are also hiring crash helmets of dubious appearance. Flash young Greek motorbike riders usually wear their 'Space Age' headgear on the handlebars, where no doubt it will protect them (that is the handlebars) from damage. A useful tip when hiring a scooter is to take along a towel. It not only provides additional padding for the pillion passenger's bottom, whilst driving on rocky roads, but saves having to sit on painfully hot, plastic seating should a rider forget to raise the squab when parked. Sunglasses are necessary to protect the eyes from airborne insets. Out of the height-of-season and early evening it tends to become very chilly, so a sweater or jumper is a good idea and females may well require a headscarf, whatever the time of day or night.

Fuel is served in litres and five litres of two-stroke costs about 320-340drs. Fill up as soon as possible as fuel stations are still in fairly 'short supply' outside the main towns. Increasingly the gap between the scooter and the car is being catered for by the provision of more sophisticated machinery, including moon-tyred and powerfully engined Japanese trials motorbikes, as well as beach-buggies.

Typical daily hire rates are: for a bicycle 250-500drs; a scooter 1500-2000drs; a car from 5000-8500drs, including full insurances and taxes but mileage may cost extra, calculated at so much per kilometre. Out of season and period hire for all forms of conveyance can benefit from 'negotiation'. Car hire companies require a daily deposit, which varies between 10,000-20,000drs per day, as well as a hirer's passport and driving licence details. Due to this large outlay it is almost mandatory to pay by credit card, which most car hire companies 'gratefully grab'.

Be very careful to establish what (if any) insurance cover is included in the rental fees, and that the quoted hire charges include any compulsory taxes. One contentious area that causes unpleasant disputes is the increasing habit of the hire companies to charge comparatively expensively for any damage incurred, and I mean any damage, however slight. A hirer's detailed reasons for the causes of an accident, the damage and why it should not cost anything falls on deaf ears. Furthermore it is no use threatening to involve the police as they will not be at all interested in the squabble. It is noticeable that I and many readers regard car hire as a legalised rip-off.

Several other words of warning might not go amiss. Taking into account the uncertain state of the roads, do not hire a two-wheeled conveyance if not thoroughly used to handling one. There are a number of very nasty accidents every year, involving tourists and hired scooters. Additionally the combination of poor road surfaces and usually inadequate to non-existent vehicle lights should preclude any night-time scootering. Anyone intending to hire two wheeled transport must ensure they are fully covered for medical insurance, including an unscheduled, *Medicare* flight home, prior to departing for the holiday. And do ensure that a general holiday policy does not exclude accidents incurred on hired transport, especially scooters.

The glass-fronted metal framed shrines mounted by the roadside are graphic reminders of a fatal accident at this or that spot. Incidentally, on a less macabre note, if the shrine is a memorial to a man, the picture and bottle often present (more often than not of Sophia Loren and whisky) reputedly represent that person's favourite, earthbound desires.

But back to finger-wagging. The importance of the correct holiday insurance cover cannot be over-stressed. The tribulations I have encountered in obtaining inclusive insurance, combined with some readers' disastrous experiences, has resulted in an all-embracing scheme being featured in the Guides. This reminder should be coupled with the strictures in **Chapter One** also drawing attention to the policy devised for readers of the Candid Guides. Enough said!

## More useful names & addresses
**Clyde Surveys Ltd**, Reform Road, Maidenhead, Berks SL6 8BU     Tel 0628 21371

# Useful Greek

| English | Greek | Sounds like |
|---|---|---|
| Where can I hire a... | Που μπορώ να νοικιάσω ένα | Poo boro na neekeeaso enna... |
| ...bicycle | ποδήλατο | ...pothilato |
| ...scooter | σκούτερ | ...sckooter |
| ...car | αυτοκίνητο | ...aftokinito |
| I'd like a... | Θα ηθελα ένα | Tha eethela enna... |
| I'd like it for... | Θα το ήθελα για | Tha dho eethela ghia... |
| ...a day | μία μέρα (or: μιά) | ...mia mera |
| ...days | **μέρες** | ...meres |
| ...a week | μία εβδομάδα | ...mia evthomadha |
| How much is it by the... | Πόσο κάνει την | Poso kanee tin... |
| ...day | μέρα | ...mera |
| ...week | εβδομάδα | ...evthomadha |
| Does that include... | **Συμπεριλαμβάνονται σ' αυτό** | Simberilamvanonte safto |
| ...mileage | τα χιλιόμετρα | ...tah hiliometra |
| ...full insurance | μικτή ασφάλεια | ...meektee asfaleah |
| I want some | Θέλω | Thelo |
| ...petrol (gas) | βενζίνης | ...vehnzini |
| ...oil | λάδι | ...lathi |
| ...water | νέρο | ...nero |
| Fill it up | Γεμίστε το | Yemiste to |
| ...litres of petrol (gas) | **... λίτρα βενζίνης.** | ...litra vehnzinis |
| How far is it to... | Πόσο απέχει | Poso apechee |
| Which is the road for... | **Ποιος είναι ο δρόμος για ...;** | Pios eene o thromos ghia |
| Where are we now | Που είμαστε τώρα | Poo eemaste tora |
| What is the name of this place | **Πώς ονομάζεται αυτό το μέρος;** | Pos onomazete afto dho meros |
| Where is... | Που είναι | Poo eene... |

## Road Signs

| | |
|---|---|
| ΑΛΤ | STOP |
| ΑΠΑΓΟΡΕΥΕΤΑΙ Η ΕΙΣΟΔΟΣ | NO ENTRY |
| ΑΔΙΕΞΟΔΟΣ | NO THROUGH ROAD |
| ΠΑΡΑΚΑΜΠΤΗΡΙΟΣ | DETOUR |
| ΕΛΑΤΤΩΣΑΤΕ ΤΑΧΥΤΗΤΑΝ | REDUCE SPEED |
| ΑΠΑΓΟΡΕΥΕΤΑΙ Η ΑΝΑΜΟΝΗ | NO WAITING |
| ΕΡΓΑ ΕΠΙ ΤΗΣ ΟΔΟΥ | ROAD REPAIRS |
| ΚΙΝΔΥΝΟΣ | BEWARE (Caution) |
| ΑΠΑΓΟΡΕΥΕΤΑΙ ΤΟ ΠΡΟΣΠΕΡΑΣΜΑ | NO OVERTAKING |
| ΑΠΑΓΟΡΕΥΕΤΑΙ Η ΣΤΑΘΜΕΥΣΙΣ | NO PARKING |

*'Is the lady nearest the camera wearing a pair of trousers on her head'?*

*It is difficult to comprehend that Kavos is only an olive stone's throw away. The location is Kritika, Bastatika, Neochori or Dragonita, Corfu!*

# 6 Island Drink, Food & Medical Care

*Let us eat and drink, for tomorrow we die. Corinthians*

It is a pity that many tourists, prior to visiting Greece, have, in sundry 'replica' tavernas throughout Europe and North America, 'experienced' the offerings masquerading as Greek food. Unfortunately, neither food or drink cross the borders very well, in fact I don't think it is possible to recreate the unique quality of Greek cooking in foreign lands. Perhaps this is because they owe much of their taste to, and are in sympathy with, the very air, laden with the scent of the flowers and herbs, the very water, clear and chill, the very soil of the plains and scrub clad mountains, the ethereal and uncapturable quality that is Greece. Incidentally, many critics would postulate that it was impossible to recreate Greek food, full stop, but be that as it may...

Salad does not normally send me into ecstasy but, after a few days in Greece, the very thought of a peasant salad of endive leaves, sliced tomatoes and cucumber, black olives, olive oil and vinegar dressing, all topped off with feta cheese and sprinkled with oregano, parsley or fennel, sends me salivating to the nearest taverna.

Admittedly, unless you are lucky enough to chance across an outstanding taverna, the majority are surprisingly unadventurous and the choice of menu limited. Mind you there are one or two restaurants serving exciting and unusual meals, if the spelling mistakes are anything to go by. For instance I have observed, over the years, the following no doubt appetising dishes: *omeled, spachetti botonnaise, shrings salad, bowels entrails, lump cutlets, limp liver* (I know what they mean), *mushed pot, shrimps, crambs, kid chops, grilled meatbolls, spar rips, wine vives, fiant oven, swardfish, pork shops, staffed vine leaves, wild greens, string queens, wildi cherry, bater honi, gregg goti (!), mate with olive oil, bruised meat, forced meat balls, Creek salad, lamp kebab ....with rise, personal shrimps, mutton bowels served with pice, beef shoup, lame liver, intest liver, cububer, scorpines, chickey, greef beans, fried pataroes, bems giauts, veal roast in kettle, loveubrawn, walout kake, honey boiles, scruffed tomatoes*, (a fish called) *drowns, various complex* (in the coffee section) and *et cetera* – don't they sound interesting!

On a more positive note, whilst the usual dishes will be known to readers, a recommendation, a mention of a dish I haven't seen before and a couple of 'musing's' may not go amiss. As to the recommendation, where an eating house serves a good, creamy tzatziki and a Greek salad it makes a very refreshing dish to combine the two. Latterly I came across an offering I have not encountered previously, *pikileea*. This is a very tasty dish, originally a distinctive mezes, a meatless selection of appetisers. Diners lucky enough to locate a restaurant that serves *pikileea*, usually now as an hors d'oeuvres, will be served a plate including, for example, tomatoes, various dips, beetroot, aubergines, sweet peppers and kalamares. With regard to the musings, the ruminations, the brown studies, they relate to the humble potato and veal. Why, oh why, taking into account the copious plates of *patatas* available (thus proving the existence, in quantity, of the aforesaid tuber), are there no variations on the theme? Where are, oh where are mashed, roast or creamed potatoes to usurp the omnipresent, universal chip, just once in a while? Perhaps of course, the veal available in Greece is not the same veal as obtainable in the United Kingdom. I more than occasionally have an inkling that the meat labelled 'veal' may, only may be old beef or goat. One thing is for definite, there certainly aren't enough cows grazing 'in all of Greece' to 'grow' the amount of veal offered in the restaurants.

**A FEW HINTS & TIPS** Do not insist upon butter, the Greek variant is not very tasty to the European palate, is expensive and, in the heat, tends to dissolve into greasy pools.

Sample the retsina wine and after a bottle or two a day, for a few days, there is every chance you will enjoy it. Moreover, retsina is beneficial (well that's what I tell myself), acting as a splendid anti-agent to the comparative oiliness of some of the food.

Bread is automatically served with a meal – and charged for – unless a diner indicates otherwise. It is very useful for mopping up excess olive oil and thus requires no butter to make it more greasy. It has become a noticeable and regrettable feature, in recent years, that the charge for bread has increased to between 10 and 30drs per head, and I have seen it as high as 50drs. Naughty! Many eateries have developed the nasty habit of lumping an extra tax calculation in with the bread charge, that is extra to the usual tax inclusive prices listed on the menu. This reminds me to point out that all establishments selling drink and food are Government controlled, the prices supposedly being listed and displayed for all clients to inspect. It is to be regretted that it is becoming increasingly evident that more and more establishments are 'failing' to carry out this simple task. Moreover, an increasing number of restaurants and tavernas are even omitting to supply clients with any menu, let alone a priced one. This 'naughty little' habit may not be unconnected with the diminished role of the Tourist police. Price lists should state the establishment's category and the price of every item served. When they do, two prices are shown. The first, being net, is not really relevant, whilst the second, detailing the price actually charged, includes all service charges and taxes.

Greek food tends to be served on the 'cool' side. Even if the meal started out hot, and by some mischance is speedily served, it will arrive on a thoroughly chilled plate. The selection of both food and drink available is usually rather limited and unenterprising, unless diners elect to frequent the more international restaurants (but why go to Greece?). On the other hand the choice of establishments in which to eat and drink is almost limitless, in fact the profusion is such that it can prove very confusing. If in doubt about which particular restaurant or taverna to patronise, use the well tried principle of picking one frequented by the locals. It is generally a waste of time to ask a Greek for guidance in selecting a good taverna or restaurant as he will be reluctant to give specific advice, in case the recommendation proves unsatisfactory.

Diners must not be shy and should assert their traditional right to look over the kitchen to see 'what's cooking'. If denied this traditional right, especially in the more rural areas, it would be best for clients to be on their guard. The food may well be pre-cooked, tasteless and plastic, particularly if the various meals available are displayed in a neon-lit showcase. Do not order the various courses all at once, as would be usual at home. If you do, they will probably be served simultaneously and or, worst, in the wrong sequence. Try to order course by course and take your time, everyone else does.

It is best for diners to appreciate that they are not being ignored or continually disregarded if the waiter does not approach the table for anything up to 20 minutes. He is probably overworked and taking his time. It certainly makes a visitor's stay in Greece very much more enjoyable, as well as helping to maintain a normal blood pressure, if all preconceived ideas of service can be forgotten. Lay back and settle into the glorious and indolent timelessness of the locals' way of life. When in a hurry, settle up as the order arrives for, if under the impression that it took a disproportionate time to be served, just wait until it comes to paying! It will probably take twice as long to extract the bill (*logariasmo*) as it did to receive the food.

Many meat dishes, and certainly chicken, are, more often than not, served with some chips. This should be borne in mind when making an order, if only to save having plate upon plate of the wretched things come forth. Fish appears expensive, in comparison with European prices, so readers can imagine the disparity with the cost of other Greek food. When ordering fish it is normal to select the choice from 'the ice' and, being priced by weight, it will be put on the scales prior to cooking. This is the reason that fish is listed at so many drachmae per kilo, which does reduce the apparently outrageous price, just a little. If seeking 'cost conscious' meals, and wishing for a change from the ubiquitous moussaka, beef steak, or for that matter, chicken and chips, why not plump (!) for squid (*kalamares*). They usually provide a filling, tasty, low budget cost meal at 300-400drs. It has to be admitted that demand has resulted in the more popular locations and areas serving imported Mozambique squid. These can often be recognised by their regular shape and sweet taste – probably suiting many palettes very well. From the late summer months, locally caught *kalamares* tend to be large and knobbly.

Food is natural and very rarely are canned or frozen items used, even if available. When frozen foods are included in the meal, the fact must be indicated on the menu by addition of the initials *KAT*. The olive oil used for cooking is excellent, as are the herbs and lemons, but it can take time to become accustomed to the different flavours these impart to the food. Before leaving the subject of hints and tips, remember that olive oil can be pressed into service for removing unwanted beach tar from clothes.

A most enjoyable road, quayside or ferry-boat breakfast is to buy a large yoghurt (*yiaorti*) and a small pot of honey (*meli*), mix the honey into the yoghurt and then relish the bitter-sweet delight. If locally produced, natural yoghurt (usually stored in cool tubs and spooned into a container) cannot be purchased, the brand name *Total* is a very adequate substitute, being made from cow's or sheep's milk. I prefer the sheep derived product and, when words fail, break into a charade of 'baa-ing'. It keeps the other shoppers amused, if nothing else. The succulent water melon, a common and inexpensive fruit, provides a juicy, lunchtime refreshment.

Apart from waving the tablecloth in the air, or for that matter the table, it is usual to call *parakalo* (please). It is also permissible to say *gharkon* or simply 'waiter'.

A disturbing habit, which is becoming increasingly prevalent in recent years, is the use of the word *Special/Spezial*. This is simply a ruse enabling establishments to charge extra for a dish, or offering, that would have, in the past, been the 'norm'. A good example is *Special souvlaki pita*, which is nothing more than that which was previously a conventional giro meat souvlaki. The now *Standard souvlaki* may well be an inferior substitute, nothing more than a slab of meat. That's improvement for you!

## THE DRINKS

**Non-alcoholic beverages** Being a cafe (and taverna) society, coffee is drunk at all times of the day and night. Greek coffee (*kafe*) is in fact a leftover from the centuries long Turkish influence. The thick, grouty infusion is served without milk in small cups and always with a glass of deliciously cool water. Unless specified otherwise Greek coffee will be served sickly sweet or *varigliko*. There are many variations but the three most usual are *sketto* (no sugar), *metrio* (medium) or *glyko* (sweet). Be careful not to completely drain the cup, the bitter grains will choke an imbiber.

Except in the most traditional establishments (*kafeneions*), a client can ask for *Nes-kafe* or simply *Nes* which, as would be expected, is an instant coffee. This home-grown version often has a comparatively muddy taste. Those who require milk with their coffee must request *(Nes) meh ghala*. A most refreshing version is to order Nes chilled or *frappé*, which is served in a tall glass with ice cubes. French coffee (*ghaliko kafe*), served in a coffee pot with a separate jug of hot milk, espresso and cappuccino coffees are found in the larger, provincial towns, ports and international establishments. However, having made a detailed request, you may well receive any permutation of all the possibilities listed above, however carefully you may think you have ordered.

Tea, (tsai), perhaps surprisingly, is quite freely available, made of course with the ubiquitous teabag, which is not so outrageous since they have become universally commonplace. In more out of the way places herbal tea may be served.

**Drinking Water** It is sad to have to report that the once unquestionably superb, island drinking water supplies have, on many islands, become very suspect (with some notable exceptions). So much so that, in my opinion, at a few locations the situation is at a crisis level, when the demand is greatest. The cause is quite simply because the traditional shortages have been exacerbated by the overwhelming demands of tourism and the consequent, seemingly continuous construction of hotels, apartments and villas necessary to cope with the influx. Rumour has it that, at some resorts and in desperation, the resources have been topped up with questionable supplies during the height of summer months.

In many locations, the original water installations, never a byword of other than mediocrity, have suffered from less than exacting civil engineering standards, on being extended and expanded. Imperfections have even resulted in the unfortunate, unintentional 'marriage' of water and effluent. I can only advise holidaymakers, planning to visit the places in question, to pack some *Milton* as well as water purification tablets. Where the drinking water is at all suspect, it is absolutely essential to only drink bottled water, the cost of which is anything between 50-85drs for a $1\frac{1}{2}$ litre bottle. Brand names include *Loutraki, Nigita*, and *Sariza*.

Bottled mineral waters include *Sprite*, which is fizzy, and *lemonade/lemonatha*, a stillish lemonade. Orangeade (*portokaladha*), *visinatha*, a cherry flavoured soft drink, and various fruit juices are all palatable and sold, as often as not, under brand names, as is the universal *Koka-Kola*. A word of warning comes from a reader who reported that, in the very hot summer months, some youngsters drink nothing but sweet, fizzy beverages. This can result in mouth ulcers caused by fermenting sugar, so drink some water every day.

**Alcoholic beverages** They are generally sold by weight. Beer comes in 330g tins and bottles, or, more usually, the larger 500g bottle. Purchase the 500g bottle, it is a good value measure and note that when purchasing to take-away, there is a deposit on the bottle of between 8-15drs. Wine is sold in 340/430g (a half sized bottle), 680/730g (1.1 pints) and 950g ($1\frac{3}{4}$ pints) sized bottles.

**Beer** Greek brewed or bottled beer represents good value except when served in cans. The latter are the export version and, in my opinion, a 'swindle'. This western European style of packaging should be resisted, if for no other reason than it means the cost, quantity for quantity, is almost double. The most widely available bottled beers are *Amstel, Henninger* and *Kaiser*. Draught lager is insidiously creeping into various resorts and should be avoided, not only for purist reasons, but because it is comparatively expensive, as are the imported, high alcohol content, bottled lagers. No names, no pack drill but *Carlsberg* is one that springs to mind. A small bottle of beer is referred to as a *mikri bira* and a large bottle as a *meghali bira*.

**Wine** Unresinated (*aretsinoto*) wine is European in style and palatable. Popular brands include red (*kokino*) and white (*aspro*) *Demestica, Cambas* or *Rotonda*. More refined palates may approve of the dry red and white wines of selected islands. On the other hand, Greek wines are not exactly famed for their quality, but if quantity of brands can make up for this, then the country will not let anyone down. When possible, red wine (*krasi kokino*), dark wine (*krasi mavro*) and white wine (*krasi aspro*) are best ordered draught (*huna*) or from the barrel (*apo vareli*), if for no other reason than they are much less expensive than the increasingly overpriced bottles.

Retsina, or resinated wine is achieved, if that can be considered the expression, by the barrels, in which the wine is fermented, being internally coated with pine tree resin. Most retsina is white, with a rosé (*kokkineli*) version sometimes available. Some consider the overall taste to be similar to chewing wet, lead pencils, but this is patently obviously a heresy. Retsina is usually bottled, and asking for *kortaki* ensures being served the traditional, economically priced, small bottle, rather than the comparatively expensive, full sized bottle. Rumour has it that the younger retsinas are more easily palatable, but that is very much a matter of taste. A particularly palatable brand of kortaki retsina is *Levkos Xnpos*, the white label of which is decorated with a maple leaf. Some tavernas serve 'open' (*apo vareli*) retsina (in metal jugs), which adjective is used to describe retsina available on draught, or more correctly, from the barrel. When purchasing for personal consumption, retsina can be found dispensed (into any container a client might like to press into service) from large vats, usually buried in side-street cellars. Whatever and wherever, a good 'starter' kit is to drink a bottle or two, twice a day, for three or four days and if the pain goes...

**Spirits & others** As elsewhere in the world, sticking to the national drinks represents good value. *Ouzo*, much maligned and blamed for other excesses, is, in reality, a derivative of the aniseed family of drinks (which include *Ricard* and *Pernod*). Taken with water, ouzo is a splendid 'medicine', traditionally served with *mezes* (or *mezethes*) – the Greek equivalent of Spanish tapas. These are small plates of, for instance, a slice of cheese, tomato, cucumber, possibly smoked eel, octopus and an olive. When served, mezes are charged for, costing some 20 to 50drs, but the tradition of offering them is disappearing in many tourist locations. Customers not wishing to be served mezes should request *khores mezes*. *Raki* is a stronger alternative to ouzo, more often than not 'created' in Crete. *Metaxa* brandy, available in three, five and seven star quality, is very palatable, but with a certain amount of 'body', whilst the *Otys* brand is smoother. Greek aperitifs include *Vermouth, Mastika* and *Citro*.

**DRINKING PLACES** Prior to launching into the various branches of this subject, I am at a loss to understand why so many cafe-bar and taverna owners select chairs that are designed to cause the maximum discomfort, even suffering. They are usually too small, for any but a very small bottom, too low and with a seat of wickerwork or raffia that painfully impresses its pattern on the sitter's bare (sun-burnt?) thighs.

**Kafeneion** (ΚΑΦΕΝΕΙΟΝ) A cafe, serving only Turkish, whoops, Greek coffee. Very Greek, very masculine and in which women are rarely seen. They are similar to a British working man's club, but with backgammon, worry beads and large open windows allowing a dim view of the smoke-laden interior.

**Ouzeries** (ΟΥΖΕΡΙ) As above, but the house speciality is (well, well) ouzo.

**Cafe-bar** (ΚΑΦΕΜΠΑΡ) As above, but serving alcoholic beverages as well as coffee, and women are to be seen.

**Pavement cafes** Rather French in style, with outside tables and chairs sprawling over the pavement, as well as the road. Open from mid-morning, throughout the day, to one or two o'clock the next morning. Snacks and sweet cakes are usually available.

Inside any of the above, the locals chat to each other in that peculiar Greek fashion which gives the impression that a full-blooded fight is about to break out, at any moment. In reality, they are probably just good friends, chatting to each other. Admittedly voices have to be raised to be heard over the blaring noise of the omnipresent television set, which is probably broadcasting a football match, a (sickly) American soap or a (ghastly) English 'comic' programme, the latter two with Greek subtitles.

Drinks can always be obtained at a taverna or restaurant, but a customer may be expected to eat, so read on. It is of course, possible to 'sip' at hotel cocktail bars, but why leave home!

**EATING PLACES** At the cheapest end of the market, and more especially found in Athens, are pavement-mounted stands serving doughnut-shaped bread (*koulouri*), which make for an inexpensive nibble, costing between 10-20drs

**Pistachio nut & ice-cream carts** The vendors push their wheeled trolleys around the streets, either selling a wide variety of nuts in paper bags, for 100-150drs, or ice-creams in a variety of flavours and prices.

**Corn on the cob BBQ's** Increasingly appearing on the pavements of resorts. The proprietors crouch over their simple tray of charcoal toasting' cobs of corn.

**Galaktopoleio** (ΓΑΛΑΚΤΟΠΩΛΕΙΟ) Shops selling dairy products, including milk, butter, yoghurt, bread and honey. Sometimes they serve omelettes and fritters with honey (*loukoumades*) for consumption on the premises or 'take-away'. A traditional, but more expensive, alternative to a restaurant/bar at which to purchase breakfast.

**Zacharoplasteion** (ΖΑΧΑΡΟΠΛΑΣΤΕΙΟΝ) Shops specialising in pastries, cakes (*glyko*), chocolates and soft drinks as well as, sometimes, a small selection of alcoholic drinks.

**Galaktozacharoplasteion** A combination of the two previously described establishments.

**Snackbars, Souvlatzidika & Tyropitadika** Snackbars are not so numerous in the less touristy areas, often being restricted to one or two in the main town. They represent good value for a stand-up snack. The most popular offering is *souvlaki pita*. This is pita bread (or a roll) filled with grilled meat or kebab (*doner kebab* – slices off a rotating, vertical spit of an upturned cone of meat, also called *giro*), and garnished with a slice of tomato, chopped onion and a dressing, all wrapped in an ice-cream shaped twist of greaseproof paper. Be careful, as *souvlaki* is not to be muddled with *souvlakia* which, when served at a snackbar, consists of wooden skewered pieces of lamb, pork or veal meat grilled over a charcoal fire. Confusingly, these are almost indistinguishable from *shish-kebab*, or *souvlakia*, served at restaurants or tavernas, where a plateful of metal-skewered meat pieces are interspersed with vegetables. Note increasingly, in tourist locations, the adjective *Special*, when applied to souvlaki pita, usually indicates an average, correctly made offering for which a comparatively extortionate price is charged. The cheaper alternative will simply be a slab of meat in place of the slices of giro meat.

Other 'goodies' include *tiropites* – hot flaky pastry pies filled with cream cheese; *boogatsa* – a custard filled pastry; *spanakopita* – spinach filled pastry squares or pies; a wide variety of rolls and sandwiches (*sanduits*) with cheese, tomato, salami and other spiced meat fillings, as well as toasted sandwiches (*tost*). This reminds me to point out to readers that if 'toast' is ordered, it is odds on that a toasted cheese sandwich will be served.

**Milk-shake bars** Glitzy, neo-American milk-shake, soda pop and ice-cream emporiums – all stainless steel and chromium plate with bar stools and neon-lit pictures of the offerings available (Ugh!). Another symptom of Greek youths unbridled honeymoon with the American dream, as represented by Hollywood films of the 1960s.

**Creperies** These are intruding in the most concentrated package tourist resorts. Compared to the more traditional establishments, they serve very expensive sandwiches, pies and other 'exotica' including thin pancakes or crepes – thus the name.

They are a rather chic, smooth, smart version of their chromium, brightly neon lit 'cousins', the:-

**Fast food joint** A surely unwelcome import, selling ice-creams, hot-dogs and hamburgers. They also display garish, neon lit illustrations of the delights available.

**Pavement cafes** Snacks and sweets.

**Pizzerias** Seem to be on the increase and are, as one would expect, restaurants specialising in the Italian dish. They usually represent very good value and a large serving often feeds two.

**Tavernas** (ΤΑΒΕΡΝΑ), **Restaurants** (ΕΣΤΙΑΤΟΡΙΟΝ), **Rotisserie** (ΨΗΣΤΑΡΙΑ) **& Rural Centres** (ΕΞΟΧΙΚΟΝ ΚΕΝΤΡΟΝ) Four variations on a theme. The traditional Greek taverna is a family concern, frequently only open in the evening. More often than not, the major part of the eating area is outside, sheltered by a vine trellis covered patio, spreading along the pavement and or on a roof garden.

Restaurants tend to be more sophisticated than tavernas, are often open all day, as well as evenings, but the definition between the two is rather blurred. The price lists may include a 'chancy' English translation, the waiter might be smarter and the tablecloth and napkins could well be linen, in place of the taverna's paper table covering and serviettes.

As tavernas often have a spit-roasting device 'tacked' on the side, there is little discernible difference between a rotisserie and a taverna. A grilled meat restaurant may also be styled ΨΗΣΤΑΡΙΑ.

The Rural Centre is a mix of cafe-bar and taverna in, you've guessed it, a rural or seaside setting.

**Fish tavernas** (ΨΑΡΟΤΑΒΕΡΝΑ) Establishments specialising in fish dishes.

**Hotels** (ΞΕΝΟΔΟΧΕΙΟΝ). ΞΕΝΟΔΟΧΕΙΟΝ ΥΠΝΟΥ is a hotel that does not serve food, ΠΑΝΔΟΧΕΙΟΝ is a lower category hotel and ΧΕΝΙΑ, a Government-owned hotel. Xenias are usually well run, the food and drink international, the menu written in French with the prices reflecting all these 'attributes'.

In the more popular holiday resorts, an extremely unpleasant manifestation (to old fogies like me) is the prolification of menus, Greek bills of fare set out Chinese restaurant style. You know, 'Set Meal A' for two, 'Meal B' for three and Meal 'C' for four and more...!

**THE FOOD** A summary of traditional dishes extolled in the past include:-
ΜΠΟΥΡΕΚΑΚΙΑ or *bourekakia*, which are long, thin tubes of battered ham filled with feta cheese and *saganaki*, a very tasty dish of scrambled eggs/omelette, in which are mixed sliced bacon and or sausage, prepared in an olive oil greased 6" pan.

**MEDICAL CARE** As has been pointed out in Chapter One, 'matters medical' require some preplanning. Travellers unfortunate enough to require the services of a doctor, must look out for the sign ΙΑΤΡΕΙΟΝ. This indicates a doctor's clinic or surgery. On larger islands, dialling 100 will, or should, whistle up an ambulance. The sign for a hospital, probably self-evident by its size alone, is ΝΟΣΟΚΟΜΕΙΟ.

The following represents a selection of the wide variety of menu dishes available.

## Sample menu

| | |
|---|---|
| Ψωμί (Psomi) | Bread |
| ΠΡΩΙΝΟ | BREAKFAST |
| Αυγά τηγανιτα με μπέικον και τομάτα | Fried egg. bacon & tomato |
| Τοστ βούτυρο μαρμελάδα | Buttered toast & marmalade |
| Το πρόγευμα (to pro-ye-vma) | English (or American on some islands) breakfast |
| ΑΥΓΑ | EGGS |
| Μελάτα | soft boiled |
| Σφικτά | hard boiled |
| Τηγανιτά | fried |
| Ποσσέ | poached |
| ΤΟΣΤ ΣΑΝΤΟΥΙΤΣ | TOASTED SANDWICHES |
| Τοστ με τυρί | toasted cheese |
| Τοστ (με) ζαμπόν και τυρί | toasted ham & cheese |
| Μπούρκερ | burger |
| Χαμπουρκερ | hamburger |
| Τσίσμπουρκερ | cheeseburger |
| Σάντουιτς λουκάνικο | hot dog |

| ΟΡΕΚΤΙΚΑ | APPETIZERS/HORS D'OEUVRES |
|---|---|
| Αντσούγιες | anchovies |
| Ελιές | olives |
| Σαρδέλλες | sardines |
| Σκορδαλιά | garlic dip |
| Τζατζίκι | tzatziki (diced cucumber & garlic in yoghurt) |
| Ταραμοσαλάτα | taramosalata (a fish roe pate) |

| ΣΟΥΠΕΣ | SOUPS |
|---|---|
| Σούπα φασόλια | bean |
| Αυγολέμονο | egg & lemon |
| Ψαρόσουπα | fish |
| Κοτόσουπα | chicken |
| Ντοματόσουπα | tomato |
| Σούπα λαχανικών | vegetable |

| ΟΜΕΛΕΤΕΣ | OMELETTES |
|---|---|
| Ομελέτα μπέικον | bacon |
| Ομελέτα μπέικον τυρί τομάτα | bacon, cheese & tomato |
| Ομελέτα τυρί | cheese |
| Ομελέτα ζαμπόν | ham |
| Ομελέτα ουκωτάκια πουλιών | chicken liver |

| ΣΑΛΑΤΕΣ | SALADS |
|---|---|
| Ντομάτα Σαλάτα | tomato |
| Αγγούρι Σαλάτα | cucumber |
| Αγγουροτομάτα Σαλάτα | tomato & cucumber |
| Χωριάτικη | Greek peasant/village salad |

| ΛΑΧΑΝΙΚΑ (ΛΑΔΕΡΑ*) | VEGETABLES | |
|---|---|---|
| Πατάτες | potatoes ** | |
| Πατάτες Τηγανιτές | chips (french fries) | |
| φρέσκα φασολάκια | green beans | |
| Υιγαντες | (large) white beans | |
| Σπαράγκια | asparagus | *indicates cooked in oil. |
| Κολοκυθάκια | courgettes or zucchini | **usually served up as chips |
| Σπανάκι | spinach | |

Note various methods of cooking include:
Baked – στο φούρνο; boiled – βραστά; creamed – με ασπρη σαλτσα; fried – τηγανιτα; grilled – στη σχαρα; roasted – ψητά; spit roasted – σούβλας.

| ΚΥΜΑΔΕΣ | MINCED MEATS |
|---|---|
| Μουσακάς | moussaka |
| Ντομάτες Γεμιστές | stuffed tomatoes (with rice or minced meat) |
| Κεφτέδες | meat balls |
| Ντολμαδάκια | stuffed vine leaves (with rice or minced meat) |
| Παπουτσάκια | stuffed vegetable marrow (rice or meat) |
| Κανελόνια | canelloni |
| Μακαπόνια με κυμά | spaghetti bolognese (more correctly with mince) |
| Παστίτσιο | macaroni, mince and sauce |
| Σουβλάκι | shish-kebab |

| ΡΥΖΙ | RICE |
|---|---|
| Πιλάφι | pilaff |
| Πιλάφι (με) γιαούρτι | with yoghurt |
| Πιλάφι συκωτάκια | with liver |
| Σπανακόριζο | with spinach |
| Πιλάφι κυμά | with minced meat |

| ΠΟΥΛΕΡΙΚΑ | POULTRY |
|---|---|
| Κοτόπουλο | chicken, roasted |

| | |
|---|---|
| Πόδι κότας | leg of chicken |
| Στήθος κότας | chicken breast |
| Κοτόπουλο βραστό | boiled chicken |
| Ψητο κοτοπουλο στη σούβλα | spit-roasted chicken |
| **ΚΡΕΑΣ** | **MEAT** |
| Νεφρά | kidneys |
| Αρνï | lamb† |
| Αρνίσιες Μπριζόλες | lamb chops |
| Παιδάκια | lamb cutlets |
| Συκώτι | liver |
| Χοιρινδ | pork† |
| Χοιρινές Μπριζόλες | pork chops |
| Λουκάνικα | sausages |
| Μπιφτέκι | steak (beef) |
| Μοσχαρίσιο | veal |
| Μοσχαρίσιες Μπριζολες | veal chops |
| Μοσχάρι | grilled veal |
| Ψητό Μοσχαράκι | roast veal |

† often with the prefix suffix to indicate if roasted or grilled as above.

| | |
|---|---|
| **ΨΑΡΙΑ** | **FISH** |
| Σκουμπρί | mackerel |
| Συναγριδα | red snapper |
| Μαρίδες | whitebait |
| Οκταπόδι | octopus |
| Καλαμάρια | squid |
| Μπαρμπούνι | red mullet |
| Κέφαλος | mullet |
| Αυθρίνι | grey mullet |
| **ΤΥΡΙΑ** | **CHEESE** |
| Φετα | feta (goat's-milk based) |
| Γραβιέρα | gruyere-type cheese |
| Κασέρι | cheddar-type (sheep's-milk based) |
| **ΦΡΟΥΤΑ** | **FRUITS** |
| Καρπούζι | water melon |
| Πεπόνι | melon |
| Μήλα | apple |
| Πορτοκάλι | oranges |
| Σταφύλια | grapes |
| Κομπόστα φρούτων | fruit compote |
| **ΠΑΓΩΤΑ** | **ICE-CREAM** |
| Σπέσιαλ | special |
| Παγωτό βανίλλια | vanilla |
| Παγωτό σοκολάτα | chocolate |
| Παγωτό λεμονι | lemon |
| Γρανίτα | water ice |
| **ΓΛΥΚΙΣΜΑΤΑ** | **DESSERTS** |
| Κέικ | cake |
| φρουτοσαλάτα | fruit salad |
| Κρέμα | milk pudding |
| Κρεμ καραμελέ | cream caramel |
| Μπακλαβας | crisp pastry with nuts & syrup or honey |
| Καταίφι | fine shredded pastry with nuts & syrup or honey |
| Γαλακτομπούρεκο | fine crispy pastry with custard & syrup |

| Γιαούρτι | yoghurt |
| Μέλι | honey |

**ΑΝΑΨΥΚΤΙΚΑ** — COLD DRINKS/SOFT DRINKS

| Πορτοκάλι | orange |
| Πορτοκαλάδα | orangeade |
| Λεμονάδα | lemonade made with lemon juice |
| Γκαζόζα (Gazoza) | fizzy lemonade |
| Μεταλλικό νερό | mineral water |
| Κόκα κολα | Coca-cola |
| Πέψι κολα | Pepsi-cola |
| Σέβεν-απ | Seven-Up |
| Σόδα | soda |
| Τονικ | tonic |
| Νερό (Nero) | water |

**ΚΑΦΕΔΕΣ** — COFFEES

| Ελληνικός (Καφές) | Greek coffee (sometimes called Turkish coffee ie. Toupkikos Καφε) |
| σκέτο (skehto) | no sugar |
| μετριο (metrio) | medium sweet |
| γλυκό (ghliko) | sweet (very) |

(Unless stipulated it will turn up 'ghliko'. Do not drink Turkish coffee before the grouts have settled.)

| Νες καφέ | Nescafe |
| Νες (με γαλα) (Nes me ghala) | Nescafe with milk |
| Εσπρέσσο | espresso |
| Καπουτσίνο | cappuccino |
| φραπέ | chilled coffee is known as 'frappe' |
| Τσάι | tea |
| Σοκαλάτα γάλα | chocolate milk |

**ΜΠΥΡΕΣ** — BEERS

| ΦΙΞ (ΕΛΛΑΣ) Μπύρα | Fix (Hellas) beer |
| φιάλη | bottle |
| κουτί | can |
| ΑΜΣΤΕΛ (Αμστελ) | Amstel |
| ΧΕΝΝΙΝΓΕΡ (Χέννινγκερ) | Henninger |

(300g usually a can, 500g usually a bottle)

**ΠΟΤΑ** — DRINKS

| Ούζο | Ouzo |
| Κονιάκ | Cognac |
| Μπράντυ | Brandy |
| Μεταξά | Metaxa |
| 3 ΑΣΤ | 3 star |
| 5 ΑΣΤ | 5 star |
| Ουίσκυ | Whisky |
| Τζιν | Gin |
| Βότκα | Vodka |
| Καμπάρι | Campari |
| Βερμούτ | Vermouth |
| Μαρτίνι | Martini |

**ΚΡΑΣΙΑ** — WINES

| Κόκκινο | red |
| Ασπρο | white |
| Ροζε Κοκκινέλι | rose |
| Ξηρό | dry |
| Γλυκό | sweet |

| Ρετσίνα | resinated wine |
| e.g. Θεόκριτος | Theokritos |
| Αρετσίνωτο | unresinated wine |
| e.g. Δεμέστιχα | Demestica |

340g is a ½ bottle, 680g is a bottle, 950g is a large bottle

## Useful Greek

| English | Greek | Sounds like |
| --- | --- | --- |
| Have you a table for... | Εχετε ένα τραπέζι για | Echete enna trapezee ghia... |
| I'd like... | Θέλω | Thelo... |
| We would like... | Θέλουμε | Thelome... |
| a beer | μιά μπύρα | meah beerah |
| a glass | ένα ποτήρι | ena poteeree |
| a carafe | μιά καράφα | meea karafa |
| a small bottle | ένα μικρό μπουκάλι | ena mikro bookalee |
| a large bottle | ένα μεγάλο | ena meghalo bookalee |
| bread | ψωμί | psomee |
| tea with milk | τσάι με γάλα | tsai me ghala |
| with lemon | τσάι με λεμόνι | me lemoni |
| Turkish coffee (Greek) | Τούρκικος καφές | Tourkikos kafes |
| sweet | γλυκός | ghleekos |
| medium | νέτριος | metreeo |
| bitter (no sugar) | πικρό | pikro |
| Black coffee | Nescafe xwpis γάλα | Nescafe horis ghala |
| Coffee with milk | Nescafe με γάλα | Nescafe me ghala |
| a glass of water | ενα ποτήρι νερό | enna poteeree nero |
| a napkin | μιά πετσέτα | mia petseta |
| an ashtray | ένα σταχτοδοχείο | enna stachdothocheeo |
| toothpick | μιά οδοντογλυφίδα | mea odontoglifidha |
| the olive oil | το ελαιόλαδο | dho eleolatho |
| Where is the toilet? | Που είναι η τουαλέττα | Poo eene i(ee) tooaleta? |
| What is this? | Τι είναι αυτό | Ti ine afto |
| This is... | Αυτό είναι | Afto eene |
| cold | κρύο | kreeo |
| bad | χαλασμένο | chalasmeno |
| stale | μπαγιάτικο | bayhiatiko |
| undercooked | άψητο | apseeto |
| overcooked | παραβρασμένο | paravrasmeno |
| The bill please | Το λογαριασμό παρακαλώ | To loghariasmo parakalo |
| How much is that? | Πόσο κάνει αυτό | Poso kanee afto? |
| That was an excellent meal | Περίφημο γέυμα | Pereefimo yevma |
| We shall come again | Θα ξανάρθουμε | Tha xanarthoume |

*'Maybe it's the Grand Union Canal, maybe not'.*

*River Himaros, Potami, Corfu.*

# 7 Shopping & Public Services

*Let your purse be your master. Proverb*

Purchasing items in Greece is still quite an art form or subject for an *Open University* degree course. The difficulties have been compounded by the rest of the western world becoming nations of supermarket shoppers, whilst the Greeks have tended to favour the old-fashioned, traditional shops selling a fixed number of items and sometimes only one type of a product. On the other hand Greece is adopting many of the (retrograde?) consumer habits of its Western European neighbours. Nowadays, in the more cosmopolitan towns, cities and tourist exposed islands, credit cards, including *Visa, Access Mastercharge, Diners* and *American Express*, may well be accepted at tavernas and restaurants as well as by gift/souvenir shops.

The question of good and bad buys is a rather personal matter but the items listed below are highlighted on the basis of value for money and quality. Clothing and accessories that are attractive, and represent good value, include embroidered peasant dresses, leather sandals, woven bags, tapestries and furs. Day-to-day items that are inexpensive take in Greek cigarettes, drinks including *ouzo*, brandy and selected island wines. Suitable gifts for family and friends include ceramic plates, sponges, Turkish delight and worry beads (*komboloe*). Disproportionately expensive items embrace camera film, toiletries, sun oils, books and playing cards. Do not forget to compare prices and preferably shop in the streets and markets, not in airport and hotel concessionary outlets, which are often more expensive.

Try not to run short of small change, everybody else does, including bus conductors, taxi drivers and shops.

**Opening hours** Strict or old-fashioned summer shop hours are:
Mon, Wed & Sat: 0830-1400hrs; Tues, Thurs & Fri: 0830-1330hrs & 1730-2030hrs. Generally, during the summer months, shops in tourist areas are open Mon to Sat, from 0800-1300hrs. They then close for the siesta until 1700hrs, after which they open again until at least 2030hrs, if not 2200hrs. Sundays and Saints' days are more indeterminate, but there is usually a general shop open, somewhere. In very popular tourist resorts and busy ports, many shops open seven days a week.

**Drink** Available in the markets, at delicatessen meat/dairy counters, from 'off licence' type shops or from zacharoplasteions.

**Smokers** Imported French, English and American cigarettes are inexpensive, compared with European prices, at between 150 and 200drs for a packet of twenty. Greek cigarettes, which have a distinctive and different taste, are excellent. Try *Karellia*, which cost 100drs for twenty, and note that the price is printed around the edge of the packet. Even Greek cigars are almost unheard of on the islands, while in Athens they cost 15-25drs each. Dutch cigars work out at 35-50drs each, so, if a cigar smoker, take along your holiday requirements.

**Newspapers & magazines** The *Athens News* is published daily, except Mondays, in English and costs 60drs. Foreign language newspapers are available up to 24 hours after the day of publication and quality English papers cost 200drs.

Note that all printed matter is comparatively expensive.

**Photography (Fotografion – ΦΩΤΟΓΡΑΦΕΙΟΝ)** Photographers should carry all the film possible as, being imported, it is comparatively expensive. For instance, a roll of 35mm, 36 exposure colour film will cost a minimum of 1000drs, but more probably

1200drs. Despite the allure of the instant print shops that have sprung up on the more popular islands, it is probably best to wait until returning home. The quality of reproduction and focus of the development is 'variable'. That is not to say that the back-at-home, 'bucket-print' outfits, whose envelopes fall out of almost every magazine one cares to purchase, are infallible. I had a long drawn-out experience with a Shropshire company who managed to 'foul up' the development of five rolls of film. The problem is that a holiday-maker, who only has two or three films to develop and receives back the complete batch rather blurred, might consider it to be an 'own goal'. It is equally possible that the print company have botched the job.

When using colour film, blue filters should be fitted to the lens to counter the very bright sunlight in the height of summer months.

**Radio** To receive English language, overseas broadcasts, tune to 49m band on the *Short Wave*. In the evening, try the *Medium Wave*. English language news is broadcast by the Greek broadcasting system at 0740hrs on the *Medium Wave* (AM), somewhere between 700-800 Khz.

**Tourist Guides & Maps** Shop around before purchasing either, as the difference in price of the island guides can be as much as 150drs, that is between 350-500drs. Island maps cost from 100-150drs. Some major ports and towns have one authentic, well stocked bookshop, usually positioned a little off the town centre. The proprietor often speaks adequate English and courteously answers most enquiries.

## SHOPS
**Bakers & bread shops** (ΑΡΤΟΠΟΙΕΙΟΝ, ΑΡΤΟΠΩΛΕΙΟΝ or ΠΡΑΤΗΡΙΟΝ ΑΡΤΟΥ) Bread shops, as distinct from bakers, tend to be few and far between. For some obscure reason bakers are nearly always difficult to locate, often being hidden away in or behind other shops. A pointer to their presence may well be a pile of blackened, twisted olive wood, stacked to one side of the entrance, and used to fuel the oven fires. They are almost always closed on Sundays and Saints days, despite which the ovens are often used by the local community to cook their Sunday dinners. Both bakers and bread shops may also sell cheese and meat pies. The method of purchasing bread can prove disconcerting, especially when sold by weight. Sometimes the purchaser selects the loaf and then pays but the most bewildering system is where it is necessary to pay first then collect the goods. Difficult if the shopper's level of Greek is limited to grunts, 'thank you' and 'please'! Greek bread has another parameter of measure other than weight, that is a graduation in hours – 1 hour bread, 4 hour bread and so on. After the period is up, the loaf is usually completely inedible, having transmogrified into a rock-like substance.

**Butcher** (ΚΡΕΟΠΩΛΕΙΟΝ) Similar to those at home, but the cuts are quite different (surely the Common Market can legislate against this deviation!).

**Galaktopoleio** *et al.* Cake shops (*Zacharoplasteion*) may sell bottled mineral water (ask for a cold bottle). *See* **Chapter Six**.

**Markets** The smaller ports and towns may have a market street and the larger municipalities often possess a market building. These are thronged with locals and all the basic necessities can be procured relatively inexpensively. Fruit and vegetable stalls are interspersed by butchers and dairy/delicatessen shops. During business hours, the proprietors are brought coffee and a glass of water by waiters from nearby cafes. The cups and glasses are carried, not on open trays but in round, aluminium salvers with a deep lid, held under a large ring handle, connected to the tray by three flat arms.

**Mini-Market** The nomenclature usually indicates a well stocked store in a small building.

**Supermarkets** (ΥΠΕΡΑΓΟΡΑ/ΣΟΥΠΕΡΜΑΡΚΕΤ) Very much on the increase and based on small town, self-service stores but not to worry, they inherit all those delightful, inherent Greek qualities, including quiet chaos. It has to be admitted, every so often, one does come across a 'real supermarket', recognisable by the check-out counters. Fortunately they no more than imitate their Western European equivalents, remaining 'organised' shambles.

**Speciality shops** Chanced upon in some big towns and Athens, whilst pavement browsing. Usually little basement shops which can be espied down steep flights of steps and specialising, for instance, in dried fruit, beans, nuts and grains.

**Street Kiosks (Periptero/ΠΕΡΙΠΤΕΡΟ)** These unique, pagoda-like huts stay open remarkably long hours, often from early morning to well after midnight. They sell a wide range of goods including newspapers, magazines (sometimes, surprisingly, in the larger cities, pornographic literature), postcards, tourist maps, postage stamps, sweets, chocolates, cigarettes and matches. Ownership is often a family affair – vested as a form of Government patronage and handed out to deserving citizens. Additionally they form the outlet for the pay phone system and, at the cost of 5drs, a local call may be made. It is rather incongruous, to observe a Greek making a possible important business call, in amongst a rack of papers and magazines, with a foreground of jostling pedestrians and a constant stream of noisy traffic in the background.

**Alternate ways of shopping** Then there are the other ways of shopping: from handcarts, their street-vendor owners selling, respectively, nuts, ice-cream, milk and yoghurt; from the 'back' of a donkey loaded down with vegetable-laden panniers or from two wheeled trailers drawn by fearsome sounding, agricultural rotovator power units. Often the donkey or trailer has an enormous set of scales mounted on the back end, swinging like a hangman's scaffold. If the vegetable/fruit is being sold by 'gypsy-types', then it is advisable to only purchase from those who have their prices on display, usually on a piece of cardboard. Even locals admit to being 'ripped off' by roadside merchants and these free market entrepreneurs are often prosecuted for breaking the law.

Frequently used shops include:
ΒΙΒΛΙΟΠΩΛΕΙΟΝ – bookshop; ΚΡΕΟΠΩΛΕΙΟΝ – butcher; ΙΧΘΥΟΠΩΛΕΙΟΝ – fishmonger; ΟΠΩΡΟΠΩΛΕΙΟΝ – greengrocer; ΠΑΝΤΟΠΩΛΕΙΟΝ – grocer; ΚΟΥΡΕΙΟΝ – hairdresser; ΚΑΠΝΟΠΩΛΕΙΟΝ – tobacconist. Readers may observe the above all have a similar ending and it is worth noting that shop titles which terminate in 'ΠΩΛΕΙΟΝ/πωλειον' are selling something, if that's any help!

## SERVICES
**The Banks (ΤΡΑΠΕΖΑ) & money** The minimum opening hours are 0800-1330hrs Mon-Thurs and 0800-1300hrs on Friday. Some banks, in the most tourist ravaged spots, open for exchange transactions in the evenings and or even on Saturdays. Some smaller towns, villages or, for that matter, islands do not have a bank. Where this is the case there may be a local money changer acting as agent for this or that country-wide bank but, if not, the Post Office has increasingly become an option (*See* **Post Offices**). Do not forget that a passport is almost always required to change travellers' cheques. In the larger cities, personal cheques may be changed at selected banks when backed by a *Eurocheque* (or similar) bank guarantee card. A commission of between $\frac{1}{4}-1\frac{1}{2}$% is charged on all transactions, depending upon I know not what! Whereas Eurocheques used to be changed in sums of no more than £50 (English sterling), the arrangement now is that a cheque is cashed in drachmae, up to a total of 25,000drs. As the charges for changing cheques are based on a sliding scale, weighted against smaller amounts, this new arrangement helps save on fees.

Generally the service varies from absent minded inattention, curt discourtesy to downright rudeness. Averagely only one employee, if at all, reluctantly speaks English. Ensure the correct bank is selected to carry out a particular transaction (such as changing a personal cheque), a task made easier by their displaying a window sticker indicating which tourist services are transacted. There is nothing worse, after queuing for half an hour or so, than to be rudely told to go away. I once selected the wrong bank to carry out some banking function, only to receive a loud blast of abuse, that followed me through the swing doors, about a long-departed foreigner's bouncing cheque. Most embarrassing.

Change offices cash travellers cheques, as do the larger hotels, but at a disadvantageous rate compared to the banks. For instance, the commission charged may be 2%, or up to double that charged by the banks. Ouch! *See* **Post Office** for another interesting and less expensive alternative.

The basis of Greek currency is the drachma. This is nominally divided into 100 lepta and occasionally menus still show a price of, say, 62.60drs. As prices are rounded up (or down) and devaluation has considerably reduced the value of one drachma, in practice, the lepta is never encountered. Notes are in denominations of 50, 100, 500 and 1000drs and coins in denominations of 1 and 2drs (bronze), 5, 10, 20drs (nickel), and 50drs (goldy bronze). Do not run out of change, it is always in demand. Repetitious I know, but well worth remembering.

**Museums** The following is a mean average of the information available, but each museum is likely to have its own peculiarities. In the summer season (1st April-31st Oct) they usually open daily 0845-1500/1900hrs, Sun & holidays 0930-1430/1530hrs and are closed Mon or Tues. They do not open for business on 1st Jan, 25th March, Good Friday, Easter holiday and 25th Dec. Admission costs range from nothing to 100/250drs, whilst Sundays and holidays are sometimes free.

**Post Offices** (ΤΑΧΥΔΡΟΜΕΙΟΝ/ΕΛΤΑ) Stamps can be bought from kiosks (plus a small commission) and shops selling postcards as well as from Post Offices. In 1988 postage rates for cards to the United Kingdom were up to 60drs for a postcard. Post boxes are scattered around, are usually painted yellow, are rather small in size and often difficult to find, being fixed, high up, on side-street walls. When confronted by two letter-box openings, the inland service is marked ΕΣΩΤΕΡΙΚΟΥ/*Εσωτερικου* and the overseas ΕΞΩΤΕΡΙΚΟΥ/*Εξωτερικου*.

Most major town Post Offices are modern and the counter staff's attitude is only slightly less rude than that 'handed out' by bank employees. They are usually open Mon-Fri between 0730-2030hrs for stamps, money orders and registered mail; 0730-2000hrs for poste restante and 0730-1430hrs for parcels, which have to be collected. Letters sent poste restante will require sight of a passport for them to be handed over.

In recent years the range of Post Office services has been expanded to include cashing Eurocheques and Travellers Cheques, in addition to currency exchange. All but the most out-of-the-way island offices now offer these facilities. This can prove very useful knowledge, especially on busy tourist islands where the foreign currency desks of the banks are usually subject to long queues. More importantly the commission charged can be up to half that of the banks. Another interesting source of taking currency abroad, for United Kingdom residents, is to use *National Giro Post Office* cheques, which can be cashed at any Post Office in Greece. Detailed arrangements have to be made with the international branch of Giro.

**Telephone Office (OTE)** A separate organisation from the Post Office. One way to make an overseas or long-distance telephone call is to proceed to the OTE office. Here are a number of booths and the counter clerk indicates which compartment is to be used. Alongside him are mounted the instruments to meter the cost. Ensure that the meter is zeroed prior to making a connection. Long queues often form at offices in busy locations. Payment is made after completion of the call, at a current rate of 7drs per unit. Opening days and hours vary enormously. Smaller offices may only open weekdays for say 7 hours between 0830-1530hrs, whilst some of the larger city offices are open 24 hours a day, seven days a week.

As the Greek telephone system improves there is an increase in the number of kafeneions and tavernas, which possess a metered telephone, from which overseas calls can be made.

**Overseas dialling codes**

| | |
|---|---|
| Australia | 0061 |
| Canada & USA | 001 |
| New Zealand | 0064 |
| South Africa | 0027 |
| United Kingdom & Ireland | 0044 |
| Other overseas countries | 161 |

**Inland services**

| | |
|---|---|
| Directory enquiries | 131 |
| Provincial enquiries | 132 |
| General information | 134 |
| Time | 141 |
| Medical care | 166 |
| City police | 100 |
| Gendarmerie | 109 |
| Fire | 199 |
| Tourist police | 171 |
| Roadside assistance | 104 |
| Telegrams/cables | 165 |

To dial England, drop the '0' from all four figure codes. Thus to make a call to, say, Portsmouth, for which the code is 0705, dial 00 44 705 ...

The internal service is both very good and reasonably priced. Local telephone calls can be made from some bars and the pavement kiosks (periptero) and cost 5drs, which is the 'standard' coin. Some phones take 10 and 20drs coins. The presence of a telephone is often indicated by the sign ΕΔΩΤΗΛΕΦΩΝΕΙΤΕ, a blue background denoting a local phone, and an orange one an inter-city phone. Another sign, Εδω Τηλεφωνειτε (the lower case equivalent), signifies 'telephone from here'. The method of operation is to insert the coin and dial. If a connection cannot be made, on placing the receiver back on the cradle, the money is returned.

Telegrams may be sent from either the OTE or Post Office.

## Useful Greek

| English | Greek |
|---|---|
| Stamps | ΓΡΑΜΜΑΤΟΣΗΜΑ |
| Parcels | ΔΕΜΑΤΑ |

| English | Greek | Sounds like |
|---|---|---|
| Where is... | Που είναι | Poo eenne... |
| Where is the nearest... | Που είναι η πλησιέστερη | Poo eenne i pleesiesteri |
| baker | ο φούρναρης/ψωμας | foornaris/psomas |
| bakery | Αρτοποιείον | artopieeon |
| bank | η τράπεζα | i(ee) trapeza |
| bookshop | το βιβλιοπωλείο | to vivleeopolieo |
| butchers shop | το χασάπικο | dho hasapiko |
| chemist shop | το φαρμακείο | to farmakio |
| dairy shop | το γαλακτοπωλείο | galaktopolieon |
| doctor | ο γιατρός | o yiahtros |
| grocer | το μπακάλης | o bakalis |
| hospital | το νοσοκομείο | to nosokomio |
| laundry | το πλυντήριο | to plintirio, (plintireeo, since i = ee) |

| liquor store | το ποτοπωλείο | to potopolio (potopoleeo) |
| photographic shop | το φωτογραφείο | to fotoghrafeeo |
| post office | το ταχυδρομείο | to tahkithromio |
| shoe repairer | το τσαγκαράδικο | to tsangkaradiko |
| tailor | ο ραπτης | o raptis |
| Have you any... | Εχετε | Ekheteh... |
| Do you sell... | Πουλάτε | Poulate... |
| How much is this... | Πόσο κάνει αυτό | Posso kanee afto... |
| I want... | Θέλω | Thelo... |
| half kilo/a kilo | μισό κιλό/ένα κιλό | miso kilo/ena kilo |
| aspirin | η ασπιρίνη | aspirini |
| apple(s) | το μήλο/μήλα | meelo/meela |
| banana(s) | η μπανάνα/μπανάνες | banana/bananes |
| bread | το ψωμί | psomee |
| butter | το βούτυρο | vutiro |
| cheese | το τυρί | tıree |
| cigarettes (filter tip) | το τσιγάρο (με φίλτρο) | to tsigharo (me filtro) |
| coffee | καφές | cafes |
| cotton wool | το βαμβακι | to vambaki |
| crackers | τα κρακεράκια | krackerakia |
| crisps | τσιπς | tsseeps |
| cucumbers | το αγγούρι | anguree |
| disinfectant | το απολυμαντικό | to apolimantiko |
| guide book | ο τουριστικός οδηγός | o touristikos odhigos |
| ham | το ζαμπόν | zambon |
| ice-cream | το παγωτό | paghoto |
| lemons | το λεμόνια | lemonia |
| lettuce | το μαρούλι | to marooli |
| map | το χάρτης | o khartis |
| a box of matches | ενα κουτί σπίρτα | ena kuti spirta |
| milk | το γάλα | to ghala |
| pate | πατέ | pate |
| (ball point) pen | το μπικ | to bik |
| pencil | το μολύβι | to molivi |
| pepper | το πιπέρι | to piperi |
| (safety) pins | μια παραμάνα | mia (meea) paramana |
| potatoes | οι πατάτες | patates |
| salad | η σαλάτα | i salatah |
| salami | το σαλάμι | salahmi |
| sausages | το λουκάνικα | lukahniko |
| soap | το σαπούνι | to sapooni |
| spaghetti | σπαγγέτο | spayehto |
| string | ο σπαγκος | o spangos |
| sugar | η ζάχαρη | i zakhahree |
| tea | το τσάι | to tsai |
| tomatoes | η ντομάτες | domahdes |
| toothbrush | η οδοντόβουρτσα | odhondovourtsa |
| toothpaste | η οδοντόκρεμα | odhondokrema |
| writing paper | το χαρτι γραψίματος | to kharti grapsimatos |

# 8 Greece: History, Mythology, Religion, Present-day Greece, Greeks, Animals & National Holidays

---

*All ancient histories, as one of our fine wits said, are but fables that have been accepted. Voltaire*

**HISTORY** Excavations have shown the presence of Palaeolithic man up to 100,000 years ago. Greece's history and mythology are, like the Greek language, formidable to say the least, with legend, myth, folk tales, fables and religious lore often inextricably mixed. Interestingly archaeologists have increasingly established that at least some mythology is based on ancient facts.

Historically Greeks fought Greeks, Phoenicians and Persians. With Alexander the Great at the helm they conquered Egypt and vast tracts of Asia Minor. Then they were in turn conquered by the Romans. After the splitting of the Roman Kingdom into Western and Eastern Empires, the Greeks, with Constantinople as their capital, were ruled by the Eastern offshoot. They then fell into the hands of the Franks, about AD 1200, who were followed by the Turks. During this latter period the Venetians, Genoese and, finally, the Turks ruled most of the islands.

In 1821 the War of Independence commenced, which eventually led to the setting up of a Parliamentary Republic in 1829. Incidentally, Thessaly, Epirus, Macedonia, Thrace, the North East Aegean islands, Crete and the Dodecanese islands remained under Turkish rule. By the time the Dodecanese islanders had thrown out the Turks, the Italians had taken over. If you are now confused, give up, because it gets even more difficult to follow.

The Greek monarchy, which had come into being in 1833 and was related to the German Royal family, opted, in 1913, to side with the Axis powers. The chief politician Eleftherios Venizelos, disagreed, was dismissed and set up a rival government, after which the King, under Allied pressure, retired to Switzerland. In the years following the end of the First World War the Turks and Greeks agreed, after some fairly bloody fighting, to exchange a total of one and a half million people.

In 1936 a General Metaxas became dictator and achieved immortal fame by booting out Mussolini's representative. This came about when, in 1940, Mussolini demanded permission for Italy's troops to traverse Greece and received the famous *Ochi* (No). This day became a national festival known as *Ochi Day*, celebrated on 28th October. The Italians demurred and marched on Greece, the soldiers of whom, to the surprise of everybody, including themselves, reinforced the refusal by routing the invaders. The Italians were only saved from total humiliation by the intervention of the Germans, who then occupied Greece for the duration of the Second World War. At the end of hostilities, all the Italian held Greek islands were reunited with mainland Greece. As the wartime German ascendancy declined, the Greek freedom fighters split into royalist and communist factions and proceeded, in the first civil war, to knock even more stuffing out of each other than they had out of the Germans. Until British intervention, followed by large injections of American money and weapons, it looked as if Greece would go behind the Iron Curtain. A second civil war broke out between 1947 and 1949 and these two internal conflicts were reputed to have cost more Greek lives than were lost during the whole of the Second World War.

In 1951, both Greece and Turkey became full members of NATO, but the issue of the ex-British colony of Cyprus was to rear its ugly head, with the resultant, renewed estrangement between Greece and Turkey. The various political manoeuvrings, the involvement of the Greek monarchy in domestic affairs and the worsening situation in Cyprus, led to the *coup d'etat* by the *Colonel's Junta*, in 1967, soon after which King Constantine II and his entourage fled to Italy. The extremely repressive dictatorship of the Junta was apparently actively supported by the Americans and condoned by Britain. Popular country-wide feeling and, in particular, student uprisings between 1973-1974, which were initially put down in Athens by brutal tank attacks, led to the eventual collapse of the regime in 1974. In the death-throes of their rule, the Colonels, using the Cyprus dream to distract the ordinary people's feeling of injustice, meddled and attempted to overthrow the vexatious priest, President Makarios. The net result was that the Turks invaded Cyprus and made an enforced division of that unhappy, troubled island.

In 1974, Greece returned to republican democracy and in 1981 joined the EEC (God help them). Greek elections are an eye-opener to citizens of other European countries, being accompanied by a certain amount of violence and dynamite throwing.

**RELIGION** The Orthodox Church prevails everywhere but there are small pockets of Roman Catholicism, as well as very minor enclaves of Muslims on the Dodecanese islands and mainland, western Thrace. The schism within the Holy Roman Empire, in 1054, caused the Catholic Church to be centred on Rome and the Orthodox Church on Constantinople. The Turkish overlords encouraged the continuation of the indigenous church, probably to keep their bondsmen quiet, but it had the invaluable side effect of keeping alive Greek customs and traditions during the centuries of occupation. This nationalism was fostered by the inmates of the various religious orders operating *Krifo Scholio*. These were illegal, undercover schools at which the local children were introduced to the intricacies of the Greek religion and way of life.

The bewildering profusion of small churches, scattered 'indiscriminately' throughout the countryside, is not proof of the church's wealth, although the Greek people are not entirely convinced of that fact! It is, in fact, evidence of the piety of the families or individuals who paid to have them erected, in the name of their selected patron saint, as thanksgiving for God's protection. The style of religious architecture changes between the island groups. Many churches only have one service a year, on the name day of the particular patron saint, and this ceremony is named *Viorti* or *Panayieri*. It is well worth attending one of these self-indulgent extravaganzas to observe and take part in celebratory village religious life and music. One and all are welcome to the carnival festivities, which include eating and dancing in, or adjacent to, the particular churchyard.

The words *Byzantine* and *Byzantium* crop up frequently, with especial reference to churches and appertain to the period between the fourth and fourteenth centuries AD. During this epoch Greece was, at least nominally, under the control of Constantinople (Istanbul), built by the Emperor Constantine on the site of the old city of Byzantium. Religious paintings executed on small wooden panels during this period are called *Icons*. Very, very few original icons remain available for purchase, so beware if offered an apparent 'bargain'. Icons usually depict a holy person or personages. If legends and folklore are to be believed, during the Middle Ages the Mediterranean would appear to have been almost awash with unmanned rowing boats and caiques, mysteriously ferrying icons hither and thither.

Inside the churches, the altar area is separated from the worshippers by a 'screen' of timber or stonework, usually honeycombed by a number of doors, varying from the very simple to the most ornately carved and fretworked constructions. Especially noticeable are the pieces of shining, thin metal placed haphazardly around or pinned to wooden carvings. These *tamata* or *exvotos* represent limbs or portions of the human body and are purchased by worshippers as an offering, in the hope of an illness being cured and or limbs healed.

Male and female visitors to all and every religious building must be properly clothed. Men should wear trousers and a shirt. Ladies clothing ought to include a skirt, or if unavoidable trousers, a blouse and, if possible, a headscarf. Many monasteries simply will not allow entrance to scantily or 'undressed' people. With that marvellous duality of standards the Greeks evince, there is quite often a brisk 'clothes hire' business transacted on the very entrance steps, but it is not wise to rely on this arrangement being in force.

**GREEKS** In making an assessment of the Greek people and their character, it must be remembered that, perhaps even more so than the Spaniards or the Portuguese, Greece has only recently emerged into the twentieth century. Unlike other countries 'discovered' in the 1960s by the holiday industry, they have not, except in the most tourist swamped islands, degraded or debased their principles or character, despite the onrush of tourist wealth. For a people to have had so little and to face so much demand for European 'necessities', would have subverted the character of a less right-minded and sober people.

The country's recent emergence into the western world is evidenced by the still patriarchal nature of their society, a view supported, for instance, by the oft-seen spectacle of men lazing in the kafeneion whilst their womenfolk work in the fields (and why not?).

More often than not, even the smallest village, on the remotest island, manifests an English-speaking islander who has lived abroad at some time in his life, earning a living through seafaring, as a hotel waiter or as a taxi driver. Thus, while making an escape from the comparative poverty at home, for a period of good earnings in the more lucrative world, a working knowledge of English, American or Australian will have been gained. 'Greek strine' (used to describe the sounds of a Greek with the overtones of an Australian accent) or, as usually contracted, 'grine', simply has to be heard to be believed.

The greatest hurdle to comprehending the national character is undoubtedly the language barrier, a difficulty compounded by Greek often seeming unable to communicate with fellow Greek! Certainly, on occasions, they appear not to understand each other and the subject matter has to be repeated a number of times. Perhaps that is the reason for all that shouting!

There can be no doubt that the traditional Greek welcome to the *Xenos* or *Singrafeus*, now increasingly becoming known as *Touristas*, has become rather lukewarm in the more 'besieged' areas. It is often difficult to reconcile the shrugged shoulders of a seemingly disinterested airline official or bus driver, with being stopped in the street by a gold-toothed, smiling Greek proffering some fruit. But remember, the bus driver has probably weighed the difficulty of overcoming the language barrier, may be very hot, has been working long hours earning a living and is not on holiday. Sometimes a drink appears, mysteriously, at one's taverna table, the donor being indicated by a nod of the waiter's head, but a word of warning here. Simply smile and accept the gift graciously. Any attempt to return the kindness, by 'putting one in the stable' for your new-found friend, only results in a 'who buys last' competition, which will surely be lost. I know, I am speaking from 'battle-weary' experience. Whilst Greeks are very welcoming, and may invite a tourist to their table, do not expect more. They are reserved and have probably had previous, unhappy experiences of ungrateful, rude, overseas visitors.

Women tourists can travel quite freely in Greece without fear except, perhaps, from other tourists. On the other hand, females should not wear provocative attire or fail to wear sufficient clothing. This is especially so when in close social contact with Greek men, who might well be inflamed into 'action', or Greek women, whom it will offend, probably because of the effect on their men! Certainly all the above was the case, until very recently, but the constant stream of 'available', young tourist ladies on the more popular islands has resulted in the local lads taking both a 'view' and a chance. It almost reminds one of the *Costa Brava* in the early 1960s. The disparate moral qualities of the native and tourist females has resulted in a conundrum for young Greek women. To compete for their men's affections they have to loosen their principles (and more!) with a previously unheard of and steadily increasing number of speedily arranged marriages, if you know what I mean.

Do not miss the summer's evening *Volta* (Βολγα), the still traditional, family 'walkabout' on the square of any large settlement. Dressed for the event, an important part of the ritual is to show off the marriageable daughters. Good fun and great watching, but the Greeks are rather protective of their family and all things Greek... It is acceptable to comment favourably, but adverse criticism and familiarity should be kept to oneself.

It is interesting to speculate on the influence of the Greek immigrants on American culture. To justify this hypothesis consider the American habit of serving water with every meal, the ubiquitous hamburger (which is surely a poorly reproduced and inferior souvlaki pita – now being re-imported) and some of the official uniforms, more particularly the flat, peaked hats of American postmen and policemen.

**ANIMALS** After a letter from the worthy *Greek Animal Welfare Fund* requesting me to mention their cause, I decided not only to so do, but to air the subject from a personal viewpoint. First things first. The Fund represents all that is best in the English. (I can write this with little self-congratulatory feelings, as it is the viewpoint of an author with a mixed Celtic parentage of Southern Irish, one generation removed, and Welsh. That explains it!) The UK based society seeks to prevent cruelty to animals in Greece and I wish them every success. They deserve all animal lovers support. But, and here we come to my caveat, readers must carefully think through any instant reaction to the sight of animals subjected to inhumanity. I quickly lost count of the number of times that I had to 'mind my own business' when observing this or that particular example of cruelty and or neglect. On the other hand it is worth considering that until, say, thirty years ago, many, many Greeks lived in conditions of such poverty and deprivation that, were they to have been animals, it would have caused outcries of indignation from their Western neighbours. Another rejoinder is that the Greeks don't regard animals as having any soul, so mistreatment simply doesn't matter! I am not condoning the state of affairs but, prior to leaping up and down and berating a particular person, ponder that they regard children as sacrosanct. They find the type of sickening child abuse cases, it is impossible not to read about every day of the week in the serious British newspapers, as incomprehensible. Quite.

**THE GREEK NATIONAL HOLIDAYS** Listed below are the national holidays and on these days many areas and islands hold festivals, usually with a particular slant and emphasis.

| | |
|---|---|
| 1st January | New Year's Day/The Feast of Saint Basil |
| 6th January | Epiphany/Blessing of the Waters – a cross is immersed in the sea, lake or river during a religious ceremony. |
| The period 27th Jan to 17th February | The Greek Carnival Season |
| 25th March | The Greek National Anniversary/Independence Day |
| April – movable days | Good Friday/Procession of the 'Epitaph'; Holy Week Saturday/Ceremony of the Resurrection; Easter Sunday/open air feasts |
| 1st May | May/Labour Day/Feast of the Flowers |
| 1st to 10th July | Greek Navy Week |
| 15th August | Assumption Day/Festival of the Virgin Mary, especially in the Cycladian island of Tinos (beware travelling at this time, anywhere in the area) |
| 28th October | National Holiday/'Ochi' Day |
| 24th December | Christmas Eve/Carols Evening |
| 25th December | Christmas Day |
| 26th December | St Stephen's Day |
| 31st December | New Year's Eve carols, festivals |

In addition to these national days, each island has its own particular festivals and holidays which are listed individually under each island.

A word of warning to ferry-boat travellers will not go amiss here – DO NOT travel to an island immediately prior to one of these festivals, NOR off the island immediately after the event. It will be almost impossible to do other than stand, that is if one has not already been trampled to death in the various stampedes to and from the ferry-boats.

**Even more useful names & addresses**
Greek Animal Welfare Fund 11 Lower Barn Road, Purley, Surrey, CR2 1HY          Tel (01) 668 0548

*'I know how he feels'.*
*An excursion boat in the shade of the FB Kamelia, Gaios Port, Paxos.*

# ATHENS CITY MAP

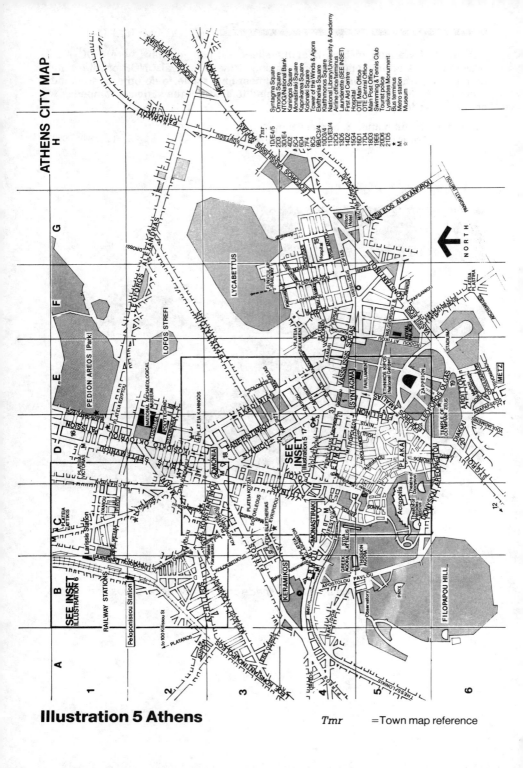

| | | Tmr |
|---|---|---|
| Syntagma Square | | 1D/E4/5 |
| Omonia Square | | 2O3 |
| NTOG/National Bank | | 3D/E4 |
| Monastiraki Square | | 4O2 |
| Kaningos Square | | 5C4 |
| Kolonaki Square | | 6D4 |
| Klafthmonos Square | | 7F4 |
| Tower of the Winds & Agora | | 8C5 |
| Eleftherias Square | | 9B/C3/4 |
| Klafthmonos Square | | 10D3/4 |
| National Library/University & Academy | | 11D/E3/4 |
| Airline Office/Terminus | | 11A |
| Launderette (SEE INSET) | | 13D5 |
| Hospital | | 14D2 |
| First Aid Centre | | 15G4 |
| OTE Main Office | | 16D1 |
| OTE Central Office | | 17D4 |
| Main Post Office | | 18O3 |
| Swimming & Tennis Club | | 19E6 |
| Lysikrates Monument | | 20D6 |
| Bus terminus | | 21D5 |
| Tourist police | | ★ |
| Metro station | | M |
| Museum | | ☆ |

NORTH

**Illustration 5 Athens**

*Tmr*   = Town map reference

# PART TWO

# 9 ATHENS CITY (ATHINA, AΘHNAI)

*There is no end of it in this city, wherever you set your foot, you encounter some memory of the past.*
*Marcus Cicero*

Tel prefix 01. The capital of Greece and major city of Attica (Illustrations 5, 6 & 7).

Previously the pivotal point for travel to most of the Greek islands (with Piraeus Port the springboard), but less so since a number of flights have become available direct to the larger islands. Experienced travellers flying into Athens airport, often try to arrange their arrival for early morning and head straight to either the West airport (for a domestic flight), Piraeus Port (*See* **Chapter Ten**), the railway station or bus terminal, so as to be able to get under way immediately.

**ARRIVAL BY AIR** International flights other than *Olympic Airways* land at the:

**East Airport** The terminal building facilities include not only the usual snackbar and toilets, but several bank counters and an NTOG (Greek Tourist Board) counter. Public transport available includes:

| | |
|---|---|
| Bus No. 18: | East Airport to Leoforos Amalias, almost as far as Syntagma Square(Sq). Going to the airport the bus stop is on the right (*Syntagma Sq. behind one*), just beyond the East Airport Olympic bus stop. Run say, every 20 mins from 0600-2400hrs and after midnight every hour on the half hour i.e. 0030, 0130, 0230hrs. Fare 120drs. Yellow express bus.* |
| Bus No. 121: | East Airport to Leoforos Olgas. Runs every 30 mins between 0630-2250hrs. Fare 120drs. |
| Bus No. 19: | East Airport to Plateia Karaiskaki/Akti Tselepi, Piraeus. Every hour from 0800-2000hrs. Fare 120drs. Yellow express bus.* |
| Bus No. 101: | East Airport via Leoforos Possidonos (coast road) to Klisovis/Theotoki St, Piraeus. Every 20 mins from 0500-2245hrs. Fare 50drs. |

* At the airport, don't jump for the bus without obtaining tickets first from the office adjacent to the bus terminus.

One correspondent advised that, for those not wanting to trek into Athens centre, it is worth considering staying in a hotel close by the airport. One drawback is the proximity of the flight-path. A recommended hotel that is a short distance away and not in a direct line with the runway is the:-

**Hotel Avra** (Class C) 3 Nireos, Paleon Faliro                    Tel 981 4064
*Directions*: Proceed north (in the direction of Piraeus) along the coastal avenue of Leoforos Vas. Georgiou B, which at Paleon Faliro becomes Leoforos Possidonos. A No. 101 bus travels the route. Proceed past the Marina to the area where the road cuts inland from the coastline, an overall distance of some 6km. Nireos St is a branch off the Esplanade Road.

The Avra is close to a beach and not outrageously expensive, in comparison to many other Athens and Piraeus hotels. Singles, sharing the bathroom, start at 1460drs & en suite 2060drs, while a double en suite costs 2600drs. These prices rise to 1760, 2480 & 3100drs respectively (1st June-31st Oct). Breakfast costs an extra 240drs.

Domestic and all Olympic flights land at the:

**West Airport** Public transport available includes:

| | |
|---|---|
| Bus No. 133: | West Airport to Leoforos Sq, Leoforos Amalias, Filellinon & Othonos Sts (Syntagma Sq). Runs every ½ hour from 0530-0030hrs. Fare 50drs. Blue bus. |
| Bus No. 122 | West Airport to Leoforos Olgas. Every 20mins between 0600-2300hrs. Fare 50drs. Blue bus. |
| Buses No. 107 & 109: | West Airport via Leoforos Possidonos (coast road) to Klisovis St, Piraeus. |

In addition there are Olympic buses connecting West and East Airports as well as Olympic buses from the West Airport to the Olympic offices (*Tmr* 12C5), on Leoforos Sygrou, and Syntagma Sq. This latter runs every 20 mins between 0600-2000hrs. Fare 100drs.

**ARRIVAL BY BUS** Inter-country coaches usually decant passengers at Syntagma Sq (*Tmr* 1D/E4/5), Stathmos Larissis Railway Station (*Tmr* B/C1) or close to one of the major city bus terminals.

**ARRIVAL BY FERRY** *See* **Chapter Ten**.

**ARRIVAL BY TRAIN** *See* **Trains, A To Z**.

**GENERAL (Illustrations 5 & 6)** Even if a traveller is a European city dweller, Athens will come as a sociological and cultural shock to the system. In the summer it is a hot, dusty, dry, crowded, traffic bound, exhaust polluted bedlam, but always friendly, cosmopolitan and ever on the move.

On arrival in Athens, and planning to stay over, it is best to seek out the two main squares of Syntagma (*Tmr* 1D/E4/5) and Omonia (*Tmr* 2/D3). These can then be used as centres for the initial sally and from which to radiate out to the other streets and squares.

There is no substitute for a city map which is issued free (yes, free) from the Tourist Office desk in the National Bank of Greece on Syntagma Sq (*Tmr* 3/D/E4). *See* **NTOG, A To Z**.

**Syntagama Square (Constitution or Parliament Sq)** (*Tmr* 1D/E4/5) Many of the city buses, as well as airport bus connections, stop here or hereabouts. It is the city centre with the most elite hotels, airline offices, international companies, including the *American Express* headquarters, smart cafes and the Parliament building, all circumscribing the central, sunken square. In the bottom, right-hand (or south-east) corner of the plateia, bounded by Odhos Othonos and Leoforos Amalias, are some very clean, attendant-minded toilets. There is a charge for the use of these 'squatties'.

To orientate, the *Parliament* building and *Monument to the Unknown Warrior* lie to the east of the square. To the north-east, in the middle distance, is one of the twin hills of Athens, *Mt Lycabettus (Lykavittos, Lykabettos* & etc, etc). The other hill is the *Acropolis*, to the south-west, and not now visible from Syntagma Sq due to high-rise buildings. On the west side of the square are the offices of *American Express* and a battery of pavement cafes, with Ermou St leading due west to Monastiraki Sq. To the north are the two parallel, main avenues of Stadiou (a one-way street down to Syntagma) and Venizelou or Panepistimiou (a one-way street out of Syntagma) that run north-west to:

**Omonia Square (Concorde or Harmony Sq)** (*Tmr* 2D3) The 'Piccadilly Circus' or 'Times Square' of Athens, but rather tatty really, with a constant stream of traffic bludgeoning its way round the large central island which is crowned by an impressive fountain. Visitors trying to escape the human bustle on the pavements, by stepping off into the kerbside, should beware that they are not mown down by a bus, taxi or car.

There is constant activity night and day and the racial admixture of people, cheek by jowl, lends the square a cosmopolitan character all of its own. On every side are hotels. These vary from the downright seedy to the better-class tawdry, housed in rather undistinguished, 'neo-city-municipal' style, nineteenth century buildings, almost unique to Athens.

Various Metro train entrance/exits emerge around the square, spewing out and sucking in travellers. The Omonia underground concourse has a Post Office, telephones, a bank and, by the Dorou St entrance, a block of 'squatty' toilets, for which the attendant charges 10drs for two sheets of paper.

Shops, cafes and booths fill the gaps between the hotels and the eight streets that converge on the Square. To the north-east side of Omonia, on the corner of Dorou St, is a taxi rank and beyond, on the right, a now rather squalid, covered arcade brimful of reasonably priced snackbars. Through this covered passageway, and turning to the left along 28 Ikosiokto Oktovriou (28th October St)/Patission St, and then right down Veranzerou St, leads to:

**Kaningos Square** (*Tmr* 4D2) Serves as a bus terminal for some routes.

To the south of Omnia Sq is Athinas St, the commercial thoroughfare of Athens. Here almost every conceivable item imaginable can be purchased, including ironmongery, tools, crockery and clothing. Parallel to Athinas St, and for half its length, runs Odhos Sokratous, the city street market during the day and the red-light district by night.

Athinas St heads due south to:

**Monastiraki Square** (*Tmr* 5C4) This marks the northernmost edge of the area known as the *Plaka* (*Tmr* D5), bounded by Ermou St to the north, Filellinon St to the east and by the slopes of the Acropolis to the south.

Many of the alleys in this area follow the course of the old Turkish streets; most of the houses are mid-nineteenth century and represent the 'Old Quarter'.

Climbing the twisting maze of streets and steps of the lower, north-east slopes of the Acropolis requires the stamina of a mountain goat. The almost primitive, island-village nature of some of the houses hereabouts is very noticeable, due, it is said, to a law passed after Independence. The Act was sanctioned to alleviate a housing shortage and allowed anyone who could raise the roof of a dwelling, between sunrise and sunset, to complete the building which then became theirs. Some inhabitants of the Cyclades island of Anafi (Anaphe) were reputed to have been the first to benefit from this new law. Other islanders followed to specialise in restoration and rebuilding, thus bringing about a colony of expatriates within the Plaka district.

From the south-west corner of Monastiraki Sq, Ifestou St and its associated byways house the *Flea Market*, which climaxes on Sunday into stall upon stall of junk, souvenirs, junk, hardware, junk, boots, junk, records, junk, clothes, junk, footwear, junk, pottery and junk. Where Ifestou becomes Odhos Astigos, and curves round to join up with Ermou St, there are a couple of extensive second-hand bookshops with reasonably priced (for Greece that is), if battered, paperbacks for sale.

From the south-east corner of Monastiraki, Pandrossou St, one of the only enduring reminders of the Turkish Bazaar, contains a better class of antique dealer, sandal and shoemaker, and pottery store.

Due south of Monastiraki Sq is Odhos Areos. The raggle-taggle band of European and Japanese drop-outs, selling junk trinkets from the pavement kerb, appear to have been replaced by a few local traders. Climbing Odhos Areos skirts the *Roman Agora*, from which various streets lead upwards, on ever upwards, and which contain a plethora of stalls and shops, specialising in leather goods, clothes and souvenirs. The further you climb, the cheaper the goods become. This interestingly enough does not apply to the tavernas and restaurants which seemingly become more expensive as one ascends.

**The Plaka** (*Tmr* D5) The 'chatty' area known as the Plaka is littered with eating places, a few good, some bad, some tourist rip-offs. The liveliest street, Odhos Kidathineon, is, at its lowest end, jam-packed with cafes, tavernas and restaurants and at night attracts a number of music-playing layabouts. The class, tone and price of the establishments improves as the street climbs in a north-eastwards direction. I have to admit to gently 'knocking' the Plaka over the years. Despite this, it has to be acknowledged that the area offers the cheapest accommodation and eating places in town and appears to have been cleaned up in recent years. Early and late in the year, once the hordes of overseas 'invaders' have dispersed, the Plaka once again becomes a 'village', a super place to visit.

The shopkeepers revert to being human, shopping returns to being inexpensive and the tavernas hark back to being 'Greek', as well as lively. In the last three weeks of February the *Apokria Festival*, a long running 'Halloween' style carnival, is centred on the Plaka. The streets are filled with dozens of revellers dressed in fancy dress, masks and funny hats who wander about, throwing confetti and creating a marvellous atmosphere. For this event all the tavernas are decorated.

To the east of Monastiraki Sq is Ermou St, initially lined by clothes and shoe shops. One third of the way towards Syntagma Sq and Odhos Ermou opens out into a small square on which there is the lovely *Church of Kapnikarea (Tmr* 6D4). Continuing eastwards, the shops become smarter with a preponderance of fashion stores, whilst parallel to Ermou St is Odhos Ploutonos Kteka, which becomes Odhos Mitropoleos. Facing east, on the right, is the City's Greek Orthodox Cathedral, *Great Mitropolis*. Built circa 1850, from the materials of about seventy old churches, to the design of four different architects, the result, not unnaturally, was a building of a rather 'strange' appearance. In strict contrast, alongside, and to the south, is the diminutive, medieval *Little Mitropolis* Church or Agios Eleftherios. This dates back to at least the twelfth century, but incorporates materials, reliefs and building blocks probably originating from as early as the sixth century AD. A little further on is the intriguing and incongruous site of a small Byzantine church, dominated by a modern office block, the very columns of which tower above and beside the tiny building.

Leaving Syntagama Sq by the north-east corner, along Vassilissis Sofias, and turning left at Odhos Irodou Attikou, runs into:
**Kolonaki Square** (*Tmr* 7F4) The most fashionable square in the most fashionable area of Athens, around which most of the foreign embassies are located. The *British Council* is located on this square, as are some expensive cafes, restaurants and boutiques. To the north of Kolonaki, across the pretty, orange tree planted Dexameni Sq, is the southernmost edge of:
**Mt Lycabettus** (*Tmr* F/G3) Access to the summit can be made on foot by a number of steep paths, the main one of which, a stepped footpath, advances from the north end of Loukianou St, beyond Odhos Kleomenous. A little to the east, at the top of Ploutarchou St, which breaks into a sharply rising flight of steps, is the cable car funicular railway. This climbs in a 213m long tunnel to emerge alongside a modern and luxuriously expensive restaurant, close by the nineteenth century chapel which caps the fir tree covered outcrop. There are some excellent toilets.

The railway service runs continuously as follows:
**Winter**: Wed, Sat & Sun 0845-0015hrs; Thurs 1030-0015hrs; Mon, Tues & Fri 0930-0015hrs.
**Summer**: As for winter, but the opening hours extend daily to 0100hrs every night.
The trip costs 65drs one-way and 100drs for a return ticket.

The topmost part of the mountain, where the funicular emerges, is surprisingly small, if not doll-like. The spectacular panorama that spreads out to the horizon, the stupendous views from far above the roar of the Athens traffic, are best seen in the early morning or later afternoon. Naturally the night hours are the time to see the city's lights.

A more relaxed climb, passing the open air theatre, can be made from the north end of Lycabettus.

Leaving Plateia Kolonaki from the south corner and turning right at Vassilissis Sofias, sallies forth to the north corner of:
**The National Garden (Ethnikos Kipos)** (*Tmr* E5) Here peacocks, waterfowl and songbirds blend with a profusion of shrubbery, subtropical trees, ornamental ponds, various busts and cafe tables through and around which thread neat gravel paths.

To the south of the gardens are the *Zappeion Exhibition Halls*; to the north-west, the Greek Parliament buildings, the (old) Royal Palace and the Tomb, or Monument, to the

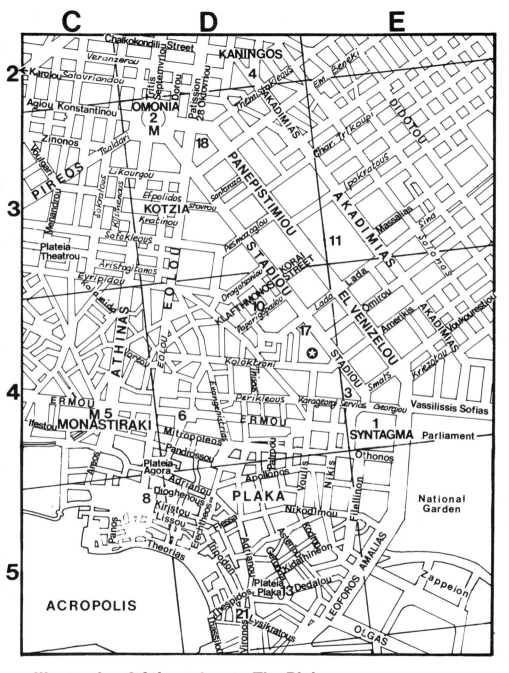

**Illustration 6 Athens inset - The Plaka**

Unknown Warrior. This latter is guarded by the traditionally costumed *Evzones*, the Greek equivalent of the British, Buckingham Palace Guards (*See* **Places of Interest, A To Z**).

South-east of the National Gardens is the *Olympic Stadium*, erected in 1896, on the site of the original stadium built in 330 BC, and situated in a valley of the Arditos Hills.

South-west across Leoforos Olgas are the Olympic swimming pool and the *Tennis and Athletic Club*. To the west of these sporting facilities is the isolated gateway known as the *Arch of Hadrian* overlooking the busy traffic junctions of Leoforos Olgas and Leoforos Amalias. Through the archway, the remains of the *Temple of Olympian Zeus* are outlined, but only fifteen of the original one hundred and four Corinthian columns remain standing.

Leaving Hadrian's Arch, westwards along Odhos Dionysiou Areopagitou, leads to the south side of:-

**The Acropolis (Akropoli)** (*Tmr* C5) A 10-acre rock rising 229m above the surrounding city and surmounted by the *Parthenon Temple* (built in approximately 450 BC), the *Propylaia Gateway*, the *Temple to Athena Nike* and the triple *Temple of Erechtheion*. Additionally, there has been added the modern Acropolis Museum, discreetly tucked away and almost out of sight.

At the bottom of the southern slopes are the *Theatre of Dionysos*, originally said to seat up to 30,000 but more probably 17,000, and the smaller, second century AD, *Odeion of Herodes Atticus*, which has been restored and is used for plays and concerts during the summer festival. It is thought provoking to consider that the Dionysos Odeion is the original theatre where western world drama, as we know it, originated.

The west slope leads to the **Hill of Areopagos (Areios Pagos)** where, in times of yore, a council of noblemen dispensed supreme judgements. Across Apostolou Pavlou St lie the other tree covered hills of:

**Filopapou (Philopappos/Mouseion)**, or **Hill of Muses**, from whence the views are far-reaching and outstanding,

**Pynx (Pynka)**, where The Assembly once met and a *son et lumiere* is now held, and the

**Asteroskopeion (Observatory)**, or the **Hill of Nymphs**, whereon stands, surprise, surprise, an observatory.

Descending from the Asteroskopeion towards and across Apostolou Pavlou St is:

**The Greek Agora** (*Tmr* B/C4) The gathering place from whence the Athenians would have approached the Acropolis. This marketplace cum-civic centre is now little more than rubble, but the glory that once was is recreated by a model.

Nearby the *Temple of Hephaistos*, or *Thission* (*Theseion*), sits on a small hill overlooking the Agora. To one side is the reconstructed marketplace, *Stoa Attalus*, the cost of which was met from private donations raised by American citizens.

A short distance to the east of the Greek Agora is the site of:-

**The Roman Forum (Agora)** (*Tmr* C5) Close by is the *Tower of the Winds* (*Tmr* 8C5), a remarkable, octagonal tower, probably built in the first century BC and which served as a combination water clock, sundial and weather vane. Early descriptions say the building was topped off with a bronze weather vane represented by the mythological Triton complete with a pronged trident. The carved eight gods of wind can be seen, as can traces of the corresponding sundials, but no interior mechanism remains and the building is now sadly used as a store for various stone antiquities.

Not far away, to the north-west, is an area known as **The Keramikos** (*Tmr* B4), a cemetery or graveyard, containing the *Street of the Tombs*, a funeral avenue laid down about 400 BC.

In a north-easterly direction from Keramikos, along Pireos St, via Eleftherias Sq Bus

Terminal (*Tmr* 9C3), turning right down Evripidou St, across Athinas and Eolou Sts, leads to:-

## Klafthmonos Square (Klathmonos) (*Tmr* 10D3/4) Supposedly the most attractive
Byzantine church in Athens, *Aghii Theodori*, is positioned in the west corner of the Square.

Looking north-east across Stadiou St, up Korai St and across Panepistimiou Ave, reveals an imposing range of neo-classical buildings (*Tmr* 11D/E3/4), fronted by formal gardens. These comprise the *University* flanked, on the left (*facing*), by the *National Library* and, on the right, by the *Academy*. Behind and running parallel to Stadiou and Penepistimiou, is Akadimias St, on which is another bus terminal. Just off Akadimias St, in Massalias St, is the *Hellenic-American Union*, many of the facilities of which are open to the general public. These include English and music libraries, as well as a cafeteria.

North-west of Klafthomonos Sq, to the left of Eolou St, is:-

## Kotzia Square (*Tmr* D3) A very large plateia around which, on Sunday at least, circle
a profusion of flower sellers' stalls.

The once paved area has been dug up by archaeologists who have unearthed a veritable treasure trove of ancient Athens city walls. The fate of the site is in the hands of the opposing and seemingly irreconcilable factions represented by the modernists, who have a vision of a vast underground car park, and the traditionalists, who quite rightly, wish to see the 'dig' preserved for posterity.

**Fokionos Negri** Actually a street, if not an avenue, rather than a square. It is somewhat distant from the city centre, almost in the suburbs to the north, and few, if any street plans of Athens extend far enough to include the full extent of the thoroughfare. To reach Fokionos Negri from Omonia Sq, proceed north along 28 Ikosiokto Oktovriou, which runs into Patission St, on past the *National Archaeological Museum* and *Green Park (Pedion Areos)*, both on the right, to where Agiou Meletiou St runs across Patission St. Fokionos Negri starts out as a fairly narrow side-street to the right, but widens out into a tree lined, short, squat avenue with a wide, spacious, centre pedestrian way once gravelled but now extensively resurfaced. Supposedly the *Dolce Vita* or *Via Veneto* of Athens but not out of the ordinary, if quiet wealth is normal. Extremely expensive cafes edge the square halfway up on the right and it certainly becomes extremely lively after nightfall.

Trolley-buses 5, 11, 12 or 13, going north, trundle past the turning.

# THE ACCOMMODATION & EATING OUT
**The Accommodation** Generally, in describing the islands, the 'haul' of accommodation detailed includes even 'E' Class hotels, but in Athens I have erred on the side of caution, sticking with 'B', 'C' and some better 'D' class hotels and pensions. No doubt there are acceptable Class 'E' hotels but... Most of the Athens pensions and lower category hotels operate a night-time curfew, usually some time between 0100-0200hrs, and an earlier than usual morning 'chuck-out', often from 1000hrs to 1100hrs, so do not forget to check.

On Adrianou St (*Tmr* D5), in the Plaka district, are a few, very cheap dormitories and students' hostels, where a certain amount of rooftop sleeping is allowed, costing upwards of 500drs per night. Unless set well back from the main road, a set of earmuffs or plugs is almost obligatory to ensure a good night's sleep.

On a cautionary note, in recent years the Greek authorities have been closing a number of the more 'undesirable', unlicensed hotels, so a particular favourite overnight stop from years gone by may no longer be in business.

Most of the detailed accommodation charges listed in this guide are priced at 1988 prices. *See* **Chapter Four** for a table outlining the various categories, with comments and guideline prices.

*See* **Arrival By Air, East Airport, Introduction.**

## SYNTAGMA AREA (*Tmr* D/E4/5)

**Festos Guest House** (*Tmr* D/E5) 18 Filellinon St        Tel 323 2455
*Directions*: From Syntagma Sq, walk up the rise of Odhos Filellinon past a number of cut-price ticket joints. The entrance is very nearly opposite Ag Nikodimos Church, on the right.
    Ethnic guest house with dormitories, triples & quadruple rooms working out at between 600 & 1000drs per person. Hot showers cost an extra 100drs, but luggage is stored free. The bar not only serves drinks but simple snacks. For the indiscriminately young at heart.

**Hotel Cleo (Cleopatra)** (*Tmr* D4) (Class D) 3 Patroou St        Tel 322 9053
*Directions*: Leaving Syntagma Sq, walk down Mitropoleos St, towards Monastiraki Sq and take the fourth turning left.
    Well recommended if threadbare. Ground floor dormitory, free baggage store. Double rooms en suite cost 1900drs, rising to 3900drs (1st May-30th Sept).
*NB The owners also have a guest house nearby in Apollonos St.*

**Pension John's Place** (*Tmr* D4) (Class C) 5 Patroou St        Tel 322 9719
*Directions*: As for *Hotel Cleo* above.
    Not surprisingly, the affable, old Papa is named John. Well looked after accommodation with singles starting at 1300drs & doubles from 1900drs (1st Jan-30th April), increasing to 1500drs & 2400drs (1st May-30th Sept) and 1300drs & 2000drs (1st Oct-31st Dec). Naturally rooms share the bathroom facilities.

**George's Guest House** (*Tmr* D4) (Class B) 46 Nikis St        Tel 322 6474
*Directions*: From Syntagma Sq, walk west along Mitropoleos St and turn down the first left-hand turning. The guest house is on the right, beyond the first side-street.
    Calls itself a *Youth Hostel with student prices*. It was recommended by four Texas college girls, met on the train to Patras, some years ago, and whose first stop in Greece this was. Shared bathroom and hot water in the evening, if you are quick. Double rooms only from 2000drs, rising to 2400drs (1st June-15th Oct).

**Hotel Kimon** (*Tmr* D5) (Class D) 27 Apollonos        Tel 323 5223
*Directions*: Midway on Apollonos St, one block down from Mitropoleos St.
    Old but renovated. Single rooms, sharing bathrooms, start off at 1400drs, increasing to 2200drs (1st June-10th Oct) & en suite 1700drs, rising to 2500drs. Double rooms, which have to share a bathroom, cost 2300drs, rising to 2600drs.

**Hotel Plaka** (*Tmr* D4) (Class B) 7 Kapnikareas/Mitropoleos Sts        Tel 322 2096
*Directions*: From Syntagma Sq proceed west along Mitropoleos. Kapnikareas St lies between Evangenistrias and Eolou Sts and the hotel is on the left.
    Listed because the hotel accepts *American Express* and or *Diners*, despite which the charges are not too exorbitant and the rooms excellent. All have en suite bathrooms with a single room costing 2000drs a night & a double 3000drs, increasing, respectively, to 2500drs & 3500/4100drs (1st April-30th June & 1st-31st Oct) and 3000drs & 4100/4700drs (1st July-30th Sept). Breakfast, which might have to be taken, is charged extra at between 320 & 400drs per head.

**YMCA (XAN)** (*Tmr* E4) 28 Omirou St        Tel 362 6970
*Directions*: From the north-east corner of Syntagma Sq, proceed along Panepistimiou St, take the third turning right and across Akadimias Avenue, on the right.
    It has been closed for renovations over the last few years but may be open in 1989... then again it may not.

**YWCA (XEN)** (*Tmr* E4) 11 Amerikis St.        Tel 362 4291
*Directions*: All as above, but second turning off Panepistimiou St and on the left.
    Don't forget, women only. Apart from accommodation there is a cafe serving breakfasts (200drs), sandwiches, a hair dressing salon, library and laundry facilities. Singles from 900drs and shared rooms 800drs per head.

**Pension Theseus** (*Tmr* D4) (Class C) 10 Thiseos        Tel 324 5960
*Directions*: From the top, north-west corner of Syntagma Sq, proceed along Odhos Karageorgi Servios, which becomes Periklious St, as far as the right-hand turning of Odhos Thiseos.
    This friendly pension is situated in a comparatively 'serene' street. All rooms share the bathrooms with a single costing 2000drs & a double 2500drs, which charges increase to 2500drs & 3000drs (1st May-31st Oct).

## OMONIA AREA (*Tmr* 2D3) Any hotel or pension rooms, facing out over Omonia Square, must be regarded as very noisy.

**Hotel Omonia** (*Tmr* D3) (Class C) 4 Omonia Sq. Tel 523 7210
*Directions*: Just stand on Plateia Omonia, swivel round and on the north side of the Square.
The reception is on the first floor, as is a cafe-bar and terrace, overlooking the square and its action. Modern but 'worn international' look to the place. Clients may well have to take demi-pension terms. All rooms have en suite bathrooms. Singles start at 1500drs & a double room 2100drs, rising, respectively, to 1750drs & 2100drs (1st April-14th July & 15th Sept-31st Oct) and 2000drs & 2600drs (15th July-14th Sept). Breakfast costs 270drs and a meal from 950drs.

**Hotel Banghion** (*Tmr* D3) (Class C) 18b Omonia Sq. Tel 324 2259
*Directions*: As for *Hotel Omonia*, but on the south side of the square.
Elegant but aging. Rooms sharing a bathroom cost 1500drs for a single & 2350drs for a double room and with en suite bathrooms 2200drs & 3000drs. These charges rise, respectively, to 1800/2850drs & 2650/3600drs (16th July-15th Sept). Breakfasts costs 350drs, increasing to 400drs.

**Hotel Carlton** (*Tmr* D3) (Class C) 7 Omonia Sq. Tel 522 3201
*Directions*: As for the *Hotel Omonia*.
Very Greek, provincial and old fashioned. All rooms share bathrooms, with single rooms charged from 1500drs & double rooms 1800drs, increasing to 1700drs & 2000drs (1st April-31st May) and 1800drs & 2300drs (1st June-31st Dec).

**Hotel Europa** (*Tmr* D2) (Class C) 7 Satovriandou St Tel 522 3081
*Directions*: North of Omonia Sq and in the second main street along, tracking east/west. This is often listed as Chateaubriandou St but the local authorities either have, or have not been notified of the change. Whatever, the street is now a pedestrian precinct.
Another 'Greek provincial' hotel, the remarkably ancient lift of which creaks its way up and down to the various floors. The rooms are adequate but dingy, there are wardrobes and the floors are covered with brown linoleum. If matters are still as they were, to use the shower it is necessary to ask the concierge for the relevant key. This may have to be in mime, if a guest's Greek is as sketchy as the staff's knowledge of English. When produced, this key might well be adjudged large enough to open the doors of the Bastille. Weighted down by the 'instrument', the moment of truth is about to dawn. When the door is opened, sheer disbelief may well be the first reaction, especially if it is the first ever stopover in Athens, as it was mine many years ago. A cavernous and be-cobwebbed room reveals plumbing that beggars description. Enough to say the shower is most welcome even if the lack of a point to anchor the shower head, whilst trying to soap oneself down, requires interesting body contortions. The rate for a single room is 1500drs & for a double 2000drs, sharing the bathrooms and the shower...

**Hotel Alma** (*Tmr* D2/3) (Class C) 5 Dorou Tel 524 0858
*Directions*: Dorou St runs north from the north-east corner of Omonia Sq.
Modern and the rooms with a balcony are on the seventh and eighth floors. Single rooms, sharing a bathroom, start at 1500drs & en suite 1800drs, while double rooms start from 1800drs & 2500drs. These rates rise, respectively, to 1700/2200drs & 2300/3000drs (1st April-15th Oct) and 1800/2000drs & 2000/2800drs (16th Oct-31st Dec).

**Hotel Orpheus** (*Tmr* C/D2) (Class C) 58 Chalkokondili St Tel 522 4996
*Directions*: North of Omonia Sq.
Stolid, studentish and provincial in character. Very well recommended and reasonably priced, with a mix of accommodation available. For 1988 rooms (& rates) include single (1300drs), double (1800drs), triple (2400drs), quadruple (2800drs), quintuple (3000drs) & dormitory (500drs per person). These charges increase by 500drs for the months of June-Oct. There is a TV lounge, outdoor patio and bar. Continental breakfast is available for 250drs and an English breakfast costs 400drs. Bar prices are reasonable with a Nes meh ghala costing 90drs, an ouzo 60drs, Metaxa 3 star brandy 60drs and an Amstel beer 100drs. Overseas telephone calls can be made.

**Hotel Eva** (*Tmr* C2) (Class D) 31 Victoros Ougo Tel 522 3079
*Directions*: West of Omonia, as far as Plateia Karaiskaki, and to the north, parallel with and two blocks back from Ag Konstantinou.
Well recommended, all rooms have en suite bathrooms. Single rooms start at 1300drs & double rooms 2300drs, rising to 1700drs & 3000drs (1st June-30th Sept). Breakfast costs 300drs.

**Hotel Marina** (*Tmr* C3) (Class C) 13 Voulgari                    Tel 523 7832/3
*Directions*: South-west from Omonia Sq, along Odhos Pireos and 4th turning to the right.
   Single rooms cost from 1445drs, double rooms 1900drs, both sharing bathrooms, while rooms with en suite bathrooms cost from 1800drs & 2550drs respectively. These rates rise (16th March-30th June & 16th Oct-31st Dec) to 1550drs & 2100drs (single & doubles sharing) and 1900drs & 2700drs (singles & doubles en suite) and again (1st July-15th Oct) to 1750/2250drs & 2100/3160drs. Breakfast is charged at 300drs.

**Hotel Vienna** (*Tmr* C3) (Class C) 20 Pireos                    Tel 524 9143
*Directions*: South-west of Omonia Sq.
   New, clean and noisy. All rooms have en suite bathrooms with singles starting at 2000drs & doubles 2800drs, increasing to 2300drs & 3300drs (1st July-31st Oct). A breakfast costs 300drs.

**Hotel Athinea** (*Tmr* C2) (Class C) 9 Vilara                    Tel 524 3884
*Directions*: Westwards along Ag Konstantinou and situated on one side of the small square of Agiou Konstantinou.
   Old but beautifully positioned, although cabaret night life may intrude. A restaurant and cake shop are close by, as is a taxi rank. All rooms have en suite bathrooms. A single room starts off at 1750drs & a double 2400drs, increasing to 2200drs & 2900drs (1st-25th March; 11th April-30th June & 1-31st Oct) and 2400drs & 3400drs (25th March-10th April & 1st July-30th Sept). Breakfast is priced at 450drs.

**Hotel Florida** (*Tmr* C3) (Class C) 25 Menandrou                    Tel 522 3214
*Directions*: Third turning left, south-west along Pireos St.
   Single rooms are charged from 850/1100drs & doubles 1530drs, both without a bathroom, whilst a double room en suite, costs 2000drs. These charges rise, respectively, to 1050/1400drs & 2000/2500drs (1st June-30th Sept). Breakfast is charged at 260drs.

**Hotel Alcestis (Alkistis)** (*Tmr* C3) (Class C) 18 Plateia Theatrou                    Tel 321 9811
*Directions*: From Pireos St, proceed south down either Sokratous or Menandrou Sts and across Odhos Sofokleous.
   Despite its chromium-plated appearance, all glass and marble with a prairie-sized lobby, it is a Class C hotel in a commercial square. Popular and all rooms have en suite bathrooms. Singles start off at 1350drs & doubles 1985drs, rising to 2190drs & 2800drs (15th March-30th June & 1st-31st Oct) and 2420drs & 3250drs (1st July-30th Sept). Breakfast costs 350drs & lunch/dinner 1200drs.

## MONASTIRAKI AREA (*Tmr* C4)
**Hotel Tembi(Tempi)** (*Tmr* C/D4) (Class D) 29 Eolou (Aiolu/Aeolou)                    Tel 321 3175
*Directions*: In a main street north of Ermou St, opposite the Church of Ag Irini.
   Pleasant rooms with singles sharing the bathroom starting at 1000drs, rising to 1200drs (1st May-31st Oct). Double rooms sharing cost from 1500drs & en suite 1900drs, advancing, respectively, to 1900drs & 2600drs. There is a laundry and book exchange.

**Hotel Ideal** (*Tmr* C/D4) (Class D) 39 Eolou/2 Voreou Sts.                    Tel 321 3195
*Directions*: On the left of Eolou, walking northwards from Odhos Ermou, and on the corner with Voreou St.
   A perfect example of a weather-worn, 19th century, Athens neo-classical building complete with an old fashioned, metal and glass canopy entrance and matchbox sized, wrought iron balconies. The accommodation lives up to all that the exterior promises! The management are helpful, there is a telephone, TV room, a bar and luggage can be stored. Tourist information is freely available as are battered paperbacks for guests. The rooms are clean and the bathroom facilities are shared, but there is 24 hour hot water – they promise! Singles start at 1000drs & doubles 1500drs, rising to 1200drs & 1900drs (16th May-31st Oct).

**Hotel Hermion** (*Tmr* C/D4) (Class D) 66c Ermou St                    Tel 321 2753
*Directions*: East of Monastiraki, adjacent to Kapnikarea Church/Square (*Tmr* 6D4).
   Old but clean, with the reception up the stairs. All rooms share bathrooms with the single room rate starting off at 1200drs & double rooms 1700drs, increasing, respectively, to 1400drs & 2100drs (1st May-31st Oct).

**Hotel Attalos** (*Tmr* C3/4) (Class C) 29 Athinas                    Tel 321 2801
*Directions*: North from Monastiraki Sq.
   Recommended to us by a splendidly eccentric English lady artist who should know – she has been

visiting Greece for some 20 years. Single rooms, sharing the bathroom, start from 1400drs & en suite 1715drs, while doubles cost 1715drs & 2050drs. These charges increase to (singles) 1715/2170drs & (doubles) 2170/2700drs (16th March-31st May) and 1715/2710drs & 2710/3615drs (1st June-15th Oct). Breakfast is charged at 350drs.

**Hotel Cecil** (*Tmr* C3/4) (Class D) 39 Athinas　　　　　　　　　　　　Tel 321 7079
*Directions*: North from Monastiraki Sq and two buildings along from the Kalamida St turning, on the left-hand side. This is the other side of the road from a very small chapel, incongruously stuck on the pavement. The 'informative' sign outside the hotel is no help.
　　Clean looking, single rooms costing 1275drs & a double 2000drs, both sharing the bathrooms.

# PLAKA/METZ STADIUM AREAS (*Tmr* D5 & D/E6) The Plaka is rich in accommodation, as it is in most things!
**Hotel Phaedra** (*Tmr* D5) (Class D) 4 Adrianou/16 Herephontos　　　　　Tel 323 8461
*Directions*: Situated close by a multi-junction of various streets including Lysikratous, Galanou, Adrianou and Herephontos, opposite the Byzantine Church of Ag Ekaterini and its small, attractive gardens.
　　Pretty area by day with splendid views but noisy by night. A clean, family hotel with a ground floor bar. All rooms share the bathrooms, with a single room costing 1650drs & a double 2000drs, which rates increase, respectively, to 2350drs & 2850drs (1st April-15th Oct). Breakfast costs 350drs.

**Students' Inn** (*Tmr* D5) (Class C) 16 Kidathineon St　　　　　　　　Tel 324 4808
*Directions*: On the left of the liveliest stretch of Kidathineon St, walking up from the Adrianou St junction, and almost opposite the front garden of a Japanese eating house.
　　Hostelish and classified as a pension but recommended as good value with hot showers 'on tap' (sorry) and an English-speaking owner. There is a rooftop, a passable courtyard, a snackbar, the use of a washing machine (which does not always work) and a baggage store costing 50drs per day. The clean but basic rooms, which all share the bathrooms, are complete with a rickety, oilcloth covered table and a mug. Single rooms cost 1400drs & doubles 1800drs. These rates increase to 1500drs & 2100drs (2nd May-15th Oct). Breakfast costs 300drs, but I would rather wander out to 'breathe in' the Plaka.

Left off Kidathineon Street, climbing towards Syntagma Sq, is Odhos Kodrou on which are two clean, agreeable hotels in a very pleasant area, the:
**Hotel Adonis** (*Tmr* D5) (Class B) 3 Kodrou/Voulis Sts　　　　　　　Tel 324 9737
*Directions*: As above and on the right.
　　Actually a pension so the rates are not outrageous. All rooms have en suite bathrooms with singles starting off at 1970drs & doubles 2100drs, rising, respectively, to 2500drs & 2650drs (1st July-30th Sept)
and the:

**Acropolis House** (*Tmr* D5) (Class B) 6-8 Kodrou　　　　　　　　　Tel 322 2344
*Directions*: As above and on the left.
　　Comes highly recommended and is clean, evincing old-fashioned charm. Once again officially classified as a pension, with a choice of rooms sharing or complete with en suite bathrooms. Single rooms, sharing a bathroom, cost 1600drs & en suite 2220drs, whilst doubles, sharing, cost 2350drs & en suite 2600drs (1st April-15th June & 1st Oct-31st Dec). These rates increase, respectively, to 2720drs, 3020drs, 3300 & 3645drs (16th June-30th Sept).

Closer to Kidathineon St, and on the right is the:
**Kourous Pension** (*Tmr* D5) (Class C) 11 Kodrou　　　　　　　　　Tel 322 7431
*Directions*: As above.
　　Rather more provincial than the two establishments detailed above, which lack of sophistication is reflected in the lower prices (and standards). All rooms share the bathrooms, with single room rates starting at 1300drs & a double 1900drs (1st Jan-30th April & 1st Oct-31st Dec), climbing to the dizzy heights (!) of 1420drs & 2400drs (1st May-30th Sept).

**Hotel Solonion** (*Tmr* D5) (Class E) 11 Sp Tsangari/Dedalou　　　　Tel 322 0008
*Directions*: To the right of Kidathineon St (*facing Syntagma Sq*), between Dedalou St and Leoforos Amalias. Odhos Tsangari is a continuation of Asteriou St.
　　I did start out by pronouncing I would not list any E class hotels but... Run by a rather stern faced lady who is assisted by a varied collection of part-time assistants to run the old, faded but externally refurbished building. If a guest strikes lucky the night porter will be a delightful old boy who was once

a merchant in the Greek community resident in Turkey, and caught up in the huge population resettlement of 1922/23. The accommodation is 'student provincial' quality, the rooms being high ceilinged with the rather dodgy floorboards overlaid and hidden beneath brown linoleum. The bathrooms are distinctly ethnic and Victorian in style but hot water is promised all day. On a fine day... it is possible to espy the Acropolis... well a bit of it. No single rooms are available. A double room, sharing the bathroom, costs from 1600drs, including one bath a day, which rises to 1900drs (1st April-31st Oct).

Close by the *Hotel Solonion* are the:-
**Hotel Kekpoy (Cecrops)** *(Tmr* D5) (Class D) 13 Sp Tsangari                    Tel 322 3080
*Directions*: On the same side of the road as, and similar in style to, the *Solonion*, but a building or two towards Leoforos Amalias.
   All rooms share the bathrooms, with singles costing 1500drs & doubles 1900drs (1st April-31st Oct).
and the

**Hotel Phoebus (Fivos)** *(Tmr* D5) (Class C) Asteriou/12 Peta Sts              Tel 322 0142
*Directions*: Back towards Kidathineon St, on the corner of Odhos Asteriou and Peta.
   Rather more up-market than the three previously listed hotels and all rooms have en suite bathrooms. A single room is charged at 2260drs & a double room 2980drs. These rates rise, respectively, to 2700drs & 3600drs (1st June-30th Sept). Breakfast costs 375drs.

A few side streets towards the Acropolis is:-
**Apartments Ava** *(Tmr* D5) 9-11 Lysikratous St                               Tel 323 6618
*Directions*: As above.
   I have no personal experience, but the establishment has been mentioned as a possibility and is in an excellent, central but quiet situation, although it is rather expensive. All rooms have en suite bathrooms, are heated and air conditioned. Single rooms cost from 2800drs & doubles from 3600drs. There are family suites complete with kitchen and refrigerator.

**New Clare's House** *(Tmr* E6) (Class C) 24 Sorvolou St                       Tel 922 2288
*Directions*: Rather uniquely, the owners have had a large compliments slip printed with a pen and ink drawing on the face and, on the reverse side, directions in Greek saying *Show this to the taxi driver*. This includes details of the location, south of the Stadium, on Sorvolou St between Charvouri and Voulgareos Sts. The pension is on the right, half-way down the reverse slope with the description *white building with the green shutters*. From Syntagma proceed south down the sweep of Leoforos Amalias, keeping to the main avenue hugging the Temple of Olympian Zeus and along Odhos Diakou. Where Diakou makes a junction with Vouligmenis and Ardittou Avenues, Odhos Anapafseos leads off in a south-east direction and Sorvolou St 'crescents' off to the left. Trolley buses 2, 4, 11 & 12 drop travellers by the Stadium. It is quite a steep climb up Sorvolou St, which breaks into steps, to the pretty and highly recommended area of Metz (highly regarded by Athenians that is). Plus points are that the narrow nature of the lanes, which suddenly become steps, keeps the traffic down to a minimum and the height of the hill raises it above the general level of smog and pollution.
   The pleasant, flat-fronted pension is on the right and has a marble floor entrance hall. Inside, off to the left, is a large reception/lounge/bar/breakfast/common room and to the right, the lift. Apart from the usual hotel business, the establishment 'beds' some tour companies clients overnighting in Athens, and en route to other destinations. Thus the hotel can be fully booked, so it is best to make a forward booking or telephone prior to journeying out here. The self-confident English speaking owner presides over matters from a large desk in the reception area and is warily helpful. The friendly lady receptionists do not exactly go wild in an orgy of energy sapping activity, tending to indulge in a saturnalia of TV watching. Guests in the meantime can help themselves to bottles of beer and Coke from the bar, paying when convenient to them and the receptionist. Despite the inferred aura of excellence, the usual collection of faults can crop up from time to time including: cracked loo seats; no hot water, despite being assured that there is 24 hours hot water (and for longer no doubt were there more hours in the day!); missing locking mechanism on the lavatory door; toilets having to be flushed using a length of string and the television on the blink. I do not mean to infer that these irritating defects occur all at once – just one or two, every so often. Double rooms sharing a bathroom cost 2900drs & en suite 4000drs. Incidentally, where the well appointed bathrooms are shared, the pleasant bedrooms only have to go fifty-fifty with one other room. The charges, which include breakfast with warm bread every day, may at first impression (and for that matter second and third impression) appear on the expensive side. The 'pain' might be eased by the realisation that the 4th floor has a balcony and a

self-catering kitchen, complete with cooker and a fridge, and the 5th floor a laundry room with an iron and 2 rooftop clothes lines. These facilities must of course be taken into account when weighing up comparative prices. The management creates an atmosphere that will suit the young, very well behaved student and the older traveller, but not exuberant, lager swilling rowdies. Hands are 'smacked' if guests lie around eating a snack on the front steps, hang washing out of the windows or make a noise, especially between 1330-1700hrs and after 2330hrs. You know, lights out boys and no smoking in the 'dorms'.

Clare's House was originally recommended by pension owner Alexis on the island of Kos. Certainly an old friend of ours, Peter, who 'has to put up with yachting round the Aegean waters during the summer months', almost always spends some of his winter at Clare's and swears by the place.

Before leaving the area, there is an inexpensive, intriguing possibility (accommodation that is) in a very quiet street edging the west side of the Stadium.
**Joseph's House Pension** (*Tmr* E6) (Class C) 13 Markou Moussourou           Tel 923 1204
*Directions*: From the region of Hadrian's Arch/the Temple of the Olympian Zeus (*Tmr* D6), proceed up Avenue Arditou in a north-easterly direction towards the Stadium. Odhos Markou Moussourou climbs steeply off to the right, immediately prior to the wooded hillside of Arditos. The pension is on the left, beyond Meletiou Riga St. On the other hand, it is just as easy to follow the directions to *Clare's House* and proceed east along Charvouri St until it 'bumps' into Markou Moussourou.

The bathrooms are shared, with single rooms charged at 1200drs throughout the year & doubles at 1500drs, which latter rate increases to 1800drs (1st May-30th Sept).

## THISSION AREA (THESION) (*Tmr* B/C4/5) First south-bound Metro stop beyond
Monastiraki and a much quieter area than, say, the Plaka.
**Hotel Phedias** (*Tmr* B4) (Class C) 39 Apostolou Pavlou           Tel 345 9511
*Directions*: South of the Metro station.

Modern and friendly. All rooms share en suite bathrooms with singles costing 2000drs & double rooms 2500drs, rising to 2500drs & 3000drs (1st July-31st Dec). Breakfast is charged at 300drs per head.

## OLYMPIC OFFICE AREA (*Tmr* C6)
**Hotel Karayannis** (*Tmr* C6) (Class C) 94 Leoforos Sygrou           Tel 921 5903
*Directions*: On the corner of Odhos Byzantiou and Leoforos Sygrou, opposite the side exit of the Olympic terminal office.

'Interesting', tatty and noisy, but very useful for weary travellers dumped late at night at the Olympic terminal. Rooms facing the main road should be avoided. The Athenian traffic, which roars non-stop and round the clock, up and down the broad avenue , gives every appearance of making the journey along Leoforos Sygrou via the hotel balconies, even on the third or fourth storeys. There are picturesque views of the Acropolis from the breakfast and bar rooftop terrace, even if they are through a maze of television aerials. Single rooms, with an en suite bathroom, cost 1615drs. Double rooms, sharing a bathroom, cost 2190drs & en suite 2285drs. These prices increase, respectively, to 1860drs & 2515/2650drs. Breakfast for one costs 250drs. Best to splash out for the en suite rooms as the hotel's shared lavatories are of a 'thought' provoking nature, possessing a number of the unique features detailed under the general description of Bathrooms in **Chapter Four**.

Whilst in this area it would be a pity not to mention the:-
**Super-Bar Restaurant** Odhos Faliron
*Directions*: As for the *Hotel Karayannis*, but behind the Olympic office.

Not inexpensive but very conveniently situated, even if it is closed on Sundays. Snackbar food, with 2 Nes meh ghala, a toasted cheese and ham sandwich and boiled egg costing 300drs. On that occasion I actually wanted toast...

**Youth Hostel** 57 Kypselis St & Agiou Meletiou 1           Tel 822 5860
*Directions*: Located in the Fokionos Negri area of North Athens. Proceed along 28 Ikosiokto Oktovriou/Patission St, from Omonia Sq, beyond Pedion Areos Park to Ag Meletiou St. Turn right and follow until the junction with Kypselis St. Trolley-buses 3, 5, 11, 12 & 13 make the journey.

This proclaims itself as *The Official Youth Hostel* and does fulfil the requirements of those who require very basic, cheap accommodation, albeit in dormitories. The overnight charge is 450-600drs and meals are available from 200drs.

**Taverna Youth Hostel** (*Tmr* G2) 1 Drossi St/87 Leoforos Alexandra           Tel 646 3669
*Directions*: East of Pedion Aeros Park along Leoforos Alexandra, almost as far as the junction with

Ippokratous St. Odhos Drossi is on the left. It is possible to catch Trolley-bus No. 7 from Panepistimiou Avenue or No. 8 from Kaningos Sq (*Tmr* 4D2) or Akadimias St.

Actually a taverna that 'sprouts' an 'unofficial Youth Hostel' for the summer months only.

If only to receive confirmation regarding the spurious Youth Hostels, it may be worth visiting the:-

**YHA Head Office** (*Tmr* D3/4) 4 Dragatsaniou                                                                    Tel 323 4107

*Directions*: The north side of Plateia Klafthmonos, in a street on the left-hand side of Stadiou St.

The office is open Mon-Fri, 0900-1400hrs. They advise of vacancies in the youth hostels and issue international youth hostel cards, as long as the application is accompanied by two full face photos. This latter is available in the Omonia Sq subway.

## LARISSIS STATION AREA (*Tmr* B/C1) *See* **Trains, A To Z.**

### Camping Sites include the following:-

| Distance from Athens | Site name | Amenities |
| --- | --- | --- |
| 8km | **Athens Camping.** 198 Athinon Ave. On the road to Dafni (due west of Athens). Tel 581 4101 | Open all year, 25km from the sea. Bar, shop & showers. |
| 10km | **Dafni Camping.** Dafni. On the Athens to Corinth National Road. Tel 581 1562 | Open all year, 5km from the sea. Bar, shop, showers & kitchen facilities. |

For the above: (Blue) Bus 853, Athens – Elefsina, departs from Koumoundourou Sq/Deligeorgi St (*Tmr* C2/3) (averagely) every 20 mins, between 0510-2215hrs.

| | | |
| --- | --- | --- |
| 14.5km | **Patritsia.** Kato Kifissia, N. Athens. Tel 801 1900<br>Closed 'temporarily' in 1987 & 1988, so who knows for 1989? | Open June-Oct. Bar, shop, showers, laundry & kitchen facilities. |
| 16km | **Nea Kifissia.** Nea Kifissia, N. Athens. Tel 807 5544 | Open April-Oct, 20km from the sea. Bar, shop, showers, swimming pool & laundry. |
| 18km | **Dionyssiotis Camping.** Nea Kifissia N. Athens. Tel 807 1494 | Open all year. |
| 25km | **Papa-Camping.** Zorgianni, Ag Stefanos. Tel 803 3446 | Open June-Oct, 25km from the sea. Laundry, bar & kitchen facilities. |

For the above (sited on or beside the Athens National Road, north to Lamia): Lamia bus, from 260 Liossion St (*Tmr* C1/2), departs every hour from 0615 to 1915hrs & at 2030hrs.

| | | |
| --- | --- | --- |
| 35km | **Marathon Camping.** Kaminia, Marathon. NE of Athens. Tel 0294 55577 | On a sandy beach & open all year round. Showers, bar restaurant & kitchen facilities. |
| 35km | **Nea Makri.** 156 Marathonos Ave, Nea Makri. NE of Athens just south of Marathon. Tel 0294 92719 | Open April-Oct, 220m from the sea. Sandy beach, laundry, bar & shop. |

For the above: A bus from Odhos Mavrommateon, Plateia Egyptou (*Tmr* D1), departs approximately every ½ hour from between 0530-2230hrs.

| | | |
| --- | --- | --- |
| 26km | **Cococamp.** Rafina. East of Athens. Tel 0294 23413 | Open all year. On the beach, rocky coast. Laundry, bar, showers, kitchen facilities, shop & restaurant. |
| 29km | **Kokkino Limanaki Camping.** Kokkino Limanaki, Rafina. Tel 0294 31602 | On the beach. Open April-Oct. |
| 29km | **Rafina Camping.** Rafina. East of Athens. Tel 0294 23118 | Open May-Oct, 4km from sandy beach. Showers, bar, laundry, restaurant & shop. |

For the above: The Rafina bus from Mavrommateon St, Plateia Egyptou (*Tmr* D1). Some thirty departures, between 0545-2230hrs.

| | | |
| --- | --- | --- |
| 20km | **Voula Camping.** 2 Alkyonidon St, Voula. (Just below Glyfada & the Airport). Tel 895 2712 | Open all year, by a sandy beach. Showers, laundry, shop & kitchen facilities. |
| 27km | **Varkiza Beach Camping.** Varkiza. Coastal road, Athens-Vouliagmeni-Sounion. Tel 897 3613 | Open all year, by a sandy beach. Bar, shop, supermarket, taverna, laundry & kitchen facilities. |
| 60km | **Sounion Camping.** Sounion Tel 0292 39358 | Open all year, by a sandy beach. Bar, shop, laundry, kitchen facilities & a taverna. |
| 76km | **Vakhos Camping.** Assimaki, nr Sounion. On the Sounion to Lavrio road. Tel 0292 39263 | Open July-Sept, by a beach. |

For the above: Buses from Mavrommateon St, Plateia Egyptou (*Tmr* D1), depart every hour between 0630-1730hrs & 1900hrs. *Note*: to get to **Vakhos Camping** catch the Sounion bus, via Markopoulo and Lavrio.

## The Eating Out

Apart from being such a matter of personal choice, in a city the size of Athens there are so many restaurants and tavernas from which to choose that only a few recommendations are made. In general, I can only suggest that readers steer clear of Luxury and Class A hotel dining rooms, restaurants offering international cuisine and tavernas with Greek music and or dancing*, all of which may be very good but are usually inordinately expensive.

'Gongoozling' from one of the chic establishments, such as a *Fioka's*, edging one of the smart squares has become a comparatively expensive luxury, with a milky coffee (Nes meh ghala) or a bottle of beer costing anything up to 200drs, and an ouzo 250drs. In contrast it is possible to 'coffee' in the Plaka, at, say, *Kafeneion To Mainalon* (on the junction of Odhos Geronda, also named Monisasteriou, and Kidathineon St), where prices are much more reasonable, with a Nes meh ghala or an ouzo costing about 100drs. Incidentally, it is on an inside wall of *To Mainalon* that are preserved two price lists that vividly highlight the 'heady' effect of inflation in Greece. One of them dates back to 1965 and the other to 1968. They are priced in drachmae and lepta – one hundred lepta made up one drachma. A bottle of beer cost 2.50drs in 1965 and 3drs in 1968, a good brandy 3drs and 3.50drs, respectively, and an ouzo 3drs in both years. Thought provoking!

In Athens, and the larger, more cosmopolitan, provincial cities, it is usual taverna practice to round off prices, which proves a little disconcerting at first.

With despair, it is noted that some restaurants and tavernas climbing the slopes of the Acropolis (up Odhos Markou Avriliou, south of Eolou St) are allowing 'Chinese menu' style collective categories (A, B, & C) to creep into their listings.

* *Note the reference to Greek dancing and music is not derogatory – only an indication that it is often the case that standards of cuisine may not be any better and prices usually reflect the 'overheads' attributable to the musicians' wages. But See* **Palia** & **Xynou Tavernas**.

## PLAKA AREA (*Tmr* D5)

A glut of eating houses ranging from the very good and expensive, the very expensive and bad, to some inexpensive and very good.

**Taverna Thespis** 18 Thespidos St                                    Tel 323 8242
*Directions*: On the right of a lane across the way from Kidathineon St, towards the bottom or south-east end of Adrianou St.

Recommended and noted for friendly service. The house retsina is served in metal jugs. A two hour, slap-up meal of souvlakia, Greek salad, fried zucchini, bread and two carafes of retsina costs some 1600drs for two.

**Plaka Village** 28 Kidathineon
*Directions*: On the left (*Adrianou St behind one*), in the block edged by the streets of Adrianou and Kidathineon.

Once an excellent souvlaki pita snackbar but.... the offerings are now so-so, added to which to sit down costs extra. Price lists do not make this plain and the annoying habit can cause, at the least, irritation. (This practice is also prevalent in the Omonia Square 'souvlaki arcade'). Even more alarming is the 'take it or leave it' attitude that also extends to customer's money. The staff err towards 'taking' it, having to be badgered to return any change. The home-made tzatziki is good, the service is quick and they even remain open Sunday lunchtimes.

Committed souvlaki pita eaters do not have to despair as any number of snackbars are concentrated on both sides of Mitropoleos St, at the Monastiraki Square end. Perhaps the most inexpensive souvlakis in the area are to be found by turning right at the bottom of Kidathineon St and wandering down Adrianou, in the direction of Monastiraki Sq.

ΟΥΖΕΡΙ Ο ΚΟΥΚΛΗΣ (or **PEPAVI**) 14 Tripodon St                       Tel 324 7605
*Directions*: Up the slope from the Thespidos/Kidathineon junction, one to the left of Adrianou (*facing Monastiraki Sq*), and on the left.

Recognising the establishment is not difficult as the 1st floor balcony is still embellished with two, large, antique record player horns mounted on the wrought iron balustrade. A large, stuffed heron (yes a bird) has disappeared, the owners of the taverna maintaining that it has flown away to Mykonos!

The 'HMV' style trumpets easily distinguish the old ouzerie/wine shop, on the walls of which a vine grows.

The taverna, standing on its own, evokes a provincial country atmosphere. It is necessary to arrive early as Pepavi is well supported by the locals, a popularity vouchsafed by the taverna being full prior to 2000hrs. The patronage is not surprising considering the inexpensive excellence of one or two of the dishes. These include salvers of dolmades and meatballs, as well as 'flaming sausages'. The latter cook away on stainless steel plates set down in front of the diner. They are served with a large plateful of hors d'oeuvres, amongst which are a meatball, beans, lettuce, feta, chilli, new potatoes and Russian salad, at a cost of 1000drs for two. Great value, very filling indeed but watch the napkins don't go up in flames and bear in mind that the house wine is pretty rough.

**Eden Taverna** 3 Flessa St.
*Directions*: Off Adrianou St, almost opposite Odhos Nikodimou, and on the left.

Mentioned because their menu includes many offerings that excellently cater (sorry) for vegetarian requirements. Open 1200hrs-0100hrs every day, except Tuesdays.

**Palia Plakiotiki Taverna (Stamatopoulos)** (*Tmr* D5) 26 Lissiou St          Tel 322 8722
*Directions*: Proceed up Lissiou St, which parallels Adrianou St, in the general direction of Monastiraki Sq. The open-air taverna is behind a perimeter wall to the right, on a steep slope at the junction with Erechtheos St.

Claims to be one of Athens' oldest tavernas. The large terraced area is laid out with clean gravel chippings. Not particularly cheap but a super place at which to have an 'atmospheric' evening as there is a resident group. (Note this recommendation, despite my usual caveats regarding places at which music 'is on score'. Those remarks are usually attributed to establishments that advertise 'live' bouzouki). Here it is a major attraction in the shape of a huge, spherical man, with a name to match, Stavros Balagouras. He is the resident singer/accordionist/electric pianist and draws tourists and Greeks alike with his dignified and heartfelt performance. Besides traditional, national songs there is year-round dancing on the one square metre floor space, if customers are so moved! The taverna is particularly Greek and lively at festival times, added to which the food is good and much cheaper than similar establishments. Cheese and meat dishes, with salad and wine, cost about 1500drs for two. The dolmades are stuffed with meat and served in a lemon sauce so cost 350drs and meat dishes average 450/500drs. The wine is rather expensive with a bottle of Cambas red charged at 350drs and a large bottle of retsina 292drs. A bottle of Lowenbrau costs a reasonable 92drs. and the bread and head tax works out at only 15drs.

**Michiko Restaurant** 27 Kidathineon St          Tel 324 6851
*Directions*: On the right, beyond the junction with Asteriou St proceeding in a north-east direction (*towards Syntagma Sq*), close to a small square and church.

Japanese dishes, if you must, and extremely expensive.

**Xynou/Xynos** 4 Arghelou Geronda (Angelou Geronta)          Tel 322 1065
*Directions*: Left off the lower, Plaka Square end of Kidathineon St (*facing Syntagma Sq*) and on the left, towards the far point of the short pedestrian way. The unprepossessing entrance door is tucked away in the corner of a recess and is easily missed.

One of the oldest, most highly rated Plaka tavernas and well patronised by Athenians. Evenings only and closed on Saturdays and Sundays. A friend advises me that it is now almost obligatory to book in advance, although I have managed to squeeze a table for two early on in the evening. Mention of its popularity with Athenians prompts me to stress these are well-heeled locals – you know shipowners, ambassadors and aging playboys. Added to which the Xynou is definitely on the 'hotel captains' list of recommended establishments and the tourists who eat here tend to look as if they have stepped off the stage-set of Dallas. It is not surprising that the cognoscenti gather because, despite being in the heart of Athens, the premises evoke a rural ambience. The single storey, shed-like, roof tiled buildings edge two sides of a high wall enclosed gravel area, on which are spread the chairs and tables. The food is absolutely excellent and, considering the location, the prices are not outrageous. A meal of two plates of dolmades in lemon sauce, a plate of moussaka, a lamb fricassee in lemon sauce, a tomato and cucumber salad, a bottle of kortaki retsina and bread for two costs 1530drs. It seems a pity that the bread has to be charged at 50drs, but the ample wine list does include an inexpensive retsina. Three guitarists serenade diners, the napkins are linen and the service is first class. Readers are recommended to save up and try Xynou's, at least once, for an experience that will not be easily forgotten.

**To Fragathiko Taverna** (*Tmr* D5)
*Directions*: On the left of Adrianou St (*proceeding towards Kidathineon St*) at the junction of Adrianou and Ag Andreou Sts.

Clean, reasonably priced and popular with the younger generation, some of whom may not be entirely wholesome, but their enthusiasm is not surprising considering the inexpensively priced dishes on offer. These include moussaka special 325drs; moussaka special served with 4 kinds of vegetable 425drs; lamb special served with 4 kinds of vegetable 425drs and a vegetarian dish costing 240drs.

Plateia Agora is a lovely, elongated, chic Plaka Square formed at the junction of the bottom of Eolou and the top of Adrianou and Kapnikarea Sts. The square spawns a number of cafe-bar restaurants, including the *Posidion* and *Appollon*, the canopies, chairs and tables of which edge the pavement all the way round the neat, paved plateia. Don't forget that prices reflect the square's modishness with a bottle of beer at the *Posidion* costing 200drs. There is a spotless public lavatory at the top (Monastiraki) end. The *Appollon* has a particularly wide range of choice and clients can sit at the comfortable tables for an (expensive) hour or so over a coffee (120drs), a fried egg breakfast (300drs) or a full blown meal, if anyone can afford the same. On this tack it is becoming commonplace for some of the smarter places such as the *Posidion* to display unpriced menus. Hope your luck is in and the organ grinder wanders through the square.

From the little square formed by a 'junction of the ways', adjacent to the Lysikrates Monument (*Tmr* 21D5), Odhos Vironos falls towards the south Acropolis encircling avenue of Dionysiou Areopagitou.

**Snackbar** Odhos Vironos
*Directions*: As above and on the right (*Plaka behind one*) of the street.

More a small 'doorway' souvlaki pita shop but small is indeed splendid.

**Restaurant Olympia** 20 Dionysiou Areopagitou
*Directions*: Proceed along Dionysiou Areopagitou, from the junction with Odhos Vironos, in a clockwise direction. The restaurant is on the right, close to the junction with Thassilou Lane (that incidentally climbs and bends back up to the top of Odhos Thespidos), hard up against the foot of the Acropolis. Between Thassilou Lane and the sun-blind-shaded lean-to butted on to the side of the restaurant, is a small grassed area and an underground public toilet.

The prices seem reasonable and the place appears to portend good things but....I can only report the promise was in reality, disappointing. The double Greek salad was in truth only large enough for one, the moussaka was 'inactive', the kalamares were unacceptable and the roast potatoes (yes roast potatoes) were in actuality nothing more than dumpy wedges. Oh dear! They do serve a kortaki retsina.

## STADIUM (PANGRATI) AREA (*Tmr* E/F6)
**Karavitis Taverna** (ΚΑΡΑΒΙΤΗΣ) 4 Pafsaniou (Paysanioy).
*Directions*: Beyond the Stadium (*Tmr* E/F6) going east (*away from the Acropolis*) along Vassileos Konstantinou, and Pafsaniou is the 3rd turning to the right. The taverna is on the left.

A small, leafy, tree shaded gravel square fronts the taverna, which is so popular that there is an extension across the street, through a pair of 'field gates'. Our friend Paul will probably berate me (if he was less of a gentleman) for listing this gem. Largely unknown to visitors but extremely popular with Athenians, more especially those who, when college students, frequented this jewel in the Athens taverna crown. A meal for four of a selection of dishes including lamb, beef in clay, giant haricot beans, garlic flavoured meatballs, greens, tzatziki, 2 plates of feta cheese, aubergines, courgettes, bread and 3 jugs of retsina, from the barrel, costs some 2400drs. Beat that! But some knowledge of Greek is an advantage and the taverna is only open in the evening.

Instead of turning off Vassileos Konstantinou at Odhos Pafsaniou, take the next right proceeding further eastwards.

ΜΑΓΕΜΕΝΟΣ ΑΥΛΟΣ **(The Magic Flute)** Odhos Aminda (Amynta).
*Directions*: As above and the restaurant is 20m up on the right.

Swiss dishes, including *fondue*, schnitzels and salads. Despite being rather more expensive than its near neighbours, it is well frequented by Athenians, including the composer Hadzithakis (so I am advised).

**Virinis Taverna**, Archimedes St
*Directions*: Prior to the side-streets that lead to the two restaurant/tavernas last detailed, the second

turning to the right off Vassileos Konstantinou (beyond the Stadium (*Tmr* E/F6), proceeding in an easterly direction) is Odhos Eratosthenous. This climbs up to Plateia Plastira, to the right of which is Archimedes St. The taverna is about a 100m along on the left. Incidentally, if returning to the centre of Athens from hereabouts, it is possible to continue along Archimedes St and drop down Odhos Markou Moussourou back to Vassileos Konstantinou.

A good selection of bistro dishes at reasonable prices, including, for instance, beef in wine sauce at a cost of 350drs. It has been indicated that I might find the place rather 'up market', as there aren't any souvlaki pita on offer. Cheeky! It's only that over the years, I have learnt through costly experience that, in Greece, gingham tablecloths and French style menus tend to double the prices!

## SYNTAGMA AREA (*Tmr* D/E4/5)

**Corfu Restaurant** 6 Kriezotou St                                                             Tel 361 3011
*Directions*: North of Syntagma Sq and first turning right off Panepistimiou (El Venizelou).
   Extensive Greek and European dishes in a modern, friendly restaurant.

**Delphi Restaurant** 15 Nikis St                                                             Tel 323 4869
*Directions*: From the south-west corner of Syntagma Sq, east along Mitropoleos and the first turning left.
   Modern, with reasonably priced food from an extensive menu as well as friendly service.

**Sintrivani Restaurant** 5 Filellinon St.
*Directions*: South-west corner of Syntagma Sq and due south.
   Garden restaurant serving a traditional menu at reasonable prices.

**Vassillis Restaurant** 14A Voukourestiou.
*Directions*: North of Syntagma Sq and the second turning to the right off Panepistimiou St, along Odhos Smats and across Akadimias St.
   Variety, in traditional surroundings.

**Ideal Restaurant** 46 Panepistimiou St.
*Directions*: Proceed up Panepistimiou from the north-east corner of Syntagma Sq and the restaurant is on the right.
   Good food at moderate prices.

**YWCA** 11 Amerikis St.
*Directions*: North-west from Syntagma Sq along either Stadiou or Panepistimiou St and second or third road to the right, depending which street is used.
   Cafeteria serving inexpensive sandwiches.

There are many cafes in and around Syntagma Square. Recommended, but expensive, is the:-
**Brazilian Coffee Cafe**
*Directions*: Close by Syntagma Sq, in Voukourestiou St.
   Serves coffee, tea, toast, butter and jam, breakfast, ice-creams and pastries.

## OMONIA AREA (*Tmr* D3)

**Ellinikon Taverna** (*Tmr* D2/3) Dorou St.
*Directions*: North of Omonia Sq, along Dorou St and almost immediately on the left down some steps to a basement.
   A cavernous, 'greasy spoon' well frequented by workmen and sundry officials, as well as a sprinkling of tourists. Inexpensive fare and draught retsina available.

**Taverna Kostoyannus** 37 Zaimi St.
*Directions*: Leave Omonia northwards on 28 Ikosiokto Oktovriou, turn right at Odhos Stournara to the nearside of the Polytechnic School, and Zaimi St is the second road along. The taverna is to the left, approximately behind the National Archaeological Museum.
   Good food, acceptable prices and comes well recommended. As in the case of many other Athenian tavernas, it is not open for lunch or on Sundays.

**Snackbars**
Probably the most compact, reasonably priced 'offerings', but in grubby surroundings, lurk in the arcade between Dorou St and 28 Ikosiokto Oktovriou, off Omonia Sq. Here are situated cafes and stalls selling almost every variety of Greek convenience fast food. A 'standard' souvlaki costs 70-80drs and a 'spezial', or de luxe, 90-100drs, BUT do not sit down unless you wish to be charged an extra 15-20drs per head. A bottle of beer is charged at about 90drs.

## Cafes
Everywhere of course, but on Omonia Sq, alongside Dorou St and adjacent to the *Hotel Carlton*, is a magnificent specimen of the traditional kafeneion.

Herein, Athenians sip coffee and tumble their worry beads, as they must have done since the turn of the century.

### Bretania Cafe
*Directions*: Bordering Omonia Square, on the left-hand side (*Acropolis behind one or, more easily, facing the Hotel Omonia*) of the junction with Athinas St.

An excellent, very old-fashioned, 'sticky' sweet cake shop which is rather more a galaktozacharoplasteion than a cafe. Renowned for its range of sweets, yoghurt and honey, cream and honey, rice puddings and so on, all served with sugar sweet bread and drinks until 0200hrs every morning. A speciality is 'Flower of the Milk', a cream and yoghurt dish costing 200drs per head.

Continuing on down Athinas St, beyond Plateia Kotzia, leads past the covered meat market building on the left and a number of:-

### 'Meat Market' Tavernas
*Directions*: As above and towards the rear of the building. It has to be admitted that it is necessary for prospective diners to pick their way through piles of bones and general market detritus after dark.

Open 24 hours a day and a find for those who like to slum it, in less expensive establishments of some note.

## LYCABETTUS (LYKAVITOS) AREA (*Tmr* F/G4) As befits a high priced area, these listings are very expensive.

### Je Reviens Restaurant 49 Xenokratous St.
*Directions*: North-east from Kolonaki Sq, up Patriachou Ioakim St to the junction with Odhos Marasli on which turn left and climb a flight of steps until they cross Xenokratous St.

French food, creditable but expensive. Open midday and evenings.

### L'Abreuvoir 51 Xenokratous St.
*Directions*: As for *Je Reviens*, as are the comments but even more expensive.

### Al Convento Restaurant (*Tmr* G4) 4 Anapiron    Tel 723 9163
*Directions*: North-east from Kolonaki Sq, along Patriachou Ioakim to Marasli St. Turn left and then right along Odhos Souidias and Anapiron St is nearly at the end.

### Bonanza Restaurant 14 Voukourestiou.
*Directions*: From the north-west corner of Plateia Kolonaki, take Odhos Skoufa, which crosses Voukourestiou St.

Once known as the *Stage Coach*. Not only Wild West in decor, air-conditioned and serving American style food but very expensive with steaks as a house speciality. Why not go to the good old US of A? Lunch and evening meals, open 1200 to 1600hrs and 1900 to 0100hrs.

## THE A TO Z OF USEFUL INFORMATION
**AIRLINE OFFICE & TERMINUS** (*Tmr* 12C6) The busy Olympic offices are to the left (*facing Syntagma Sq*) of the traffic frantic Leoforos Sygrou. As with other Olympic facilities the office doubles as a terminus for airport buses arriving from and departing to the East and West Airports. Passengers who land up here should note that the most convenient, combined bus stop to Syntagma Square, the centre of Athens, is (*with the building behind one*), across the busy thoroughfare and some 50m up the incline of Leoforos Sygrou. This 'hosts' any number of buses and trolley-buses, while the stop directly across the road serves only one or two trolley-buses.

**Aircraft timetables.** *See* **Chapter Three** for general details of the island airports described in this guide and the individual island chapters for details of the schedules.

**BANKS (Trapeza – ΤΡΑΠΕΖΑ)** Note that if a bank strike is under way (apparently becoming a natural part of the tourist season 'high jinks'), the National Bank on Syntagma Sq stays open and in business. However, in these circumstances, the place becomes even more than usually crowded. Athens' banks include the:

**National Bank of Greece** (*Tmr* 3D/E4) 2 Karageorgi Servias, Syntagma Sq.
All foreign exchange services: Mon to Thurs 0800-1400hrs; Fri 0800-1330hrs; Sat, Sun & holidays 0900-1600hrs. Travellers cheques & foreign cash exchange services: weekdays 0800-2000hrs; Sat, Sun & holidays 0900-1600hrs.

**Ionian & Popular Bank** (*Tmr* D/E/4/5) 1 Mitropoleos St.
Only open normal banking hours.
**Commercial Bank of Greece** (*Tmr* E4) 11 Panepistimiou (El Venizelou).
Normal banking hours.
**American Express** (*Tmr* D/E4/5) 2 Ermou St, Syntagma Sq.                    Tel 324 4975/9
Carries out usual Amex office transactions and is open Mon to Thurs 0830-1400hrs; Fri 0830-1330hrs
& Sat 0820-1230hrs.
    There are several banks in the concourse of the East Airport terminal building.

**BEACHES** Athens is not on a river or by the sea, so to enjoy a beach it is necessary to leave the city
and travel to the suburbs. Very often these beaches are operated under the aegis of the NTOG (Greek
Tourist Board), or private enterprise in association with a hotel. The NTOG beaches usually have beach
huts, cabins, tennis courts, a playground and catering facilities. Entrance charges vary from 25-100drs.
    There are beaches and or swimming pools at:

| | | |
|---|---|---|
| Paleon Faliron/ | A seaside resort | Bus No. 126: Departs from Odhos Othonos, south side of Syntagma |
| Faliro | | Sq (*Tmr* E5). |
| Alimos | NTOG beach | Bus No. 133: Departs from Odhos Othonos, south side of Syntagma |
| | | Sq (*Tmr* E5). |
| Glyfada(Gilfada) | A seaside resort | Bus No. 129: Departs from Leoforos Olgas, south side of the Zappeion |
| | | Gardens (*Tmr* E5/6). |
| Voula | NTOG beach | Bus No. 122: Departs from Leoforos Olgas, south side of the Zappeion |
| | Class A | Gardens (*Tmr* E5/6). |
| Voula | NTOG beach | Bus No. 122: As above. |
| | Class B | Admission costs: adults 60drs, children 40drs. |
| Vouliagmeni | A luxury seaside | Bus No. 118: Departs from Leoforos Olgas, south side of the Zappeion |
| | resort & yacht marina. | Gardens (*Tmr* E5/6). |
| | NTOG beach | Admission costs: adults 100drs, children 50drs. |
| Varkiza | A seaside resort & | Bus No. 115: Departs from Leoforos Olgas, south side of the Zappeion |
| | yacht marina. | Gardens (*Tmr* E5/6). |
| | NTOG Beach | Admission costs: adults 100drs, children 50drs. |

There are beaches all the way down to Cape Sounion (Sounio) via the coast road. *See*
**Bus timetables, A To Z.**

**BOOKSELLERS** Apart from the second-hand bookshops in the Plaka Flea Market (*See*
**Monastiraki Square, Introduction**), there are three or four on Odhos Nikis (west of
Syntagma Sq) and Odhos Amerikis (north-west of Syntagma Sq), as well as one on
Lysikratous St, opposite the small church (*Tmr* 21D5).
    Of all the above it is perhaps invidious to select one but here goes...
**The Compendium Bookshop (& Computers)** 28 Nikis St.                    Tel 322 1248
*Directions*: On the left of Nikis St (*facing Syntagma Sq*).
    Well recommended for a wide range of English language publications. As well as new
books they sell some good condition, 'used' books. The owner, Rick Schulein, is happy
to buy books back into stock that he has sold to a client. The *Transalpino* travel office is
in the basement.

**BREAD SHOPS** In the more popular shopping areas. For instance, descending along
Odhos Adrianou, in the Plaka (*Tmr* D5), from the Odhos Thespidos/Kidathineon end,
advances past many shops, general stores and a bread shop (or two).

**BUSES & TROLLEY-BUSES** These run variously between 0500 and 0030hrs (half an
hour past midnight), are usually crowded but excellent value with a 'flat rate' charge of
30drs. Travel between 0500 and 0800hrs is free, not only on the buses but the Metro
as well. Also *See* **Access to the Stations, Trains, A To Z.**

**Buses** The buses are blue (and green) and bus stops are marked *Stasis* (ΣΤΑΣΙΣ). Some
one-man-operated buses are utilised and a few have an honesty box for fares.

**Trolley-Buses** Yellow coloured vehicles and bus stops. Entered via a door at the front
marked *Eisodos* (ΕΙΣΟΔΟΣ), with the exit at the rear, marked *Exodos* (ΕΞΟΔΟΣ). Have the
correct money to put into the fare machine as there are no tickets or change disgorged.

**Major city terminals & turn-round points**:
include:
Kaningos Sq: (*Tmr* 4D2) North-east of Omonia Sq.

Stadiou/Kolokotroni junction: (*Tmr* D/E4). This has replaced the Korai Sq terminus, now that Korai has been pedestrianised.

Kifissou St: West-north-west of Omonia Sq. The depot on this major highway lies between the junctions of Lenorman and Leoforos Athinon.

Liossion St: (*Tmr* C2) North-west of Omonia Sq.

Eleftherias Sq: (*Tmr* 9C3) North-west of Monastiraki Sq.

Leoforos Olgas: (*Tmr* D/E5/6) South of the National Garden.

Mavrommateon St*: (*Tmr* D/E1) West of Pedion Areos Park, north of Omonia Sq.
* *This tree shaded, north-south street is lined with bus departure points.*

Egyptou Place (Aigyptou/Egiptou): (*Tmr* D1) Just below the south-west corner of Pedion Areos Park, alongside 28 Ikosiokto Oktovriou.

Ag Asomaton Square: (*Tmr* B/C4) West of Monastiraki Sq.

Koumoundourou St: (*Tmr* C2/3) West of Omonia Sq, third turning off Ag Konstantinou.

(Also *See* KTEL & OSE terminals listed at the end of this section).

**Trolley-bus timetable** Some major city routes include:

| | |
|---|---|
| No. 1: | Plateia Attikis (Metro station) (*Tmr* C1), Leoforos Amalias, **Stathmos Larissis** (railway station), Karaiskaki Place, Ag Konstantinou, **Omonia Sq**, **Syntagma Sq**, Kallithea suburb (SW Athens). Every 10 mins, from 0505-2350hrs. |
| No. 2: | Pangrati (*Tmr* G6), Leoforos Amalias (Central), **Syntagma Sq**, **Omonia Sq**, 28 Ikosiokto Oktovriou/Patission St, Kipseli (N Athens). Between 0630-0020hrs. |
| No. 10: | N. Smirni (S Athens), Leoforos Sygrou, Leoforos Amalias, **Syntagma Sq**, Panepistimiou St, Stadiou/Kolokotroni junction (*Tmr* D/E4). Between 0500-2345hrs. |
| No. 12: | Leoforos Olgas (*Tmr* D/E5/6), Leoforos Amalias, **Syntagma Sq**, **Omonia Sq**, 28 Ikosiokto Oktovriou/Patission St (N Athens). From 0630-2235hrs. |

Other routes covered by trolley-buses include:

| | |
|---|---|
| No. 3: | Patissia to Erythrea (N to NNE Athens suburbs). Between 0625-2230hrs. |
| No. 4: | Odhos Kypselis (*Tmr* E1, North of Pedion Areos Park), **Omonia Sq**, **Syntagma Sq**, Leoforos Olgas to Ag Artemios (SSE Athens suburbs). Between 0630-0020hrs. |
| No. 5: | Patissia (N Athens suburb), **Stathmos Larissis** (railway station), **Omonia Sq**, **Syntagma Sq**, Filellinon St, Koukaki (S Athens suburb). Between 0630-0015hrs. |
| No. 6: | Ippokratous St (*Tmr* E3), Panepistimiou St, **Omonia Sq**, N Filadelfia (N Athens suburb). Every 10mins, from 0500-2320hrs. |
| No. 7: | Panepistimiou St (*Tmr* D/E3/4), 28 Ikosiokto Oktovriou/Patission St, Leoforos Alexandras (N of Lycabettus). Between 0630-0015hrs. |
| No. 8: | Plateia Kaningos (*Tmr* 4D2), Odhos Akadimias, Vassilissis Sofias, Leoforos Alexandras, 28 Ikosiokto Oktovriou/Patission St. Between 0630-0020hrs. |
| No. 9: | Odhos Kypselis (*Tmr* E1, North of Pedion Areos Park), 28 Ikosiokto Oktovriou/Patission St, Stadiou St, **Syntagma Sq**, Petralona (W Athens suburb – far side of Filopapou). Every 10mins, from 0455-2345hrs. |
| No. 10: | Stadiou/Koloktoroni junction (*Tmr* D/E4), Stadiou St, **Syntagma Sq**, Filellinon St, Leoforos Sygrou, Nea Smirni (S Athens suburb). Every 10mins, from 0500-2345hrs. |
| No. 11: | Koliatsou (NNE Athens suburb), **Stathmos Larissis** (railway station), 28 Ikosiokto Oktovriou/Patission St, Stadiou St, **Syntagma Sq**, Filellinon St, Plastira Sq, Eftichidou St, N Pangrati (ESE Athens suburb). Every 5mins, from 0500-0010hrs. |
| No. 13: | 28 Ikosiokto Oktovriou/Patission St, Akadimias St, Vassilissis Sofias, Papadiamantopoulou St, Leoforos Kifissias, Labrini (just beyond Galatsi suburb – NE Athens suburb). Every 10mins, from 0500-2400hrs. |
| No. 14: | Leoforos Alexandras, 28 Ikosiokto Oktovriou/Patission, Patissia (N Athens suburb). |

**Bus timetable** Bus numbers are subject to a certain amount of confusion, but here goes! Some of the routes are as follows:

| | |
|---|---|
| No. 022: | Kaningos Sq (*Tmr* 4D2), Akadimias, Kanari, Patriarchou Ioakim, Marasli, Genadiou St (SE Lycabettus). Every 10mins, from 0520-2330hrs. |
| No. 023: | Kaningos Sq (*Tmr* 4D2), Kolonaki Sq, Lycabettus. |
| No. 024*: | Leoforos Amalias (*Tmr* D/E5), **Syntagma Sq**, Panepistimiou St, **Omonia Sq**, Tritis Septemvriou, Stournara, Sourmeli, Acharnon, Liossion St. Every 20mins, from 0530-2400hrs. |

* *This is the bus that delivers passengers to 250 Liossion St (Tmr C2), one of the main bus terminals.*

| | |
|---|---|
| No. 040: | Filellinon St (close to **Syntagma Sq** – *Tmr* D/E4/5), Leoforos Amalias, Leoforos Sygrou to Vassileos Konstantinou, **Piraeus**. Every 10mins, 24 hours a day. A green bus. |
| No. 045: | Kaningos Sq (*Tmr* 4D2), Akadimias St, Vassilissis Sofias, Leoforos Kifissias, Kefalari & Politia (NE Athens suburb). Every 15mins, from 0600-0100hrs. |
| No. 047: | Menandrou St (SW of **Omonia Sq**), Stathmos Larissis (railway station). |
| No. 049: | Athinas St (*Tmr* C/D3), (S of Omonia Sq), Sofokleous, Pireos, Sotiros, Filonos St to Plateia |

|  | Themistokleous, **Piraeus**. Every 10mins, 24 hours a day. A green bus. |
|---|---|
| No. 051*: | Off Ag Konstantinou (*Tmr* C2/3, W of **Omonia Sq**), Kolonou St, Lenorman St, Kifissou St. Every 10mins, from 0500-2400hrs. |

* *This is the bus that connects to the 100 Kifissou St (*Tmr* A2), a main bus terminal.*

|  |  |
|---|---|
| No. 115: | Leoforos Olgas (*Tmr* D/E5/6), Leoforos Sygrou, Leoforos Possidonos (coast road) to Vouliagmeni & Varkiza (S Athens coastal suburbs). Every 20mins, 24 hours a day. |
| No. 116,117 | Leoforos Olgas, Varkiza (S Athens coastal suburb). |
| No. 118: | Leoforos Olgas, Leoforos Sygrou, Leoforos Possidonos (coast road) to Vouliagmeni (S Athens coastal suburb). Every 20mins, from 1245-2015hrs. |
| No. 121,128, 129: | Leoforos Olgas (*Tmr* E6), Glyfada (SSE Athens coastal suburb). |
| No. 122: | Leoforos Olgas, Leoforos Sygrou, Leoforos Possidonos (coast road) to Voula (S Athens coastal suburb). Every 20mins, from 0530-2400hrs. |
| No. 132: | Othonos St **Syntagma Sq** – *Tmr* D/E4/5), Filellinon St, Leoforos Amalias, Leoforos Sygrou to Edem (SSE Athens suburb). Every 20mins, from 0530-1900hrs. |
| No. 153: | Leoforos Olgas, Vouliagmeni (SSE Athens coastal suburb). |
| No. 224: | Polygono (N Athens suburb), 28 Ikosiokto Oktovriou/Patission St, Kaningos Sq, Vassilissis Sofias, Democratias St (Kessariani, E Athens suburb). Every 20mins, from 0500-2400hrs. |
| No. 230: | Ambelokipi (E Athens suburb), Leoforos Alexandras, Ippokratous St, Akadimias St, **Syntagma Sq**, Leoforos Amalias, Dionysiou Areopagitou, Apostolou Pavlou, Thission. Every 10mins, from 0500-2320hrs. |
| No. 405: | Leoforos Alexandras, **Stathmos Larissis** (railway station). |
| No. 510: | Kaningos Sq (*Tmr* 4D2), Akadimias St, Ippokratous St, Leoforos Alexandras, Leoforos Kifissias to Dionyssos (NE Athens suburb). Every 20mins, from 0530-2250hrs. |
| No. 527: | Kaningos Sq, (*Tmr* 4D2) Akadimias St, Leoforos Alexandras, Leoforos Kifissias to Amaroussion (NE Athens suburb). Every 15mins, from 0615-2215hrs. |
| No. 538, 539: | Kaningos Sq, Kifissia (NNE Athens suburb). |
| No. 603: | Akadimias St (*Tmr* D/E 3/4) to Psychiko (NE Athens suburb). |
| No. 610: | Akadimias St to Filothei (NE Athens suburb). |
| No. 853, 862, 864: | Plateia Eleftherias (*Tmr* 9B/C 3/4), Elefsina (Elefsis – West of Athens, beyond Dafni). |
| No. 873: | Plateia Eleftherias, Dafni (W Athens suburb). |

**Attica buses & timetable** (orange buses) include:

Athens – Rafina: depart from 29, Mavrommateon St (*Tmr* D/E1).
Athens – Nea Makri: depart from 29, Mavrommateon St.
Athens – Marathon: depart from 29, Mavrommateon St.
Athens – Lavrio*: depart from 14, Mavrommateon St.
* *See* Athens – Sounion details following.

| Athens – | Sounion – West coast road: depart from 14 Mavrommateon St |
|---|---|
|  | Every half hour between 0600-1830hrs |
| *Return* | 0540, 0630, then every half hour between 0800-2000hrs & 2100hrs. |
|  | One-way fare 370drs, duration 1 ½hrs. |
| Athens – | Sounion – via Markopoulo & Lavrio: depart from 14 Mavrommateon St. |
|  | Every hour between 0630-1730hrs & 1900hrs. |
| *Return* | Every hour between 0730-2130hrs. |
|  | One-way fare 340drs, duration 2hrs. |
| Athens – | Vravron: Take either the Sounion bus, via Markopoulo, or the Lavrio bus, get off at Markopoulo & catch a local bus to Vravron. |

**NB For specific details of bus connections to the relevant Mainland Ports, refer to Chapter Ten.**

The rest of Greece is served by:
**1) KTEL** A pool of bus operators working through one company from two terminals. 260 Liossion St* and 100 Kifissou St**

**\* Liossion St** (*Tmr* C2) is to the east of Stathmos Peloponissou Railway Station. This terminus serves Halkida, Edipsos, Kimi, Delphi, Amfissa, Kamena Vourla, Larissa, Thiva, Trikala (Meteora), Livadia, Lamia.
**Refer to bus route No. 024 for transport to this terminus.**

**\*\* Kifissou St** (*Tmr* A2) is to the west north-west of Omonia Sq, beyond the 'steam railway' lines, across Leoforos Konstantinoupoleos and up either Leoforos Athinon and turn right, or Odhos Lenorman and turn left. This terminus serves Patras, Pirgos (Olympia), Nafplio (Mikines), Adritsena (Vasses), Kalamata, Sparti (Mistras), Githio (Diros), Tripolis, Messolongi, Igoumenitsa, Preveza, Ioanina, Corfu, Zakynthos, Cephalonia, Lefkas, Kozani, Kastoria, Florina, Grevena, Veria, Naoussa, Seres, Kilkis, Kavala, Drama, Komotini, Korinthos, Kranidi, Xilokastro.
**Refer to Bus route No. 051 for transport to this terminus.**

**2) OSE** (The State Railway Company) Their buses terminus alongside the main railway stations of Stathmos Peloponissou and Larissis. Apart from the domestic services, there is a terminal for other European capitals, including Paris, Istanbul and Munich, at Stathmos Larissis Station.

For any bus services connecting to the islands and relevant Mainland Ports detailed in this guide, also refer to the Mainland Ports, Chapter Ten, and or the relevant Island chapters.

**CAMPING** *See* **The Accommodation.**

**CAR HIRE** As any other capital city, numerous offices, the majority of which are dotted about the smarter areas and squares, such as Syntagma Sq and Leoforos Amalias. Apart from the international firms of *Avis* and *Hertz* typical is: **Pappas,** 44 Leoforos Amalias Tel 322 0087.

There are any number of car hire (and travel) firms in and around the airport, bus and train locations, as well as on the right of Leoforos Sygrou, descending from the 'spaghetti junction' south of the Temple of Olympian Zeus (*Tmr* D6).

**CAR REPAIR** Help and advice can be obtained by contacting: **The Automobile & Touring Club of Greece (ELPA),** (*Tmr* I/3) 2 Messogion St Tel 779 1615. For immediate, emergency attention dial 104.

There are dozens of back street car repairers, breakers and spare part shops parallel and to the west of Leoforos Sygrou, in the area between the Temple of Olympian Zeus and the Olympic Airline terminal.

**CHEMIST** *See* **Medical Care, A To Z.**

**CINEMAS** There are a large number of outdoor cinemas, and don't worry about a language barrier, the majority of the films have English (American) dialogue with Greek subtitles.

. **Aigli** in the Zappeion is a 'must' and is situated at the south end of the National Garden. Other cinemas are bunched together on the streets of Stadiou, Panepistimiou and 28 Ikosiokto Oktovriou/Patission.

Note that the cinemas in Athens, of which there are vast numbers, generally screen poor quality, jerky films complete with squiggly lines, scratches, hisses, long black gaps as well as loss of sound. However a recommendation is the:

**Radio City** 240 Patission St.

*Directions*: North of Omonia Sq.

Large screen, good sound and knowledgeable operators.

**CLUBS, BARS & DISCOS** Why leave home? But if you must, there are enough to go round *See* **The Eating Out.**

**COMMERCIAL SHOPPING AREAS** During daylight hours a very large street market ranges along Odhos Athinas (*Tmr* C3/4), Odhos Sokratous and the associated side streets from Ermou St, almost all the way up to Omonia Sq. After dark the shutters are drawn down, the stalls canvassed over and the 'ladies of the night' appear.

Plateia Kotzia (*Tmr* C/D3) spawns a flower market on Sundays, whilst the Parliament Building side of Vassilissis Sofias (*Tmr* E4) is lined with smart flower stalls that open daily.

Monastiraki Sq (*Tmr* 5C4) and the various streets that radiate off are abuzz, specialising in widely differing aspects of the commercial and tourist trade. Odhos Areos contains a plethora of leather goods shops; the near end of Ifestou Lane is edged by stall upon stall of junk and tourist 'omit-abilia' (forgettable memorabilia); Pandrossou Lane contains a better class of shop and stall selling sandals, pottery and smarter 'memorabilia', while the square itself has a number of handcart hawkers.

The smart department stores are conveniently situated in or around Syntagma Sq, and the main streets that radiate off the square, including Ermou, Stadiou and Panepistimiou.

Tapestries are an extremely good buy. A reliable shop is sited close to and on the far side (*From Syntagma Sq*) of Kapnikarea Church (*Tmr* 6 D4), on Ermou St.

In the area south of Syntagma Sq, on the junction of Apollonos and Pendelis Sts, close by Odhos Voulis, are three small, obliging fruit and greengrocery shops. Apollonos St is useful to shoppers because, close by the junction with Odhos Nikis and on the right-hand side, is a combined fruit and butcher's shop. Next door is a stick souvlaki snackbar and across the road an ironmongers.

*See* **Bread Shops** & **Trains, A To Z** for details of other markets and shopping areas.

**DENTISTS & DOCTORS** *See* **Medical Care, A To Z.**

**EMBASSIES**

| | |
|---|---|
| Australia: 15 Messogion Av. | Tel 775 7650 |
| Belgium: 3 Sekeri St. | Tel 361 7886 |
| Canada: 4 Ioannou Gennadiou St. | Tel 723 9511 |

| | |
|---|---|
| Denmark: 15 Philikis Etairias Sq. | Tel 724 9315 |
| Finland: 1 Eratosthenous & Vas. Konstantinou Sts. | Tel 751 9795 |
| France: 7 Vassilissis Sofias. | Tel 361 1663 |
| German Federal Republic (West Germany): 3 Karaoli/Dimitriou Sts. | Tel 369 4111 |
| Great Britain: 1 Ploutarchou & Ypsilantou Sts. | Tel 723 6211 |
| Ireland: 7 Vassileos Konstantinou. | Tel 723 2771 |
| Netherlands: 5-7 Vassileos Konstantinou. | Tel 723 9701 |
| New Zealand: 15-17 Tshoa St. | Tel 641 0311 |
| Norway: 7 Vassileos Konstantinou St. | Tel 724 6173 |
| South Africa: 124 Kifissias/latridou. | Tel 692 2125 |
| Sweden: 7 Vassileos Konstantinou St. | Tel 722 4504 |
| USA: 91 Vassilissis Sofias. | Tel 721 2951 |

**FERRY-BOAT & FLYING DOLPHIN TICKET OFFICES** Apart from the headquarters, most, if not all, ferry-boat ticket offices are located in Piraeus Port, as is the main *Ceres Flying Dolphin* booking office. Incidentally, the latter are the hydrofoils that service the Argo-Saronic and Sporades islands. There is also a *Ceres* first floor office in the building immediately to the left of the *National Bank* (*Tmr* 3D/E4) (*Syntagma Sq behind one*). Despite the staff being disinterested, they are able to hand over a comprehensive timetable and prices.

**HAIRDRESSERS** No problems, with sufficient in the main shopping areas.

**HOSPITALS** *See* **Medical Care, A To Z**.

**LAUNDERETTES** There are others but a good, central recommendation must be:
**Coin-op** (*Tmr* 13D5) Angelou Geronda.
*Directions*: From Kidathineon St (*proceeding towards Syntagma Sq*), at the far end of Plateia Plaka turn right down Angelou Geronda, towards Odhos Dedalou, and the launderette is on the right-hand side.
A machine load costs 200drs, 9 mins of dryer time 200drs and a measure of powder 50drs. In respect of the detergent, why not pop out to Kidathineon St and purchase a small packet of *Tide* for some 40drs? For customers who are busy and are prepared to leave the laundry behind, the staff supervise the wash and dry operation at an extra cost of 400drs. Open in the summer, daily 0800-2100hrs. Note that my lavatorial obsession would not be satisfied without mentioning the Public toilet sited on Plateia Plaka.
Other launderettes are situated in Odhos Psarion, north of Plateia Karaiskaki (*Tmr* B/C2), and in Didotou St (*Tmr* E3), close to the junction with Odhos Zoodochos Pigis. The more usual Athens style is for customers to leave their washing at any one of the countless laundries, collecting it next day dry, stiff and bleached (if necessary).

**LOST PROPERTY** The main office is situated at 33 Ag Konstantinou (Tel 523 0111), the Plateia Omonia end of Ag Konstantinou. The telephone number is that of the Transport police who are now in charge of lost property (or *Grafio Hamenon Adikimenon*). Another 'lost & found' telephone number is 770 5771. It is still true to say that you are far more likely to 'lose' personal belongings to other tourists, than to Greeks.

**LUGGAGE STORE** There is one at No. 26 Nikis St (*Tmr* D5) advertising the service at a cost of 50drs per day per piece, 250drs per week and 750drs per month. Many hotels, guest houses and pensions 'mind' a clients' bags, quite a number at no charge.

**MEDICAL CARE**
**Chemists/Pharmacies (Farmakio – ΦΑΡΜΑΚΕΙΟ)** Identified by a green or red cross on a white background. Normal opening hours and a rota operates to give a 'duty' chemist cover.
**Dentists & Doctors** Ask at the **First Aid Centre** for the address of the School of Dentistry, where free treatment is available. Both dentists and doctors advertise widely and there is no shortage of practitioners.
**First Aid Centre (KAT)** (*Tmr* 14D2) 21 Tritis Septemvriou St, beyond the Chalkokondili turning and on the left. Tel 150
**Hospital** (*Tmr* 15G4) Do not proceed direct to a hospital (or *Go*) but initially attend the **First Aid Centre**. When necessary they direct patients to the correct destination.
**Medical Emergency:** Tel 166

**METRO/ELEKTRIKOS (ΗΣΑΜ)** The Athens underground, or subway system, operates below ground in the heart of the city and overground for the rest of the journey. It is a simple, one track layout from

Kifissia (NE Athens suburb) to Piraeus (SW of Athens), and represents marvellous value with two rates of fare at 30drs and 60drs. Passengers must have the requisite coins to obtain a ticket from the machine, prior to gaining access to the platforms. Everyone is most helpful and will, if the ticket machine 'frightens' a chap, show how it should be operated. Take care, select the ticket value first, then put the coins in the slot and don't forget to keep the ticket so as to be able to hand it in at the journey's end. The service operates every 10 mins between 0500 and 2400hrs and travel before 0800hrs is free, as it is on the buses. Keep an eye open for the old-fashioned wooden carriages.

**Station Stops** There used to be 20 stations, but the new 'Peace Stadium' has 'acquired' a stop called *Irene*. Others include Kifissia (NE suburb), Stathmos Attiki (for the main railway stations), Plateia Victorias (N Athens), Omonia Sq, Monastiraki Sq (for the Plaka), Plateia Thission (for the Acropolis) and (Piraeus) Port. Incidentally, from the outside, the Piraeus terminus is rather difficult to locate, the entrance being in the left-hand corner of what appears to be an oldish, waterfront building. *See* **Access to the stations, Trains, A To Z.**

**MUSIC & DANCING** *See* **Clubs, Bars & Discos, A To Z, & The Eating Out.**

**NTOG (EOT)** The headquarters of the National Tourist Organisation (NTOG) or, in Greek, the EOT (Ellinikos Organismos Tourismou – ΕΛΛΗΝΙΚΟΣ ΟΡΓΑΝΙΣΜΟΣ ΤΟΥΡΙΣΜΟΥ) is on the 5th floor at 2 Amerikis St (*Tmr* E4), close by Syntagma Sq. But this office does not handle the usual tourist enquiries, although the commissionaires manning the desk do hand out bits and pieces of information.

The information desk, from whence a free Athens map, advice, information folders, bus and boat schedules and hotel facts may be obtained, is situated inside and on the left of the foyer of the: *National Bank of Greece* (*Tmr* 3D/E4) 2 Karageorgi Servias, Syntagma Sq Tel 322 2545 *See* **Banks, A To Z** for directions. Do not hope to obtain anything other than pamphlets and a snatch of guidance, as it would be unrealistic to expect personal attention from staff besieged by wave upon wave of tourists of every creed, race and colour. The Athens hotel information sheets handed out now include a list of Class D & E establishments. Open Mon-Fri between 0800-2000hrs & Sat 0900-1400hrs.

There is now a sign requesting, if there are long queues, that enquirers use the tourist information office inside the *General Bank*, situated at the junction of Ermou St and Syntagma Sq.

There is also an NTOG office conveniently sited at the East Airport.

**OPENING HOURS** (Summer months) These are only a guideline and apply to Athens (as well as the larger cities). Note that in country and village areas, it is more likely that shops will be open from Monday to Saturday, for over 12 hours a day, and on Sundays, holidays and Saints days, for a few hours either side of midday. The afternoon siesta is usually taken between 1300/1400hrs and 1500/1700hrs.

**Trade Stores & Chemists** Mon, Wed & Sat 0800-1430hrs; Tues, Thurs & Fri 0900-1300hrs & 1700-2000hrs.

**Food Stores** Mon, Wed & Sat 0800-1500hrs; Tues, Thurs & Fri 0800-1400hrs & 1730-2030hrs.

**Art & Gift shops** Weekdays 0800-2100hrs & Sun (Monastiraki area) 0930-1445hrs.

**Restaurants, Pastry shops, Cafes & Dairy shops** Seven days a week.

**Museums** *See* **Museums, Places of Interest, A To Z.**

**Public Services** (including **Banks**) Refer to the relevant **A To Z** heading.

**OTE** There are offices at: No. 85, 28 Ikosiokto Oktovriou/Patission St (*Tmr* 16D1) (open 24hrs a day); 15 Stadiou St (*Tmr* 17D4) (open Mon to Fri 0700-2400hrs, Sat & Sun 0800-2400hrs); 53 Solonos (*Tmr* E3) and 7 Kratinou (Plateia Kotzia) (*Tmr* C/D3) (open between 0800 and 2400hrs). There is also an office at 45 Athinas St (*Tmr* C/D3).

**PHARMACIES** *See* **Medical Care, A To Z.**

**PLACES OF INTEREST** Most areas are described in the **Introduction**.

**Parliament Building** (*Tmr* E4/5) Syntagma Sq. Here it is possible to watch the Greek equivalent of the British 'Changing the Guard at Buckingham Palace'. The special guards (*Evzones*) are spectacularly outfitted with tasselled red caps, white shirts (blouses do I hear?), coloured waistcoats, a skirt, white tights, knee-garters and boots topped off with pom-poms. The ceremony officially kicks off at 1100hrs on Sunday morning but seems to falter into action at about 1045hrs. Incidentally, there is a band thrown in for good measure.

**Museums** The seasons are split as follow: Winter (1st Nov-31st March) & Summer (1st April-31st Oct). Museums are closed on: 1st Jan, 25th March, Good Friday, Easter Day & Christmas Day. Sunday hours are kept on Epiphany, Ash Monday, Easter Saturday, Easter Monday, 1st May, Whit Sunday,

Assumption Day, 28th October & Boxing Day. They are only open in the mornings on Christmas Eve, New Year's Eve, 2nd January, Easter Thursday & Easter Tuesday. Museums are closed on Tuesdays, unless otherwise indicated. Students with cards will achieve a reduction in fees.

*Acropolis* (*Tmr* C5). The museum exhibits finds made on the site. Of special interest are the sixth century BC statues of Korai women. Entrance charges are included in the admission fee to the Acropolis, which costs 600drs per head and is open Summer months: weekdays 0730-1930hrs; Sun & holidays 0800-1800hrs. The Museum hours are 0730-1930hrs; Tues 1200-1800hrs; Sun & holidays 0800-1800hrs.

*Benaki* (*Tmr* E/F4) On the corner of Vassilissis Sofias and Koubari (Koumbari) St, close by Plateia Kolonaki. A very interesting variety of exhibits made up from private collections. Particularly diverting is a display of national costumes. Open Summer months: daily 0830-1400hrs & closed Tues. Entrance 150drs, with free admission Sun.

*Byzantine* (*Tmr* F4/5) 22 Vassilissis Sofias. As one would deduce from the name – Byzantine art. Open Summer hours: daily 0845-1700hrs; closed Mon. Entrance costs 300drs.

*Goulandris* 13 Levidou St, Kifissia, N Athens. Natural History. Open Summer months: daily 0900-1300hrs & 1700-2000hrs; closed Fri. Entrance costs 100drs.

*Goulandris* (*Tmr* F4) 4 Neophitou Douka St (off Vassilissis Sofias). The second or 'other' Goulandris Museum. The situation is not helped by the little quirk of some people referring to the Natural History Museum as 'Goulandris'. Help! This Goulandris, that is the *Cycladic & Ancient Greek Art Goulandris Museum*, is open daily in the Summer months: weekdays 1000-1600hrs; Sat 1000-1500hrs; closed Tues, Sun & holidays. Entrance costs 150drs.

*Kanellopoulos* (*Tmr* C5) On the corner of Theorias and Panos Sts, in the Plaka, and located at the foot of the northern slope of the Acropolis, at the Monastiraki end. A smaller version of the *Benaki Museum* open Summer months: daily 0845-1500hrs; Sun & holidays 0930-1430hrs; closed Tues. Entrance costs 200drs.

*Keramikos* (*Tmr* B4) 148 Ermou St. Finds from Keramikos cemetery. Open Summer months: daily 0845-1500hrs; Sun & holidays 0930-1430hrs; closed on Tues. Entrance to the site and museum costs 400drs.

*National Gallery & Alexandros Soutzos* (*Tmr* G4) 46 Vassileos Konstantinou/Sofias. Mainly 19th and 20th century Greek paintings. Open Summer months: weekdays 0900-1500hrs; Sun & holidays 1000-1400hrs; closed on Mon. Admission costs 30drs.

*National Historical & Ethnological* (*Tmr* D4) Kolokotroni Sq, off Stadiou St. Greek history and the War of Independence. Open Summer months: weekdays 0900-1400hrs; Sat, Sun & holidays 0900-1300hrs; closed Mon. Entrance costs 100drs, with free admission on Thurs.

*National Archaeological* (*Tmr* D/E2) 1 Tossitsa St, off 28 Ikosiokto Oktovriou/Patission St. The largest and possibly the most important Greek museum, covering a wide variety of exhibits. A must if you are a museum buff. Open Summer months: weekdays 0800-1900hrs; Sun & holidays 0800-1800hrs; closed on Mon. Entrance costs 500drs, which includes entrance to the *Santorini* and *Numismatic* exhibitions (*See* below).
Also housed in the same building are the:
*Numismatic* Displaying, as would be imagined, a collection of Greek coins, spanning the ages. Open Summer months: weekdays 0830-1330hrs; Sun & holidays 0900-1400hrs; closed on Tues. Admission is free.

*Epigraphical Collection*: Open Summer months: as for the *Numismatic Exhibition*.
*Santorini Exhibition*: Open Summer months: as for the *Numismatic Exhibition*.
and
*The Casts & Copies Exhibition*: Open Summer months: as for the *Numismatic Exhibition*.
*Popular (Folk) Art* (*Tmr* D5) 17 Kidathineon St, The Plaka. Folk art, folklore and popular art. Open Summer months: daily 1000-1400hrs; closed on Mon. Entrance costs 200drs.

*War* (*Tmr* F4/5) 2 Rizari St, off Leoforos Vassilissis Sofias. Warfare exhibits covering a wide variety of subjects. Open Summer months: daily 0900-1400hrs; closed on Mon. Entrance is free.

**Theatres & Performances** For full, up-to-date details enquire at the NTOG enquiry desk (*Tmr* 3D/E4)

(*See* **NTOG, A To Z**). They should be able to hand out a pamphlet giving a precise timetable for the particular year. As a guide the following are performed year in and year out:

*Son et Lumiere*. From the *Pynx* hillside, a *Son et Lumiere* features the Acropolis. This show is produced from early April to the end of October. The English performance starts at 2100hrs every evening, except when the moon is full, and takes 45 minutes. There are French versions at 2215hrs daily, except Tues & Fri when a German commentary is provided at 2200hrs.

Tickets and information are available from the *Athens Festival booking office* (*See Athens Festival*) or at the Pynx, prior to the outset of the show. Tickets cost 400drs (students 150drs), and are also available at the entrance of the Church, Ag Dimitros Lombardiaris, on the way to the show. Catch a Bus No. 230 along Dionysiou Areopagitou St, getting off one stop beyond the *Odeion (Theatre) of Herodes Atticus* and follow the signposted path on the left-hand side.

*Athens Festival* This prestigious event takes place in the restored and beautiful Odeion of Herodes Atticus. This was built in approximately AD 160 as a Roman theatre, seating about 5000 people and situated at the foot of the south-west corner of the Acropolis. This Festival lasts from the middle of June to the middle of September, and consists of a series of plays, ballet, concerts and opera. The performances usually commence at 2100hrs and tickets, which are on sale up to 10 days before the event, are obtainable from the Theatre one hour prior to the commencement of the show or from the Athens Festival booking office (*Tmr* D/E4) at 4 Stadiou St, Tel 322 1459.

*Dora Stratou Theatre* (*Tmr* A6) A short stroll away on *Mouseion* or *Hill of Muses*. On the summit stands the *Monument of the Filopapou (Philopappos)* and, nearby, the Dora Stratou Theatre, where an internationally renowned troupe of folk dancers, dressed in traditional costumes, perform a series of Greek dances and songs. The theatre group operates daily from about the middle of May to the end of September. The show starts at 2225hrs, that is except Wed & Sun when they perform at 2015 & 2225hrs. Ticket prices vary from 750-950drs (students reduced rates) and are available between 0900-1400hrs (Tel 324 4395) & 1830-2300hrs (Tel 921 4650).

Performances are timed to coincide with the ending of the *Son et Lumiere*, on the *Pynx*.

*Lycabettus Theatre* On the north-east side of Lycabettus Hill. Concerts and theatrical performances take place at the hillside sited open-air theatre, between the middle of June and the first week of September, from 2100hrs. Tickets can be purchased from the theatre box office, one hour before the event, or from the *Athens Festival booking office*, referred to previously under *Athens Festival*.

*Wine Festival* Held daily at Dafni, between 1900-0030hrs, from the middle of July to the end of August. Ticket price 250drs per head, students 150drs. Information and tickets from the *Athens Festival booking office*.

**POLICE** *See* **Tourist Police, A To Z**.

**POST OFFICES (Tachidromio** – ΤΑΧΤΔΡΟΜΕΙΟΞ) Weekday opening hours, as a guide, are 0800 to 1300hrs. The Central Post Office at 100 Eolou St (*Tmr* 18D3), close by Omonia Sq, is open Mon-Sat, 0730-1500hrs. Branch offices are situated on the corner of Othonos and Nikis Sts (Syntagma Sq); at the Omonia Sq underground Metro concourse and on Dionysiou Areopagitou St, at the corner of Tzireon St (*Tmr* D6).

The telephone and telegraph system is run by a separate state organisation. For details of the telephone service *See* **OTE, A To Z**.

**SHOPPING HOURS** *See* **Opening Hours, A To Z**.

**SPORTS FACILITIES**
**Golf.** There is an 18 hole course, the *Glifida Golf Club* (Tel 894 6820) close by the East Airport. Changing rooms, restaurant and refreshment bar.
**Horse Riding.** A number of stables including the *Hellenic Riding Club* (Tel 681 2506), Maroussio (NNE Athens suburb) & the *Athens Riding Club* (Tel 661 1088), Gerakas (ENE Athens suburb).
**Swimming.** There is a *Swimming (& Tennis) Club* on Leoforos Olgas (*Tmr* 19E6), across the way from the Zappeion National Gardens. *The Hilton Hotel* (*Tmr* G4) has a swimming pool but, if you are not staying there, use of it costs the price of an (expensive) meal. *See* **Beaches, A To Z**.
**Tennis.** There are courts at most of the NTOG beaches (*See* **Beaches, A To Z**), as well as at the *Ag Kosmas Athletics Centre* (Tel 894 8900), close by the West airport.

**TAXIS** (ΤΑΞ) Used extensively and, although they seem to me to be expensive, are 'officially' the cheapest in Europe. The Athens drivers are, now, generally without scruples. The metered fares cost about 30drs per kilometre. But this is subject to various surcharges, including 20drs for each piece of baggage, 250drs per hour of waiting time and 50drs for collection from, or delivery to, public transport facilities. There is also an extra charge for the hours between midnight and daylight. Prospective fares, standing at a taxi rank, must be picked up but taxis are not obliged to stop when cruising, for which there is an extra 'flag falling' charge of 25drs. The sign ΕΛΕΤΘΕΡΟΝ indicates a cab is free for hire. Passengers must ensure that the meter is zeroed at the start of any journey, for which the minimum fare is 120drs.

Sample fares include: Syntagma/Omonia Square to the East airport 500drs and to the West airport 400drs; the East airport to Piraeus 500drs and the West airport to Piraeus 350drs. The Syntagma taxi station telephone number is 323 7942.

**TELEPHONES** *See* **OTE**.

**TOILETS** Apart from the facilities sited at the various bus termini and the railway stations, there is a super public toilet on the south-east corner of Syntagma Sq, as there is a pretty grim 'squatty' in the Omonia Sq Metro concourse (which latter costs 20drs). The Plaka is well 'endowed' with one at Plateia Plaka, (on Odhos Kidathineon) and another on the Plateia Agora, at the other end of Odhos Adrianou. Visitors to Mt. Lycabettus will not be 'caught short' and the toilets there are spotless.

**TOURIST OFFICE/AGENCIES** *See* **NTOG** & **Travel Agents** & **Tour Offices, A To Z**.

**TOURIST POLICE** (*Tmr* 20D6) Despite the reorganisation of the service, the Athens headquarters remains in operation. This is situated at 7 Leoforos Sygrou (Sygrou/Syngrou/Singrou Av) (Tel 923-9224) and is open daily 0800-2100hrs. Tourist information in English is available on the telephone number 171.

There are also Tourist police offices close by and just to the north of Larissis Railway Station (open 0700-2300hrs, tel 821 3574) and the East airport (open 24 hours a day, tel 981 4093/969 9500).

**TRAINS** (Illustration 7) They arrive at (or depart from) either (a) Larissis Station (Stathmos No. 1) or (b) Peloponissou Station (Stathmos No. 2).

**Advance Booking Office**. Information and advance booking for both stations is handled at: No. 6 Sina (*Tmr* E3, tel 363 4402/4406) off Akadimias St; No. 1 Karolou (Satovriandou (*Tmr* C2, tel 524 0647/8) west of Omonia Sq & No. 17 Filellinon (*Tmr* D/E5, tel 323 6747/6273).

**Toilets** The station toilets usually, well always, lack toilet paper.

**Sustenance (on the train)** An attendant brings inexpensive drinks and snacks around, from time to time, and hot snacks are available from platform trolleys at the major railway stations.

**Railway Head office** (*Tmr* C2) Hellenic Railways Organisation (OSE), 1-3 Karolou St. Tel 522 2491 This office is one back from the far end of Ag Konstantinou, west from Omonia Sq.

**Provisions** Shopping in the area of the railway stations is made easy by the presence of the Street Market on Odhos Chiou (*See* **Larissis Station, Trains**).

**Access to the stations**
**Bus/Trolley-bus.** From the Airport, travel on the Olympic bus to the terminal at 96-100 Leoforos Sygrou (which, at a cost of 100drs, is good value). Then catch a bus (Nos. 133, 040, 132, 155, 903 and 161 amongst others) across the street from the terminus to Syntagma Sq, after which a No. 1 or No. 5 (via Omonia Sq), or a No. 11 trolley-bus, to the Stathmos Larissis Railway Station. Instead of making a change of bus at Syntagma Sq, it is also possible to walk west from the terminal on Leoforos Sygrou across Falirou and Odisseos and Androutsou Sts to the parallel street of Odhos Dimitrakopoulou. Here catch a No. 1 trolley-bus all the way to the stations.

From Piraeus Port catch the No. 40 (green) bus that 'routes' along Leoforos Vassileos Konstantinou (parallel to the quay) as far as Syntagma Sq, or the No. 049 from Plateia Themistokleous to Athinas St, close by Omonia Sq. For other possibly conflicting information *See* **Arrival by Air, Introduction; Airline offices & terminus** & **Buses & Trolley-buses, A To Z**.

**Metro** The metro station for both railway stations is Attiki, close to Plateia Attikis. From the platform, assuming a traveller has come from the south, dismount and turn right down into the underpass to come out the far or west side of the station, on Odhos Liossion. Turn left and walk to the large irregular Plateia Attikis (*with the Hotel Lydia on the right*). Proceed down Domokou St (the road that exits half-right on the far side of the square) and which spills onto Plateia Deligianni, edged by Stathmos Larissis. A more long-winded alternative is to get off the Metro at Omonia Sq, walk west along Ag Konstantinou to Karaiskaki Sq and then up Odhos Deligianni, or catch a No. 1 trolley-bus.

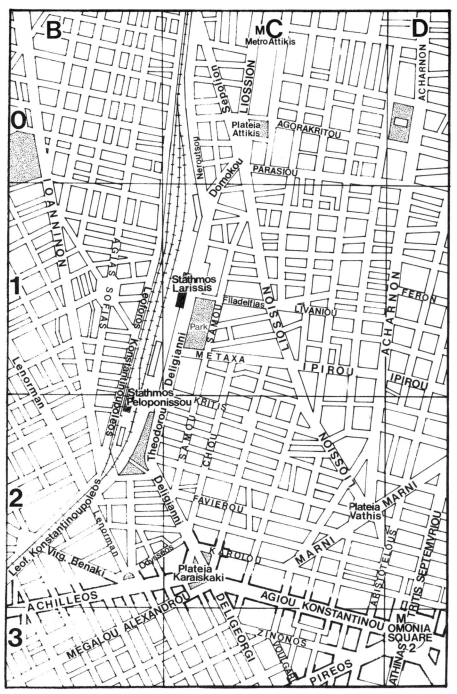

**Illustration 7 Athens inset - The Railway Stations**

**Taxis** A reasonable indulgence, if in a hurry, although it must be noted that, in the crowded traffic conditions of Athens, it is often quicker to walk than catch a cab. *See* **Taxis, A To Z**.

**Station to Station** To get from one to the other, say Stathmos Larissis to Peloponissou, it is necessary to turn right out of the station and climb the steps over the railway line, turning left at the bottom of the far side and walk some 100m to the forecourt in front of Stathmos Peloponissou. Almost, but not quite adjacent, as some guides put it, if 150m on a very hot day, laden down with cases seems contiguous.

**(A) LARISSIS STATION** (*Tmr* B/C1)                                                    Tel 821 3882
The main, more modern station of the two. Connections to the Western European services and the northern provinces of Central Greece, Thessaly, Macedonia and Thrace. The bus stop to the centre of Athens is to the right of the station (*station building behind one*). Refer to **Buses** below.

One correspondent has reminded me to reiterate that it is advisable to reserve return train seats as soon as is possible after arrival in Greece. This is done at the International 'hatch'.

Services in and around the building include:
**The National Bank of Greece**. Open Mon to Thurs 0830-1400hrs & Fri 0830-1330hrs.
**Post Office**. Open Mon to Sat 0700-2000hrs & Sun 0900-1400hrs.
**Tourist police**. There is an office just to the north of the station building. *See* **Tourist Police, A To Z**.

To the front of the station is a reasonable priced pavement cafe-bar and an elongated square – well more a widening of the road.

**THE ACCOMMODATION** Even early and late in the summer a number of the hardier stretch out on the pavements around and about the stations (and at the nearby *Hotel Oscar's* rates I'm not surprised). Arrivals, even whilst on the train, are bombarded with offers of accommodation, so much so that the touts are a nuisance.

To the right (*Station behind one*) across the concourse and on the corner, is the:
**Hotel Lefkos Pirgos** (*Tmr* C1) (Class E) 27 Leof. Metaxa/Deligianni              Tel 821 3765
*Directions*: As above.

Seedy looking establishment. All rooms share the bathrooms. Singles start off at 715drs & double rooms 1150drs. These prices increase, respectively, to 970drs & 1590drs (1st May-30th June & 16th Sept-31st Dec) and 1210drs & 1990drs (1st July-15th Sept).

**Hotel Nana** (*Tmr* C1) (Class B), 29 Leof.Metaxa                                      Tel 884 2211
*Directions*: Alongside the *Hotel Lefkos Pirgos*.

Smarter, much smarter (well it is B class) with the charges reflecting this pre-eminence. All rooms have an en suite bathroom with a single room charged at 2430drs & a double at 3400drs, rising to 3400drs & 4660drs (16th March-31st Oct).

Directly opposite the main station entrance is the:
**Hotel Oscar** (*Tmr* C1) (Class B), 25 Samou/Filadelfias                              Tel 883 4215
*Directions*: As above.

I hardly dare detail the room rates, which for a double room kicks off at 4200drs rising to 6240drs en suite, naturally. Breakfast costs 410drs. I must own up to one staying at the Oscar. But it was at the end of a long stint on the Greek islands, added to which there were a couple of other (good) reasons. Firstly they accept payment by *Amex* which, as I have written before, may be of great assistance in eking out dwindling funds, and secondly, the hotel is conveniently close to the railway and the inter-country coach station. Thus the comforts of this hotel, or similar, can be put to good use in order to build up the bodily reserves, prior to a long distance bus or railway journey! That is not to say that even this luxurious establishment does not escape some of the common faults oft experienced as a 'norm' when staying at lower classified 'cousins'. The en suite bathroom of our room had a loose lavatory seat, the bath plug had no chain attached (there was a chain, but it was not attached) and the small bathroom window was tied up with string. The sliding balcony window would not completely shut – there was no locking mechanism and the air conditioning didn't. Mind you, I must admit to making a reservation without Rosemary, who guarded our backpacks whilst I sorted out the formalities. It may have been the sight of the two, towering, aforementioned packs reversing through the swing doors into the reception that resulted in our being allocated this particular 'downtown' room, at the rear of the hotel, overlooking and overlooked by the backsides of a block of flats.

**Hotel Elena (Helena)** (*Tmr* B/C1) (Class C) 2 Psiloriti/Samou                       Tel 881 3211

*Directions*: Along Samou St, south from Leof. Metaxa St, and on the right.

Approximate rates are as follows:- single rooms, sharing the bathroom, cost 1400drs & en suite 1900drs; double rooms sharing are charged at 2100drs & en suite 2500drs.

**Hotel Louvre** (*Tmr* C2) (Class D) 9 Chiou/Favierou Sts                    Tel 522 9891
*Directions*: Next street back from and parallel to Samou St, towards the south end of Chiou St.

Greek provincial in outward appearance, despite the grand and evocative name. Single rooms, sharing a bathroom, cost 1400drs; double rooms, sharing, 1950drs & en suite 2500drs.

**Joy's Hotel** (*Tmr* D1) 38 Feron St                    Tel 823 1012
*Directions*: Proceed along Odhos Filadelfias, almost directly opposite the main station, across Odhos Liossion continuing along Livaniou St as far as Odhos Acharnon. Turn left and then first right on to Feron St.

Reputedly a good value, busy, Youth Hostel style establishment complete with a bar/cafeteria and offering accommodation ranging from a dormitory (500drs) to quadruples. A single bed starts off at 900drs and a double 1600drs. A hot shower costs an extra 100drs.

**Street Market** Whilst in this area it is worth noting that Odhos Chiou, between Kritis and Favierou Sts, is host to an extensive street market where almost everything is sold from fish to meat and hardware to clothing.

**Bread shop & Supermarket** (*Tmr* B/C1/2) On the corner of Samou St and Eratyras St. A bit disorganised but very useful.

**Snackbar** (*Tmr* B/C1) Odhos Samou.
*Directions*: Across the street from the Park, on the stretch of Odhos Samou between Filadelfias and Leof. Metaxa Sts.

A small, convenient, souvlaki pita snackbar, run by a very friendly chap. A souvlaki and a bottle of beer costs 150drs.

**Buses**: Trolley-bus No. 1 pulls up to the right of the station, as do the No's 2 & 4. The fare to Syntagma Sq is 30drs.

**(B) PELOPONISSOU STATION** (*Tmr* B1/2)                    Tel 513 1601
The station for trains to the Peloponnese, the ferry connections for some of the Ionian islands and international ferries to Italy from Patras.

**Tickets**: The concept behind the acquisition of a ticket is similar to that of a lottery. Purchasing a ticket results in the allocation of a compartment seat. In theory this is a splendid scheme but, in practice, the idea breaks down in a welter of bad tempered argument over whom is occupying whose seat. Manners and quaint old-fashioned habits of giving up one's seat to older people and ladies are best avoided. I write this from the bitter experience of offering my seat to elderly Greek ladies, only for their husbands to immediately fill the vacant position. Not what one had in mind! Find your seat and stick to it like glue and if you have made a mistake feign madness, admit to being a foreigner, but do not budge.

At Peloponissou Station the mechanics of buying a ticket take place in organised bedlam. The ticket office 'traps' open half an hour prior to the train's departure. Scenes reminiscent of a Cup Final crowd develop, with prospective travellers pitching about within the barriers of the ticket hatch, and all this in the space of about 10m by 10m. To add to the difficulty, there are two hatch 'slots' and it is anybody's guess which one to select. It really is best to try and steal a march on the 'extra-curricula' activity, diving for a hatch whenever one opens.

Travellers booking a return journey train ticket to Europe, and routing via Italy, must ensure the tickets are to and from Patras, not Athens (Yes, Patras). Then the purchase of the separate Patras to Athens (and vice versa) ticket, ensures a seat. A voyager boarding the train with an open ticket will almost surely have to stand for almost the whole of the four hour journey. Most Athens – Patras journeys seem to attract an 'Express' surcharge of between 100-150drs, which is exacted by the ticket collector.

Incidentally, the general architecture of the Peloponissou building is delightful, especially the ceiling of the booking office hall, centrally located, under the main clock face. To the left, on entering the building, is a glass-fronted information box with all the train times listed on the window. The staff manning this desk are extremely helpful. They speak sufficient English, so pose no problems in communication – the very opposite of the rushed disinterest shown at the NTOG desk in the National Bank of Greece, on Syntagma Sq.

## TRAIN TIMETABLES

**Peloponissou Station** It is easy to read the Peloponissou timetable and come to the conclusion that a large number of trains are leaving the station at the same time. On seeing the single-line track, a newcomer cannot be blamed for feeling apprehensive that it may prove difficult to select the correct carriages. The mystification arises from the fact that the trains are detailed separately from Athens to say Korinthos, Mikines, Argos, Tripolis, Pirgos and etc, etc. There is no mention that the railway line is a circular layout, with single trains circumscribing the route and that each place name is simply a stop on the journey.

Making changes for branch lines on the Peloponnese can be 'exciting'! Stations are labelled in demotic script and there is no comprehensible announcement from the guard, thus it is easy to fail to make an exit on cue!

### A. LARISSIS STATION
**Athens to Thessaloniki & on to Alexandroupoli:**

| | |
|---|---|
| Depart | 0725, 0830, 1100, 1424, 1930, 2120, 2155, 2310hrs |

**Thessaloniki**

| | |
|---|---|
| Arrive | 1450, 1558, 1757, 2213, 0350, 0538, 0614, 0745hrs |
| Depart | 1536, 1721, 1920, 2302, -- 0608, -- 0925hrs |

**Drama (for Kavala)**

| | |
|---|---|
| Arrive | 1857, 2109, -- 0256, -- 1026, -- 1331hrs |

**Alexandroupoli**

| | |
|---|---|
| Arrive | 2217, -- -- 0651, -- 1407, -- 1727hrs |

| One-way fares: | | | |
|---|---|---|---|
| | Athens to Thessaloniki | :B Class 1520drs: | A Class 2280drs. |
| | Athens to Drama | : 2030drs: | 3050drs |
| | Athens to Alexandroupoli | : 2410drs: | 3620drs |

### B. PELOPONISSOU STATION
**Athens to Patras:**

| | |
|---|---|
| Depart | 0625, 0821, 1013, 1303, 1547, 1827, 2141hrs |
| Arrive | 1055, 1218, 1446, 1708, 2024, 2200, 0159hrs |

*Return*

| | |
|---|---|
| Depart | 0230, 0628, 0809, 1101, 1400, 1647, 1854hrs |
| Arrive | 0640, 1000, 1300, 1500, 1848, 2115, 2254hrs |

One-way fare: Athens to Patras:B Class 630drs, A Class 950drs.

Surcharge on Express trains varies from 170-300drs.

**TRAVEL AGENTS & TOUR OFFICES** There are offices selling tickets for almost anything to almost anywhere, which include:

| | |
|---|---|
| **ABC** 58 Stadiou St | Tel 321 1381 |
| **American Express** 2 Ermou St | Tel 324 4975/9 |

On the first floor is an excellent retail travel service. Admittedly they are mainly involved in the sale of tours and excursions but the assistants are extremely efficient and helpful. They will, for instance, telephone round to locate all or any hotels, that accept an Amex card, to ascertain if they have a room and the cost.

| | |
|---|---|
| **CHAT** 4 Stadiou St | Tel 322 2886 |
| **Key Tours** 5th Floor, 2 Ermou St | Tel 323 2520 |
| **Viking** 3 Filellinon St | Tel 322 9383 |

The agency that was most highly regarded by students for prices and variety, was:

| | |
|---|---|
| **International Student & Youth Travel Service (ISYTS)** 11 Nikis St | Tel 323 3767 |

For FIYTO membership. The second floor office is open Mon-Fri 0900-1900hrs & Sat between 0900-1200hrs.

Two recommended offices offering helpful, inclusive and inexpensive travel options include:-

| | |
|---|---|
| **Magis Bus – International Pullman** 20 Filellinon St | Tel (Buses) 323 7471 |
| | (Flights) 322 6810 |
| and | |
| **Transalpino Travel** 28 Nikis St | Tel 322 0503 |

Located in the basement of the *Compendium Bookshop* and will also arrange accommodation.

Filellinon and the parallel street of Odhos Nikis (to the west of Syntagma Sq), all the way south and up as far as Nikodimou St are jam-packed with tourist agencies and student organisations. These include one or two express coach and train fare companies. A sample, going up the rise from Syntagma Square, includes:

**(Budget) Student Travel** (Tel 322 7993), 1 Filellinon St, on the right, opposite a church
and
**Stafford Travel** (Tel 322 4225), 20 Filellinon St, on the corner of Filellinon & Kidathineon Sts.

An example of the packaged tours on offer, in this instance from **CHAT Tours** but representative of most, includes:-
One day to Delphi from 4200drs; two days to Epidauras & Mycenae 10900drs; three days to Delphi & Meteora from 27950drs & a one day cruise to Aegina, Poros & Hydra, 4500drs.

Callers at the National Bank (*Tmr* 3D/E4/5) usually have to run the gauntlet of 'tour from touts', even if some may only be offering advice ('....I know this white woman'?). They are best brushed aside, otherwise the unwary might well be borne along on an unstoppable tide.

Sample 'charter' air & bus fares available from Athens to various European capitals include (as quoted by **Economy Travel**, 18 Panepistimiou St, Athens Tel 363 4045) the following:
*Air* to London 25000drs; Paris 24000drs; Rome 17500drs; Munich 20000; Berlin 21000drs; New York 40000drs; Stockholm 29000drs.
*Bus* to London 13000drs; Paris 12000drs; Venice 9000drs; Munich 11000drs & Istanbul 4500drs.
**YOUTH HOSTEL ASSOCIATION** *See* **The Accommodation**.

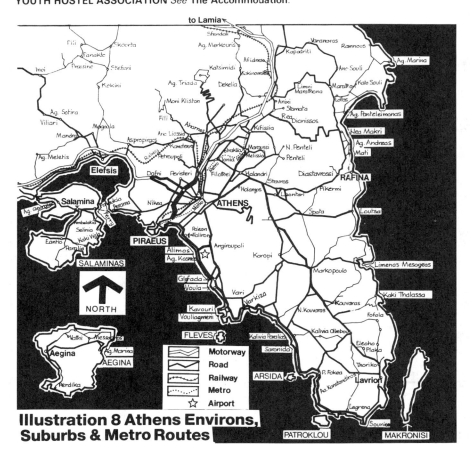

**Illustration 8 Athens Environs, Suburbs & Metro Routes**

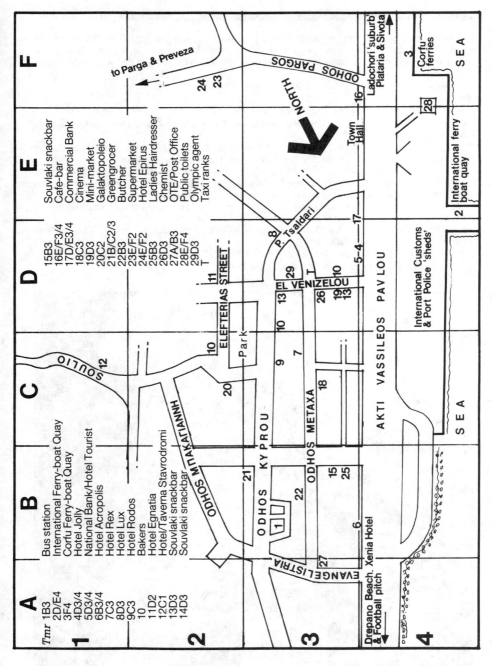

| | A | B | | C | | D | | E | |
|---|---|---|---|---|---|---|---|---|---|
| *Tmr* | 1B3 | Bus station | | | 15B3 | Souvlaki snackbar | | | |
| | 2D/E4 | International Ferry-boat Quay | | | 16E/F3/4 | Cafe-bar | | | |
| | 3F4 | Corfu Ferry-boat Quay | | | 17D/E3/4 | Commercial Bank | | | |
| | 4D3/4 | Hotel Jolly | | | 18C3 | Cinema | | | |
| | 5D3/4 | National Bank/Hotel Tourist | | | 19D3 | Mini-market | | | |
| | 6B3/4 | Hotel Acropolis | | | 20C2 | Galaktopoleio | | | |
| | 7C3 | Hotel Rex | | | 21B/C2/3 | Greengrocer | | | |
| | 8D3 | Hotel Lux | | | 22B3 | Butcher | | | |
| | 9C3 | Hotel Rodos | | | 23E/F2 | Supermarket | | | |
| | 10 | Bakers | | | 24E/F2 | Hotel Epirus | | | |
| | 11D2 | Hotel Egnatia | | | 25B3 | Ladies Hairdresser | | | |
| | 12C1 | Hotel/Taverna Stavrodromi | | | 26D3 | Chemist | | | |
| | 13D3 | Souvlaki snackbar | | | 27A/B3 | OTE/Post Office | | | |
| | 14D3 | Souvlaki snackbar | | | 28E/F4 | Public toilets | | | |
| | | | | | 29D3 | Olympic agent | | | |
| | | | | | T | Taxi ranks | | | |

*Tmr* = Town map reference
*Fsw* = Facing seawards
*Sbo* = Sea behind one
*Fbqbo* = Ferry-boat Quay behind one

**Illustration 9 Igoumenitsa**

# 10 Greek Mainland Ports & Western Coast Resorts (Epirus)

*Fortune and hope farewell! I've found the port, you've done with me; go now with others sport. From a Greek epigram.*

This guide describes Corfu and the Ionian islands, and this chapter chronicles the relevant mainland ports (*See* Illustrations 4 & 14) from which a traveller can effect a connection with the various islands.

## IGOUMENITSA: Epirus Region, NW Greece (Illustration 9) Tel prefix 0665.

Both an international and Ionian island ferry-boat port. Despite this, Igoumenitsa is not really recommended as a resort because it is more a 'frontier' port, with almost the whole of Akti Vassileos Pavlou, the sign-ridden Esplanade, occupied by 'fast' ferry-boat ticket agencies. These, in common with the other shops, stay open quite late in the evenings. Incidentally, the town 'hots up' at night, when the international ferries dock, and again in the morning, when the boats depart. Around midday Igoumenitsa becomes pretty sleepy, apart from the little flurries of activity that erupt with the comings and goings of the Corfu craft. Visitors wishing to stay in the area should consider the delights of the nearby coastal villages, described later on in the chapter.

The port is dominated by two streets, the Esplanade, Vassileos Pavlou, which finally runs out at the north end of the town, alongside the football stadium, and Odhos Kyprou, which parallels the waterfront through the main body of the town.

Some attempt has been made to beautify the quayside where there is a pleasant public garden edging the Esplanade. The generally unattractive appearance of the town is perhaps forgivable, as Igoumenitsa had to be rebuilt, after being razed to the ground, in 1944. If this were not enough an earthquake in 1979 caused a great deal of damage. Despite these calamities there are a few old houses still surviving. They edge Odhos ΜΠΑΚΑΓΙΑΝΝΗ, the poorly surfaced road on which the buses park.

To see examples of the marvellous, distinctive houses of the Epirus region, it is necessary to travel to, say, the villages of Filiates or Plessio, north of Igoumenitsa.

## ARRIVAL BY BUS

The town is well connected to other major Greek cities with a direct service to and from Athens. It is thus all the more strange that the rather 'doo-hickey' Bus office (*Tmr* 1B3) should be inconveniently hidden away, in a crescent that encircles a large building fronting on to Odhos Kyprou. It appears that the site has been created by knocking down some old cottages. On the north wall there is a fascinating but faded list of taxi fares in days of yore. They include charges of 5½drs per kilometre 'in the confines of the town' and 9drs 'outside'; flag falling 5drs; waiting at the bus station 5drs and 'indemnity' waiting 24drs per hour. Bearing in mind inflation over the years, I wonder if the vehicles were chariots?

## ARRIVAL BY FERRY

Both international craft (*Tmr* 2D/E4) and Corfu 'landing-craft' ferries (*Tmr* 3F4) dock at the port. As some of the international boats also call in at Corfu island and Patras, Igoumenitsa is a pivotal port.

## THE ACCOMMODATION & EATING OUT

**The Accommodation** Waterfront hotels include the:-

**Hotel Jolly** (*Tmr* 4D3/4) (Class C) 20 Vassileos Pavlou                    Tel 23970
*Directions:* Towards the south end of the Esplanade, opposite the International Ferry-boat sheds.

Very expensive, but all rooms include en suite bathrooms. Single rooms cost 2480drs & doubles 3780drs, increasing, respectively, to 3260drs & 5460drs (1st June-15th Sept).

**Hotel Tourist** (*Tmr* 5D3/4) (Class C) 22 Vassileos Pavlou                              Tel 22406
*Directions*: A few doors along from the *Hotel Jolly*, over the National Bank.
   Prices similar to the *Hotel Jolly*.

Much more reasonably priced accommodation is available at the:-
**Hotel Acropolis** (*Tmr* 6B3/4) (Class D) 76 Dimokratias                              Tel 22342
*Directions*: North along the Esplanade.
   Rooms share the bathrooms, with a single charged at 1200drs and a double 1800drs.

Further north of the town, alongside the Drepano Beach turning off the extended Esplanade, is the:-
**Hotel Xenia** (Class B) 2 Vassileos Pavlou                              Tel 22282
*Directions*: As above.
   Calls itself a motel, which may account for the place looking a bit of a 'chalet shambles', on stilts.
   Double rooms only, complete with en suite bathrooms, charged at 2900drs, increasing to 3600drs
(Summer months).

Odhos El Venizelou ascends from the Esplanade, starting out close by the National Bank (*Tmr* 5D3/4).
Off to the left (*Sbo*) is the:-
**Hotel Rex** (*Tmr* 7C3) (Class D) 12 Metaxa                              Tel 22255
*Directions*: Left along Odhos Metaxa, which branches off El Venizelou St, and on the right.
   Looks a bit of a dump. Rooms share the bathrooms, with a single room costing 1000drs & a double
1650drs, which rates increase, respectively, to 1250drs & 2100drs (1st April-15th Oct).

**Hotel Lux** (*Tmr* 8D3) (Class D) 16 P Tsaldari                              Tel 22223
*Directions*: From Odhos El Venizelou, turn right (*Sbo*), not left as for the *Rex*, and on the left, in the
corner of a crossroads.
   A smart, clean building. A single room costs 1085drs & a double 1805drs, both sharing bathrooms.
Bedrooms with en suite bathrooms are charged at 1355drs for a single room & 2260drs for a double.

**Hotel Rodos** (*Tmr* 9C3) (Class E) 13 Kyprou                              Tel 22248
*Directions*: El Venizelou St opens out onto Odhos Kyprou, close to a small park. This hotel is to the
left and on the left-hand side, beyond a baker (*Tmr* 10C/D3). There is an illuminated sign, *Furnished
Rooms. D. Tismouri*.
   Unkempt and provincial in appearance, which is reflected in the charges. A single room costs 900drs
& a double 1250drs, both sharing the bathrooms.

**Hotel Egnatia** (*Tmr* 11D2) 1 Eleftherias                              Tel 23648
*Directions*: The far, south side of the park.
   All rooms have an en suite bathroom with a single charged at 1300drs & a double 1850drs, which
rates increase, respectively, to 1500drs & 2800drs (1st July-30th Sept).

Next door to the *Hotel Egnatia* is a Pension charging 550drs per head, a night.

Souliou Lane steeply ascends from the far, north side of the park, climbing past the:-
**Hotel Stavrodromi** (*Tmr* 12C1) (Class E) 14 Souliou                              Tel 22343
*Directions*: As above, and on the right.
   This accommodation also 'quadruples' up as a taverna, cafe-bar and mini-market. Rustic in appear-
ance, but clean and well constructed. Rooms share the bathrooms with a single listed at 850drs & a
double 1250drs. Incidentally, by the evening the taverna food appears rather tired.

The C class *Hotel Epirus* (Tel 22504) is south of the main town (*See* **Commercial Shopping Area, A
To Z**). Along the sea hugging road, in the 'suburb' of Ladochori, are some **Rooms**, but it is a few
kilometres walk.

## Camping
**Camping Sole Mare**, Ladochori                              Tel 22105
*Directions*: A kilometre or so south of the town, in the 'suburbs' Ladochori.
   Unfortunately, in 1988, the site appeared to be thoroughly 'dead'.
   On the other hand, there are several very good sites in the area of Plataria, some 8km distant (*See.*
**Plataria** later on in this chapter).


# The Eating Out
The Esplanade ferry-boat ticket offices are interspersed with cafe-bars
and fast food outfits. The latter advertise their presence with garish neon signs which

emblazon the street to the north. Generally an Amstel beer costs some 90drs, as does a frappe coffee.

Two waterfront establishments that merit attention include the:-
**Snackbar/Cafeteria Alekos**
*Directions*: At the north end of the Esplanade, approximately across the way from the small caique harbour.

Smart, clean, professional service (with a smile). Various pizzas and meat dishes cost about 500drs per person. Seating inside and out.

Close by is:-
**Snackbar/Taverna** ΑΘΑΝΑΣΙΟΥ ΧΠΟΥ
*Directions*: As above. On the right (*Sbo*) of the taverna is a sheltered, gravel surfaced patio (more an extension of a bomb site car park).

A pleasantly extensive menu including kalamares, liver, Greek salad and kortaki retsina. A meal for two costs about 1250drs.

Odhos El Venizelou 'houses' two souvlaki snackbars. The first (*Tmr* 13D3) sells stick souvlaki, and is more a hole in the wall. The other (*Tmr* 14D3) is towards the top of the street, close by the junction with Odhos Kyprou. This is a clean, 'mother and daughter' outfit, at which a good 'giro' costs 75drs, and one down from which is an excellent, locals kafeneion, if you dare!

There is another souvlaki pita snackbar (*Tmr* 15B3) in the wide street connecting the waterfront with Odhos ΜΠΑΚΑΠΑΝΝΗ (on which the buses park). A further possibility is offered by the corn-on-the-cob BBQ's scattered along the north end of the Esplanade during the summer months.

A most convenient cafe-bar (*Tmr* 16E/F3/4) nestles down diagonally across from the Corfu ferry-boat ramp. Apart from enabling a traveller to be close to hand for a particular departure, it is great fun simply observing the antics of the passengers, many of whom are 'BPTs' enjoying an 'away day' from Corfu (Condescending S.O.B.? – yes).

# THE A TO Z OF USEFUL INFORMATION
**AIRLINE OFFICE & TERMINUS** *See* **Travel Agents..., A To Z.**

**BANKS** At least two are sited on the busiest section of the Esplanade, the **National Bank** (*Tmr* 5D3/4) and the **The Commercial Bank** (*Tmr* 17D/E3/4). They only open the usual hours but there are a number of exchange offices open every day and most of the night. There is a tendency for those bureaux associated with ferry-boat ticket offices to restrict change facilities to clients who purchase tickets. Naughty.

**BEACHES** The beach to the south of Igoumenitsa is about a kilometre walk but it is dominated by oil storage tanks and the tankers that deliver the cargo.

On the other hand all is not lost. To the north and turning left at the *Hotel Xenia*, and keeping close to the shore, leads to the magnificent:-
**Drepano Beach** Admittedly about a 6km hike but well worth it. From the Xenia turning, the road edges the backshore of a very scrubbly strip of foreshore, littered with bits of old plastic and kelp. The route continues on round the curve of the bay to a pretty peninsular on which is built a chapel. Here the road swings round to the right with a large, land trapped lagoon to the right and the very long stretch of sandy shore to the left. The beach is, in the main, narrow and bordered by a thin strip, along which trees are evenly spaced. The sea-bed shelves gently and a number of sand spits protrude into the sea. Unfortunately the shore is subject to the prevailing wind, which brings with it some seaborne rubbish, but not a lot. The lagoon and tree foliage harbour mosquitoes, but not a lot.

Adjacent to a particularly broad, very sandy section, about the middle of the beach, is a large taverna/ snackbar. This is housed in a square, rather out of place, two storey building, across the road from which are a row of changing huts and a 'Richter 8', 'starting block' squatty. To one side, close to the toilet entrance door is a rather elemental, wobbly shower head.

Despite a few comments to the contrary, motor caravans and tents informally camp beneath the backshore trees. It is interesting to note that few backpackers make it this far, on the other hand, the beach is popular with the locals and thus is busiest at the weekends.

To really appreciate the overall beauty of the setting, it is necessary to view it from across the bay, on the coast road that climbs from Igoumenitsa towards Plataria.

**BICYCLE, SCOOTER & CAR HIRE** No bicycle or scooter hire is in evidence but almost each and every tour office 'littering' the Esplanade rents cars.

**BREAD SHOP** There are two on opposite sides of the park. One (*Tmr* 10C/D3) is on Odhos Kyprou and the other (*Tmr* 10C2) is at the outset of Odhos Souliou. Yet another Baker (*Tmr* 10D3) is situated on the right (*Sbo*) of Odhos El Venizelou. The Baker on Odhos Kyprou can be recommended and the little girl 'on the counter' speaks English.

**BUSES** The Terminal (*Tmr* 1B3) and its position is described in **Arrival by Bus, Introduction**.

## Bus timetable

**Igoumenitsa to Athens** *(Tel:5125954)
Daily           0830, 1100, 1800hrs
*Return journey*
Daily           0630, 1200, 1915hrs
One-way fare: 2530drs; duration 8½hrs.
*100 Kifissou St.

**Igoumenitsa to Ioannina★**
Daily           0630, 0800, 0900, 1000, 1200, 1330, 1430, 1500
                1600, 1700, 1900, 2000hrs
One-way fare: 1330drs; duration 4hrs.

★Ioannina is a pivotal bus terminus with, for instance, services to Patras.

**Igoumenitsa to Thessaloniki**
Daily           1145hrs

**Igoumenitsa to Sivota**
Daily           0645, 1430hrs

**Igoumenitsa to Perdika**
Daily           0600, 1400hrs

**Igoumenitsa to Parga**
Daily           0600, 1115, 1315, 1715hrs

**Igoumenitsa to Preveza**
Daily           1145, 1530hrs

**Igoumenitsa to Kastrini**
Daily           0700, 1450hrs

**Igoumenitsa to Filiates**
Daily           0500, 0615, 0730, 0845, 1015, 1100, 1300
                1500, 1815hrs

**Igoumenitsa to Paramithia**
Daily           0515, 0750, 1130, 1300, 1430, 1830hrs

**Igoumenitsa to Kokkinia**
Daily           0630, 1320hrs

**Igoumenitsa to Mazdakia**
Daily           0630, 1400hrs

**Igoumenitsa to Polineri**
Daily           0645, 1330hrs

**Igoumenitsa to Scorpiona**
Daily           0645, 1430hrs

**Igoumenitsa to Ag Vlasios**
Daily           0630, 0800, 0830, 1000, 1215, 1315, 1345,
                1445, 1600, 1800, 2030hrs

**CINEMA** (*Tmr* 18C3) On the left (*Waterfront on the left hand*) of Odhos Metaxa.

**COMMERCIAL SHOPPING AREA** Not only is there no central market, but the general standard of the shops is not very high. The Mini-market (*Tmr* 19D3), at No 3, on the left (*Sbo*) of Odhos El Venizelou is recommended. The owner, who speaks English, is very helpful, the shop is clean and well stocked with drinks and goods. On the north side of the park is a Galaktopoleio (*Tmr* 20C2); on the right (*Waterfront on the left-hand*) of Odhos Kyprou is a Greengrocer (*Tmr* 21B/C2/3) and on the right (*Waterfront on the left-hand*) of the parallel street of Odhos Metaxa is a Butcher (*Tmr* 22B3).

Despite the busy, day in, day out, activity, most of the shops close for Sunday. An exception to this rule is the 'shambles' of a small Supermarket (*Tmr* 23E/F2) on the left of Odhos Pargos. The old man who runs it is a character and speaks some English. A little further on is the *Hotel Epirus* (*Tmr* 24E/F2). Incidentally, there are any number of peripteros.

**FERRY-BOATS** Not only 'domestic' connections but international ferries link with the Italian ports of Brindisi, Bari, Ancona and, at the height of season, with the Yugoslavian ports of Dubrovnik, Rijeka, Split and Zadar. This aspect of the port's activity necessitates a whopping great quay.

For details of the international ferries *See* **Chapter Two** and note these include boats that proceed on to Patras.

**Ferry-boat timetable**

**Igoumenitsa to Corfu (Kerkyra)**
Daily          0530, 0630, 0800, 0930, 1030, 1230, 1400, 1600,
               1730, 1900, 2000, 2100, 2200hrs
*Return*
Daily          0530, 0700, 0730, 0930, 1100, 1230, 1400, 1500,
               1600, 1730, 1900, 2000, 2130hrs
One-way fare: 330drs; duration 1hr 55mins.

**FERRY-BOAT TICKET OFFICES** Oh my goodness yes, any number of them, but be careful. The port officials scrutinise tickets and any discovered to have been sold beneath the statutory listed prices will be confiscated and the unfortunate purchaser made to go and buy correctly priced replacements. Oh dear!

**HAIRDRESSER** There is a ladies hairdresser (*Tmr* 25B3).

**MEDICAL CARE**
**Chemists/Pharmacies** Many, including one (*Tmr* 26D3) on the corner of El Venizelou and Metaxa Sts.
**Hospital** 15 Odhos Filiates.

**OTE** (*Tmr* 27A/B3) Unusually, the OTE is combined with the Post Office. The OTE is open for business weekdays, between 0700-2400hrs and Sat 0730-1510hrs.

**PETROL** Numerous petrol stations.

**POLICE**
**Tourist** Over the Town police office.
**Town** To the south along the Esplanade, beyond the Town Hall and the signposted road to Parga, Preveza, on the left.

**POST OFFICE** (*Tmr* 27A/B3) Shares the OTE building, on the right (*Sbo*) of Odhos Evangelistrias, at the junction with Odhos Metaxa. Normal weekday hours.

**TAXIS** Apart from the two ferry-boat points, there is a rank (*Tmr* TD3) at the junction of El Venizelou and Metaxa St and another adjacent to the Bus station (*Tmr* 1B3).

**TELEPHONE NUMBERS & ADDRESSES**
Hospital 15 Filiates St                                                    Tel 22205
Police, tourist                                                            Tel 22302

**TOILETS** There are a couple of convenient public toilets, one at the Bus station (*Tmr* 1B3) and another (*Tmr* 28E/F4) down a tree lined path between the International and Corfu ferry-boat docking points.

**TRAVEL AGENTS & TOUR OFFICES** Dozens of offices line Akti Vassileos Pavlou, the Esplanade. Most are combined with ferry-boat ticket agencies.

The Olympic agent (*Tmr* 29D3) is situated at No 10A, Odhos El Venizelou.

Rather than stay in Igoumenitsa, travellers might well consider the delights of nearby Plataria, Sivota, the not so adjacent Arilia or even Parga.

From Igoumenitsa the main coastal road to the south curves round the bay, beyond the fuel storage tanks, prior to ascending the mountainside. The route passes a neatly constructed, cliff edging park from whence there are excellent panoramic views of the bay, the port and far Drepano Beach. On the other side of the bluff, the road sweeps by the angled lane down to:-

**Camping Kalami Beach** (8km from Igoumenitsa)                                    Tel (0665) 71211
Buses slog over from Igoumenitsa to both Plataria and Sivota and a taxi costs about 500drs.
   This established, extremely well facilitated campsite is in a lovely setting on the edge of a small bay. The narrow, fine shingle beach gently slopes into the sea and trees grow almost all the way down to the backshore. The complex includes a clinic, bar-restaurant, mini-market, a shower block (with 24hr hot water), washing machines and kitchen. Charges are: per head 410drs & per tent 330drs. There is a closely printed set of regulations, which I suspect are disobeyed only under the threat of transgressors having their hands cut off. Achtung!

A kilometre or so further along the Plataria road is another turning off to the right that steeply descends, for a 100m or so, on a concrete surfaced track, to a fork. To the right advances to:-

**Plataria Beach Hotel** (Class B)                                                Tel 71287
All rooms have en suite bathrooms, with a single costing 2500drs & a double 3700drs, which rates rise, respectively, to 3000 & 4500drs (1st June-31st Aug).
and to the left to:-

**Helena's Beach Camping**                                                        Tel 71414
This campsite has only been established for a few years. The family owners certainly knew a thing or two when selecting the location for this is a beautiful setting, edging a small curve of a large bay and pleasantly wooded right down to the edge of the narrow, fine shingle, very clean beach. A disadvantage is that the sea-bed shelves very steeply.
   There are showers, a restaurant and store. Although the facilities are perhaps not so comprehensive as those of *Camping Kalami*, I suspect the atmosphere and regime is rather more informal. Nod, nod...

**PLATARIA (Approx 12km from Igoumenitsa)** This is a very pleasant spot, even if it would appear that the Corfu travel agents, not content with despoiling their own island, dispatch tour buses to pore (or paw!) over the mainland. The fishing village is set down on the nearside of a large, semi-circular bay. The settlement, which evinces signs of gathering development, is backed by a flat plain, rimmed by distant, large mountainsides, the horns of which curve round to enclose the turquoise gulf.
   To the right (*Fsw*), beyond the formal gardens around which the centre of the village clusters, is a small caique harbour and pier. There are at least four *Rooms*, a number of bars, a taverna/restaurant or two (specialising in fish dishes), a baker and a couple of peripteros.
   The coastal road to Sivota stretches away to the left (*Fsw*) edging a long, straight backshore of fine shingle, pebbly, kelpy and quite steeply shelving beach. There are a few sandy spits and some effort is made to clean away the kelp, as manifested by the heaps gathered together on the middle shore.

At the far end of the bay the road climbs and winds round the horn of mountain to:-

**SIVOTA (Mourtos) (Approx 24km from Igoumenitsa)** (Tel prefix 0665) A very pretty, fishing boat hamlet. Not many years ago Sivota was only accessible by boat or over rough tracks. Now a good surfaced road has been engineered and Sivota has been 'discovered'. Despite this, (or more realistically due to sympathetic development) the location has, to date, remained largely unspoilt.
   The short, final approach to the waterfront is down a right-hand turning off the main road (*Plataria behind one*), which abruptly terminates on a small, irregular, rough surfaced square. From here it is only a stride or five to the waterfront quay, along an alley between the huddle of buildings that edge the wide spread of the 'Esplanade', some 15-20m from the water lapped coping stones of the sea wall.
   The jumble of Esplanade buildings house amongst their number, and ranged to the left (*sic*), *Peters Flea Market*, a supermarket (more a general store), *Joseph's Restaurant*, *George's Restaurant* and a tourist type shop. The tables and chairs of the taverna

restaurants are prettily spread about across the Esplanade. The last in the row is an inexpensive family run taverna, still unspoilt by the tourist influx. They serve ample portion, piping hot meals. There is no menu but the daughter, when present, speaks English. Around the corner from this latter establishment is **Rooms**, behind a Grill Restaurant. Not much further to the left (*Fsw*) of the last Esplanade taverna and the quay runs out on the edge of a very small, kelp covered smidgin of sandy beach. Beyond this is a square, two storey, red roof tiled building, hosting *Jannis Taverna* and a *Boats For Rent* business. On the far side of the building is an expansive patio necessary, I guess, to cope with evening hungry party groups. A track winds up behind Jannis Taverna on to a surprisingly large, tree covered headland, which is being steadily covered with villas.

The main quay hosts a number of fishing boats, a 'Daily Cruise' trip boat, that at the height of the season connects with the islands of Corfu and Paxos, and yachts stretching away to the right (*Fsw*).

Back at the aforementioned square is:-

**Sivota Travel** 46.100 Sivota                                                Tel 93264
'General Toyrist Office' (*sic*), run by two pleasant, kind, helpful chaps, one of whom speaks English (Stamatis, I think). Apart from selling tickets for the cruise caique, they vend postcards, stamps, Greece-Italy ferry-boat tickets; rent **Rooms**, apartments, hotel rooms and villas as well as exchanging money.

Close to the junction with the main road, there is a Clinic and, in the direction of Plataria, *Camping Sivota* (Tel 31483).

The road to Arilia ascends the hillside and is, in effect, a loosely knit High St. It passes a butchers and **Rooms** on the right, and, on the left, a tourist office sporting a *Budget Rent A Car* sign with some scooters and bicycles lined up outside. The street then crosses a French style village square, shaded by a couple of very large trees and edged by a locals taverna, on the left. From hereon passes a vegetable shop; a rather out of place, luxurious cafe-bar/restaurant, and, on the right, a supermarket and BP Petrol Station. The supermarket is more a general store but in this case a regular Aladdin's cave of a place with food, drink and an extremely wide selection of reasonably priced items littering the dexion shelves. Still ascending sweeps by on either side, for instance, a bakery, *Rent A Bike*, in the bottom half of an incomplete dwelling and over which is **Rooms** (*Apartments Dumas Stratis* – Tel 91465), the *Restaurant Pizzeria*, **Rooms** above a mini-market, *Hotel Long Summer Apartments*, with a terracotta roof, followed by the *Hotel Akropolis*.

Beyond the latter hotel is a little slip road down to a small cove, with a sandy beach and sea-bed. Some *ad hoc* camping takes place in the olive grove that borders the inlet. On the far side of this turning is an older *House To Let* (Tel 0651 32137), prettily located on a bluff overlooking the surrounding coves.

About a kilometre further on, beyond a sign to another hotel, there is a 100m of beach set in a lovely if cramped inlet, edged by a clean beach made up of a fine mix of pebbles, sand and fine shingle. The backshore is fringed by a small olive grove, in which may well be parked one or two motor caravans.

There is yet another, even smaller cove with some 30-40m of beach off to the right of the main road.

To sum up, and if not prepared to use the good services of Sivota Travel, accommodation, apart from **Rooms**, includes:-

**Long Summer Apartments** (Class B)
Suites start at 3930drs, increasing to 4300drs (16th July-30th Aug).

**Hotel Beta Vraka** (Class B)                                                Tel 91461
All rooms have en suite bathrooms with singles starting at 1880drs & doubles 2390drs, increasing

to 1900drs & 2620drs (28th May-17th June & 18th Sept-1st Oct) and 2935drs & 4880drs (18th June-17th Sept).

**Hotel Sivota** (Class C)                                                                        Tel 91497
Once again all rooms have bathrooms en suite. Single rooms are charged at 2000drs & doubles 2500drs, rising to 2500drs & 3000drs (21st June-10th Sept).

**Hotel Mikros Paradissos** (Class D)                                                        Tel 91201
The rooms have en suite bathrooms with singles costing 1800drs & doubles 2250drs, advancing to 1500drs & 3000drs (1st July-31st Aug).

**Hotel Acropolis** (Class E)
Double rooms only, those sharing bathrooms are priced at 1800drs & en suite 2000drs, increasing, respectively, to 2000drs & 2500drs (21st June-10th Sept).

The coastal route from Sivota to Arilia, which winds around the contours of the sea hugging mountainside some 50m above sea-level, must be one of the most beautiful drives in Greece. Despite many map indications to the contrary, the road, is metalled all the way.

At the signpost for Perdika straight on, take the right to:-

**ARILIA (Arila, Arrilia, Aiailla – approx 34km from Igoumenitsa)** Apart from the loveliness of the immediate surroundings, in the far distance is the southern coastline of Corfu island. The road emerges from the hillsides revealing a stunning view out over a long, slow crescent of beach set in a lovely, tree covered cove. There is accommodation in a private house, prior to descending to the shoreline, close to which the road surface finally becomes unmetalled. Along a slip track angling off the approach road is a restaurant specialising in fish. A certain amount of informal camping is evident in amongst the olive trees that grow right down to the backshore of the grey, fine, thick sand beach, which spreads out to either side.

Standing on the backshore, to the left (*Fsw*) is a well shaded, counter service taverna, where they serve a morning breakfast and meals all day long. The lemonade available is the very pleasant *HPN* and a beer costs 100drs. On the right is a shower head.

Despite the signs urging visitors to keep the place tidy, the beach is subject to a certain amount of seaborne rubbish, bits of log and some stones. Horseflies tend to be a menace, despite which this is a very pleasant spot.

To proceed southwards it is necessary to backtrack to the main road and pass through:-

**PERDIKA (approx 34km from Igoumenitsa)** A two donkey-droppings, rustic hamlet spread around an elongated square. There are a number of tavernas, and an estiatorion, at any one of which it might be interesting to eat.

On this northern approach to Parga, the route passes through the village of **Ag Kiriakis**, where there are *Rooms*, as there is on the descent to sea-level. Approximately 3km beyond Ag Kiriakis, and having descended some way down the mountainside, the route passes a turning to **Lichnos Beach** (*See* this chapter, following the Parga description).

On the outskirts of Parga are Apartments, Flats and *Rooms*, followed by *Camping Elia*, a BP Petrol Station and *Parga Camping*, beyond which the road forks. The right-hand turning curves and rises into Upper Parga, close to the Bus station (*Tmr* 1D2/3), and the left, lower turning descends past the town beach, Krioneri, into the waterfront and port quarter of:-

**PARGA: Epirus Region, NW Greece** (Illustration 10) Tel prefix 0684. This small, picturesque seaside town, crowded and hemmed in by steep, heavily wooded foothills, is rather 'Lindos flavoured'. The settlement had a convoluted history in which the Venetians, Turks, Russians, French, British and Turks all had a hand (and in that order), controlling the area until it was reunited with Greece, as late as 1913.

The port area is hunched and spread around the waterfront, from which the Old Quarter

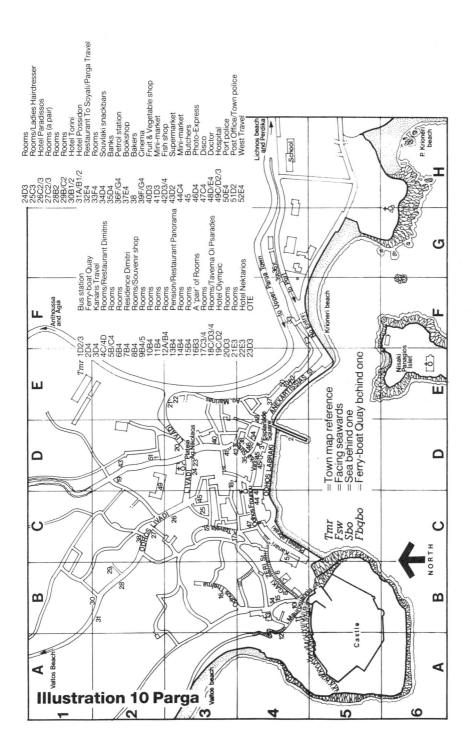

Illustration 10 Parga

of whitewashed houses winds up a fortress capped spur, in a maze of narrow streets and unexpected steps, rather in the fashion of a Cornish fishing village. The upper town spreads gently round the inland flank of the hillsides.

The beautiful cove, around which Parga sprawls, is hemmed in by prominent, tree covered, rocky islets, one complete with a whitewashed chapel and small dwelling. Beyond the castle topped promontory is a much larger bay, with a long, sandy shore (Valtos Beach) set at the foot of a steep, wooded backdrop.

The beauty of the overall scene, a landscape artist's dream, ensures that the locale, popular with both Greeks and tourists alike, is rather crowded in the summer months.

Back at the fork in the main road, the progress of vehicles along the left-hand, seafront turning is barred (between 1100-0400hrs) by a couple of 'no-entry' signs. These are 'dug in' approximately adjacent to the small, crescent shaped, 'town' beach. This is encircled by rather large lumps of rock which might be chunks of mountainside dropped into the sea, perhaps by a celestial hand. The street curves and drops round to the right, becoming a restaurant and taverna edged Esplanade, Anexartissias St. This runs out on an informal waterfront square, from which projects a small, concrete, ferry-boat finger pier (*Tmr* 2D4).

The right-hand fork off the main road winds round, following the contour of the foothills, on the way to Anthoussa village, north of Parga. From this road, a left-hand turning (Odhos Livada) sweeps down to the 'crossroads square' of Plateia Ag Nikolaos. The turning to the left from this plateia wanders and narrows down to the waterfront; straight on continues up Odhos Livada and the street to the right ascends past the Bus station (*Tmr* 1D2/3) and the combined Post Office/Police station.

Parga was once rather more expensive than most of the other western mainland coastal resorts, and popular with British and Italian holiday-makers. Nowadays prices are not much out of line, and the resort is still popular with the British and Italians.

## THE ACCOMMODATION & EATING OUT

**The Accommodation** There are any number of *Rooms*, most of which are situated along the length of the steeply climbing hillside street, Odhos Gaki Zeri, that finally peters out up against the Castle walls. Despite this plethora of accommodation, the owners do not mob new arrivals, so it is necessary to search out a bed. Double rooms, sharing a bathroom, cost from 1500drs and with an en suite bathroom are charged from 1800drs. In addition, there are quite a few hotels.

Starting out from the Ferry-boat Quay (*Tmr* 2D4), it is probably best to turn left alongside Kanaris Travel (*Tmr* 3D4) in order to zig-zag along the streets of Vaska and Frouriou to reach the hill-scrambling Odhos Gaki Zeri.

Accommodation includes *Rooms* (*Tmr* 4C/D4), over *Restaurant Dimitris* and opposite the small church in front of which is a fountain. It is a climb before the next house with beds.

At a fork, the 'High St', Odhos Gaki Zeri, starts out on the 'serious' climb to the right and a cul-de-sac, Odhos Kanari, dips down to the left and along which are *Rooms* (*Tmr* 5B/C4).

Continuing climbing the steps of Odhos Gaki Zeri leaves *Rooms* (*Tmr* 6B4), at No 9, on the left in a house of ethnic appearance. Not much further on is *Residence Dimitri* (*Tmr* 7B4 – tel 31694), at No 21, a relatively new house of smart appearance, advertising *Rooms with private toilet, balcony and sea view*. On the opposite side of the lane are *Rooms* (*Tmr* 8B4), above a souvenir shop, the (only) Greek speaking lady owner of which is smiley, even if Papa does lurk in an inner sanctum, bellowing instructions!

At the top of the climb, a lateral path, Odhos Maurogiannis, edges the foundations of the Castle. Turning right, and keeping to the left, opposite a turning off to the right, is *Rooms* (*Tmr* 9B4/5 – tel 31543), the bedrooms of which have en suite bathrooms and a terrace. Opposite is a house (*Tmr* 10B4 – tel 31048) with accommodation, as there is another **Rooms** (*Tmr* 11B4 – tel 31543), back on the left-hand side of the lane. These latter three are all 'housed' in nice looking buildings.

Occupying an enviable position, a few more strides onwards and now descending, is **Rooms** (*Tmr* 12A/B4 – tel 31460). The bedrooms have en suite bathrooms, but the major plus point is the splendid view out over Valtos Beach.

Taking a turning to the right off Odhos Mauragiannis, prior to the last mentioned accommodation, leads to *Pension/Restaurant Panorama Grill Bar* (*Tmr* 13B4 – tel 31147). Once again there is an excellent prospect out over Valtos Beach from the terraces of the accommodation, which are beyond the basement kitchen. The building edges an irregular square. By keeping round to the right (*Valtos Beach behind one*) and returning towards the top of the 'High St', leaves, to the left, two houses (*Tmr* 14 & 15B4) with accommodation.

Back at the *Pension Panorama* (*Tmr* 13B4), following the lane to the left and turning right down Odhos Thelma, passes, on the left, two side-by-side houses (*Tmr* 16B3) with accommodation.

Other **Rooms** in this area are at No 1 Odhos K. Tzavela (*Tmr* 17C3/4 – tel 31121), and those advertised in the window of the *Fish Taverna Oi Psarades* (*Tmr* 18C/D3/4 – tel 31033), on the little Plateia Ag Cosma.

Another area from which to spread out in search of accommodation is the Bus station (*Tmr* 1D2/3). Proceeding north along the street, and leaving the Bus station on the right (*Town Beach behind one*), ascends to the:-

**Hotel Olympic** (*Tmr* 19C/D2) (Class C)                    Tel 31360
*Directions*: As above.

Single rooms share the bathrooms and cost 2260drs, whilst double rooms sharing are available for 2670drs & with en suite bathrooms 2890drs. These rates increase, respectively, to 3010, 3615 & 4065drs (1st July-15th Sept).

Back to Plateia Ag Nikolaos and ascending east along Odhos Livada, towards the Anthoussa road, leaves **Rooms** (*Tmr* 20D3 ) on the left, **Rooms** (*Tmr* 21E3) on the right, as well as the:-

**Hotel Ag Nektarios** (*Tmr* 22E3) (Class D)                    Tel 31150
*Directions*: As above and in the corner of the junction of Livada and Ag Marinas Sts.

Single rooms, sharing a bathroom, cost 1555drs & en suite 1745drs and double rooms sharing 2045drs & en suite 2570drs. These charges increase, respectively, to 1950/2010drs & 2240/2830drs (16th May-30th June) and 2285/2675drs & 2970/3625drs (1st July-10th Sept).

Returning to Plateia Ag Nikolaos, Odhos Livada climbs away to the west, eventually to terminate at Valtos Beach. Not many steps beyond the OTE office (*Tmr* 23D3) is, on the left, **Rooms** (*Tmr* 24D3), at No 19, with the entrance squeezed in between a pair of ice-cream parlours. A pace or ten further on is an irregular square, on the left, about where the street bends round to the right. The topmost lane off this plateia has **Rooms** (*Tmr* 25C3), above a ladies hairdresser on the left.

**Hotel Paradissos** (*Tmr* 26C2/3) (Class D)                    Tel 31229
*Directions*: On the left (*Town Beach behind one*) of Livada St.

This hotel possesses an international metered telephone.

A little way beyond the *Paradissos*, and on the same side of the road, are a 'pair' of **Rooms** (*Tmr* 27C2/3), at No 39 and No 43. There is **Rooms** further along the same street as there are, yet more **Rooms** (*Tmr* 28B2 & 29B/C2), almost opposite each other, even higher up Odhos Livada. The right-hand house is down a cul-de-sac, just beyond the town's Fire Station.

**Hotel Torini** (*Tmr* 30B1/2) (Class C)                    Tel 31219
*Directions*: Further north-west on Odhos Livada and on the right.

All rooms have en suite bathrooms with a single room costing 2710drs & a double room 3160drs, which prices increase, respectively, to 3615drs & 4515drs (1st July-31st Aug).

**Hotel Possidon** (*Tmr* 31A/B1/2) (Class E)                                                    Tel 31058
*Directions*: Diagonally across the road from the *Torini*.

All rooms have en suite bathrooms, with a single charged at 1850drs & a double 3250drs, rising, to 2250drs & 3650drs (21st June-20th Sept).

Almost opposite both the *Torini* & *Possidon* are **Rooms**, although those across the way from the *Torini* are labelled *Villa Parga* and *Sun Med*. The accommodation opposite the *Possidon* is in the same building as the *Grill/Cafe-bar Toxotis*.

Another 'source' of accommodation is beside the Esplanade. The 'old' *Hotel Bacoli* (*Tmr* 32E4) is, or possibly more correctly was, above the *Restaurant To Soyli* and Parga Travel, but this is a bit of a mystery for the upper rooms appear to be nothing more than an empty dump. I can only presume the hotel has been relocated, somewhere! Once round the corner of the Esplanade, and heading away from the sea, there is accommodation (*Tmr* 33F4) hidden behind a large restaurant building. Those not prepared to traipse around the town might try the ever helpful **Kanaris Travel** (*Tmr* 3D4).

Another alternative is to consider the merits of the **Rooms** scattered on either side of the road to Anthoussa. This courses along the tree covered mountainside, high above Valtos Beach on the way to Agia. It does seem a long way out of town, even if it is a very pretty area overlooked by a one-time, hill topping Venetian castle.

For other accommodation *See* **Valtos Beach, Beaches, A To Z**.

**Camping** There at least two sites on the main road approach to Parga:-

**Parga Camping**                                                                               Tel 31161
*Directions*: Just out of town, prior to the BP Petrol Station.

Well recommended and comparatively inexpensive, but the situation is the major attraction as it edges the small P. Krioneri Beach. Open April to the end of October
and

**Elea Camping**                                                                                 Tel 31010
*Directions*: Beyond the BP Petrol Station.

Also *See* **Valtos Beach, Beaches, A To Z**.

**The Eating Out** The 'main thrust' is massed along the waterfront Esplanade, at the left (*Fsw*), uphill end. Here are a row of 'average' restaurants with their raised, awning shaded terraces across the road, edged by the Town beach sea wall. The benches and tables are reached up small flights of steps.

For simpler fare, there are two side-by-side giro pita snackbars (*Tmr* 34D4) (well they would be adjacent, wouldn't they?), across the street from the bottom of the steps up to the first floor office of Kanaris Travel. The left-hand one (*Sbo*) is *Grill Bar, Giro, Fish Taverna. The beautiful Parga*. Yes, well. The owner, Nikos Stelios, is not above schlepping and I have even observed him chin-chucking a pram bound baby in an effort to drum up trade! The establishment next door is the *Grill Bar Three Stars* .

The bar, located in the ground floor of the building in which Kanaris Travel (*Tmr* 3D4) occupies part of the first floor, is conveniently situated, close to the Ferry-boat Quay. Apart from the toilets (of which there is a 'town shortage'), it possesses a metered telephone. Merely a hint, but it is possibly best to check any change due here!

The English presence in the resort is proclaimed by those Esplanade establishments which offer 'Full English Breakfast'.

## THE A TO Z OF USEFUL INFORMATION

**BANKS** Two side-by-side (*Tmr* 35D4), but only the **National Bank** is of any use to tourists as the other is an Agricultural Bank\*. Apart from the usual hours, during the height of summer frenzy, the National Bank opens weekday evenings for exchange purposes, between 1830-2030hrs.
\*In one or two locations the Agricultural Banks are widening their duties to include tourist services.

**BEACHES Town Beach (Krioneri)** Not over-large and rather hemmed in by a substantial sea wall. Some sand but mainly pebble with little outcrops of rock here and there. About 4m into the water and the sea-bed is covered with sea grass. Seemingly almost within touching distance, the pretty islet of Nisaki Panagias dominates the view. Pedaloes are marshalled on the shore's edge.

**Valtos Beach** A brisk walk or a circuitous drive to the north-west side of the Castle outcrop. The motor road passes through old olive groves, the tree trunks of which are tortured and gnarled with age. Incidentally, a taxi ride costs 75drs. The backshore of much of this beach is edged by a metalled track, the narrow width of which is often reduced by a 'litter' of parked cars. The beach is an attractive, extremely long, gently curving, fairly wide sweep of grit and sand. To top up the crowds, caiques ferry passengers to and from the Town Esplanade. Pedaloes and water sports are complemented by deck chairs (200drs a day) and sun umbrellas (150drs a day), but there is a total absence of beach showers. For those who wish to supplement the various delights, a signboard, some three quarters of the way along the beach road, proclaims *Every day boat trips in (sic) the River Styx. Visit Hades Oracle of the Dead, Necromanteion. Visit inside the Blue Aphrodites, caves. Swimming at Lichnos Beach. Depart Parga 9am, Return 1330hrs. Info (from) Boat Gregorakis and Soragio or Parga Tourist office* Well, that says it all really. The beach road terminates in a sprawl of tree shaded businesses dedicated to assuaging the various desires of beach visitors. One proclaims *Valtos by Night Cafe-bar/cocktail, pizza, spaghetti bolognese*. Beyond this, edging the backshore and enclosed by a fence, is *Parga Beach Bungalows Chryssoyali*. The bungalows are rather 'Portacabin like' and one wonders if the fence is to keep the occupants in? *Valtos Camping* (Tel 31287) is open April to September.

**BICYCLE, SCOOTER & CAR HIRE** Scooters are for rent from the same block of buildings as is the accommodation (*Tmr* 20D3), on Odhos Livada. Alongside the petrol station (*Tmr* 36F/G4), bordering the Esplanade, is **Rent A Bike**.

**BOOKSELLERS** (*Tmr* 37E4) A shop on the Esplanade stocks a limited range of international newspapers and English language books.

**BREAD SHOPS** Two Bakers 'lurk' close to the 'Esplanade Square', one alongside the National Bank (*Tmr* 35D4) and the other (*Tmr* 38D3/4) on the right (*Sbo*) of Odhos Vaska. Yet another Baker (*Tmr* 38C2) is situated at No 36, on the right of Odhos Livada, beyond the *Hotel Paradissos*.

**BUSES** The Bus station (*Tmr* 1D2/3) is on the right (*Sbo*) of the street that ascends from Plateia Ag Nikolaos.

## Bus timetable

**Parga to Athens** (Tel 5129252)
Daily            0715, 1000, 1415hrs
*Return journey*
Daily            0700, 1330, 2000hrs

**Parga to Igoumenitsa**
Daily            0715, 1245, 1430, 1830hrs
Saturday       0715, 1430, 1830hrs
Sunday         0730, 1645hrs
*Return journey*
Daily            0600, 1115, 1315, 1715hrs
Saturday       0600, 1315, 1715hrs
Sunday         0630, 1530hrs

**Parga to Preveza**
Daily            0710, 1015, 1430, 1600hrs
Saturday       0710, 1015, 1400, 1600hrs
Sunday         0710, 1015, 1600hrs
*Return journey*
Daily            0500, 0645, 1045, 1415, 2000hrs
Saturday       0500, 0800, 1045, 1415, 2000hrs
Sunday         0500, 0800, 1415, 2000hrs

**Parga to Anthoussa & Agia**
Daily            0830, 1300, 1615hrs

**CINEMA** (*Tmr* 39F/G4) A building edging the Esplanade.

**COMMERCIAL SHOPPING AREA** There isn't a central market or particular street, the shops being spread around the town. A strict siesta is in force between 1400-1700hrs, but naturally enough this does not extend to many of the tourist orientated businesses.

In the street that descends from Plateia Ag Nikolaos, south towards the waterfront, there is a well stocked Fruit and Vegetable shop (*Tmr* 40D3), a Mini-Supermarket (*Tmr* 41D3) and a Fish shop (*Tmr* 42D3/4).

Beyond the Bus station (*Tmr* 1D2/3), and on the same side of the street, is a Supermarket (*Tmr* 43D2), whilst on the left of Odhos Frouriou is a Mini-Market (*Tmr* 44C4). There are two Butchers (*Tmr* 45D4), close together, across the street from the Banks, and another (*Tmr* 45C3) in a small square off Odhos Livada.

Almost across the way from the bottom of the steps up to Kanaris Travel is **Photo Express** (*Tmr* 46D4), which stocks a useful range of films and batteries. The kafeneions, restaurants, tavernas and pizza places which line the Esplanade, Odhos Anexartissias, are interspaced by the occasional chemist, as well as gift and souvenir shops, all the way up to the No Entry Signs.

**DISCOS** At least one (*Tmr* 47C4), on the right of Odhos Frouriou.

**FERRY-BOATS** For a ferry to thread its way through the rocky surrounds of the small, irregular bay would appear to be a difficult task, which it may well be. The small inter-island craft, which connect with Paxos, moor to the finger pier (*Tmr* 2D4) that juts out from the Esplanade. A caique departs at 0930hrs every day, and in the height of season, a 1700hrs boat is a possibility.

**FERRY-BOAT TICKET OFFICES** *See* **Travel Agents & Tour Offices, A To Z**.

**HAIRDRESSER** There is a Ladies Hairdresser (*Tmr* 25C3) on Odhos Livada, diagonally across from the baker's.

**LAUNDRY** No launderette but there is a Laundry, at No 4, close to the junction of the Town and Beach roads.

**MEDICAL CARE**
**Chemists & Pharmacies** One or two spaced out along the Esplanade, Odhos Anexartissias.
**Dentist** To the right (*Esplanade behind one*) off Odhos Frouriou, immediately prior to a disco.
**Doctor** (*Tmr* 48D/E4) 'Dr George Dimchristou, MD Physician, specialised (*sic*) in internal medicine'. He practices from a clinic in a narrow lane that branches off 'Esplanade Sq'.
**Hospital** (*Tmr* 49C/D2/3) A large building reached along Odhos Livada, from beyond Plateia Ag Nikolaos.

**OTE** (*Tmr* 23D3) On Plateia Ag Nikolaos and open weekdays only, between 0730-2200hrs.

**PETROL STATIONS** One filling station (*Tmr* 36F/G4) is situated close to where the Esplanade is stopped off to traffic and the other, a BP Petrol Station, is towards the main road outskirts of Parga.

**PLACES OF INTEREST** Obviously the Castle, which dominates the town and surrounding coastline, must be included in the list, if only for the view. The edifice, now a shell, was originally built by the French, with each and every successive occupying force making use of the structure. Climb the steps from the upper village. Open daylight hours.

The tour and travel offices offer a fascinating excursion into Greece's mythological past, with boat trips to the River Acheron, known by the ancients as the Styx. This is followed by a walk to the Necromanteion of Ephyra (oracle for the dead) and the Sanctuary of Persephone and Hades. One cannot help occasionally day-dreaming about this or that relative making the one-way trip...

The town elders have initiated the construction of an intriguing Piazza which stretches along the waterfront to the base of the Castle topping outcrop. The nicest approach is via the tunnel-like archway off Odhos Frouriou, opposite a disco (*Tmr* 47C4). There are a couple of interesting buildings edging the paved area. One is a classical, three storey mansion with dull red coloured walls and prominent iron railed balconies. It is a pity that the prospect is criss-crossed with the usual spaghetti of cables. At the other end of the spectrum is a relic, a hillbilly dwelling squeezed in between its smarter neighbours and occupied by a black clothed old dear and her daughter. The entrance way is filled by cut stone blocks and the front 'garden' wall is topped with neatly stacked firewood. The front yard appears to be an integral part of the living area.

**POLICE**
**Port** (*Tmr* 50E4) Close to the 'Esplanade Sq'. The entrance is off the narrow alley between the offices of West Travel and Parga Travel.
**Town** (*Tmr* 51D2) Next door to the Bus station, above the Post Office.

**POST OFFICE** (*Tmr* 51D2). Alongside the Bus station.

**TAXIS** Plentiful, and rank throughout the town.

**TOILETS** As they are noticeable only by their total absence, it is necessary to utilise those of convenient cafe-bars.

**TRAVEL AGENTS & TOUR OFFICES**
**Kanaris Travel** (*Tmr* 3D4)                                                         Tel 31490
*Directions*: Up a flight of stone steps and located in the first floor of a large building on the west side of 'Esplanade Sq'.
 Represents *Sun Med*. Callers will indeed be lucky if Katerina is on duty. She is extremely helpful and speaks excellent English.
**West Travel** (*Tmr* 52E4) 10 Anexartissias St                                       Tel 31223
*Directions*: A stride of twenty, ascending the slope of the Esplanade, from 'Esplanade Sq'.
 Sells ferry-boat tickets and offers trips to the River Archeron. The office hours are 0900-1300hrs & 1800-2100hrs, daily.
**Parga Travel & Tourist Office** (*Tmr* 32E4) 9 Anexartissias St                       Tel 31580
*Directions*: Across an alley from West Travel.
 They flog the River Archeron trips, amongst other goodies. Sample prices for various excursions include: Ioannina (City) 3200drs, Greek Night Out 3500drs, Fish Picnic 3200drs and the Ancient City of Nikopolis 2200drs. For more details of this latter, star turn read on.

**LICHNOS BEACH** The signposted turning down to the beach is about 2km from Parga, along the route back to the main Igoumenitsa/Preveza road.
 It is quite a long, steep descent to the bay. About half-way down, metal surfaced tracks lead to *Enjoy Camping* (Tel 0684 31371) and some apartments, whilst the track to the beach becomes unsurfaced. Close by this 'junction', there are a number of 'twee' villas as well as *Rooms*.
 The road decants to the left (*Fsw*) of the bay on a rather restricted, flat area bordering the backshore. Further to the left are an array of holiday flatlets and their grounds, which sweep down to the edge of the beach. To the right are a couple of neat, almost squeaky clean tavernas and beyond them some chalets and the campsite grounds.
 Although the development here is fairly low key, it has only left a narrow 'bridgehead' to the beach. This is an aggreeable, wide, clean, steeply shelving sweep of fine shingle. The sole showers are those in the area of the chalets. An outfit called Thomas Watersports has the franchise for... guess what?
 The relative tranquillity of the location is disturbed daily by trip boats which motor round from Parga.

The coastal road between Igoumenitsa and Preveza, south of the turning off to Parga, is open to traffic, if rather perilous in places where subsidence has destroyed much of the surface. Apart from the undoubted scenic attractions, this route enables a traveller to call in at the seaside village that stands on the mouth of the legendary River Archeron, that is:-
**AMOUDIA (approx 49km from Igoumenitsa)** The road from the north looks down over and loops round the large, almost circular, fertile plain that edges the sea. This broad area is latticed with drainage ditches and is intensively cultivated. As the route proceeds southwards it descends towards sea-level and at the far end there is a flyover crossroads. The turning inland, signed Preveza and Athina (Athens), leads to the inland village of Messopotamos. To the right is crudely signposted Amoudia.
 The arrow straight, 3km or so of road to the sea starts out across a quarry, beyond which it is pleasantly tree lined with, on the left, the River Archeron, sluggishly paralleling the road. The Archeron is, by the way, the Styx, the river of hell of Greek mythological fame along which it is possible to advance towards the Necromanteion, or Oracle (Temple) of the Dead.
 From a distance the seaside location appears to be rather attractive, with a broad

sweep of beach edging a 'U' shaped bay, but reality is rather a disappointment. The embryonic, rather doo-hickey development is criss-crossed with a grid layout of streets. Rudimentary Amoudia may be, but it has all the hallmarks of becoming a full-blown resort in a year or ten. Scattered amongst the new buildings erected, and those in the course of construction, are a few hillbilly farmyards. There is a *Hotel Glaros*, 'Breakfast quickly meals', a ticket office shed, *Pension Cafe Bar Papas*, a petrol station that's either permanently closed or about to open, a 'Laden Shop' which sells fresh bread (it proclaims) and a cigarette hut.

The quite broad, oily green, tree shaded Archeron drifts past a distinctly seedy line of cafe-bars to discharge into the sea across a weedy mess of marshland, at the far left-hand side (*Fsw*) of the bay. The rather strange thing is that there is no port or harbour, nor even a finger pier. The clean beach, which is up to 30/40m wide, is very sandy, as is the sea-bed. There isn't any kelp but there is a 'high water' mark, as well as some seaborne bits and pieces and a scattering of seaweed. The backshore is edged by a broad swathe of spindly gum trees bordered by a roadway. Some *ad hoc* camping is evident in the summer months.

Back on the main road, there is a choice of routes. Travellers can proceed directly to Preveza or route inland to Arta and Amfilokhia via:-

**MESSOPOTAMOS (approx 51km from Igoumenitsa)** This pleasant, busy, agricultural village, with a baker and goodness knows what else, is the site of ancient Ephyra. Nearby and signposted is the:-

**Necromanteion, Oracle of the Dead & Sanctuary of Persephone and Hades** The ruins of this sacred site are located on a hill, whereon also the 18th century Monastery of St John. The building was a labyrinth of chambers and passageways along which those who wished to make contact with the dead were led by the priests. The gruesome ceremony took a number of days, during which the supplicant was put in the correct frame of mind to be able to conjure up the spirits of the deceased. To facilitate this process, the visitor had to eat selected, possibly hallucinatory food, be cleansed and purified, both magically and by bathing. When the priests adjudged the time was right, the petitioner was led into a room in which the spirits appeared.

Excavations have led archaeologists to suspect that the priests were not above helping matters along as finds have included wheels and winches. No doubt they were used to lower, raise and jiggle corpses in order to heighten the illusion.

The Necromanteion was probably erected in the 4th century BC and razed by the Romans sometime between 165-170BC. Close by is the confluence of the Rivers Archeron and Kokytos and the banks of the now dry Lake Acherousian.

One of the joys of this route is that it passes, via Arta, through:-

**AMFILOKHIA (approx 159km from Igoumenitsa)** A busy, agricultural, neat, 'spa' town and a pleasant place at which to stop-over. It is situated on Amvrakikos Gulf, at the furthest point from the 'mouth' (across which ply the Preveza-Acteon ferry-boats). Despite this, Amfilokhia rather has the feel of being on the edge of a large inland lake.

A formal stone parapet embankment circles the clear waters of the bay, from which the High St ascends, towards the south, a layout rather similar to the handle of a frying pan. At the bottom of the High St (*Fsw*), the Arta road is to the right. This leads past private houses, the occasional restaurant, taverna and bar, the *Hotel Helena* and *Amvrakhia*, a petrol station, towards the (surely) jokily signed Accapulco Beach. This is a small, fine pebble and shingle shore on which lurks one or two pedaloes.

Back at the roundabout (*High St behind one*), the left-hand Esplanade advances past a row of cafe-bar restaurants, the Post Office, over which is the *Cafe Le Roca Pub*(!), the Police station, the *Hotel Oscar* and, where the road divides, a tiny harbour and another petrol station.

Prior to ascending the High St, the taverna cafe-bar edging the Esplanade, immediately on the right (*Sbo*), is one of the most popular and convenient. A few metres along the High St, also on the right, is an excellent souvlaki pita bar sandwiched (oh dear) in between a butcher and women's accessories shop. The fare here must rate as some of the best I have 'gorged' in Greece. The proprietor cooks the meat on sticks and then folds the pita bread round the filling, adding some chips and charges 65drs. Don't tell everybody.

Almost directly across the High St is a narrow lane which curves round, approximately parallel to the Esplanade. This contains a clinic, a bread shop, the *Hotel Zefiros* and lots of shops, including some selling fruit and vegetables and one tapestries.

Back on the High St, on the left (*Sbo*) is a chemist and supermarket, over which towers the *Mistral Hotel*. About a 100m from the Esplanade, and on the right, is the Ionian and Popular Bank, yet another bank, a second baker, the *Hotel Oscar*, and petrol stations to left and right, after which the road crests a rise to run on in a southerly direction.

Note, siesta is strictly observed and the greatest excitement will be preparing the formula, for mixing the chemicals necessary to make the paint, which can be watched drying...

From Amfilokhia the route passes through Agrinion to bypass:-
**MESSOLONGI (approx 235km from Igoumenitsa)** (Tel prefix 0631) From the main road take the second signposted turning, the middle one of three. Quite frankly, unless determined to drop in and have a look round, travellers are advised to give the place a miss. It certainly isn't attractive and the outskirts are depressingly drab. Additionally, it is a garrison town, very few of which, anywhere in the world, could be deemed anything but cheerless. Whenever I visit Messolongi, it seems to be raining.

The town is famed for its association with Lord Byron, the poet, during the Greek War of Independence. Despite his energetic support, in both effort and money, the locals continually managed to quarrel amongst themselves. Byron fell ill from a serious fever in the month of February 1824, not surprisingly considering the low-lying, marshy nature of the surrounding land. Consequent upon the usual letting of blood prescribed by the medics, Byron died on the 19th April, in the same year. As a result of his heroic encouragement for the Hellenic cause, Byron (or Vironos as his surname translated) became greatly respected, if not revered, by the Greeks.

In 1826, the desperate citizens of Messolongi attempted to break through the Turkish siege by rushing the main gate. Supposedly they were betrayed, detected and slaughtered. On the other hand, I am unable to conceive this storming out of the major entrance resulting in anything else but detection.

Unfortunately the house in which Byron lived was destroyed, but there is a museum on the edge of the Main Square, in which are exhibited various memorabilia relating to Byron and the War of Independence. Perhaps he had a presentment of his death when he wrote 'Seek out – less often sought than found –
A soldiers grave, for thee the best;
Then look around, and choose thy ground,
And take thy rest'.

The approach road to the town edges the old, 3m high outer wall, on which canons are still positioned in the embrasures. Once through the Main Gate, the way divides into two streets of about 'equal' weight. The right-hand choice passes the very large *Liberty Hotel* and a side-street off to the right is signed *To The Heroes Tomb*. This advances to a park or Garden of Heroes, which is planted out with palm trees and shrubs, and enclosed by stout looking brick piers and iron railings. A 'fancy' building is visible through the vegetation and there is a statue to Byron, beneath which is buried his heart. Unfortunately, the gates are locked, more often than not.

The original town is a messy warren of narrow, crowded, traffic-ridden streets that criss-cross the Old Quarter. There are quite a few 19th century houses still in existence and the street lights are attractively set in leaves fashioned from wrought iron.

The actual size of the place is obscured by the cramped nature of the inner town, in the middle of which is a very large Main Square. Outside of the tightly packed centre, the sprawling development is encircled by massive port facilities which have a very abandoned air.

The town's saving grace is the extremely long causeway that seems to stretch away into the shallow sea, forever. At the outset is the *Xenia Hotel* and either side are fish catching enclosures. The outstanding feature must be the large, now rickety, fishermans' wooden houses (or *Feluccas*) mounted on wooden columns sticking out of the water. At the far end of this raised roadway is a 'Canvey Island' like area of land named Tourlida. Hereon are a number of modern-day, holiday home shacks, also supported on piles, despite being built on dry land, and a couple of fish tavernas. This causeway is paralleled by another, also festooned with similar buildings.

There are local buses, in addition to the KTEL national bus service.

Back at the Amoudia, Messopotamos area, for those wishing to make a more direct run, it is best to keep to the coast road. Close to Preveza, it is possible to turn off to the left to marvel at the remains of:-

**Nikopolis** : 'Victory City' was the brainchild of the Roman Emperor Augustus. It was built to commemorate a famous sea victory over forces led by Anthony and Cleopatra, off Actium (present day Acteon) in 31BC. Nikopolis was destroyed by an earthquake, in AD 375, but was rebuilt again as a Byzantine settlement. The site must have covered hundreds of acres as there are lumps, bumps and outcrops of masonry spread around for miles. Apart from the Roman Odeion, or theatre, and lengths of impressive city walls, the site tends to 'attract to deceive', as closer inspection can prove disappointing.

Unfortunately, being Roman, the authorities would appear, until recently, to have rather disregarded the remains. But in 1988 the walls were being cleared of vegetation and self-sprouting trees, prior to repointing of the brickwork. There is a museum displaying finds from the site.

## PREVEZA: Epirus region NW Greece (Illustration 11) Tel prefix 0682. A
bustling, cosmopolitan, commercial harbour town situated on the tip of a peninsula, which juts down into the entrance to the Gulf of Amvrakikos. Preveza, whilst not unattractive, has little to commend it to the island traveller but, due to vagaries of the local bus services, an overnight stop might be necessary.

Founded in 290 BC by King Pyrrhu, the town and its surrounds are steeped in history. It is close to the site of the Roman city of Nikopolis, as well as the remains of an aqueduct, baths, amphitheatre, basilica and several Roman roads which are dotted around the area.

In common with other towns in the region, there was a convoluted series of overlords and until 1912, Preveza was on the border between Greece and the Ottoman Turkish Empire. Mute testament to these troubled times are manifested by the ruined Venetian Fort.

The town radiates out from the long, north-south waterfront Esplanade. The landing craft style ferries, that connect to Acteon (across the narrow neck of the water), tie up at the southern end of the Esplanade (*Tmr* 1C/D3), while to the north is the commercial port. A number of restaurants, tavernas and cafes line the Esplanade, together with banks and the Post Office. There is a Market building (*Tmr* 2E2/3), whilst the main shopping area is located in Odhos Ethniki Antitasis, the street which runs one block back and parallel to the waterfront road. The Bus terminus (*Tmr* 3F1/2) and Police station (*Tmr* 4F1) are located at the western end of the town.

Much of the old town is still crumbling away amongst the more modern buildings, it only being necessary to wander along a few of the side-streets to see Preveza of yesteryear.

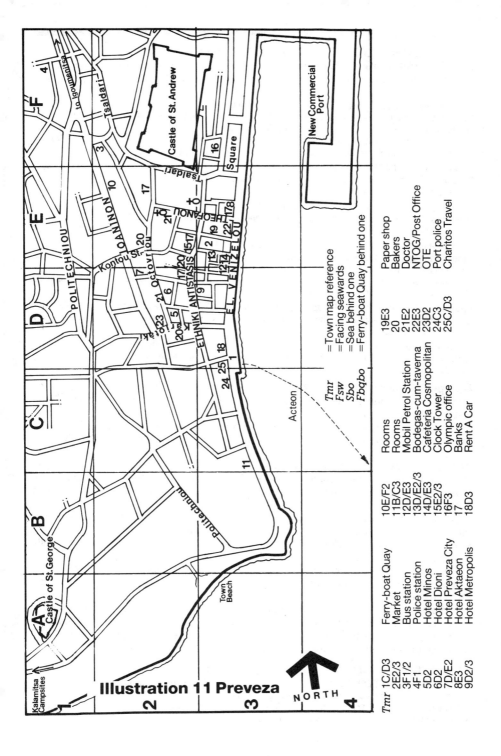

**Illustration 11 Preveza**

NORTH

Kalamitsa Campsites

Castle of St. George

Castle of St. Andrew

New Commercial Port

Town Beach

Square

POLITECHNIOU
IOANNINON
HEROANOU
EL. VENIZELOU
ETHNIKI ANTISTASIS
21 Octovriou
Koptou St.
Ploraki
Tsaldari

to Igoumenitsa

Acteon

| Tmr | 1C/D3 | Ferry-boat Quay | | 10E/F2 | Rooms | | 19E3 | Paper shop |
|-----|-------|-----------------|---|--------|-------|---|------|-----------|
| | 2E2/3 | Market | | 11B/C3 | Rooms | | 20 | Bakers |
| | 3F1/2 | Bus station | | 12D/E3 | Mobil Petrol Station | | 21E2 | Doctor |
| | 4F1 | Police station | | 13D/E2/3 | Bodegas-cum-taverna | | 22E3 | NTOG/Post Office |
| | 5D2 | Hotel Minos | | 14D/E3 | Cafeteria Cosmopolitan | | 23D2 | OTE |
| | 6D2 | Hotel Dioni | | 15E2/3 | Clock Tower | | 24C3 | Port police |
| | 7D/E2 | Hotel Preveza City | | 16F3 | Olympic office | | 25C/D3 | Charitos Travel |
| | 8E3 | Hotel Aktaeon | | 17 | Banks | | | |
| | 9D2/3 | Hotel Metropolis | | 18D3 | Rent A Car | | | |

*Tmr* = Town map reference
*Fsw* = Facing seawards
*Sbo* = Sea behind one
*Fbqbo* = Ferry-boat Quay behind one

## THE ACCOMMODATION & EATING OUT

**The Accommodation** There are only a few *Rooms* in the town and the majority of the hotels are housed in very smart, high rise buildings. Certainly the following are comparatively luxurious:-

**Hotel Minos** (*Tmr* 5D2 (Class C) No 11, 21st Oktovriou                          Tel 28424
*Directions*: From the Ferry-boat Quay (*Tmr* 1C/D3), walk along Odhos Kariotaki and turn right or, from the Bus terminal (*Tmr* 3F1/2), proceed south along Odhos Ioaninon.

All rooms have en suite bathrooms with a single room charged at 2100drs & a double 2750drs, increasing, respectively, to 2850drs & 3600drs (1st July-30th Sept).

**Hotel Dioni** (*Tmr* 6D2) (Class C) 4 I. Kalou                          Tel 27381
*Directions*: Only just down a side-street from the *Minos*.
The rates are as for the *Minos*.

**Hotel Preveza City** (*Tmr* 7D/E2) (Class C) 81-83 Ioaninon St                          Tel 27370
*Directions*: On the side of the 'High St', which connects the Bus terminus and Ferry-boat Quay.
Charges are as for the *Minos*.

More old-fashioned and, thus, more realistically priced, is the:-
**Hotel Aktaeon** (*Tmr* 8E3) (Class C) 1 Kolovou                          Tel 22258
*Directions*: Towards the north end of the Esplanade.
Rooms share the bathrooms with a single costing 1200drs & a double 1800drs, increasing to 1540drs & 2260drs (1st July-31st Dec).

Apart from the Class C *Hotel Metropolis* (*Tmr* 9D2/3 – tel 22235), there are **Rooms** (*Tmr* 10E/F2 – tel 27123), in close proximity to the Bus terminus, and **Rooms** (*Tmr* 11B/C3), fairly close and south of the Ferry-boat Quay.

It must be pointed out that there are any number of *Rooms* sprinkled about the outskirts, including *Furnished Rooms* (Tel 26290 & 27069) down a gravel track off the road round to *Kalamitsa Camping* (*See* **Camping**).

**Camping** *Camping Indian Village* is some 3¼km south along the coastal road, past the Town beach, beyond St George's Castle. And do not turn right, along the nearside castle walls, but keep straight on.

Another campsite, *Kalamitsa Beach* (Tel 22335), is located at the location of the same name, but it is extremely difficult to find as the signs run out. It is also a long walk.

**The Eating Out** There is an abundance of restaurants, tavernas, cafes and bars spread along the length of the Esplanade, which bustles with activity in the evening. One of the most popular of these is the restaurant situated next door to the Mobil Petrol Station (*Tmr* 12D/E3).

My own favourite is a 'Bodega-cum-Taverna' (*Tmr* 13D/E2/3) (there is a Greek word but it is almost unpronounceable – Oinopoleio). The cellar-like room is across the narrow street from the Market building. A very 'local' local serving retsina with plates of fish, from early morning onwards.

The rather inappropriately named *Disco Club Cafeteria Cosmopolitan* (*Tmr* 14D/E3) is a most conveniently situated cafe-bar for 'Esplanade gongoozling'... and don't be put off by the name!

A drably painted restaurant, edging the Esplanade and in front of the Market building (*Tmr* 2E2/3), is a good value eatery, specialising in souvlakia. They also offer breakfast.

Unfortunately there are no souvlaki pita snackbars, but the baker, squeezed in between the clock tower (*Tmr* 15E2/3) and a bank, is very popular for its cheese pies.

## THE A TO Z OF USEFUL INFORMATION

**AIRLINE OFFICE & TERMINUS** The Olympic office (*Tmr* 16F3) is on the west flank of a small park, at the north end of the Esplanade. The office opens daily, between 0900-1800hrs.

The airport is on the Acteon side of the Gulf, but labelled Preveza... To catch a bus, first take the ferry to Acteon where the connection can be made.

**Aircraft timetables** (Mid-season)
Preveza to Athens (& vice-versa)
Mon, Wed, Thurs, Sat & Sun   1720hrs
Tues & Sun                   1540hrs
*Return*
Mon, Wed, Thurs, Sat & Sun   1540hrs
Tues & Sun                   0840hrs
One-way fare: 5290drs; duration 65-80mins.

**Preveza to Athens**
Tues & Sun                   1005hrs
*Return*
Tues & Sun                   1445hrs
One-way fare: 4400drs; duration 45mins.

**BANKS** There are at least four, one (*Tmr* 17D2), in the street almost opposite the *Hotel Dioni*, another (*Tmr* 17E3) towards the northern end of the Esplanade, one (*Tmr* 17E2/3), close by the clock tower on the edge of the 'Market' St, and yet another (*Tmr* 17E2) at the northern end of Odhos 21st Octovriou.

**BEACHES** The town beach is 10-15 minute walk south along the coast road, nearly as far as St George's Castle. Apart from not being very salubrious, it has been 'manufactured', although the authorities are attempting to make something of the site. There is a scraping of sand, some 'dead' showers and changing rooms, as well as the remains of thatched sun shades.

**BICYCLE, SCOOTER & CAR HIRE** Two firms slug it out in the small square behind the *Disco Club Cafeteria Cosmopolitan* (*Tmr* 14D/E3), despite which they appear to share a signboard. **Rent A Motor** offers bicycles and motorbikes, as does **Jannis Rent A Motobice** (*sic*) or **sigle** (*sic*) (Tel 24865).
   Cars are for hire from the offices of **Rent A Car** (*Tmr* 18D3), situated on the Esplanade, across the road from the Ferry-boat Quay.

**BOOKSELLERS** There is a shop (*Tmr* 19E3), opposite one of the Market building entrances, on Odhos M. Palkou, which sells foreign language newspapers and some English language paperbacks.

**BREAD SHOPS** There are several on Odhos Ethniki Antistasis, the 'Market' St, one of which is squeezed in between the clock tower (*Tmr* 15E2/3) and a bank; another (*Tmr* 20D/E2/3) further south along the same street, on the same side of the road; one (*Tmr* 20E2) on Odhos Oktovriou and yet another (*Tmr* 20D2) on the left (*Sbo*) of Odhos Kariotaki, in between a pharmacy and a church.

(**BUSES** There are daily services, to a wide number of destinations, that start out from the Bus terminus (*Tmr* 3F1/2 which is located towards the northern end of the 'High' St, Odhos Ioaninon. This building 'houses' a snackbar and possesses, a toilet 'out back', which is regularly washed down.

**Bus timetable**
**Preveza to Athens***(Tel.5129252)
Daily          0910, 1300, 1830hrs
*Return journey*
Daily          0700, 1330, 2000hrs
One-way fare: 21250drs; duration 7hrs.
*100 Kifissou St.

**Preveza to Ioannina**
Daily          0600, 0720, 0845, 1015, 1100, 1200, 1300, 1400,
               1500, 1615, 1745, 1930hrs
*Return journey*
Daily          0600, 0700, 0900, 1000, 1100, 1200, 1330, 1445,
               1515, 1600, 1715, 1910hrs

**Preveza to Arta**
Weekdays       0700, 1000, 1230, 1430, 1630hrs
Sat & Sun      1000, 1230, 1430, 1630hrs
*Return journey*
Weekdays       0630, 1000, 1230, 1430, 1715hrs
Sat & Sun      1000, 1230, 1430, 1715hrs

**Preveza to Igoumenitsa**
Mon to Sat     1100, 1530hrs
Sun            1100, 1515hrs
*Return journey*
Daily          1145, 1530hrs

**Preveza to Parga**
Weekdays       0500, 0645, 1045, 1415, 2000hrs
Sat            0500, 0800, 1045, 1415, 2000hrs
Sun            0500, 0800, 1415, 2000hrs
*Return journey*
Weekdays       0700, 1015, 1415, 1600hrs
Sat            0700, 1015, 1400, 1600hrs
Sun            0700, 1015, 1600hrs

There are a number of other destinations including:-
Thesprotiko, Polistasilio, Padates, Kranaia, Kasiopi, Cheemadio, Mitika, Ag Forma, Sinopi, Samsiois, Frisola, Skiada & Opopo.

**COMMERCIAL SHOPPING AREA** Meat and fish are sold from a large but rather sad Market building (*Tmr* 2E2/3). Odhos Ethniki Antistasis, which parallels the Esplanade, is the 'Market St', stretching from Odhos Kariotaki, in the south, all the way to Odhos Tsaldari, in the north. It contains shops of all sorts, shapes and sizes, including vendors of fruit and vegetables, diagonally across from the clock tower (*Tmr* 15E2/3).

Some traditional, old-fashioned traders, including a cobbler, who still makes boots, metal workers and tailors, are located on 21st Octovriou St, in the area of the crossroads with H. Kontou St (*Tmr* E2). Plenty of peripteros are spread along the Esplanade and there are an unusual number of wet fish shops dotted throughout the town. The high prices of the latter's offerings tends to confirm that restaurants are not making an undue profit from their piscatorial dishes.

**FERRY-BOATS** The Acteon craft dock (*Tmr* 1C/D3) is at the southern end of the Esplanade.

**Ferry-boat timetable** (Mid-season)
Daily          Every half hour between 0600-2200hrs &
               every hour between 2200-0600hrs
*Return*
Daily          As above, but 10 minutes later.
One-way fare: 30drs; duration 5 mins.

**FERRY-BOAT TICKET OFFICES** Tickets are sold from a hut on the quayside, close by where the ferries moor, or, if closed, on the ferry itself.

**MEDICAL CARE**
**Chemists & Pharmacies** Quite a few are spaced out along the streets of Kariotaki and Ethniki Antistasis.
**Doctor** (*Tmr* 21E2) More a microbiologist (of whom the Greeks appear inordinately fond) situated alongside a 'dead' church, both of which are opposite a 'dead' cinema, in Odhos Theofanou.
**Hospital** Off the town map, north of the Commercial port and close to the waterfront road.

**NTOG** The town has a rather 'twee', but very helpful information office (*Tmr* 22E3) located in an administration building, towards the north end of the Esplanade.

**OTE** (*Tmr* 23D2) On the right, of Odhos Kariotaki, the 'High St' that right-angles off the southern end of the Esplanade, almost opposite the Ferry-boat Quay. Open weekdays between 0700-2400hrs and weekends 0730-1510hrs.

**PETROL** There are two petrol stations on the Esplanade.

**POLICE**
**Port** (*Tmr* 24C3) The officers work from a glass sided hut, south of the Ferry-boat Quay. This is despite one particular town plan that 'inks' the office in what I am fairly sure is a defunct lavatory block.
**Town** (*Tmr* 4F1) Off to the left of the 'High St', Odhos Ioaninon, and beyond the Bus terminus.

**POST OFFICE** (*Tmr* 22E3) Located in the local government office block, towards the northern end of the Esplanade, beyond the cafe-bar/taverna 'gauntlet'.

MAINLAND PORTS 131

**TAXIS** The ranks are plentifully scattered about the town, including one adjacent to the Ferry-boat Quay and another close to the Bus terminus.

**TELEPHONE NUMBERS & ADDRESSES**

| | |
|---|---|
| Bus terminus (*Tmr* 3F1/2) | Tel 22213 |
| Hospital | Tel 22871 |
| Olympic office (*Tmr* 16F3) | Tel 28343 |
| Police (*Tmr* 4F1) | Tel 22281 |
| Taxi ranks | Tel 28030, 22887, 28470 |

**TOILETS** *See* **Bus Station, A To Z**.

**TRAVEL AGENTS & TOUR OFFICES**
**Charitos Travel** (*Tmr* 25C/D3) 9 El Venizelou      Tel 25881
*Directions*: Opposite the (Acteon) Ferry-boat Quay.
   Provides the usual mix of information and offers, which include excursions to such delights as Zalongo, Kassiopi, Necromanteion, Nikopolis and Ioannina.

**The Lefkas connection** Lefkas is the least accessible of the Ionian islands, from the standpoint of conventional ferry-boat, inter-island travel. Apart from 'rumours' and tenuous Vassiliki (Lefkas) possibilities, travellers approaching from the north must take the ferry from Preveza to Acteon and then catch the bus to Lefkas Town.
   The bus between Preveza and Igoumenitsa takes about 2 hours and passes through some truly beautiful and, at times, dramatic countryside. From Preveza, the bus travels east, following the line of the bay, before swinging north and climbing over the densely wooded coastal mountains. It then drops down to the shores of the Ionian Sea, which it follows for several miles, as far as Loutsa. After this the route cuts inland again, across a fertile plain to Kanalaki, the first sizeable community since leaving Preveza. The journey continues along a long valley grazed by sheep. There are fields of corn, olives and cotton, whilst roses and lime trees grow in profusion in the cottage gardens. Beyond the village of Gliki, the road crosses a rickety Bailey bridge over the oft swollen River Acheron. The narrow valley is edged with rugged, steep scree slopes and cloud-capped mountains to the right whilst, to the left are gentle, rolling hills, which irresistibly remind one of a colony of slumbering hippos. At the end of the valley, the route joins the road from Parga, after which it switchbacks over the lower slopes of the mountains, passing through the village of Paramithia, before descending steeply through a pass to a wide plain. Here it connects with the main Ioannina to Igoumenitsa highway, from whence the road follows the line of the wide River Thiamis before gently climbing, once again, over red sandstone to yet another fertile valley. Finally the road rises over a further range of hills before dropping gently down to the sea and the port of Igoumenitsa.

Back to Preveza, and catching one of the shuttle ferry-boats, crosses over to:-
**ACTEON (Action, Akteon)** This is an archetypal way-station with only a Ferry-boat Quay, a couple of ticket offices, various sheds, castle remains, more castle bits and pieces, some bored, tired looking officials and a few more shacks.

About a kilometre out of Acteon is a petrol station whilst Preveza airport is about two kilometres from Acteon, on the side of the road to Vonitsa.

For those not turning off for Lefkas island, and continuing south along the coastline, there are a couple of seaside villages worthy of a mention. They include:-
**PALAIROS (approx 32km from Acteon)** A very busy, large, farming community with a small harbour 'flavoured' by flotilla yachtsman – thus the *Old Mill Tavern*.

The road from Palairos corniches along the coastline and is remarkably attractive. On the distant horizon can be seen the islands of Lefkas, Meganisi, Kalamos, Arkoudi and Atokos, as well as a speckling of islets closer to the shore. Not only are the sea views unexpectedly alluring but wild life is plentiful, as are the free ranging domestic herds of goats, sheep and pigs.

**MITIKAS (approx 49km from Acteon)** An attractive, if slovenly way-station of a settlement dominated by the inshore island of Kalamos. The village is reached from the bypass along a slip road, which skirts a crescent of pebbly foreshore. Unfortunately it is almost entirely covered with kelp and edged by bamboos.

Almost immediately there are two signs pronouncing *Rooms*, followed by a pizzeria, a church, a Main Square, more *Rooms*, the *Restaurant Glaros*, another *Rooms*, *Dionyssis Restaurant* and the expensive:-

**Hotel Simos** (Class C)                                                            Tel 81380
All rooms have en suite bathrooms with a single costing 3000drs & a double 3500drs, increasing, respectively, to 3800drs & 4500drs (1st July-15th Sept).

The hotel is followed by a baker and a narrow, busy High St in which are located a pharmacy, another restaurant and the much more reasonably priced:-
**Hotel Akroyali** (Class E)                                                         Tel 81206
Rooms share the bathrooms with a single room charged at 1700drs & a double 1900drs.

Incidentally there are two other (E class) hotels, the *Alisia* (Tel 81232) and *Kymata* (Tel 81258). The latter's rooms all have en suite bathrooms, a single room costing 2000drs and a double 3000drs.

Continuing through the village passes a fruit and vegetable shop, a kafeneion, a number of souvenir shops, a chandlery-cum-gift shop, the Post Office and a clinic, opposite which is a house with *Rooms*, followed by a boat quay. From the far end of the village, there stretches an initially lovely looking, fairly narrow sweep of foreshore. Unfortunately, the shore is made up of medium sized pebbles, spoilt by quite a lot of seaborne rubbish, and the sea-bed is rather slimy.

**ASTAKOS: Epirus region, NW Greece** Tel prefix 0646. A busy, bubbling, small Greek resort and port. In strict contrast to Mitikas, the (southern) approaches are distinctly unattractive. The shadeless countryside has a moth-eaten appearance, despite the presence of scattered cypress trees. The impression of scrubbliness is not diminished by the presence of an informal scrapyard of wrecked cars and lorries. Additionally, there is an ambience of dusty, concrete construction, of shuttering and reinforcing rods.

On the outskirts there are two petrol stations, followed by a curve of waterfront, despite which there is no beach about which to write home. The settlement's Health Centre is signposted, prior to passing a sports field.

The Bus turn round point and high ceilinged, flyblown ticket office are at the outset of the town.

**Bus timetable** (Mid-season)
**Astakos to Athens** *(Tel.5129293)
Daily          0815, 1430hrs
*Return journey*
Daily          0700, 1330hrs
One-way fare: 1610drs; duration 5hrs.
*100 Kifissou St.

**Astakos to Agrinio**
Daily          0630, 1200, 1400, 1600, 1915hrs

**Astakos to Agrimalia**
Daily          1330hrs

**Astakos to Kayoyna**
Daily          0630, 1200, 1400, 1600hrs

**Astakos to Litsiania**
Daily          1330hrs

To the left of the Bus terminus (*Sea on the left*) is the waterfront Esplanade and, to the right, a 'High St', which parallels the shore. In this latter, on the right and just before a bakery, is the Ferry-boat ticket office. The helpful young lady, who 'mans (!) the desk, speaks some English. The ferry-boats are half-sized craft and comparatively expensive.

**Ferry-boats timetables**

| Day | Departure time | Ferry-boat | Ports/Islands of Call |
|---|---|---|---|
| Daily | 1400hrs | | Vathi (Ithaca),Ag Evfimia (Cephalonia) |
| One-way fares; to Ithaca | | 440drs; duration 1hr 45mins | |
| to Cephalonia | | 590drs; duration 3½hrs | |

Beyond the ticket office, and on the other side of the road, is a cellar-like, low ceilinged, 'barrels in the roof', 'greasy' taverna. Well worth a peep,if not a bite.

In the second street back from the Esplanade, and also paralleling the waterfront, is a Post Office, a National Bank, a pharmacy, another baker and plenty of shops. It certainly is a great place in which to purchase fish as there are plenty of shops selling the catches.

The paved Esplanade is blocked off to traffic by the tables and chairs of the cafe-bars, which line the stretch between the Ferry-boat ramp and the fishing boat quay. Beyond this latter quay is a pebbly beach.

Hotels listed include the *Stratos* (Class B, tel 41096), where accommodation, with en suite bathrooms, is charged at 4500drs for a single and 4900drs for a double; the *Akti Beach* (Class D, tel 41135), which only has double bedrooms, sharing bathrooms, at a cost of 2000drs and the *Byron* (Class D, tel 41516).

## PATRAS (Patra, Patre, Patrai): Peloponnese (Illustration 12) Tel
prefix 061.

## RELIGIOUS HOLIDAYS & FESTIVALS include: the Patras Carnival which
lasts for some three weeks in February and early March. The festival officially starts ten days before Lent. Great goings on and good fun. On the 30th November there is a feast to celebrate St Andrew, the city's patron saint.

## GENERAL The modern city was rebuilt in a grid layout, in the 1820s, after the Turks
had razed it to the ground, in 1821.

Bearing in mind that Patras is the third largest city in Greece, as well as being a commercial centre, international seaport and railway terminal, it is not surprising that the place has an industrial, cosmopolitan, bustling, noisy ambiance. The majority of a traveller's immediate needs are spread along the Esplanade, Odhos Othonos Amalias, across the way from and parallel to the quay wall, alongside which the railway line ranges. To add to the general confusion, and the continuous stream of traffic, a shunting train shares the Esplanade road with the tangled traffic of cars and humans. Keep an eye and ear open.

It is quite possible that a visit to Patras will only occur in order to change ferries or disembark from bus or train to embark on a ferry. The key to the town is the Esplanade, which sweeps from the north end of Patras' waterfront, where it is named Iroon Politechnou, past the North Harbour (*Tmr* 1A2), the NTOG offices (*Tmr* 2A2), the main Bus terminal (*Tmr* 3A/B3) and the Railway station (*Tmr* 4A4). The Tourist police office (*Tmr* 6A/B3/4) is conveniently located, diagonally across the road from the Railway station, which is also almost adjacent to Plateia Trion Symmahon.

Trion Symmahon Square is a palm-tree'd square at the hub of Patras and is edged by cafes, restaurants and newsagents. From the far, south-east side of Plateia Trion Symmahon, Odhos Ag Nikolaou runs straight and true to a flight of steps to one side of the Acropolis of Patras. After dark, Plateia Trion Symmahon comes alive and families stroll across the paved area, whilst others sit beneath the spreading branches of the trees, drinking coffee or ouzo served from one of the many small cafes that line the periphery of the square. A pleasant after dinner walk is to perambulate along the jetty (*Tmr* A4), opposite the square, watching the old men fishing – no rod, just a line resting through their fingers, using bread as bait.

South along Leoforos Othonos Amalias stretches past the private yacht moorings to the South Harbour.

## THE ACCOMMODATION & EATING OUT

**The Accommodation** There are a profusion of *Rooms*, pensions and hotels in an area radiating out from the Railway station. Being an epicentre for travellers, accommodation tends to be rather expensive with 'C' class hotels charging, on average, 3500drs and 'D' class 2200drs for a night in a double room.

Many owners of accommodation lift room prices to the 'height of summer' rates for Carnival weeks (Feb/March). If there is no differential between the seasons, then the carnival charges are increased by between 300-500drs per night for a double room.

The Tourist police (*Tmr* 6A/B3/4), conveniently across the Esplanade from the Railway station, supply accommodation details, but 'No Rooms, only hotels'. Another drawback is the officers' limited English.

A last point to bear in mind, is that the streets and buildings of Patras are on a large scale. On the plan a distance might appear a few paces but may well prove to be a ten minute trudge.

**Hotel Rannia** (*Tmr* 22B3/4) (Class B) 53 ΑΝΑΡ ΜΙΧΑΛΑΚΟΠΟΤΛΟΤ                  Tel 220114
*Directions*: From the Railway station, turn left (*Sbo*) along the Esplanade as far as the corner with Koloktroni St, on which is the *Hotel Acropole*. The Rannia is in the third block along Koloktroni St, on the right.

All rooms have en suite bathrooms, with a single room priced at 2400drs & a double 4000drs, increasing, respectively, to 2650drs & 4400drs (1st July-31st Aug).

**Hotel Adonis** (*Tmr* 7B3) (Class C) Zaimi/9 Kapsali Sts                  Tel 224213
*Directions*: Behind the main bus terminal, alongside the English church of Ag Andreas in the area where, across the Esplanade, the quayside wall of the North Harbour turns sharply.

Clean, modern and all rooms have en suite bathrooms. A single room costs 2400drs & a double room 2800drs, increasing to 2750drs & 3200drs (1st June-30th Sept).

**Hotel Splendid** (*Tmr* 8A/B3/4) (Class D) 28 Ag Andreou                  Tel 276521
*Directions*: Almost opposite the Railway station and one street back.

Splendid it may have been, but not now... Rather a 'sleazy', despite which the Splendid is not inexpensive any more. A single room costs 2015drs & a double 2425drs, both sharing the bathroom, whilst a double room, with an en suite bathroom, is charged at 3655drs.

**Hotel Anglias** (Class D) 26 Ag Andreou                  Tel 277916
*Directions*: Next door to the *Splendid*.

Definitely a 'sleazy', with only double rooms, sharing the bathrooms, available at a cost of 1650drs.

**Hotel Acropole** (*Tmr* 9A/B3/4) (Class C) 39 Othonos Amalias                  Tel 279809
*Directions*: Diagonally across the Esplanade from the Railway station.

All rooms have en suite bathrooms, with a single charged at 2000drs & a double 3200drs, increasing to 2650drs & 3800drs (1st July-30th Sept).

**Hotel Delphi** (Class D) (*Tmr* A/B4) 63 Ag Andreou                  Tel 273050
*Directions*: Bordering Plateia Trion Symmahon. Depending on one's viewpoint, unclean and noisy, or dirty and downright clamorous!

Singles start at 850/1000drs & double rooms 1085/1300drs, which charges increase, respectively, to 1000/1200drs & 1300/1560drs (1st June-30th Sept), all sharing the bathrooms.

**Hotel Hellas** (*Tmr* 19B4) (Class D) 14 Ag Nikolaou                  Tel 273352
*Directions*: On the right (*Sbo*) of the street that climbs off Plateia Trion Symmahon.

Another 'down at the heel' and thus inexpensive hotel. A single room costs 1200drs & a double room 2100drs, all sharing the bathrooms.

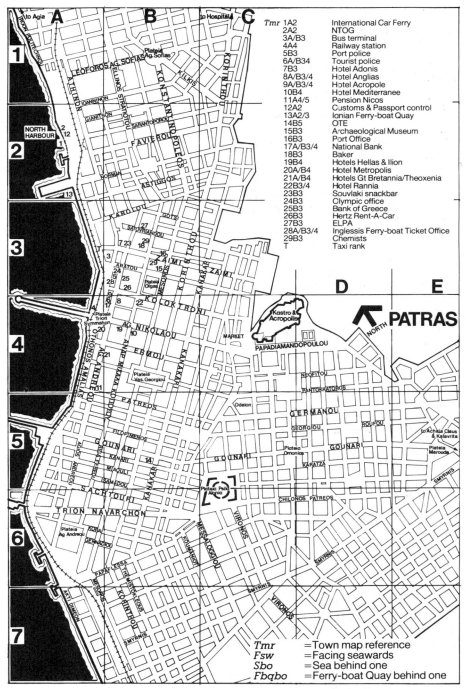

| Tmr | 1A2 | International Car Ferry |
|---|---|---|
| | 2A2 | NTOG |
| | 3A/B3 | Bus terminal |
| | 4A4 | Railway station |
| | 5B3 | Port police |
| | 6A/B34 | Tourist police |
| | 7B3 | Hotel Adonis |
| | 8A/B3/4 | Hotel Anglias |
| | 9A/B3/4 | Hotel Acropole |
| | 10B4 | Hotel Mediterranee |
| | 11A4/5 | Pension Nicos |
| | 12A2 | Customs & Passport control |
| | 13A2/3 | Ionian Ferry-boat Quay |
| | 14B5 | OTE |
| | 15B3 | Archaeological Museum |
| | 16B3 | Port Office |
| | 17A/B3/4 | National Bank |
| | 18B3 | Baker |
| | 19B4 | Hotels Hellas & Ilion |
| | 20A/B4 | Hotel Metropolis |
| | 21A/B4 | Hotels Gt Bretannia/Theoxenia |
| | 22B3/4 | Hotel Rannia |
| | 23B3 | Souvlaki snackbar |
| | 24B3 | Olympic office |
| | 25B3 | Bank of Greece |
| | 26B3 | Hertz Rent-A-Car |
| | 27B3 | ELPA |
| | 28A/B3/4 | Inglessis Ferry-boat Ticket Office |
| | 29B3 | Chemists |
| | T | Taxi rank |

| | |
|---|---|
| Tmr | =Town map reference |
| Fsw | =Facing seawards |
| Sbo | =Sea behind one |
| Fbqbo | =Ferry-boat Quay behind one |

**Illustration 12 Patras**

**Hotel Ilion** (Class D) 10 Ag Nikolaou                                                                     Tel 273161
*Directions*: As for the *Hellas*, but nearer the waterfront and separated from the *Hellas* by a cinema, Cine Elite.
Much as for the *Hellas*, but even less expensive with single rooms priced at 850/1100drs & double rooms 1300/1500drs.

**Hotel Mediterranee** (*Tmr* 10B4) (Class C) 18 Ag Nikolaou/ΑΝΑΡ ΜΙΧΑΛΛΑΚΟΠΟΤΛΟΥ Sts
                                                                                                             Tel 279602
*Directions*: From Plateia Trion Symmahon proceed along Ag Nikolaou St and the hotel is on the right.
Well appointed, comfortable and all rooms have en suite bathrooms. A single room costs 2100drs & a double 2850drs, increasing, respectively, to 2500drs & 3650drs (1st June-15th Oct).

**Hotel Metropolis** (*Tmr* 20A/B/4) (Class D) Plateia Trion Symmahon                         Tel 277535
*Directions*: On the south side of the square.
A single room cost 1100drs & a double 2000drs, all sharing the bathrooms.

**Hotel Gt Bretannia** (*Tmr* 21A/B4) (Class E) 95 Ag Andreou                                 Tel 273421
*Directions*: From Plateia Trion Symmahon, proceed south-west along Ag Andreou St, which runs parallel to the Esplanade but one back.
As befits a Patras E Class hotel, rather decrepit, but clean, with a single room priced at 1200drs & a double room 2200drs, all sharing the bathrooms.

Next door at No 97 is the *Theoxenia*, a D class hotel (Tel 222962).

**Pension Nicos** (*Tmr* 11A4/5) 3 Patreos/121 Ag Andreou                                     Tel 276183
*Directions*: South, or right (*Sbo*) from Plateia Trion Symmahon, along Ag Andreou St and on the corner of the third turning left.
An ethnic, forbidding, hostel atmosphere. Callers find themselves in a gaunt, dark brown coloured, high roofed hallway, decorated with a couple of huge travel posters, from the rear of which ascends a broad flight of stairs. A sign instructs enquirers to ring the bell for assistance. Any inclination to proceed to the upper storey is stopped short by a 'charming' sign which declares "It is strictly forbidden for those who are not resident to stay or come upstairs according to the 976028134012,19,77 decision of the Department of Law and Order". It is so nice to be made welcome, isn't it? The cost of a bed for the night starts off (to where may I ask?) at about 600drs per head. Oddly enough, the patron accepts payment by *Visa* credit cards.

**Youth Hostel** 68 Iroon Politechnou                                                        Tel 427278
*Directions*: Turn left on leaving any ferry and proceed along the quayside northwards for between ½-1km, depending on the point of outset.
The old, but restored Victorian style house was once used by the Germans as an HQ, during the Second World War. Inexpensive, if a bit of a squeeze, with cheap meals and laundry facilities available. A dormitory bed costs 500drs (but guests must bring their own sheets).

## Camping
**Agia-Patras Camping**                                                                      Tel 424131
An NTOG site five kilometres north-east from Patras, situated at Agia (Patron), on the coast road to Rio. Pleasantly located convenient to a bus stop, by a sandy seashore with lawns, trees, car parking, showers, laundry, a bar, restaurant and shop.

**The Eating Out** Tavernas and restaurants are grouped along and around Othonos Amalias, Ag Nikolaou and Plateia Trion Symmahon (what isn't?). Despite the competition, the average cost of a meal tends to be expensive, especially those served by the establishments lining the dusty, dirty Esplanade. There are a pair of side-by-side, souvlaki pita snackbars (*Tmr* 23B3), in the narrow street behind the *Hotel Adonis*.

Another good hunting ground for tavernas is in the area of the upper-town market, two-thirds of the way along Odhos Ag Nikolaou, on the way to the Acropolis.

## THE A TO Z OF USEFUL INFORMATION
**AIRLINE OFFICES & TERMINUS** There is an Olympic office (*Tmr* 24B3) set in the rear of the *Hotel Astir* building, on the corner of Aratou and Ag Andreou Sts.

**BANKS** The **National Bank of Greece** (*Tmr* 17A/B3/4) is conveniently situated in the same row as the Tourist police, across the Esplanade from the Railway station. They change Eurocheques. The

**Bank of Greece** (*Tmr* 25B3) is to the left (*Sbo*) of the Railway station, on Odhos Andreou, one street back and parallel to the Esplanade.

**BEACHES** None in town, it being necessary to travel five kilometres north-east along the coast to Agia (Patron), where there is also a NTOG campsite.

**BICYCLE, SCOOTER & CAR HIRE** I'm not sure about bikes and scooters, but car hire is available from, for instance, **Hertz Rent A Car** (*Tmr* 26B3), on the left (*Sbo*) of Odhos Koloktroni.

**BOOKSELLERS** One, **Papachristou**, at 16 Ag Nikolaou and another, **Calitas**, on Ermou St.

**BREAD SHOPS** There is a Baker (*Tmr* 18B3) on the left (*Sbo*) of Odhos Zaimi. **Patisserie Pakalos** is a very good shop, located on the nearside of *Hotel Ilion* (*Tmr* 19B4), at the outset and on the right (*Sbo*) of Ag Nikolaou St, which runs off from the far side of Plateia Trion Symmahon. There is also a fruit and vegetable grocer, that sells rolls, in the same building as the *Hotel Metropolis* (*Tmr* 20A/B4).

**BUSES** Apart from the main routes to Athens, Ioannina, Volos, Thessaloniki and down the west coast of the Peloponnese (for Killini, Pirgos, Pilos and Kalamata), there are local services to Rio. The journey to Killini is direct and connects with the ferry to the island of Zakynthos.

The major Bus terminal (*Tmr* 3A/B3) is situated on the far side of the Esplanade, opposite the point at which the quay takes a left turn. There is an information office in the large building, which opens daily at 0700hrs, and the staff speak basic English.

## Bus timetable

**Patras to Athens** *(Tel.5124914)
Daily          0615, 0630, 0700, 0815, 0900, 1030, 1100, 1200, 1300, 1400,
              1530-2130 every hour
*Return journey*
Daily          0630-1330 every hour, 1415, 1500, 1630, 1730, 1800, 1900,
              2000, 2115hrs
One-way fare: 1130drs; duration 3½hrs.
*100 Kifissou St.

**Patras to Ioannina**
Daily          0815, 1430hrs
*Return journey*
Daily          0900, 1430hrs
One-way fare: 1330drs; duration 4hrs.

**Patras to Kalamata** (S.Peloponnese)
Daily          0700, 1430hrs
*Return journey*
Daily          0800, 1400hrs
One-way fare: 1220drs; duration 4hrs

**Patras to Thessaloniki**
Daily          0830, 1030, 1500, 2100hrs
*Return journey*
Daily          0830, 1300, 1700, 2100hrs
One-way fare: 2560drs; duration 9½hrs.

**Patras to Volos** (E.Thessaly)
Daily          1030, 2100hrs
*Return journey*
Daily          1315hrs (Yes I know, where is the other bus?)
One-way fare: 1550drs; duration 6hrs.

**Patras to Zakynthos** (via Killini)
Daily          1245, 1600, 1930hrs
*Return journey*
Daily          0800, 1230, 1500hrs
One-way fare: 425drs (+ferry-boat fare); duration 2½hrs.

*Note that* **OSE** (as compared to the **KTEL** buses), that is the Railway company buses, also run services from outside the Railway station (*Tmr* 4A4) to various major destinations.

**CINEMAS** There is the **Cine Elite**, located between the Hotels *Ilion* (*Tmr* 19B4) and *Hellas*.

**COMMERCIAL SHOPPING AREA** The main district is sited in the upper town, half-way along Odhos Ag Nikolaou. But as that is a long stride, the following gives an idea of shops closer to the Railway station and Esplanade.

There are a clutch of fruit and vegetable, fish and butchers shops on or close to the crossroads of the streets of Zaimi and ΑΝΑΡ ΜΙΧΑΛΛΑΚΟΠΟΤΛΟΥ (previously named Riga Fereou) (*Tmr* B3). In the same building as the *Hotel Metropolis* (*Tmr* 20A/B4) are a general store and a fruit and vegetable shop, which supply most items. Peripteros are plentiful, especially on the main squares.

**CUSTOMS** (*Tmr* 12A2) Customs and passport control are both in one single storey block, at the north end of the Harbour, where the international ferries berth.

**ELPA** (*Tmr* 27B3) North of the Bus terminal, on Odhos Satovriandou.

**FERRY-BOATS** Berth at the North and South Harbours. The International (*Tmr* 1A2) and the Ionian (*Tmr* 13A2/3) ferry-boats dock at the North Harbour end of the waterfront.
*See* **Chapter Two** for the international ferry-boat details.

### Ferry-boats & timetables

| Day | Departure time | Ferry-boat | Ports/Islands of Call |
|---|---|---|---|
| Daily | 1330hrs | Kefalinia | Sami(Cephalonia),Vathi(Ithaca). |
| | 2200hrs | Ionis/Ionian Glory | Poros(Cephalonia),Vathi(Ithaca),Gaios(Paxos), Igoumenitsa(M),Corfu. |

| One-way fare: | Patras | to Cephalonia | 1050drs; duration 3½hrs |
|---|---|---|---|
| | | to Ithaca | 1050drs; duration 5½hrs |
| | | to Paxos | 1860drs; duration 9hrs |
| | | to Corfu | 1860drs; duration 10¼hr |

| Daily* | 1300, 1616, 1945 | | Zakynthos |
|---|---|---|---|

*This is a possible!

**FERRY-BOAT TICKET OFFICES** These 'gather' along the Esplanade, mostly in the stretch between the Railway station and the North Harbour.

Some of the offices appear to be run with a total disregard for the ferry-boat companies' life blood, that is the passengers. In 1988 my experiences concerning the Fragline office and boarding their ship, the **CF Ouranos**, were almost unbelievable. Enough to summarise the events as follows:-

> arrived at the office early in the afternoon of the evening boat's departure to find the office besieged by potential passengers. The reason for the disorderly crush became apparent when it was realised that, despite a total of five staff, only one was engaged in issuing tickets. For most of the hour it took to reach the front of my particular queue (simply to establish if there was room on the craft for our 'shed' - as our van is affectionately nicknamed), the ship's captain benignly watched over the utter chaos, probably muttering 'let them eat cake', in Greek. If this were not enough, the hour of embarkation turned out to be a tense, nail-biting experience with lorry drivers jostling cars for places and some unlucky, ticket holding motorists being left on the quayside!

Incidentally, this office, the central one for the Fragline companies' Ionian island ferries is:-
**Inglessis Bros** (*Tmr* 28A/B3/4) 12 Othonos Amalias                     Tel 277676

**LUGGAGE STORE** Try the Railway station (*Tmr* 4A4). They charge approx 50drs a day, per piece of luggage, and the office is open 24 hours a day.

### MEDICAL CARE
**Chemists & Pharmacies** There are a couple (*Tmr* 29B3) at the north end of ΑΝΑΡ ΜΙΧΑΛΛΑΚΟΠΟΤΛΟΥ.
**Hospital** A University facility north, north-west of the town.
**Hospital** A University facility north, north-west of the town.

**NTOG** (*Tmr* 2A2) The office is in the new complex at the North Harbour, as are the Customs and Passport controls.

**OTE** (*Tmr* 14B5) On the corner of Odhos Gounari and Kanakari and open daily between 0730-2200hrs.

**PETROL** Plentiful.

**PLACES OF INTEREST**
**The Acropolis** (*Tmr* C4) At the top, south-east end of Ag Nikolaou St are the huge flight of access steps. In the early Middle Ages, a fort was built on the site of the ancient Acropolis but has been the subject of much alteration over the years.

**The Odeion** (*Tmr* C5) To the south-west of the Acropolis, or immediate left (*Fsw*), is the theatre, re-discovered in the 1800s. Subject of heavy 'restoration' due to the acquisitive nature of local builders, who used much of the original stonework for their own jobs!

**Archaeological Museum** (*Tmr* 15B3) Three blocks back from the Esplanade, on Aratou St, Plateia Olgas. Not outstanding.

**The Church of Ag Andreas** (*Tmr* A6) Overlooking Plateia Ag Andreou, at the far, south-west end, down around the corner of the waterfront. A modern but colourful church dedicated to St Andrew and the repository of his gold and silver encased head. He was martyred on a crucifix erected in the form of an X.

**Achaia Clauss** Admittedly a few kilometres (actually nine) from Patras, but the site of the renowned winery that 'grapes' some well-known bottles. Good for a 'free' wine tasting sojourn. The 'bar' opens daily between 0900-1300hrs & 1600-1830hrs.

**POLICE**
**Port** (*Tmr* 5B3) To the left (*Sbo*) of the Railway station, on the Esplanade and next door to the *Hotel Astir*.
**Tourist** (*Tmr* 6A/B3/4) Almost directly across the Esplanade from the Railway station. A lack of English and commitment might make the NTOG office a better bet.

**POST OFFICE** (*Tmr* 16B3) Located on Odhos Zaimi, close to the corner with Mesonos St.

**TAXIS** (*Tmr* T) Rank at various 'hot spots' around the town, including the Bus terminus and Railway station.

**TELEPHONE NUMBERS & ADDRESSES**

| | |
|---|---|
| Hospital | Tel 222812 |
| NTOG (*Tmr* 2A2) | Tel 420304/5 |
| Police, tourist (*Tmr* 6A/B4) | Tel 220902/3 |

**TRAINS**
**Railway Station** (*Tmr* 4A4) Bounded by the quayside and Odhos Othonos Amalias, diagonally opposite Plateia Trion Symmahon. There is an information office inside the booking hall (open daily between 0800-1300hrs), where the young lady speaks reasonable English.

**Train timetable**
**Patras to Kavasila Junction (for Killini Port) & on to Kalamata**
Daily: depart   1055, 1218, 1446, 1708, 2245, 0159hrs
One-way fare about 300drs, duration about 1½hrs.

**Patras to Athens**
Daily: depart   0203, 0628, 0809, 1101, 1400, 1647, 1854hrs
      arrive   0640, 1000, 1300, 1500, 1848, 2115, 2254hrs
One-way fare: 2nd class 630drs; duration 3½-4hr 40mins
            1st class 950 drs.

**YOUTH HOSTEL** *See* **Accommodation.**

**KILLINI (Kilini, Kyllini): Peloponnese** (Illustration 13) Tel prefix 0623. A scruffy, fly-blown, messy, rather god-forsaken port, but the sole* ferry-boat connection to the island of Zakynthos, as well as a link with the better served Cephalonia. The harbour, formed by the upside down 'L' shaped quay, not only hosts the ferry-boats but is the home port for a fair number of medium sized, high prowed and sterned fishing boats.
* I know there is a Cephalonia/Zakynthos summer months connection, for which refer to the relevant island's **Ferry-boats, A To Z.**

**ARRIVAL BY BUS** Buses pull up on the Ferry-boat Quay (*Tmr* 1D3/4).

**ARRIVAL BY FERRY** It is an immense Harbour for the size of the settlement. The Ferry-boats moor stern to the main Quay (*Tmr* 1D3/4).

Another method of alighting at Killini port is:-
**ARRIVAL BY TRAIN** Really a story on its own, for the train journey to Killini involves an interesting ride on the Pelopponese, Athens to Pirgos line (*See* **Athens, Chapter Nine**). The journey requires a change of train at Kavasila junction which, incidentally, is not detailed on most of the official, small scale maps. It is vital to realise when the train has arrived at Kavasila, for it is all too easy to pass through and proceed on round the Peloponnese. The halt (the word 'terminus' would give a false impression of grandeur) is rather reminiscent of the scenes of the South American railways, so beautifully portrayed in the film *Butch Cassidy and The Sundance Kid* – dusty, desolate, deserted and dilapidated. You now should have the picture.

The branch line train lurks in a siding, usually with the occasional chicken hopping in and out of the cab. The driver, friends and travellers may well be found playing cards or backgammon on rickety tables and stools scattered about the actual railway line. Travellers can be forgiven for not realising that the seemingly immobile piece of machinery is the passport and carriage to the shores of Killini, but there you go...

The Station Master is a short but important man, topped off with a red-banded, peaked hat. Unfortunately, he speaks no English and loses interest, as well as concentration, after a verbal exchange of any length. He also appears to be the ticket collector, station clerk and general factotum.

The train hurtles down the single line track, stopping at the occasional halt, finally coming to a halt at the deserted, end-of-the-line Killini station. The train occasionally proceeds on to the Ferry-boat Quay, but on what basis I cannot advise.

On descending from the train, it is necessary to take off diagonally to the right (*Train behind one*), across the sandy station environs, left along a short hedgerowed lane, then right on the main road, prior to spilling out on to the sprawling, rather disjointed layout that is the port and settlement. To the right is the huge quay, whilst the rest of Killini straggles away to the left.

## THE ACCOMMODATION & EATING OUT
**The Accommodation** There are two hotels and a number of simple *Rooms*.

**Hotel Ionion** (*Tmr* 2B1) (Class C)                                   Tel 92318
*Directions*: Towards the far side of Killini, overlooking the broadest section of the beach and the backshore (on which a number of vans informally park most nights).
   A single room, sharing the bathrooms, costs 2500drs & a double sharing 3100drs, whilst a double room, with an en suite bathroom, costs 3600drs.

**Hotel Glarentza** (*Tmr* 3A5/6)                                   Tel 92397
*Directions*: About 200m along the road out of the port, and on the right (*Port behind one*).
   A surprisingly modern but drab dwelling, with a single room priced at 2200drs & a double room 3200drs, all rooms with en suite bathrooms.

There are a number of *Rooms* set back from the waterfront. The house on the right (*Sbo*) (*Tmr* 4A2) is in a smart building, those to the left (*Sbo*) (*Tmr* 4A3) appear rather ethnic. A number of houses spread along the main road out of Killini offer accommodation.

**Camping** A NTOG campsite is listed at and named Killini, but it is actually situated some 5km away, at Vartholamia, thus may well be of no practical use for an overnight stay.

**The Eating Out** There are a row of restaurants, tavernas and cafeterias (*Tmr* 5B3) parallel to the waterfront, about 100m from the entrance to the Ferry-boat Quay.
   One of the most inexpensive Kafeneion/snack-bar's (*Tmr* 6C2/3) is on the left (*Fsw*) of the final approach to the Ferry-boat Quay. Housed in a small shed, a couple of coffees with milk (admittedly pretty thick) and a brandy cost 200drs. Another noteworthy

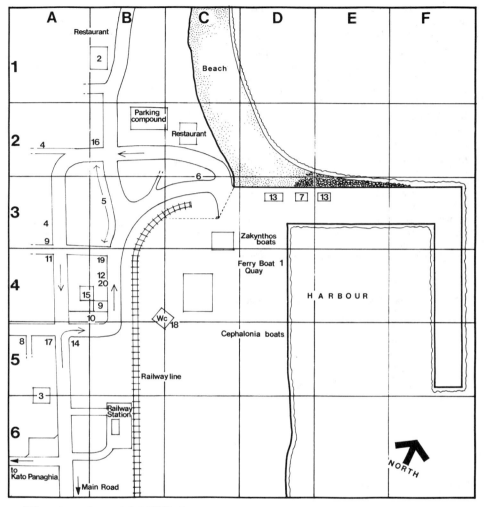

## Illustration 13 Killini

| Tmr | 1D3/4 | Ferry-boat Quay | | 16A/B2 | Police station |
|---|---|---|---|---|---|
| | 2B1 | Hotel Ionion | | 17A5 | Post Office |
| | 3A5/6 | Hotel Glarentza | | 18B/C4/5 | Toilets |
| | '4 | Rooms | | 19B4 | Kafeneion |
| | 5B3 | Restaurants, tavernas & cafeterias (a row of) | | 20B4 | Snackbar |
| | 6C2/3 | Kafeneion 'shed' | | | |
| | 7D3 | Snackbar hut | | | |
| | 8A5 | Bakery | | | |
| | 9 | Butchers | | | |
| | 10A/B4/5 | General store | | | |
| | 11A3/4 | Store | | | |
| | 12B4 | Fruit & Vegetable store | *Tmr* | =Town map reference | |
| | 13D3 & E3 | Ferry-boat ticket huts | *Fsw* | =Facing seawards | |
| | 14A5 | Chemist | *Sbo* | =Sea behind one | |
| | 15A/B4 | Petrol station | *Fbqbo* | =Ferry-boat Quay behind one | |

Snackbar (*Tmr* 7D3) is the hut, on the left of the Ferry-boat Quay, from which the patron sells acceptable cheese pies and doughnuts. The fruit and vegetable store is straddled by a Kafeneion (*Tmr* 19B4) and a Snackbar (*Tmr* 20B4).

# THE A TO Z OF USEFUL INFORMATION

**BEACHES** There is a surprisingly noteworthy sweep of sand. It is at its widest adjacent to the harbour wall, from whence it stretches away for about 250m. The beach is a dirty grey colour, with quite a lot of kelp spread about, and the sea-bed is sandy. In fact the beach would be very attractive if it were kept clean of rubbish – there are litter bins ranged along its length.

**BREAD SHOP** One, a Bakery (*Tmr* 8A5) on the far side of the Post Office.

**BUSES** *See* **Patras,** for details of a connecting bus (that continues on to Zakynthos island), and **Athens, Chapter Nine**.

**COMMERCIAL SHOPPING AREAS** There are sufficient shops, including two Butchers (*Tmr* 9A3 & 9A/B4); a General store (*Tmr* 10A/B4/5), which also sells milk and cheese, and in which most of the goods are stacked on the floor; a small Store (*Tmr* 11A3/4), with very few goods on the simple shelving, but which possesses, importantly, a metered telephone; as well as a Store (*Tmr* 12B4), selling fruit and vegetables.

**FERRY-BOATS** The port services both Cephalonia and Zakynthos, but inconveniently this does not extend to a scheduled ferry-boat connection between the two islands. That is not to say there is no link. Unfortunately, the boats that 'perform' the trip are smaller, 'private enterprise' craft, only operating a height of summer season schedule, for details of which *See* the relevant island chapters.

**Ferry-boat timetable**

| Day | Departure time | | Ports/Islands of Call | |
|---|---|---|---|---|
| Daily | 1015hrs | | Zakynthos. | |
| | 1145hrs | | Poros(Cephalonia). | |
| | 1330hrs | | Argostoli(Cephalonia). | |
| | 1430hrs | | Zakynthos. | |
| | 1715hrs | | Poros(Cephalonia). | |
| | 1730hrs | | Zakynthos. | |
| | 2100hrs | | Zakynthos. | |
| | 2130hrs | | Poros(Cephalonia). | |
| Tues & Fri | 2115hrs | | Argostoli(Cephalonia). | |
| One-way fare: | Killini to | Argostoli (Cephalonia) | 875drs; duration 2¾hrs | |
| | to | Poros (Cephalonia) | 540drs; duration 1½hrs | |
| | to | Zakynthos | 420drs; duration 1¼hrs | |

Please note out of the height of season months, these services are severely curtailed.

**FERRY-BOAT TICKET OFFICES** Well, more huts (*Tmr* 13D3 & 13E3) really, on the left (*Fsw*) of the Ferry-boat Quay. If not open all day, they certainly 'lift the hatches' prior to a particular craft's departure.

**MEDICAL CARE** Not a lot, but there is a **Chemist** (*Tmr* 14A5).

**OTE** A small store (*Tmr* 11A3/4) has a metered telephone.

**PETROL** There is a petrol station (*Tmr* 15A/B4), where the entrance road swings round towards the waterfront.

**POLICE** Yes, an office (*Tmr* 16A/B2), on the corner of a crossroads, which looks out over the ugly shambles of a wire mesh enclosed vehicle park (Ugh).

**POST OFFICE** (*Tmr* 17A5) In the corner of the village's major crossroads.

**TOILETS** A quite clean, 'squatty' block (*Tmr* 18B/C4/5) plonked down towards the south end of the Ferry-boat Quay. Nearby is the skeletal outline of a large, two storey building. One cannot but wonder what it will become?

# PART THREE

# 11 Introduction to the Ionian Islands

*An isle under Ionian skies, beautiful as a wreck of Paradise. Shelley*

Compared with other Greek island groups, not only are the Ionian widely spaced out, but they are off the western coast of the Greek mainland, set in the sparkling blue Ionian Pelagos. Inter-island travel is not always easy, it being more difficult to get from, say, Cephalonia to Zakynthos than from Italy to Corfu.

The islands grouped together and described in this third edition include, from north to south, Corfu, Paxos, Antipaxos, Lefkas, Meganissi, Cephalonia, Ithaca and Zakynthos. Additionally the description of the adjacent mainland has been greatly expanded to incorporate the coastal strip of Epirus and Central Greece, as well as the relevant section of the Peloponnese. Those mainland ports that service the islands, including Igoumenitsa, Parga, Astakos, Patras and Killini, are described in detail. It is usual to find Kithira incorporated in guide books of this grouping, but I have included it in **GROC's Candid Guide to the Mainland Islands** (Argo-Saronic & Sporades), as it has never been considered one of the Ionian, other than as an administrative manoeuvre during a period of colonial administration. Perhaps more importantly, Kithira cannot be reached directly from any of the other Ionian islands. It is arguable that Lefkas is, strictly speaking, not an island. The ancient cutting separating Lefkas from the mainland is a man-made channel, excavated in the fifth century BC and deepened in the nineteenth century AD. Notwithstanding, Lefkas is included.

Scheduled ferry-boat transport between the islands and the mainland is reasonably easy, with the exception of Zakynthos, for which island it is necessary to travel to and from the Peloponnese port of Killini, no inter-island ferry-boats making the connection. It has to be admitted, there is a height of season boat that plies between Cephalonia and Zakynthos.

Air travel can be utilised to reach Corfu, Cephalonia and Zakynthos from Athens and there is also an airport at mainland Preveza (well, Acteon really), from which Lefkas can be attained. It is now possible to fly direct from Corfu to Cephalonia, Preveza and Zakynthos. Various bus services and the Peloponnese train circuit also make connections, using the ferry-boat links. However, the frequency of all forms of travel depends on the time of year. Outside the months of June, July, August and September, schedules may only operate two or three times a week, and some are suspended altogether.

Owing to their location on the western side of the mainland, the Ionian islands do not constantly reflect Turkish historical intrusion. They are more a mirror reflecting the expansionist nature of the European colonial powers, France, the United Kingdom and Venice. For example, the *Cantades*, a Venetian based folk music, is one of the pointers to the different cultural heritage and certainly is a welcome change to the ubiquitous bouzouki.

As a result of the earthquakes, that have devastated the islands over the ages, much of historical note has been damaged or destroyed beyond practical use, serving only as a basis for archaeological enquiry. Corfu, Paxos and Lefkas have possibly suffered less, but Cephalonia, Ithaca and Zakynthos lie adjacent to a geographical fault or faults and have experienced a number of sizeable earthquakes over the last four or five hundred years. The most recent, serious tremors, in 1953, destroyed up to seventy per cent of the buildings of the last three mentioned island's. This explains the lack of old houses and, conversely, the rather twentieth century, prefabricated look of many of the buildings. They have had to be constructed with an eye to withstanding future seismic disturbances, rather than aesthetic considerations. A pity, but practical.

Naturally, a sizeable chunk of the Ionian islands' prosperity is now related to tourism. On the other hand, there is a very strong agricultural prop to their economies, based on grapes, olives, currants, almonds, vegetables, dairy herds, sheep and goats whilst commercially, shipping has and does play an important part in the various budgets.

The member of the wild life family most likely to bother a tourist is the mosquito, although the islands do sport the occasional jackal, and snakes are in evidence, but are not renowned for any poisonous powers. Care should be taken if marching about wild countryside, not only for snakes, which seem much more interested in evading one's approach than in any aggressive intent, but also in respect of the very seldom seen scorpion. Bird life takes in golden orioles, hoopoes, kingfishers and birds of prey including buzzards, kestrels, the golden eagle and osprey. Turtles come ashore to lay their eggs on certain Zakynthos beaches, at the appropriate season.

Overall the islands are exceptionally green, compared to their Aegean counterparts, and pine, olive and cypress trees are abundant. Underfoot vegetation, including bracken, is thick and lush, even at the height of the hottest summer months. One of the reasons for the luxurious nature of the flora is the comparatively heavy rainfall experienced in the winter months. Even in the summer season it is not unusual to experience short, heavy and sometimes prolonged rainstorms, which are occasionally accompanied by the most spectacular lighting and deafening thunder. But it is 'warm' rain.

Naturally, due to the connections with Homer's Odyssey, the islands have received more than their fair share of mythological and archaeological attention. Incidentally, during the period between 1800 and the early 1900s, it must have been difficult to avoid tripping over wild-eyed chaps, wielding trowels and shovels and every so often shouting 'Eureka' (or the archaeological equivalent). Despite all this scholarly activity certain Homeric questions and various island claims, to this or that, have not been finally clarified or unequivocally substantiated. If anything, this has saved possibly embarrassing inter-island strife breaking out, and the islanders can each claim that which suits them, with various amounts of 'tongue in cheek'.

The Corinthians were in occupation during the eighth century BC, but by the sixth century BC, Corfu decided to go it alone and won the subsequent sea-battle with their overlords. During the fifth to third centuries BC, Athens and the Peloponnese (in the Spartan camp) had a long, drawn out scrap, with Athens gaining the support of the Ionian islanders. The Romans were invited to take over the administration of Corfu about 230BC and slowly, during the next hundred years, took over the rest of the group. All was fine until the Romans decided to have their own internecine squabbles, into which the various islands were drawn on one side or the other, with unfortunate consequences for those who backed the loser. Fortunately the last years of the decline of the Roman Empire were comparatively peaceful for the Ionian. From AD 300 to 1100, they were part of the Byzantine domain, suffering bouts of pillaging from various piratical groups. About 1100 the thrustful Normans were expanding their Western European Kingdom. To help keep the Normans at bay the Greeks sought an alliance with the City State of Venice, in exchange for freedom of trade and various concessions. As a result of 'misunderstandings' between the Allies, the Normans slipped in and occupied Corfu, Cephalonia, Ithaca and Zakynthos. By AD 1200 the Byzantine Empire had collapsed, due to the usual amount of double dealing. Between AD 1200 and 1500 the Venetians, although nominally in control of the Ionian, left the various feudal families to run them as their own personal fiefdoms. The increasing threat of the advancing Turks decided the Venetians to formalise their control and administer the islands directly, but they still suffered severe savaging at the hands of raiders, over the next 300 years.

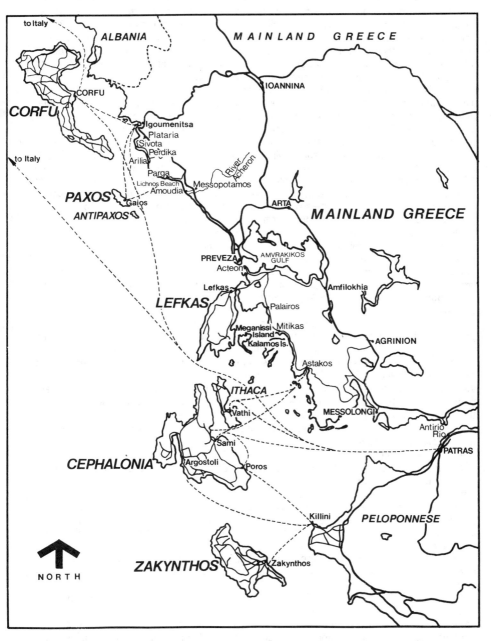

**Illustration 14 The Ionian Islands & Western Coast of Greece**

In 1797 Napoleon Bonaparte, after overcoming the Venetians elsewhere in the European theatres of war, decided once and for all to take the Ionian islands under his wing. As soon as he achieved this feat, a Russo-Turkish coalition overthrew the French, leaving the Russians in control. It is interesting to note that the Czars were running a school of insurgency, as long ago as the 1770s, which dissident Cephalonians, Corfiots and Zantiots attended. Is nothing new? In the meantime (1803) Britain and France declared war (on each other) and Napoleon repossessed the Ionian islands as part of his global strategy. This brought the British into this part of the world and by 1807 they had taken Cephalonia, Ithaca and Zakynthos, followed by Lefkas in 1811. Corfu was extremely strongly garrisoned by the French and, to save unnecessary bloodshed, the British haphazardly blockaded the island for the next six years. At a meeting of The Great Powers (Great Britain, Austria, Prussia and Russia), following the final defeat of the French in Europe, the administration of the Ionian islands was formally granted to Britain, who ruled until 1864. Lasting monuments to British rule, (or misrule, according to your viewpoint) must include encouraging the island farmers to implement comparatively revolutionary advances in agriculture. These were coupled with the necessary and complementary land drainage, extensive road building, some administrative buildings of note and British cemeteries. Corfu alone benefited from the added delights of cricket and ginger beer. After various 'misadventures', Lord Palmerston handed over the Ionian islands to the Greeks, in 1864. As is often the case, the locals had been vociferous in their wish to rid themselves of the 'appalling and oppressive' British. Sadly, once the 'Brits' departed, the islands suffered heavy emigration due to the rapid decline of the agricultural underpin to the economy. Incidentally the British, had sneakily taken over Cyprus, thus storing up big problems for the future.

The Second World War brought in its train further dramatic upheavals. The Germans gave the Italians administrative control in 1941, but seized it back in 1943, after some fairly bloodthirsty events, when the Italians sided with the Greek freedom fighters. Fortunately the islanders were little involved in the Civil War uprisings, which erupted at the end of the Second World War. Unhappily they did not escape scot-free for, in 1953, a horrendous earthquake laid waste Cephalonia, Ithaca and Zakynthos. The most recent pages of Ionian history are dominated by the upsurge of tourism. This really took off in the 1960s, was given a fillip during the 'Colonels' regime and is now, seemingly, proceeding headlong, if not almost totally out of control. It is interesting to note that Italian holiday-makers now invade the Ionian islands, almost block booking everything in the month of August.

The dominant religion is Greek Orthodox, but there is a thriving Catholic enclave on Corfu, a few Jews scattered about several of the islands (remnants of previously large ghettos) and one or three Anglicans.

There are very few Byzantine churches standing, due to the centuries of earthquakes, but the later Ionian version is better represented. The separately constructed bell towers, or more correctly walls pierced by bell arches, topped off with small, overhanging, tiled roofs are named *Campaniles*.

At the end of this chapter there is an alphabetical list of the islands included in the book, their major town and port(s), as well as a quick reference resumé of ferry-boat connections.

The island chapters follow a format, which has been devised and developed over the years, to make the layout as simple to follow as is possible, without losing the informative nature of the text. Each island is treated in a similar manner, allowing the traveller easy identification of his (or her) immediate requirements. The text is faced by the relevant port and town maps, with descriptions tied into the various island routes.

## Symbols, Keys & Definitions

Below are some notes in respect of the few initials and symbols used in the text, as well as an explanation of the possibly idiosyncratic nouns, adjectives and phrases, to be found scattered throughout the book.

Where and when inserted, a star system of rating indicates my judgement of an island, and possibly its accommodation and restaurant standards, by the inclusion of one to five stars. One star signifies bad, two basic, three good, four very good and five excellent. I must admit the ratings are carried out on whimsical grounds and are based purely on personal observation. For instance, where a place, establishment or island receives a detailed 'critique' I may consider that sufficient unto the day... The absence of a star, or any mention at all, has no detrimental significance and might, for instance, indicate that I did not personally inspect this or that establishment.

**Keys** The key *Tmr*, in conjunction with grid references, is used as a map reference to aid easy identification of this or that location on port and town plans. Other keys used in the text include *Sbo* – 'Sea behind one'; *Fsw* – 'Facing seawards'; *Fbqbo* – 'Ferry-boat quay behind one'; *BPTs* – 'British Package Tourists' and *OTT* – 'Over The Top'.

**GROC's definitions, 'proper' adjectives & nouns**: These may require some elucidation, as most do not appear in 'official' works of reference and are used with my own interpretation, as set out below:

**Backshore:** the furthest strip of beach from the sea's edge. The marginal rim separating the shore from the surrounds. *See* **Scrubbly**.

**Benzina:** a small fishing boat.

**Chatty:** with pretention to grandeur or sophistication.

**Dead:** an establishment that appears to be 'terminally' closed, and not about to open for business, but...

**Donkey-droppings:** as in 'two donkey-droppings', indicating a very small, hamlet. *See* **One-eyed.**

**Doo-hickey:** an Irish based colloquialism suggesting an extreme lack of sophistication and or rather 'daffy' (despite contrary indications in the authoritative and excellent *Partridges Dictionary of Slang!*).

**Downtown:** a rundown/derelict area of a settlement – the wrong side of the 'railway tracks'.

**Ethnic:** very unsophisticated, Greek indigenous and, as a rule, applied to hotels and pensions. *See* **Provincial.**

**Gongoozle:** borrowed from canal boat terminology, and is the state of very idly and leisurely, but inquisitively staring at others who are involved in some busy activity.

**Greasy spoon:** a dirty, unwholesome cafe-bar, restaurant or taverna.

**Great unwashed:** the less attractive, modern day mutation of the 1960s hippy. They are usually Western European, inactive loafers and layabouts 'by choice', or unemployed drop-outs. Once having located a desirable location, often a splendid beach, they camp under plastic and in shabby tents, thus ensuring the spot is despoiled for others. The 'men of the tribe' tend to trail a mangy dog on a piece of string. The women, more often than not, with a grubby child or two in train, pester cafe-bar clients to purchase items of home-made jewellery or trinkets.
Note the above genre appears to be incurably penniless (but then who isn't?).

**Grecocilious:** necessary to describe those Greeks, usually bank clerks or tour office owners, who are making their money from tourists but are disdainful of the 'hand that feeds them'. They appear to consider holiday-makers are some form of small intellect, low-browed, tree clambering, inferior relation to the Greek homo-sapiens. They can usually converse passably in two or three foreign languages (when it suits them) and habitually display an air of weary sophistication.

**Hillbilly:** another adjective or noun, similar to 'ethnic', but applied to describe countryside or a settlement, as in 'backwoods'.

**Hippy:** those who live outside the predictable, boring (!) mainstream of life and are frequently genuine, if sometimes impecunious travellers. The category may include students or young professionals taking a sabbatical and who are often 'negligent' of their sartorial appearance.

**Independents:** vacationers who make their own travel and accommodation arrangements, spurning the 'siren calls' of structured tourism, preferring to step off the package holiday carousel and make their own way.

**Kosta'd:** used to describe the 'ultimate' in development necessary for a settlement to reach the apogee required to satisfy the popular common denominator of package tourism. That this state of 'paradise on earth' has been accomplished, will be evidenced by the 'High St' presence of cocktail or music bars, discos, (garden) pubs, bistros and fast food. 'First division' locations are pinpointed by the aforementioned establishments offering inducements, which may include wet 'T' shirt, nightdress or pyjama bottom parties; air conditioning, space invader games and table top videos, as well as sundowner, happy or doubles hours.

**Local prices:** *See* **Special prices.**

**Mr Big:** a local trader or pension owner, an aspiring tycoon, a small fish trying to be a big one in a 'small pool'. Despite being sometimes flashy with shady overtones, his lack of sophistication is apparent by his not being Grecocilious!

**Noddies or nodders:** the palpable, floating evidence of untreated sewage which is being discharged into the sea.

**One-eyed:** small. *See* **Donkey-droppings.**

**Poom:** a descriptive noun 'borrowed' after sighting on Crete, some years ago, a crudely written sign advertising accommodation that simply stated POOMS! This particular place was basic with low-raftered ceilings, earth-floors and windowless rooms, simply equipped with a pair of truckle beds and rickety oilcloth covered washstand – very reminiscent of typical Cycladean cubicles of the 1950/60s period.

**Provincial:** usually applied to accommodation and is an improvement on **Ethnic.** Not meant to indicate, say, dirty but should conjure up images of faded, rather gloomy establishments with a mausoleum atmosphere; high ceilinged, Victorian rooms with worn, brown linoleum; dusty, tired aspidistras as well as bathrooms and plumbing of unbelievable antiquity.

**Richter scale:** borrowed from earthquake seismology and employed to indicate the (appalling) state of toilets, on an 'eye-watering' scale.

**Rustic:** unsophisticated, unrefined.

**Schlepper:** vigorous touting for customers by restaurant staff. It is said of a skilled market schlepper that he can 'retrieve' a passer-by from up to thirty or forty metres.

**Scrubbly:** usually applied to a beach or countryside and indicating a messy, shabby area.

**Special prices:** A phrase employed to conceal the fact that the price charged is no more, no less than that of all the other bandits, no, no competitors. **Local prices** is a homespun variation designed to give the impression that the goods are charged at a much lower figure than that obtainable elsewhere. Both are totally inaccurate, misleading misnomers.

**Squatty:** A Turkish or French style ablution arrangement. None of the old, familiar lavatory bowl and seat. Oh no, just two moulded footprints edging a dirty looking hole, set in a porcelain surround. Apart from the unaccustomed nature of the exercise, the Lord simply did not give us enough limbs to keep a shirt up and control wayward trousers, that constantly attempt to flop down on to the floor, awash with goodness knows what! All this has to be enacted whilst gripping the toilet roll in one hand and wiping one's 'botty' with the other hand. Impossible! Incidentally, ladies should (perhaps) substitute blouse for shirt and skirt for trousers, but then it is easier (I am told) to tuck a skirt into one's waistband!

**Way-station:** mainly used to refer to an office or terminus, stuck out in the sticks and cloaked with an abandoned, unwanted air.

## Ionian Islands described include:-

| Island name(s) | Capital | Ports (at which inter-island ferry-boats & Flying Dolphins dock) | Ferry-boat/Flying Dolphin connections (FB=ferry-boat;FD=Flying Dolphin; EB=excursion boat;M=Mainland). |
|---|---|---|---|
| Antipaxos | | Agrapidias | EB:Paxos.<br>FB:Gaios(Paxos). |
| Cephalonia | Argostoli | Ag Evfimia | FB:Vathi(Ithaca),Astakos(M). |
| | | Argostoli | FB:Lixourion,Killini(M). |
| | | Fiscardon | FB:Vassiliki(Lefkas).Frikes(Ithaca),<br>Nidri(Lefkas),Meganissi.Sami(Cephalonia). |
| | | Lixourion | FB:Killini(M). |
| | | Pesada | FB:Korithi(Zakynthos). |
| | | Poros | FB:Vathi(Ithaca),Gaios(Paxos),<br>Igoumenitsa(M),Corfu.<br>Killini(M).Patras(M). |
| | | Sami | FB:Vathi(Ithaca),Gaios(Paxos),<br>Igoumenitsa(M),Corfu.Fiscardon<br>(Cephalonia),Vassiliki(Lefkas).Patras.<br>Brindisi(Italy). |
| Corfu | Corfu Town | Corfu Town | EB:Gaios(Paxos).<br>FB:Igoumenitsa(M).<br>Igoumenitsa(M),Gaios(Paxos),Vathi<br>(Ithaca),Sami(Cephalonia),Patras(M).<br>Ancona,Bari & Brindisi(Italy).Dubrovnik<br>(Yugoslavia). |
| Ithaca | Vathi(Ithaca) | Vathi | FB:Ag Evfimia(Cephalonia),Astakos(M).<br>Sami(Cephalonia),Patras(M).Gaios<br>(Paxos),Igoumenitsa(M),Corfu(M).<br>Astakos(M). |
| | | Frikes | FB:Nidri(Lefkas),Meganissi. |
| Lefkas | Lefkas Town | Lefkas | EB:Nidri(Lefkas).Meganissi. |
| | | Nidri | FB:Spartochori & Vathi(Meganissi).<br>Fiscardon(Cephalonia),Frikes(Ithaca). |
| | | Vassiliki | FB:Fiscardon & Sami(Cephalonia). |
| Meganissi | The Chora | Spartochori<br>Vathi | FB:Nidri(Lefkas),Fiscardon(Cephalonia),<br>Frikes(Ithaca). |
| Paxos | Gaios | Gaios | EB:Parga(M).Corfu.<br>FB:Corfu.Lakka & Logos(Paxos).Vathi<br>(Ithaca),Sami(Cephalonia),Patras(M).<br>Igoumenitsa(M).Antipaxos.Parga(M). |
| | | Lakka | FB:Corfu.Logos & Gaios(Paxos). |
| | | Logos | FB:Lakka(Paxos),Corfu.Gaios(Paxos). |
| Zakynthos | Zakynthos Town | Korithi Port | FB:Pesada(Cephalonia). |
| | | Zakynthos | FB:Killini(M).Patras(M). |

Corfu and surrounding islands

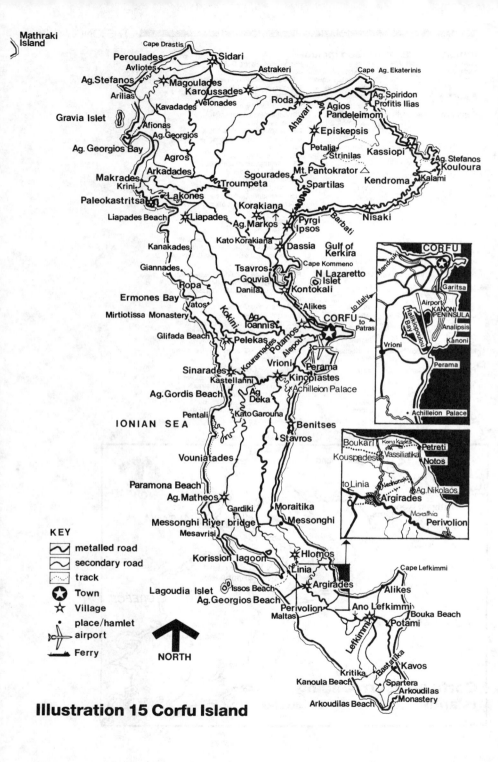

**Illustration 15 Corfu Island**

# 12 CORFU (Kerkira, Kerkyra, Korfu, Corfou)
## Ionian Islands

The 'Kosta'd Resorts ★
Most of the Island ★★
Some of the west coast ★★★★

*Women should be beaten like an olive tree; but in Corfu neither the women nor the olive trees are beaten - because of the laziness of everyone - an island proverb*

**FIRST IMPRESSIONS** Traffic congestion in Corfu Town; harbour pong & smell of drains; clamour of clashing brass band & pop music; swifts & swallows; tall, once gracious, crumbling buildings resulting in a 'touch of the Maltas'; green countryside, olive-tree & fern covered.

**SPECIALITIES** Mandolato nougat; the liquer *Coum Cout*; *Koummkuat* candy; pastit-sada (spiced, braised veal & macaroni); sofrito (spiced, fried & subsequently baked meats); Edward Lear; the Durrell family; the English language, island newspaper, Corfu News.

**RELIGIOUS HOLIDAYS & FESTIVALS** include: 21st May – Ionian islands union with Greece; 6th August – Panaghia, Mouse island; 14th August – Assumption of the Holy Virgin, Mandouki (suburb of Corfu Town); Palm Sunday, the following Saturday, the 11th August and the first Sunday in November – Church services and Corfu Town processions, accompanied by the remains of St Spirodon.

**VITAL STATISTICS** Tel prefix 0661. The island is 56km long, has a maximum width of some 27km and an area of around 593sqkm. The overall population is about 99,000, of which approximately 32,000 live in Corfu Town.

**HISTORY** Due to a quirk of history, the British administered the Ionian islands as a Protectorate, from as early as 1809, only relinquishing control in 1864. This period of administration, which in the case of Corfu occupied the years 1815-1864, resulted in some lasting peculiarities. These include the *Malta* ambience of much of Old Corfu Town; a number of fine buildings; brass bands; the cricket pitch (albeit of sandstone) on the Esplanade; the large British cemetery, as well as the availability of ginger beer. The island is also remarkable for the presence of a thriving Roman Catholic population.

**GENERAL** Corfu island may come as a pleasant surprise. Despite the years of exposure to tourism, it would not be unreasonable to expect the island, its people and their culture, to have wilted under the strain. Not so! Naturally, much of the coastline development has intruded on areas of natural loveliness, previously only visited by the more adventurous travellers. And where building growth has not been possible, coach-trip exploitation has ensured spoilation of certain beauty spots. Apart from some appalling, 'Kosta'd' resorts and a constantly nagging odour of sewage present in and around Corfu Town, probably the most annoying evidence of the tourist invasion is the ability of waiters to politely hear out halting Greek efforts, only to respond in excellent English, American or German!

Still in evidence is the peasant's traditional dependence on the donkey as a beast of burden. Even nowadays it is not an uncommon sight to observe women sitting side-saddle on well-laden, clip-clopping burros. In the country areas the people are friendly and hospitable.

The island presents an amazing kaleidoscope of the best, and worst, of nearly all Greek countryside. The blend includes mountains, verdant valleys, precipitous cliffs, sandy shores, picturesque inland and coastal villages, as well as highly developed (and ravaged) tourist areas, some squalor and urban sprawl. The only surprising omission is the paucity of archaeological remains but the Kasfiki dig, on the Kanoni peninsula, might alter all that.

It is a pity that Gerald Durrell, naturalist and zoologist brother of author Lawrence, and once involved in a long-running orgy of mutual admiration with the island and its people, is now being vilified by the authorities. The reason is that he supposedly 'blew the gaff' on Corfu's present-day shortcomings, in a Sunday Times Colour Supplement article (January 1988). In this, Durrell expressed his dismay at the spoilation bought about by mindless tourist exploitation. Rather like Canute, the relevant civil servants misguidedly deny the damning contents, instead of taking to heart the undeniable kernel of truth in his criticisms. Instead of owning up, they simply blame his comments for the fall off in tourism – the symptoms not the cause. As Noel Coward put it, "I love criticism just so long as it's unqualified praise"!

## CORFU: capital town, main port & airport (Illustration 16) The town
varies from 'modern squalid' to old-fashioned beautiful, with an interesting blend of Venetian, French and British architecture. The Old Quarter, built on a headland hill with, all round, lovely seascapes, is a maze of narrow streets, lanes and alleyways piercing the tall, eighteenth century buildings. High above the pavements, washing lines, and their cargoes of clothes, haphazardly criss-cross the gap between the cast-iron balustrades, similar to massed cats-cradles of crochet. Caged birds trill in the deep shadows of the shabby, careworn facades of the houses. Streets and lanes quite often come to an abrupt end at a flight of steps. These, in turn, spill on to unexpected, small squares squashed in by vintage tenement buildings and often abandoned, ruined churches.

Corfu possesses a surprisingly large number of brass bands. The discordant noise of their practising has not only to compete with the shrieking, diving, swooping swifts and swallows, but actually manages to drown the muffled beat of pavement pop music, the hubbub of the crowds and the chatter of side-street printing presses.

The island can be reached by scheduled, domestic and international buses, ferries and flights.

## ARRIVAL BY AIR The airport is close to Corfu Town, having been constructed in
Halikiopoulou Bay, or lagoon. This bay is formed by a tongue of land to the south of the town, the Paleopolis peninsula, usually referred to as Kanoni, and the Perama headland. There is no city bus to and from the airport terminus building, only various hotel buses and an Olympic coach. It has to be pointed out that the City Buses No 5 (to and from Kastellani & Kouramades) and No 6 (to and from Perama & Benitses) run along the main road from which branches the long, wide, rather grand, airport access road. Travellers requiring door-to-door transport, and arriving on a charter flight, will have to hail a taxi. Unfortunately the fare costs 1000drs, which is exorbitant. The most inexpensive advice to the impecunious, or the thrifty, is to walk, a pleasant stroll which will take little more than 20-30 minutes.

## ARRIVAL BY BUS London and the other major European capitals spawn a number
of coach operators, of a varying degree of professionalism, who journey to Corfu island, transhipping from Italy or Igoumenitsa (Greek mainland). For instance the *National Express Co* operates a twice weekly service to Corfu in the months of April, May, June and September and daily in the months of July and August. In 1988, the one-way fare cost £79.

There is a scheduled service from Athens via Rio-Antirio and Igoumenitsa, from whence the journey is completed on a ferry-boat (*See* **Buses, A To Z**).

## ARRIVAL BY FERRY There are two ports, the Old and the New. The Old Port (*Tmr*
F1), at which the Igoumenitsa(M) and Paxos island ferries dock, is to the east of the New Fort. The New Port (*Tmr* B/C1), where the Patras inter-island ferry-boats, the international craft and cruise liners tie up, is to the west of the New Fort.

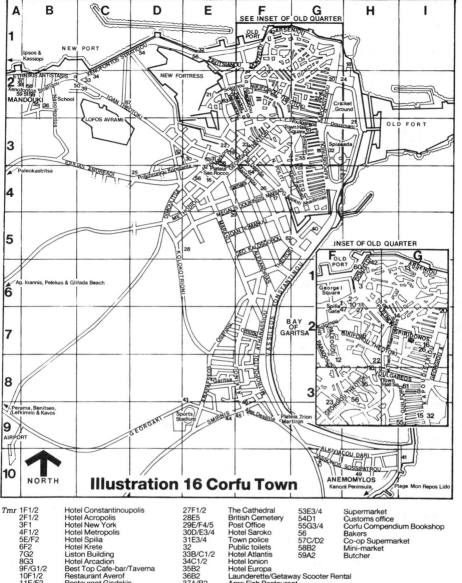

**Illustration 16 Corfu Town**

**Old Port** (*Tmr* F1) To the left (*Sbo*) of the Ferry-boat Quay, Donzelot Parade rises quickly from sea-level, following the cliff-edge around the headland to merge into Arseniou Parade. Akti Donzelot is lined by a number of tourist offices renting rooms, scooters, boat trips, and goodness knows what else.

**New Port** (*Tmr* B/C1) The area, apart from the Old Quarter of Mandouki (to the west along Odhos Xenofontes Stratigou), is a rather dusty, unattractive jungle of concrete buildings. If arriving late at, or planning to make an early departure from the New Port, it may be necessary to seek accommodation in the Mandouki.

## THE ACCOMMODATION & EATING OUT

**The Accommodation** There is a plethora of accommodation, including many *Rooms*. The NTOG office (*Tmr* 20G/H1/2) now only hands out lists of hotels and does not advise enquirers of private house rooms.

Those travellers who disembark at the New Port (*Tmr* B/C1) have quite a wide choice, including two modern hotels:-

**Hotel Atlantis** (*Tmr* 33B/C1/2) (Class C) Xenofontos Stratigou          Tel 35560
*Directions*: Across the junction of the ways from the entrance gates to the New Port.
   All rooms have en suite bathrooms, a single room being priced at 1800drs & a double room at 2500drs increasing to 3000drs & 3600drs (16th June-20th Sept)
and the
**Hotel Ionion** (*Tmr* 34C1/2) 46 Xenofontos Stratigou          Tel 39915
*Directions*: A stride or ten, further east along the Esplanade.
   Less expensive than the *Atlantis*. All rooms have en suite bathrooms, with a single room costing 1310drs & a double 1925drs, which prices rise to 1800drs & 2260drs (1st July-30th Sept).

A more reasonably priced, more hostelish alternative is the:-
**Hotel Europa** (*Tmr* 35B2) (Class D)          Tel 39304
*Directions*: It is easiest to proceed west along Xenofontos Stratigou from the roundabout junction. Then turn left (south) on Odhos Napoleontos, leaving a school on the left, beyond which take the first right and right again. The hotel is a few metres down the alleyway, on the left.
   Clean, cluttered and friendly with a television room and snackbar. Single rooms share the bathrooms at a cost of 1500drs. Double rooms, sharing, cost 2500drs & with an en suite bathroom 3000drs, increasing to 3000drs & 3500drs (16th March-15th Sept). The owner, an old lady, is no walkover, but will negotiate rates. She also runs a launderette, diagonally across the street, next door to her son George's business, Getaway Scooter Rental (*Tmr* 36B2) (*See* **Bicycle, Scooter & Car Hire, A To Z**). The launderette, once the only facility in town, is now rather expensive at a 1000drs a load (*See* **Laundry, A To Z** for a much better value alternative).

There is private accommodation in the Old Quarter of Mandouki. It is best reached from the New Port road, Ethnikis Antistasis. Turn down the narrow alley, crowded in by the 'cruiseliner' smart *Argo Fish Restaurant* (*Tmr* 37A/B2), on the right (*Sbo*), and a ruined building of almost classical appearance, on the left.
**Rooms** (*Tmr* 38A/B2)
*Directions*: As above, and on the right (*Sbo*), in an old mews terrace. Well signposted from a number of directions (but none on the house) and owned by an honest, caring, middle-aged couple (sounds like one of those lonely hearts ads, doesn't it?)
   Despite the antiquated nature of the accommodation, (the ceilings are matchboard), it is squeaky clean and more the size of an apartment. The bedroom two is spacious, the bathroom is a separate room and there is a kitchen, not a kitchenette. (Okay Geoff, cut the waffle, how much? Sorry?) One night costs 1800drs, for three nights this is reduced to a total of 5000drs and must be the best value in town. It has to be mentioned that the beds reminded me of sleeping on the horse, not the hair...

One other rather doo-hickey option is:-
**Rooms** (*Tmr* 39B/C2) No 124 Ioan Theotoki.
*Directions*: From the 'New Port' roundabout, ascend Odhos Ioan Theotoki (once Avramiou) in the direction of Plateia San Rocco (Theotoki). The accommodation is on the right, beyond a row of shops, the last of which is a Rent A Scooter/Car outfit. Well advertised by crude, red lettering on cardboard, which also proclaims 'Luggage Storage'. To the nearside is a garden adjacent to the oldish house which butts onto a new, many storeyed building.

---

The owner is a wizened old boy, aged about 60, who hobbles around his property. He demands a mid-season price of 1800/2000drs for the positively ethnic double rooms, but emphatically guarantees hot water showers.

Those travellers wishing to get to the centre of the town, should continue along Odhos Ioan Theotoki to Plateia San Rocco.

Across the wide quay from the Old Port is a very large, grass square, named after King George II. Behind this 'scrambles' the Old Quarter, wherein lie numerous houses with **Rooms**. Many of the owners 'cull' obvious clients, carrying them off to their particular nook of the maze.

Hotels in this area include the:-

**Hotel Acropolis (Acropole)** (*Tmr* 2F1/2) (Class D) 3 C. Zavitsianou          Tel 39569
*Directions*: In the street parallel to and immediately opposite the ferry-boat quayside, from which it is separated by George II Sq.

Clean but seedy, late (Greek) Victorian hotel (two classes better than its counterpart, traditionally featured in those 1950, black and white films). All rooms share the bathrooms. A single room costs 1100drs & a double 2700drs, increasing to 1300drs & 2900drs (15th June-30th Sept).

**Hotel Constantinoupolis** (*Tmr* 1F1/2) (Class D) 11 C. Zavitsianou          Tel 39826
All as for the *Acropolis*, from which it is separated by an alleyway.

**Hotel New York (Nea York)** (*Tmr* 3F1) (Class D) Donzelot Parade or 21 Ypapantis          Tel 39922
*Directions*: Instead of crossing George II Sq from the Old Port quayside, turn left (*Sbo*) towards Donzelot Parade, which doubles back on the harbour, ascending to follow the cliff round the bluff of the Old Quarter headland. The hotel is across the road, almost opposite the outset of Donzelot.

Charges are approximately as for the *Acropolis*.

**Hotel Metropolis** (*Tmr* 4F1/2) (Class D) 24 Leoforos Konstantinou          Tel 31156
*Directions*: In a small side-street/square/off Zavitsianou St, at the foot of the steps up to the Cathedral.

**Hotel Spilia** (*Tmr* 5E/F2) (Class E) 2 Solomou St          Tel 34097
*Directions*: On the right-hand side of Odhos Solomou, approaching from the New Fortress Bus Square (*Tmr* 21E2). The entrance is actually in an alley off Solomou St, 4th Parodos, the one closest to the Bus Sq being 3rd Parodos – it's a popular alley name hereabouts, there being at least four.

A typical E Class, rather sleazy hotel, but quite adequate for an overnight stop. Only double rooms available, sharing the bathrooms, which cost 1600drs, increasing to 1800drs (1st July-30th Sept).

**Hotel Krete (Criti)** (*Tmr* 6F2) (Class E) 43 Nikiforou Theotoki          Tel 38691
*Directions*: They should sound easy, nevertheless actuality blunts the clarity of my descriptive powers, but here we go. Plateia George II is split north/south by an avenue. This joins Zavitsianou St, the other side of which is a narrow side-street. The latter jinks right and then left and is the outset of Odhos Nikiforou Theotoki. The street runs south for two blocks. It then climbs steeply to the left, in a south-east direction, at the Square of the Church of St Andrew and St Anthony. Beyond a row of shops set amongst a colonnaded walkway, on the right, Nikiforou Theotoki widens out. On the left is another small, colonnaded shopping arcade, above which is the hotel. Phew! Incidentally, across the street is a lovely, church campanile dated AD 1867.

Despite the somewhat dilapidated external appearance of this rather unique, rustic provincial, wooden window shuttered, E Class hotel, it smells clean and nice (as Rosemary so olfactorily put it). A double room, sharing the bathrooms, cost 2000drs per night. The pleasant, refined lady owner is not adverse to bargaining, well out of season, but has little English.

Also in this area is an excellent hotel, the:-

**Hotel Cyprus** (*Tmr* 12F2/3) 13 Ag Pateron St          Tel 30032
*Directions*: Best to locate the National Bank (*Tmr* 16F/G2/3), which is close to the junction of Georgiou Theotoki and Voulgareos Sts. With the bank on the left (*Facing the Old Fort/Liston*), proceed along the lane on the near or Plateia San Rocco side of the bank. Then, turning left, circle around to the right, past the sound of a daytime chattering printing press hidden away in some building. The hotel is on a 'sort of' hillock around which the street winds. Across the road is the ruined Church of Ag Pateres.

Pleasantly old-fashioned and owned by a courteous lady, originally from Athens and who speaks English. The well equipped double bedrooms have matchboard ceilings, share the bathrooms and start off at 1800drs, which rate increases to 2200drs (1st April-31st July & 1st-30th Sept) and 2500drs (1st-31st Aug). A laundry sign advises that a machine load costs 800drs. Its a thought.

Continuing west on Odhos Voulgareos 'bumps' into the transverse Kapodistriou St, which edges the 'backside' of The Liston building (*Tmr* 7G2). To the right, and on the right, is the:-

**Hotel Arcadion** (*Tmr* 8G3) (Class C) 44 Kapodistriou St                              Tel 37671
*Directions*: As above.

A splendid location looking out over the Spianada. A single room, sharing a bathroom, is priced at 1600drs & en suite 2050drs. Double rooms en suite cost 2250/2650drs. These prices increase, respectively, to 1850drs, 2500drs & 2700/3200drs (1st April-20th June & 11th Oct-31st Dec) and 2160drs, 2760drs & 2930/3450drs (21st June-10th Oct).

Other hotels in the centre of town include the: smart *Olympic* (*Tmr* 17F4 – Class B, tel 30532); clean, Greek in character *Hermes* (ΕΡΜΗΣ) (*Tmr* 19E/F3 – Class C, tel 39321), with single rooms sharing from 1810drs & doubles 2260drs, single rooms en suite 2260drs & doubles 2710drs increasing, respectively, to 2620drs & 3160drs and 2970drs & 3430drs (1st April-30th Sept), and the *Saroko* (*Tmr* 30D/E3/4). Hotels that overlook the picturesque, if rather smelly, Bay of Garitsa are the very swanky, luxury *Corfu Palace* (*Tmr* 40G5, tel 39485) and, on the far headland, the *Manna* (*Tmr* 41H10).

There are dozens of private houses offering lodgings, the majority of which are in the Old Town or Quarter, a veritable rabbit-warren of streets and buildings. Unfortunately the NTOG no longer issues lists of these, but aid is at hand, it only being necessary to locate the:-

**Tourist Bureau** (*Tmr* 42F1) 43 Arseniou St                              Tel 22101
*Directions*: From the Old Port, climb headland hugging Donzelot Parade past the *Hotel Astron* and a National Bank. Proceed about another 100m and the office is on the right, set in the ground floor of one of the buildings that line the street.

This 'Rooms Agency' is run by 'Billy' Katsaros, a helpful, energetic, grizzled, middle-aged man who appears to speak almost any language other than English. The office opens seven days a week between 0800-1300hrs & 1600-1900hrs. The accommodation he represents is charged at prices ranging from 1000drs to 1500drs, per night, for a double room, depending upon the facilities.

For those travellers approaching Corfu Town from the airport, once close to the large Football/Sports Stadium, there are, in fairly rapid succession, the:-

**Hotel Bretagne** (*Tmr* 43D/E8/9) (Class C) 27 Georgaki                              Tel 30724
*Directions*: As above and on the left.

All rooms have en suite bathrooms, with a single starting at 2000drs & a double 2500drs, which rates increase to 3000drs & 3600drs, at the height of season,
and the

**Pension Phoenix** (*Tmr* 44E9) (Class B) 2 Ch Smirnis                              Tel 42290
*Directions*: As above, and continuing eastwards, past a church on the left. The pension is on the right.

All rooms have en suite bathrooms, with a single room costing 2300drs & a double 3000drs, rising to 2800drs & 3800drs (1st April-31st May & 1st-31st Oct) and 3000drs & 4100drs (1st June-30th Sept).

Not much further on is *Rooms* (*Tmr* 45E/F9) at No 6. Across the other side of the crossroads is the *Inter Cafe Agoris* (*Tmr* 46E/F9), which advertises information, stamps, maps & *Rooms*. None of these will be quiet, as the road from the airport remains constantly busy.

One last area of accommodation, if rather distant for new arrivals, is the Kanoni Peninsula, whereon are various hotels and houses with lodgings. The hotels tend to be luxurious and it is doubtful if 'room will be found at the inn', even for manifestly well-heeled, middle-class independents clutching suitcases and sporting cravats and brogues. Mind you, once established, it might be worth a foray to inspect the offerings (*See* **Lido 3, Beaches, A To Z**).

## YHA & Camping
There are none in or adjacent to Corfu Town but the two Youth Hostels and various island campsites are listed under the island text description of:-

| | | |
|---|---|---|
| **Kontokali** | Camping | 7km NW of Corfu Town, on the east coast (Route One). |
| **Tsavros (Limni)** | YHA & Camping | 10km NW of Corfu Town, on the east coast (Route One). |
| **Ag Ioannis** | YHA | 9km W of Corfu Town, inland (Route Four). |
| **Dassia/Kato Korakiana** | Camping | 12km NW of Corfu Town, on the east coast (Route One). |
| **Ipsos/Pyrgi** | Camping (3 sites) | 16½km NW of Corfu Town, on the east coast (Route One). |
| **Roda** | Camping | 37km N of Corfu Town, on the north coast (Route One). |
| **Astrakeri/** | Camping | 36km N of Corfu Town, on the north coast (Route One). |

| **Karousades** | | |
|---|---|---|
| **Afionas Beach/** | Camping | 35km NW of Corfu Town, on the north-west coast (Route Two). |
| **Ag Georgios** | | |
| **Paleokastritsa** | Camping | 25km NW of Corfu Town, on the west coast (Route Three). |
| **Vatos** | Camping | 15km W of Corfu Town, 2km inland (Route Three). |
| **Pelekas Beach/** | Camping | 15km W of Corfu Town, on the west coast (Route Four). |
| **Sinarades** | | |
| **Messonghi** | Camping | 23km S of Corfu Town, on the east coast (Route Five). |

**The Eating Out** It is often the case that large, popular island, main towns possess any number of establishments, but few, reasonably priced tavernas with an imaginative menu. In fact Corfu is well serviced, even if the options are rather spaced out. Additonally, there can be few cafe-bar locations as splendid as those gathered in amongst the colonnades of The Liston (*Tmr* 7G2).

For travellers who require a reliable breakfast service then there is no need to proceed any further than the:-
**Best Top Cafe-bar/Taverna** (*Tmr* 9F/G1/2) 33 Filelinon St, Upper Cathedral Sq          Tel 24010
*Directions*: Situated at the very north, Old Port end of Filelinon St, in the little square to one side of the Cathedral. Perhaps one of the best spots at which to soak up the ambiance of the Old Quarter. This small plateia is kissed by the sun, for those breakfasters who do not 'repas' too early in the day. There is a choice of stools in the narrow, crowded interior, or tables and chairs on the square. For those who choose to lounge outside, it is a delight to swivel round and imbibe the bubbling, busy local life. Worthy citizens, bent on their daily round, emerge from and disappear into the narrow alleys that spill onto the square. This is hemmed in by tall, three to five storey high, 18th century buildings. They are French provincial in style with slate tile roofs, ormolou windows, chipped and cracked plasterwork revealing old brickwork, once brightly painted but now a faded ochre colour, peeling paintwork, rotting doors and shutters, in and around which are strung and draped a profusion of washing lines, telephone wires and power cables. During business hours, a printing press chatters away on one side of the square, in the direction of a competitor, *Grill Room Mon Ami*, which we shall now forget (bigoted, but at least loyal to old friends!).
     Spiros, the engaging, friendly, tireless proprietor serves a goodly English breakfast for 200drs. A cup of Nes meh ghala costs 75drs and a 3 star Metaxa 50drs. Incidentally, they can offer properly boiled eggs but no 'soldiers', only toast. That is not all, as Best Top stays open all day and evening, serving a full gamut of food which includes toasted sandwiches and omelettes, starting at 185drs, various 'with meat added' dishes, such as spaghetti bolognese, stuffed tomatoes or peppers, all costing 285drs, chicken 260drs, moussaka 330drs and veal cutlet 462drs. A helping of French fries costs 41drs, a Greek salad 190drs, a bottle of beer 50drs, and a bottle of retsina (a rather pricey) 147drs. In addition, there are ice-creams, cakes, fruit juices and an interesting fish dish labelled *Drowns* – but I thought that's just what they didn't do!

Fairly close by is the:-
**Creperie Asterix** (*Tmr* 14G2) Odhos Sof Dousmani
*Directions*: Half-way up the steps climbing from the junction of the streets of Ag Spiridonos, Philarmonikis and Filelinon, and on the right, opposite the Church of Ag Nikolaos.
     Worth bearing in mind as an (expensive) alternative to the ubiquitous moussaka, especially an early or late evening snack. An excellent selection of traditional (from 300drs) and savoury (from 500drs) crepes. Salads start at 90drs for a tomato dish but rise to 400drs for an 'Asterix' salad. It should be very special at that price.

The steps continue to steeply ascend to Plateia Elenis. This is completely surrounded by lovely, if faded, 18th century buildings, most with the original balconies still in place, and in the middle of which is a mature palm tree. The riveting, historical footnote is that the Church of Ag Nikolaos (opposite the *Creperie Asterix*) became the focal point and church to a Serbian community that fled to Corfu, in December 1916. They numbered some 150,000, and included the King and his minsters. Up to that year, Serbia had been an independent country, the demise of which was 'written large' after a Serbian citizen assassinated Archduke Francis Ferdinand, heir to the Austrian throne, in June 1914. Naturally, the Austro-Hungarian forces put Serbia to route, thus the mass migration. Incidentally, this historic killing of a royal personage put in motion the onset of the First World War. For a few years, prior to the creation of Yugoslavia of which Serbia became a founder state, Corfu Town hosted the Serbian government in exile. Unfortunately an epidemic ran through the community, reducing their numbers by at least a third.

In the lower, main Cathedral Square, and across the way from the *Hotel Metropolis* (*Tmr* 4F1/2), is *Kostas*. This is a very convenient kafeneion, popular with the younger Corfiots who idle away the late night hours making a beer, coke, lemonade or coffee last for hours on end.

For more substantial fare there are a number of taverna/restaurants in the area of the old Spilia Gate (*Tmr* E/F1/2), which overlooks George II Square. These include the:-

**Restaurant Averof** (*Tmr* 10F1/2)
*Directions*: On the corner of Anipou and Prossalendou Sts, conveniently reached by slipping down the alleyway between the *Hotels Acropolis* and *Constantinoupolis*.

Once inexpensive, but the Averof, and its competitor opposite, are now rather high priced with, for instance, a Greek salad costing 300drs and kalamares 650drs. If price is not a restraint, the Averof is a truly Greek restaurant operating with the obligatory arm-waving and shouting. No shortage of waiters here and the service is excellent. The whole performance is reigned over by a seated Mama and Papa overlooking and supervising proceedings from behind the raised cash register. Sitting outside, under the passageway awning, a diner can watch the continuing battle with the *Pantheon* for passing custom. Both restaurants employ a waiter to 'influence' the 'punters'.

,A less expensive and popular alternative is just along the transverse alleyway that almost parallels Odhos Zavitsianou. (This starts out as Prossalendou and moving to the right (*Sbo*) becomes Odhos Dona). On the left, towards the far end is the:-

**Restaurant O Dionysos** (*Tmr* 47F1/2) 17 Dona St                    Tel 24072
*Directions*: As above.

The proprietor, Spiros Krasakis, and his wife are well respected, old hands serving unexceptional if typical taverna offerings. An average meal for two costs about 1400drs. Dishes include taramosalata, tzatziki and spaghetti (175drs), chicken (260drs), spaghetti bolognese and stuffed tomatoes (274drs), pizza (360drs), moussaka (375drs), various veal dishes (445drs), fried potatoes (60drs), gigantes (beans - 295drs) or a Greek salad (250drs).

**Grisdakis** (*Tmr* 11E/F2) 20 Solomou St
*Directions*: From St George's Sq, progress along the outset of N Theotoki St and branch right (*Sbo*) onto Odhos Solomou, in the direction of the main Bus Sq.

The family and their formica-topped restaurant tables lack charm, but the establishment appears popular.

In this area are a number of utterly forgettable eating houses, which must include the self-service, fast food *Edem*, sporting chrome cabinets and garish pictures portraying the gourmet delights within.

For those requiring an inexpensive bite, there is:-

**Giro Souvlaki** (*Tmr* 48E/F2/3) No 54 Parodos Alley
*Directions*: A cellar snackbar at the end of Odhos Parodos, a side alleyway off to the left (*Facing the Bus Sq*) of Odhos Solomou.

Not out of the 'top souvlaki pita draw', but serves both stick and giro at a cost of 85drs, for take away, or 95drs for those who perch on a stool. A bottle of beer costs 85drs and kortaki retsina is on sale.

An intriguing possibility, for those who are prepared to 'slum it', is the dark, low ceilinged, front room taverna on the corner, diagonally across the street. No menu and very popular with local artisans.

Just around the corner from Solomou St, and ascending Odhos Ag Sophia permits further choice including a 'Stick Souvlaki' outfit on the left, at No 45, a Cafe-bar on the right, popular with the *cognoscenti* and, further along the street, again on the right, a vegetarian Cafe/Snackbar, whose offerings include a vegetarian pizza.

Fairly close by, across the road from the *Hotel Krete* (*Tmr* 6F2), is:-

**Makis Grill Bar** 38 St Vasileos St
*Directions*: As above, on the parallel side-street to Odhos Nik. Theotoki, to the west of the front entrance of Ag Vasiloy and Stefanou Church.

John Makis and his wife, Koula, assisted by their two daughters, Mary and Marinella, operate a souvlaki and grill taverna. Unlike a lot of the smarter restaurants, where most of the food is prepared using modern equipment, John's dishes are cooked in the traditional manner, over charcoal. Only open evenings and the prices are reasonable.

Further to the west is the 'Cubby Hole Bar', popular with clients who..., well, who wish to drink in a place called the Cubby Hole Bar?

In the smarter, east section of town, where the road borders the far end of the Esplanade and overlooking the canal and the Old Fort, there are a number of fashionable, cafe-bar/restaurants. Naturally their location is reflected in the prices. A charming diversion is to take refreshment at one of the cafe-bars located in the Old Fort side of The Liston (*Tmr* 7G2). From beneath the classical colonnades, waiters scurry to clients seated on the far side of the broad sweep of pedestrian way. Here it is possible to sit and watch the *Volta* of the Corfiots, and tourists, endlessly wandering backwards and forwards along the parade of Georgiou A. The tables and chairs which edge the Esplanade are five or six deep. Admittedly a coffee costs about 160drs and an ouzo 145drs, but where else in the world is it possible to laze away an hour or three, of an evening, in such marvellous surroundings so comparatively inexpensively? And the coffees are served with a jug of hot water that allows yet another cup. One intrusive factor is the drains, the smell of which make their presence known, even here.

Incidentally, the roads that encircle the Esplanade and the pathways that run through the park, are thronged with ambling couples and families on most summer evenings.

Another magnificent location, exploited by two or three restaurants, is the Arseniou cliff-top road, which looks out over Potamos Bay with Vidos island in the near distance. The tables and chairs of these establishments border the cliff-edge under awnings, whilst the kitchens are across the road. Let's hope none of the staff are knocked down by the passing traffic, it could make the meal very drawn out!

One of the leading contenders is:-
**Pizza Pete** (*Tmr* 13G1)
*Directions*: As above.

The years have 'encouraged' the owners to bask in a welter of self-adulation. So much so that there is a separate folder containing congratulatory comment extolling the virtues of the place. I hope readers do not have the unworthy thought that this unreserved panegyric encouraged me to destroy the illusion, but I will admit to considering some realism might not go amiss. Not one, but two schleppers convince the uncommitted that Pizza Pete's is the answer to a gourmet' prayers. The kitchen is clean and the waiters are almost obsequious in their attention but... the menu includes picture representations of many of the dishes. Prior to departing, after our meal, I left a note, the gist of which, perhaps, encapsulates my conclusions:-

"Dear Pizza Pete

Noting your self esteem and numerous laudations, I hope you will excuse the observations of a couple of old hand, Greek island travellers. Even if you do, here goes.

1. I am disappointed your wine list does not include a kortaki retsina.

2. I am more than a little annoyed when the only salad available, despite the number listed in the menu, is a fruit salad bowl of 'Special Salad', at double the cost of the more mundane, less expensive alternatives. Admittedly this was a very nice salad and the waiter had the decency to be embarrassed at the omission.

3. The tzatziki was enjoyable, even if the introduction of carrot seems to stray from the more usual interpretation of this traditional dish.

4. The 'Special' ( that word again) Pete's Pizza was good, and might well join the list of memorable pizza's enjoyed over the years, but no more.

Geoff O'Connell

PS The bread, although inexpensive, was just a few slices."

A meal for two of special pizza (770drs), tzatziki (160drs), two beers (at 94drs each), bread & service (30drs) costs some 1148drs.

Further on round Odhos Arseniou, towards the Esplanade and down by the 'Old Fort Lido', is:-
**Mr Chans, Faliraki** (*Tmr* 18H1/2)
*Directions*: As above.

The only thing that has changed over the years are the prices. A set meal for two now costs about 2500drs, for three 3500drs and for four 4500drs. The least expensive wine is 'extorted' at 700drs.

Mr Chans opens daily between 1200-1430hrs & 1830-2330hrs, but is closed Sunday lunch-time... probably to count the money.

The stretch of Esplanade between the Old and New Ports 'hosts' a number of eateries. For instance a Cantina caravan is parked alongside the Old Port (*Tmr* F1) quay wall and stays open until late at night, whilst at the far, New Port end, at the outset of Odhos Ioan Theotoki, which rises back to Plateia San Rocco, is a:-

**Souvlaki Snackbar** (*Tmr* 50B/C2)
*Directions*: As above, on the right (*Sbo*), with tables and chairs spread along the pavement, and hedged in by car hire and travel offices.

The friendly owner serves a stick souvlaki, as well as beers and coffee.

Down at the New Port, and in the Mandouki area, the *Restaurant Orestes* (*Tmr* 51A/B2) is on the left (*Sea to the right*) of the 'now' back street Xenofontos Stratigou. Despite catching the eye, the menu is rather expensive.

Almost at the San Rocco Sq end of Ioan Theotoki St, and on the right (*Sbo*), alongside 'The' Launderette (*Tmr* 52D/E3), is:-

**Louka's Snackbar**
*Directions*: As above.

A narrow fronted establishment, serving reasonably priced food with a souvlaki pita costing 55drs and a plate of chips 42drs. Other offerings include spit roasted 'this and that'. Why not pop your clothes into the launderette and, whilst waiting, enjoy a snack or meal.

On the left (*New Port behind one*) of nearby San Rocco Sq is a very popular pie shop, close to a Supermarket (*Tmr* 53E3/4). There are other pie snackbars in the maze of market alleys (*Tmr* 22F/G2/3) off to the left (*Facing The Liston*) of Georgiou Theotoki/Voulgareos Sts, namely Odhos Michael Theotoki (also known as Doughnut Lane) and Ag Vassiliou/Fish Lane. One is on the small square, Plateia Vraklia Oti, and the other at the bottom, Port end, of M. Theotoki.

I hope readers will excuse me saving the best for last. The first, *Taverna* O ΓΙΑΝΝΗΣ, must rate as a five star entry, both for menu content and price, whilst the *Chicken Shack* or (*Yanni's*) is included for quality and price. Why not try both.

**Taverna O ΓΙΑΝΝΗΣ** (*Tmr* 49H10) Iassonos Sossipatrou St          Tel 31066
*Directions*: At the far, south end of the Bay of Garitsa. By the Plateia Trion Martiron angle right, rather than keeping to the waterfront lane. Take the second left along the ever narrowing Iassonos Sossipatrou (a one-way street, thus these detailed directions), past the lovely Byzantine church, of the same name as the street. The taverna is on the right. It is easy to pass by the front garden of the establishment without realising, as there is no advertising material, not even a menu on display. Mind you, there aren't any menus, full stop.

The kitchens must be inspected to divine exactly what is on offer but be assured there is a vast choice. Dishes might include meat balls, sausages, liver, stiffado, octopus, lamb, pork meat wrapped in intestines, veal and a full range of vegetables, yes, vegetables, including Brussel sprouts and mixed vegetables. Retsina from the barrel washes about and an outstanding meal for two costs about 1500drs. Mind you, the locals have heard of the place and tend to leave little room for latecomers. I must admit that I would visit Corfu on the strength of this taverna alone.

Before leaving the area, the aforementioned church (Saints Jason and Sosipatros) dates back to the 11th century and is named after two of St Paul's disciples who incepted the conversion of Corfu to Christianity, despite the ruling Roman's displeasure.

### The 'Chicken Shack' (Yanni's)
*Directions*: Take the main road that passes the Airport, after which proceed beyond a large supermarket, a Mobil Petrol Station and a sign for **Rooms**, all on the right. At the end of a slow descent, about 2km out of town, and also on the right, is a single storey shack (thus the nickname) edging the busy road and shaded by three large trees. This is it.

The fame of Yanni's was due to the previous owner, who ran it for ten years. Towards the end of 1988 a friendly family of expatriate Australian Greeks took over, but will they stay? One can only hope so, because, for the impecunious and hungry, this is an ideal location. The bill of fare is simple, being restricted to spit roasted lamb or chicken, accompanied by a basic choice of salad, chips, bread and barrel retsina. They serve take-away or sit-down meals. A night out for two of ½kilo of lamb, chips, a large salad, plentiful bread and a bottle of retsina cost about 1500drs. A kilo of chicken costs 630drs (take-away) or 800drs (sit-down) and lamb (1800drs (T.A.) or 2000drs (S.D.). Can't be bad, if rather basic.

Before leaving the overall subject of eating and drinking, whilst scanning my collection of Greek memorabilia, I spotted a Forward by Beverley Nichols to the 1969 edition of *Corfu – Venus of the Isles*\*. This referred to *The Spoty (sic) Dog*, adjacent to *The Mimosa* (or, as it had become known, *Dirty Dicks*), and situated "on the casual, rambling waterfront... a pub ... small and decorous." Where, oh where had I seen them. Then it came in a flash *Dirty Dicks*, no misnomer this, is still located in the ground floor of the *Hotel New York*, and bless it, next door is no other than *The Spoty Dog*. The thrust of Beverley Nichols mention was the spelling, which he was unable to bring himself to point out to the owner. I cannot recall whether it is now spelt with one or two 't's'. Can somebody advise me?

\* Published by East Essex Gazette, then of 95 Pier Ave, Clacton-on-Sea, Essex.

## THE A TO Z OF USEFUL INFORMATION
**AIRLINE OFFICES & TERMINUS** The Olympic office (*Tmr* 15G3/4) is towards the south end of Kapadistriou St and opens daily between 0800-1600hrs. Note that nearby, across the road on the edge of the Esplanade, is a public toilet, a relatively rare Ionian facility. It is rather hidden from view behind a hedge and underground.

### Aircraft timetable

**Corfu to Athens** (& vice versa)
A Minimum of 3 flights a day:-
Daily            0705, 1950, 2315hrs
From 19th June, additionally:-
Tues, Thurs,  0830hrs
  Sat & Sun
*Return*
A minimum of 3 flights a day:-
Daily            0535, 1820, 2145hrs
From 19th June additionally:-
Tues, Thurs,  0700hrs
  Sat & Sun
One-way fare: 7680drs; duration 50mins.

**Corfu to Cephalonia**
Tues & Sun  1110hrs
*Return*
Tues & Sun  1355hrs
One-way fare: 5100drs; duration 50mins.

**Corfu to Zakynthos**
Tues & Sun  1110hrs
*Return*
Tues & Sun  1255hrs
One-way fare: 6650drs; duration 1hr 25mins

**AIRPORT** The taxi fare is a steep 1000drs. As there are no buses, the other choice is 'shanks pony' – and it is only some 20-30 minutes from the centre of Corfu Town.
The football field sized piles of unclaimed lost baggage, that once lined the runway, have been replaced by unsightly heaps of rubbish. I wonder where the luggage has gone?

**BANKS** There are at least four or five major banks. Probably the most convenient are the **National Bank of Greece** (*Tmr* 16F2/3), to one side, and the **Commercial Bank** (*Tmr* 16F3), on the other side of Odhos Evangelistrias Voulgareos. This is where the street divides around an old church bell tower in the middle of the road. Incidentally, the tower is all that remains of a 14th century Catholic church destroyed by World War II combat. The church was the repository for various commemorative items in respect of the Venetian victory over the Turkish navy, in 1571, at the Battle of Lepanto. During the summer season, in addition to the usual banking hours, the National Bank opens weekday evenings, between 1730-1900hrs.
Another useful Bank (*Tmr* 16G2), which cashes Eurocheques, is situated on Kapodistriou St, close by the junction with Spiridonos St. The **Bank of Crete** and the **Ionian Bank** have branches on the north side of Plateia San Rocco, and **Barclays Bank** (*Tmr* 16E4), is located diagonally across the same square. There are a couple of banks on nearby Odhos Alexandras.

**BEACHES** Corfu Town does not have any beaches, just three lidos.

**Lido 1** (*Tmr* 18H1/2): Situated to the south of the small headland overlooked by the north side of the Old Fort and its little yacht harbour. Where Arseniou Parade joins Kapodistriou St, there is a sharply downwards inclined, short, metalled path, leading to a blockhouse of some description. At the bottom, turning left through the arch (or St Nicholas' Gateway) gives access to a small open area. To the left is a 'terrace' of buildings including, end-ways on to the sea, a fish-packing factory, or similar, then a ruined church or chapel, the landward end of which has been converted into an extremely expensive Chinese restaurant (*See* **Mr Chans** (*Tmr* 18H1/2) **The Eating Out**). On the right is a rather shabby, tree sheltered lido. There is no beach, simply access to a buoyed-off area of sea by way of a set of steps. The sea-bed is hard sand, and fairly clean. There are changing rooms, open-air showers, toilets and sunbathing beds, in an area bounded by a crumbling, low-columned parapet. A small cafe sells drinks and a limited range of food. Admission costs 40drs.

The central part of the area is free, with its own steps into the sea. The latter recall the fact that this was the site of the Venetian landing steps. They gave access to the town via one of the four original gateways, St Nicholas, through which the lido path still 'ducks'. The aforementioned church also dates back to the Venetians.

**Lido 2** (*Tmr* H10) **Plage Mon Repos:** This is situated around the corner of the far southern headland of the Bay of Garitsa. Despite the imposing encircling wall, the rows of tree shaded changing huts and the large play area, the 80m or so of wide, gritty sand is disappointing and kelp covered. The gently shelving sea-bed is weed covered, rather slimy and rocky in places. A high, rickety, wooden pier juts out into the sea from which it is possible to swim. There are showers and the gate is administered by a rather off-beat gentleman. Admission costs 50drs.

**Lido 3**: Located at the foot of the cliff, on the top of which is the *Hilton Hotel*, at the far end of the Kanoni Peninsula. The main, one-way road forks at about sea-level. Close by are *Rooms*, the *Hotel Salvos* (Class C, tel 32001), scooter hire, and *Jimmy's 'Bar –'* 'Garden Pub, music bar, exotic cocktails and snacks, open between 0700-0300hrs' (despite which, out of the height of season, it closes midday). Drinks advertised amongst the plethora of other exotica include 'Planders Punch' & 'Harvey Wallbarger' (*sic*). The right-hand, sea-level lane, with the quagmire created by the airport runway away to the right, runs out alongside the causeway that bridges the sea-end of Halikopoulou swamp – sorry, Lake. Straight ahead, just offshore, are the tiny, beautiful twin islets of Vlachernon Monastery and Mouse, probably the single most photographed scenic view in all of Greece, let alone Corfu. The closest islet supports Vlachernon Monastery, the campanile of which dates back to the 17th century. This is not really an island, as a narrow causeway connects the peninsula to the rock edged, concrete platform. The further islet, Mouse or Pontikonisi, is a little larger, with a pretty clump of trees almost obscuring the 12th century chapel. To the left, (*Fsw*) at the base of the cliffs, is a beach bar and rough surfaced car park. There is a tiny triangle of shingle and coarse sand alongside the causeway to the monastery, but unfortunately it is piled high with kelp. Boats can be hired. Around the corner, it is possible to clamber over the rocks to a lido concrete quay on which are plonked down some conical, thatched sun shelters and rows of sun-beds. The 'beach' is man-made but is quite pleasant, the water clean and there is a kiosk bar selling a selection of hot snacks and ice-cream at quite reasonable prices, reasonable considering it is run by the *Hilton Hotel*.

Back at the junction the left fork climbs steeply to the environs of the *Royal Hotel*. This hotel has a cafe-bar with an extensive patio terrace. Steps from beside the cafe-bar tumble down to sea-level. People flock to the Royal Hotel patio to look out over the panorama, which takes in such disparate sights as the lovely sea view and the dirty, messy, swampy outset of Corfu airport runway. Incidentally, many, many visitors simply come to watch the, admittedly dramatic, arrival and departure of the passenger aircraft. This occurs about every 10 minutes. When all this activity proves too tiring it is possible to catch a bus back to Corfu Town from alongside the *Hotel Royal See* **Buses, A To Z**.

A few metres further on along the anticlockwise, one-way system, and also headland topping is the *Hilton Hotel*.

There is a turning off this ring road to the region of Kanoni known as Analipsis which takes in the Royal Palace of Mon Repos (*See* **Places of Interest, A To Z**). The side road comes to an end at a series of no entry gateways and an unsurfaced, 'frying pan' of a turn-round. This pleasant, wooded, eastern side of the headland looks out over the sea, way below. There are some smart houses here and the *Top of the Hill Restaurant*.

To complete the journey round the peninsula, the road descends to the east side of Kanoni, past various, snackbars, mini-markets and hotels of varying degrees of plushness. In the main, tree covered

Kanoni is a strange mix of doo-hickey farming, fashionable apartments, unfashionable apartments and hotels. Unhappily the smell of lavatories even lingers out here.

**BICYCLE, SCOOTER & CAR HIRE** There are numerous establishments hiring all three modes of transport. They are, in the main, grouped around the New and Old Ports, the Esplanade between them, Xenofontos Stragigou and the streets of Ioan Theotoki, the Plateia San Rocco end of Leoforos Alexandras, as well as Arseniou. Prospective hirers should shop around, ensuring that they are seen to be doing just that by the various proprietors. It is possible to achieve a reduction off the 'opening price', especially in out of the height of season months, particularly once an operator has observed a visit to one of his competitors!

Out of the plethora of businesses I can do no better than highlight one or two musings and some hard facts. In respect of scooters, I rather favour **Getaway Bike Rental Co.** (*Tmr* 36B2 – tel 41231) c/o *The Europa Hotel*. If for no other reason, the owner, George, is tucked out of the way and is an affable chap who speaks excellent English. Other firms that may grab your attention in this area, if only for their individual names, include 'Scooters For The Lazy Bones', and 'Rent a Scooter Jamaica'.

There are rather less car hire firms, than scooter operators, but quite enough to choose from including:- **Hertz**, close to the Customs office (*Tmr* 54D1), **Avis**, adjacent to the *Hotel Ionian* (*Tmr* 34C1/2), yet another **Avis**, alongside an Agricultural Bank, on the left (*San Rocco Sq behind one*) of Leoforos Alexandras and an **Olympus Rent A Car**, almost opposite the *Hotel Bretagne* (*Tmr* 43D/E8/9), on the road from the Airport to Corfu Town. One car hire firm I would avoid is the **Budget Rent A Car** office at the New Port end of Odhos Ioan Theotoki. Not so much the firm, as the individual who is in charge. Apart from displaying Grecociliouness and some vanity, I watched from a nearby Cafe-bar (*Tmr* 50B/C2) as he balled out some British lads whose motor caravan had broken down close to his shop front. Admittedly it was causing some inconvenience to the orderly flow of the larger lorries but the bellowed tirade of invective was totally out of order! To make matters worse and further massage my prejudice, observing me staring at him during this diatribe, he proceeded to give me an earful, in excellent English. Most embarrassing.

Corfu Town is an expensive location from which to hire a scooter, with an average one day charge of 2000drs and a three day rate of 5000drs. Ouch! Incidentally, light fingered tourists have resulted in most scooters being supplied with cable locks. Car hire averages about 6000-8000drs for three days, depending on the model, and do not forget the disproportionate deposit requested.

**BOOKSELLERS** Being a large and cosmopolitan town, there are a number of booksellers with an 'international' flavour including a Book (& stationery) shop close to the National Bank (*Tmr* 16F2/3) and a periptero stocking foreign language newspapers in front of the San Rocco Sq supermarket (*Tmr* 53E3/4). At the outset and on the right of Odhos Nikoforous Theotoki (*From The Liston end – Tmr* 7G2) is located an overseas language newspaper shop.

The real bonus is the existence of an English bookshop, the:-

**Corfu Compendium** (*Tmr* 55G3/4) 40 Guilford St                    Tel 41512
*Directions*: The most delightful route to take is to turn left (*The Liston behind one*) off Odhos Voulgareos, along a narrow street that almost immediately widens out onto the very neat, airy, large, sloping 'Town Hall Square'. On the left is the Roman Catholic Cathedral. Odhos Guilford branches off from the far, left-hand corner, paralleling Odhos Kapodistrou. Interestingly, the street is named after the eccentric Lord Frederick North, the fifth Earl of Guilford (1769-1828), who some said was singular, to the point of madness. He founded Corfu University in 1823 (unfortunately closed by 1864) and was regarded as an integrated member of the island community. The bookshop is on the right, almost directly behind the Olympic office (*Tmr* 15G3/4).

An excellent choice of English books as well as an antiquarian section and some French, German, Italian and Greek titles. As elsewhere in Greece, books are expensive but savings can be made by making use of their second-hand book exchange. The shop's hours are the old-fashioned opening times. The owner, Pippa Hughes, is the Honorary British Consul.

One other very interesting, old-fashioned bookshop, if only stocking Greek language books, is on the left of a cul-de-sac along The Liston side of the *Hotel Kriti* (*Tmr* 6F2). Incidentally, this dead-end alley terminates in front of a pleasing, tall building with lovely windows, to the left of which is sited the unattractive *Cafe Bar Yannis*. That is unattractive to all except those potential clients who enjoy tabletop video games and the presence of staff whom have the look and 'weight' of bouncers. The cafe displays a sign " Telephone for long distance telephone calls" – a metered, international telephone.

There is even a book, '*The Rogue's Guide To Corfu*', written by, and about, long-standing overseas expatriates, published on the island. Lastly, but not least, is the most useful and informative monthly newspaper for English speaking visitors. This is the free issue **Corfu News** available from the NTOG office (*Tmr* 20G/H1/2). The proprietors, Mary-Jane Carreyette and Howard Wells, include topical articles as well as a plethora of extremely useful information in respect of bus and ferry-boat travel, places of entertainment, eating establishments, museums, lists of dentists, doctors and chemists, as well as names and addresses of the various sports clubs. It is more than worthwhile winkling out a copy.

**BREAD SHOPS** A Baker (*Tmr* 56E3/4) is situated at the junction of Odhos Markora and San Rocco Sq. In this area there is also an excellent outfit (*Tmr* 56D/E4) on the left (*San Rocco Sq behind one*) of Dimoulitsa St. It is down some steps and on the right. Off to the right (*Facing The Liston*) of Georgiou Theotoki St is a Baker (*Tmr* 56F3), on the right. One 'lurks' in Michael Theotoki St, close by the street market (*Tmr* 22F/G2/3) (Theotoki is a most common and confusing street name, there must be a dozen or so). Yet another Baker is located in Odhos Philarmonikis, at the corner with Odhos Ag Spiridonos. Mention of this latter street reminds me that it 'hosts' a very old, lovely but bedraggled church with a splendid bell tower topped off by a cracked, red coloured cupola (*See* **The Church of St Spiridon, Cathedrals & Churches, Places of Interest, A To Z**). From 'Best Top Sq' (*Tmr* 9F/G1/2), the narrow alley Ag Theoloras branches off to the left (*Cathedral behind one*), a few metres along which, on the left, is a small Baker.

From the Old Port (*Tmr* F1), a line of shops edges the Esplanade, Akti Zavitsianou, one of which is a Baker (*Tmr* 56E1), who also sells pies. From the New Port (*Tmr* B/C1) it is necessary to stride along Xenofontos Stratigou on the right of which, in the Mandouki, are two Bakers (*Tmr* 56B2 & 56A/B2).

Alongside the 'Airport' road is a Baker, on the right, just before an excellent supermarket (*See* **Commercial Shopping Area, A To Z**), and yet another on the road into Corfu Town, on the right of Odhos Anapafseos.

**BUSES** Three bus terminals accommodate the island's buses.

### Bus timetables (Height of season)
**Corfu Town to Athens***
Daily          0900, 0930, 1800, 1830hrs
*Return journey*
Daily          0700, 1930, 2000, 2030hrs
One-way fare 2565drs ( +ferry fares)
*100 Kifissou St,Tel 5129443

### From (Esplanade) Cricket Sq (*Tmr* 21H2/3)
**Corfu Town to Mandouki & Kanoni** (Suburbs of Corfu Town)
Bus No.2 Daily  From 0700hrs every ½ hr until 2245hrs
Sun & Holidays From 0700 to 2245hrs
*Return journey* 30mins later.

**Corfu Town to Vassilli**
No.3 Daily          From 0730hrs every ½ hr until 2100hrs
Sun & holidays From 0930-2100hrs.
*Return journey* 30mins later.

### From San Rocco Square (*Tmr* 21E3/4)
**(Plateia G Theotoki - close by the Bank of Crete.)**
**Blue Buses**
**Corfu town to Potamos, Evropouli, Tebloni** (NW of Corfu Town).
No.4 Daily          0545, 0700, 0900, 1030, 1130, 1300, 1350, 1430, 1630,
                    1800, 2000, 2130hrs.
Sun & holidays 0900, 1000, 1200, 1700, 2100hrs.
*Return journey* 45mins later, Evropouli 30mins later.

**Corfu Town to Kastellani & Kouramades** (NSW of Corfu Town).
No.5 Daily          0615, 0700, 0800, 0900, 1100, 1300, 1450, 1600, 1800,
                    1900, 2100, 2200hrs.
Sun & holidays 0700, 1100, 1300, 1515, 1600, 1900, 2100hrs
*Return journey* 25mins later.

**Corfu Town to Perama & Benitses** (S of Corfu Town)
No.6 Daily        0700-2230hrs, every 30mins
Sun & holidays 0700-2200hrs, every 60mins
*Return journey* 30mins later.

**Corfu Town to Kontokali & Dassia** (NWN of Corfu Town)
No.7 Daily        From 0700-2230hrs, every 30mins
*Return journey* 30mins later.

**Corfu Town to Achilleion & Gastouri** (S of Corfu Town)
No.10 Daily        0700, 1000, 1200, 1415, 1700, 2000hrs
*Return journey* 20mins later.

**Corfu Town to Pelekas** (W of Corfu Town)
No.11 Daily        1000, 1200, 1415, 1600, 1700, 1800, 2000hrs
Sun & holidays 1000, 1200, 1700, 2100, 2200hrs
*Return journey* 30mins later.

**Corfu Town to Ag Ioannis, Afra** (W of Corfu Town)
No.8 Daily        0600, 0700, 0800, 0920, 1000, 1200, 1300, 1415, 1600,
                  2030, 2200hrs
Sun & holidays 0730, 1000, 1200, 1515, 1700, 1900, 2100hrs
*Return journey*
Daily        0720, 0830, 0930, 1030, 1230, 1330, 1445, 1540,1630,
             1830, 2230hrs
Sun & holidays 0800, 1030, 1230, 1535, 1730, 1920, 2130hrs

## From the New Fortress, Old Port (*Tmr* 21E2)
**Corfu Town to Kavos** (S of the island)
Daily        0500, 0630, 0900, 0930, 1030, 1130, 1230, 1330, 1500,
             1530, 1600, 1815, 1930hrs
Sun & holidays 0500, 0915, 0930, 1030, 1530, 1600, 1930hrs
*Return journey*
Daily        0615, 0800, 1045, 1115, 1215, 1345, 1400, 1530, 1645,
             1715, 1730, 1945, 2100hrs
Sun & holidays 0615, 1115, 1600, 1745, 2100hrs

**Corfu Town to Messonghi** (SE Coast)
Daily        0830, 0930, 1030, 1230, 1700, 1800, 1930hrs
Sun & holidays 0930, 1100, 1300, 1600, 1800, 1930hrs
*Return journey*
Daily        0730, 0915, 1015, 1115, 1330, 1615, 1745, 1845, 2015hrs
Sun & holidays 1015, 1200, 1345, 1645, 1845, 2000hrs

**Corfu Town to Ag Georgios & Argirades** (SW of Corfu)
Daily        0845, 1000, 1230, 1700, 1800, 1930hrs
Sun & holidays 0930, 1600, 1930hrs
*Return journey* (from Ag Georgios)
Daily        0945, 1100, 1330, 1800, 1900, 2030hrs
Sun & holidays 1030, 1800, 2030hrs

**Corfu Town to Ag Georgios & Sinarades** (W coast of Corfu)
Daily        0600, 0800, 0915, 1045, 1300, 1430, 1600, 1730, 2000hrs
Sun & holidays 0900, 1030, 1600, 1730hrs
*Return journey* (from Ag Georgios)
Daily        0630, 0830, 1000, 1130, 1345, 1515, 1645, 1815, 2045hrs
Sun & holidays 0945, 1115, 1645, 1815hrs.

**Corfu Town to Sidari & Cape Ag Stephanos** (NW coast of Corfu)
Daily        0530, 0900, 1100, 1300, 1530, 1930hrs
Sun & holidays 0930, 1600hrs
*Return journey*
Daily        0700, 1045, 1215, 1445, 1700, 2100hrs
Sun & holidays 1700, 1715hrs

**Corfu Town to Ag Georgios & Pagi** (WNW coast of Corfu)
Daily              0630, 1000, 1330hrs
*Return journey*
Daily              0730, 1130, 1500hrs

**Corfu Town to Karousades & Astrakeri** (N coast of Corfu)
Daily              0600, 0900, 1400hrs
Sun & holidays 0930hrs
*Return journey*
Daily              0700, 1030, 1530hrs
Sun & holidays 1700hrs

**Corfu Town to Afionas & Cape Arilla** (NW coast of Corfu)
Daily              0530, 1400hrs
*Return journey*
Daily              0645, 1530hrs

**Corfu Town to Kassiopi** (NE coast of Corfu)
Daily              0545, 0730, 0900, 1000, 1100, 1200, 1430, 1615, 1815hrs
Sun & holidays 0930, 1030, 1400, 1630hrs
*Return journey*
Daily              0700, 0830, 1030, 1100, 1200, 1315, 1600, 1730, 1930hrs
Sun & holidays 1200, 1500, 1730hrs

**Corfu Town to Roda & Aharavi** (N coast of Corfu)
Daily              0530, 0900, 1030, 1330, 1600, 1815hrs
Sun & holidays 0900hrs
*Return journey*
Daily              0645, 1015, 1145, 1515, 1715, 1915hrs
Sun & holidays 1730hrs

**Corfu Town to Vatos** (W coast of Corfu)
Daily              0700, 0900, 1430, 2000hrs
Sun & holidays 0900, 1900hrs
*Return journey*
Daily              0745, 0930, 1500, 2020hrs
Sun & holidays 0930, 1930hrs

**Corfu Town to Glifada** (W coast of Corfu)
Daily              0700, 0900, 1000, 1030, 1100, 1130, 1200, 1230,
                   1300, 1430, 1530, 1600, 1730, 1900, 2000hrs
Sun & holidays 0900, 0930, 1030, 1100, 1130, 1200, 1300, 1430,
                   1530, 1600, 1730, 1900hrs
*Return journey*
Daily              0730, 0945, 1045, 1115, 1145, 1215, 1245, 1315,
                   1345, 1550, 1615, 1645, 1815, 1945, 2045hrs
Sun & holidays 0945, 1015, 1115, 1145, 1215, 1245, 1345, 1515,
                   1615, 1645, 1815, 1915hrs

**Corfu Town to Ipsos, Pyrgi & Barbati** (NE coast of Corfu)
Daily              0715, 0900, 0930, 1030, 1130, 1200, 1300, 1400,
                   1500, 1700, 1815, 1900, 2100, 2200hrs
Sun & holidays 0830, 0930, 1030, 1130, 1200, 1300, 1400, 1500,
                   1700, 1900, 2100, 2200hrs
*Return journey*
Daily              0745, 0930, 1015, 1115, 1215, 1230, 1330, 1430,
                   1545, 1745, 1930, 2030, 2130, 2230hrs
Sun & holidays 0900, 1000, 1200, 1230, 1330, 1430, 1530, 1730,
                   1930, 2130, 2230hrs

**Corfu Town to Paleokastritsa** (NW coast of Corfu)
Daily              0830, 0900, 0930, 1000, 1030, 1100, 1130, 1200, 1230,
                   1300, 1430, 1530, 1600, 1700, 1730, 1800, 1900hrs
Sun & holidays 0900, 1000, 1030, 1100, 1130, 1200, 1300, 1430, 1530,
                   1600, 1700, 1730, 1800, 1900hrs

*Return journey*
Daily          0915, 0945, 1015, 1045, 1115, 1145, 1215, 1245, 1315,
               1345, 1515, 1615, 1645, 1745, 1815, 1845, 1945hrs
Sun & holidays 0945, 1045, 1115, 1145, 1215, 1245, 1345, 1515,
               1615, 1645, 1745, 1815, 1845, 1945hrs

**CAMPING** *See* **The Accommodation**.

**CINEMA** (*Tmr* 22F3) At least one, the **Pallas**, on the left (*San Rocco Sq behind one*) of Georgiou Theotoki St. Usually shows English, American, Germans or French films, with Greek subtitles.

**COMMERCIAL SHOPPING AREA** The layout of Corfu Town is rather confusing till certain major streets are absorbed into the geographical part of the memory. Plateia San Rocco (or Geo Theotoki) (*Tmr* E4) is a worthwhile starting point. The square is bordered by shops which include a large, well stocked Supermarket (*Tmr* 53E3/4), alongside the Bank of Crete. There is an excellent cheese counter at the far rear of this store. A little further along (*Towards the Port end of the square*) is a Butcher beyond which is a Drink shop selling bulk supplies. From the south-east side of Plateia San Rocco, the main street, Georgiou Theotoki, runs north-east and is edged by a number of large department type stores. The second turning to the left off Georgiou Theotoki is Ag Sofias. This ascends to the elongated 'Fire Station Sq', whereon is located the 'Cabbage Market' (*Tmr* 22E/F3), a large, unsophisticated, 'tin roof' street market. Where trees trunks interfere with the run of the corrugated lean-to roofs, the stallholders simply cut the tin to shape. On sale are, fish, fruit and vegetables.
   Georgiou Theotoki St runs into Odhos Evangelistrias Voulgareos. Selecting the left-hand fork, beyond the National Bank (*Tmr* 16F/G2/3), bears onto a small square, Plateia Vraklia Oti, with colonnaded shops on the left. The buildings tower skywards, overshadowing the very narrow market side-streets of Ag Vassiliou/Fish Lane and Michael Theotoki (*Tmr* 22F/G2/3). I write narrow, but every so often a vehicle will, improbably, squeeze its way out of one of the narrow alleyways, reminding me irresistibly of a released champagne cork. Both these lanes are cluttered with vegetable, fruit, fish and meat shops, as well as the occasional, most welcome, snack and pie counter.
   At the bottom of Odhos Michael Theotoki, across Nikif Theotoki St, is Odhos Philarmonikis, once packed with old-fashioned stores but now increasingly being taken over by souvenir and gift shops. One or two businesses are still *in situ* including a butcher, a coffee shop and a small general store selling some fruit and vegetables. At the end of the constantly climbing Philarmonikis St, beyond the Odhos Ag Spiridon turning, a few steps climb to the narrow entrance to Filelinon Lane, which curves off to the left. The junction of the two aforementioned streets and the steeply stepped Odhos Sof Dousmani is bordered by an informal display of fruit and vegetables 'boxed' up the steps. On the right of Sof Dousmani is a cobbler & leather shop. Both the lanes of Ag Spiridon and Filelinon are lined by gift and souvenir shops. The narrow, claustrophobic Filelinon is the busier. also housing tape and record stores, clothes, boutiques and fur shops. Where Filelinon spills onto 'Best Top Sq', the narrow alley Ag Theoloras, to the right, 'boasts' a small cigarette shop.
   Probably the smartest, most expensive street is the paved Odhos Voulgareos which stretches from The Liston (*Tmr* 7G2) to the junction with Georgiou Theotoki. It is lined with 'awfully' smart, gold, jewellery and fur shops. Yes, well.
   The most consistently busy area must be the waterfront that stretches between the Old and New Ports. At the Old Port end, there is Spiros Cava Off Licence, on the nearside of the *Hotel New York* (*Tmr* 3F1), but the most active section is from the outset of Akti Zavitsianou proceeding towards the New Port. The single storey, rather ugly row of shops that border the quayside road include a restaurant, drinks, souvenirs, fruit, a baker, a store, scooter hire, souvenir & gifts, an ironmonger, a yacht chandler, bulk feta cheese, another chandler, marine engine repairs, yet another chandler, scooter hire, a further chandler, a travel office, scooter hire and, at the apex, a smart, expensive restaurant, across the road from which is its pretty, awning covered patio. The Esplanade now angles back past a travel office, car hire, scooter hire, a petrol station and the Customs office (*Tmr* 54D1). Beyond the latter, the thoroughfare becomes rather dusty.
   A wide street branches off to a junction with the main, New Port road of Ioan Theotoki, in the angle of which is a largish, quite well organised and reasonably priced Co-operative Supermarket (*Tmr* 57C/D2). Turning right descends to the waterfront along Ioan Theotoki. This busy road is edged by a row of two storey buildings in which are located a snackbar, travel office and outboard and scooter sales, all on the left, whilst on the other side of the road is a scooter hire and 'Luggage Storage Deposit'. Back on the left of the street are several more scooter hire businesses, a private house with

accommodation (*Tmr* 39B/C2), scooter & car hire, a snackbar (*Tmr* 50B/C2), a yacht cruise office, a souvenir/gift shop, a bank, bar and more souvenirs. At the junction with the Esplanade, to the left (*Fsw*) the original street, Xenofontos Stratigiou, winds through the Mandouki Old Quarter. Herein a Fruit & Vegetable Store/Mini-Market (*Tmr* 58B2), followed by a Butcher (*Tmr* 59A2) and a store.

The other commercial area of shops, stalls and even a hardware shop is around the New Fortress Bus Square St (*Tmr* 21E2).

For those with transport, the best and cheapest Supermarket is beyond the Airport access carriageway, on the right of the Benitses road, about 1½km out of town. This has an enormous range of inexpensively priced food.

**DISCOS** One publication advises that 'Discos abound'! I'm sure they do, although most are in the northern 'suburbs', between lkm and 3km distant.

**ELPA** The 'Greek A.A.' maintain (oh dear) a caravan on the side of the road (*Tmr* F1) that divides the park-like George II Sq, the Old Port.

## EMBASSIES, CONSULATES & VICE CONSULS

| | |
|---|---|
| Belgium | Tel 33788 |
| Denmark | Tel 39481 |
| France | Tel 30067 |
| Germany, West | Tel 31755 |
| Holland | Tel 39900 |
| Italy | Tel 37351 |
| Norway | Tel 32423 |
| Spain | Tel 39620 |
| Sweden | Tel 29469 |
| United Kingdom 2 Alexandras Ave, | Tel 30055 |

## FERRY-BOATS

**Old Port** (*Tmr* F1) Only Igoumenitsa(M) and Paxos ferry-boats dock here. The Igoumenitsa 'landing craft' fill most of the waterfront with the Paxos bound **FB Kamelia** tucked away on the far right (*Fsw*). Note that Patras(M) ferries, which call in at Cephalonia and Ithaca, berth at the New Port, (*Tmr* B/C1).

Much of the unfathomable, inscrutability attributable to the Greek ferry-boat system is nowhere better illustrated than by those that ply the Ionian Sea, so please bear in mind all the strictures listed in Chapter Three.

It is marvellous to report that the **FB Kamelia** (despite reports of its untimely demise, to invoke Mark Twain) still ploughs a furrow (to mix my metaphors) to and from Paxos island.

### Local Ferry-boat timetable (Mid season)

| Day | Departure time | Ferry-boat | Ports/Islands of Call |
|---|---|---|---|
| Daily | 0845hrs | Theologos | Gaios(Paxos) via Igoumenitsa(M). |
| Mon | 1630hrs | Kamelia | Lakka(Paxos),Logos(Paxos),Gaios(Paxos). |
| Mon & Tues | 1700hrs | Anna Maria | Gaios(Paxos). |
| Tues,Thurs & Fri | 1430hrs | Kamelia | Gaios(Paxos). |
| Wed & Sat | 1400hrs | Kamelia | Lakka(Paxos),Gaios(Paxos). |
| Fri | 1500hrs | Anna Maria | Gaios(Paxos). |
| Sun | 1300hrs | Anna Maria | Gaios(Paxos). |
| | 2000hrs | Anna Maria | Gaios(Paxos). |

One-way fare 550drs; duration 3hrs +(depending on number of Port calls).
*See* **Places of Interest, A To Z & Sidari (Route Two)** for day-trip caique excursions to the offshore islets of Othoni, Erikoussa and Mathraki.

**New Port, Xenofontos Stratigou** (*Tmr* B/C1) Both the Ionian inter-island and international ferries dock here. To check if any of the latter craft also call in at any other islands *See* **Chapter Two**. But note that travellers may not be able to disembark from international ferries at will. Some shipping lines do not allow stopover or a break in the journey, despite the fact that they make a port call, whilst others will only allow it if the ticket is purchased with this in mind.

Typical of the international ferries that make 'domestic' calls are the **CF Ionian Star** and **CF Ionian Glory**, of Strintzis Lines, *en route* from Patras(M) to Brindisi (Italy), which take in Sami (Cephalonia), Igoumenitsa(M) and Corfu.

**Inter-island Ferry-boat timetable** (Mid-season)

| Day | Departure time | Ferry-boat | Ports/Islands of Call |
|-----|------|------|------|
| Daily | 0645hrs | Ionis/Ionian Glory | Igoumenitsa(M),Gaios(Paxos),Vathi(Ithaca), Sami(Cephalonia),Patras(M). |

One-way fare: Corfu to Patras 1862drs; duration 10½ hrs.

**FERRY-BOAT TICKET OFFICES** A number of ferry-boat ticket agencies are located at the right-hand side of the Old Port (*Fsw*), in the wall created by Donzelot Parade as it sweeps up the hillside (rather similar to walled-in railway arches). Do not forget that each office usually only deals with one particular ferry company, will not advise in respect of competitors' sailings AND remember to ask more than once! A short flight of steps climbs from the Old Port quay to Odhos Donzelot.

One particular agency I can unequivocally recommend is:-

**Nicos Bonelos & Son** (*Tmr* 60F1) No 4 Old Port — Tel 39778

*Directions*: At the foot of the sweep of Arseniou Parade.

Mr Nicos is the charming, personable, extremely helpful owner who speaks impeccable English, as well as a number of other languages. He also accepts payment by Eurocheque, which can save the 'drachmae drain'.

As a last resort, tickets for the international ferries can be purchased at the time of travel, from the kiosks inside the New Port terminal building BUT there is invariably a crush of people. It is rather less bruising to obtain tickets in advance. For those travellers 'going foreign', do not forget that to the cost of the tickets must be added the price of the boarding pass/port dues, which may cost about 800drs per head.

**HAIRDRESSERS** Sufficient unto the day thereof..., including a Ladies Hairdresser on the right (*Facing north*) of San Rocco Sq, between Georgiou Theotoki and Markora Sts.

**HORSE DRAWN CARRIAGES** *See* **Monipo**.

**LAUNDRY** The Hotels *Europa* and *Cyprus* operate a laundry service (*See* **The Accommodation**). But the best option in town is the:-

**Launderette** (*Tmr* 52D/E3) Ioan Theotoki St.

*Directions*: From San Rocco Sq, proceed along Ioan Theotoki St towards the New Port. The launderette is on the left, beyond the first side-street to the left and next door to *Loukas Snackbar*.

The owner is very helpful and hard-working. A five kilo machine load costs 500drs, which includes the use of the dryer and the washing powder. Customers short of time might like to leave their washing behind. The proprietor will look after the process for an extra 150drs, which includes folding the clothes. Open seven days a week between 0900-2100hrs, but out of the height of season the shop closes at 1500hrs.

**LUGGAGE STORE** There are two at the New Port end of Ioan Theotoki. One is at the old man's **Rooms** (*Tmr* 39B/C2), on the left (*Fsw*), the other, the **Luggage Storage Deposit** is a little further towards San Rocco Sq, on the other side of the street.

**MEDICAL CARE**

**Chemists & Pharmacies** There are any number, including one Pharmacy across the street from the main OTE office (*Tmr* 26F4), in N Mantzarou St, and another on San Rocco Sq. They operate a rota system outside normal hours and each shop displays advice as to which Chemist is open.

**Casualty Clinic** On Plateia Scaramanga, to the rear of the Commercial Bank (*Tmr* 16F3) and reached down the lane to the right, on the nearside of the bank (*San Rocco Sq behind one*).

**Dentists & Doctors** A number in the town, the addresses of which can be obtained from perusing the directory page of *Corfu News* or from the NTOG office (*Tmr* 20G/H1/2).

**Hospital** (*Tmr* 25C/D3/4) From the north end of Plateia San Rocco proceed along Odhos Polichroniou Konstanta, which runs into Ioulias Andreadi. The hospital is on the right. There is a 24hr casualty service, in addition to which English is spoken.

**MONIPO** These extremely colourful, horse-drawn, brightly painted, Victorian carriages are 'ranked' alongside George II Sq, at the Old Port. Their horses are 'decked out' with an assortment of brasses and ornaments and are quite often 'straw be-hatted', with holes cut out for their ears. The controlled charges are calculated by the hour or trip but must be checked prior to hiring.

**NTOG** (*Tmr* 20G/H1/2) The small office is presently located in the west wing of the Palace of St Michael & St George (as are the Tourist police). A much less grand set-up than the previous, palatial location and now a rather a low-key operation, with limited information available but no less helpful. For instance the lists of accommodation only detail hotels, no private rooms. The office is open Mon-Sat, inclusive, between 0700-2000hrs.

**OTE** There are two offices. The main OTE (*Tmr* 26F4) is on the left (*San Rocco Sq behind one*) of N Mantzarou St and opens seven days a week, between 0600-2400hrs. The other office (*Tmr* 26G2) is on Odhos Kapodistriou, close to the junction with Spiridonos St and opens weekdays only, between 0730-2230hrs.

**PETROL** Petrol is obtainable on Leoforos Alexandras, south of Plateia San Rocco, and there are several filling stations on Xenofontos Stratigou, in the area of the New Port.
  'Out of town' supplies are patchy. Fuel is fairly frequently available north of Corfu Town as far as Pyrgi, on the east coast, and there are also filling stations at, for instance Nisaki, close by Kassiopi, Karoussades, Ag Spiridon, Roda, Sidari, Armenades, Liapades, Vatos, Linia, Argirades, Perivolion, Potami, Kavos and Moraitika.

**PLACES OF INTEREST** The continual involvement of the island, and more especially the town, in acts of war, over the centuries, has tended to reduce the number of early remains. On the other hand, the military character of Corfu Town has resulted in some architecturally interesting buildings and forts. Possibly the most eye-catching area, probably established as a clear field of fire, is:
**The Esplanade** (*Tmr* G/H2/3) This is divided into two. The sandy Plateia, whereon are arranged the rather unexpected cricket matches, and the grassy Spianada. On the latter are sited a wrought iron bandstand, where some of the town's many bands perform, and an Ionic rotunda, a memorial to Sir Thomas Maitland, a governor of Malta and first High Commissioner of Corfu (1816-1824). It was said of Sir Thomas that he was discourteous, dirty and drunk! Unfortunately, the cricket ground outfield appears to be under pressure from car parking.

To the east of the Esplanade is the:-
**Old Fort or Citadel** (*Tmr* H2/3) Truly a magnificent sight from the sea and perhaps best viewed from the Corfu to Paxos ferry-boat. Despite the propaganda advising the edifice is being restored, the overall impression is of overgrown, neglected ruins. I consider the single, most impressive building to be the Parthenon like British Garrison Church, built in 1830 on the south side of the fortifications. It is a shame that the basic structure appears to be seriously faulted. The other, eye-catching structure is a ruined, square, Venetian clocktower, if only because the clock face hands are stopped for ever. Young bushes and saplings sprout from the arches of the building, completing the air of abandoned dilapidation.
  Entrance to the large site is free between 0800-1900hrs. There is a *Son et Lumiere* show. This is presented nightly in the fortress during the summer months, between 15th May-30th Sept, at 2145hrs. Admission costs 300drs and students 100drs. The English commentary show is on Mon, Tues, Wed, Thurs & Fri nights. The sound and light display is preceded by an exhibition of Folk Dances daily, except Sunday. These performances commence at 2100hrs. Admission to both costs a total of 350drs and students 150drs.

On the western side of the Esplanade is:-
**The Liston Building** (*Tmr* 7G2) French inspired, designed and constructed (1807-1814) with large colonnades and arcades, supposedly after the style of the Rue de Rivoli building, Paris. The builder was the father of de Lesseps, constructor of the Suez Canal. Fashionable cafes and cafe-bars line the Esplanade facing ground floor and great lamps are suspended from above the arches.

To the north of the Esplanade is the:-
**Palace of St Michael & St George** (*Tmr* 24G/H1/2) A very impressive, if solid pile, complete with triumphal arches, a flank of which is pierced by the road off the Esplanade. It was built by the British (1819-1825) as an administrative building, an official residence of the High Commissioner and the headquarters of the Order of St Michael & St George. This order was created, in 1819, to honour British civil servants who served with distinction in both Malta and the Ionian Island Union. After Independence, the Greek Royal family took over the Palace and used it as a residence until 1913, after which it fell into disrepair. The building has now been restored and a museum and public library are located within the Palace. The oriental collection of an erstwhile Greek ambassador makes a rather incongruous, if interesting, exhibition.

## Cathedrals & Churches

*The Greek Orthodox Cathedral (Tmr 27F1/2)* Approached by a flight of steps from the top end of Plateia Konstantinou, off the left-hand corner *(Sbo)* of Plateia King George II. The Cathedral, built in 1577, is the repository for the headless remains of St Theodora and at most times of the day there are constant comings and goings. Look out for the small, coloured plates over the green painted doors (No 23 & 24) of a now coffin maker's workshop, to the right of the Cathedral *(Sea still behind one)*. This was most likely a tavern during the British occupation and the signs, bearing the words 'Beer House', probably represent soldiers and regimental colours from this period.

*The Church of St Spiridon (Tmr G2)* On the left of Ag Spiridonos St *(Esplanade behind one)*. Construction of this lovely church began in 1589 and deserves a mention, if only because it houses the remains of the much revered St Spiridon, which are paraded around the town four times a year. He is credited with having saved the Corfiots from death and destruction on numerous occasions but the four processions date back to specific events. The tradition of Palm Sunday hails back to 1630, when the Saint was purported to have stopped a plague; the Easter Saturday event dates from 1574, when Spiridon delivered Corfu from famine; the 11th August celebrations herald the Saint's intervention in the Turkish siege of 1716 and the November custom relates to a famine and plague in the 17th century, both sorted out by the intercession of St Spiridon. The Saint's 'bits and pieces' are said to be minus an arm which is supposed to have finished up in Rome, some 160 years ago. Not surprisingly, Spiro is an extremely popular Christian name for Corfiot males.

*The Catholic Cathedral of St James (Tmr 61G3)* Borders the Town Hall Square and constructed in 1632, but severely damaged in 1943 by aerial bombing. Many of the men who carried out the repairs, at the end of the Second World War, are supposed to have been descendants of the Maltese workmen originally 'imported' during the British rule.

Incidentally, the Town Hall was originally built as a Venetian loggia for merchants, became a theatre and was only turned over to administrative duties in the early 1900s.

**The New Fort** *(Tmr D/E1/2)* Built about 1580 to improve the town's fortifications and the subject of late improvements by the British, immediately prior to their rather swift departure. It fell into disuse until taken over by the Greek Navy. As they are still in occupation, the Fort is not open to the public.

## Museums

*The Archaeological Museum (Tmr 62F/G5)* 5 Vraila St. Sited to the south side of the *Corfu Palace Hotel*, close to Vassileos Konstantinou, the Garitsa Bay Esplanade. It contains several unique exhibits. These include a famed Gorgon western pediment and a 7th century BC, crouching lioness associated with Menacrates Tomb, as well as a varied and interesting range of other items. Well worth a visit and open daily between 0930-1600hrs, except Tuesdays. Admission costs 200drs.

*The Solomos Museum (Tmr G1)* In a narrow lane off Arseniou Parade. Dionysios Solomos (1795-1857), a famous poet, was a native of Zakynthos but settled and died on Corfu, living in the house which has been rebuilt and is now a museum to his memory.

**The British Cemetery** *(Tmr 28E5)* Reached by turning down Odhos Dimoulitsa, from the top west corner of Plateia San Rocco. Two hundred metres or so along, on the left, is Kolokotroni St. A few more metres south on Odhos Kolokotroni, and on the left, again, is the paint covered, steel entrance door to the cemetery. The grounds contain many interesting headstones of British sailors and soldiers, who served during the British Protectorate, and members of the Armed Forces who fell during and after the two World Wars, as well as a few civilians. They are set out in a tranquil, tree-shaded, beautifully kept English garden. George Psailas is the current caretaker. He took over stewardship on his father's death, when he was 17 years old and George and his wife still live in the house at the entrance to the grounds. For his 44 years dedicated service, he was awarded the BEM, in 1988. The most evocative, poignant graves must be those commemorating the 44 British sailors of the Destroyers Saumarez and Volage. They were killed on 22nd October 1946 when Albanian mines, illegally laid in the Corfu Channel, sunk their ships.

Visitors should take mosquito cream as the vicious little..........., that swarm amongst the tombs, appear determined to increase the number of the cemeteries incumbents. There is a visitors' book and donation tray.

**Vido island** Prettily set in the sea to the north of Corfu Town and a fifteen minute 'voyage'. For a boat enquire at the Old Port. Despite the apparent tranquillity of this now Corfiot picnic location, the islet's history has been far from peaceful. Prior to the various authorities realising the potential for besiegers, it was regularly used by attacking forces as a stepping stone. The island's original fortifications were added to and strengthened until the departure of the British, who 'rubbled' the defences here, as they did those of the Old Fort. More recent use was as a prison but now Vido is a beauty spot.

**Mon Repos** To the south of Garitsa Bay, in the Anemomylos area, and still a 'royal' villa with park-like gardens. Mon Repos was built, in 1831, as the summer residence of the British High Commissioners. It became the property of the Greek Royal Family and (perhaps of particular interest to British tourists) the Duke of Edinburgh was born here. I write 'still' a royal residence as, despite the enforced exile of the ex-Greek King Constantine after the Colonel's Junta, the Palace still belongs to him.

Even more engrossing, in recent years, archaeological digs have established that the gardens of Mon Repos, which spread atop of the Hill of St Pandeleimon, probably overlays part of the site of Ancient Corcyra. At present the Kasfiki dig is being actively pursued and is bound to keep turning up interesting finds over the forthcoming years.

Whilst in the area, for details of the beautifully sited twin islets south of Kanoni peninsula (*See* **Lido 3, Beaches, A To Z**).

Various areas of the town are of interest. The association of Plateia Elenis and the Church of Ag Nikolaos with Serbia has been touched upon (*See* **Creperie Asterix, The Eating Out**).

There was a Jewish community, which thrived under the Venetian occupation and was based around Odhos Velissariou. In fact, there is still a Synagogue (*Tmr* 63E2) which serves the few Jews left. Their present-day lack of numbers starkly compares to the 5000 or so that were resident up to a fateful day, early in June 1944. The Nazis caused them to be rounded up and dispatched to various German death camps. Only a hundred or so lived to tell the tale.

The Mandouki, then a village, but now close to the New Port and through which Xenofontos Stratigou runs, was settled by mainlanders from Parga. This was in 1822 when Corfu was under British rule and Parga was about to be taken over by the Turks. The inhabitants chose Corfu and the 'Brits', rather than the infamous Pasha.

Danilia Village is described under Route Four. The offshore islands of Mathraki, Othoni and Erikoussa are detailed under Sidari, Route Two. During the height of season months, I believe I am correct in saying that a boat, the Alexandros KII, departs from Corfu Old Port, at 0630hrs, on Tuesday and Saturday, commencing the return trip, at 1230hrs, on the same day.

Apart from 'Places of Interest' there are 'Sounds of Interest' which must include:-

**The Philarmonic Societies** The first society was formed in 1840 to accompany religious processions, there now being, possibly, as many as ten or twelve bands. One street, Odhos ΘΙΛΑΡΜΟΝΚΗΣ, salutes their importance and anyone ambling down that, or the associated lanes of Ag Spiridonos and Filelinon, may well hear one or other band practising, often managing to drown out the chords of modern-day pop. This Philarmonic tradition is one shared with Lefkas Town.

**Corfu Festival** A month long, classical music festival sponsored during September and October. The events are held at the Municipal Theatre (*Tmr* 64F4).

## POLICE
**Port** More a customs and passport office at the New Port (*Tmr* B/C1), as well as an aluminium and glass hut on the Old Port quayside (*Tmr* F1).

**Tourist** (*Tmr* 20G/H1/2) The main office is in the western wing of the Palace of St Michael & St George. There is also a smart, glass sided shed signed 'Tourist Police Information' at the Old Port, but this may only flash into existence at the height of season.

**Town** (*Tmr* 31E3/4) On the left (*San Rocco Sq behind one*) of Odhos Geo Markora (or Geo Samaptzh – take your choice).

## POST OFFICE (*Tmr* 29E/F4/5) The main office, which is on the right (*San Rocco Sq behind one*) of Leoforas Alexandras, is open Mon-Fri between 0730-2000hrs.

## SPORTS FACILITIES Corfu island is very well endowed, almost awash, with sporting facilities for the energetic visitor. I consider lifting a glass briskly is usually quite enough activity...

**Cricket** Played on the Esplanade, east of The Liston (*Tmr* 7G2). For any details telephone Pipos Kondegeorgos (Tel 39469).

**Diving** *See* **Water Sports**.

**Gambling** (Is this a sport?) *See* **Achilleion Palace** (Tel 56210), Route Five.

**Golf** *See* **Corfu Golf Club** (Tel 94220), Vatos, Route Three. There is also a course nearby Ipsos (*See* **Route One**).

**Horse Riding** *See* **Alikes** Route One and **Vatos**, Route Three.

**Recreation Centre** (*Tmr* D/E4/5) Roi Mat, 6 Metropolitan Methodiou (Tel 37068). Chess, back-gammon, music, pool and snacks.

**Squash** *See* **Korkyra Beach Hotel** (Tel 30770), **Gouvia**, Route One.

**Stadium** (*Tmr* D9) Beside the Airport road from Garitsa Bay.

**Tennis. The Corfu Tennis Club** (*Tmr* F5), Ioannou Romanou St has four courts, a bar and changing rooms. Various of the smarter hotels throughout the island possess a tennis court or two.

**Ten Pin Bowling** *See* **Hilton Hotel** (Tel 36540), **Lido 3**, **Beaches, A To Z**.

**Water Sports** Take your choice of the more popular seaside resorts. For Diving *See* **Paleokastritsa & Ermones Beach**, Route Three.

**TAXIS** Various ranks including those on Plateia George II (*Tmr* E/F1/2), Plateia San Rocco (Geo Theotoki) (*Tmr* E4) and the New Port (*Tmr* B/C1). *See* **Monipos, A To Z**.

**TELEPHONE NUMBERS & ADDRESSES**

| | |
|---|---|
| British Consulate, 11 Leoforos Alexandras St | Tel 30055 |
| Harbour Master, The Old Port | Tel 32655 |
| Hospital (*Tmr* 25C/D3/4), Ioulias Andreadi St (off Plateia San Rocco) | Tel 30562 |
| NTOG (*Tmr* 20G/H1/2), Palace of St Michael & St George | Tel 39730 |
| Police, tourist (*Tmr* 20G/H1/2), Palace of St Michael & St George | Tel 30298 |

**TOILETS** Public WCs are comparatively rare on the Ionian islands, thus worthy of note. There are clean, but smelly underground amenities (*Tmr* 32E3/4), at the north-west end of Plateia San Rocco, some underground toilets (*Tmr* 32G3), across the road from the Olympic office and an above ground facility (*Tmr* 32E1), at the west end of the Old Port. This latter is watched over by a middle aged couple who set up their table and chairs to entertain friends. Lidos 1 and 2 have toilets (and showers) (*See* **Beaches, A To Z**).

**TRAVEL AGENTS & TOUR OFFICES** Apart from the ferry-boat ticket offices jammed together at the Old Port, there are any number of agencies strung out along Arseniou, Kapodistriou and Xenofontos Stratigou Sts.

One of the better organised firms is:-
**Charitos Travel** (*Tmr* G1) 35 Arseniou Parade                                    Tel 44611
*Directions*: From the Old Port ascend Donzelot Parade and continue round the headland.
   Excursions, tours, daily cruises, boat trips on the **MS Romantica**, as well as car and scooter hire.

One other office that catches the eye is:-
**Greek Sky**, across a narrow side-street from the Olympic office (*Tmr* 15G3/4). Worth a mention if only because they act for *American Express*.

# ROUTE ONE
## To Karoussades via Kontokali, Ipsos, Kassiopi & Roda (41km)North of Corfu

Town (well, north-west due to the curve of the bay), the main road from the New Port hugs the coastline and can be followed all the way round the outline of the island, as far as the seaside village of Roda.

   Once past the New Port, the immediate surrounds are appalling, a jumble of mangled wrecks and disused building sites. The route passes by a boatyard, a boat wreckers yard, and in amongst this nightmare, a bit of sandy beach. This is close to a gypsy encampment, with all that one of those entails. The *Hotels Zorba* and *Salina* are based in this 'delightful setting'. Once over a summer full river, the large *Kerkyra Golf Hotel* and a (horse) riding school are to the right, set down in an absolute wasteland. To the left is much industrial enterprise and, to the right, the *Hotel Sunset*, followed by a petrol station. Incidentally, filling stations are so plentiful on this stretch that each and everyone will not be detailed. To add to the scenic delights there is a petrol refinery.

   The Gulf of Kerkira is a lovely bay, but the road out past **Alikes**, as far as Kontokali, has experienced rather cheap, ramshackle and tatty semi-industrial building, as well as 'rapid-rise' hotel development. The traffic is comparatively heavy as far as Tsavros, a major road junction beyond Gouvia. I feel very sorry for those package holiday-makers on this stretch, especially where the hotel is the opposite side of the highway to the water's edge. Not only is there traffic noise to contend with, but the job of crossing the road is quite enlivening (or not, if you see what I mean). In addition the sea-shore is both muddy and reedy.

Beyond the refinery, down a spur to the right, is the first major settlement.
**KONTOKALI (Kontokalion, Kondakali) (7km from Corfu Town)** Possibly once a village but long ago 'Kosta'd', having been subject to the very worst speculative development. A pot-holed road is lined by villas and apartments; 'traditional' Greek tavernas, pubs, charcoal grills, restaurants and cafe-bars (which include 'Harry's', 'Wine House Cosy', 'Restaurant Fat's', 'Piggys Fast Food' and the 'Navigators'); scooters for rent 'In Cheap' (*sic*); 'Bakery roast bred (*sic*) for toast'; a charming, old-fashioned bicycle hire business and an elderly building; a supermarket and numerous travel agencies, all cheek by jowl and overlaid with a pervading smell of drains, frying chips and shish-kebabs, as well as sun-blistered bodies. Not a lot to do with a traditional Greek village really, and could well be chosen to represent the unacceptable face of Corfu.

Beyond a more scattered spread of houses, shops and some wasteland, the vast, rather messy and dusty Gouvia yacht marina dominates the Kontokali seafront. Incidentally, an NTOG office is sited in the marina, to cater for boat-borne visitors, as is a flotilla fleet.

Opposite the entrance to the marina is the *Villa Christos, Apartments and Rooms To Let*. To the north are little bits of shoreline here and there.

Hotels include: the *Kontokali Palace* (Class L, tel 38736), *Pyrros* (Class C, tel 91206), *Telessila*, *Hariklia* (Class D), *Panorama* (Class D, tel 91239), *Aleka* (Class E).

Campsites include: *Kontokali Beach International* (Tel 91202), open April-October.

The country lane from Kontokali progresses to:-
**GOUVIA (8km from Corfu Town)** A better class of tat (than Kontokali) borders this High St, which embraces 'The Old Barrel Pub', various cocktail bars, the 'Cuckoo's Nest', travel offices, supermarkets, beach bars, *Villa Maria Carmen* (rooms to let with private bathroom & kitchen), Flats To Let, 'Bessie's Bit of Everything' (!), 'Gouvia Shopping Centre' (yes a shopping development – so Greek), 'Cafe-bar Silver Knight' and a ladies hairdressing saloon (the building of which resembles a public lavatory). Across the bay is a prettily located church mounted on a low, rocky promontory, rather Mouse island like.

Hotels include:- the *Grecotel Corcyra Beach* (Class A, tel 30770), *Angla* (Pension Class B, tel 91336), *Aspa* (Pension Class B), *Molfetta Beach* (Class B, tel 91915), *Park* (Class B, tel 91530), *Artemis* (Class C, tel 91509), *Constantinos* (Class C), *Galaxias* (Class C, tel 91223), *Gouvia* (Class C), *Iliada* (Class C, tel 91360), *Maltezos* (Class C), *Pheacion* Class C, tel 91497), *Sun Flower* (Class C, tel 91568), *Hariklia* (Class D), *Louvre* (Class D, tel 91443), *Orfeas* (Class D, tel 91436), *Sirena* (Class D, tel 91458) & *Ormirkon* (Class E, tel 91471).

Gouvia Bay, on which both Kontokali and Gouvia are situated, was where Suleiman the Magnificent, the Turkish sultan, landed his troops in 1537. A seaman of Kontokali, one Christoforos, was a sea captain with the Venetian navy and captured a Turkish ship during the Battle of Lepanto (1571) (*See* **Banks, A To Z, Corfu Town**). The Venetians established a naval base in the bay and caused to be built three Arsenals (boat sheds), the roofless remains of which still bear mute testament to their extensive sea power. The Arsenals stand to the side of the road between the marina and the centre of Gouvia.

At the far, north side of Gouvia village, the slip loop road rejoins the main thoroughfare. The Kontokali/Gouvia bypass routes past several *Rooms* and the *Pension Avagalios*. There are squash courts and an equestrian establishment at the *Korkyra Beach Hotel*. Hereabouts are scattered holiday developments and a couple of campsites prior to:-
**TSAVROS (Limni) (10km from Corfu Town)** This is the site of a road junction, close by a supermarket furniture centre. Left advances towards Paleokastritsa and right follows the coastline past still more holiday activity, boats for rent, apartments to let and, amidst a mish-mash of bits and pieces, a turning off to the *Astir Palace Hotel*. There are two campsites and the rumour of a *Youth Hostel*.

**DASSIA (Kato Korakiana) (12km from Corfu Town)** Not so awful as Kontokali, in fact, by comparison, it is almost wholesome. There is a 'ginormous' *Chandris Dassia Hotel*, which lifts the tone, if concrete can achieve that, and then the equally smart and massive *Corfu Chandris Hotel*. Not so strange to relate that, 'only the other day', I observed a bent-backed shepherd goading his three sheep across the busy main road, the lead animal drawn on a length of knotted string.

Several arrow straight turnings give access to the beach through old olive groves, now sprinkled with 'discreet' hotels, restaurants, tavernas and cafe-bars, the tree shaded patios of which stretch down to the backshore. Additionally, there are one or three discos, 'space invaders', beach gear, gift and Greek 'original' art shops as well as tour buses and an all-pervading, swampy, frying oil smell. The tracks decant up against a neat concrete wall edging the seemingly endless, thin ribbon of gritty, shingle beach upon which are stretched rows of peeling tourists. The occasional English voice breaks through the continuous hubbub. Landing stages and finger piers jut into the constantly churned, muddy blue sea, from which operate a constant stream of caique trip craft as well as water and para-skiing power boats.

Dotted about the coastal strip is the occasional, extremely expensive tree and beach surrounded hotel, recognisable by the canopy under which air conditioned Pullman coaches and taxis disgorge their well groomed occupants.

Hotels include: the *Elea Beach* (Class A, tel 93490), *Margarona Corfu* (Class A, tel 93742), *Paloma Bianca* (Class B, tel 93575), *Sofia* (Pension, Class B), *Amalia* (Class C, tel 93520), *Dassia* (Class C, tel 93224), *Dassia Margarita* (Class C), *Galini* (Class C), *Laskaris* (Class C), *Primavera* (Class C, tel 91911), *San Remo* (Class C), *Tina* (Class C, tel 93664) & *Scheria* (Class D, tel 93233).

There is a shore edging campsite, the *Karda Beach* (Tel 93595), which opens between April-October. Whilst in the area I mustn't forget the *Curry House*!

Beyond Dassia is a turning to the left, signposted to the inland village of Kato Korakiana, close to which is the *Dionyssos Campsite* (Tel 91417), open between May-October.

**IPSOS & PYRGI (14.5 and 16km from Corfu Town)** Once upon a time, small hamlets tucked away at either end of a, long, sweeping bay bordered by a narrow (no more than 6-8m wide), undulating, fine shingle foreshore. The kelpy beach is subject to the occasional outbreak of rock, usually covered with rubbish.

Ipsos proper is tucked away to the near, south side of the bay, almost angled back from the main road but the original settlements of both Ipsos and Pyrgi have now been developed into a continuous 'fishing village holiday resort'. The inland side of the coastal road, once a plain covered in olive groves and a few farmhouses, has been swamped with ribbon development. This 'sunset-strip' is now most attractive at night, especially when viewed from above. In amongst the plethora of businesses, flats, apartments and villas, I would like to compliment the well stocked Ipsos Supermarket Platanos. This shop sells English language newspapers and some of the cheapest camera film on the island, if not many islands. One of the more 'committed' haunts sponsors a 'Mr Wet Y-fronts Competition'. The mind boggles. Signposts indicate the proximity of the *Corfu Golf & Tennis Club*.

About centre of the bay is a rather pathetic little concrete and rock mole, once utilised by local fishermans' benzinas, but now overflowing with tatty fibreglass speedboats. Towards the north, Pyrgi end of the bay, are the water sports which include para-skiing and a ski club outfit. As the main road climbs the steep hillside, away from the sea's edge, holiday inducements include the Pig & Whistle Taverna, and the Shamrock Original Irish Bar.

Hotels include: the *Ipsos Beach* (Class C, tel 93232), *Doria* (Class C), *Ionian Sea* (Class C, tel 93241), *Jason* (Class C, tel 93583), *Mega* (Class C, tel 93208), *Platanos* (Class C, tel 93240), *Costas Beach* (Class D, tel 93205), *Pyrgi* (Class C, tel 93209), *The Port* (Class C, tel 93293), *Ionia* (Class D, tel 93349), & *Theo* (Class D).

Campsites include: *Ipsos Camping* (Tel 93243), *Kerkyra Camping* (Tel 93246), & *Paradise Camping* (Tel 93282), all open between April-October.

Beyond Pyrgi are two turnings to the left, and a petrol station. The first junction leads, on a lovely route around the southern base of the Pantokrator mountain range, to the village of:-

**AG MARKOS (& on to Korakiana)** At Ag Markos is a chapel constructed circa 1075, with icons dating from the 11th century, as well as a 16th century church with wall paintings of the same period.

The second turning embarks on a serpentine scramble, seemingly for the roof of the world. The route passes through the mountain hugging village of **Spartilas**, which, naturally, hosts a *Panoramic Bar*, and reputably dates back to Ancient Greece. The road continues to climb very, very steeply as far as a turning to the right, signed **Petalia**. Straight on proceeds to the north coast road at Ahavari, via Episkepsis. Those wishing to scale Mt Pantokrator should follow the Petalia sign. In the main, this is a surfaced road across a small, fertile plain, overlooked by a rather imposing church , as far as:-

**STRINILAS (circa 28km from Corfu Town)** An extremely pretty, tree shaded, if rather tidy mountain village, which is on the coach trip schedules. Thus the *Elm Tree Restaurant* serves, amongst other delights, pizza, moussaka, chips, omelettes, souvlakia, chops and salads.

Immediately beyond Strinilas, the route becomes unmetalled, although there appears to be plans to lay a tarmacadam finish. After some ½km it is necessary to bear right for the 'final assault' on:-

**Mt Pantokrator** This takes place over a wide, increasingly poorly surfaced track which is battered across acceleratingly hostile countryside. The route deteriorates to a boulderous granite, barren, lunar landscape. Hereabouts, dramatically into view hoves the stark, bare, monastery capped mountain summit, above which impossibly rears a red and white painted, 'Eiffel tower' of a radio beacon.

The road narrows down, prior to the ultimate ascent, which is an extremely steep, scrabbling climb over an increasingly uncertain surface. Drivers should watch out for the strands of reinforcing rod that dangerously poke through the surface of the track. The much modified monastery is not only ugly, but totally dominated by the spread-eagled feet of the meccano-like communications mast which are plonked down on the courtyard. Round the back of the building, one of the wells has a new pail and drinking mug. Very thoughtful, but Rosemary was of the opinion that, for those foolhardy enough to make the journey, the well should dispense Metaxa brandy – seven star. As can be imagined, the views are phenomenal. One or two, surely deserted, hamlets stand out as outcrops of green, enveloped in the surrounding, surprisingly arid, rolling mountain folds. On 'a very clear day' observers are supposed to be able to see a smidgin of the coastline of Italy. Certainly the views do include the islands north of Corfu, the Albanian coast and the Lake of Butrinto, the Greek mainland beyond the Albanian headland, the island of Paxos and, of course, much of the island of Corfu.

Back on the coastal road, from Pyrgi the road pleasantly corniches through hill-hugging olive groves that grow all the way down to sea-level. The route tracks along the steep mountainside slopes, between 100 and 500m above the rocky coastline down below and to the right. The inland, bare flanks climb quite sharply towards the craggy peaks. This is 'Villa' country, but the buildings are fairly well scattered, and usually discreetly out of sight. The only indication of their presence are the smart signboards, neat gates and surfaced driveways. The coastline (and road) continues to skirt Mt Pantokrator, which dominates this part of the island.

The route descends, past a track to the right signposted through the olive groves 'To the beach, boat trips to Ipsos every 30mins', towards:-

**BARBATI (18km from Corfu Town)** This new hamlet, still some 100m above sea-level, possesses a taverna, mini-market, *Rooms*, *Villa Margarita*, Mini-Market Giannis, signs to 'Motorboats and Pedaloes', villa this and villa that. Barbati beach is pebble. It is interesting to note that, in this area, where the holiday homes are a considerable distance from the beaches, there is a trend towards bars having swimming pools as part of the ensemble. Towards the far, north end of Barbati is the *Hotel Alexiou* (Class B, tel 91383), as well as a very modern looking construction on the inland hillside.

Other hotels include: the *Barbati* (Class C, tel 93594 & the *Poseidon* (Class C, tel 93620).

Next on the itinerary is:-
**GLYFA (20km from Corfu Town)** A path descends to another pebble beach and the *Taverna Glyfa*, prior to the outskirts of:-

**NISAKI (22km from Corfu Town)** On the right of the tree lined, southern approaches is some freelance camping amongst the olive trees, followed by a scattering of villas, much new construction, a surgery on the left, a mini-market (the signs of which will convince passers-by that there's little they won't do), the Supermarket Katerina Bakery and a beach signpost "The community gives you free entrance". That is as long as pedestrians can face the long walk down and, conversely, the even more arduous climb back from the shingle beach.

Nisaki 'High St' passes the *Asprochori Village*, which are furnished apartments, more villas, another 'free entrance' beach road, the *Taverna Bar Vitamins*, which is what walkers may need if they have tracked up and down to sea-level, *Rooms*, another mini-market, the *Coffee Shop Giannia*, a boutique, international phone, an entrance to *Club Med Helios*, scooter and car hire, as well as a sign proclaiming "Rent a car, souvlaki, a scooter, a moped, a bicycle, 500m at the Shell" (Can one 'rent a souvlaki...?). Nisaki is a rather polite location, the olive groves are neater, the villas more twee, the stone walls tidier and most things are trimly signposted. Despite the continuously steep sided hillsides down to the distant sea, there is yet another free entrance beach path, followed by a supermarket, a rent a car sign, the *Taverna Panorama*, which dispenses the souvlaki, and the Shell Petrol Station.

The contour following road still gently chicanes in and around the folds of the mountain. The coastline, which is now some 250/300m down below, reveals the occasional, tiny, pebble cove. Beyond *Rooms* (Tel 91269), there is yet another community indication to a free (pebble) beach. This cove is bordered by the very large, if somewhat bleak, *Hotel Nisaki Beach*, complete with swimming pool, restaurant, bar and almost every water sport known to man. Then, officially, the Nomarch, the Community of Nisaki ceases, because a sign says so!

The road, once a Venetian mule path, commences to head away from the coastline, now some 500/600m above sea-level, on the way to the olive grove surrounded village of:-
**KENDROMA (25km from Corfu Town)** Although it is a prodigiously long way down, one or two small hotels allow access to their private beach, even if it is on foot. There are *Rooms* to let.

The road ascends to Kendroma after which it gently descends to:-
**GIMARI (Guimari), (26km from Corfu Town)** Signs indicate *Rooms* and " To the sea free access". The beach is kelpy pebble. Gimari also houses a bakery, mini-market, surgery, kafeneion and a police station. Far off Kalami Cove is clearly visible, in the distance.

The road from Pyrgi to Gimari traces a lovely, if somewhat downwardly distant shoreline. If the thought of the long walk either way is too much for a traveller (and for whom would it not be?) then there is no need to fret. A few kilometres beyond Gimari, in what is now nicknamed *Durrell Country*, a (right-hand) turning descends to a fork.

To the right, along a poorly surfaced road, progresses to:-

**KALAMI (30km from Corfu Town)** Once an extremely pleasant, small, caique fishing village wherein only a dozen old houses (some rather grand), a couple of reasonably priced restaurant bars and a taverna (let into the side of a larger dwelling house) situated on the edge of a shingly beach. The long threatened development has now taken place with, on the right of the approach, Adonis Mini-Market, the *Restaurant Bar Kalami Beach* on the left, as well as *Rooms*. A sign advises "Free access for pedestrians only" and the road terminates beyond a private parking lot. The houses are still pleasantly set in the trees but fences are everywhere, as are the holiday-makers' accommodation. These include *Villa Rita* and 'We rend (*sic*) rooms & apartments, Kalami Tourist Services'. There is scooter rental and parking signs for this hotel and that villa. There are *Rooms* at No 7, towards the far right-hand end of the bay.

It remains a lovely, curving bay framed by hillsides, which are dotted with cypress trees. The coastline of Albania appears to shut out the seaward background. The large pebble beach is not very attractive for bathers and there is a distinct kelp line with a certain amount of rubbish scattered about. The horn of headland to the far right of the bay is pretty, with the trees actually toppling over the edge of the cliff.

To the left, at the fork, descends to:-

**KOULOURA (30km from Corfu Town)** This tiny hamlet is on the northern side of the headland that separates it from Kalami, unlike which it remains an enchanting spot. A small, slanted bay edges the hillside and there are still a dozen or so craft moored bow on to the cliff side. It has to be admitted that the original mole, forming a small, attractive mooring for local fishing vessels has been replaced by a fairly large harbour. The taverna and church are, to this day, separated by a row of terraced houses, even if these have been extensively refurbished and are now holiday apartments. On the way down to the port, an appallingly surfaced track keeps on, at the last, sharp right-hand bend, advancing to a small length of pebble shore, edged by a ruined house set in thickly tree'd surrounds.

Both Kalami and Kouloura, as other deeply set, eastern coast seaside locations in the shadow of Mt Pankokrator, lose the sun quite early in the afternoon and thus cool down quickly.

As indicated these last two hamlets have been labelled Durrell Country, the family having lived hereabouts in the 1930s, as depicted in the 1988 television film of Gerald's book *My Family and Other Animals*. The authorities responsible for tourism have roundly castigated Durrell for bemoaning the tourist rape of Corfu, in the Sunday Times. They maintain that his criticisms in respect of human and vegetable pollution, amongst other complaints, are those of a jealous lover who has lost his beautiful lady. Well, all I can say is that if the shock and doubts I experienced over a period of some ten years are anything to go by, what on earth Mr Durrell must have felt over a span of 55 years... doesn't bear thinking about.

The hills above the road from the Kalami/Kouloura junction, as far as the Ag Stefanos turn-off, are much gentler, while the coastline is very beautiful. The route winds upwards, past a turn off to the left to **Vigla**. At the village of **Agnitsini** a track descends to a shingle beach set in a largely undeveloped, beautiful setting.

Less than ½km from a handful of houses and a bakery, a signpost indicates the fairly circuitous, alternately metalled and unsurfaced road which branches off to the right, descending over fire damaged hillsides and looking out over the lovely, deep bay of:-

**AG STEFANOS (circa 35km from Corfu Town)** Perhaps the extent of tourist penetration is telegraphed by the signs for the tourist office. These appear long before reaching the well established, well-heeled, well-groomed, settlement that spreads around the informal waterfront at the bottom of the bay. Albania is at its closest and almost seems to blank off the sea inlet. It will not have been that many years ago that Ag Stefanos was only accessible by boat, that is apart from a rugged ride on a donkey or mule.

The approach road emerges at the left-hand (*Fsw*) side of the 'U' of the bay, alongside the smart and clean *Restaurant Bar Eucalyptus*, beyond which the shore peters out. To the right, the unsurfaced, 'informal' backshore Esplanade edges a pebbly, kelp covered seashore from which juts any number of small jetties, with the 'threat' of some water sports. About centre of the settlement's waterfront, and standing back from the sea's edge, are the very smart *Restaurant Caparelli*, the *Taverna Gallini* and, in the ground floor of a two storey, purpose built building, the *Coffee Bar Dameanos* – no local kafeneion this. Further on round, once again housed in a large, substantial, expensive construction, are a large supermarket, Stefanos Travel and the *Restaurant Bar Delfini*. At the far side are some young trees prettily spaced out round the edge of a small quay.

This really is an upwardly mobile holiday resort where 'BPTs' change for drinkies and the restaurant menus include Wiener schnitzel.

Hotels include: the *Nafsika* (Class C) & the (*Saint Stefanos* (Class C, tel 31254).

The main road continues to angle inland across the headland, through **Kariotiko**, beyond which is a petrol station and terraced olive groves on the left. Without any apparent reason, there is an outbreak of houses, a taverna and a 'dead' disco and prior to **Rodolakkos** 'proper', a signpost to the right to:-

**Avlaki Beach (Dimitris Boats) (35km from Corfu Town)** This whole area will become a planned holiday villa resort, courtesy *Manos Michael Angelo Village Development*, but until then... Proceed along the unmade track, which threads through olive groves being eroded by a steady building programme. Turn right at the fork in the road, which bumps along to an unspoilt, dramatic, great sweep of bay. This is bordered by a 5m wide strip of rather dirty, kelpy, pebble beach with a scrubbly plant backshore, edged by an encircling track, the inland side of which is fringed by dense tree growth. About centre of the bay is a small cottage and at the nearside, where the approach road spills onto the backshore of the bay, there is a summer months only taverna and the Dimitris Boat water sports operation. Until the holiday village is completed, Avlaki Beach is an ideal bolt-hole. Being a conscientious developer, Mr Manos has installed rubbish bins but they are not emptied...

Rodolakkos and Kassiopi merge in a messy, straggling sprawl, wherein the occasional villa 'rubs shoulders' with random farmsteads, on the outskirts of:-

**KASSIOPI (36km from Corfu Town)** Perhaps the road down to the large, almost circular harbour says it all. In amongst an enthusiastic building programme, there is a bar with swimming pool, bakery, surgery, supermarket, another baker, the *Taverna Istoni*, various 'happy hour' bars, 'space invader UFO', scooter hire, *Oasis Taverna* and **Rooms**.

The wide, spacious and picturesque quay is edged by a miscellany of bars, scooter hire firms, restaurants, tavernas and tour offices. There is even a Post Office 'hut'. One shop of note is Aleka's Lace House, round to the right (*Fsw*), and patronised by English royalty in the shape of Princess Margaret, who has friends in the vicinity.

The municipality is very keen to point out, on a number of strategically placed signs, that all the Kassiopi shops are equally good and prospective clients had better be on the look out for those (wicked) entrepreneurs paying commission to schleppers who make successful introductions!

One or two of the travel/tour offices, most of which are manned by pleasant, helpful personnel, will supply details of private accommodation. There are also a number of notices indicating the whereabouts of **Rooms**.

Perhaps the extensive history of the location is the most interesting feature of this once quiet backwater, which has been 'treated' to become a 'typical' fishing village resort, possessing all the trappings and paraphernalia necessary to cope with the package holiday industry. Punters will be delighted to hear that excursions available include, for instance:

Nimfes Greek Night, Grand Island Tour, Corfu by Boat, Corfu by Night, Corfu Shopping, Danilia Village, Beach BBQ, Paxos, Ipsos Disco Alley, Sidari Boat, Ericusa Treasure Island, Football, Kassiopi By Night, Feast of the East and, last but not least, Scuba Doo!

Back to history. Supposedly founded in 360 BC, settlers who made an impact were Greeks who also colonised mainland Necromantion (Parga) and Kassope (near Preveza) and thus, possibly, the name. Other migrants were rumoured to have been refugees from the dictat of the Emperor Augustus. It is said that he decreed that everybody in the vicinity of Preveza should be relocated in his (then) modern city of Nikopolis. This bald pronouncement would have had a similar reaction, I should imagine, to that of informing the inhabitants of modern-day Woburn Sands that they had to relocate in nearby Milton Keynes. Shipborne visitors are supposed to have included such august chaps as Emperor Nero, Pliny, Cicero and Mark Anthony.

The ruined castle, on the western headland of Cape Kassiopi, was the site of Roman, then Norman, followed by Venetian fortifications. The track round here continues on to the town's long, featureless, shadeless, steeply sloping, wide, pebble and shingle beach. The shore is subject to some kelp, many sun-beds as well as various water sports and the sea-bed is, in the main, pebble.

The Church of Kassopitra, close to the Harbour, is probably built over a Roman temple dedicated to Jupiter. An icon achieved sufficient fame to warrant a mandatory salute from passing ships but the miracle of the blinded boy did more for the promotional image. After a night spent in the church, his sight was restored, causing a bit of a hoo-ha.

Hotels include: the *Oasis* (Class D). Most of the other likely looking establishments are furnished apartments.

The coast road north-west of Kassiopi skirts the main beach (previously described) and one or two attractive, small, white pebble coves, even if the inland scenery is rather unappealing.

The next stretch of the route skirts the long, flat Gulf of Apraos. This is a rather strange area of gently shelving salt flats, from whence it looks possible to walk out for miles. The far end, signposted **Kalamaki Beach**, is very sandy, whereon evidence of pedaloes, some small boats pulled up on the shore and a rather swampy stream meandering onto the backshore, with some buildings scattered about.

The next settlement, a doo-hickey way-station, is:-
**PROFITIS ILIAS (47km from Corfu Town)** Here are a few holiday villas set in olive groves (but it is some way from the sea), a 'fruit market' and a petrol station.

Almost immediately beyond this hamlet is a turning off to the right, through more olive groves. Either side of the metalled lane, and spaced out amongst the trees, are set down a scattering of chalets, some villas and a number of large, old houses, surrounded by a fairly rudimentary farming community. There is a hotel (with a car park for residents only) and a taverna housed in an old building.
**AG SPIRIDON (50km from Corfu Town)** The church (of Ag Spiridon) is to the left (*Fsw*), in front of which is a sweep of sandy beach. Some deck chairs and a few tired pedaloes indicate a possible height of season flurry of activity. This beautiful shoreline is spoilt by piles of kelp. The surroundings to the coastline are low-lying with an outcrop of jagged rock just offshore. Away to the left is an attractive sea inlet bordered by reed beds and netted for fish. A track edges the lagoon-like inlet of the sea to rejoin the main coast road.

The somewhat flat, monotonous, low-lying, sand-duney countryside is pleasant enough. Alongside a tar making plant is a sign for:-
**Almiros Beach** There are also indications for *Rooms* and a taverna. At this east end of an enormous, 15m wide sweep of gritty sand beach, is a network of tracks which criss-

cross the flattish, scrub bearing landscape, linking the scattered villas. The sea's edge is, in the main, shelving biscuit rock.

The shore continues on beyond distant **Achavari**, from whence the tempo of beach chalet and villa building increases. The landward side of the road is pleasantly tiered, gentle hills. To the right the area backing the beach is still low-lying and marshy in places, with tangental tracks making off to the Hayling Island like, sea's edge – and the foreshore is sand, not biscuit rock, with some fine pebble. There are apartments, villas, the occasional hotel but no **Rooms**, so far. Out of the blue appears a roundabout, from which an inland road to Ag Pandeleimon, a petrol station and an increasingly built-up suburb, prior to yet another roundabout off which branches the main 'High St' to:-

**RODA (37km from Corfu Town, via the inland village of Troumpeta or 56km, via the coast road)** Tel prefix 0663. The 'High St' hosts a Post Office van, a doctor, *Rooms* and a butcher prior to making a junction with the beach tracking Esplanade, at the left-hand end (*Fsw*). The pleasant, sandy beach spreads along to the right in a series of sweeping curves, varying in width from almost nothing to 15/20m. Some of the first metre or so of the sea-bed is pebbly. At the far right or east end of the waterfront, the shore is almost all pebbles. The inland side of the Esplanade is edged by an almost unbroken row of low-rise development.

Roda is a very English resort, a fact borne out by the style and type of businesses that edge the road. One enterprising restaurant even offers mashed potatoes.

Hotels include: the *Roda Beach* (Class B, tel 93202), *Aphroditi* (Class C), *Mandylas* (Class C), *Milton* (Class C), (*Silver Beach* (Class C, tel 93134). *Village Roda Inn* (Class C, tel 93358) & *Ninos* (Class E, tel 93291).

There is a campsite 1km from the beach, the *Roda Beach* (Tel 93120), open between April-October.

From Roda, in a westerly direction, the road climbs off the coastal plain through a countryside of brambles and olive trees. One or two villas are scattered about. They will no doubt be joined by more of the same. The route links with:-

**KAROUSSADES (34km from Corfu Town)** This pleasant, inland town overlooks a fertile plain, hasn't been inflicted with villas and possesses a filling station.

From Karoussades there is a road to the north which leads to:-

**ASTRAKERI (36km from Corfu Town)** A rather scruffy, busy little place with a large factory, two hotels, the *Antzela Beach* (Class B) and the *Astrakeri Beach* (Class C, tel 31238), a campsite, *Karoussades* (Tel 31394), and a few houses. The settlement is at the east end of a large, flat bay bordered by a huge sweep of shore, possibly best seen from the west.

To observe this a signed track, further from Karoussades, branches down to:-

**AG ANDREAS BEACH (36km from Corfu Town)** The initially surfaced lane rises steeply, prior to descending through backyard farming communities and becoming unsurfaced. It peters out on a strip of greensward, alongside a small homestead farm, set in a forest of olive trees, on a low headland. This is about 50m above and to the far west of the glorious sweep of wide sand that stretches away to the right. To the nearside is a large area of rather messy water, trapped behind the middleshore. The beach is bordered by low cliffs of varying heights, there is some kelp in areas and the sea-bed shelves very slowly. About the middle of the bay, the sand turns into a spit topped off by a quay, alongside which berth a few, largish fishing boats. The sweep of shore continues on in another curve, but now with a stony backshore all the way back to Astrakeri.

Returning to the main road, there is yet another side-lane, this one signposted 'Sidari Beach Hotel and Ag Ionnis'. The metalled track serpentines through pleasantly tree planted countryside. The conifers and undergrowth of bracken and ferns results in almost English like surroundings, if it weren't for the gnarled and tortured olive trees. Despite the lane becoming unsurfaced, plans are obviously afoot to asphalt the rest. There are signs for apartments to rent, prior to the approach running out on the backshore of the shore.

To the left (*Fsw*), the coastline extends in a slow curve all the way to Sidari. It is a pity that the beach is nothing much to write home about, only being a 10m strip of shingle, with at least a metre of shallow shelving, pebble sea-bed. The backshore and undulating dunes are rather scrubbly and untidy. The hourly hire rate for a pedalo is 500drs, for a canoe 300drs, whilst the day charge for a sun-bed or umbrella is 200drs.

Those adventurers who continue westwards along the main thoroughfare will discover that not only does the surface disappear, but so does the road! A signpost to the right advises 'Gold Beach, umbrellas, sun-beds', whilst crudely written signs indicate a very rough track to the left. This crosses parkland like countryside prior to joining the Velonades-Sidari main road. For Sidari, *See* **Route Two**.

## ROUTE TWO

**To Lakones, via Troumpeta, Sidari, Peroulades, Ag Stefanos, Afionas, Ag Georgios & Krini (circa 80km)**The inland journey from Corfu Town, directly to the north-west coast of the island, passes through lovely countryside. The route remains totally unspoilt, beyond the left turn at the Tsavros junction. Towards the village of **Troumpeta**, the road climbs steeply over the spine of a hill range, which runs all the way from the bottom corner of Mt Pantokrator to Paleokastritsa. There are magnificent views of the east coast, with Corfu Town still visible in the distance.

One or two of the villages and their settings on this route are very reminiscent of the French Dordogne. Close to the summit of the hill range, the road forks right to Roda (*See* **Route One**) and left for Sidari. From the high ground (certainly scenic if not moral), the north-west coast and sea beyond hoves into view. In very fine conditions, so do the small islands of Mathraki (to the left), Othoni (to the centre) and Erikoussa (to the right). The pleasant route now descends, via **Arkadades**, **Athanasios** and **Velonades**, in a northerly direction. Close to the seaside resort (of Sidari), the road crosses a Bailey bridge, fording a sluggish stream, before entering the flat grasslands on the outskirts of:-

**SIDARI (37km from Corfu Town)** (Tel prefix 0663) Villas and apartments are spaced about the 'suburbs', there is a filling station, *Rooms* (Tel 95304), 'Full English Breakfast', a surgery, quite a few *Three Brothers* this, that and the other, a coffee shop – 'The only coffee shop with local prices', a small park, *Rooms*, a football ground and *Nikos House*. This latter is a pleasant looking building, towards the west end of the beach, which advertises 'A place to stay and relax, rooms and apartments, day and weekly rates. Ring our bell any time.'

Sidari is, in the main, a low-rise, low density but vigorous and crowded holiday resort radiating out from a straggling 'High St'. There is little, if any, 'old village' infrastructure. On the other hand, the resort possesses a splendid, wide, clean, sandy, beach with a shallow shelving, sandy sea-bed. Water sports, sun-beds and umbrellas predominate, but there aren't any beach showers. The left-hand (*Fsw*) end of the bay, where the sand is at its widest, terminates in a low, distinctive sandstone, sea eroded spur.

Hotels include: the *Afroditi Beach* (Class C, tel 95247), *Astoria* (Class C, tel 31315), *Mimoza* (Class C, tel 31363), *Three Brothers* (Class C, tel 31242) & *Sidari* (Class D, tel 31239). Incidentally, there are more **Rooms**, several hundred metres to the west of Sidari.

Enquire at the Sidari tour offices for day boat trips to the offshore, westernmost Greek islands of:-

**Mathraki** (8km sea voyage from Sidari); **Othoni** (20km sea voyage from Sidari), the largest and most attractive of the group, with a couple of tavernas and a store at the hamlet port of Othoni, and **Erikoussa** (9km sea voyage from Sidari), with a small taverna at the anchorage of Erikoussa. This latter island 'had' an exciting Second World War as it was both a staging post for Allied escapees and a resistance group HQ.

From Sidari a westwards, countryside road advances towards **Avliotes**, from whence a right-hand turning leads to the beautifully Old Corfiot village of:-
**PEROULADES (40km from Corfu Town)** On the left of the approach is a 'Rooms To Let' sign, nailed to a tree, in front of a broken down shack of a place. It is quite possible that the smarter building. to the rear, is the accommodation. There is at least one other house with accommodation and the sleepy settlement possesses a number of nice cottages and low, two storey houses with pleasant stonework. On Sundays the village women often sit on their front doorsteps dressed in traditional Corfiot 'get up'.

At the far side of Peroulades is a sign 'To the Sunset Taverna'. This surfaced track, off to the right of a country lane, passes a couple of strategically positioned tavernas, prior to abruptly terminating on a car park, some 150m above sea-level. A steep footpath descends to beautifully sandy, if narrow beaches that lie to either side, at the foot of towering cliff faces. An extremely pleasant, if shaded spot, which becomes rather crowded with locals at weekends. They know a good thing when they see it.

The adventurous can follow the track from the village, in a northerly direction, for a 20minute walk to the staggering beautiful Cape Drastis.

From Peroulades travellers may either retrace the route back to the main road or keep to the aforementioned country lane from which the 'landslip' Sunset Taverna was indicated. This latter curves back round to rejoin the road to:-
**AVLIOTES (40km from Corfu Town)** A surprisingly large village, with a modern cafe-bar, a number of shops, kafeneions and some **Rooms**.

Ag Stefanos is signposted from the far end of Avliotes, a route that advances through lovely countryside, even if the road's surface becomes 'indeterminate'. Beyond a number of villas, seemingly stuck out in the middle of nowhere, and the view looks out over the bay. The very poorly surfaced road hereabouts commences to wind down, past a number of holiday apartments, to:-
**AG STEFANOS (44km from Corfu Town)** Corfu, in common with other Greek islands, has a 'naughty little habit' of using similar names for places miles apart. Ag Stefanos (west coast) vis-a-vis Ag Stefanos (north-east coast) highlights this confusing custom.

When I first researched the guide, this Ag Stefanos possessed a magnificent sweep of sandy beach, with gentle breakers rolling in across the slowly shelving shore. That has not changed, but I wrote at the time "the surrounding coastal plain, fishing boat mole and church are being overtaken by the slow but steady encroachment of newly constructed tavernas, restaurants, a mini-market, villas and apartments. All well spread out at the moment, but one fears for the future". Well it has come to pass. In the intervening years the haphazard, if still well spaced out, development has continued apace. There are **Rooms**, but most of the accommodation is holiday villas. 'Support facilities' now include signposts to a filling station (which I couldn't locate), scooter-hire, gift shops and snackbars – advertising English breakfast. This latter gourmet bias is natural enough as the resort is slanted towards the United Kingdom travel companies – no Greek spoken here, only English.

Next door to the Supermarket Ag Stefanos is a popular cafe-bar, separated from the beach backshore by a bamboo grove or three. They serve reasonably priced dishes – the most expensive of which is charged at 450drs. A meal for two costs about 800drs. A tomato and cucumber salad is priced at 66drs, a Greek salad 148drs, a plate of chips 66drs but the only beer is canned Amstel, expensive at 95drs, whilst a lemonade is an acceptable 40drs.

The beach is amazingly wide, but there is an outcrop of centrally situated, kelp covered rocks. The kelpy, south end foreshore, at the small caique harbour side, is shelving biscuit rock overlooked by a headland. In the proximity of the harbour is a beach taverna and the gently shelving sweep of shore hosts lines of sun-beds, umbrellas and water skiing. Some ten years ago there was a 'beach lurking' JCB digger used to gather up the kelp for removal by lorry. It is comforting to see it is still in position.

From the 'heights' above Ag Stefanos, sea views take in the nearby islet of Diaplo and the offshore, more distant Mathraki island. In the most popular summer months, trip boats make the excursion to one or both.

Hotels include: the *Nafsika* (Class C) & *St Stefanos* (Class C, tel 31254).

Back at the turning down to Ag Stefanos, to the left advances towards Arilias, across scrubby countryside dotted with holiday villas and apartments. At the next road junction, whence views out over the islet of Gravia, turn right (left leads back to Magoulades) for **Arilias**, which village hosts a mini-market and a pub(!). Straight on heads for Afionas and right (again) descends to:-

**ARILIAS BEACH (circa 41km from Corfu Town)** The thoroughfare runs out on the transverse, tarmacadamed Esplanade, alongside the *Hotel Marina*. Arilias Beach is somewhat unappealing – perhaps the lack of any tree cover or, for that matter, vegetation aggravates the state of affairs. Furthermore it is an incomplete, 'green fields' seaside development with some delusions of grandeur, if the totally out of place street lighting is any indicator. The beach is not nearly so attractive as nearby Ag Stefanos, being very narrow, with a pebbly backshore. The water's edge and a metre or so of the foreshore is sandy. The view to sea is dominated by the craggy, uninhabited islet of Gravia. Despite any drawbacks, one or two UK package holiday companies are present and Rent A Bike keeps the punters mobile.

One hundred metres to the right (*Fsw*) is the *Flamingo*, a trendy little development with gardens, a restaurant, swimming pool and bar serving cocktails. To the left of the concrete quay is a rocky section of sea-bed. Incidentally 'The Beach' would not be complete without a *Coconut Cocktails Bar*, would it?

Hotels include: the *Arilla Beach* (Class C, tel 51201) & *Marina* (Class C, tel 31400).

Returning to the Afionas road, **Rooms** are passed and the countryside becomes attractive as the route climbs. A signpost to the left indicates Ag Georgios, but that is not strictly accurate. This track descends, increasingly steeply, to the west of the centre of the great sweep of Ag Georgios Bay and there is no road connection with the main, south-eastern end of the bay, where Ag Georgios village is sited. Read on for more details... Continuing along the Afionas road passes a sign **Rooms**, in the first storey of a mini-market store, beyond which the route continues to climb, past another track plunging down to the left and signed Afionas Beach (of which more later), as far as:-

**AFIONAS (circa 45km from Corfu Town)** A large, sprawling, agricultural headland settlement situated high up on the cliff-top. The road climbs past a baker, a taverna with accommodation and **Rooms** to terminate on a small, irregular square. Despite the relatively isolated nature of the village, *Timsway* have a number of holiday cottages situated here.

Straight ahead from the square, some 30m, is **Rooms** on the left. Beyond the accommodation, a rough track enables walkers to gain a vantage point from which there are stunning views out over Ag Georgios Bay, with the massive headland of Cape Falakron forming a splendid backdrop.

To the right, from the square, steps climb through the village, past a scrubbly, doohickey farmstead onto pastureland. From there are wonderful seascapes to the right (*Fsw*) but an even better viewpoint can be gained by dropping down and then climbing along the neck of land that connects to the large headland of Cape Arilias. Set into the headland cape at sea-level is a large inlet with a sand and pebble beach bordered by a 'temporary' fishing boat hamlet, but once a place of some import.

That aforementioned view over Ag Georgios confirms that the once undeveloped, almost empty bay has not escaped the attentions of the holiday industry.

From Afionas village it is possible to tumble down the remarkably well maintained track, previously mentioned, to:-

**AFIONAS BEACH (circa 46km from Corfu Town)** This is not a separate beach, more the north-west sector of Ag Georgios Bay. The track runs out on the backshore alongside *Rooms* on the right *(Fsw)*, as well as a couple of beach tavernas. The fine, gritty sand beach is very broad but becomes tiny pebble towards the sea's edge. A few pedaloes languidly await a hirer or two, there is some rubbish and a midshore, winter storm driven, low ledge of kelp. Along the beach towards Ag Georgios, beyond the backshore bordering *Rent Rooms Studio Spiro*, is a 'false start' of a track, which climbs the hillside, only to fall back again. Despite vehicles not being able to get through, walkers can (possibly scooters even), as it is only the lack of an adequate track that precludes progress.

Instead of returning by the Afionas track, it is worth climbing out on the aforementioned turning signed 'To Ag Georgios'. This steep track passes *Rooms*, near the top, and on the right, *St George Camping* (Tel 41384), a tidy, neat campsite.

Heading back northwards along the main Magoulades road, there is almost immediately an angled turning off to the right. This route crosses lovely countryside, sprinkled with cypress trees, and passes through the villages of **Kavadades**; scrubbly but pretty **Armenades** and backwoods **Dafni**, set in hillsides covered with old but still harvested olive trees and beyond which is a petrol station. The road continues past the incongruously sited chalet buildings of *Hotel Bella Vista*, followed by **Aspiotados** village, a smidgin of a place, even smaller **Manatades**, all set in lovely, terraced olive groves, amongst which are scattered numerous small farmsteads. At **Agros**, the main Sidari road is joined. To the north is:-

**AG ATHANASIOS (27km from Corfu Town)** Both Agros and Ag Athanasios, which almost merge, are sizeable, time-worn, hillside village communities, the older ladies of which still wear traditional costume. Ag Athanasios boasts a large, roadside drinking water tank, a snackbar and cafe-bar, whilst Agios possesses a water tap, a small bar, complete with a telephone, a general store, a mini-market, grandly labelled 'Supermarket', a baker, the 'Sweet Taste' Zacharoplasteion and a pharmacy.

There is accommodation in a nice looking house, about one kilometre south of Agios, beyond which is **Arkadades** village, wherein, off to the right, is the signposted turning to Ag Georgios.

This winding road almost returns a traveller to the Corfu of yesteryear, passing through terraced olive groves and rather 'scrapyard' homesteads. The sights might well include an old lady clothed from head to foot in black, tethered with a bit of string to a lead goat or sheep and followed by their tumbling flock; her 'cousin', accompanied by the inevitable donkey, crouched on a hillside with a distaff around which she is winding the wool or simply a 'huddle of crones', resembling a flight of foraging crows.

Villages *en route* include **Vationes** and **Kontatagi**, the latter hosting at least two bakers, a store and a super kafeneion. The narrow way is well signposted in Kontatagi, and no wonder. The traffic is all one way down in the mornings and all the other way out in the evenings.

The presence of a settlement becomes apparent on the last section of the route and a scattering of new apartment buildings, set down in the olive groves, heralds:-

**AG GEORGIOS (circa 35km from Corfu Town)** This once deserted, grand sweep of a bay has 'suffered' possibly the worst example of haphazard, partial development I have seen. The road simply runs out on an informal car park, towards the left end of the beach.

Around this are grouped and spread out a higgledy-piggledy collection of buildings which include *Mary's Place*. This is a cafe-bar with pretensions to grandeur, and the nearest thing to a local kafeneion – and that's not very adjacent, if the *Cafe-Bar Possidon* is not open. There is also a mini-market, the *Restaurant Bar Marma* and the Lola Beach Supermarket but don't forget there isn't a local kafeneion.

Away to the right (*Fsw*) stretches the great sweep of fine grit and sand beach, which spreads all the way down into the sea. The sea-bed of sand, a band of rounded boulders, sand and some more boulders, at first shelves, then noticeably rises before falling away again. The sea is beautifully clean and clear. A tiny bit of kelp is thinly scattered along the shore, as are sun-beds. The backshore is a mish-mash of paths and tracks. These are at first, edged by a number of unco-ordinated two and three storey apartments and then widely spaced out taverna/restaurants, set into the quite steeply shelving, moth-eaten hillsides which are almost devoid of any vegetation.

At night, those intending to trek to this or that eating spot will require a torch as there isn't any street lighting – naturally as there aren't any streets. It is necessary to wander up, down and along the edge of the sand from one track or path to another. It is rather similar to scrambling about in one of those small chalk pits, once so beloved by cyclists but now by bikers.

The saving grace is the spaciousness, an attribute somewhat eroded by the lack of any tree cover. Holiday-makers should note that mosquitoes are a menace here. Water sports predominate with a profundity of wind surfers as well as a water skiing school, which also hires jet ski machines.

From Ag Georgios, instead of cutting back to Corfu Town, it is possible to continue south to Paleokastritsa (*See* **Route Three**). Rather than climbing all the way back to Arkadades, turn right (*Coast behind one*) for the village of **Prinilas**. From here a very, very rough, wide mountain track forks off for the 2km trek towards Makrades. This choice of route is for the stout of heart only, but is wildly attractive and allows amazing views back out over Ag Georgios Bay.

**MAKRADES** (30km from Corfu Town) A recent phenomena is the informal stalls run by the villagers from where they sell local wines and herbs. The more enthusiastic, enterprising younger traders forcibly stop vehicles in order to make a trade.

From Makrades follow the road to:-
**KRINI (31km from Corfu Town)** There's a fountain and a cul-de-sac slip road to the body of the village. A wide path winds, from the main square, past houses with accommodation, to:-
**The Castle of Angelo Kastro** This Byzantine fort, is dramatically sited on a mountain spur, some 325m above sea-level and from the ruined remains of which are fabulous views. The castle was the traditional refuge for the villagers of Paleokastritsa. During a number of sieges, over the years, the inmates were, for instance, able to hold out in excess of a year against the Genoese, as well as withstanding a series of vicious Turkish assaults. It is said that the incumbents could send signals to Corfu Town.

Do not be tempted to scramble down the path to an apparently, beguiling beach cove. Apart from the necessity to abseil some of the way, it simply isn't worth all the effort.

The main road continues on (signed Angelokastro) past the *Restaurant Grill Room Panorama, Rooms To Let* as well as accommodation, next door, in the *Villa Evridiki* and the *Bella Vista*. This latter is a beautifully sited taverna overlooking Paleokastritsa. The establishment boasts 'Where the Kings of Greece have eaten as well as the Kaiser, Tito and Nasser'. A rather expensive, spick outfit where a couple of coffees and a brandy cost 330drs, but the view...

**LAKONES (25km from Corfu Town)** This narrow streeted, mountainside hugging village may be named after a migration of Spartans (from their Peloponnese city of Laconia). There is a butcher, the *Cafe Olympia*, a zacharoplasteion, a cafe-bar and *Rooms Tsimis*. The views are not very good, despite some suggestions to the contrary, due to the juxtaposition of an 'inconvenient' hillside.

Beyond Lakones is the *Fantasia House Rooms, S. Amthinmos*, after which the narrow, poorly surfaced road serpentines down through terraced olive groves, on the lower slopes of which are apartments, *Rooms*, a campsite and a general bustle of activity that heralds the outskirts of Paleokastritsa (*See* **Route Three**).

## ROUTE THREE
### To Paleokastritsa & on to Liapades, Giannades, Ermones Beach & Vatos
**(circa 39km)**The road from the Troumpeta village junction to Makrades, via Alimatades (*See* **Route Two**), is similar to driving across a hot, Welsh mountain road (if such a thing is possible). The views over the hillsides to the northern coast and to the south-west over Kerkira Bay, are nothing short of spectacular. The little villages and hamlets are, in the main, untouched by the great tourist explosion, which has intruded along much of the coastal region. The inhabitants gentle way of life is only disturbed by the klaxons of the tour-buses as they transport their air conditioned occupants from one 'beauty-spot' to the next. From Makrades proceed to Lakones (*See* **Route Two**), the latter section taking in a few villages covered in Route Two.

It is without doubt the most dramatic approach to what must be one of the loveliest panoramas on Corfu, if not the Ionian. The view is sensational. The Monastery of Paleokastritsa appears to hang out over the sea's edge, being built on a 100m high promontory. Of the five or six coves overlooked by the monastery, some form a clover leaf-like shape. Unfortunately, the hotels, villas and general development associated with tourism have detracted from the overall beauty of:-

**PALEOKASTRITSA (25km from Corfu Town)** Tel prefix 0663. Once the main road is joined, on the outskirts, the 'fun' really starts. This thoroughfare is bordered by a disco, *Rooms*, olive groves being torn up for yet more buildings, a supermarket, Rent A Bike, Rent A Car, English breakfast, *Rooms*, naturally every water sport known to mankind, tourist offices, Rent Rooms, a Tourist Information centre, the Unique Gift shop, *Villa Theodore Rooms*, *Villa Tonia Rooms*, *Caterina Pension*, *Rooms to Let Green House*, *Elipa Taverna Rooms*, *Rooms Verna Kalm* (which Paleokastritsa certainly isn't), *Restaurant Bar Astacost* and *Rooms*. In amongst this row, one gem of a shop is the Supermarket Nicholas. The kindly owner speaks English as well as changes money and there are a number of *Rooms* in the buildings surrounding his establishment. Beyond the *Restaurant Astacost*, the first of the bays is to the left.

Paleokastritsa is, alas, a typical example of how uncontrolled package tourism can 'transform' a once, truly, idyllic spot. Even the relative solitude of the little sandy coves across the bay has been destroyed, due to the flotilla of water taxis. These ply constantly back and forth with their cargoes of tourists, ever hopeful that they will find a few, free square metres of sand on which to blazon their multi-hued, multi-shaped bodies. Apart from the usual 'deluge' of water sports, there is a diving school.

It is perhaps noteworthy that Edward Lear, whilst living on the island, commented that he would have to flee the scene of Paleokastritsa, due to the impending arrival of picnic parties, and that was sometime in the 1860s. Well, well.

The harbour is a very ancient settlement dating back to at least 1000 BC, when it may have been the site of a royal palace.

The first bay, adjacent to the roadway, has a sandy beach but pebbly sea's edge and the next bay is pebbly. Beyond this, a steep road curves up to a tree shaded, surfaced, circular 'square', bordered by the beautifully positioned:-

**Paleokastritsa Monastery** Originally constructed in the 13th century, possibly using stonework from adjacent ruins. Genoese soldiers ransacked the monastery, in the early 1400s. After rebuilding, the Turks, the rotters, 'rubbled' the place in 1537. Subsequently it was once again reconstructed in 1572, with further modifications and enlargements over the centuries.

The chapel and tower are set in a paved square surrounded by the monks and nuns' cells and protected by a fortified wall. The monastery possesses a number of icons, some dating back to the 17th century. In addition to these, the museum contains books and relics, some of which are rather strange. If the depredations of the invading Genoese, Turks and Russians *ad nauseam* were not enough, during the Second World War, the Germans turned the square into a garrison. To the right of the entrance gate (*Facing the monastery*) is a Russian canon set in the embrasure of the parapet, from alongside which is an interesting view. The monastery opens seven days a week between 0700-1300hrs and 1500-2000hrs. Entrance is free, despite which, the friendly, English speaking priest, who beckons and encourages 'prospects' into his lair, plainly expects visitors to show their appreciation – about 200drs fills the bill. Tourists must be respectably dressed and are advised to arrive early as the Monastery area (and town for that matter) is abuzz with scooters, cars and numerous trip coaches by mid-morning.

Across the square from the monastery is a small cafe where two Nes meh ghala cost 200drs, which is not expensive, considering the location. That is not to say that the rest of Paleokastritsa is inexpensive – far from it.

Hotels include: the *Akrotiri Beach* (Class A, tel 41275), *Oceanis* (Class B, tel 41229), *Paleokastritsa* (Class B, tel 41207), *Pavillion Xenia* (Class B, tel 41208), *Apollon* (Class C, tel 41211), *Odysseus* (Class C, tel 41209), *Hermes* (Class D, tel 41211), *Zephros* (Class D, tel 41244), *Fivos* (Class E) & *Paleo Inn* (Class E, Tel 41220).

There are any number of *Rooms* and a campsite, *Paleokastritsa Camping* (Tel 41204), open between April-October.

From Paleokastritsa keep to the right for Pelekas at the Lakones junction, beyond which is *Nikos Rooms To Let*. This is a pleasant looking place with impressive gates and floodlights.

The countryside of farms and small groves of olive trees, opens out, the road passing several *Rooms* and a bakery.

**LIAPADES (22km from Corfu Town)** This widespread, rather scrubbly village lacks trees. The main street reflects the growing intrusion of tourists and 'houses' Bikes To Rent Nikos, a 'dead' travel office, *Rooms*, more *Rooms* and a market, on the left.

Signposts 'urge' travellers to fork right. This road threads past a pharmacy, a very eye-catching church campanile, across the way from a rather moth-eaten football ground, *Villa Mike*, *Rooms*, *Villa Akilias*, *Rooms To Let and Kitchen*, *Villa Papa Oulas* and the *Villa Elini*. A few package tourist apartments border the very poorly surfaced, steeply descending, rather hemmed in road, as does a *Cricketer's Taverna*. Beyond some more smart apartments is:-

**Liapades Beach (23km from Corfu Town)** A beautiful cove edged by a small, stony shore of pebbles and grit with the pebbles running into the sea. Little of the beach surface is visible as most is obscured by pedaloes, rent a boat outfits, sun-beds and a few sun umbrellas. Most water sports are catered for, including para-gliding. Any spare space is more than fully occupied by the crowds that gather here, even outside the height of season months. This beach must have been idyllic, once upon a time...

The road south of Liapades passes over a plain, with mountains to the left and hills to the right, on which is some industry as well as a Shell Petrol Station. After a couple of kilometres, a countryside road off to the right is bordered by scrubbly farmland on which the occasional, 'flash' new villa has been built. Between **Kanakades** and **Mamaro** are more olive groves, after which the terrain is almost meadowland. A taverna, the *Cool Sun*, with a bandit-like 'corral' of locals, marks the junction of the Marmaro, Giannades and Vatos roads.

From Giannades village square there is a lovely view out over the English like countryside of the Ropa Valley.

The unmetalled road to Vatos, the one closest to the coast, crosses attractive scenery to join the major Ermones Beach to Vatos Pelekas road.

The road to Ermones Beach is parallelled by an unmade road, to which it is connected by an old bridge fording a deep river gorge. The south, unmade road and the bridge are overlooked by the *Pension Taverna Katerina*, which might well be worth a second or third look. Both roads edge the banks of the wide gorge all the way down to:-

**ERMONES BEACH (17km from Corfu Town)** Homer has it that Ulysses was washed ashore here but I don't think he would recognise the spot now.... On the heights of the steep hillside to the right (*Fsw*) are the very smart, landscaped chalets of the *Ermones Beach Hotel*, whose pampered guests descend to the beach by a funicular railway. To gain access to the beach from this side, ordinary mortals must use the steps of the *Poseidon Club*. This latter establishment is almost 'blue chip' smart and includes a very chic snackbar and a diving school.

The main beach is gritty sand with a wide band of small pebbles and a strip of sandy foreshore, beyond which the sea-bed is made up of small pebbles. Once upon a time it was necessary to cross a tumble down bridge of wood to ford the summer trickle of the stream that bisected the shore. Not now, oh no. The surface has been bulldozed flat, resulting in a man-made pond (or swamp) up against the backshore. Beach and water 'distractions' include pedaloes, wind surfing, sun-beds and umbrellas. The far, left-hand (*Fsw*) hillside supports two tasteful cafe-bar restaurants. The price of drinks and meals are not cheap, not impossible but not cheap.

The ambience is dignified and expensive, no 'cheapo lager dregs' here. On the other hand I cannot help wondering what is pumped through the pipes that emanate from the *Hotel Ermones* and snake along the sea-bed, out to sea?

From Ermones Beach the road to Vatos crosses rather flat, featureless countryside whilst the thoroughfare is subject to nasty, unheralded stretches of subsidence. At the junction with the Ropa village/Vatos road, the entrance to *Corfu Golf and Country Club* is straight ahead, whilst to the right the route swings over a modern bridge towards:-

**VATOS (15km from Corfu Town)** On the approach is a petrol station, *Rooms* and a cafe grill bar. There is *Rooms* along a branch road to hill mounted Vatos village 'proper' and around the corner, close to the Pelekas and Beach Myrtiotissas roads, more accommodation and the turning left to some horse riding stables. This is followed by another *Rooms*.

## ROUTE FOUR
**To Ag Gordis via Ag Ioannis, Danilia Village, Pelekas, Glifada Beach, Monastery (& Beach) of Mirtiotissa, Pelekas Beach & Sinarades (circa 23km)**The road westwards from Corfu Town proceeds towards Vatos, via **Alepou**, where there are a number of *Rooms*, and on past the turning to **Kombitsa**, a monastery hamlet of some appeal. Beyond this detour, and standing back from the road, is a large Venetian mansion mounted on a knoll. About 1½km further westward is a junction. To the right leads along the Ropa valley road, through:-

**AG IOANNIS (9km from Corfu Town)** A turning to the right leads to a *Youth Hostel*, housed in a faded but converted mansion. There are also *Rooms* to let in the village.

The other side of Ag Ioannis and 3km beyond **Kefalovrysso** (12km from Corfu Town), is a minor road to the right. This crosses the island back to Corfu Town via **Potamos**. About half-way along its length, east of **Tembloni** and on the right is:-

**Danilia Village & Folklore Museum** Despite a multiplicity of signposts and a blitz of advice that a visit is a must, the road via Potamos, from Corfu Town, is not very clearly indicated. Casual callers are not really catered for, the 'experience' being orientated towards group and party trips. I must admit it makes me very sad that it has been necessary to 'recreate' a typical Corfiot village. One would have hoped there were plenty of the real thing... I am advised that the most enjoyable way to partake of the experience is to join an '... Evening Out'. I shall write no more except to say the project is well executed, the museum, worth visiting and opening hours are between 1000-1300hrs & 1800-2200hrs, but closed on Sundays.

Returning to the junction, instead of taking the Ag Ioannis road, the western, left-hand route passes through **Ag Nikolaos** to:-

**PELEKAS (13km from Corfu Town)** For no apparent reason this large, hilltop village is very popular with the young in heart. Because of this or because of their presence, Pelekas evokes a rather freebooting, frontier town ambiance – one feeds off the other.

Prior to the swinging 60s, 70s and 80s (that's decades, not age) the village was famed for the views, more particularly those of the setting sun. The seal of approval was stamped on the beauty of the setting due to Kaiser Wilhelm II, the German King of Achilleion Palace fame, popularising the viewing platform. This latter 'spiral of fire escape' is well signposted, 'To The Sunset', up the a steeply climbing street that sets out from between the church and *Skippy's*, about centre of the village, opposite *Antonis*.

To return to the outskirts. From the turning off the Vatos/Sinarades 'highway', the olive grove bordered road climbs the village High St past *Martini Rooms*, *Galaktios Rooms*, *Dukakis Rooms*, Alamo Travel, *Rooms*, a small mini-market, posing as a supermarket, Kritikos Tours and a mini-market.

On the left-hand of the High St (*approaching from the south*) is the centrally located *Pension Restaurant Bar Antonis* across the road from the side-street which climbs to the Kaisers View. The family owners are rather laid back but there's a convenient balcony, sea views and, apart from good if unimaginative meals, accommodation with hot and cold water. A plenteous meal for two, of chicken and chips, an adequate Greek salad and a bottle of beer costs 950drs.

Diagonally across the Main St from *Antonis* is the quaintly labelled *Skippy's Cafe Snackbar Fast Food San Nichola Australian Man*. To the left of 'Kaisers View St' is the 'Super Market The Folia' incongruously set into the side of a church, the campanile of which crowns the store. Mr Kontis, the owner, also carries a 'Rooms For Rent' sign, which refers to his pension in the northern High St.

Beyond *Antonis* is a little alley, off to the left, which leads to the side-by-side *Restaurant Acropolis* and *Panorama*. They both possess a rooftop eating area and the signs hysterically advise prospective clients which are the 'correct' concrete steps to reach their particular upstairs panoramic terrace. It must be fun while the two patrons scrap it out.

Continuing along the Main St passes Lena's Travel, which office changes almost any colour and type of currency known to mankind, scooter hire, exchange, *White Horse Bar*, Pension Spiros Kontis (he of The Folia Supermarket), *Ghetto Snackbar*, *Jimmy's* and *San Nicholas* (the last two being competing taverna/pension owners), more *Rooms*, a disco, *Snackbar Pizzeria Pension Paradisos Petros* and *Rooms Mexa*. From hereon the houses begin to space out with accommodation scattered about, up to 2km from the centre of the village. Close and to the north of Pelekas, off the Vatos road and to the left, is the turning down to:-

**GLIFADA BEACH (Glyfada) (Circa 14½km from Corfu Town)** The approach descends past the *Pension/Restaurant Michaelis Grill Room* to finish up at the far, right-hand side (*Fsw*) of the great sweep of this magnificent, sandy beach. The shore is hemmed in by once olive tree clad, rolling hills. I write once, because the groves have been uprooted to make way for the holiday industries' buildings. The backshore is rather uneven and duney.

Unfortunately, the location is extremely crowded, with people as well as sun-beds and umbrellas, even during the out of the season months. This is not surprising because the original *Grand Hotel*, at the left-hand end, the centrally located self-service snackbar and smart taverna up against the right horn of the bay, have been energetically infilled with serried ranks of tasteful, if small holiday apartments, restaurants and another hotel, the *Glyfada Beach*. The development has not been such as to reduce the rather expensive, refined aura of the location. Hire of canoes cost 250drs and pedaloes 500drs, per hour. To enjoy more advanced water sports, simply take the side road down to an 'all encompassing' mini-market. Alongside is a beach path passing the *Grand Hotel*, in the grounds of which is the Top Sail Club.

Apart from the crowds, holiday-makers are rather 'locked in' this resort, although there is an excellent bus service to and from Corfu Town.

Whilst on the Vatos road it is worth continuing to the poorly indicated, 1½km dirt track that angles off to the left to:-

**The Monastery (& beach) of Mirtiotissa** This route is narrow, winding and often traffic bound! The last ½km section should not be attempted in a car and there are quite often 'scenes' caused by thoughtless drivers inconsiderately parking their cars. The now very rough, rutted track passes a steep path down to the left, to **Rooms** and *Snackbar Soula*, both almost hidden by olive trees. The main route crests the hillside, the vista from which is beautiful, if not breathtaking. The small, very sandy, crowded beach is almost encircled by large pumice stone type rocks. The far right (*Fsw*) section is for the nudists and further on, along a track, is the Monastery. The beach was larger but rumour has it that the illegal extraction of sand for building purposes has reduced its size. Oh dear.

Returning to the Vatos/Sinarades road, south of Pelekas, and proceeding towards Sinarades, a turning off to **Sfraida** descends past the 'Gift Shop Georgie Porgie', amongst other delights, ending up at the pink and yellow *Yaliskari Palace Hotel*. The hotel, built in a defile, blocks off the steeply shelving, pebbly beach. To the right a really very rough, 'tank track' of a passage switchbacks to a fork, just above the nearside of:-

**PELEKAS BEACH (15km from Corfu Town)** The left path, incongruously signposted 'Free Parking', tumbles down to a sandy shore sprinkled with rocks, as is the inshore sea. To the left (*Fsw*) is a small, rocky mole encircled harbour and some 'wild' camping. To the immediate right, against the backshore, is the *Captain Maria Beach Taverna*, a large, shack of a place, beyond which is a full-blown bay and a lovely stretch of sandy beach – and two more beach tavernas. Most people walk down here including some who 'get over the wire' from the *Yaliskari Palace*. The owner of the *Captain Maria Taverna* runs an 'off the cuff' jeep service back to civilisation, at about 1700hrs in the evening. The isolation is already threatened, as the right-hand turning at the fork, above the nearside of the beach, is signed 'Apartments To Let'. Also 'on the beach' is *Pelekas Vatos Camping* (Tel 94393), open between April-October.

From the main route, a branch road detours to:-

**SINARADES (13km from Corfu Town)** A large, lovely, country village, with washing strung across the streets. A pleasant admixture of *Apartments To Let*, a taverna, kafeneion, a store with a metered telephone, a pharmacy, **Rooms**, a baker, surgery, even a Philarmonic Building and a museum.

South of Sinarades, the route rejoins the main road, from which the sea becomes visible, as does:-

**AG GORDIS BEACH (17km from Corfu Town)** Tel prefix 0663. The steeply descending approach passes various enterprises edging the road, including *Vicki's Apartments*, Space Bikes All New Models, a small mini-market, *Dinas Apartments*, Supermarket Robolo and Supermarket Spiros. Hereabouts the 'High St' narrows down and abruptly terminates on the beach backshore. Those householders who used to let out their front gardens for car parking have, in the main, put the space to better use and erected buildings, from which to run small businesses.

The vines still spread right down to a strip of bamboos which separate them from the sandy beach, that is where they have not been uprooted to make way for new construction. The wide, sandy beach has a sprinkling of pebbles, the water's edge is fine pebbles, with a scattering of small rocks, and the sea-bed is mainly pebble. The beach narrows at each end. To the right *(Fsw)* is a Cantina, and to the far right the beach becomes totally pebble, then rocky, beyond which Plitiri Point rears up in the background. To the left is a small beach bar and a large hotel overhanging the beach. A towering islet marks that end of the bay.

Where the road runs out, up against the beach, an operator hires out sun-beds and umbrellas whilst water skiing and para-gliding are available, for the energetic.

Apart from the magnificence of the surrounding scenery, Ag Gordis is not pretty. As a 'downmarket Glifada Beach', it has little to recommend it, being rather reminiscent of the more popular, south Cornish harbour village beauty spots – you know, absolutely nowhere to park and double yellow lines down both sides of the street.

Hotels include: the *Ag Gordis* (Class A, tel 36723), *Pension Alonakia* (Class B, tel 30407), *Chrysses Folies* (Class C, tel 44750), *Diethnes (International)* (Class D, tel 44744), *Pink Paradise* (Class E) & *Pink Paradise II* (Class E).

On the way down to Ag Gordis Beach, there is a turning left up to **Kato Garouna**, for details of which *See* **Route Five**.

## ROUTE FIVE
**To Kavos via Korission Lagoon, Ag Matheos, Linia, Issos Beach, Argirades, Ag Georgios, Korakades, Petreti, Perivolion, Kaliviotes Beach, Maltas Beach, Lefkimmi, Potami, all the beaches & back via Messonghi, Moraitika, Benitses, Achilleion Palace & Perama. (circa 150km)**South-west from Corfu Town, the 'centre of the island' roads pass through **Kinopiastes** and **Kastellani**. To observe and enjoy probably the last area of the old, 'Durrell Corfu', turn left in Kastellani for **Ag Theodori** and Ag Matheos. About 15km from Corfu Town, turn right off the main road, at the outset of some magnificent, cypress and other tree clad, mountainous countryside, and right again for:-

**KATO GAROUNA (16km from Corfu Town)** There is accommodation at the *Cafe-bar Grill Martha Theo's* as well as *Rooms*.

To continue south, backtrack through Kato Garouna and keep right, leaving the branch road back to the main thoroughfare on the left, whilst heading for:-

**KATO PAVLIANI (17km from Corfu Town)** A lovely, beautifully clean, well-shaded hillside village. Even the grass beneath the olive trees appears to have been mown. It is startlingly apparent that the villages and their inhabitants, in this area, reflect an age that has past, a time prior to sun oil, sun-beds and umbrellas, fast food snackbars, lager, cocktails, happy hours, running hot and cold water, en suite bathrooms, in fact, all the regrettable paraphernalia of the tourist led boom. The residents are delighted to welcome visitors simply for their effort to call in or pass through. This is the island Greece of the shyly proffered plate of fruit or a glass of wine, not the Greece of frenzied peasants thrusting bags of herbs or bottles of wine under the noses of passers-by, in exchange for money, more money. This is a region of busy agriculture and fishing, but where there is always time to linger over a Greek coffee in the local kafeneion. Viva this Greece.

Beyond Kato Pavliani there is a fork. Left detours to **Ano Pavliana** and right, a serpentine but metalled road, descends through a delightful scenery of cypresses, heather and olive trees to:-

**PENTALI (23km from Corfu Town)** One of the best times of year to visit these mountainside settlements is when the grape harvest is being collected and the wine made. All hands are to the 'press' and, even if the product is hardly up to Apellation Controlée standards, enthusiasm certainly makes up for snobbery. I say lead me to the nectar.

Fortunately, the signposting is good. A very rough road to the right sheers off back to Ag Gordis, not a track I would fancy, whilst left bears south. The road, the surface of which becomes unmetalled hereabouts, drops down to parallel the coastline, with the sea on the right and massed olive trees to the left. Even here is *Rooms*, in a farmhouse, and then a deserted hamlet. To sea, an offshore reef comes into view and the track passes by apartments to let, prior to the waterfront of:-

**AG MATHEOS BEACH (Paramona Beach) (28km from Corfu Town)** Unfortunately, a disappointment as the flat, featureless curve of the bay is edged by a possibly sandy shore which is almost entirely covered in kelp. The middle beach is small pebble. The *Hotel Restaurant Sunset* is certainly very conveniently situated. To the left (*Fsw*) is a spit of rocks, beyond which is another pebble shore bay bounded, on the south side, by a reef of seaward jutting rocks.

From the waterfront the main, now surfaced, road heads inland, past a mini-market and *Rooms*, on the right, to a divergence in the ways. To the left heads towards Ag Matheos and to the right continues to run south, becoming a rough, unsurfaced track again. Keeping to the latter choice, almost immediately there are *Rooms* on the left, after which the track meanders through an almost magical forest, the boughs of the old olive trees almost obscuring the way ahead. Despite rather informative, if old-fashioned road signs, the tracks and paths are not easy to follow and the shadowy darkness does not help. There are a number of turnings off to the right, to **Skidi**, **Kanouli Beach** (and *Katerina Villa*) and **Stelato**. Of these, Skidi is the best to select (if you can locate it!), for this sandy length of shore is easily the best of the beaches on this section of coastline. The countryside over which these excursions cross is rather strange, being intensely cultivated and ending on sandy cliffs. In amongst the agriculture are the occasional, sometimes amazing villas, often for rent. One single storey building, at Stelato, has a driveway floodlit by lights that would not go amiss on either side of a landing strip. The now sandy route bears round towards the coast and an enormous, inland lake, the:-

**KORISSION LAGOON (circa 29km from Corfu Town)** The track from the north makes a 'T' junction with the surfaced Gardiki to Mesavrisi road. To the right is signed 'Mesavrio Beach Bar Taverna'. This latter choice passes, on the left, a placard pointing skywards in the direction of a small dolls house of a shed, on stilts, labelled 'Villa Costes', and the *Taverna Nicola*. The track then runs out at the north end of Lake Korission, a metre or so from the sea-shore which borders the great sand dunes dividing the sea from the lake. It is not true to indicate that the track completely runs out, because it does curve round to the north, no doubt to rejoin the informal mish-mash of unsurfaced paths criss-crossing the area. The first 100m or so of the shoreline to the south is rather unappealing, being narrow with some kelp and pebbles. But then it embarks, adjacent to a beach taverna (of which more later), on a staggering sweep of sand and beach, which goes on and on forever, well at least as far as Issos Beach. Incidentally, about half-way along this 6km stretch, is a canal linking the lagoon and sea.

The lagoon, still used to net fish, and now a nature reserve, is rather reminiscent of Norfolk, if it were not for the distant heights of Ag Matheos and Hlomos. But then many

Corfu environs remind one of other locations in the world. Certainly Lake Korission and the parallel beach must be one of the most unspoilt sectors of Corfu.

Mesavrisi is actually a widespread scattering of homesteads. The referred to beach taverna, which resembles a doo-hickey yacht signal station, is labelled 'Boring Bora' and is the rather ramshackle *Mesavrio Beach Bar Taverna*, with cabin apartments stuck on the side. Rumour suggests it is advisable to establish prices, prior to 'troughing'. You have been warned.

On the way back to the junction with the main highway at Gardiki, the road surface becomes surfaced. The intensive agriculture hereabouts may favour plastic greenhouses, but is still very old-fashioned in ambiance, with young girls riding donkeys and the eardrum shattering clatter of juddering rotovator trucks renting the air.

**GARDIKI (23km from Corfu Town)** The site of very old settlements and a cave shelter dating back some 25000 years. Were they early *Thomson* apartments?

About a ½km before the main road junction there is a turning to the right to:-
**Gardiki Castle** Probably built in the 13th century, now only the overgrown walls, the main gate tower and the eight towers of the octagonal layout are left standing.
   Those who approach the Gardiki turn off to the Lake, from the direction of Ag Matheos, should note that the correct route is signed 'Taverna Nicola/Lake Korission'.

Travellers wishing to return to Corfu Town, should head for:-
**AG MATHEOS (Ag Mathias) (21km from Corfu Town)** This pleasant village is domi-nated by the oak tree clad Mt Ag Matheos (463m), which is topped off by a monastery. There is a choice of two footpaths, either of which takes about 30mins. The more northerly of the two requires turning left towards the village church, where turn left again after which follow the well worn track, keeping round to the left. The southern path starts the mountain climb from the village outskirts, turning right beyond an (engineers) shop and keeping to the main track. The views from the Monastery out over Lake Korission are truly splendid.

Back at the 'starting blocks', for the other, more eastern centre of the island' roads, from Corfu Town proceed to **Kinopiastes** and then **Ag Deka**. This route prettily winds down the centre of the island to **Ano Messonghi** (the Messonghi River bridge – about 22km from Corfu Town). Prior to crossing over the bridge there is *Rooms*, on the right, and a road to the left heads back round to the main coastal route from Messonghi to Corfu Town, but more of that later. Once over the bridge, a turning to the right curves back through **Vranganiotika**, whence petrol, through New Forest type countryside (if olive trees can be substituted for English hardwoods) towards the north and Gardiki.
   Ignoring these diversions, the road to the south continues down the centre of the island, through **Hlomotina**, wherein are *Rooms*. The countryside is, in the main, quite attractive with groves of olive trees scattered about, as is new building development.

**LINIA (28km from Corfu Town)** A way-station crossroads. Most of the development is on the north side of the hamlet and includes a petrol filling station, cafe-bar, mini-market, travel office (a what?), baker and *Rooms*.

To the right, at the crossroads, is a side road, the surface of which deteriorates, beyond *Pension Villa Jimmy*. It meanders, through countryside, to the huge expanse of:-
**ISSOS BEACH (29½km from Corfu Town)** The track runs out on a large, backshore turning circle, obviously used for informal gatherings as there are some tatty chairs and tables scattered about. Oh dear! Straight ahead is a majestic sweep of sandy beach. To the left (*Fsw*) runs all the way to distant Ag Georgios. To the right, and backed by huge, mountainous, Sahara like dunes, the beach goes on and on and on... all the way to Mesavrisi. Lagoudia islet is offshore. Behind the dunes is a great sandy plain, which peters

out in the waters of the southern end of Lake Korission. This expanse provides grazing for the occasional, shepherd accompanied flock. But a word of warning, a note of caution must advise that this truly marvellous location is absolutely shadeless. Worse, it is polluted. The middle-shore rubbish drums, thoughtfully provided, remain unemptied, with the contents sprawled about their surrounds. A few manky sun-beds remain stacked.

Back at Linia, the road to Hlomos is unsurfaced, while the south-eastern route continues on past more *Rooms* and a restaurant to:-
**ARGIRADES (30km from Corfu Town)** There's a filling station, pharmacy, some shops, including a fruit and vegetable store, and a baker.

Opposite the *Pension Restaurant Bar La Coste* is a side road to the right. This passes *Rooms*, opposite a bamboo grove, *Pension Villa Eli* and *Studio Rooms Helena*, prior to:-

**AG GEORGIOS (31½km from Corfu Town)** The rather soulless Esplanade extends to either side, parallel to but some 50km back from the straight coastline. The beach is, in effect, a continuation of the Lake Korission sweep, but rather narrow and rocky in spots, with the central section entirely boulderous. Only some four or five years ago Ag Georgios was an embryonic resort, but it was obvious that the unsatisfactory jumble of bars, restaurants, holiday apartments and villas would result in a tawdry 'strip'. Admittedly not yet complete, sadly the outcome of the development to date is entirely forgettable. There are blue signs indicating this or that 'delight'.

Across the Esplanade from the junction is a scooter hire business. To the right (*Fsw*) are *Rooms*, Rent A Bike George, a travel office, Save Centre Supermarket, some villas, after which the shore continues all the way to Issos Beach (Perhaps it is the ever lively, 'Enjoy a beach night out' tourists of Ag Georgios who cause the rubbish at Issos Beach). To the left stretches a long way and is rather Hayling Island like, mirroring the right-hand of the Esplanade, but with many chalets and more open spaces between the street and the shore. There is a mass of *Rooms*. At the far end is an extremely long, sandy beach, even if the nearside has a pebbly sea-bed.

The overall development would appear to have overtaken the main services. The electricity supply is indeterminate and often, even early and late in the season, the water is shut off at about 1700hrs (I bet the holiday brochures do not include that little gem of information!). Another problem Ag Georgios shares with similar, comparatively new resorts, set down some distance from the main road, is that it is often necessary to walk many kilometres to catch a bus. In the case of Ag Georgios this requires a 2km hike to Argirades.

Returning to Argirades, the left, north turning off the main highway drops down to an olive-groved plain, with a rather confusing road system. A few kilometres beyond the large but featureless village of **Neohoraki**, to the left leads to:-
**KOUSPADES (32km from Corfu Town)** Noted for the Mini-market Spiros.

From this village, a turning to the left descends steeply to the small cove of:-

**BOUKARI POINT (33km from Corfu Town)** The winding, surfaced road borders a summer dry river gorge, past the 'flash' *Hotel Hellios*, on the left, and the *Hotel Boukari* (Class C, tel 22687), on the right, prior to spilling on to the quay of a beachless but pretty, tree shaded location. A backshore track meanders off in both directions and a wooden quay juts into the sea. As in years gone by, the two taverna owners, one on each side of the road, battle for clients. Due to difficulties in getting to Boukari, the establishments rely on passing trade, in this case the trip boat caiques who clip past the headland, morning and night, on their way out and back from this or that distant delight.

Neither the *Taverna Boukari*, owner Spiros Karidis and on the right (*Fsw*), or the *Taverna To Limani*, on the left, are inexpensive. If pressed, I must plump for 'Spiros', and those who observe his rather rotund shape, may share my little joke. There is also a *Hotel Penelope* (Class C).

Right in Kouspades sallies forth to the villages of **Vassiliatika** and **Korakades**. The latter is a lovely, old settlement with a cement rendered, rock 'High St'. It is possible, by persevering along a track from the top end of the village, to wind down through a heavily wooded plantation and emerge at the port of Petreti.

Returning to the junction the north side of Neohoraki, close by is a pharmacy and *Rooms*. The right-hand, narrow road advances through pretty, spaced out, aged olive trees, vines and scattered settlements. Flocks of sheep and goats graze the meadowland, on which some private villas are being constructed. A fork to the right progresses to the village of **Ag Nikolaos**. The fork to the left leads to:-

**NOTOS (34km from Corfu Town)** A small bay edged by a muddy, kelpy shoreline backed by olive groves. Offshore is a tiny islet. There is *Rooms* and the *Panorama Snackbar*. To the left is a beach. At the end of a dusty track and to the right is a signpost to the *Pension Sailor's Restaurant*. This is about 1½km distant, following the coastline, but about 20m above sea-level.

By backtracking, the route continues on to:-
**PETRETI (35km from Corfu Town)** A messy development in a lightly wooded, flat plain, scattered about which are a number of buildings, including accommodation in a nice looking house, and a butcher. On the way to the waterfront is a new football pitch. There is a surprisingly large fishing boat quay and the surrounding area has been tarmacadamed. A number of caiques are randomly chocked up on the shore. The seashore is muddy, seaweedy and scruffy and, were if not for the heat and the sprawling taverna, the scene could well be the Cornish Helford river, at middle tide. The *Taverna Dimitrios*, still a 'watering hole' for the rather piratical locals, has replaced the marquee with an asbestos and tiled outbuilding to cover the terrace. Dimitrios is not now without some competition as across the way is a smart restaurant, but I wouldn't cross the road. A village supermarket offers accommodation whilst along the shoreline, to the right (*Fsw*), and accessible from the village 'High St', is the *Pension Bar Restaurant Egrypos*. Further to the right is an attractive cove, a stark contrast to the village's immediate shoreline.

Leaving this area, from Argirades, the main road continues on to:-
**PERIVOLION (35km from Corfu Town)** A large, busy village with a friendly community and an increasing awareness of the business possibilities available by supplying tourist services. Thus the to be expected stores and services, which include a hardware shop, baker and clinic, are now supplemented by apartments for rent, Rent A Bike and *Rooms*.
A turning to the left advances along a metalled road, which is in danger of losing its tarmacadam surface, past the *Pension Adriani*, a new apartment building, the *Pension Christos* and a number of buildings 'in construction' amongst the olive groves, to:-

**KALIVIOTES BEACH (36½km from Corfu Town)** There is a taverna, a picturesque but mud shore, set in a series of coves, and a small quay. What shore is not mud, is big pebble, on both sides of the quay.

Back at the centre of Perivolion, at the crossroads alongside a campanile and pointing to the right, is a sign 'To The Beach'. Following this progresses through pretty countryside, past *Rooms*, beyond which the road's surface becomes unmetalled. There is a signpost to accommodation to the right, more *Rooms*, some two storey package holiday apartments, more apartments, a large souvenir shop and then:-

**MALTAS BEACH/ST BABARA (37½km from Corfu Town)** Must be rated as the best of the Corfu package holiday seaside resorts. Apart from being neat and clean, the beach is superb, there are sufficient pensions and tavernas to make life interesting and the package holiday exploitation is at an acceptably low level. Only two companies are in attendance, one English *Sunvil Holidays* (an interesting tour operator) and one German.

As the number of apartments is very few, their clients do not swamp the place. That in itself would be difficult as, to the right (*Fsw*), the splay of golden sand beach seems to stretch on forever... gradually narrowing down. It must extend almost as far as Ag Georgios. Back at the 'core' of the hamlet, a stream has cut a shallow channel across the surface of the beach. There are some sun-beds, umbrellas and pedaloes 'masterminded' by a couple of local entrepreneurs. The gently shelving sea-bed is sandy and the central surface of the beach is raked daily. To the left a darker, narrower beach undulates along at the foot of the cliffs, for about 3km.

My favourite establishment is in a prime position, on the right (*Fsw*), and adjacent to where the road spills on to the backshore. This is the:-

**Pension Restaurant Bar Saint Babara**
*Directions*: As above.

Lefteras, the manager, is a strong, capable man who runs a tight ship. A room with breakfast costs 2000drs a night. The reasonably priced beach bar/taverna is combined in a single storey, asbestos roofed building.

There are two other backshore tavernas but the comparative quietness of the location might not suit everybody. The lack of public transport is a drawback, it being necessary to walk the 2½km to and from Perivolion in order to catch a bus. Incidentally, the fare to Kavos costs 55drs and Corfu Town 190drs.

South of Perivolion, on the road to Lefkimmi, a sign to the right indicates **Vitalades** and a beach, but this is a hamlet with a path down to a continuation of the Maltas Beach. Beyond a BP Petrol Station, the road has been re-engineered, being wide and in good order all the way to **Ano Lefkimmi** and **Lefkimmi** (40km from Corfu Town). Lefkimmi is a large, dusty, sprawling settlement. At Ano Lefkimmi, a turning to the left sheers off to:-

**ALIKES (42½km from Corfu Town)** Not to be confused with the 'north of Corfu Town' Alikes. There are two, dusty approach roads, the other closer to Potami, which join up near to Alikes. There is a plethora of *Rooms*, which is very mystifying because this Alikes and its surrounds are an absolute dump.

To the right (*Fsw*) is a working salt extraction business, the pans of which occupy a large area. The headland is topped off by a small harbour, to the right of which extends an indescribably filthy foreshore, covered in kelp and stinking seaweed.

Prior to the headland, and to the left, a sign indicates 'Petrakis Beach', along a narrow street. Beyond the 'dead' Disco Victoria, a mini-market and bakery, this wide path comes to end alongside a large hotel/restaurant. To the left stretches another appalling foreshore, similarly covered in kelp. A number of fishing boats are randomly moored in the primeval swamp. This can only be a Greek resort because nobody in their right mind would voluntarily visit the place.

From Lefkimmi a turning to the right, unmetalled from the outset, is signposted Neochori. This wanders through another relatively unspoilt region of Corfu, possibly made all the more attractive in comparison to nearby Kavos. At the outset the countryside is very scrubbly but becomes more appealing and parkland in nature. The unaffected nature of the area is indicated by the remarkable number of donkey-borne women. At the lovely village of **Kritika**, the road surface is metalled. At the junction turn left for less attractive **Bastatika** (46km from Corfu Town), which seems to go on forever, possessing a clinic, baker and a water fountain. Next is **Neochori**, a small settlement set in lovely countryside, which is followed by **Dragotina** (48½km from Corfu Town), a quite large village wherein the road surface is tarmacadamed. There is a clinic, kafeneion, a taverna or two and a drinking water fountain. A signpost indicates:-

**KANOULA BEACH (50km from Corfu Town)** The track, is rather rough and 'bottoms out' close to a spit, on the right (*Fsw*). This terminates in rocky, shallow water. In the far lee of the outcrop, a number of fishing boats are drawn up. The beach certainly is sandy but much of the sea's edge is biscuit rock and subject to kelp infestation. The coastline is a series of sandy coves set at the base of savagely eroded cliffs. The overall setting is wild but shadeless, the steep hill slopes only being sparsely vegetated.

To the right, the shoreline is edged by a backshore track. To the left is a sea-lapped, low, rocky outcrop set in angled, shelving slabs, edged by a rough roadway that peters out alongside a tiny, harbour. By tramping along the foot of the cliff-face (also to the left), it is possible to scramble over and round the rocks all the way to the spectacular, pebble and sandy **Arkoudilas Beach**. Whow!

Back at Dragotina village, a metalled road heads for small **Spartera** (50km from Corfu Town), where are *Rooms*. Beyond Spartera, the now appalling, unsurfaced road treks through a forest of trees to a junction on the outskirts of Kavos. (*See* later on in the Route). To delay the inevitable awfulness of Kavos, don't turn left, but angle back to the right and strike out for the:-

**Monastery Panaghia Arkoudilas (51km from Corfu Town)** This is approximately a 35-45 minute walk along a well-worn path. The route is set in trees which include cypress and oak. The campanile gateway of the walled monastery peeks through stately cypress trees. The original chapel is a ruin and the more recent building is vandalised. Beyond the monastery it is possible to scramble on in order to look out over the cliffs, with Arkoudilas Beach down below.

Back at Lefkimmi, the main highway proceeds eastwards, past another Alikes turning, to:-
**POTAMI (Potamos) (41km from Corfu Town)** Tel prefix 0661. The village possesses a fine Bailey bridge. This crosses a prettily tree lined cutting resembling a canal, but which is in fact the River Himaros. The scene is most surprising, for there are caiques and small boats lineally moored to both sides of the river, a sight that puts one in mind of Holland or a very hot Midlands canal scene, not Corfu.

Incidentally, in 1985, the local residents blockaded the bridge for a few days, cutting off road communications to Kavos. This 'theft of the highway' was in protest at height of summer water shortages, which were blamed on the tourists. As an 'ill wind' doesn't blow everybody a storm, the local boat owners made a financial killing by ferrying the Kavos based package holiday-makers to and from Corfu Town and the airport. In 1988, at the end of September, Kavos tourists had another nasty shock. An island wide strike (in respect of a proposal to jettison untreated sewage in the sea at Igoumenitsa) left the incoming visitors foodless, for days. Only the timely intervention of the Honorary British Consul, who interceded with the Mayor of Kavos, saved the day... and the holiday-makers hunger pangs.

From the 'western' outskirts, there are apartments for rent, general stores, a pharmacy, baker, a filling station and then the Bailey bridge, across which are *Rooms*. The river banks 'host' some kafeneions and tavernas, in the vicinity of the bridge, at the chairs and tables of which a number of more undesirable visitors gather, daily.

Hotels include: the *Pension Elvira* (Class B, tel 91995), *Zorbas* (Class D, tel 37654) & *Spyros* (Class E, tel 32979).

On the far, 'east' side of the bridge, a river quay edging street to the left becomes an unmetalled wide track. This borders the banked river all the way to the coast at:-
**Bouka Beach (42½km from Corfu Town)** To the right of the long breakwater, that protects the river mouth, is a very sandy, if small beach with a sandy sea-bed. The beach quickly narrows down to a long grass, duney backshore, in the direction of Kavos. There is some kelp. The delightful thing is the infrequented air of peace and tranquility, in comparison to 'that other place', which can be 'sensed', if not viewed, away in the

distance to the right (*Fsw*). The almost total lack of people compares rather favourably with the 'few million' based at Kavos.

From Potami, the road passes through a plain, heavily wooded with olive trees and groves, to:-
**KAVOS (Cavos) (47km from Corfu Town)** Tel prefix 0662. The original settlement has been swamped. The long, tree shaded 'High St' is lined by a fly-blown mess of villas, apartments, fast food, 'slow food', discos, restaurants, hotels, souvenir and gift shops, mini-markets, supermarkets, foreign language book and paper shops, travel and currency exchange offices. On the other hand, there aren't any banks, bakers, nor a Post Office. Incidentally, bread is sold by the supermarkets. The 'High St' runs parallel to and about 100m back from the 20m wide, beautifully sandy beach which extends for 'miles'. There is some kelp at the south end of the shoreline. Unfortunately this lovely shore, with a slowly shelving, sandy sea-bed, is covered with people, sun-beds and umbrellas. The expensive beach and hotel bars that border the backshore do a roaring trade. They are divided into informal blocks by haphazard, wide swathes of undeveloped land which link the High St and the beach. Late night, beach revellers leave a scattering of bottles, glasses and fire ashes as a mute reminder of their bacchanalian merry-making. As the shore progresses northwards, it narrows down and becomes comparatively quieter, due to the less densely packed holiday accommodation.
 Hotels include: the *Pension Roussos* (Class B, tel 22122), *Saint Marina* (Class B), *Alexandra Beach* (Class C, tel 22281), *Cavos* (Class C, tel 22107), *Morpheas* (Class C), *Cavo Palace Alexandra* (Class D), *Panela Beach* (Class D, tel 61328) & *Spyrou* (Class E).
It is a great pity that it is with Kavos that the description of the southern tip of Corfu must end.

Returning to the Messonghi River bridge, once again, the road to the east advances to the major, north-south coastal highway and the most intense development on Corfu, stretching all the way from Messonghi to Perama. A side-road to the right advances to:-

**MESSONGHI & MIRANGI BAY (23km from Corfu Town)** Tel prefix 0661. Rather more 'serene' than Benitses, the 10m wide strip of sandy beach with pebbles at the sea's edge, stretches to the right (*Fsw*) for some two hundred metres. Most sea sports and 'beach support facilities' are available. The 'High St' approximately parallels the shore, but unusually is almost toally separated from it by various businesses and villas beside which it is necessary to squeeze. At the far, south end are **Rooms**. There are a number of 'Free Parking' signs, despite which the resort remains attractive, probably because the inland side of the main street has not been developed. Almost as soon as the immediate environs have been left behind, it is countryside...
 Hotels include: the *Gemini* (Class B, tel 55398), *Maria House* (Class C, tel 38684), *Melissa Beach* (Class C, tel 55229), *Rossis* (Class C, tel 55352) & *Roulis* (Class C, tel 55353).
 There is *Sea Horse Camping* (Tel 25735), which is open mid April-mid October.

Off to the left (*Messonghi behind one*) of the approach to Messonghi, a metalled road climbs the foothills of the Hlomos Mountain to:-
**SPILIO (25km from Corfu Town)** A pleasant, sprawling hillside village with a couple of **Rooms** and some holiday apartments. Travellers should avoid Tasso's *Bella Vista Bar Grill*, which is about 75 steps up the hill and on the right. If the surly, slow service were not enough, menu's are only noticeable by their absence. This allows mine host, a handsome man of Cretan appearance, who carries out a shouting (and slanging) match with a disembodied voice in the bowels of the basement, to 'massage' the bill. A lunchtime snack for a couple of two plain omelettes (200drs each), a tzatzaki (250drs – ouch!), a salad without feta (250drs – double ouch!), a Henninger beer (120drs), bread and service (150drs – yes, 150drs) totalled 1170drs. This was reduced to 1150drs when sheer

disbelief was expressed. But I refused to pay more than 1000drs, which all caused a certain amount of unseemly disagreement.

From Spilio a road does continue on to Hlomos village. From this mountain settlement an unmade, serpentine track descends through forests to Linia, with super views out over Lake Korission.

From Messonghi there are still some olive groves bordering the coast road as far as:-
**MORAITIKA (20km from Corfu Town)** The 'High St' of this 'Kosta'd' resort is about 100m distant from the shore. Apart from the usual package holiday 'back-up' facilities of bars and mock tavernas, there is a pharmacy, a clinic and a filling station. Perhaps the sign, to one side of the 100m long, narrow track to the beach says it all. This proudly announces 'The Best English Tea In Corfu'.

There is about 300m of beach with a pebbly sea's edge and a sandy sea-bed. Various water sports help to entertain the hordes.

Hotels include: the *Motel Delfinia* (Class A, tel 30318), *Albatross* (Class B, tel 55315), *Alkyonis* (Class B, tel 55201), *Delfinakia* (Class B, tel 55450), *Messonghi Beach* (Class B, tel 38684), *Pension Solonaki* (Class B), *Margarita* (Class C, tel 55267), *Prassino Nissi* (Class C, tel 55379), *Sea Bird* (Class C, tel 92348), *Three Stars* (Class C, tel 92457), *Pension Fontana* (Class D) & *Moraitika* (Class E, tel 952378).

The coastal road gently corniches northwards, at or at about sea-level, passing a pebble beach and, opposite the **Strogili** turning, a long, olive tree shaded, man-made, free entry beach, complete with thatched sun shelters and some kelp. The coastline becomes rocky and weedy and the flanks of the inland hillsides display signs of a serious forest fire.

**BENITSES (12½km from Corfu Town)** Well, yes! Benitses used to be billed as a genuine Corfiot fishing village – which it was, many, many years ago. I can remember watching a 'mother-ship' caique set out to sea, towing a clutch of rowing boats, from the stern of which were hung the large, sardine attracting lanterns - but that was ten years or more past.

Unfortunately 'Kosta'd' Benitses now epitomises all that is worst in the Mediterranean holiday resort industry. Sufficient to advise that it is the playground of countless numbers of British lager dregs, determined to enjoy themselves!

From south to north, a brief rundown of some of the 'delights' might graphically reveal the state of play. The Benitses Go Kart Club is followed by a pleasant coastal strip, a sign for 'Free Safety Deposit Boxes' (Yes, safety deposit boxes...), **Rooms**, Lonely Rooms, 'Sunday lunch, Roast Beef', a section of concrete contained, man made beach, an undeveloped strip, the now by-passed High St, a pocket handkerchief of beach in the angle of a small quay, 'English Chef', 'Fish and Chips' and the caique quay, which marks the end of the finish.

Hotels include: the *San Stefano* (Class A, tel 36036), *Belvedere* (Class B, tel 92411), *Eugenia* (Class B, tel 92064), *Potamaki* (Class B, tel 30889), *Bavaria* (Class C, tel 92592), *Bella Vista* (Class C, tel 92087), *Corfu Maris* (Class C, tel 92381), *Kamares Benitson* (Class C), *Le Mirage* (Class C), *Loutrouvia* (Class C, tel 92258), *Avra* (Class D, tel 92424), *Benitsa* (Class D, tel 39269), *Eros* (Class E, tel 92393) & *Riviera* (Class E, tel 92258).

It is a well founded rumour that one Benitses hotel caters exclusively for Germans. In order to marshall their guests, the management have installed loudspeakers, not only in the hotel, but strategically placed throughout the grounds. When necessary the *Musak* is faded out for the instructions and propaganda to be broadcast. Achtung!

From Benitses, it is only a kilometre to the angled turning that climbs to the:-
**ACHILLEION PALACE (10km from Corfu Town)** Built for Empress Elizabeth of Austria, in 1891. When this out-of-the ordinary lady was assassinated, in 1898, by an Italian anarchist, the palace was subsequently owned by the German Kaiser. He was a regular visitor between 1908 and 1914, after which the outbreak of the First World War curtailed

his movements. The palace was expropriated, finishing in the ownership of the Greek Government. Now part of the building is used as a casino which is only open to non-Greeks, so punters should take along their passport.

The architecture is often airily criticised and one pile of 'neo' this or that does look much like another (does it not?). Be that as it may, I admit the palace attracts me, even if it does resemble a large wedding cake decoration. Sadly, on closer inspection, the structure, which houses a museum, has an aura of faded and unrepaired grandeur. Less prosaically, the setting provided a scene in the James Bond film *For Your Eyes Only*. The palace attracts numerous guided tour coach parties and an interesting diversion is to listen and watch the cruise liner contingents. Admission costs 200drs, there are super toilets and outside the main gates is the mandatory snackbar.

Back on the coast road, and proceeding towards Corfu Town, the route corniches past unattractive, rather weedy trees, a *Rooms*, close to *Snackbar Fattys Club*, and then the remains of the **Kaisers Bridge** (circa 8km from Corfu Town). Obviously it was once a rather grand structure but is now minus its *raison d'etre* – the span. The bridge was part and parcel of a quay, to which the illustrious owner of the Achilleion Palace, the Kaiser, moored his private yacht.

The road climbs away from sea-level towards:-
**PERAMA (7km from Corfu Town)** No 'lager strip', more a dignified, pretty location with plenty of tree cover through which the main road advances in a series of fast loops. From here can be viewed the much photographed, twin islets of Kanoni. Perama is connected to the Kanoni peninsula by a causeway which allows pedestrians and scooterists to cross the mouth of Halikiopoulou lagoon. A trip boat plies hither and thither.

Hotels include: the *Alexandros* (Class A, tel 368557), *Akti* (Class B, tel 39445), *Oasis* (Class B, tel 38190), *Aegli* (Class C, tel 39812), *Continental* (Class C, tel 33113), *Fryni* (Class C, tel 36877), *Pontikonissi* (Class C, tel 36871) & *Perama* (Class E, tel 33167).

Perhaps the Corfiot character is best summed up by a notice, once pinned to some olive trees on the outskirts of an island village. This was reprinted in a national English newspaper some years ago. In essence this politely requested tour buses to turn around and leave the village and its inhabitants to their own devices, so as not to spoil the intrinsic character of their life. Nice that!

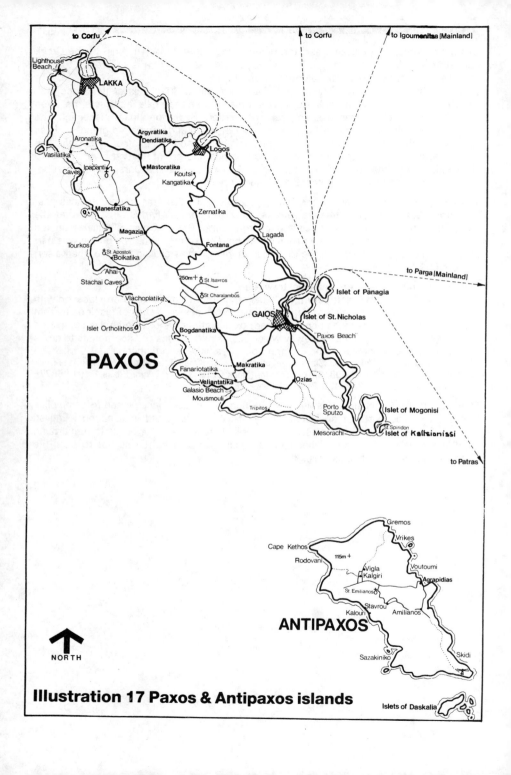

Illustration 17 Paxos & Antipaxos islands

# 13 PAXOS (Paxoi, Paxi) & Antipaxos

## Ionian Islands

Dinghy sailors ★★★★★
island ambiance ★★★
Beach lovers ★

---

*Paxos - Greek for a spell in the slow lane. - A quotation from the brochure of 'Friends of Paxos Ltd'.*

**FIRST IMPRESSIONS** Busy ports (yes, ports – three of them); boulder strewn hillsides & dry river beds; olive groves; narrow, olive-blackened roads; old, ruined buildings; the smell of olive dross; saline drinking water ('glypha' – brackish water); a damp island out of the height of summer months; few sandy beaches; wasps 'in season'.

**SPECIALITIES** Olives, olive oil & the wine of Antipaxos.

**RELIGIOUS HOLIDAYS & FESTIVALS** include: 15th August – Assumption (Dormition) Day, Gaios Port.

**VITAL STATISTICS** Tel prefix 0662. The island is approximately 10½km long, 4½km wide with an area of about 19sqkm. Paxos has about 2500 inhabitants of which some 500 live in Gaios port.

**HISTORY** Mythology advises us that the Greek god of the sea, Posidon (the Roman Neptune), tiring whilst travelling between Corfu and Lefkas, struck the sea with his trident and the island of Paxos bubbled up out of the waves.

The island's oldest recorded churches date back to the 6th century AD and are located in the Ozias region, reputably the earliest settled area of Paxos. One was at the port of Ozias, which surely must have been in or around Porto Sputzo?

Naturally the history of Paxos closely mirrored that of Corfu. The Venetians constructed the castle on the Gaios harbour islet of St Nicholas. The islanders were a plucky lot, rising up against their then French masters, in 1810. It is interesting to note that a member of the well-known island family of Grammatikos was involved. One Laskaris Grammatikos, a Francophile, was put to death by the patriots, along with the island's governor.

**GENERAL** Paxos, like Ios in the Cyclades, is a reasonably priced island, probably for the same reasons – a preponderance of British tourists. The 'Brits' tend to be rather less free-spending than their European cousins, or just more careful, depending upon your viewpoint. Although averagely inexpensive, a few items are noticeably more costly, probably because nearly all supplies, including groceries, have to be 'imported'.

The Paxos countryside is very different from any of the other Ionian islands. There is an 'enchanted forest' milieu when travelling between centres. The olive-blackened roads and tracks wind up and down through boulder strewn, rambling, cool, shady, olive groves. Many of the extensive olive groves are extremely old and the individual tree trunks are gnarled, twisted and of immense size. An evocative mirror image can still be observed along the south-west coastal strip of Corfu island.

In common with most of the other Ionian islands, Paxos is extremely verdant, due to the comparatively high winter rainfall experienced. This fact is evidenced by the deep, summer-dry, rocky river-beds, which interweave with the roads and are criss-crossed by stone built bridges, an unusual sight on a Greek island.

The island's agriculture is almost entirely based on the olive. Prior to harvest time, the rolled up nets are tucked into the forked branches of the trees. When the olives are 'in season', the nets are opened out and laid on the ground beneath the spreading boughs. A curious sight are the large bells strapped to, and hanging down from convenient branches. These are to sound a warning, in case of fire, of which the islanders are truly very apprehensive, no, terrified. For this reason random camping is strictly forbidden, a stricture which must be obeyed.

Apparently, derelict buildings and long abandoned olive presses are littered about amongst the forests of olive trees, imparting an ethereal overlay to the cool, fairy-tale, almost medieval atmosphere. It may take a little time to realise that the often comparatively massively constructed houses of dressed stone, which are scattered about the countryside, are unusually, not painted white.

A number of factors combine to make Paxos a difficult island on which to find accommodation, and an independent traveller's nightmare, at the height of season. For instance, the few Gaios hotels usually listed are block-booked by a sailing school and a tour operator. To make matters more difficult for short-term stopovers, the three main towns (port/villages really) are family, holiday-villa territory. The various specialist tour companies have staked out nearly all the houses and flats with every nook and cranny exploited to create even more accommodation of this type. These drawbacks do not interfere with the waves of day-trippers from Kavos, Ipsos and even Kassiopi (all Corfu locations), as well as Parga, Sivota and Igoumenitsa (all mainland ports), who, in the height of season months, swarm, mainly over Gaios and its surrounds. Terrific!

Unlike Corfu, the few government officials speak very little, if any, English but a high percentage of islanders understand some.

## (Porto) GAIOS (Paxi): capital & main port (Illustration 18) Gaios town
and harbour borders a small bay into which the large islet of St Nicholas fits, leaving a wide channel running all the way round the quay. The New Port is at the far, north end of the harbour and is separated from the main port and waterfront by a curving road.

Gaios spreads along the quayside and radiates out from the attractive town square over the narrow, sea-level valley. The settlement is rather beguiling and many a traveller, planning a short visit, might well stay on and on and on.... The preponderance of relatively well behaved, middle class, villa and sailing school tourists, speaking well modulated, perceived English (hey, what dat man!), has resulted in a rather Home Counties, Sunday drinkies ambience. (Some say the greater 'yuk-yuk' bird can be heard at cocktail time, but I cannot comment).

Vessels of all types anchor gunwale to gunwale, bow or stern on to the quayside, which they fill from end to end. They include trip boats, small tramp-like ferries, luxury motor cruisers, excursion caiques, high speed trip boats, yachts and caiques. On the way round from the New Port, the sailing school dinghies are the first craft to be encountered. They are followed by larger vessels and the local ferries. The bigger, excursion trip caiques and high speed craft are centred alongside the Main Square section of the quay. The private yachts, smaller fishing boats and caiques are berthed towards the east end of the 'Esplanade'.

This is definitely a 'Greek town', as defined towards the end of Chapter Three. The rubbish is still collected, during the week, by a bell ringing character, a look-alike for Zorba's father, who bestrides a Greek cross between a dumper truck and a motorised pallet cart.

## ARRIVAL BY FERRY The larger inter-island ferries dock at the New Port or quay.
On disembarking turn left (*Ferry-boat behind one*) for the 200 to 300m walk to the heart of the port.

The smaller, local ferries dock (*Tmr* 1C4/5), conveniently, to the north of the Main Square. Following the harbour wall round to the left leads, after only three or four blocks (or another 150m), to the Main Square. In addition to the ferries, there are a number of high speed, dory style water taxis that run to a schedule.

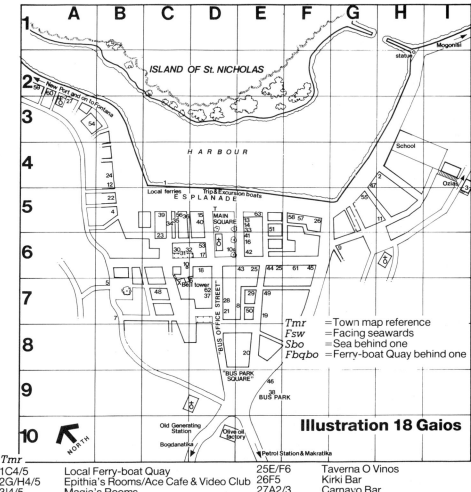

**Illustration 18 Gaios**

| Tmr | | |
|---|---|---|
| 1C4/5 | Local Ferry-boat Quay | |
| 2G/H4/5 | Epithia's Rooms/Ace Cafe & Video Club | |
| 3I4/5 | Magia's Rooms | |
| 4B5 | Rooms/Supermarket | |
| 5B7 | Rooms sign | |
| 6C/D7 | Rooms sign | |
| 7B7/8 | Rooms | |
| 8D/E7 | Rooms | |
| 9G6 | Rooms | |
| 10 | Peripteros | |
| 11G/H5 | Police station | |
| 12B4/5 | Makris Scooter & boat hire/Rooms | |
| 13E5 | Cafe-bar Anesis | |
| 14E5 | Cafe-bar Gaios | |
| 15D5 | Kafeneion | |
| 16E6 | Volcano Cafe-bar Restaurant | |
| 17D6 | Cafe-bar/Taverna | |
| 18D6 | Spiros Taverna | |
| 19E7 | Taka-Taka Restaurant | |
| 20E8 | Gaios Grill Taverna | |
| 21D7 | OTE | |
| 22B5 | Bar Naftaki | |
| 23C5/6 | Grill Rex | |
| 24B4 | Restaurant Grill Alexandros | |
| 25E/F6 | Taverna O Vinos | |
| 26F5 | Kirki Bar | |
| 27A2/3 | Carnavo Bar | |
| 28D7 | Baker/store | |
| 29E7 | Ice cream & pastry shop/Clinic | |
| 30C6 | Chandler/change office | |
| 31C6 | Laundry | |
| 32C/D6 | Hardware shop/change office | |
| 33D/E5/6 | 'Popular Art'/change office | |
| 34C5 | Scooter hire | |
| 35C5 | Scooter hire | |
| 36C5 | Tohatsu Boat Hire | |
| 37D7 | Bus ticket office | |
| 38E9 | Bus park | |
| 39C5 | Bulk olive oil warehouse | |
| 40D5 | A pair of stores | |
| 41D/E5/6 | Tobacconist | |
| 42E6 | Drink shop/store | |
| 43E6/7 | Fruit & Vegetable store | |
| 44E5/7 | Butcher | |
| 45F6/7 | Fruit & Vegetable store | |
| 46E9 | Fruit & Vegetable store | |
| 47G/H4/5 | Butcher | |

Within the map:

Tmr = Town map reference
Fsw = Facing seawards
Sbo = Sea behind one
Fbqbo = Ferry-boat Quay behind one

## THE ACCOMMODATION & EATING OUT

**The Accommodation** The lop-sidedness of the tourist development, concentrating as it does on villa-lets, has distorted the normal island mix of accommodation. Bearing in mind the previous remarks in respect of the availability (or more correctly the lack of availability) of accommodation, it shouldn't come as a surprise that there are no queues of welcoming house owners. But we may well be able to overcome this difficulty. For a start, those arriving on the **FB Kamelia** may refer to the notice displayed in the craft's saloon. This announces 'If you require accommodation in Paxos, please see the captain of the Kamelia

At the height-of-summer, the lack of sufficient accommodation has occasioned the authorities to insist that independent travellers must have guaranteed accommodation, prior to purchasing a ferry ticket to Paxos. 'Naturally', to ease the difficulties occasioned by this stipulation, there are 'Rooms For Sale' desks, close to the Corfu Old Port ferry-boat departure point. Their service does cost more than would a freelance enquiry, on landing.

**Hotel Paxos Beach** (Class B)                                                                    Tel 31211
*Directions*: This chalet complex is in a most attractive situation, about 1½km distant to the east of Gaios and on the left-hand side of the road to Mogonisi island (*See* **Route Two**).
The olive tree covered hillside, in which the buildings nestle, steeply slopes down to a tiny, pebbly beach and fringes a clear, blue-water, crescent-shaped bay. The management have opened their bar and beach to outsiders, between 0900-2400hrs. Prospects with a weak heart should think again, as it is a very abrupt climb back to the road. Anyone intending to 'book in' has to face up to the expense, as the owners insist that guests must have breakfast and the evening meal. This increases the double room chalet cost from 2600drs, or 4300drs (16th June-30th Sept), by some 3300drs! Several travel companies include the hotel in their brochures.

Back to town and reality! My first choice if only for sentimental (and thus the wrong?) reasons is:-
**'Epithia's' Rooms** (*Tmr* 2G/H4/5)
*Directions*: The house is situated towards the east end of the Esplanade and into the front of which is set the *Ace Cafe & Video Club*.
The very smiley Mama, who doesn't speak English, has simple, clean rooms. The house is splendidly sited bordering the Esplanade and overlooking the east portion of the harbour, where the local fishing boats and caiques moor. Due to the configuration of the harbour wall, most of the town's activity can be viewed from the narrow balconies of the first floor, front rooms. There are two drawbacks. The construction of the ground floor cocktail bar, which the '20th century', English speaking daughter runs, must make the location noisy. Furthermore, access to the excellent bathroom and shower, positioned on the ground floor, is via the family kitchen, which is usually jam-packed 'with somebody'. A double room costs from 1500drs a night.
On one occasion, whilst lazing on the balcony sipping the day away, I chanced to observe a caique pull up to the quay wall. Tethered to the small foredeck were a family of goats. The pantomime that ensued, in order to get the animals ashore, was worth the room rent alone. On the same day, a fisherman and his wife dragged from the hold of their small caique a recently caught, enormous flat fish. It wasn't many minutes before hordes of villagers gathered around to shout at each other, and the fish, for the next few hours, all just beneath us.

If Epithia has no accommodation available, she will probably direct enquirers to:-
**Magia's Rooms** (*Tmr* 3I4/5)
*Directions*: Proceed to the end of the alley, alongside Epithia's, jink left and right at the school, climb a flight of steps and cross the Ozias road.
To recommend or not? The careworn, elderly lady, who owns the place, almost always looks worried and obviously has to work from dawn to dusk. She is usually to be seen scurrying hither and thither during daylight hours. I usually prefer to hand over my money to someone who needs it (patronising git), but Magia's accommodation manifests almost all the room and bathroom faults outlined in Chapter Four, and some more! These digs are really priceless but they are basically clean. The bedrooms are pleasantly airy and lofty, with a chandelier, over-bed 'chandelierlettes' and a bedside lamp. I've dreamt of bedside lamps. Incidentally, the chandeliers are Woolworths imitation, rather than Harrods' cut glass but... It may be necessary to ferret out any blankets required.

The area of thought provoking eminence is the dark, shared bathroom. Loo rolls may well be in short supply, the water is cold (from both taps) and very saline, the door won't lock, the light lacks a globe, the toilet chain emerges from a hole in the roof, the vanitory unit is falling off the wall and the shower won't drain away. Beat that. A mid-season double room costs 1500drs.

Returning to the area of the local Ferry-boat Quay (*Tmr* 1C4/5), there is *Furnitured* (sic) *Apartments & Rooms* (Tel 31555) above a general store/supermarket (*Tmr* 4B5); a sign **Rooms** (*Tmr* 5B7) on the wall of the pleasant, tree shaded square, south-west of the quay; **Rooms** (*Tmr* 7B7/8); a sign **Rooms** (*Tmr* 6C/D7) in the alley alongside the 'bell tower' church; **Rooms** (*Tmr* 8D/E7) & **Rooms** (*Tmr* 9G6).

The port's two peripteros, (*Tmr* 10D/E6 & 10C/D6) advertise details of accommodation. One kiosk is at the top, left-hand (*Sbo*) corner of the Main Square, the other is down the lateral street, to the right of the first kiosk.

The police (*Tmr* 11G/H5) have a list of house owners with accommodation, but the officers are reluctant informants.

The scooter and bike hire operation (*Tmr* 12B4/5), directly opposite the local Ferry-boat Quay, is run by Spiros Markris, a now more rounded, if still rather taciturn young man, and his bubbly, cuddly sister Georgia. They speak English and Spiros has a house with accommodation in Makratika (the first village out of Gaios). Prices for a double room start from 2000drs per night. Additionally, Georgia should have her own accommodation ready for the 1989 season. This is on the outskirts of Gaios.

The tourist agencies will be able to offer advice (*See* **Travel Agents & Tour Offices, A To Z**).

**The Eating Out** There are many more establishments nowadays and the Main Square is adequately endowed with cafe-bars and their awning shaded patios, including the:-
**Cafe-bar Anesis**(*Tmr* 13E5)
*Directions*: The first cafe-bar, on the left (*Sbo*).

They serve reasonably priced fare, including a plate of eggs and bacon which can, after months abroad, prove a welcome and nostalgic alternative to the rather bland, Greek version of a French Continental breakfast. A Henninger costs 90drs, a liberal ouzo 60drs, a 3 star brandy 110drs and a Nes meh ghala 75drs. As the packet of Nes, the jug of hot water and a carton of milk makes at least 1½cups, it is extremely good value, considering the prime location. Eavesdropping hereabouts can prove amusing... "... and I bought my (goat) bells in Nepal".

Next door is the look-alike *Cafe-bar Gaios* (*Tmr* 14E5) and the opposite side of the Square is a 'men-only' Kafeneion (*Tmr* 15D5). Further along the Square, and on the same side as the *Anesis*, is the *Volcano Cafe-bar Restaurant* (*Tmr* 16E6), mentioned if only because their menu commences 'Momentary'?

Diagonally across the Main Square from the Volcano; on the south-west corner is the:-
**Cafe-bar Taverna** (*Tmr* 17D6)
*Directions*: As above.

Apart from drinks and a limited range of food, they serve a large 'stick in a pita' souvlaki, costing 90drs, and a plate of chips, 60drs. These are 'sit-down' prices. A bottle of Henninger beer is priced at 90drs.

Across the street is:-
**Spiros Taverna** (*Tmr* 18D6)
*Directions*: As above, in a rather pokey, mankey building.

During the day there are only a few tables and chairs outside but at night they spread out behind the periptero, filling the small square. The menu lists a number of interesting dishes including soup, fresh swordfish, special pizza and veal stew. A meal for two of bean soup, (excellent – 218drs), chicken (good – 250drs), chips (60drs), veal stew with green beans (very good – 368drs), a Greek salad (passable, but awful olives which, considering this is an island speciality, seems shoddy – 152drs), a bottle of kortaki retsina (expensive – 119drs) and bread (for which there was no charge) cost 1167drs.

**Taka-Taka Restaurant** (*Tmr* 19E7)
*Directions*: From the Main Sq, proceed up 'Bus office' St, turn left (*Sbo*) at the first lateral turning, beyond the OTE (*Tmr* 21D7), and left again down the next main street. The establishment is directly across the road.

Rather expensive and no retsina listed.

**Gaios Grill Taverna** (*Tmr* 20E8)
*Directions*: Diagonally south-west from *Taka-Taka*. The large terrace stretches up the hillside, edging the road.

Very popular with the villa and apartment set, which is understandable, as the place offers good value food. A filling meal, for two, of green beans and ratatouille (both hot, if salty), spiced lamb with rice (excellent), moussaka (appetising), patatas, bread, a bottle of mineral water and a kortaki retsina cost 1370drs. The waiter totalled the damage on a calculator – better than an abacus I suppose.

Other establishments include the *Restaurant Grill Alexandros* (*Tmr* 24B4); the *Bar Naftaki* (*Tmr* 22B5), run by a nice, old lady and a quieter place, even if a coffee does cost 80drs; *Grill Rex* (*Tmr* 23C5/6) and the *Taverna O Vinos* (*Tmr* 25E/F6), rather seedy but, invitingly, wine barrels are stacked on racks. Next door is the *Kafeneion Irine*.

For those requiring rather smarter surroundings, in which to sip a cocktail, there are a couple of establishments, towards the east end of the port. The *Kirki Club* (*Tmr* 26F5), which is not so flash as the *Ace*, more a yachtsmans' rendevous, and the previously mentioned *Ace Cafe & Video Club* (*Tmr* 2G/H4/5). At the opposite end of the Esplanade is the *Carnavo Bar* (*Tmr* 27A2/3), the *Sun Med*, 'happy hour' watering hole. For simpler fare, try the bakers (*Tmr* 28D7 ). They sell a tasty, but not cheap, cinnamon pie at a cost of 80drs. The sweet-toothed might consider the small confectionery/ice-cream/wine/spirits/tarts and pastry shop (*Tmr* 29E7), over which is a Doctor's surgery.

It is inevitable to draw price comparisons between Gaios and the rather look-alike Fiscardon, at the north end of Cephalonia island (*See* **Chapter Fifteen** – what is he on about readers will, no doubt, be muttering). Tassou, he of *Captain's Cabin* fame, and a most likeable, charming man, stoutly defended the Fiscardon charges. There a Nes meh ghala costs 90drs, an ouzo 100drs, a 3 star brandy 150drs and the average meal for two a minimum of 1600drs, if not 2000-2500drs. I think the rogue 'ingredient' is flotilla yachts, the presence of which, I have always maintained, pushes up prices. Paxos doesn't 'harbour' any (oh dear), Cephalonia does.

## THE A TO Z OF USEFUL INFORMATION

**BANKS** There are no banks, only money-changers representing various major banks. Don't forget the Post Office (*Tmr* 55G5). 'Change alley' is set behind some colonnades, to the right (*Sbo*) from the far end of the Main Sq, and on the right. At the far left (*Fsw*) is a Chandlery store (*Tmr* 30C6), which acts for the National Bank of Greece. Next but one to the right is the original change office, a Hardware shop (*Tmr* 32C/D6) which acts for the Commercial Bank. This latter 'bank' is run by an earnest, round-faced man, complete with steel-rimmed spectacles. He operates from a counter in the dark and dusty interior. The 'Popular Art Shop' (*Tmr* 33D/E5/6), on the Main Sq, represents the Ionian and Popular Bank.

**BEACHES** There is no port beach, it being necessary to take to the Mogonisi Island road (*See* **Route Two**). Beyond the town statue, is a tiny, pebbly beach and a few hundred metres further on, another pebble cove. Mind you, apart from Mogonisi beach and those of Antipaxos, the island's pebble edged bays and coves are a disappointment. An air-bed is almost a must in order to comfortably laze on the shores.

The track that continues on beyond the New Port Quay, towards Fontana village, passes by two or three attractive, but pebble beaches.

**BICYCLE & SCOOTER HIRE** There are a number of bicycle and scooter operators, but, to date, no cars for hire.
**Makris Scooter & Boat Hire** (*Tmr* 12B4/5) Tel 31769.
*Directions*: Situated across the Esplanade from the ramp for the **FB Kamelia**.

This is my favourite firm, run by the brother and sister team of reticent Spiros and effervescent, friendly Georgia Makris. They are an interesting pair with whom to while away the time, and Spiros may acquiesce to a hirer helping him repair one of the two-wheeled conveyances or a boat. They also hire boats and have *Rooms*. Spiros will not negotiate rates, which for a scooter are 1500drs a day, plus the cost of petrol.

Other firms include two (*Tmr* 34C5 & 35C5), in adjacent lanes that branch off the local ferry section of the Esplanade.

**BOOKSELLERS** There is no bookseller, but two or three of the travel offices operate book-swop (*See* **Travel Agents & Tour Offices, A To Z**).

In the busy summer months English newspapers are available from the kiosk in the Main Square (*Tmr* 10D6).

**BOAT HIRE** More correctly, fibreglass dinghy hire. A day boat, suitable for four and complete with an eight horse-power outboard motor, costs from 4000drs, plus the cost of the petrol. The beauty of the Paxos and Antipaxos coastlines is so dramatic that it is well worth considering hiring a craft. In a day there is time and enough fuel to journey completely round Paxos or out to and around Antipaxos (but not both!).

There are two firms:-
**Makris** (*Tmr* 12B4/5). They of scooter hire fame
and
**Tohatsu Boat Hire** (*Tmr* 36C5)
*Directions*: Across the Esplanade from the local ferry-boat section of the quay – 'Renta Boat and Sea Taxi'.

Not only dinghy hire, but they also operate the 'Paxos Express' which speeds to and from various destinations including Corfu Town, Kavos (Corfu), Parga(M) and Sivota (Mourtos)(M).

**BREAD SHOPS** (*Tmr* 28D7) on the left (*Sbo*) of the 'Bus Office' St. They also have a general store and sell pies.

**BUSES** The ticket office (*Tmr* 37D7) is on the right (*Sbo*) of the main street that gently climbs south-west from the Main Sq. This is a quaint, little cupboard of a store, labelled 'The Bus Office', which also appears to sell other tickets, various. The buses park (*Tmr* 38E9) on the edge of the town, where the two main island roads climb away from Gaios.

The timetables are stuck up all over the place, including in the cabin of the **FB Kamelia** and on various telegraph posts. On is prominent, at the outset of the 'Bus office' St.

**Bus timetable**
**Gaios Port to Lakka via Logos**
Mon-Sat          1000, 1100, 1330, 1730, 2000, 2230hrs
*Return journey*
Mon-Sat          0630, 1030(direct), 1130, 1400(direct), 1830, 2100, 2230hrs.
One-way fare 70drs.

**COMMERCIAL SHOPPING AREA** There isn't a market or particular shopping street. Locals quite often 'set up stall' on the high, stone bench, across the way from the periptero (*Tmr* 10C/D6), in front of the colonnades. For such a small place there are plenty of shops. At the north end of the Esplanade, diagonally across from the local ferry-boat quay is a Supermarket (*Tmr* 4B5), more a general store, with a contraceptive dispenser labelled 'Against Aids' (of no interest to me, honest, I had the 'bricks' years ago). Walking along the harbour quay passes a bulk olive oil business (*Tmr* 39C5), which must account for the olive press waste, or dross, which drains into the harbour at this point, with the resultant, distinctive smell. Close to the north corner of the Main Sq, next door to a kafeneion, are a pair of side-by-side Stores (*Tmr* 40D5). On the opposite flank of the Main Sq is a Tobacconist (*Tmr* 41D/E5/6), a Drink shop/store (*Tmr* 42E6), next door but one, and across the lateral street, a Fruit & Vegetable store (*Tmr* 43E6/7). To the left (*Sbo*), along this latter street and on the same side, is a Butcher (*Tmr* 44E5/7) and a Fruit & Vegetable shop (*Tmr* 45F6/7). Around to the right, and close to the 'Bus Park' Sq, is another Fruit & Vegetable store (*Tmr* 46E9). A Butcher (*Tmr* 47G/H4/5) is located towards the east end of the harbour, close to the *Ace Cocktail Bar* and yet another Butcher (*Tmr* 50E7) in the area of the 'Bus Park' Sq. Apart from a couple of Hardware shops (*Tmr* 32C/D6 & 48C7), there is a Dress & Shoe shop (*Tmr* 49E7) and a very smart, tasteful but not inexpensive souvenir gift shop (*Tmr* 63E5).

**FERRY-BOATS** The island is served by the larger inter-island ferry-boats which dock at the New Port (*See* **Ferry-boats, A To Z, Patras, Chapter Ten** and **Ferry-boats, A To Z, Corfu, Chapter Twelve**). Additionally there are the local ferry-boats. Of these the **FB Kamelia** is a most interesting craft as it is representative of the average inter-island ferry-boat, prior to the mid l970s, but now an antique tiddler compared to the modern-day giants. The small, flush stern deck may have crammed in place two or three cars and a truck stacked high with household contents (which almost always seem to consist of old bedsteads). Additionally, there might well be a number of goats tethered to the taffrail and a few crates holding chickens. The pokey main cabin's on the same level as the deck and accommodates, within the low deckhead, dark interior, the purser, a snackbar, bolted down tables, padded bench seats and squatty loos.

**Local Ferry-boat timetable** (Mid-season)

| Day | Departure time | Ferry-boat | Ports/Islands of Call |
|---|---|---|---|
| Daily | 1400hrs | Theologos | Igoumenitsa(M),Corfu Town. |
| Mon | 0730hrs | Kamelia | Logos(Paxos),Lakka(Paxos),Corfu Town. |
| | 0900hrs | Anna Maria | Corfu Town. |
| Tues | 0730hrs | Kamelia | Corfu Town. |
| | 0900hrs | Anna Maria | Logos(Paxos),Corfu Town. |
| Wed | 0730hrs | Kamelia | Lakka(Paxos),Corfu Town. |
| | 1000hrs | Anna Maria | Logos(Paxos),Antipaxos*. |
| | *(Return from Antipaxos 1700hrs) | | |
| Thurs | 0730hrs | Kamelia | Corfu Town. |
| Fri | 0700hrs | Anna Maria | Lakka(Paxos),Corfu Town. |
| | 0730hrs | Kamelia | Corfu Town. |
| Sat | 0730hrs | Kamelia | Lakka(Paxos),Corfu Town. |
| | 0800hrs | Anna Maria | Logos(PAxos),Lakka(Paxos),Parga(M)*. |

**Inter-island Ferry-boat timetable** (Mid-season)

| Daily | 0900hrs | Ionis/Ionian Glory | Vathi(Ithaca),Sami(Cephalonia),Patras(M). |
|---|---|---|---|

*(Return from Parga at 1600hrs).

One-way fare: to Corfu 550drs; duration 3hrs plus
Return fare: to Antipaxos 1590drs
to Parga 1590drs
One-way fare: Gaios to Patras 1862drs; duration 8hrs.         Also *See* **Taxis, Water, A To Z.**

**HAIRDRESSERS** A ladies (*Tmr* 51E/F5/6) is hidden away in a narrow lane running parallel to the Esplanade.

**LAUNDRY** (*Tmr* 31C6) Squeezed in between two money change offices.

**MEDICAL CARE**
**Chemists & Pharmacies** (*Tmr* 52E6). Bordering the lateral street to the left (*Sbo*) of the 'south' end of the Main Sq.
**Clinic** (*Tmr* 29E7) Above an ice-cream, pastry shop, in a 'shambles' of alleys.
**Doctor** (*Tmr* 53D6) Costas Karaburnriotis is the Town doctor, who I am pleased to advise specialises in 'intern medicine' (*sic*).

**OTE** (*Tmr* 21D7) The office opens weekdays between 0730-1510hrs.

**PETROL** The petrol station is on the outskirts of Gaios, bordering the main Makratika road.

**PLACES OF INTEREST** Paxos is not over-endowed with dramatic, or for that matter, any ancient ruins.
    The town's statue (*Tmr* H1/2), at the outset of the Mogonisi road, is in honour of one Georgios Anemoyiannis. He was an islander and sailor, who the Turks captured in 1821, whilst he was trying to 'fire' their fleet, moored in Nafpaklos harbour. The ever 'gentle' Turks reciprocated by 'barbecuing' the brave fellow. Incidentally, the statue is mounted on a small plaza jutting out into the sea, adjacent to the harbour's eastern mole. I am on intimate terms with this flagstone square having, many years ago, spent a night huddled on the unyielding surface. I would have written slept, but the Gaios mosquitos made sure that the night's rest was rather fitful.
    Beyond the statue, beside the Mongonisi road, is an aquarium. This 'phenomena' is spreading throughout the more tourist populated islands.
    The *Greek Island Club* sponsor a Cultural Festival, about the third week of July. Performances are staged at Gaios, Logos and Lakka.
    The island of St Nicholas, which forms the channel of Gaios harbour, is topped off by a Venetian castle built in 1423 and restored by the French in the early 1800s. Close by are the remains of a windmill.
    The Islet of Panaghia, adjacent to and east of St Nicholas, is ringed by a whitewashed wall and host to a church and lighthouse. Panaghia is famed for the pilgrimage that takes place on the 15th August, after which festivities continue long into the night on the Main Square of Gaios.
    On the left of the road around to the New Port, is a most impressive building erected for the British Residency (*Tmr* 54A/B3) and now housing port officials.
    The varied and numerous island churches are rather lovely, if simple.
    The island's several sea caves, on the north-west coast, are set at the base of dramatically towering

cliff-faces which awesomely plunge into the sea. The most celebrated of the caverns is perhaps Ipapanti. This serves as a 'pit-stop' for seals and was large enough, so it is rumoured, to be used as a natural submarine pen by the Greeks, during World War Two. Other natural phenomena, all on the west coast, include the triple sea-caves at Stachai, Ortholithos, the high pillar of rock, which towers some 30m above the sea, opposite Petriti cave, and lastly the flying buttress of rock at Tripitos.

Did you know... Aristotle Onassis is rumoured to have paid for the island roads to be tarmacadamed, supposedly in gratitude for the islanders' friendliness. Is my scepticism showing, or was the gesture to alleviate the threat of a tax bill or ameliorate central government, revenue enquiries?

**POLICE**
**Town** (*Tmr* 11G/H5) In the same block as the Post Office, but at the rear, on the edge of a pretty little plateia.
**Port** (*Tmr* 54A/B3) As previously described, their offices are located in the architecturally prominent building that was the British Residency.

**POST OFFICE** (*Tmr* 55G5) East of the Main Square, along the Esplanade. Services include changing Eurocheques.

**TAXIS** They rank on the quayside of the Main Sq.

**TAXIS, WATER** The old-fashioned caiques are being shouldered aside by a selection of large, high speed or 'Express', dory style craft. Apart from various excursions, which include Kavos (Corfu), Corfu Town, Parga(M) and Sivota (Mourtos)(M), Gaios Travel (*Tmr* 56C5), operates a scheduled, 'busy summer months' service to Corfu with a craft named 'Pegasus'.

**Water Taxi timetable**
**From Paxos to Corfu Town**
| | |
|---|---|
| Wed, Thurs | 0830hrs |
| Sun | 0800, 1700hrs |
| *Return* | |
| Wed, Thurs | 1500hrs |
| Sun | 1300, 2000hrs |

It has to be pointed out that *Sun Med* clients take preference, but there might occasionally be space.

One of the caique excursions on offer is 'Inside blue grotes (*sic* – I'm sure it is), each person 300drs, 1 hour go and come back.' The average price for the return caique trips to Antipaxos is 400drs (depart 1000hrs, return 1700hrs). There is a water taxi service to Mogonisi beach.

**TELEPHONE NUMBERS & ADDRESSES**
| | |
|---|---|
| Clinic | Tel 31466 |
| Police, town (*Tmr* 11G/H5) | Tel 31222 |
| port (*Tmr* 54A/B3) | Tel 31259 |

**TOILETS** (*Tmr* 59A2) At the far, north end of the town, alongside the New Port road. Unfortunately they are in an appalling condition.

An old, radial aircraft engine, probably dredged up by a fisherman's nets. lies on its side, on the way round to the toilets, beneath the small chapel, next door to the Customs office (*Tmr* 60A2/3).

**TRAVEL AGENTS & TOUR OFFICES** In the past there weren't any, the town's periptero's acting as unofficial information offices. Not any more.
**Gaios Travel** (*Tmr* 56C5)                                                    Tel 31823
*Directions*: Edges the Esplanade, across the way from where the local ferry berths.

Agents for *Sun Med* and staffed by a helpful staff. There is a general information office handbook, which is useful for telephone numbers and other queries. Another bonus point is their book exchange. Most excursions on offer cost 500drs per person, including round the island and around Antipaxos. In common with travel offices at Logos and Lakka, Gaios Travel offers for rent a number of houses and villas, in this case, mainly centred in and around Gaios.

It would be unfair not to mention that there are other tour offices. These include **Paxos Tourist Enterprises** (*Tmr* 57F5, tel 31675), **Flying Horse Tourist Office** (*Tmr* 58F5), with limited book exchange, and **Paxos Sun Holidays** (*Tmr* 61F6). This latter office represent Olympic Airways and their office is open Mon-Sat, between 0930-1300hrs & 1830-2100hrs. Jammed in between the Baker (*Tmr* 28D7), and the OTE (*Tmr* 21D7) is **Paxos Holiday Agency** (Tel 31381). One last office of note is that of **Greek Islands Club** (*Tmr* 62D7), on the right (*Sbo*) of the 'Bus Office' St.

**WATER** Sadly the islands drinking water is often saline. For instance, the tap close to the Main Sq church is definitely not for use, other than washing. There is a water tap, between Makris Scooter Hire (*Tmr* 12B4/5) and Bar Naftaki (*Tmr* B5 ), which delivers an acceptable drink, even if it is from a rainwater 'sterna'. Unfortunately the supply is only turned on two or three times a week.

## EXCURSIONS TO GAIOS PORT SURROUNDS

**Excursion to Lagada Beach (circa 2kms)**In days of yore, the New Port road was a cul-de-sac. It has now been extended round the headland in an unsurfaced swathe that hugs the coastline. At the outset this route passes the town's rubbish dump, positioned where else but on the cliff edge! At a fork, the right-hand choice drops down to edge the angled, rocky coastline about 20m above sea-level, passing two small, pebbly coves prior to:-

**LAGADA BEACH** A quite large cove of white pebble, backed by a pleasant olive grove. To the left (*Fsw*) is a sympathetically constructed, white, cut stone house and outbuildings.

From Lagada Beach a very wide, steep, unsurfaced track climbs inland, without the benefit of any tree cover, prior to cutting through mountainside olive groves to the village of Fontana (*See* **Route One**).

**Excursion to Ozias & back (circa 5km)** This is a lovely, tree shaded, route that sweeps up to the hamlet of **Ozias**. The road winds past the huddle of dwellings at **Tramakatika** to a 'spaghetti junction', close by the settlement of **Zenebisatika**. To the left is signposted **Veliantatika**, whilst curving round to the right joins the Gaios/Makratika road. At this latter junction, to the right descends back to Gaios, to the left towards Lakka (*See* **Route One**).

## ROUTE ONE

**To Lakka (circa 11km), or via Logos (circa 14km)**The signposting of the island's few routes is rather confusing. Most of the villages are enveloped by captivating, enchanted forests of olive trees, the great twisted and gnarled trunks of which are so distorted as to resemble lattice work. The olive groves are contained by stone terraces, across which grows an almost lawn-like grass and which are divided by endless rock wall edged tracks. Most of the roads have, over the years, been stained black with the juice of fallen olives crushed beneath the hooves of donkeys or the tyres of vehicles. The majority of the countryside is also blanketed by massed olive trees, in amongst the spreading branches of which are a sprinkling of large, grey, cut stone farmhouses.

The main road from Gaios to the north Paxos coastal resort and port of Lakka runs along the elevated spine of the island, with various roads running off, like the bones of a fish.

The section of the road climbing out of Gaios, towards the village of Makratika, initially runs alongside a deep, summer-dry river-bed which snakes through the trees.

The Ozias road branches off to the left, prior to Makratika 'proper'.

**MAKRATIKA (2km from Gaios Port)** Here are a number of fine, large buildings and a sizeable church, with a tall, eye-catching campanile.

The shorter, right fork from Gaios joins the main road, beyond Makratika. It is a rather more typically Greek island road, winding through boulder-strewn, shadeless foothills.

From **Bogdanatika** a side track to the left advances to **Vlachoplatika**. The main road beyond Bogdanatika breaks out of the olive groves into cypress tree and boulder strewn hills. About 2km on, a turning to the right sallies forth to:-

**FONTANA (circa 3½km from Gaios Port)** This prettily situated village hosts the *Cafe-bar Fontana*.

From Fontana, to the right descends to Lagada Beach (*See* **Excursions to Gaios Port Surrounds**). To the left, the road progresses through the hamlets of **Zernatika** and **Kangatika**, past the large, pebble cove of Logos beach, to Logos.

Continuing along the main road towards Lakka, immediately prior to **Arvanatatika** (the name of which is longer than the hamlet), and close to the roadside, are the ruins of a picturesque, old wine press. Beyond Arvanatatika, almost on the outskirts of Magazia, there is an angled, yellow sign indicating the turning left to:
**Ag Apostoli Church (8km from Gaios Port)** The initially old-fashioned but surfaced road is hemmed in by stone walls. There are even a few holiday villas edging the route, that is prior to olive trees overwhelming the landscape and the road's surface deteriorating. At a fork another yellow sign guides travellers to the right along the rather wildly undulating track. After passing through somebody's backyard, it comes to a dead end in a spaced out wood of olive trees. Perhaps visitors might attempt to start the old army truck that moulders away on the right.
It is necessary to ascend some steps to the grounds of the small, unembellished church. Entry is through a metal gate, on which is fixed an exhortation to 'Please Shut The Gate'. The doors of the building are locked nowadays which is unfortunate as the interior, despite being rather stark, is captivating, if only because of its simplicity. From the graveyard, planted with trees and complete with a water cistern, there is a stunning view of the towering, chalky cliffs of Erimitis. Someone has thoughtfully provided a picnic table beneath a clump of firs. Well worth the dusty, stony trip.

Immediately north of the Ag Apostoli turning, the main road progresses through the very spread out village of:-
**MAGAZIA (6km from Gaios Port)**. This is beautifully set in the inevitable sea of olive trees, which even spread throughout the settlement. There are one or two prominent buildings, a couple of shops, a village store ambitiously labelled 'Super Market' and an angled turning back towards Fontana.

On the far side of Magazia, about ½km beyond the road to Fontana, there is a route to the left that winds off and round, only to rejoin the main Lakka road at **Aronatika**. This detour routes via the village of Manesatika, Ipapanti Church and several back gardens, on a distinctly 'Z' class road or 'C' class donkey track. The magical downhill journey passes through tree-covered hillsides, about which are dotted many large, old and dilapidated houses, finally combining with the main road, lower down on the Lakka valley plain. The extremely interesting, twin domed Church of Ipapanti was built in 1600 and contains some relics. The pleasing bell tower was built in the 1770s.

Back at the main Gaios to Lakka road, the route to **Mastoratika** is at quite a height, following, as it does, the raised, rocky backbone of the island, with the countryside falling away on each side. Beyond Mastoratika, the road diverges on its final approach to Lakka.
Selecting the right-hand, Lakka road passes, almost immediately, a turning to the right, which branches off alongside a very large apron for collecting rainwater/combined with a storage tank ('Sterna'). 'Interestingly' the local women do their washing on the angled water gathering platform. This latter, lovely country lane descends quickly down the valley, past a ruined Martello tower and bordering a tree-shaded, dry river-bed, all the way to the pretty port of:-

**LOGOS (Loggos) (circa 10km from Gaios Town)** On the outskirts the road meanders between old buildings, allowing snatched views of mainland Greece. It then makes a junction with the harbour quay road that edges the deeply indented bay.
Most of the development is around to the right (*Fsw*), while to the left the road fairly quickly turns inland, away from the waterfront, to curve round in a loop, past the port's rubbish dump, prior to rejoining the main road. Hardly an ideal location, one would conjecture, to erect holiday villas, close to the tip, but there are a few... Also to the left is the port's beach, a scrubbly, pebbly stretch, with, in the background, a rather ugly, abandoned factory sporting a tall chimney. To the left of the two factory bays is a smaller

building with an incongruously formal frieze topped by a statue. I believe a foreigner has purchased the site with the intention to restore the buildings.

**ARRIVAL BY FERRY** The **FB Kamelia** berths once a week on its way from Corfu Town to Gaios.

Back at the junction with the Esplanade, on the left (*Fsw*) is the:-
**Loggos Tourist Company**                                                                          Tel 31710
*Directions*: As above.

The business is owned by an English/Greek partnership established in 1981 and is something of a Logos phenomena, for there is at least one other tourist related business with an English connection. The unusual combination has resulted in their company actively promoting holiday apartments and villas, based in and around Logos as well as Antipaxos. This latter inclusion hurts me, for I had hoped this idyllic island would remain outside the orbit of all but day-trippers. The properties appear to be quality and ideal for those holiday-makers who wish to step outside the turgid banality of the 'fast package' offerings. That is as long as the pocket is deep enough - excellence costs money and I own up that I might cough once or twice at the prices. The office staff are extremely helpful and there is a massive book exchange. Office hours are Mon-Sat 0845-1300hrs & 1800-2100hrs; Sun 1000-1200hrs & 1800-2000hrs. The UK address is 51 High St, Newport, Gwent Tel (0633) 842225.

Beyond this office is the *Grill Yianni's*, while to the right of the junction is *Taverna Vassilis*, which edges the narrow quay road for some 30m, after which the water front opens out a little. A short, narrow walkway runs down to a back alley that rejoins the quay road, beyond the single story, ochre coloured taverna, another 30m on.

In this 'hidden quarter' warren is a *Greek Island Club*, 'hole in the wall' office wherein money exchange, day trips, book swap, a metered telephone and stamps for sale. Further round to the left is the *Snackbar Kacarantzas*. Prospective clients must ignore the omnipresent TV set, which appears to be switched on as soon as the doors open. It may well be worth it just to enjoy a full range of breakfast options. I own up to greed and paying 300drs for a full scale gluttony of 2 lumps of fried bread, 2 eggs, 2 slices of ham, 2 sausages and tomatoes. Somewhat on the greasy side but excellent value. (PS I did buy Rosemary a similar meal). The young man who runs the establishment is pleasant and speaks 'soap' (a linguistic mishmash as uttered by American and English actors in the likes of 'Dysentery' and 'The Street').

Next door is the small:-
**Gamal Shop** HQ for 'Friends of Paxos'                                                            Tel 31929
*Directions*: As above.

An apartment, house and villa holiday agency. The UK agent is Ron Allen, 84 Algers Road, Loughton, Essex 1G10 4ND (Tel 01 508 3371). Prices are less expensive than their big brother competition but do not include the airline fare or any other associated travel costs. They are friendly and may well direct independent travellers, looking for accommodation, to *Rooms Magdalena*. This is about 150m up the hillside, ascending the path alongside the adjacent church. Magdalena's is a pleasant house with a large terrace, wherein a double room costs between 2000-2500drs. The shop also sells souvenirs, clothes, cards, stamps, cigarettes as well as other bits and pieces.

Returning to the Esplanade, at the outset of the side alley, and proceeding along the waterfront passes a grocer, with a sign in the window 'Renting Houses Informations (*sic*) In This Shop. Takis Dendias Tel 31597'; a gift souvenir shop, sporting a sign for 'Rooms' and which appears to hire scooters, followed by the *Cafe-bar Europi*. This latter watering hole is a pleasant spot at which to while away an hour or so beneath the shade of a conveniently sited tree.

Beyond the *Europi*, the quay opens out into an informal square and is bordered by a taverna/restaurant and the wine cellar *Oinomageipeion O Gaios* which serves 'ocktapas' (*sic*). The quayside road then narrows down past *Logos Grill Room*, and another *Greek Islands Club* office. Hereabouts the coast road branches off to the right, to climb the side of the hill over and down to Logos Beach. The harbour Esplanade curves round to the left, past the 'Bakery Market' and Roxy Bar, to end on a stumpy ferry-boat quay, which is topped off with a harbour entrance light.

On Sundays, when the baker is closed, bread is sold on an informal basis from a restaurant table edging the port square, close to the church.

Despite almost every other house appearing to be a holiday let, Logos remains an extremely pleasant, pretty, if rather gushy, one time fishing boat port – irresistibly recalling the Cornish village of Boscastle, even if it is externally bathed in summer sunshine.

There are a number of small bays to either side of Logos. The road that tracks over the right-hand (Fsw) hillside, in the direction of Fontana village, passes the track down to the nearside of close by:-

**Logos Beach** Labelled 'Welcome To Logos To The Beach'. The attractively situated, pebble beach is edged by a large olive grove in which lurks an untidy Cantina. Despite the sign 'Please No Litter, No Fires, No Nude Bathing', there is a certain amount of rubbish scattered about the trees. Unusually, there are a couple of holiday apartments, discreetly tucked away in the trees, on the far side. Concrete steps ascend the south hill bluff but the way is barred by locked gates. Water sports are catered for and an inshore tethered bathing platform facilitates water skiing.

Returning to the Gaios/Lakka road, to the fork in the two routes that descend to Lakka, the more attractive is the right-hand one (Facing Lakka). This choice is bordered by a scattering of chapels, single storey houses, as well as the occasional grand house, all set in olive trees 'fenced off' by stone walls which wander off to left and right.

The outskirts of Lakka, on either route, are depressingly dirty and ramshackle, which squalor spreads out into the lower olive-grove covered foothills.

## LAKKA (about 11km from Gaios Port) The northern port and village of Paxos.

The very pleasant harbour bay is almost totally enclosed by the horns of the encircling headlands. The narrowness of the mouth, or entrance to the bay is emphasized by a stone mole built out from the right hillside (Fsw). Dusty Lakka, criss-crossed by a network of poorly surfaced streets, has a 'recently erected' ambiance and the drains smell. The village is, to some extent, dominated by *Greek Island Sailing Club*, who, in addition to apartments and villas, operate an RYA recognised, sailing and wind surfing centre.

English is well spoken and understood, not only because of the high level of British tourists, but due to the presence of a scattering of English expatriates domiciled here.

## ARRIVAL BY FERRY (Tmr 1B/C4/5) The FB Kamelia, which connects with

Corfu Town, calls in on Lakka three times a week, in the summer months.

## THE ACCOMMODATION & EATING OUT

**The Accommodation** As elsewhere on the island, the high percentage of 'villa lets' has reduced the available accommodation to a trickle. The couple of establishments that used to be conventional hotels/pensions have, in part, thrown in the towel and allowed their rooms to be block booked by the various holiday companies.

Apart from the 'nod and a wink', later on in this section, it is probably best to head for:-
**Routsis Holidays** (Tmr 2E/F4) Lakka, 49082                                        Tel 31807
Directions: The office is at the far, left end (Fsw) of the Ferry-boat Quayside.
  Readers must understand that my masochistic partiality for this business is based mainly on familiarity (and you know what that breeds). The partners, John and George Grammatikos come from a famous island family. John possesses a splendid, 'RAF' handlebar moustache, is watchfully shrewd, chatty, friendly and speaks excellent English. To expand the business, from a family pension into a full-blown tourist office, John's brother, George, joined the enterprise. Enough to say that George is almost the antithesis of John, clean shaven, maladroit, taciturn, aloof and possessing less linguistic skill. I'm sure you have the point! John Grammatikos is married to Nancy, a smiley, middle-west, American lady,

who does the hard work – don't women everywhere? The brothers may well be able to offer rooms in their:-

**Pension Lefcothea** (*Tmr* 3C/D3)
*Directions*: One block back from the Ferry-boat Quay.

It is best to go directly to the office, as no one is resident. The construction is that which I 'shorthand' as 'resounding door'. This indicates that whenever a door is opened or closed, the sound reverberates throughout the building. The bathroom facilities are shared, but each floor only possesses one toilet compartment and one shower cum toilet. The shower arrangement is to be 'recommended', for it has added a new variable to my register of bathroom foibles. For some unfathomable reason, it is necessary to bob up and down to keep the trickle of hot water running. Why, the reader may ask? Because, if the shower head is raised above shoulder height, the hot water ingredient goes missing, resulting in the unfortunate bather being 'scalded' by a trickle of cold water. Thus it is necessary to constantly knees bend. Thank goodness no one can see. The bedroom doors may require locking simply to keep them shut, but there is an alternative house 'fall back' – a doubled up cigarette packet to wedge under the door! A double room is charged at between 2200-2500drs.

Another establishment is the:-

**Hotel Ilios** (*Tmr* 4C/D3/4)                                                              Tel 318008
*Directions*: Towards the quay end, on the left, of a long, narrow street that stretches down from the Main Sq.

Now block booked by the *Greek Island Club*, so it may well be best to approach:-

**Planos Holidays Travel office** (*Tmr* 5C/D4)
*Directions*: Facing on to the Ferry-boat Quay, on the corner diagonally across from the ramp.

Act for 'GIC'.

Readers may be interested to hear of another possibility, only a possibility, that is:-

**Marianthi's Shop** (*Tmr* 6D1/2)
*Directions*: From the Main Square proceed along the first, nearside street to the left (*Bus & Taxi Park behind one*).

Marianthi is a most attractive woman and married to Costas. She owns a wool, gift and overseas newspaper shop and if approached without a lot of fuss, may be able to arrange accommodation, be it *Rooms* or a villa. None are in the port.

One last option is the white cottage (*Tmr* 7A2) set about half-way up a steeply terraced olive grove, enclosed by a wire fence bordering the harbour road round to the right (*Fsw*). An olive tree mounted sign advises 'The House In This Estate For Rent. Tel 31439/066522363'.

## The Eating Out
The presence of many yachting orientated 'Brits' tends to ensure menu prices are on the 'high side of high'. There are a number of quality tavernas, few basement sleazys and an excellent 'local', the:-

**Kafeneion** (*Tmr* 8C/D1/2)
*Directions*: Borders the Main Square.

Almost barn-like inside, with a wooden ceiling but little outdoor seating. Apart from the normal kafeneion functions, the cold cabinet and refrigerators contain, amongst other items, yoghurts and ice-creams. There are some racked snacks and, most importantly, two metered telephones. The friendly, smiley, old patron reminds me a little of Mr. Mole. The atmosphere is that of a local community centre, if it weren't for the foreigners bawling and shouting into the overseas phones. Happily the prices are reasonable. A bottle of beer costs 90drs, a 3 star brandy 100drs, a limon 50drs, a Nes meh ghala 80drs and an ouzo 60drs. On the other hand bottled water is comparatively expensive at a cost of 100drs, having paid as little as 50drs on the mainland.

Directly across the Main Square is the reasonably priced *Kafeneion Diogenisi* (*Tmr* 9C/D2), which has a spread of chairs and tables outside.

**Taverna La Piazza** (*Tmr* 10C2) No 4
*Directions*: East of the Main Sq, across the main road in a small, simple, tile roofed, single storey building with a garden. The authentic, rather grand name is actually 'Restaurant Bar La Piazza'.

A plain meal, for two, of tomato salad (75drs), tzatziki (dear on this island – 170drs), stuffed aubergines with sauce (quite nice – 232drs), 2 beers (85drs each), bread (sufficient) and service cost 700drs.

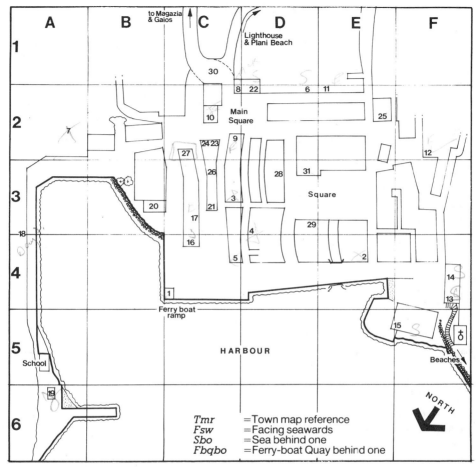

**Illustration 19 Lakka**

To the left (*Fsw*) of the Main Sq, in the first narrow street, is:-
**Taverna Grill Horiatis** (*Tmr* 11E1/2)
*Directions*: As above and on the left.

A popular location and rightly so. One sign advises 'Established 1950' and another 'If you are going to have a party at your villa just give us a call a day before you do a party. In other words you can take away food from the special Taverna Horiatis. Family taverna with low prices. Come and try us. Local wine'. There is no doubt that Dimitri, the Klinger look-alike (MASH anyone?) restaurant owner serves a magnificent range of menu alternatives, and there are no lunchtime leftovers. The only problem is that, as the evenings tempo and excitement increases, Dimitri gets more stimulated and expansive, as do the bills! His wife Eleni is not so high spirited. On our last visit it was fortunate that pretty young Julie was serving in the taverna. She is a Paxiot lass, whose family lived in Antipodes for many years and thus speaks almost 'perfect' Australian. Julie is willing to translate a customer's more obscure, philosophical thoughts. I find these musings become more and more abstruse as the evening wears on – almost in direct relation to the amount of retsina consumed. Apart from lobster and plates of fish (from 800drs), a meal might include bean soup (300drs), meatballs with briam (an enormous helping – 500drs), stifado with briam (super – 700drs), moussaka with vegetables, including beans, carrots and other bits and pieces (500drs), a plate of chips (a pricey 100drs), a bottle of kortaki retsina (an expensive 150drs) and bread and service (an almost unacceptable 50drs per head). It has to be admitted that prices wavered between a lower and upper limit. Another disconcerting little habit is that a diner might well be served various plates of unrequested but delicious hors d'oeuvres, such as garlic potatoes and Paxos cheese, and then be charged! A meal for two costs between 1700-2700drs. But don't heed my carping about financial trifles, grab a table and enjoy yourself. Julie finds the pricing inconsistencies almost as bemusing as do the clients.

Edging another square, not many twists and turns distant, is the:-
**Ubu Bar Taverna** (*Tmr* 12F2/3)
*Directions*: In the southern corner of the village.

Italian cooking AND prices! This emphasis probably reflects the summer surge of Italian holiday-makers. The menu is very interesting, if expensive, and includes spaghetti with lobster sauce 1000drs, spaghetti arrabbiata 450drs, spinach gratin with mushrooms 450drs, home-made onion soup 300drs, risotto with chicken 600drs, pork chop a la pitsaela 600drs and beef fillet in mushroom sauce 1200drs. If readers aren't salivating, they should be.

At the far, south end of the Ferry-boat Quay are:-
**Cafe Zytomoleion** (*Tmr* 13F4/5)
*Directions*: As above.

A 'sort of' cocktail bar serving special ice-cream, special fruit salad punch, special this, that and the other. How very Greek.

**Taverna Kapodistria** (*Tmr* 14F4)
*Directions*: As above and next door.

Rather more conventional than the *Zytomoleion* serving special Paxos pizza as well as breakfast and 'scrambled' (*sic*) eggs. A rumour portends a change in management for 1989, which it is suggested should auger well for both the new patron and prospective clients
and

**Bastas Cafe Bar** (*Tmr* 15E/F5)
*Directions*: Attractively situated on a patio which juts out into the sea, almost directly across the quay road from Routsis Holidays.

Not cheap but then the position is all important. A coffee costs 100drs and a (large) brandy 150drs. You pays your money and makes your choice... The *Sun Med* representatives 'huddle' here.

A number of side-streets which branch off the quay road, decant on a large Square 'hidden' in the centre of the village. There are at least three tavernas edging this Plateia, including the *Butterflies Taverna* (*Tmr* 31D/E2/3).

At the other end of the quay, almost directly across the way from the Ferry-boat ramp and behind the conveniently located *Harbour Lights Cafe Snack Bar* (*Tmr* 16C3/4), is the:-
**Taverna Restaurant Dionyssos** (*Tmr* 17C3)
*Directions*: As above.

For some reason, the Dionyssos is not as popular as the reasonably priced and extensive menu should warrant. Moussaka cost 250drs, stuffed tomatoes 220drs, spaghetti with mincemeat 220drs,

PAXOS 219 

veal with potatoes 360drs, lamb with potatoes 290drs, stifado 360drs, string beans 180drs, chicken 235drs, veal chops 515drs, pork chops 490drs, lamb chops 412drs, souvlakia 450drs, squid 260drs, tzatziki 180drs, shrimps 1000drs, special pizza 490drs, a kilo of chicken 955drs, 350gm of lamb 450drs and so on.

A favoured daytime alternative is the:-

**Taverna Cafe-bar Nautilus** (*Tmr* 18A3/4)
*Directions*: On the walk round the harbour to the right (*Fsw*), *en route* to the GIC sailing club.

It's public acclaim may have a lot to do with the most attractive location, looking out over the bay towards the main quay.

## THE A TO Z OF USEFUL INFORMATION
**BANKS** *See* **Post Office** and **Travel Agents & Tour Offices, A To Z.**

**BEACHES** Beach sun worshippers 'posted' to Lakka are advised to take along an air-bed The very attractive beaches are almost entirely large pebble.

There is a smidgin of sand tucked into the side of the quay that juts into the sea, close by Rose Cottage (*Tmr* 19A6), the Greek Island Club House. Unfortunately, the rest of the shore in front of the cottage is pebble. Equally unfortunately, the free standing shower, situated alongside the retaining wall of the cottage balcony, is for the club's use only. Those of an indolent nature will find this a rather tiring spot. This is due to there being lots of 'chaps and chapesses', displaying boundless energy and valour whilst testing their character and mettle against the vagaries of the elements whilst seated in a dinghy or standing on a sailboard. A signboard advertises 'Escape From Lakka Bay'. Why?

The main beaches are to the left (*Fsw*) of the port, accessed by ascending the steps behind *Bastas Cafe bar* (*Tmr* 15E/F5), leaving a church and its small, simple bell tower on the left hand.

**Beach 1** A very small cove of medium sized pebbles on which are 'cliffs of kelp'. The backshore is attractively bordered by an olive tree grove terraced up the hillside. Despite the bins, the rubbish is not collected on a regular basis. A sign warns 'Please Do Not Swim Beyond The Red Buoys – Risk of Accident'. These markers bob up and down about 75m offshore.

The path dips down to the backshore of this beach, only to climb up and over, past an old water well, now steadily being filled with tourist litter, to:-

**Beach 2** A long, sharply shelving, large pebble beach about 10m wide. Here again olive trees swarm all over the terraces of the steeply graded slopes that back the cove, growing all the way down to the edge of the beach. Towards the far end is a block of changing huts, currently employed as rubbish tips, thus the beach is quite clean. There are a number of pedaloes and wind surfers in evidence. Sadly the late afternoon sun dips out of sight, leaving the beach in the shade. This necessitates decamping to Beach No 1, where only the flat rock surfaces, at the port end, capture the sun for much longer.

The sea-bed of both beaches is pebble and the waters of the bay have a rather murky consistency.

There is yet another beach:-

**Lighthouse Plani Beach** Either about ½km walk along a path off the Disco Aloni road out of Lakka or a boat trip.

There are other beaches to the right (*Fsw*) of Lakka, but a local advised that strong shoes, a compass and guide are necessary.

**BICYCLE & SCOOTER HIRE** (*Tmr* 20B/C3) Operate from a 'lean-too', set back from the Ferry-boat ramp. 'Mopeds To Hipe (*sic*), Special Prices'. They also hire dinghies. The office opens daily between 0830-1400hrs & 1500-2100hrs, but the business does not appear to function outside of the busy summer months.

**BOOKSELLERS Marianthi's Shop** (*Tmr* 6D1/2) sells English language newspapers in the summer months.

**BREAD SHOP** (*Tmr* 21C3) The Baker also sells a range of drinks.

**BUSES** The buses informally park (*Tmr* 30C1) at the junction of the two roads out of Lakka.

**Bus timetable**

| Mon-Sat | 0630hrs Logos, Gaios. | 2100hrs Logos, Gaios. |
|---------|----------------------|----------------------|
|         | 1030hrs Gaios.        | 2230hrs Logos, Gaios. |
|         | 1130hrs Logos, Gaios. |                      |
|         | 1400hrs Gaios.        |                      |
|         | 1830hrs Logos, Gaios. |                      |

**COMMERCIAL SHOPPING AREA** There are a number of shops scattered about, including Steve's Market (*Tmr* 22C/D1/2), which is a fruit and vegetable store, despite the hype proclaiming 'International Grocery, Yacht Stores', and a Mini Market (*Tmr* 23C2). This latter store, which also sells fruit and vegetables, appears to be part of the adjacent Post Office and assures passers by that 'Shopping Here Is a Pleasure'. There is a Hardware shop (*Tmr* 25E/F2), a Butcher (*Tmr* 26C3), a Store/Patisserie (*Tmr* 27C2/3) and a 'Hole-In-The-Wall' periptero (*Tmr* 28D3) possessing a public telephone, distinguished by a prominent Marlborough cigarette sign and run by a smiley lady. On the same Square is a Shawl & Rugs shop (*Tmr* 29D/E3/4) and a couple of Souvenir/Gift shops.

Note Lakka shuts on Sunday.

**DISCOS** The Disco Aloni borders the right-hand (*Sbo*) road out of Lakka and is owned by a prominent citizen who is reputed to open the doors on impulse.

**FERRY-BOATS** For scheduled Ferry-boats, See **Ferry-boats, A To Z, Gaios**.

**MEDICAL CARE** See **Medical Care, A To Z, Gaios**.

**OTE** See **The Main Square Kafeneion** (*Tmr* 8C/D1/2), **The Eating Out**.

**PLACES OF INTEREST** There is an Aquarium on the outskirts of Lakka and visitors, in the third week of July, might look forward to the GIC sponsored Cultural Festival. Events are performed in Lakka, Logos and Gaios.

**POST OFFICE** (*Tmr* 24C2) More a private enterprise outfit than a government operated unit.

**SPORTS FACILITIES** Apart from the 'overwhelm' of boating activity, there is a Tennis Court close by the right-hand (*Sbo*) road leaving Lakka.

**TAXIS** (*Tmr* 30C1) They park at the junction of the two main roads out of Lakka.

**TRAVEL AGENTS & TOUR OFFICES**
**Routsis Holidays** (*Tmr* 2E/F4)                                                    Tel 31807
*Directions*: At the far, south end of the Ferry-boat Quay.

Their *Room* activities have been narrated, See **The Accommodation**. In addition the 'Good Brother Grammatikos' can supply almost everything to everybody. These activities include currency and travellers cheque exchange, hire of outboard powered boats (3000drs a day), as well as their speciality of renting apartments and villas in and around Lakka.

**Planos Holiday Travel Office** (*Tmr* 5C/D4)
*Directions*: On the corner diagonally across from the Ferry-boat ramp.

The owner, Panioytis, is the GIC manager, thus the joint use of the premises. Tickets can be booked for an Antipaxos Sunday excursion, departing at 1030hrs. The office is open daily between 0830-1330hrs & 1800-2030hrs and the staff are friendly and helpful.

Prior to 'putting Lakka to bed', it is worthwhile noting that the right-hand (*Sbo*) road that climbs out of Lakka is unmetalled and poorly surfaced almost all the way to the crossroads with the other, left-hand road out of Lakka. The junction is beyond a truly enormous school building.

# ROUTE TWO
## Gaios Port to Porto Sputzo, Mogonisi island & beach (3km)
From the eastern end of Gaios harbour, beyond the town statue, a poorly surfaced road edges a tiny, pebbly beach and, a few hundred metres on, another small cove. This is overlooked by a bar/taverna set in groves of olive trees. The road surface rapidly deteriorates as it climbs past the *Cliff Taverna*. This establishment diffidently, almost shyly proclaims 'Attention, The Big Surprise Of The Month. On Friday A Greek Fantastic Night And Dancing Show. Ask For Taverna Cliff. Beautiful Cliff Top Views. A Warm Welcome Awaits You'! Next is the *Hotel Paxos Beach* (*See* **The Accommodation, Gaios Port**.

Between half and two-thirds of the way to Mogonisi, there are some rather nice, private villas edging a small, pebble cove. This is rather polluted with rubbish and set in a slab rock bordered bay. Mogonisi island hoves into view beyond a fenced off smidgin of pebble beach, where the electricity supply comes ashore. The road finally peters out alongside a small, pebbly strip of sea-shore. A quite wide, if rocky track makes off for the Mogonisi causeway. The path edges some pleasantly shelving, flat slabs of rock suitable for sunbathing or from which to swim – but do not fail to observe the sea urchins. Continuing to sidle along the now hillside donkey track leads to a causeway of rocks. This allows access to:

**THE ISLAND OF MOGONISI (3km from Gaios Port)** Causeway walkers might have to remove their footwear. The minimal rise and fall of the Ionian Sea is enough to submerge most of the rocks to ankle height, on the flood. Once across, a path to the left skirts the sea's edge, crossing the patio of a 'dead', rather ugly cafe-bar. On the far side is the beach bar and beach which look out over the pretty 'bay' formed by the Paxos 'mainland' and Mogonisi island.

The beach, on which there are some sun-beds for hire, is narrow but sandy, even if there are some pebbles. The south end is made up of fine grit. The sea-bed is sandy towards the right-hand side *(Fsw)*. On the right is a low quay to which the various trip and excursion craft moor. An express dory craft runs a water taxi service to and from Gaios Port, the last 'bus' departing at 1700hrs.

The well established beach bar and its terrace sprawl over the lower slopes of the olive tree planted hillside. The 'knowing' bar staff can only offer Lowenbrau bottled beer (110drs) and a lemonade costs 50drs. No doubt 'Brits' will be estatic to hear that the menu includes a breakfast of bacon, eggs, fried bread and baked beans.

The restaurant above and to one side of the beach bar appears 'dead'. A hand painted sign indicates a toilet up the hillside, somewhere amongst the olive trees.

The location now wears a rather abandoned, run down air. Years ago it was an all action spot. The beach used to be crowded and the water was abuzz with dinghy sailors, sailboats, wind surfers and water skiing, but the water sports activities appear to have departed. The beach still hosts a fair number of sun worshippers and swimmers. Trip boats still call from as far away as Kavos (Corfu island). A good time of day to visit is late afternoon. Many of the visitors have departed and the beach doesn't lose the sun's rays until almost dusk. There is a lovely, blue sea-water cave on the south-east side of Mogonisi island.

Separated from Mogonisi by a channel, wide and deep enough for a yacht to cruise through, is **Kaltsionissi Islet**. This has a small, isolated, one time-time hermit's chapel, built beside the water's edge.

# ANTIPAXOS (Antipaxoi, Andipaxi) Three sq km in area with a population of about 150. The speciality is the island wine.

The 2km straits between the southern end of Paxos and Antipaxos can be crossed by a small boat in 15 to 20 minutes. In the main, the rocky coastline of the island is cleft by narrow strips of rocky, pebbly or sandy beaches. As on Paxos, the east coast consists of comparatively gentle hillsides encircling a series of bays, whilst the west coastline is much more dramatic, with towering cliff-faces plunging into the deeps of the Ionian sea. It is a pity for the serenity of the island, and its wonderful coastline, that high speed excursion craft shuttle hordes of day-trippers to and from Antipaxos. The delightful bays are also host to a number of yachts. If this were not enough, there are now two, simple villas for rent. This has been made possible by the arrival of mains electricity. There are three tavernas but no stores. To avoid the crowds, arrive early, leave late or keep moving as far south as is necessary.

Along the east coast from the headland of Gremos are a number of lovely, isolated bays starting with **Vrikes**, whereon the backshore of which is a simple summer-time taverna.

The second, main bay is that of **Voutoumi**. This is absolutely beautiful, perhaps one of the loveliest in Greece, with a clean, golden sand beach and sea-bed and clear, clear water. A rustic beach bar/taverna caters for the inner man, and woman.

Prior to reaching Ormos Agrapidias, there are two more lovely bays, with sandy sea-beds, but round pebble foreshores. **Ormos Agrapidias** is the small harbour of Antipaxos with a low, rocky mole, a number of fishing boats and two tracks to the interior.

Towards the far end of the island, stony **Ormos Skidi** gives access, via a winding track, to the pretty lighthouse and adjacent dwelling, complete with, surprise, surprise, an ornamental garden. Rounding the southernmost headland of Antipaxos, in the channel created by the outlying islets of Daskalia, is rather awe-inspiring and reminiscent of Lands End, in calm seas. The water is startlingly clear and the outlines of the great shelving slabs of rock that form the sea-bottom can be seen, with frightening clarity.

Around 'the corner' is a small, stony bay and, a few minutes further on, a large, pebble and sandy cove between the headlands of **Sazakiniko** and **Kontazi**.

Perhaps almost the last of the western seaboard backdrops says it all. Three pebbly coves have been scoured and eroded out, over the aeons, between the headlands of **Alikes** and **Rodovani**. A lofty, mountainous islet, set in this incredibly dramatic scene soars skywards with seagulls wheeling and screaming in their endless aerial rough and tumble.

*'Mill's closed now....but hardly the West Riding!*

*Logos shore, Paxos.*

*'Anyone for a swim?'*

*Logos Beach, Paxos.*

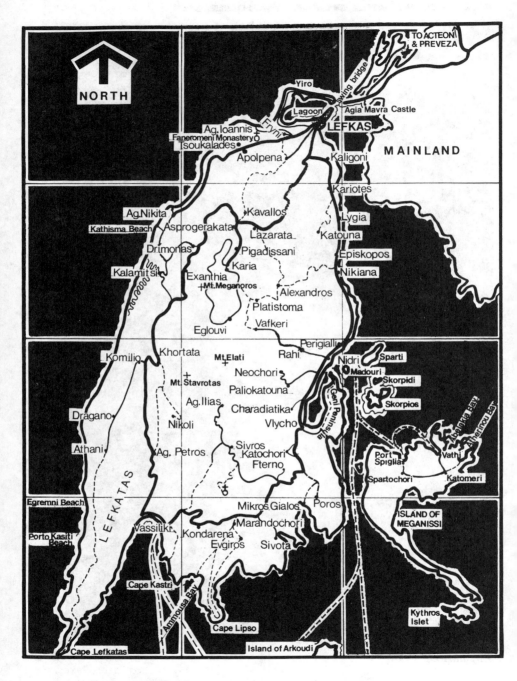

**Illustration 20 Lefkas & Meganissi Islands**

# 14 LEFKAS (Lefkada, Levkas) & Meganissi
## Ionian Islands

Water sports ★★★★
★★★

---

**FIRST IMPRESSIONS** Tin reinforced, wooden buildings; mountainous country-side; wonderful beaches; beautiful countryside; womens' brown dresses; French spoken; smelly drains & 'dodgy' drinking water in Lefkas Town; a now discovered but still quintessential, Greek island.

**SPECIALITIES** Honey; mandolato, an almond sweetbread; pastelli, a sesame seed & honey pastry; island brandy & retsina (especially tasty).

**RELIGIOUS HOLIDAYS & FESTIVALS** include: Fifty days after Easter – Panaghia, followed by dancing and feasting, Faneromeni Monastery (Fryni); 11th August – Festival in honour of St Spiridon, Karia; the last two weeks of August – Music and folk dance festival*.

* *See* **Places of Interest, A To Z, Lefkas Town.**

**VITAL STATISTICS** Tel prefix 0645. The island is 38km long, up to 16km wide with an approximate area of 300sqkm. The population numbers some 22,000, of which total up to 7,000 live in Lefkas Town.

**HISTORY** Historically, and mythologically, the island of Lefkas has a 'lot going for it'. The old cutting, separating the island from the mainland, was a man-made channel excavated in the fifth century BC and deepened in the nineteenth century AD. A Mr Dorpfeld, a German archaeologist, rushed about excitedly, at the turn of the 1900s, loudly proclaiming that Lefkas was in fact the ancient Ithaca of Homeric connections. On the road between Lefkas Town and Nidri there is the site of one of his 'digs'.

At the southernmost tip of the island is Cape Lefkatas. The mythological poetess Sappho, having been spurned in love, is reputed to have thrown herself over those cliffs', with the resultant 'dashing' death. Certainly during the period of Apollo worship, 'socially unacceptable' types were sacrificed by 'urging them' to imitate lemmings. Callow Roman youths are supposed to have developed the art a stage further, indulging in a historical hang-gliding, jumping over the edge with birds feathers strapped to their bodies. Survivors were plucked (oh, no) from the sea by craft standing off. Perhaps they were sponsored!

**GENERAL** Fortunately the outstandingly beautiful island of Lefkas has, to date, avoided the worst tourist excesses. The outbreaks of exploitation have been isolated to a number of specific centres, namely the 'villa country' stretch of coast between Kariotes and Nidri, Nidri itself, Mikros Gialos, Sivota and Vassiliki. The development is more specialised than the more usual lager belt, 'gang-bang' of hotels.

Whichever came first, Lefkas is now much more easily accessible by air, land and sea. Still ignored by the large, scheduled ferry-boats, island travellers will be delighted with the availability of 'landing craft' style car ferries running to an organised timetable. These link Nidri with Ithaca and Cephalonia. The more usual excursion craft maintain a Lefkas Town hook-up with the aforementioned islands and a caique passenger boat also operates a height-of-summer connection between Vassiliki, Ithaca and Cephalonia.

Those of us selfish enough to deprecate the expanding awareness of any of our island favourites will, of course, resent the increased popularity of Lefkas. At least it is a discriminating, selective growth in the spheres of water sports and villas, rather than Kosta strips of package hotels.

## LEFKAS (Lefkadas): capital & main port (Illustration 21) The town is
vaguely reminiscent of Cowes on the Isle of Wight with a long, active waterfront which
hosts commercial boats as well as private and flotilla craft. It certainly possesses immense
charm and generates infinite interest. In fact the very long, gently meandering Main St is
similar to that of Limnos and provides a fascinating view of a Greece not yet submerged
in a welter of fast food shops and cocktail bars. That is not to say that some manifestations
of the modern-day holiday industry have not bludgeoned their way into the lower, port
end of Odhos Dorpfeld. A number of the buildings that line the High St, many of them
the old, single storey variety, manifest an intriguing range of architectural styles and
building materials. These include stone; stone built ground floors with wooden, overhanging upper works; timber frames with brick infill and wooden frames plated with tin
and or galvanised corrugated iron. The toy-town look to some of the metropolis owes a
lot to a long history of earthquakes, culminating in the big 'shake-up' of 1948. Other little
oddities include the church clocks being mounted on skeletal iron frameworks (similar to
the water windmills of Crete), the open gully drains and the traditional dress of the women.
These costumes consist of a brown bodice and shawl and similarly coloured, pleated
skirt.
The High St is barred to traffic during the night hours.

**ARRIVAL BY AIR** There are flights from Athens to Preveza airport. In actuality the
runway is close to Acteon, not Preveza. (*See* **Acteon**, **Chapter Ten**). The cheapest
method of reaching Lefkas is take a taxi for the 2km drive to Acteon, from whence catch
the bus to Lefkas. The profligate will catch a taxi all the way from the airport to Lefkas
Town.

**ARRIVAL BY BUS** There is a regular service from Athens as well as Acteon, which
latter connects by ferry to Preveza, from whence buses link with, for instance, Parga and
Igoumenitsa.
The last kilometre or two of the mainland approach road, to the island, skims the sea's
edge. A long sliver of land offshore creates the impression of a large, shallow lagoon.
Solitary fishermen pole their punts about the water's surface, laying and tending their
nets. This spectacle is best observed early morning, when gentle mists wreath both the
elongated islet and the fishermen in ethereal wraps. The road passes one fort, and then
another, Agia Mavra, close by the 20-25m canal, which separates the mainland and the
island. Until 1986, the cutting had to be crossed on one of the two parallel chain-ferries
that plied backwards and forwards, across the narrow channel. Now a fabricated swing
bridge is in place, the steel ribbed surface of which makes for a juddering drive. The
bridge opens for ships, and thus closes to road traffic, every hour between 0800-2200hrs.
Between 2200-0800hrs it opens when necessary.
Agia Mavra Castle (Santa Maura) derives its name from a chapel built within the walls
by the wife of Orsini the Venetian, who constructed the original fort, in about 1300. The
ownership of the castle mirrors the island's history over the last 700 years. The Turks
and Venetians swopped 'the real estate' during a 500 year period, followed by the French
(1797-8), then the Russians for the next nine years, the French again for four years and
the British, between 1811 and 1864.
The road bridges the shallows to Lefkas Town, on a causeway. Another road loops
around the large, rectangular lagoon to the right (*Facing Lefkas Town*), beside a sparse,
long, shingly beach, some forlorn windmills and then back through rather marshy, rubbish
strewn surrounds into the Town.

**ARRIVAL BY FERRY** No inter-island ferry-boats dock. On the other hand there are
a couple of smaller, landing craft style ferries and a number of passenger boats that run
scheduled services to the islands of Meganissi, Cephalonia and Ithaca (*See* **Ferry-boats,
A To Z, Lefkas Town, Nidri and Vassiliki**).

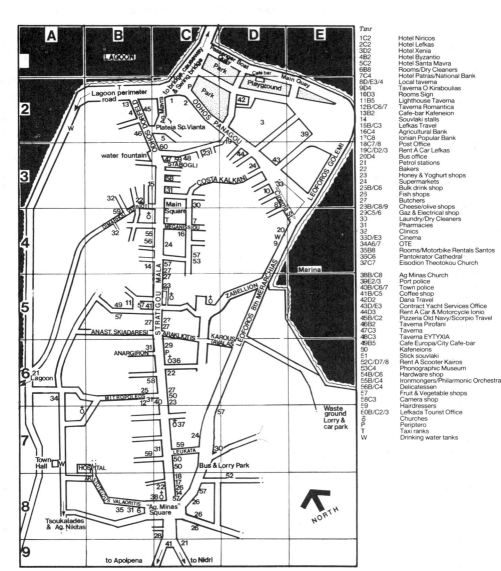

Tmr
| 1C2 | Hotel Niricos |
| 2C2 | Hotel Lefkas |
| 3D2 | Hotel Xenia |
| 4B2 | Hotel Byzantio |
| 5C2 | Hotel Santa Mavra |
| 6B8 | Rooms/Dry Cleaners |
| 7C4 | Hotel Patras/National Bank |
| 8D/E3/4 | Local taverna |
| 9D4 | Taverna O Kiraboulias |
| 10D3 | Rooms Sign |
| 11B5 | Lighthouse Taverna |
| 12B/C6/7 | Taverna Romantica |
| 13B2 | Cafe-bar Kafeneion |
| 14 | Souvlaki stalls |
| 15B/C3 | Lefkas Travel |
| 16C4 | Agricultural Bank |
| 17C8 | Ionian Popular Bank |
| 18C7/8 | Post Office |
| 19C/D2/3 | Rent A Car Lefkas |
| 20D4 | Bus office |
| 21 | Petrol stations |
| 22 | Bakers |
| 23 | Honey & Yoghurt shops |
| 24 | Supermarkets |
| 25B/C6 | Bulk drink shop |
| 26 | Fish shops |
| 27 | Butchers |
| 28B/C8/9 | Cheese/olive shops |
| 29C5/6 | Gaz & Electrical shop |
| 30 | Laundry/Dry Cleaners |
| 31 | Pharmacies |
| 32 | Clinics |
| 33D/E3 | Cinema |
| 34A6/7 | OTE |
| 35B8 | Rooms/Motorbike Rentals Santos |
| 36C6 | Pantokrator Cathedral |
| 37C7 | Eisodion Theotokou Church |
| 38B/C8 | Ag Minas Church |
| 39E2/3 | Port police |
| 40B/C6/7 | Town police |
| 41B/C5 | Coffee shop |
| 42D2 | Dana Travel |
| 43D/E3 | Contract Yacht Services Office |
| 44D3 | Rent A Car & Motorcycle Ionio |
| 45B/C2 | Pizzeria Old Navy/Scorpio Travel |
| 46B2 | Taverna Pirofani |
| 47C3 | Taverna |
| 48C3 | Taverna EYTYXIA |
| 49B5 | Cafe Europa/City Cafe-bar |
| 50 | Kafeneions |
| 51 | Stick souvlaki |
| 52C/D7/8 | Rent A Scooter Kairos |
| 53C4 | Phonographic Museum |
| 54B/C6 | Hardware shop |
| 55B/C4 | Ironmongers/Philarmonic Orchestra |
| 56B/C4 | Delicatessen |
| 57 | Fruit & Vegetable shops |
| 58C3 | Camera shop |
| 59 | Hairdressers |
| 60B/C2/3 | Lefkada Tourist Office |
| ô | Churches |
| P | Periptero |
| T | Taxi ranks |
| W | Drinking water tanks |

# Illustration 21 Lefkas Town

| Tmr | =Town map reference |
| Fsw | =Facing seawards |
| Sbo | =Sea behind one |
| Fbqbo | =Ferry-boat Quay behind one |

## THE ACCOMMODATION & EATING OUT

**The Accommodation** At the north peak of the town, behind the small park close by the bridge, there are, side by side, the *Hotel Lefkas* and *Niricos* as well as, to the left (*Sbo*), the *Hotel Xenia*. They are not inexpensive!

**Hotel Niricos** (*Tmr* 1C2) (Class C) Ag Mavra                                    Tel 24132
*Directions*: As above.
   All rooms are en suite and pricey at about 2400drs for a single room & 3800drs for a double, increasing to 2800drs & 4500drs (1st July-15th Sept).

**Hotel Lefkas** (*Tmr* 2C2) (Class B) 2 Panagou                                    Tel 23916
*Directions*: As above.
   All approximately as for the Niricos. One night a week (Saturday in 1988, Wednesday in 1987) the hotel puts on a display of Greek dancing. Non residents only have to buy a coffee and brandy and they are in.

**Hotel Xenia** (*Tmr* 3D2) (Class B)                                    Tel 24762
*Directions*: As above.
   Only double rooms en suite at a cost of 2900drs, increasing to 3450drs (July-Sept).

At the other end of the standards and prices spectrum, and perhaps more in line with the usual recommendations espoused in the Candid Guides, are the:-

**Hotel Byzantio (Vyzantion)** (*Tmr* 4B2) (Class E) 40 Odhos Dorpfeld                Tel 22629
*Directions*: On the right (*Sbo*), at the outset of the long High Street that gently snakes through the town.
   Simple and clean. Rooms share the bathrooms with a single costing 1000drs & a double 1600drs.

**Hotel Santa Mavra** (*Tmr* 5C2) (Class C) 2 Sp Vianta                            Tel 22342
*Directions*: A few metres along the High Street and to the left, edging a small square, some 150m from the waterfront.
   A correspondent advises that the *Mavra* is a first-class, friendly hotel, well situated next door to an excellent restaurant. All rooms have en suite bathrooms. A single room is charged at 2000drs & a double 3000drs.
   Note that both the *Byzantio* and *Santa Mavra*, allow other than guests to 'take a shower' at a cost of about 150drs.

Regrettably the delightfully traditional Greek hostelry, the hotel at No. 4, has 'died'.

**Hotel Patras** (*Tmr* 7C4) (Class E) 1 Meganissiou                                Tel 22359
*Directions*: Overlooking the Main Square and in the ground floor of which is the National Bank of Greece.
   Rooms share the bathrooms, with a single priced at 1000drs & a double 2000drs.

Still in the main quay, north end of the town, there is a sign *Rooms To Let* Tel 24167 (*Tmr* 10D3), almost directly across the street from the Cinema. For more details enquire of Philippa, at Rent A Car & Motorcycle Ionio (*Tmr* 44D3) or her father, at Rent A Car Lefkas (*Tmr* 19C/D2/3). Philippa owns accommodation 200/300m along Leoforos Golemi. A double room, sharing the bathroom, costs 2000drs in the busy summer months, with en suite rooms charged at 2500drs.

At the south end of the High St is 'Ag Minas' Square, a 'confluence' of the ways. To the right (*Sbo*) is Odhos Aristotelous Valaoritis on the left of which are:-
**Rooms** (*Tmr* 6B8) No 19                                    Tel 22375
*Directions*: As above and in the ground floor of which is a Dry Cleaners shop
and:-

**Rooms** (*Tmr* 35B8)
*Directions*: As above, a few metres down the street, over 'Santas Motorbike Rentals'.
   Both are rather spartan and ethnic with separate bathrooms. A double room cost from 1800drs a night.

For a more distant but close to a beach option *See* **Beaches, A To Z**.

**Camping** None in the town or suburbs. *See* **Kariotes (6km), Circular Route**.

**The Eating Out** Unfortunately the flotilla yachts have tended to sky-rocket prices in those tavernas and restaurants within 'yellow wellie' walking distance of the waterfront. Generally the quality of the offerings reflects these higher charges.

**Cafe-bar Kafeneion** (*Tmr* 13B2).
*Directions*: At the outset of Odhos Dorpfeld. The small, single storey, red roof tiled hut is to the right (*Sbo*) and the awning covered patio to the left of the street. One of those 'whoops, who ran over the waiter' locations.

In this case it is a waitress who battles on despite often appearing tired. The place gets crowded with both locals and tourists and no wonder. The situation is pleasant, the prices reasonable, and service quick. A couple of very drinkable Nes meh ghala cost 150drs, and water is served automatically. Despite not stocking Amstel, a small bottle of Lowenbrau only costs 70drs.

Continuing up Dorpfeld St leaves the *Pizzeria Old Navy* (*Tmr* 45B/C2) on the left, which serves other dishes than pizzas. On the same side of the street is a very chatty ice-cream parlour and a little further along, on the right, is the *Taverna Pirofani* (*Tmr* 46B2). More a restaurant with high-backed Spanish chairs set out beneath a blind covered patio - twee, terribly touristy... and they accept credit cards. How Greek. More in keeping, if predictable, are two tavernas, one (*Tmr* 47C3) on the left of the High St and the other, the *Taverna* ΕΥΤΥΧΙΑ (*Tmr* 48C3), in the adjacent side-street. Further along this latter lane is the *Pub Barbarossa*, hardly a traditional, local cafe-bar.

Bordering the eastern waterfront is the:-
**Taverna Restaurant O Karaboulias** (*Tmr* 9D4)                          Tel 23367
*Directions*: Across Leoforos Golemi from the Marina.

Unbuckle your belts for a splendid meal, from a most interesting menu at acceptable prices. It is always a delight to find an establishment that serves an unusual dish. Here the talented owner/chef offers clients *Pikileea*, a meatless mezes (or more realistically an hors d'oeuvres), the constituents of which include kalamares, tzatziki, aubergine dip, beetroot, tomatoes, fried aubergines, olives and sweet peppers. A super dish, costing about 120drs a head. Main courses include whitebait with a beetroot side plate, oven chicken with patatas and beef in a tomato sauce with rice. A meal for two including pikileea, main dishes, water, two bottles of Lefkas retsina and two large coffees cost about 1400drs. Not inexpensive but a splendid meal accompanied by excellent service. (I have not been able to be exact for each item, because we were fortunate enough to share the evening with Dorothy, an English yacht owner's wife who kindly introduced us to this find).

From the *O Karaboulias*, left (*Fsw*) past the Bus office (*Tmr* 20D4) progresses to the lateral 'Cinema' St, on the left of which is a very 'local' taverna (*Tmr* 8D/E3/4), with an awning covered patio across the wide, dusty street.

Still on the Esplanade, Leoforos Golemi, and twenty or so paces to the north, moored stern on to the quay wall, is a Walt Disney cartoon, 'two storey', poop deck boat. This floating restaurant owes its Heath Robinson looks to the inexpert addition of the second floor.

From this area, along Odhos Panagou, towards the main bridge, is the:-
**Taverna Agriveli**
*Directions*: As above, in the stretch between Rent A Car Lefkas (*Tmr* 19C/D2/3) and *Hotel Lefkas* (*Tmr* 2C2), and fronted by wrought iron gates.

Highlighted as, in the late evening, traditional singers are accompanied by bouzouki and mandolin, with a special performance on Saturday nights. Despite the 'music hall', prices are average, that is Lefkas Town average – not cheap.

The Main Square is edged by various cafe-bar restaurants.

The old-fashioned 'Greek fast food' snackbar is represented by a souvlaki stall, about a third of the way along the High Street, on the right (*Tmr* 14B4).

**Light House Taverna** (*Tmr* 11B5)
*Directions*:Down a side-street, to the right (*Sbo*) of the High Street, and left along an alley.

The proprietor Steve, who speaks excellent American, is a product of his own success. Not only is he somewhat tired but I regret to report, so is the food. The Lighthouse is unfortunately a victim of the flotilla yacht custom, because it was only three or four years ago that we had occasion to heap praise on the establishment. There is a faint but noticeable smell of frying oil and menus do not overwhelm diners. The proprietor was heard to opinion that 1988 had been his best year, and at these (high) prices I am not surprised. A meal for two of tzatziki, Greek salad, kalamares (440drs), a shish-kebab (500drs), both served with soggy chips, a big helping of bread, 2 bottles of beer (no retsina available) and a bottle of water cost a hefty 1660drs.

Just around the corner is the *Cafe Europa/City Cafe Bar* (*Tmr* 49B5), which, despite its rather grand title, is nothing more than a rather sleazy kafeneion.

**Taverna Romantica** (*Tmr* 12B/C6/7) Odhos Mitropoleos.

*Directions:* Further along the High Street, and off to the right (*Sbo*), close to the Police station and on the left. Signed 'Green Garden (behind)'.

Plusher than the *Light House Taverna.*

Towards the upper (south) end of the High St is a small, local's Kafeneion/Snackbar (*Tmr* 50C6/7), on the left, and two more (*Tmr* 50C7/8) also on the left, beyond Odhos Leukata. The most southerly, with a few chairs outside and distinguished by a somewhat twee, wooden fascia, is a popular rendezvous.

## THE A TO Z OF USEFUL INFORMATION
**AIRLINE OFFICES** (*See* **Scorpio Travel, Travel Agents & Tour Offices, A To Z**).

For timetables *See* **Aircraft timetable, A To Z, Preveza, Chapter Ten.**

**BANKS**
**National Bank of Greece** (*Tmr* 7C4)
Located on the edge of the Main Sq, in the ground floor of the *Hotel Patras*. They change personal cheques backed by a Eurocard.

Diagonally across Odhos Meganissiou is the **Agricultural Bank** which, most unusually (to date, that is) services tourist currency requirements and cashes Eurocheques. The **Ionian and Popular Bank** (*Tmr* 17C8) is almost at the far, south end of the High St, next door to the Post Office.

**BEACHES** It is necessary to proceed along the Lagoon perimeter road, for about 2km. The sea facing shore stretches all the way around the inland sea. Unfortunately a shadeless and unattractive expanse of tar and rubbish polluted fine pebble. This is interspersed by angled biscuit rock and edged by a couch grass and prickly shrub supporting backshore.

The good news is that the south-west corner becomes a magnificent sweep of sandy beach, which continues west along the north facing coast. The bad news is that this seashore is edged by sporadic, spasmodic, rather doo-hickey development and is polluted by piles of kelp and some rubbish. That is except for the far west end, where there is a Cantina hut. This latter section is popular with the windsurfing enthusiasts who cannot afford, or do not wish to join the more well heeled *aficionados* at squeaky-expensive Vassiliki. About 400m inland from the backshore track are 'Rooms & Bungalows To Let' (Tel 24397). Incidentally, to access this western sector of the beach, it is necessary to turn left (*Town behind one*), off the lagoon perimeter road, along a dirt track, past a derelict restaurant. The rough surfaced road borders the backshore towards Ag Ioannis and is edged by the occasional private home.

**BICYCLE, SCOOTER & CAR HIRE** Odhos Panagou is the 'Rent A Conveyance' street. Of all the businesses in this stretch, and which include 'Broumis' Rent A Car & Motorcycle System... I nominate the family team. Father runs **Rent A Car Lefkas** (*Tmr* I9C/D2/3) and Philippa, the daughter, operates **Rent A Car & Motorcycle Ionio** (*Tmr* 44D3).

There are other, possibly less expensive scooter firms at the more unfashionable, south end of town. These include **Rent A Scooter Kairos** (*Tmr* 52C/D7/8) and **Santas Motorbike Rentals** (*Tmr* 35B8).

**BOOKSELLERS** Rather tucked away, alongside the Phonographic Museum (*Tmr* 53C4), is an International Newspaper & Bookshop. An interesting Lefkas Town quirk is that newspapers are sold from handcarts spaced out along the High St.

Contract Yacht Services (*Tmr* 43D/E3) operate a large selection, English language book exchange.

**BREAD SHOPS** The bakers tend to 'hide their light under a bushel'. There are a few spaced out along the town's length. They include a splendid example (*Tmr* 22B3/4) down the narrow lane of Dimarhou Verrioti, one (*Tmr* 22C6) further south, on the left of the High St, who also 'Oven Pies', and another (*Tmr* 22B/C7/8), close to Plateia Ag Minas, on the other side of the street.

**BUSES** The Athens bus may drop passengers at the Main quay end of the High St. The new Bus office (*Tmr* 20D4) is conveniently located, towards the north end of Leoforos Golemi. Despite the modernity, the large waiting room encompasses all those qualities that help make a Greek bus terminal unforgettable. These include chaos, an air of expectancy, a cacophony of sounds, the shambles of a floor area 'mined' with suitcases, cardboard boxes (tied with string), a litter of assorted backpacks amongst and around which are cluttered bundles of black costumed Greek ladies, nose-picking men and a seemingly uncontrollable horde of well dressed young children. The snacks counter serves odds and ends of food as no Greek can approach the portals of any transport system without compulsively eating. Perhaps it is a form of masticatory supplication?

The building exhibits an excellent display board depicting a large outline of the island, with arrows indicating details of bus (and boat) services from each major centre. It is a wall mounted, 'tourist office all-in-one map/guide'. Unfortunately it is sometimes difficult to follow... but let me not complain. Would it be that each and every office had such a facility.

## Bus timetable
**Lefkas Town to Athens***
Daily          0830, 0930, 1230, 1630hrs
*Return journey*
Daily          0700, 1300, 1630, 2045hrs
One-way fare 2000drs, duration 7hrs
*100 Kiffissou Tel 5133583

**Lefkas Town to Acteon** (M)
Daily          0715, 0910, 1100, 1510hrs
For return details See Acteon, Chapter Ten.

**Lefkas Town to Vassiliki via Ag Petros** (S coast)
Daily          0630, 1030, 1345, 1900hrs

**Lefkas Town to Ag Nikitas via Tsoukalades** (NW coast)
Daily          0710, 1000, 1200, 1415, 1715hrs

**Lefkas Town to Vlycho via Kariotes, Lygia, Paradisos, Episkopos, Nikiana & Nidri** (E coast)
Daily          0540, 0615, 0700, 0800, 1030, 1130, 1230, 1315, 1345, 1700, 1900hrs

**Lefkas Town to Sivota** (SE coast)
Daily          0615, 1330hrs

**Lefkas Town to Ag Ilias** (South of inland centre of island)
Daily          0540, 1330hrs

**Lefkas Town to Karia** (North of inland centre of island)
Daily          0550, 0650, 1000, 1205, 1345, 1515, 1700hrs

**Lefkas Town to Eglouvi** (Centre of island)
Daily          0630, 1345hrs

**Lefkas Town to Poros** (SE coast)
Daily          0640, 1330hrs

**Lefkas Town to Paliokatouna** (West of Nidri), **Rahi & Geni** (Peninsula)
Daily          0645, 1345hrs

**Lefkas Town to Athani via Dragano** (SW coast)
Daily          0610, 1340hrs

**Lefkas Town to Katouna** (W of Ligia)
Daily          0740, 1205hrs

**Lefkas Town to Nikoli via Manasi** (East of Dragano)
Daily          1420hrs

**Lefkas Town to Kalamitsi** (W coast)
Daily          0600, 1430hrs

**Lefkas Town to Kavallos** (Inland, south of Lefkas Town)
Daily          0630, 1300hrs

**Lefkas Town to Katochori** (S of Vlycho)
Daily          0615, 1330hrs

**Lefkas Town to Sivros** (South of centre of island)
Daily          0615, 1330hrs

**Lefkas Town to Vafkeri** (West of Nidri)
Daily          0630, 1515hrs

**Lefkas Town to Plagia**(?)
Daily                 0645, 1300hrs

The map advises the return bus times from the particular destination.

**CINEMA** (*Tmr* 33D/E3) An open-air example.

**COMMERCIAL SHOPPING AREAS** No central area but the town is very well 'stocked' with a varied range of shops, some of which are excellent. Depending on one's viewpoint, it is to be regretted that the inhabitants have clasped supermarkets to their collective bosoms. Examples include the largest Supermarket 'in town' (*Tmr* 24C7), across the way from the Bus and lorry park; a capacious unit (*Tmr* 24D3), round the corner from the Bus office and yet another (*Tmr* 24C4) on the left (*Sbo*) of the High St. Despite this onslaught, a Mini-market survives, alongside a shop (*Tmr*) 29C5/6) selling Gaz cylinders and Siemens domestic electrical goods.

Fortunately, not all the bygone age outlets have yet disappeared. Gems must include the specialist, Lefkas honey shops which include a honey only, small 'corner shop' (*Tmr* 23C/D2/3) at No. 6, alongside the Pub Barbarossa, and a simply splendid, High St Yoghurteria (*Tmr* 23B/C5), which also sells honey and is presided over by an old crone, who reeks of mothballs. A honey shop is across the alley from the *Light House Taverna* (*Tmr* 11B5) and a Yoghurteria (*Tmr* 23C6/7) edges the High St, almost opposite the outset of Odhos Mitropoleos.

Butchers 'abound' and noteworthy examples include two (*Tmr* 27C4/5) prior to the Yoghurteria (*Tmr* 23B/C5) (*Proceeding south along the High St*), the most southerly highlighted, if only for the middle-aged owner's distinctive 'duck's arse' hairstyle; a clutch of three (*Tmr* 27B/C5/6) straddling the Main St, the one closest to Odhos Arakliotis being an old-fashioned butcher who might be closing, as well as a combined poultry and butchers shop (*Tmr* 27C6), almost opposite Odhos Mitropolis.

There are a surprising number of Fish shops (*Tmr* 26C8) gathered in a small area close to Plateia Ag Minas, with two almost side-by-side on the left (*Sbo*) of the High St.

Unusual shops include one (*Tmr* 28B/C8/9) retailing cheeses and olives, one alongside a butcher, across the street from the Post Office (*Tmr* 18C7/8), selling goat's bells and tanned skins, an old-world store (*Tmr* 41B/C5) grinding coffee beans and a Delicatessen (*Tmr* 56B/C4). Apart from a Hardware shop (*Tmr* 54B/C6) and an Ironmongers/Shipstore/Chandlery (*Tmr* 55B/C4), there are a couple of second-hand/antique businesses.

One drink shop nestles close by the *Hotel Byzantio* (*Tmr* 4B2) and another on the south-west corner of the Main Sq on the corner of Meganissiou and the High St. But the 'king' must be the outfit (*Tmr* 25B/C6/7) on Odhos Mitropoleos which advertises, 'We make our drinks the same way since 1945, ask to try them', and backs this up with an invitingly barrelled interior.

Fruit and vegetable shops are plentiful with a local 'hole-in-the-wall' (*Tmr* 57B5) in the *Light House Taverna* lane, a pair (*Tmr* 57C8) at the south end of the High St and two (*Tmr* 57C8 & C/D6/7) spaced out on the right (*Fsw*) of Leoforos 8th Merarchias.

In the line of buildings behind the High St water fountain (*Tmr* B/C2/3) is a large Souvenir cum sports shop. Also in the High St, but on the other side of the road, beyond or south of the water fountain, are a pair of side-by-side Camera shops (*Tmr* 58C3). Souvenir and gift shops are not in short supply. Odhos Ag Mavra (*Tmr* B/C2) is lined with them, from the Esplanade to Plateia Sp Vianta.

**FERRY-BOATS** Goodness only knows why Lefkas is not incorporated in the scheduled inter-island ferry-boat timetables. Fortunately, nowadays there are various island services to mainland destinations and other Ionian islands. Lefkas Town travellers only have the use of passenger boats operating from the Main Quay (*Tmr* D1), in the summer months. Craft include the **Margarita** and **Caterina**, connecting with Ithaca and Cephalonia, and even small boats which ply to and from Nidri and Meganissi island. For details of the itinerary *See* **Dana Travel, Travel Agents & Tour Offices, A To Z.**.

For all the year round, schedules car ferry services to Meganissi, Ithaca and Cephalonia islands, *See* **Ferry-boats, A To Z, Nidri, Circular Route.**
**HAIRDRESSERS** A ladies Hairdresser (*Tmr* 59B3/4) lurks on the right (*High St behind one*) of Odhos Dimarhou Verrioti. A couple of men's Barbers (*Tmr* 59B/C7 & 59C7) are located, one each, in side lanes off to either side and at the south end of the High St. Another (*Tmr* 59C3) is squeezed in the side-street off the High St, almost opposite the water fountain.

**LAUNDRY** Unfortunately there aren't any launderettes, but there are a number of Dry Cleaners (*Tmr* 30C3/4, 30C/D7 & *Tmr* 6B8).

## MEDICAL CARE
**Chemists & Pharmacies** There are more than sufficient, mostly gathered towards the top, south end of the High St (*Tmr* 31B/C6, 31B/C6/7, 31B/C7 & 31B8), as well as one next door to the Post Office (*Tmr* 18C7/8).

**Clinics** (ΙΑΤΡΕΙΟΝ) Two (*Tmr* 32B3/4 & 32B4), close together and in narrow lanes off to either side of Odhos Dimarhou Verrioti.

**Dentist** A surgery is on a High St corner, in the area of the water fountain, on the north side of a Taverna (*Tmr* 47C3).

**Hospital** (*Tmr* A/B7/8) To the right (*Sbo*) of Plateia Ag Minas, along Odhos Aristotelous Valaoritis. The hospital is on the right, immediately beyond the kink in the road. Alternatively, turn down Odhos Mitropoleos and keep round to the left.

**NTOG** The Community of Lefkada Tourist Information office (*Tmr* 60B/C2/3) is (or was) sited at the north end of the High St, on the right (*Fsw*) of Odhos Dorpfeld. I insinuate a past tense because, on my last visit, the 'cupboard was very bare'. As elsewhere, what is left of the Tourist police are ensconced with the Town police (*Tmr* 40B/C6/7).

**OTE** (*Tmr* 34A6/7) The modern building is to the north of the Town Hall, in a very dusty, modern part of the town. Turn right (*Sbo*) off the High St, either along Odhos Mitropoleos or Aristotelous Valaoritis. Open weekdays between 0700-2400hrs and weekends between 0730-2230hrs.

**PETROL** One (*Tmr* 21C8/9) is on the south side of Plateia Ag Minas, to the left (*Sbo*) at the outset of the Nidri road, whilst another (*Tmr* 21A6) is situated east of the OTE office.

## PLACES OF INTEREST
**Ag Mavra Castle** *See* **Arrival by Bus**.

### Cathedrals and Churches
*Pantokrator Cathedral Tmr* 36C6) Built in 1684 but subject (as have been most older Lefkas buildings) to constant reconstruction due to earthquake damage over the years.

*Church of Eisodion Theotokou* (*Tmr* 37C7) Cream and white with railings fencing off the front.

*Church of Ag Minas* (*Tmr*38B/C8) Prior to earthquake damage, a very fine church, built in 1707, but now most noticeable for the angle-iron, meccano-like clock tower to one side.

**Festival, Annual** Once a year, during the last two weeks of August, the island hosts an international festival of drama, folk-dance, singing and speech which attracts entries from many countries. The participants perform nightly, in Lefkas Town, and tour the island villages, as well as partaking in a parade of boats. The first seven days are of a more serious tenor. During the second week the festival breaks loose, with a 'conga' of the participants through the town's streets. This finishes up on the park, to the fore of the *Hotel Lefkas* (*Tmr* 2C2). The town's evening performances are staged towards the west end of Odhos Anastassiou Skiadaresi. Tickets can be pre-purchased from the travel agents or the Main Sq sited festival hut.

### Museums
*Archaeological (or Dorpfeld)* Borders the Tsoukalades road out of town. Small, unimpressive and only labelled in German and Greek.

*Folklore* Close by the Town Hall (*Tmr* A7) and exhibits an interesting display of clothes, costumes, a loom, models and weaving.

*Phonographic* (*Tmr* 53C4) As would be imagined, a collection of antique gramophones.

**Philarmonic Orchestra** An active, enthusiastic, amateur band which has its very own first floor practice room, 'Filamoniki Lefkadas 1850', above an ironmongers (*Tmr* 55 B/C4). The band hold a parade once a month. In addition, they join in all official activities, be it an army or navy function, and any funeral. The latter can prove quite an 'interesting spectator event'. Anything can happen including the corpse falling out of the coffin!

One item of interest (or more correctly sight) is the replica of Jason's Argonaut. This was built in recent years for a rerun of the mythological hero's voyage. Now, sadly, it 'eyes' onlookers from the boatyard islet offshore of the Main Quay.

## POLICE
**Port** (*Tmr* 39E2/3) Located where would be expected, close by the main quay.

**Town (& Tourist)** (*Tmr* 40B/C6/7) In the first floor of a building on the corner of the High St and Odhos Mitropoleos. Proud possessors of a prowl car which cruises up and down the 'main drag'. When not in use, the vehicle is neatly parked opposite their office.

**POST OFFICE** (*Tmr* 18C7/8) On the left, almost at the south end of the High Street, close to the Ionian and Popular Bank.

**TAXIS** They rank (*Tmr* T) at various strategic points throughout the town, which include close by the junction of the main causeway and the outset of the Lagoon road, as well as both sides of the Main Sq (*Tmr* C3/4).

**SPORTS FACILITIES** Not a lot, but there is always Fagotto Pool & Pinball Arcade (*Tmr* C7), on the junction of Leoforos 8th Merarchias and Odhos Leukata. Well, I only thought I would mention it. One other place of note is *Taverna Akritiri* on the Faneromeni Monastery road. This is supposed to possess a skating rink.

**TELEPHONE NUMBERS & ADDRESSES**

| | |
|---|---|
| Hospital (*Tmr* A/B7/8) | Tel 22336 |
| Police (*Tmr* 40B/C6/7) | Tel 22322 |
| Taxis | Tel 24600 |

**TRAVEL AGENTS & TOUR OFFICES**
**Dana Travel** (*Tmr* 42D2)                                                  Tel 23629/24650
*Directions*: South of the Main Quay, beyond a park and hemmed in by the *Hotel Xenia*.

The town's 'top' office, which offers almost every service possible including apartments, hotels, villas, taxis, excursions and tickets.

Other High St offices include **Scorpio Travel** (*Tmr* 45B/C2) sited over the *Pizzeria Old Navy*, who act for Olympic Airways, and **Lefkas Travel** (*Tmr* 15B/C3).

**WATER** Scattered about the town are a number of large, bulk drinking water tanks including one (*Tmr* W D/E4), close to the Bus office, one (*Tmr* W A2) bordering the Lagoon perimeter road, and another (*Tmr* W A7) in front of the Town Hall. The reason for their presence is that a few years ago a decision was made to replace and extend the drinking water supply. The trenches were dug and the new pipes left out 'to dry', for a whole summer. Unfortunately, when the job of completing the installation was restarted, the channels were not properly lined. As a result, the ultra-violet affected water pipes cracked, which allowed the ingress of sewage from nearby and also fractured conduits. This 'infusion' resulted in large numbers of Lefkas Town inhabitants being carted off to hospital – since when they don't trust the usual water supply and thus the above ground storage tanks.

**YACHT REPAIRS**
**Contract Yacht Services** (*Tmr* 43D/E3).
*Directions*: Behind and in the same block as the Port police.

An English run and staffed yacht service business. Apart from an book-swop scheme, they may help out with totally disinterested advice. If an enquirer owns a boat they perk up, a bit. Rates charged are those levied in England and some of the work I observed was adequate, just. There is a drinking water tap outside the office.

A competitor has set out his stall:-
**Lefkas Marine Service** 4 Leoforos Golemi                                      Tel 22976
*Directions*: The business, started in 1988, operates from a shop close to the Bus office (*Tmr* 20D4).

Teo (Theodore) Georgakis, an engaging young man, used to work for Contract Yacht, but felt the urge to be his own boss. He is very friendly and keen to please, a pleasant alternative to his erstwhile employers. Best of luck to him.

# A CIRCULAR (CLOCKWISE) ROUTE
## To Vassiliki via Nidri, Poros & on round to Lefkas Town via Ag Petros & Tsoukalades (80km)
From Ag Minas Square, at the top or south end of the High Street, select the main, left-hand fork. Initially this route meanders across a confusion of suburbs, cultivation and olive groves.

Beyond **Kaligoni** some Ancient Lefkas excavations hove into view, on the right, lurking, in a low, dark, tree shaded grass meadow. These and other 'digs' were the result of one Herr Dorpfeld, a German archaeologist. He was obsessed with the theory that Lefkas, not Ithaca, was the 'fatherland' of Homer's Ulysses (Odysseus). All that is to show for Dorpfeld's undoubted energy is an abundance of remains, including this jumble of large cut and unworked stone blocks.

To the left is a track down to some Alikes, or saltings. The Lefkas end of the sea channel is rather confusing, not altogether surprisingly considering the centuries long adjustments carried out by the various world powers, during their particular suzerainty. An islet in the channel is capped by the unusual remains of a Russian built fort, a relic of their short occupation.

**KARIOTES** (5km from Lefkas Town) A spaced out straggle. *Camping Kariotes Beach* (Tel 23594, open 15th May-Sept) is on the right and certainly not 'on the beach', which is to the left of the road. Also on the right are several *Rooms*.

Kariotes almost merges with:-
**LYGIA (6km from Lefkas Town)** On the approaches to this seaside hamlet is the *Hotel Benaki*, at least four *Rooms*, a petrol station and a mini-market. Close to the centre of Lygia is more *Rooms*. A very small, fine shingle beach and sizeable quay are followed by at least three more *Rooms* and a circular cove with a shingly shore bordered by tall gum trees.

The route now edges the mainly rocky coastline. The overall setting is pretty with the mainland looming up across the sound, imparting a Norwegian fjord milieu.

After about 8km, on the outskirts of **Episkopos**, the road passes *Camping Episkopos*, on the left, followed by *International Camping Beach*, on the right, *Camping Episkopos Beach* (Tel 23043, open June-Sept), on the right, 'Blucher Flats To Let' and *Rooms*.

The thoroughfare continues to hug the shoreline, in which are a scattering of little, shingly beach coves, and is bordered by *Rooms* and apartments, to left and right.

**NIKIANA (9km from Lefkas Town)** Contains a mini-market with a metered telephone, restaurants, an Express Market, over which are *Rooms*, a *Restaurant Giovani*, more accommodation in private houses, on both sides of the road, Rent A Motorbike, close to *Rooms*, the *Taverna Dionnisos, Rooms De Luxe* and the *Alexandros Restaurant/Taverna*.

As the route proceeds through olive groves south of Nikiana, the coast is some 50m to the left. Signs exhort 'No Camping' and advise of *Rooms* on both sides of the road. Sparti islet hoves into view, prior to the very expensive *Gallini Apartments* (Class B, tel 92431) where a double room apartment kicks off at 6000/7500drs, increasing to 9000/1100drs. A track branches up to two *Rooms*, one in *Jimmy's House*. The aroma of pine trees is particularly noticeable hereabouts and the road, once again, drops towards sea-level.

**PERIGIALI (14km from Lefkas Town)** The small beach hosts a burgeoning tumult of windsurfing. The settlement possesses a mini-market, a petrol station, *Rooms*, the *Hotel Knossos, Perigaiali Beach Rooms*, more *Rooms*, Rent A Car Motorcycle, *Rooms*, a disco and a cafeteria.

At about Perigiali, the island's central range of mountains rear up in the distance as the route, and coast, swings west. The outskirts of Perigiali are only a donkey dropping or three from the approaches to:-

**NIDRI (Nydri) (17km from Lefkas Town)** (Illustration 22) The beautiful situation of this attractive fishing port would have ensured its continued popularity, without the rise in villa holiday tourism. For many years *Cricketers Holidays* alone, specialised in bringing the discerning to the delights of Lefkas island. Their pioneering spirit and enterprise have been 'rewarded' by a crush of competitors and there are now an abundance of *Rooms*, apartments, bungalows and villas to rent.

Quite frankly, during the height of season, Nidri is a destination that independent travellers might well consider avoiding. The British presence is so overpowering that even the German tourists gutteral utterings are muted, if not swamped, by the 'yuk yuk' of the yachties and the general murmur of the 'BPTs'.

To seawards, the various inshore islands are delightfully speckled about the sound with the bulk of the mainland forming a backdrop. To the south, the beautiful, fjord-like bay of

Vlycho cuts into the island, the eroded land forming a thick, crooked, mountain finger. The waters are awash with wind surfers, motorboats and yachts. It irresistibly reminds one of the more popular reaches of the Broads or Thames... on a very hot day. The number of boats is not surprising as the port hosts at least two flotilla fleets, which appear to spend most of their time in and or around the location.

The long, arrow straight 'High Street' is not a 'cocktails happy hour', Kosta'd sunset strip. Somehow it has retained a village 'innocence', even retaining one or two older, Lefkian style buildings. Mind you, there is almost everything a tourist might want. It may be something to do with the air but it is rumoured that, at one or two shops, ladies will have to check their 'chastity belts'.

Parallel to the High Street is a very pleasant, long waterfront from which a large quay juts into the bay. The restaurants, tavernas and cafe-bars, which line this 'Esplanade', shut the strand off from the main road, vehicle access being along two transverse, narrow lanes. A number of alleys also cut through from the High St. To the left-hand (*Fsw*) is the tree and bamboo bordered Mithos beach. Not only is it small, but it is narrow, the main body of which is shingle, whilst the fairly steeply shelving foreshore is sand and tiny pebble. Considering the crowds of people, the beach is kept quite clean. The quay front has the occasional, green, top loading garbage bins with handwritten signs rightly urging disposers of rubbish to 'Dispose Garbage Inside'.

Onassis family trusts probably still own the 'James Bond' film set, adjacent islets of Skorpios and Skorpidi. Potential visitors to these lovely, mysterious playthings of the fabulously wealthy, are actively discouraged by gun-toting minders and their guard dogs, sentinels that only an overpowering amount of money could, or would wish to buy. For those who look on with envy, it is thought-provoking to remember that Aristotle Onassis had to 'buy' his last wife, his only son was killed prematurely in a private aeroplane crash, being buried in the Skorpios family vault, and the unhappy Christina died precipitately, in mysterious circumstances. Money might buy the trappings but in this fated family's case it didn't seem to guarantee either happiness or longevity.

The most intriguing of the islets must surely be the closest, the tree-covered Madouri. On the Nidri facing shore is an imposing, Palladian fronted building set in apparently close-cut, green lawns. It was built for and or by the nationally famous poet Aristotle Valaoritis who died in 1879. His family still own the islet, to which callers are also forbidden.

**ARRIVAL BY FERRY** A splendid, year round, small, car ferry link between Nidri and the islands of Meganissi, Cephalonia and Ithaca. It has to be admitted that the Cephalonia and Ithaca ports are the relatively unfashionable Fiscardon and Frikes.

## THE ACCOMMODATION & EATING OUT
**The Accommodation** There are any number of houses with private accommodation, a few pensions and a hotel. Prices reflect the popularity of the resort.

**Hotel Gorgona** (*Tmr* 2A3) (Class E)                                                 Tel 92268
*Directions*: Along the fourth side-street to the right (*Lefkas Town behind one*) of the High St.
   All rooms have en suite bathrooms. Single room rates commence at 3000drs & doubles 3300drs, increasing to 3620drs & 4600drs (6th June-10th July & 27th Aug-20th Sept) and 6000drs for either (11th July-26th Aug).

**Pension Nydrion Akti** (*Tmr* IC1) (Class B)                                          Tel 92400
*Directions*: First left (*Lefkas Town behind one*) off the High St, at the outset of the development.
   All rooms have en suite bathrooms with a single costing 2200drs & a double 2500drs, which prices rise to 2500drs & 3000drs (1st April-14th June & 16th Sept-31st Oct).

A private accommodation double room (*Tmr* 4), with en suite bathroom, costs a minimum 2500drs, take it or leave it. Amongst that available are **Rooms** (*Tmr* 5C4 – tel 92200), in the ground floor of which is a souvenir shop; **Rooms** (6C8 – tel 92252), over a souvenir shop; **Rooms** (*Tmr* 7B9 – tel 92337), luxurious rooms with bathroom, 'For information apply opposite or to the pastry shop';

# Illustration 22 Nidri

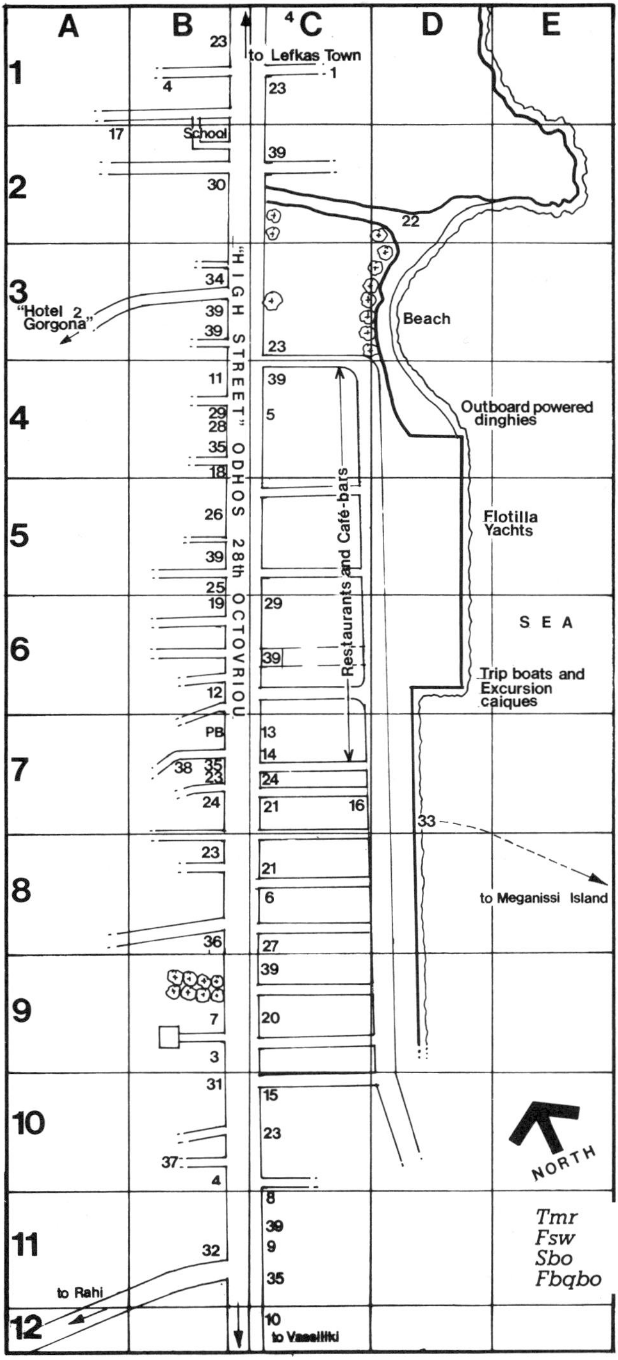

Grid labels: A B C D E (columns), 1–12 (rows)

to Lefkas Town

School

"Hotel 2 Gorgona"

Beach

HIGH STREET - ODHOS 28th OCTOVRIOU

Restaurants and Café-bars

Outboard powered dinghies

Flotilla Yachts

SEA

Trip boats and Excursion caiques

to Meganissi Island

NORTH

to Rahi

to Vaseliki

*Tmr*

| | |
|---|---|
| 1C1 | Pension Nydrion Akti |
| 2A3 | Hotel Gorgona |
| 3B9/10 | Pastry shop |
| 4 | Rooms |
| 5C4 | Rooms/Souvenir shop |
| 6C8 | Rooms/Souvenir shop |
| 7B9 | Rooms |
| 8C10/11 | Rooms |
| 9C11 | Rooms |
| 10C12 | Rooms |
| 11B3/4 | Fast Food Nidri |
| 12B6/7 | Kafeneion |
| 13C7 | The Bistro |
| 14C7 | Bar de Paris |
| 15C10 | Restaurant/Taverna Heavens Gardens |
| 16C/D7 | Nick the Greek's |
| 17A/B1/2 | Homers |
| 18B4/5 | Fragoulis Rent A Motorbyke |
| 19B5/6 | International Paper Shop |
| 20C9 | 'Pub' |
| 21 | Bakers |
| 22D2 | Kavos Beach Cafe-bar |
| 23 | Mini-markets/Supermarkets |
| 24 | Market/Fruit & Vegetable stores |
| 25B5/6 | Fruit & Vegetable shop |
| 26B5 | Butcher |
| 27C8/9 | Fish shop |
| 28B4 | Drink store |
| 29 | Tobacconists |
| 30B2 | Nidri Yacht Club |
| 31B9/10 | Bora-Bora Cocktail Bar |
| 32B11 | Ouzerie |
| 33D7/8 | Ferry-boat Quay |
| 34B3 | Dry cleaners |
| 35 | Chemists |
| 36B8/9 | OTE |
| 37B10 | Port police |
| 38B7 | Post Office |
| 39 | Travel offices |
| PB | Post Box |

| | |
|---|---|
| *Tmr* | =Town map reference |
| *Fsw* | =Facing seawards |
| *Sbo* | =Sea behind one |
| *Fbqbo* | =Ferry-boat Quay behind one |

*Rooms* (*Tmr* 8C10/11 – tel 92361), 'The Beautiful View'; *Rooms* (*Tmr* 9C11), behind a one time cafe-shop which now appears to contain motorbike parts, and *Rooms* (*Tmr* 10C12), along a narrow alley, an ideal situation if it were not almost exactly opposite the 'Disco Alexanders - Air Conditioned'. Incidentally, on the left-hand side of this disco is No 7, the pleasing presence of a traditional wooden building, possibly now unoccupied.

## The Eating Out
Drinks and meals are comparatively expensive and, naturally, the waterfront Esplanade is lined with cafe-bars and restaurants. A Nidri speciality is monumental ice-creams. A number of concerns spring to mind, not for any other reason than some quirk or idiosyncrasy, and a mention does not indicate an endorsement!

Establishments listed under this caveat include *Fast Food Nidri* (*Tmr* 11B3/4), which sells doughnuts; a Kafeneion (*Tmr* 12B6/7), housed in a meritorious old building with a corrugated iron upper storey; *The Bistro* (*Tmr* 13C7), which reckons it serves the first and best English breakfast with offerings that include scrambled eggs, bacon and tomato and serves 'Special Meals For Children'; the very smart *Bar de Paris* (*Tmr* 14C7), specialising in ice-creams and drinks; *Restaurant/Tavern Heavens Gardens* (*Tmr* 15C10); *Kavos Beach Cafe-Bar* (*Tmr* 22D2); the *Nidri Yacht Club* (*Tmr* 30B2), hardly the Royal Yacht Squadron, I can assure you; the *Bora-Bora* (*Tmr* 31B9/10), where cocktails and spirits 'only' cost 300drs between 7pm-10pm (and then probably decrease in cost!); an Ouzerie (*Tmr* 32B11), and, I nearly forgot, the *Pub* (*Tmr* 20C9).

I feel honour bound to mention *Nick the Greek* (*Tmr* 16C/D7), one of the original, long serving, now rather tired cafe-bar/tavernas. The owner, Nick (surprise, surprise), is no shy, retiring violet and he shamelessly promotes himself. He and his taverna's fame dates back to the erstwhile patronage of Aristotle Onassis and his clan. The taverna's walls are lined with very faded photographs of these days of super stardom. Maybe my slightly patronising tone is due to the fact that, in the intervening years, Nick remains as sleek as ever and almost always appears to have a good looking lady in close attendance. I'm not sure of the whereabouts of his large motor cruiser, emblazoned with his name, which used to moor against the adjacent quayside, but he certainly owns a caique.

Even today, every so often in amongst the dazzling array of establishments that face on to the quayside is a family who has stuck it out, still living in comparative squalor. During the summertime a number of corn on the cob BBQs are set out, towards the south end of the waterfront.

## THE A TO Z OF USEFUL INFORMATION
**BANKS** *See* **Post Office, A To Z.**

**BICYCLE, SCOOTER & CAR HIRE** General daily rates are 1000/1350drs for a 50cc Honda/Vespa scooter, 5500drs for a 2CV or sedan, 7000drs for a Jeep and 8000drs for a soft top vehicle. Apart from the Travel offices, businesses include **Homer** (*Tmr* 17A/B1/2) and **Fragoulis Rent A Motorbike (& Tsakalos Rent A Motorboat)** (*Tmr* 18B4/5).

**BOOKSELLERS** More exactly an International paper shop (*Tmr* 19B5/6), bordering the High St.

**BOAT HIRE** Tsakalos Rent Motorboat (*Tmr* 18B4/5) have a High St office (shared with Fragoulis Rent A Motorbike). Their operatives also lurk in the tree lined alley close to the beach. The small, outboard powered dinghies are moored at the very north end of the flotilla yacht quay.

**BREAD SHOPS** The original Nidri Baker (*Tmr* 21C7) was headed up by a once bouncing octogenarian, with 'hands' for the ladies, but he now, sadly, appears to be falling foul of *anno Domini*. The shop also sells cakes and stays open all day. The competition (*Tmr* 21C8) also ignores the siesta. A Pastry/Patisserie (*Tmr* 3B9/10) acts as an informal information desk for some adjacent accommodation, as well as selling drinks.

**BUSES** *See* **Buses, A To Z, Lefkas Town.**

**COMMERCIAL SHOPPING AREA** The High St is lined by various shops which include a number of Mini-markets and Supermarkets (*Tmr* 23B1, 23C1, 23C3/4, 23B7, 23B8 & 23C10); Mini-market fruit & vegetable stores (*Tmr* 24C7 & 24B7); a Fruit & vegetable shop (*Tmr* 25B5/6); a Butcher (*Tmr* 26B5); a Fish shop (*Tmr* 27C8/9); a Drink store (*Tmr* 28B4); a Tobacconist (*Tmr* 29B4), as well as a Tobacconist which sells camera film (*Tmr* 29C5/6); a boutique and a number of Souvenir/Gift shops.

**FERRY-BOATS** In effect, Nidri is the Ferry-boat port of Lefkas with a daily 'landing craft' car ferry service to the islands of Meganissi, Ithaca and Cephalonia.

## Ferry-boat timetable

| Day | Departure time | Ferry-boat | Ports/Islands of Call |
|---|---|---|---|
| Daily | 0700hrs | Meganisi/Lefkas | Spartochori Port(Meganissi).* |
| | 0830hrs | Meganisi/Lefkas | Fiscardon(Cephalonia),Frikes(Ithaca). |
| | 1400hrs | Meganisi/Lefkas | Spartochori Port(Meganissi).* |
| | 1945hrs | Meganisi/Lefkas | Spartochori Port(Meganissi).* |

One-way fare: to Meganissi       185drs
to Fiscardon/Frikes400drs
*Meganissi-bound ferries also call in at Vathi(Meganissi) but on what basis I am not sure.

**FERRY-BOAT TICKET OFFICES** Tickets can be purchased on board but are also available from the appropriate Travel Agent. For instance the **CF Meganissi** is represented by Fragoulis (*Tmr* 18B4/5).

**LAUNDRY** More a Dry-cleaners (*Tmr* 34B3) where 'English Spoken'.

## MEDICAL CARE
**Chemists & Pharmacies** A number (*Tmr* 35B4, 35B7 & 35C11/12) spread out along the High St.

**OTE** (*Tmr* 36B8/9) A pleasantly doo-hickey office, with only one cubicle and open weekdays, between 0800-1230hrs & 1700-2100hrs.

**PETROL** South of Nidri.

**PLACES OF INTEREST** Apart from excursion boat trips 'round the bay' and to Meganissi island (*See* this chapter), there are 'Donkey Safaris' – A peaceful (*degrading* – Author's note), traditional way to see the panoramic view of the Ionian islands. Ride through shady, aromatic citrus and olive groves with frequent stops to water the donkeys at mountain springs plus cool drinks for the riders. Then a leisurely lunch at a shady spot before an amble back down the mountain. Treks daily departs (*sic*) 10am, returns 5pm approx. Information and booking from Kartanos Grocery!' Yes, well!

**Dimosari Gorge Waterfall** Select the Rahi road from Nidri High St. In Rahi village follow the track signed to the right, for the ¼hr walk. The summer-dry river-bed path curves right at a small cascade to the main waterfall pool.

## POLICE
**Port** (*Tmr* 37B10).

**POST OFFICE** (*Tmr* 38B7) The unit is along a narrow, unsurfaced alley indicated at the High St outset with a large sign. Fortunately they exchange currency, travellers cheques and Eurocheques. Open weekdays between 0800-1500hrs.

## TELEPHONE NUMBERS & ADDRESSES
| | |
|---|---|
| Clinic | Tel 31216 |
| Taxis (unreliable) | Tel 92528 |

**TRAVEL AGENTS & TOUR OFFICES** Many of the offices hire scooters and cars and will locate accommodation. In the past I had occasion to praise **Georges Tourism** (*Tmr* 39C3/4) but I can only report as I find. If George has left his abusive, arrogant, unspeakably rude young man in charge – then why run the gauntlet of his appalling manners? ('Shut your mouth'!).

Diagonally across the High St (*Tmr* 39B3/4) is a very kind, helpful gentleman who will field most questions, even if he cannot actually sell 'an enquirer anything. This office is the nearest to Georges, there being another business a few metres further north. I hope readers will patronise him.

Apart from a number of High St firms, which include **Fragoulis** (*Tmr* 18B4/5), the largest office is:-

**Nidri Travel** (*Tmr* 39B5)                                              Tel 92256
*Directions*: As above, across the street from yet another, splendid, tin clad first storey building.

The firm is the *Falcon Sailing* agent – 'Beach BBQ, Free Wind Surfinge' (*sic*). A most helpful staff, of which 'Girl Friday' is Vassiliki, an extremely pleasant young Greek lady who speaks excellent English. An interesting thing about this office is that next door is a kafeneion. To save the unnecessary walk out of the office on to the Main St and into the kafeneion, there is an inter-connecting door, and why not.

**WATER SPORTS** Yes. *See* **Nidri Travel, A To Z**. As *Falcon*, amongst others, operate from Nidri, the waterfront is abuzz with most variations on all and every theme.

South of Nidri, the route passes several petrol stations and yet more *Rooms*. The views are stunning. The inland sea or, more correctly, the Bay of Vlycho is backed by the mountainous Geni peninsula. To the right, the inland perspective is dominated by a steep mountain range, topped off by the 1150m high Mt Elati.

Almost a part of Nidri now is:-
**MEGALO AVLAKI & VLYCHO (18/20km from Lefkas Town)** This combined village stretches along the stony seashore of the bay in a narrow, extremely elongated straggle bounded by the two roads of the one-way traffic system (sounds like home doesn't it?). Fishing boats are moored along the shore and there is a mini-market, a restaurant and the occasional private house accommodation. In contrast to the main body of the bay, which is beautiful, the south end is not particularly attractive, resembling a pine tree edged, stagnant lake.

From Vlycho a turning to the left runs out around the edge of the bay. At the far end a right fork crests a col to *Desimi Beach Campsite* (Tel 95225, open May-Oct), sited above a small, shingle beach.
    The left fork climbs the spine of the hilly headland of Geni peninsula. The unsurfaced track initially 'ducks and weaves' on its winding way towards the Churches of Apostoloi and Kryiaki. The lane breaks out of the profuse tree mantle of the lower slopes to the more patchily covered hilltop, from whence there are enchanting views of the bay, on the one side, and the in-shore islands, on the other.
The main road from Vlycho steeply climbs the hillside, in a series of serpentine loops, advancing past the short side road to the village of **Katochori** At a fork, the left-hand road curves off, past a track down to Mikros Gialos Beach, to end up in:-

**POROS (27km from Lefkas Town)** A mellow, provincial village, with lovely roofs, edging narrow, winding lanes between the crowded houses, the whole set on the mountainside clad in groves of mature olive trees.
    From the Poros road, a winding track descends steeply to the Bay of Rouda on the edge of which is:-
**Mikros Gialos Beach (Ag Marina, Poros Beach) (31km from Lefkas Town)** Two-thirds of the way down is a nice-looking house to let (Tel 95386), but transport would be required. Close to the shore of the bay are the portals of the well situated, agreeably laid out *Camping Poros Beach* (Tel 23203, open June-Sept). A large signboard indicates the wide range of facilities and activities, which include 'Danse'. The site is actually a mix of Camping Bungalows and pitches for tents, caravans and motor caravans. The pleasant girl, Irene, explains all, in respect of charges (410drs per person, 265drs per car and 640drs per tent) and the facilities, which include a mini-market, a dandy restaurant, playground and the aforementioned dancing. There are super views out over the bay.
    Beyond the campsite are *Rooms*, on the right; a 'Pub', more a tin bunker, the signboard of which indicates that there are few items that the establishment cannot offer; a scattering of houses, one of which, on the right, offers accommodation prior to decanting on to the nearside of the backshore of a clean 150m sweep of broad but shadeless, pebble beach. Idyllic looking from the heights above, the pebbles extend into the sea. There is evidence of a serious oil spillage with a 'high water' tar line as well as numerous blobs of tar scattered about the shore.
    The metalled road, which runs along the edge of the beach, is substantial enough to give a similar impression to that gained at many an embryonic Spanish resort in the 1960s – all roads and street lights. This recollection is heightened by the attempt to create formal gardens between the road and the backshore. An ice-cream van is parked against the kerbside. In addition to another snackbar, at the far end, on the right, is the *Porto Leoni Cafe/Restaurant* – '25m Parking in the shade'. Oh dear me. *Poros Community Camping* (Tel 95475 – open April-Oct) is also present.

Back on the main route, the road continues to climb across olive tree clad, granite mountains on the road to Vassiliki. A right-hand road sheers off to **Sivros**, a substantial village nestled up against the southern foothills of Mt Elati. Some private houses offer accommodation. Beyond Sivros it is another 7km mountainside ascent to **Ag Ilias**, where the paved road runs out and from whence tracks wander off into the peaks.

At about the Sivros branch turning, the countryside becomes rather softer. Another three kilometres on, a narrow track to the left, wanders down to the bay and hamlet of:-
**SIVOTA (Syvota) (31km from Lefkas Town)** This once beautiful, fairy-tale fishing inlet is now on the way to becoming a full blown, 'undiscovered, get-away-from-it-all, villa brochure find'. The original grass growing, shingly sweep of shore, at the bottom of the deep fjord-like bay, has been buried under an infill of builders rubble.

One of the reasons for the expansion of this previously isolated location, is the presence of a flotilla fleet of yachts. They are moored to a concrete quay beyond two nearside tavernas, to the right (*Fsw*) of the bay. From the balcony patios of these tavernas, small wooden jetties project into the sea. The far taverna is the original *Cafe-bar Stavros*. A road loops round behind these eateries to the flotilla and boat quay bordered by a smart cafe-bar.

On the left-hand side of the 'U' of the bay is the uncharacteristically neat *Restaurant Ionian*, also with a wooden patio extended out over the sea-water I suspect one or all three tavernas stage 'Greek Evenings'. Between the two sides of the bay is a greensward planted with olive trees, under the spreading branches of which are often pitched the occasional tent or three. There are a number of villas as well as a steady building programme. A double room with en suite bathroom costs 2000drs a night.

Incidentally, the German archaeologist Dorpfeld believed it was at Sivota that Odysseus came ashore, after his fifteen year sea voyage. Just where he made his landfall is hard to say. It certainly wasn't on the beach marked on the map for, despite much rock clambering around the bay, it is and was difficult to locate ever a smidgin of sand or shingle.

Another 1¼km further along the main route, is:-
**MARANTOCHORI (circa 32km from Lefkas Town)** A spaced out country village encompassing a 'Grill Market', a square church clock tower, the face of which lacks any hands, a railway carriage bus shelter, a bread shop, a very new kafeneion cum fish restaurant and, prior to a petrol filling station, a side road off to the left, signed *Camping Kastri*.

**Cape Kastri** This unmade track, which is hard going in places, initially crosses arid fields. I hesitate to write meadowland as there is little or no grass, despite which there are plenty of domestic farm animals. In 1988, a charcoal man and his smouldering mounds were hereabouts. After about 1½km an irritating decision has to be made at an unsigned fork. Keep right, as the left-hand choice is an extremely rough 12km track that loops right down to Cape Lipso and back to Marantochori. Very strange.

Back on the right-hand track, the surface becomes most 'indeterminate', in places. Fifty metres prior to the backshore of a narrow, pebble cove, at the end of Ammousa Bay, are some large olive trees, beneath which, apparently fairly long term, *ad hoc* tents are positioned. These are followed by a substantial water well set in an apron of concrete.

From the cove backshore a sign to the right (*Fsw*) indicates 'Camping Kastri soon'! Only a madman (or woman) would expect potential clients to make this god-forsaken, 6km trek. It appears that any would-be customers have voted with their feet, as Camping Kastri, which blocks off the route, is now 'dead', windblown and abandoned. Immediately prior to the campsite entrance is a rather magnificent, but unfinished house – perhaps it is owned by the same dreamer who conjured up the idea of the Camping Kastri?

In the nearside of Cape Kastri is a tiny, shingle and pebble cove.

The southern island section of the main route is peppered with yellow bus shelters, which seem to be 'flavour of the minute', down this end of the island. West of **Kondarena** hoves into view a most beautiful panorama out over Vassiliki plain and bay, with the long mountain finger of Cape Lefkatas forming a majestic backdrop.

**VASSILIKI (36km from Lefkas Town)** (Illustration 23) The once totally relaxed, fishing village community has been shaken out of its torpor, into the 20th century, by the location becoming a renowned, if not international wind surfing centre.

The main road from Kondareno skirts the village, branching right to parallel the majestic sweep of beach as it crosses the agricultural valley plain. The street to the settlement's waterfront is straight ahead round the one-way system, at the junction formed by the main road, the 'High Street' and the 'Port St'.

The extremely spaced out nature of Vassiliki almost completely conceals the actual size of the resort. If development continues apace along the wide swathe of land 'trapped' between the beach backshore and the Ag Petros road, as well as across the valley fields the inland side of that road, then, without doubt, it will become the largest, single island settlement. That is, excluding Lefkas Town. Notwithstanding, there are still a number of timber-framed buildings, with brick infill and or corrugated and tin cladding.

Beyond the Ferry-boat Quay, a bay hugging road heads towards the hills, in the general direction of Agiophilia Beach. Beyond small outcrops of development, which include the *Hotel Apollon*, across from which is a tiny smidgin of shingly beach, and a breakfast snackbar, adjacent to another very small, pebbly cove, the surface 'goes' unmetalled and boulderous. But only for a short stretch, prior to running out on the mountainside slopes. I think its easier to catch the excursion boat to Agiophilia!

## THE ACCOMMODATION & EATING OUT

**The Accommodation** Much of that available has been appropriated by the travel companies, but not all is lost. For a start, there are a number of hotels, one or two of which may have room at the inn. They include the:-

**Hotel Lefkatas** (*Tmr* 1C9/10) (Class C)                                                  Tel 31305
*Directions*: On the right (*Fsw*) of the High St, close to the main road.

Almost absurdly smart, dominating as it does this top end of the narrow main street. The hotel is almost exclusively reserved by package holiday firms. If space is available it is not inexpensive. All rooms have en suite bathrooms. A single room is charged at 2500drs, a double room 4100drs, increasing to 3500drs & 5500drs (16th June-15th Sept).

**Hotel Apollon** (Class B)                                                                  Tel 31122
*Directions*: South of the 'roundabout' at the end of the Ferry-boat Quay and on round the curves of the 'Agiophilia Beach' shore road.

All rooms have en suite bathrooms. A single room costs 2000drs & a double room 2500/3500drs, increasing to 2500drs & 3800/4800drs (1st July-3rd Aug).

**Hotel Paradissos** (Class E)                                                              Tel 31256
*Directions*: At the south end of the village, up a short but steep hill and smothered by trees and flowering shrubs.

A single room, sharing a bathroom, starts at 1100drs, a double sharing 1500drs & 2200drs for a double with en suite bathroom. These rates increase, respectively, to 1500drs & 1900/2700drs.

The greatest concentration of accommodation is in the area of the Ferry-boat Quay 'roundabout'. Most of these *Rooms* are in fairly modern, tidy, beflowered houses. They include 'Let Independence Rooms' (*Tmr* 2B3/4); *Rooms* (*Tmr* 4B4 & 4B4/5); a Mini-market (*Tmr* 12B/C4), with a 'Rooms for Rent' sign, and a:-

**Pension** (*Tmr* 3B3)
*Directions*: Just around the corner from the Ferry-boat Quay, along the 'Agiophilia path' road.

A family run pension in another modernish building which advertises 'Motorbike Rentals, Rooms, Hot bath showers for passenger sailing boats'. A double room, sharing the bathroom, is priced at

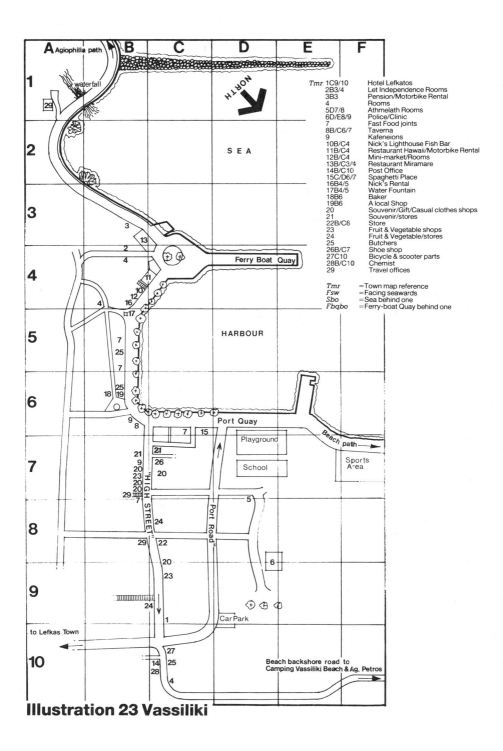

**Illustration 23 Vassiliki**

2000drs, which might be negotiated downwards in the quieter months. Sailors (or anybody else for that matter) are charged 150drs for the use of a shower.

My choice would be:-

**Athmelath Rooms** (*Tmr* 5D7/8)

*Directions*: Behind the Port Quay, on the edge of a 'backyard' road that runs up to the Police/Clinic building (*Tmr* 6D/E8/9). The school is to the left.

The friendly, round, rosy cheeked lady doesn't speak English. Her double rooms have the use of a kitchen and in mid-season cost 1000drs.

Close to the main road junction is **Rooms** (*Tmr* 4C10), 'Rent Rooms with Kitchen'. Another fruitful area is on the way to and at the north-west end of the bay, along the Ag Petros road. These include **Rooms**, 'with kitchen', opposite the Petrol Filling station, and at the far side of the bay, in a very small and, as yet, localised outbreak of restaurants, houses, cafes – 'Full breakfast, lunch', are **Rooms** and **Rooms Alexis**. At the outset of this distant, Vassiliki 'suburb' is the Falcon Sailing apartment block, named the *Windsurfing Centre*.

## Camping On the left and about half-way down along the 'bay backing' road is:-

**Camping Vassiliki Beach**            Tel 31308

*Directions*: As above, on a large plot running down to the beach. The sign says 'Camping, Restaurant International Cuisine. No need to be resident. English breakfast, friendly advice, Cocktail Bar'.

The impression that this site is favoured by Germans is given credence by a comprehensive set of 'camp ground rules', displayed at the main gate, of which more later, and reinforced by the card advising 'Ideal for Surfen'. Mmh! A well maintained, tidy set up with a nice shower, washroom and laundry area, and a neat restaurant. The site rules. Oh yes. They insist:- 'Max speed 10km. Campsite must be vacated 12 noon. Campground gates will close at 0030hrs, beach gate at 2300hrs. Any form of noise strictly prohibited past 0030hrs. Persons must park outside and walk in. Dogs must be kept on a leash. Please don't allow pets to foul the camp, if so you are responsible for cleaning up (*and a jolly good thing too...*). All cleaning, laundry, cooking to be done in facilities provided, not with outside hoses. Playground hours 1000-1400hrs & 1800-2100hrs. Children to be supervised (*otherwise we will gas them...*). We take no responsibility... No ball games. Non residents must obtain permission for use of the facilities other than the restaurant. Please park in the parking lot in front of the gate. Thank you'. Lest I forget, the charges for Low Season (with High Season (June-mid Sept) in brackets) are as follows:- Adults 350drs (450drs), children 220drs (300drs), a car 220drs (300drs), a tent 350drs (450drs). Use of an iron costs 120drs and cooking facilities 120drs, per half hour.

## The Eating Out The rather lopsided, wind surfing bias to the 'BPT' trade has resulted in an outbreak of chromium plated, fast food joints. Examples include a small, brightly coloured place (*Tmr* 7B/C7/8), only open midday and evenings. Additionally there are a number of Esplanade firms such as *The Penguin* (*Tmr* 7C6/7), breakfast and ice-creams, *Zeus* (*Tmr* 7B5/6), a cocktail type bar, and a milkshake, breakfast cafe-bar (*Tmr* 7B5), where a Nes meh ghala costs 62drs. The fast food establishments usually only serve canned beer and soft drinks, it being necessary to patronise the tavernas for bottled drinks. As the season draws to a close, staff often fall into a bored torpor. Even the more traditional restaurants display uncooked doner kebabs (souvlakias), already skewered in batches. Most of the Esplanade bordering establishments have attractively awning covered patios on the tree shaded quayside – even if the harbour water is rather murky.

At the junction of the High St and the 'Port Quay' Rd, are the two original Vassiliki places of entertainment. One is a Taverna (*Tmr* 8B/C6/7) and the other a Kafeneion (*Tmr* 9B6/7). This latter is still jealously 'guarded' by the locals – and why not? Further along the Esplanade, close by the Ferry-boat Quay roundabout, is *Nick's Lighthouse Fish Bar* (*Tmr* 10B/C4), next door and south of which is the *Restaurant Hawaii, George Hortis* (*Tmr* 11B/C4). Incidentally, George doubles up with motorbike rental. On the south side of the 'roundabout' is my Vassiliki choice, the:-

**Restaurant Miramare** (*Tmr* 13B/C3/4).

*Directions*: As above.

There is a pleasant, plum tree and awning shaded terrace which edges the curve of the road. Citing the tree reminds me to mention that end of season diners should watch out for falling fruit. There is a full range of plentiful fare at reasonable prices (that is for Vassiliki). A minor snag is that the restaurant employs wind surfing and sail board groupies as night-time waiters. Those clients tempted to parade their Greek will get a shock as the lads minds are attuned to English. Any misunderstanding will result in an interesting combination of yours and the waiter's ideas of what a diner's order actually was. A meal for two of omelettes (200drs each), a Greek salad (265drs), a plate of giants (140drs), a kortaki retsina (113drs), bread and service (25drs each) cost 968drs. A plate of stuffed tomatoes cost 250drs, a spaghetti bolognese 350drs, briam 150drs and a bottle of beer 85drs. The helpings are substantial and the location convenient from which to observe most of the port's comings and goings, including those buses that turn round on the adjacent quay.

Other firms include *Spaghetti Place* (*Tmr* 15C/D6/7), bordering the 'Port Quay' and which only opens in the evening, as well as a snackbar out on the Agiophilia 'road'. This latter serves toast, coffee, ice-creams, drinks and cocktails and is beyond the *Hotel Apollon*, between two very small coves of pebble and sand.

# THE A TO Z OF USEFUL INFORMATION
**BANKS** None. *See* **Post Office, A To Z**.

**BEACHES** Oh yes. A magnificent, 3km sweep of beautiful sand, which shelves very slowly for a 100m or so. There are occasional, small outbreaks of kelp. But if the beach is superb, the bay is recognised by experts as one of the best in the world, let alone Greece, for wind surfing enthusiasts. This eminence is reflected in the 100m swathe, stretching along the backshore and bounded by the main road, being developed at an 'unhealthy' rate. It will not be many more years before it is completely infilled.

**BICYCLE, SCOOTER & CAR HIRE** Apart from businesses which divide their efforts, including *Pension/Motorbike Rentals* (*Tmr* 3B3) and *Restaurant Hawaii/Motorbike Rental* (*Tmr* 11B/C4), there is the 'dedicated':-

**Nick's Rental** (*Tmr* 16B4/5)
*Directions*: Edging the south end of the Esplanade just beyond the village's water fountain.
Nick is an engaging and charming character who advertises 'Enjoy idyllic ride round the island with one of our cars, motorbikes, mopeds and automatics as well as bicycles. Best at special prices'. One of his two seater, automatic mopeds costs 900drs a day.
Along the Ag Petros road, on the right and prior to the campsite, is **Georges Rental Motorcycles**, which set-up is probably associated with the *Restaurant Hawaii*.

**BOOKSELLERS** None but a number of the travel offices and the *Hotel Lefkatas* operate a book swop.

**BREAD SHOPS** (*Tmr* 18B6) The original shop has 'enjoyed' a face-lift and is now approached across a paved patio.

**BUSES** *See* **Buses & Bus Timetables, A To Z, Lefkas Town**. Then enquire at the *Hotel Lefkatas* or the travel offices, for specific times of the outward journey.

**COMMERCIAL SHOPPING AREA** One of the most engaging shops, is housed in a shed (*Tmr* 19B6) from which an old boy sells a 'scattering' of fruit, vegetables and honey. There is a Mini-market (*Tmr* 12B/C4), bordering the Harbour Esplanade, which sells camera film, drinks and bottled water. The High St contains the to-be-expected souvenir/gift and casual clothes shops (*Tmr*20), as well as a number of souvenir/stores, one (*Tmr* 21B/C7) of which, on the right (*Sbo*), sells stamps. The well stocked Store (*Tmr* 22B/C8), located in a single storey building, possesses a couple of metered telephones in booths – useful to know as there is no OTE. Note a number of other establishments advertise metered telephones. There are a few small, local fruit and vegetable shops (*Tmr* 23), but the best (*Tmr* 24B/C9) is combined with a general store. Two Butchers (*Tmr* 25B5 & 25B6) are close by each other, on the Esplanade, whilst another (*Tmr* 25B/C10) lurks, at the far end of the town, alongside the Ag Petros road. This latter shop advertises 'We speak English'. A Shoe shop (*Tmr* 26B/C7) is to be to the left (*Sbo*) of the High St. One dusty, old-time business (*Tmr* 27C10) operates from a shed close to the main road junction. It stocks bicycle and scooter parts and the proprietor also 'tin bashes'.

**FERRY—BOATS**
Despite my remarks to the contrary, there is a scheduled, 'landing craft' car ferry link with

Fiscardon(Cephalonia) and Sami(Cephalonia). I write despite, that since writing Chapters Twelve to Fourteen, 'I chanced' upon the wretched thing. There also 'Height of season' excursion craft to Ithaca and Cephalonia *See* **Travel Agents & Tour offices, A To Z.**

### Ferry-boat timetable

| Day | Departure time | Ferry-boat | Ports/Islands of Call |
|---|---|---|---|
| Daily | 1200hrs | | Fiscardon(Cephalonia). |
| | 1800hrs | | Fiscardon(Cephalonia),Sami(Cephalonia). |

**LAUNDRY** None, unless visitors want to emulate the natives and use the communal wash place on the right of the Agiophilia 'road'.

**MEDICAL CARE** There is a Chemist (*Tmr* 28B/C10) and a Clinic (*Tmr* 6D/E8/9).

**PETROL** A station borders the Ag Petros road.

**PLACES OF INTEREST** *See* **Travel Agents..., A To Z.**

**POLICE** (*Tmr* 6D/E8/9) Shares a building with the Clinic.

**POST OFFICE** (*Tmr* 14B/C10) Transacts currency matters and is open weekdays between 0730-1430hrs.

### TELEPHONE NUMBERS & ADDRESSES

| | |
|---|---|
| Clinic (*Tmr* 6D/E8/9) | Tel 31216 |
| Police (*Tmr* 6D/E8/9) | Tel 31218 |
| Taxis | Tel 31300 |

**TRAVEL AGENTS & TOUR OFFICES** There are three offices spaced out throughout the settlement. Note they close for siesta.

**Vassiliki Travel** (*Tmr* 29B/C8)
*Directions*: About midway up (or down) the High St and on the left (*Fsw*).
   A busy, large office, some of the staff of which are English. They are able to organise most 'BPTs' requirements and represent *Sun Med*.

**Lefkas Travel** (*Tmr* 29B7/8)                                                  Tel 22430
*Directions*: Prettily located in the High St, up a very steep flight of steps and surrounded by older buildings, with wooden frames and infill, as well as corrugated iron and tin clad upper storeys.
   Appear to cover most holiday-makers activities.

**Travel Sideris** (*Tmr* 29A1)                                                   Tel 31261
*Directions*: Up an incline from the Agiophilia 'road' and occupying the ground floor of a holiday studio apartment building.
   A modern, smooth, general tourist agency. The offices tout various excursions which include boat trips to Agiophilia Beach, at a cost of 400drs, the outward boat departing at 1200hrs and returning at 1600hrs and infinitely easier than the walk; Porto Katsiki (west coast of the Lefkatas Peninsula) priced at 1200drs, but only if the sea state is calm and the Ithaca/Cephalonia connection at a cost of 330drs, but only in the months of July, August and early September.
   The unreliability of the latter is highlighted by one of the staff in Vassiliki Travel disparagingly commenting 'The boat is there but the captain isn't'! This in a genuine Cockney accent. The same chap denied the existence of the Porto Katsiki trip, despite the signboard outside extolling the delights of the same! As the offices handle different excursions, it is necessary to shop around.

**WATER** It is a delight to report that Vassiliki's water remains in excellent condition. There is a water fountain (*Tmr* 17B4/5), dating back to 1904 and down a few steps beside the Esplanade. In fact, there is so much mountain water that it rushes down the hillside edging the Agiophilia 'road'.

**WATER SPORTS** The beach based 'Watersports Club' charges as follows: wind surfers per hour 1000drs, per morning (or afternoon) session 2000drs and for a day 4000drs. Instruction for windsurfing costs 5000drs for a three mornings course of 3hrs a day and a waterski flip round the bay is priced at 1500drs.

At the far, west end of the bay, the main road commences a steep ascent to the scrubbly, hill-hugging village of:-

**AG PETROS (37km from Lefkas Town)** Pleasantly uninterested in tourism, possessing a private house with accommodation, a baker, several cafe-bars, a supermarket, narrow, moth-eaten roads and a taxi rank.

At about 6km north of Ag Petros, to the left of the route, is the village of **Komilio** (30km from Lefkas Town), wherein a clearly signed metalled road to Athani. This excursion stretches all the way down to Cape Lefkatas through:-

**DRAGANO (34km from Lefkas Town)** A one-eyed hamlet, despite which there is a *Cafe/Fish Restaurant* which advises 'English and European meals cooked freshly, taste the best-English spoken'. By the time a traveller has read the sign they will be out through the other side of the dusty place.

**ATHANI** (36km from Lefkas Town) The direction is now clearly signposted. Local wine is on sale, English is spoken, there are a few *Rooms* and a cafeteria, as well as a mini-market.

Beyond Athani the road's surface becomes unmetalled but the signposting continues to remain adequate.

**Egremni Beach (circa 38km from Lefkas Town)** Not only is the swathe of track to the right indicated, but the junction is clearly marked by a, now totally defunct, bailer/combine harvester that lies rotting in the angle of the roads. As in years gone by, the wide, unsurfaced road terminates quite suddenly on the cliff face, goodness knows how many hundred of metres above sea-level. Do not, repeat do not, drive down to the very last 50m section. The chalky, boulderous surface is so loose that it can prove difficult to back up. There are various steep, uncertain, sometimes almost impassable, paths down to the shadeless but beautiful sweep of cliff edged, golden sand. Not surprisingly, there aren't any 'beach support facilities'.

Back on the Cape Lefkatas route, the surrounding hillsides are now treeless and rather bare.

**Porto Katsiki (circa 41km from Lefkas Town)** The way is clearly indicated and the road terminates about 100m from the shore, on a broad, bulldozed, irregular, red coloured, stony and packed earth square. This is overlooked by two, not one, Cantinas who compete for the business. How Greek.

The scenery, views and wilderness are most impressive and the sea-water has an almost milky blue appearance. It seems a pity to have ploughed a road to the spot. There are about a hundred concrete steps down to the nearside of the glorious sand bounded by the undercut cliff face. To the right (*Fsw*) is a col across to a boulder of land with more steps. At the far end are breathtaking panoramas along the cliffs, the sea's edge and back over the beach. One drawback not mentioned by the publicity, is the windiness of the location, on all but the calmest days.

Once this far, why not continue on the increasingly poorly surfaced, rocky road to:-

**Cape Lefkatas (circa 50km from Lefkas Town)** This is the Cape from which Sappho and others were reputed to have performed their desperate leap. The track finally opens out on to an attractive, almost circular, heavily cultivated, saucer-shaped depression. To the far right is the lighthouse, impossibly topping the towering, chalky cliffs that plunge a few hundred metres into the boulder bestrewn, ever active sea, far below. From here, on a clear day.... It is extremely pleasant to watch the ferry-boats plough past on their way to the islands of Cephalonia and Ithaca, easily discernible in the middle distance. I am informed the night views are out of this world, with the liners and ferries' lights supplemented by the massed glow-worm-like specks of fishing boat lamps appearing to be suspended twixt sea and sky. This is a second-hand impression because the overall beauty of this darkened world is, in my mind, outweighed by the horrors of the return journey, in the dark.

Returning to the main route from Komilio, it is only a few kilometres to:-

**KHORTATA (27km from Lefkas Town)** On this side of the island the women not only commonly wear the brown garb but, as in days of yore, carry large loads balanced on their heads. I have also observed, a little further on up the coast, two donkeys in tandem pulling a very simple, wooden dagger plough to turn the unyielding, stony soil.

The views in this area are really most dramatic with the central island mountains ranging north-south and the shimmering blue Ionian Sea stretching away to the left. The main road passes across glorious mountain scenery, and although metalled, is narrow and, in places, rather difficult to drive along.

Keeping straight on progresses through **Exanthia** (21km from Lefkas Town), a remarkably attractive settlement clinging to the mountainside, and followed by **Drimonas** (19km from Lefkas Town). This is a large village with the old houses nestling in a hollow. Whilst in this area it may be worth noting there is a petrol filling station in the village of **Lazarata**.

Instead of driving on to Drimonas, there is a turning off to the left, about 5km beyond Khortata, to the messy, rubbish bestrewn outskirts of:

**KALAMITSI (26km from Lefkas Town)** For the time being the settlement, surrounded by vineyards, is a lovely, doo-hickey mix of old roof tiles, tin plate and corrugated iron, with many of the 'watchful' inhabitants lining the streets, and the kafeneions bulging with the men of the village. Prior to the *Cafe-bar To Ionio* – 'Steak house, Breakfast, Tourist Information', there is a sign in red to 'Free Parking' which leads on to an irregular, concrete surfaced area. Progress is obviously on its way. Kalamitsi hosts another shambles of a cafe-bar.

At the southern entrance to the village, a narrow, averagely bad, unmetalled track is signposted off to the left. As this descends the mountainside, so the surface deteriorates until it becomes boulder-strewn and deeply potholed, with a gradient on the inside of the numerous hairpins which exceeds one in three. This is not a drive for the faint-hearted, or, come to that, anyone with a strong will to live. Those insane or reckless enough to continue to sea-level will be richly rewarded with one of the most magnificent beaches on the whole island. A long, wide, shallow crescent of sand and shingle backed by towering, tree covered mountains. It is a truly idyllic spot.

North of the Kalamitsi, the road's surface become unmetalled and, on the left, an old Austin A35 motor car lies rotting, minus a wheel, engine and most of its windows. This route is undergoing major civil engineering reconstruction and is now straightened and regraded, with vast storm drains in position. Once complete, that may well be the end of the isolation of Kalamitsi and its beaches.

A mere kilometre on and a branch road climbs, to the right, back up to Drimonas. To the left bears off towards Ag Nikita, along another road under complete reconstruction, almost all the way to the turning to the left for:-

**Kathisma Beach (14km from Lefkas Town)** Now a surfaced road serpentines down to the far, north end of this splendid sweep of sandy beach. A small strip of vineyard borders the olive tree supporting, once ancient terracing that struggles up the gradual slopes of the mountainside. Still no 'tourist support facilities', not even a Cantina, but some 'wild' camping spaced along the backshore.

Prior to the Kathisma Beach turning, the road reverts to the 'norm' – that is a sensibly proportioned, narrow and wandering thoroughfare advancing through olive groves, even if it is surfaced.

Prior to the turning down to Ag Nikita there is, to the left, signposts for a rural, rustic, open-air disco and the track muddles its way on to the seashore, where there is an excellent, sandy beach with some facilities. A campsite lurks in the olive groves on the right.

**AG NIKITA (12km from Lefkas Town)** A pretty, small, rather chi-chi Greek look-alike for a Cornish fishing village, with only one road in, and the same road out. This street tapers down gradually between the buildings that 'hedge' in the thoroughfare, only to come to a dead end on the backshore of a mainly fine pebble, exposed beach of about 70-80m in length. If the sea is rough, the last few metres of the street are cluttered with a few pedaloes and various glass fibre dinghies. To either side of the main street buildings is much of the original village, but it is necessary to snoop about. Ag Nikita is a tourist centre and there are any number of pensions and plenty of **Rooms**, as well as the usual proliferation of restaurants, cafes and bars.

The narrow cul-de-sac road into the seaside resort descends past the *Pension Austria/Taverna Bar*, close to the junction; **Rooms**, on the right; *Argos Rooms* (Tel 22102)'... with private bath'; a lot of new construction in the scrubbly outskirts; a 'No Entry' sign; **Rooms** and more **Rooms**, combined with a snackbar, both on the right; **Rooms**, 'low prices'; *Pension Restaurant Elena* and *Taverna Clementaria*, on the left; *Restaurant Korali*, also on the left; *Mistral Rooms*, up a lane to the right; a restaurant to the right; a mini-market to the left; a snackbar up a lane to the left; *Spiti Lagadi*, 'Furnished Rooms St Nikitas', a brown painted, older building on the right; *Taverna Portoni*, a chromium plated, twee little set-up and finally a bar, both on the left.

The main road to the north skirts Ag Nikita and a large, if somewhat messy, exposed beach of sand and shingle, which extends for nearly 3km and is serviced by a few small tavernas. A number of boulders are scattered along this length of the seashore.

Despite the map-makers indicating otherwise, the extremely long ascent from Ag Nikita is on a tarmacadamed, if 'gnawed', patchily edged road. This heads towards:

**TSOUKALADES (6km from Lefkas Town)** The village is rather spaced out and hillbilly. Despite this, almost in the middle of nowhere is the most incredibly smart *Hotel Adonis*, several **Rooms**, the *Pension Gabrini Cocktail Bar* and a 'snappy' mini-market. The village is surrounded by doo-hickey homesteads as well as thickly set olive groves and many stone walls.

From the heights there are unsurpassed views over the north of the island, especially the Lagoon, and the adjacent mainland. This is an area rich in enchanted glades of wild flowers, which include pink orchids and wild cyclamen. The road commences to descend steeply down to the plain surrounding Lefkas Town.

About half-way down is the path off to:-

**Faneromeni Monastery (3km from Lefkas Town)** Built on the site of an ancient temple, and said to have been founded by St Paul. In the third century a full-blown monastery was erected. The various buildings suffered from the outbreaks of fire over the centuries. The present structure, now home to only one monk, was extensively rebuilt in the 1970s.

# Meganissi (Meganisi)

Dedicated Island lovers ★★★★★
Happy hour, cocktail bar swingers -----

Is there a conspiracy of silence not to mention Meganissi? Certainly, of all the islands I have visited, this has remained one of the most delightfully Greek and, without doubt, must rate as a find. Most of the women still dress in the Lefkiot habit, but with black trimmings, and it is a common sight to see them portering loads balanced on their heads. Looms are much in evidence and forget the twin-tub for washing clothes – it's a washboard and or the rocks.

As there isn't any public transport, independent visitors might consider bringing a scooter, but not a car – The Chora roads are rather narrow and twisting.

**PORT SPIGLIA: port of Spartochori** Readers must not be misled by the grand sounding name. This quiet, sleepy port is set on the extreme right (*Sbo*) of a very large, deep, irregular shaped bay and is overlooked by the Chora dwellings, which peep over the vertical cliff-face that shuts off the inland side. It comprises a Ferry-boat ramp, enhanced by a notice 'Garbidge are not allowed on the harbour'; a broad sweep of concrete quay, to which are moored small fishing craft and on which are usually heaped a quantity of building materials, and the subsequent sweep of road. This curves round to the left past a muddle of backshore and an olive grove. Close to the 'dolls house' shrine is a cast iron housed water tap.

On the right is a simple cafe-bar taverna, grandly titled *Restaurant Marme Ross*, specialising in fish and grill house snacks. The owner, Costas, is a quiet, dignified gentleman. There is a rumour that his family were at the forefront of the local wartime resistance. It is also said that they hid fleeing servicemen in a cave on their grounds. This story achieved credibility, and notoriety, when Costas allowed an American tourist to see the location. The visitor, left to his own devices, stumbled upon a wartime revolver and some ammunition, left behind by the escapees. To repay his host's kindness, the Yank blabbed the story with the result that the authorities showed more than a passing interest, causing not a little bother for mine host. Perhaps it is all gossip, and certainly best left uncommented upon, so I shall not write a word.

On the left, where the Port to Chora concrete road commences its steep and winding ascent, is the:-

**Taverna Porto/Spiglia**                                    Tel 51439 & 51233
*Directions*: as above and advertises 'English Breakfast, Chicken Grills, Steaks, Souvlakia, Fresh Fish. Rooms To Let'.

This establishment sprawls along the backshore of a section of fine pebble, steeply shelving beach. There is a large, covered terrace and they must hope to cater for excursion boat parties. Unfortunately, most of these appear to 'steam' on down to a taverna at the bottom of the bay. This 'skulduggery' causes the small, worried looking owner, Vassali, to become apoplectic at times. The upset is such that he quite often retires to the kitchen, in the privacy of which stabbing motions are enacted. Asimo, his wife, who appears painfully thin, has lost one eye and is pathetically eager to please. In her enthusiasm to generate business, Asimo often frantically waves at possible clients in a sort of Greek semaphore siren call, even if they are as far away as the Ferry-boat Quay. Vassali and Asimo are deliberately, nobly; massively and ponderously assisted by Babi, their son who speaks both English and American. The food is generally absolutely excellent, even if the menu is understandably rather limited. A meal for two of stuffed tomatoes, some potatoes, an adequate Greek salad and two bottles of beer cost 850drs. Probably best in the evenings to order dishes that have not simmered on from the lunchtime session. The basic toilets are kept very clean. The accommodation is in The Chora and a double room with en suite bathroom cost 1500drs, increasing to 2000drs in the height of season months.

The main beach is to the nearside of the referred to taverna, at the bottom of the bay. The shore is pebble and subject to some pollution by seaborne rubbish driven on by the prevailing wind. This establishment appears to specialise in 'A Lunch/Night out on an undiscovered island' and probably has made a deal with the Nidri travel offices. Certainly, much to Papa Vassali's undisguised fury (he of *Taverna Porto Spiglia*), the excursion caiques shuttle to and forth the place. Fortunately, apart from the occasional visiting yachtsman, this is almost the sum total of the tourist invasion. The setting is attractive with the backshore bordered by a small plain beyond which are olive groves, after which the mountainsides close in.

It is a 1km ascent to:-

**SPARTOCHORI (The Chora)** This is an eye-opener and must rank with some of the other, magical, bygone age, island Choras, too few of which are now left unspoilt. The village is a labyrinth of dwellings, lanes and alleys. The drinking water wells are topped up by the roof gathered rainwater.

Spartochori is not medieval in character, more reminiscent of, say, the 1930s. The settlement bubbles with a contented, vibrant village life, almost totally untouched and unruined by 20th century tourism. It has to be admitted that the ambience of well-being is probably greatly aided by the number of comparatively well-heeled expatriates who have returned to spend the last years of their life on the island of their birth.

There are several kafeneions and two or three tavernas. The port road climbs into the centre of The Chora where, on the right, is the laid back *Snackbar Gacia*. Here a Metaxa, Nes meh ghala and lemonade costs 200drs. The disinterested son, Nico, is involved in price setting.

The star in The Chora's eating houses is round the back of *Gacia's*, almost a circular walk. This is *Chicken Billy's*, run by an ebullient, friendly almost waggish character and his quieter, more thoughtful wife. There are only a few chairs in the narrow street and the interior is a delightful, if somewhat greasy, jumble of table and chairs, shelves, bottles, embroidery and lace covered furniture, kitsch *objet d'art*, messages, notices, faded newspaper cuttings and the spit. The fame of the taverna is based on their chicken meals and that Christine Onassis danced here till she was sick – and Billy was still going.

Hospitality can get totally out of hand. Anyone dining more than once, may well wish they had not, as drink tends to flow rather freely from the locals. A very 'dangerous' location. A meal for two of six, good, special, stick souvlakis, a bottle of beer and several ouzos cost 460drs, after which the evening faded into a blur... Billy confirmed that many of the inhabitants have returned to Meganissi after making their fortune somewhere else in the world. He and his wife spent nine years in Johannesburg, from whence his passable English, and now all he wants is to be surrounded by his friends and a few clients... Incidentally, he sells postcards.

Despite the lack of a bank, OTE or Post Office, there are some five, dark, dusty, gloomy, poorly stocked, general stores. One of the largest, which is opposite *Chicken Billy's*, acts as an agent for the National Bank of Greece, as well as being the unofficial Post Office. The 'dry as a stick' old boy who runs the store does not exactly break into a sweat, so be prepared for delays.

In the area of the *Snackbar Gacia* small posters are stuck to the walls with the various car ferry timetables to and from Meganissi.

To proceed to Katomeri, keep left past *Snackbar Gacia*. The metalled road advances across rock and stone strewn countryside, which also supports spaced out olive trees, some of great age. As the road gently climbs there are beautiful views to the right out over Kolopoula Bay, with a backdrop of the island's prehensile tail-like peninsula curving around to enclose the southern sea. This very long tongue of land has a number of deep sea caves, one of which is supposed to have been a wartime hideout for a Greek submarine. But so have a number of other caves throughout the Greek islands...

**KATOMERI (3km from The Chora)** A large hill village. It is another maze but not so photogenic as Spartochori. Many of the people are concerned with the fishing trade and nets are spread out all over the place, either simply drying or after repair. Incredibly there is a petrol station, the *Taverna lagas*, the doo-hickey 'Californian Supermarket', which doubles up as a den-like-cafe-bar, a souvlaki shop and a relatively organised supermarket.

Beside the Vathi road, northern outskirts and to the right, is a baker. The young man who minds the shop speaks excellent English, learnt in the USA. A rough track between the baker and a church progresses some 50m to the large skeletal outline of the embryonic *Hotel Meganissi*, proprietor Jim Politis. Thus pronounces the signboard facing down the Vathi road. The young baker hopes that the building will be completed in time for the 1989 tourist season, but the final tranche of a Government loan is awaited...
A track allows a ½hr walk down to the picturesque **Atherinou Bay**.

From beyond the bakers, the metalled road descends for a kilometre to:-

**VATHI (Vathe, Vathy) (4km from The Chora)** A 'perfect' but dusty fishing boat port set at the bottom of a 'U' shaped bay. At least half a dozen workmanlike caiques are berthed in the harbour. The houses of the port are evenly spread around the bay and up the hillsides. The Ferry-boat ramp and large quayside is on the right-hand (*Sbo*) of the port. Bordering the quay is a rather pleasant, turn-of-the-century church. This is followed by the conveniently situated *Restaurant/Cafeteria Mouragio*, then the Post Office, another taverna and **Rooms** (Tel 51553 & 51397), as well as a supermarket (well, more a shop that calls itself a supermarket). *Rose's Taverna* may or may not spring into life, and there aren't many roses in the garden.

If there are English registered vehicles parked by the small park, at the centre of the village, it is not so strange, as a donkey track heads eastwards to **Abelakia Bay**. Here has been constructed a 'Club Med' look-alike of eighteen cabana 'woven or wood' huts with a beach-bar-cum-taverna. The location is leased from the Greek government by a flotilla yacht business.

**Ferry-boat timetable** (Mid-season)

| Day | Departure time | Ferry-boat | Ports/Islands of Call |
|---|---|---|---|
| Daily | 0830hrs | Meganisi | Nidri(Lefkas),Fiscardon(Cephalonia), Frikes(Ithaca),Nidri(Lefkas),Meganiss. |

Note both Meganissi island ports of Spartochori & Vathi are included in the schedule, but on what basis I know not.

One-way fares: Meganissi to Fiscardon 400drs;  duration 2hrs
to Frikes  400drs;  2hrs 40mins.

'Whow!'

*A view from Porto Katsiki towards Cape Lefkatas, Lefkas.*

*'Bother the filling, when do we start the emptying?'*

*Sivota, Lefkas.*

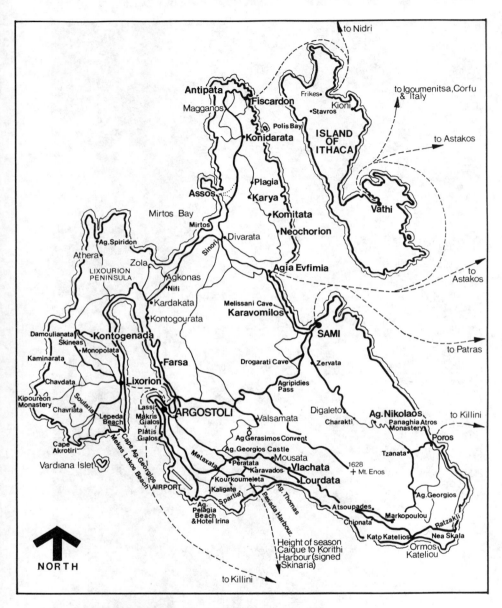

**Illustration 24 Cephalonia Island**

# 15 CEPHALONIA (Cefalonia, Kefalonia, Kefallinia, Kephallenia,) Ionian Islands

South & west island ★★
North island ★★★★

**FIRST IMPRESSIONS** Dramatic, forest clad, mountainous scenery; prefabricated buildings; massed cypresses.

**SPECIALITIES** Lemonda; Robola wine (white & light); Monte Nero wine (red & dry); an overall lack of retsina – usually found where there are island wines; thyme-scented honey; bacaliaropitta (codfish pies); tserepes (spiced meat in a casserole); mandolato nougat.

**RELIGIOUS HOLIDAYS & FESTIVALS** include: 17th July – Feast Day, Ag Marina, Vlachata; 15th August – Our Lady Day, Lixourion; 15th August – Assumption of the Virgin, Markopoulou; 22nd August – Our Lady of Loutra, Sami; 8th September – Feast Day of Theotokos Poros.

**VITAL STATISTICS** Tel prefix *See* individual towns & villages. The island has an area of 782sqkm, is up to 35km long, 33km wide with a total population of about 30,000, of which some 6,000 or so live in or around Argostoli Town.

**HISTORY** The east coast port of Sami perpetuates the Homeric name of the island, Same. Later the island was titled after a local tribe. An archeological item of note are the Mycenaean 'bee hive' tombs.

Subsequent to a period of supreme wealth and power (circa 1200BC), there were four city states: Sami, close by the present port of the same name; Krani, at the bottom of Koutavos Gulf, on the west side of which is Argostoli Town; Pali, 1½km north of Lixourion Town and Pronni, inland and south of Poros port. Once the Romans had managed to take Sami Port, in about 190BC, the island followed the historical route of much of the Ionian.

In comparatively recent years, one of Cephalonia's most famous citizens was General Metaxas, Prime Minister and dictator of all Greece. His eminence was firmly established, on 28th October 1940, in a famous, but very terse speech. Apocryphally he is supposed to have advised Mussolini 'Ochi' (No), after Il Duce had demanded the right of passage for his troops across Northern Greece. This day is now one of the country's public holidays.

That fate is fickle (or more prosaically 'There's nowt so strange as life') is no better illustrated than by the lot of a crack force of 7,000 Italian troops. They had occupied the island for three years, during the Second World War. On Mussolini's death, they refused to obey the orders of the German High Command and the erstwhile oppressors became the island people's heroes. After a week long battle against overwhelming odds, the 3,000 or so Italian soldiers, who finally surrendered, were murdered in a three day frenzy by the Germans. Some thirty Italians escaped, with the help of the islanders, through a medieval, 8km long tunnel between Ag Georgios Castle and the lagoon, at the southern end of Argostoli Bay. The tunnel was subsequently destroyed by the 1953 earthquake, although the castle end of the entrance can still be seen.

**GENERAL** Panoramically the island is extremely dramatic, with the majority of the land taken up by mountain ranges. Despite the majestic beauty of the scenery, visitors may well have to persevere with Cephalonia, a number of tourists leaving, almost as soon as they arrive. There are a number of drawbacks. The main city of Argostoli was unsympathetically reconstructed after the devastating earthquake of 1953; the roads that hug the edges of the hills are very mountainous and last, but not least, although the bus system is widespread, due to the distances involved, it is often difficult to get back to the departure point on the same day. If this were not enough, Cephalonia is rather unusual in that the capital is not the main port, the inter-island ferry-boats docking at either Poros or Sami.

Effectively the island is split into three segments – the main, southern island mass; the western Lixourion peninsula and the northern tip of the island. Stick it out, visit the Lixourion peninsula and under no circumstances miss the northern end of the island.

**ARRIVAL BY AIR** The airport is situated some 14km south of Argostoli Town, on the coast road, close by Svoronata. A brand new terminal building is under construction, the old facilities being quite unable to cope with the present-day traffic. Argostoli Town buses do not call but the Kourkoumeleta bus (also signed *Irina Hotel*) passes the side turning down to the airport (*See* **Bus timetable, Buses, A To Z, Argostoli Town**). An Olympic bus makes the connection to the capital and there is a special rank for Argostoli taxis. For those travellers who can't be bothered to plough on, a couple of hundred metres along the airport approach road is the *Rooms Studio Errieta* (Tel 41588). At the junction with the main road is the *Villa Evita, Rooms for Rent* (Tel 41357).

**ARRIVAL BY BUS** There are at least two daily connections between Athens and Cephalonia. Note that some proceed via Patras(M) to Sami Port, thence to Argostoli and on to Lixourion, whilst others proceed via Killini(M) to Poros and Argostoli. For details *See* **Bus timetable, Buses, A To Z, Argostoli**.

**ARRIVAL BY FERRY** Apart from the main ports of Poros and Sami, Argostoli is now linked to mainland Killini, in addition to the landing craft ferries which shuttle back and forth to Lixourion. Furthermore there are ferry-boats between Ag Evfimia and Astakos(M), Nidri(Lefkas) as well as a high-season Pesada connection to Korithi Port (Zakynthos).

## POROS (Porros): port (44km from Argostoli) Tel prefix 0674. One of the main reasons for the importance of Poros was the ferry-boat connection with mainland Killini, but this has been supplemented by a direct Killini to Argostoli link.

**ARRIVAL BY FERRY** Travellers who have decided not to stay at Poros, will find it useful to locate the green Pullman, Athens to Argostoli Town bus. Having travelled over on the ferry, it draws up on the square to take on more customers.

**Ferry-boat timetables** (Mid-season)
**Poros to Killini**
Daily            0900, 1500, 1930hrs
*Return*
Daily            1145, 1715, 2130hrs
One-way fare 540drs; duration 1½hrs.

At the southern outset of the settlement is the Ferry-boat Quay and harbour, across from which are some 'BPT' holiday apartments. What beach there is here is pebble, with a number of small boats usually pulled up on the shore. Quayside 'services' include a couple of cafe-bars, one which advertises **Rooms**, a Post Office and Ferry-boat Ticket office. An unsurfaced, lovely, 'standard' Greek island track follows the coastline round to Skala (*See* **Route One**).

The main development is reached along the road climbing round the hillside between a cocktail bar, on the left, and the prettily situated *Hotel Hercules*, on the opposite side. Beyond the hotel, the way drops down to sea-level again, to smart and scrubbly 'Poros proper'. Here are formal gardens edging a pebble beach, across from a parade of buildings which include a self-service restaurant. This latter establishment advertises local forthcoming events which might include such delights as a football match – 'Locals v All Stars, anybody can play', or 'Parties Saturday & Sunday at the Preluna Bar, everybody is welcome for the best dance, drink of the Island'.

A backshore track parallels the sea round to the right. The High St, which swings away to the left, is edged by, for instance, a supermarket, shops, a petrol station, across from which is Poros Rent A Car & Motorbike, a butcher, another supermarket, a pharmacy, a Unisex hairdresser and a Ford Rent A Car. At the top of the High St, the road forks. To the left advances to Argostoli Town. To the right crosses a Bailey bridge, past *Pension Lefteras*, – 'First & Second Class Rooms To Let' and yet more **Rooms**, to 'Esplanade' a shadeless, 300-400 metre shingle and pebble beach, possessed of a sandy sea's edge. There is a para-sailing outfit as well as pedaloes, sun-beds and umbrellas, which can be hired from *Angelos Snackbar*. On the left is a scattering of houses, hotels, apartments, as well as a tennis court and, at the north end, the *Restaurant To Akrogiali*, which advertises **Rooms**.

The referred to unsurfaced backshore track, curves to the right round a bluff and then back to join the outset of the main beach Esplanade. Initially it sallies forth past *Poros House Hotel*, next door to which is a baker, more **Rooms**, in a fairly modern building, and a Post Office, in the basement of a block of flats.

I own up to being underwhelmed by Poros.

Hotels include: *Pension Hercules* (Class B, tel 72351), where rooms, with en suite bathroom, cost 2800drs for a single & 3500drs for a double; *Hotel Atros Poros* (Class C, tel 72205), with en suite bathrooms and a single room priced at 1310drs & a double 2100drs; *Kefalos* (Class C, tel 72139), with en suite bathrooms, a single costing 2040drs & a double 2900drs, increasing to 2700drs & 3850drs (1st June-15th Sept); *Galini* (Class E, tel 72353), single rooms with en suite bathroom priced at 1000drs & double rooms en suite 1500drs; *Poros House Hotel* (Class E, tel 72417), all rooms having en suite bathrooms with a single costing 1950drs & a double 2050drs, rising to 2150drs & 2300drs (1st July-31st Aug), and the *Riviera* (Class E, tel 72327), where a single room sharing the bathroom costs 1690drs, a single room with en suite bathroom 1800drs & a double room en suite 1900drs, increasing, respectively, to 1790/1900drs & 2180drs (1st July-31st Aug).

# ROUTE ONE
## Poros to Argostoli Town (44km)
At the outset of the Argostoli main road, a track to the north advances a couple of kilometres to the **Monastery Panaghia Atros**, sited on the sea side of Mt Atros and dating back to AD1260. The first section of the road is 'Pyrennean mountain pass' type countryside and generally is as frightening as it is dramatically beautiful. The bus drivers have a disturbing habit of carrying on intense, high pitched conversations with a number of the passengers, who are usually seated towards the rear of the bus. The alarming thing is that any discourse can only be carried out by the driver facing the people involved, and this whilst the bus hurtles along dynamited rock faces, with precipitous cliff sides to the right and horrifyingly steep drops to the sea-bounded plain on the left. The lovely scenery of olive and cypress-tree covered slopes can be somewhat marred by both the ride and the cacophony of sound resulting from the driver's hands apparently being glued to the horn. Quite frankly, it is best, if of a nervous disposition, to take a paper bag and some boiled sweets, as the journey irresistibly reminds one of a low altitude flight and all this on a road of normal Greek island inconsistency in quality, general line of construction and lack of width.

**TZANATA (4km from Poros Port)** This small village is where an uphill, unmade turning to the right, signposted *Camping Karavamilos Beach*, makes off across beautiful, rugged countryside to Sami Port. The main road continues on to Argostoli.

Selecting the diversion, the Sami road passes through **Ag Nikolaos**, a very pretty, little mountain village. Here a turning to the right descends to **Lake Avithos**, a small but unusual sight on the islands as it is constantly topped up by mountain water. Cypress trees and vines abound on the rolling, terraced, green hillsides across which this route advances but much road reconstruction is in evidence. The next village is **Charakti** (yes Charakti) followed by **Digaleto**, despite the maps indicating them the other way round. Beyond Digaleto, and a water fountain, the road commences on the long descent on a now metalled surface to distant Sami. From the highest point of the route are marvellous views but for outstanding panoramas a track to the left progresses towards the summit of Mt Enos.

Returning to the main route to Argostoli at Tzanata, the mountain hugging road descends suddenly, passing through a rock bestrewn landscape. Shortly, at about **Ag Georgios**, the scenery changes again to the 'Greek island norm' – undulating hillsides peppered with flat topped houses built amongst olive trees, set in grass and granite rock wastelands. Amongst the grasses, the occasional strip of cultivated and tilled land unexpectedly appears, the raw earth contrasting starkly with the worn, scrub-covered , unyielding surroundings. Here and there villages crop up, haphazardly. Equally unpredictably, the road rushes past great areas gouged out of the hillsides, presumably for yet another prefabricated concrete filling station or house.

**MARKOPOULOU (28km from Argostoli Town)** The village church and its environs here experience a rather mysterious, strange occurrence on the 15th August, the Virgin Mary's day. The building and surrounds are invaded by small, reputedly harmless snakes, with black crosses on their heads. They are regarded as having healing powers, so much so that some pilgrims clasp them to their breasts. Well if you must, you must. Interestingly, these snakes are not seen at any other time.

To the west of **Atsoupades**, where petrol is available, there is an acute turning (24km from Argostoli Town), back towards the extreme south-east of the island.
**Detour to Nea Skala via Kato Katelios (14km)** Some of the little villages, nestling on the south facing hillsides, are pretty and well cared for, with a profusion of flowers covering the walls of the houses. The area is predominantly agricultural and the road to Nea Skala has been widened and resurfaced, for the most part. **Chionata** surrounds have suffered fire damage.

The next stop *en route* perfectly highlights the crass fallibilities, the inexhaustible and voracious appetites of the package holiday companies in their eternal quest for ever new locations, to despoil – sorry develop. As the limited supply of suitable sites diminishes, so is increasingly highlighted the unsuitability of some of the havens press-ganged into becoming the latest Elysian holiday spot. No more so than:-

**KATO KATELIOS (32km from Argostoli Town)** A one-time, one-eyed, isolated fishing boat hamlet that has become a hillbilly seaside holiday resort. The still scrubbly, scattered settlement is situated to the nearside of a large bay edged by a great swathe of shingle and some sand. Further on round the bay, to the east and rather inaccessible, are miles of golden sands as subsequently described.
 Along the inland side of the dirt High St are ranged a number of smartish taverna/restaurants and holiday apartments, with nary a kafeneion in sight. At Kato Katelios stupendous ice-creams arrive complete with fizzing sparklers and customers order cocktails... Establishments include *Seafood Jimmy's Restaurant Bar*, in the ground floor of which is displayed a stuffed seabird standing over an egg. There are **Rooms** over this emporium. A store is to the left (*Fsw*) and more **Rooms** off an alley, to the rear of the hamlet. A swathe of tree planted ground infills the space between the 'main, dirt thoroughfare' and the untidy, rocky mole protected harbour. In amongst the 'struggling chic', nibbling goats and pecking chickens wander in a ceaseless search for food.
 The eastward end of the waterfront peters out alongside a grove of trees amongst which is an informal, untidy, Greek occupied camp and caravan site, one or two of the

tents forming very large corrals. Beyond this 'bivouac', the hard-packed backshore track is crossed by a stream before it runs out on the long, narrow plain which borders the large bay. In the main the beach is shingle with some sand at the sea's edge and a lot of kelp towards the village end.

Kato Katelios seems to me to be an ideal away-from-it-all, independent travellers haunt, but hardly a package holiday sanctuary.

Continuing eastwards, the still surfaced road rises up from Kato Katelios, rimming the low cliffs which hem in Kateliou Bay.

**RATZAKLI (35km from Argostoli Town)** A sleepy inland village possessing some *Studio Rooms*, a bungalow on stilts, a small kafeneion, *Rooms*, a cafe-bar and not much else.

Beyond this small community, a narrow, initially concrete surfaced path descends to the right from the Skala road. This becomes a somewhat alarming, rough, loosely surfaced donkey track. It emerges alongside an electricity substation amongst the backshore dunes of a most spectacular, long, wide and sandy beach – undoubtedly one of the best on the island. Even in September it can be totally deserted and is devoid of any amenities. There is some sea and windblown bits and pieces and a thin moustache of kelp. The backshore is bordered by a background of low sand hills, bamboo and low bushes, including oleanders. A short but hairy detour to reach a superb location.

The road east from Ratzakli winds dramatically down around the cypress tree covered hillside, with tantalizing glimpses of the beach, to:

**NEA SKALA (38km from Argostoli Town)** Still a quiet, low-level, seaside village situated above a long, wide, pebble and shingle beach.

On the outskirts of Skala there is a Clinic, on the left; 'Welcome Disco & Bistro' housed in a neo Spanish style building; *Rooms* on the left; a Ford Rent A Car office on the left, opposite which is Bikes To Rent; and by the junction with the Main Street, a periptero and small campanile. The Main St, is edged by a number of single storey, prefabricated wooden buildings as it gently descends towards the sea. 'High St' businesses include a butcher, a general store-cum-souvenir shop on the left, *Restaurant Sirroco* on the right, *Scandinavian Cafeteria Snackbar Pizzeria* (which title must cover most eventualities) and the *Restaurant Grillroom Miabeli* on the left. A baker's van calls daily and the village store stocks fresh rolls and bread, towards the rear of the shop.

Prior to the street running out above the shore in amongst formal gardens, there are signs to the right in the direction of 'Penguins Sea Club' and 'Yanni's Water Sport – Pentaloes(sic), Wind Surfing, Water Ski School, Canoes, Skala Beach'. Between the gardens and the beach is a wide, pine tree clad slope in which are displayed 'No Camping' notices, beneath and around which are dotted a number of tents and camper vans! Much of the beach is edged by pine trees, rather set back. The beach bar has a drinking water tap. Sun-beds and umbrellas are spaced out with regimental neatness.

In the area are the remains of a sixth century BC temple and a second century AD Roman villa with mosaics.

From Skala a 6km, unmade track heads off towards Poros, initially zig-zagging along the edge of the wide beach, past the pleasantly sited *Tara Beach Bungalows*. The road's surface is irritatingly 'corrugated', which gives a juddering drive. In 1988 the route was being surveyed, so is probably due for civil engineering works. The boulderous hillsides are covered with low bushes, plants as well as olive and fig trees. Wild life abounds, especially hawks. About half-way round, the lie of the land allows sea views of Ithaca island. Hereabouts the track drops to sea-level, passing smidgins of fine shingle but rubbish strewn beaches. To seawards of yet another pebble cove, a noticeable number of substantial boulders are scattered about in the shallows.

Returning to the main Poros to Argostoli route, the road is dominated by the cloud-capped:-

**Enos Mountains** The mountainside, to which the road clings, is a pine tree covered Central Massif. It is thought that many of the Greek islands were similarly tree clad prior to massive deforestation, which possibly started as long ago as the Hellenic/Greco-Roman periods (1000 BC to AD 300) and continued, in fits and starts, up to the fifteenth century. What timber the boat builder didn't appropriate, the depredations of the goat may well have ravaged.

**VLACHATA (17½km from Argostoli Town)** Here are a petrol station, *Studio Rooms* and a:-
**Detour to Lourdata Beach via Lourdata (18½km)** The poorly surfaced road descends in a series of loops through a mix of tree covered hillsides and new buildings. The latter include *Buena Vista Studios – Rooms To Let With Kitchen* (Tel 28703); *Rooms For Rend (sic), Lourdas Studios* (Tel 31276); *Ocean Front Studios 77, Rooms With Kitchen For Rent* (Tel 31252) and *Rooms For Rent-Information Here*, in a house on the edge of **Lourdata** village. This settlement straggles down the hillside and takes in *Rooms For Rent* (Tel 31206); *Rooms*, in a hillbilly taverna; a cafe-bar, and *New World & Rent Rooms*, beyond which the village peters out, despite still being some way above the beach. The hillsides hereabouts are well covered with vegetation and numerous cypress trees.

**Lourdata Beach (18½km from Argostoli Town)** The approach junctions with a wide backshore track alongside a taverna, close by a filling station style sign proclaiming *Rooms For Rent Cut Price*. The inland side of the 'Esplanade' is edged by smallholdings of intensely cultivated land, from which have been carved a scattering of buildings. One of these, about centre of the frontage, houses the *Restaurant Clematis* which has a shower. To the right (*Fsw*) of the 'road junction taverna', is a small beach bar. The long beach is contained by a substantial concrete sea wall 'scaled by a number of steel 'siege' steps. These give access to a pebble middle shore and a sandy foreshore, but in no way is it the best on the island, as some maintain. The sea is turquoise, clear and there is very little rubbish. During the height of the summer, various water sports are promoted.

Returning to the main route, the next main village is:-
**MOUSATA (15km from Argostoli Town)** Here is a baker, a mini-market and a *Room With A Bed Sitting Room*.

Prior to, at and beyond Peratata a number of side roads turn off to the south-west corner of Cephalonia (*See* **Excursions to Argostoli Town Surrounds**).

**PERATATA (9km from Argostoli Town)** This village was extensively ruined in the 1953 earthquake (what was not?). Peratata's claim to fame is its proximity to the site of the old Venetian capital of San Giorgio. Additionally it lies in the shadow of the extensive and impressive, mountainside remains of the castle of Ag Georgios (St George), towering above the village. Incidentally, this medieval settlement was destroyed by an earthquake, in the sixteenth century.

Peratata has dozens of *Rooms* and some apartments. The village is almost enjoined to **Travliata**, where is petrol and the *Hotel Nova*.

The main road becomes quite decent, if not over wide, on the approach to:-
**ARGOSTOLI (Argostolion): capital & (minor) port** (Illustration 25) Tel prefix 0671. Argostoli is built on a thick finger of land that projects into the Gulf of Argostoli and the sea reaches well inland, giving the appearance of being a large lake, rather than an inlet. The town, which had to be rebuilt after the 1953 earthquake and was reconstructed on a sterile, gridiron layout, is not attractive. Looking around Argostoli makes one realise what a splendid job the citizens of Zakynthos (Zante) island made in rebuilding their capital town.

**Illustration 25 Argostoli**

| Tmr | | |
|---|---|---|
| 1C/D4/5 | Market/Bus terminus | |
| 2C3 | Plateia Valianou Metaxa | |
| 3C/D2 | Lixourion Ferry-boat Quay | |
| 4C/D2/3 | Cruise Liner Quay | |
| 5C/D2/3 | Hotel Cephalonia Star | |
| 6C2 | Cafe-bar/Rooms | |
| 7C4 | Hotel Moukis | |
| 8C5 | Restaurant Kalafatis | |
| 9C5 | Antonatos Supermarket | |
| 10C3 | Rex Cinema | |
| 11C3 | Port of Cefalos Restaurant | |
| 12C4/5 | Tzivras Bros Rooms/Restaurant | |
| 13B/C5 | Taverna H Kambana | |
| 14C4 | Airline office | |
| 15C4/5 | National Bank | |
| 16C3 | Bank of Greece | |
| 17C3/4 | Ionian & Popular Bank | |
| 18C/D3 | NTOG | |
| 19B/C3/4 | OTE | |
| 20C6 | Hospital | |
| 21C3/4 | Archaeology Museum | |
| 22C3/4 | History/Culture Museum | |
| 23C4 | Post Office | |
| 24C/D5/6 | Scooter hire | |
| 25C5 | Fina Petrol Station | |
| 26C4 | Foreign language Newspapers | |
| 27C4 | 'Bakety' Pastry shop & Zacharoplasteion | |
| 28C4 | Camera shop | |
| 29C4 | Doctor | |
| 30C/D3 | Port police | |
| 31C/D2/3 | Town police | |
| 32C4 | Seven Islands | |

It must be pointed out that the authorities have, north of the Market building, caused to be planted palm trees along the Esplanade. This is night-time lit by attractive, old-fashioned style lamps.

The paved main square, Plateia Valianou or Metaxa (*Tmr* 2C3 & inset), is extensive in size and rather barren in appearance, although the palm trees have now matured. Cafes and restaurants edge its perimeter. A bewhiskered gentleman sometimes 'sets up shop' on the square. He erects his Victorian, mobile portrait studio, complete with painted backdrop and an enormous, ancient plate camera. He also copies photos of loved ones with an attachment clipped to the front of his plate camera. After dark the Main Square bustles with activity as tourists and locals promenade up and down, pausing for a while to drink coffee or ouzo at one of the many cafes. At night Odhos Diadhohou Konstantinou/Valianou is closed to traffic and also has its fair share of perambulating residents and visitors. The citizens of Argostoli evince a very liberated attitude towards their young and during the *Volta*, female teenagers stroll about in groups, displaying the latest fashions to the delight of the young men.

Despite the lack of any adjacent beaches (it being necessary to travel some 3km) and the lack of intimate atmosphere, the proximity of the airport has resulted in the town becoming a package tourist resort. For the life of me I cannot see what attractions the town has for batches of holiday-makers requiring a swinging environment and sandy beaches, but there you go.

**ARRIVAL BY AIR** *See* **Introduction**.

**ARRIVAL BY BUS** The Bus station is combined with the Town Market (*Tmr* 1C/D4/5). The building is constructed in the form of a flat 'W' on a part of the quay that juts out into the sea, on the right-hand side of the road, approaching from the south.

**ARRIVAL BY FERRY** Killini(M) and Lixourion ferries dock at the quays (*Tmr* 3C/D2 & 4C/D2/3) north of the Market.

## THE ACCOMMODATION & EATING OUT

**The Accommodation** The lampposts that edge Akti I. Metaxa, the Esplanade, and adjacent to the many side-streets, have signs clamped to them with the name of the hotels in that street. Apart from hotel accommodation being comparatively expensive, the majority are taken over by the numerous tour companies which now offer package holidays in Argostoli.

**Hotel Allegro** (*Tmr* C4) (Class D) 2 Andrea Choida St                    Tel 22268
*Directions*: Conveniently to hand as this side-street is directly opposite the top or north end of the Market/Bus Station (*Tmr* 1C/D4/5). The hotel is on the right-hand side.

If the garrulous, English-speaking, hotel-owner's comparatively expensive accommodation was half as good as his chat, then it would be an excellent establishment. As it is, the rooms are acceptable, the beds have sprung mattresses but the bathrooms leave much to be desired. The overall management style is 'dismissive laid back'. A single room with en suite bathroom, costs 2500drs, a double room sharing a bathroom 2500drs & with en suite bathroom 3100drs, rising, respectively, to 2800drs & 2800/3900drs (1st June-15th Sept).

Moving south from the side-street of Andrea Choida 'mines' a reasonably rich seam of handy, if varied accommodation.

**Hotel Tzivras Bros (Restaurant) Rooms** (*Tmr* 12C4/5) 1 Vasiliou Vandorou          Tel 22628
*Directions*: On the left (*Sbo*) of the Esplanade side-street, two down from Odhos A. Choida. 'We Rent Rooms Abova (*sic*) of the Restaurant', which says it all really.

A 'sleazo', with rather unpleasant, shared bathrooms. The first floor 'hosts' an antique, communal fridge. Despite the careworn, rather unkempt state of the place, a sign requests 'Please Keep Cleanliness of Bathroom & Dont Knock Doors'. A mid-season room is charged at 2000drs.

In strict contrast to the *Tzivras* is:-
**Rooms Anatolitis** (*Tmr* C5) Akti Ioannou Metaxa                    Tel 22534

*Directions*: Facing out over the Esplanade, above a restaurant beside and to the south of Antonatos Supermarket (*Tmr* 9C5).

Very clean accommodation with a mid-season double room, sharing the bathroom facilities, priced at 2000drs.

Moving north along the Esplanade, beyond the Market/Bus station, gives more choice including:-

**Hotel Mouikis** (*Tmr* 7C4) (Class C) 3 Vironos St            Tel 23032
*Directions*: As above and fourth side-street along. The hotel is on the junction with Odhos Kritis, the first street parallel to the Esplanade.

A modern building with all rooms having an en suite bathroom. A single room is priced at 2100drs & a double room 3120drs, increasing to 2880drs & 4080drs (16th June-20th Sept). Readers must bear in mind that most of the better class hotels are block-booked by tour operators.

**Hotel Tourist** (*Tmr* C3/4) (Class C) 94 Akti I. Metaxa St           Tel 22510
*Directions*: Bordering the Esplanade, alongside the Ionian & Popular Bank (*Tmr* 17C3/4).

Fully occupied with package tourists in the height of season months. Single rooms, sharing a bathroom, start at 1500drs & with en suite bathroom 2000drs, whilst double rooms, sharing, cost 2200drs & en suite 2800drs, increasing, respectively, to 2000/2800drs & 3000/3800drs (1st June-30th Sept).

Further north is Odhos 21st Maiou which leads to Plateia Valianou and more (expensive) accommodation, including:-

**Hotel Aegli** (*Tmr* N Inset) (Class C) 3, 21st Maiou St           Tel 22522
*Directions*: On the left-hand side of 21st Maiou, on the corner with Odhos Kavalia, walking towards the Main Square, Plateia Valianou.

Strangely enough, all rooms share the bathroom facilities. A single room is charged at 1060drs & a double 1800drs, increasing to 1300drs & 2200drs (1st April-30th June) and 1800drs & 3000drs (1st July-30th Sept).

To the left (*Sbo*) of the *Aegli*, along Odhos Kavalia and on the right is:-

**Rooms** (*Tmr* O Inset) (Class A) 32 Kavalia St           Tel 28415
*Directions*: As above.

A modern building, rather resembling a block of flats. A charming sign, in a door window, round the back, advises 'If you would like to rent a nice room with private toilet & shower, see Ms Maria on (*sic*) next building. Thank you. The Management'. A double room costs from 2500drs.

On Odhos 21st Maiou a sign informs 'First class Rooms to Rent, 3 Metaxa St. Tel 28919', whilst other boards advise of **Rooms** at 24 Argostoli St, Tel 28460 & 27 Pilarinion St, Tel 28297.

At the junction of Odhos 21st Maiou and Plateia Valianou, on the right, is the:-

**Hotel Aenos** (*Tmr* M Inset) 11, 21st Maiou           Tel 28103
*Directions*: As above.

Another modern building in which all rooms have en suite bathrooms. A single room is priced at 1900drs & a double room 3000drs, increasing to 2400drs & 3800drs (1st July-15th Sept).

**Hotel Kastello** (*Tmr* D Inset) (Class C) Valianou Sq           Tel 23250
*Directions*: In the far, top right-hand (*Sbo*) corner of the square, when approached from the Esplanade along 21st Maiou St.

Plush, and all rooms have en suite bathrooms. A single room is priced at 2100drs & a double 3120drs, increasing to 2880drs & 4080drs (16th June-20th Sept).

**Hotel Cephalonia Star** (*Tmr* 5C/D2/3) (Class C) 50 Akti I. Metaxa        Tel 23180
*Directions*: Further north along the Esplanade, opposite the Ferry-boat Quay.

When rooms with en suite bathrooms are available, they cost 2100drs for a single & 3120drs for a double, increasing to 2880drs & 4080drs (16th June-20th Sept).

**Cafe-Bar Rooms** (*Tmr* 6C2) Akti I. Metaxa           Tel 28017
*Directions*: North of the *Cephalonia Star* and one block beyond, bordering the Esplanade.

The years of tourism have enabled the old shack to be replaced by a three storey, provincial building with a cafe-bar in the ground floor and accommodation above. To the side is a vine trellis shaded patio enclosed by bamboo screening and at the rear is a large garden. Still owned by Spiros Rouhotas, a very smiley, small, round man with no English. Remains probably the best value in town, with the double rooms sharing four, jolly clean, separate showers and toilets. There is a big communal fridge on the landing. A mid-season double is charged at 1700drs.

There are two, not one, official tourist offices to help enquirers. The NTOG (*Tmr* 18C/D3), which 'stocks' lists of accommodation, has an office conveniently located on the large Cruise Liner Quay. But this is a rather beleaguered facility which, apart from a spurt in August, is only open Mon-Fri, between 0800-1500hrs. Too bad for weekend callers. The other office is the grandly titled Argostoli Council Tourist Board Information Centre (*Tmr* H. Inset). Staffed by extremely friendly, helpful (and pretty) girls. The office opens weekdays between 0800-1430hrs & 1730-2100hrs, as well as weekends between 0800-1300hrs & 1730-2100hrs. Very sensible.

Along the northern road out of Argostoli Town, which encircles the Lassi Peninsula, and approximately opposite a boatyard, alongside a junction, is *Rooms - Dhomatio Marina*.

## Camping

**Argostoli Campsite** , Fanari, Argostoli                                        Tel 23487
*Directions*: Situated some 2km north of the town, along the coast road and in the 'mess of development' that litters the Lassi Peninsula, alongside a 'mini' Albert Hall, signed Noufaro Music Hall. The Sea Mills rotunda is just beyond the campsite.

A nicely laid out facility shaded by widely spaced, low trees. The per person cost is 350drs and a tent is charged at 250drs. The site is open April-October.

## The Eating Out
Generally speaking the Main Square restaurants and cafe-bars are expensive and firmly entrenched in the tourist trade. A once 'average Joe' cafe/grocer on the north of the square has been brought bang-up-to-date and is now a 'rinky-dinky', chromium plated *Cafe-Bar/Local produce Boutique* (*Tmr* B Inset). In deference to the 'BPTs' there are a number of Pubs. Oh dear! For instance, in the ground floor of the *Hotel Aenos* is the *Corner Pub*. The *Imperial Restaurant* (*Tmr* D Inset) is impossibly... Imperial, with a splendidly sited terrace on the Main Square.

**Cottage Greek Taverna** (*Tmr* L Inset)
*Directions*: Beyond the top, left-hand (*Sbo*) side of the Main Square, across the street from the public gardens.

Has averagely priced, interesting menu which includes *pikileea* and bean soup. 'Chatty' with a pleasant garden alongside.

A recommended Main Square eating house is the:-
**Kefalos Restaurant** (*Tmr* S Inset)
*Directions*: Named after the First King of Cephalonia and to the left-hand (*Sbo*) side of Plateia Valianou, on the corner of Odhos Valianou, facing the side of the long Government building.

Average fare at average Main Square prices.

Just off the Main Square, towards the Esplanade, in the side-street Odhos Kavalia is:-
**Taverna Dionyssos** (*Tmr* Q Inset)
*Directions*: As above.

Apart from a garden to the rear of the building, the interesting menu is reasonably priced. Offerings include saganaki (195drs), liver (226drs), sugling pig (*sic*) (646drs), chicken & patatas (245drs), Greek salad (150drs) and an Amstel beer (80drs).

**Souvlaki Cafe-bar** (*Tmr* I Inset)
*Directions*: On the right (*Sbo*) of Odhos 21st Maiou.

Apart from souvlaki pita, 'English is Spoken'.

North along the Esplanade is the:-
**Port of Cephalos Restaurant** (*Tmr* 11C3)
*Directions*: As above.

Very pricey and smart, serving 'foreign' food and much frequented by BPTs. It has to be admitted the dishes are extremely good, but so they should be at these unprintable prices.

Beyond the *Cephalonia Star*, is the aforementioned:-
**Greek Cafe** (*Tmr* 6C2)
*Directions*: As above.

Offers simple meals at reasonable prices. 'BBQ chicken, we served, breakfast, Kokoretsi'. This latter item is sheep's entrails (No thank you). Alongside is a large, bamboo enclosed, vine shaded patio.

The Market/Bus terminus (*Tmr* IC/D4/5) buildings have a number of kafeneions. Across the Esplanade, to the south of Odhos Metaxa and next door to Antonatos Supermarket (*Tmr* 9C5), is the *Restaurant Diana*. The *Diana* is separated by a butchers shop from the favourably mentioned, nicely appointed *Restaurant Kalafatis* (*Tmr* 8C5), the outside tables and chairs of which are spread along the wide pavement. This is an excellent spot from which to watch the endless comings and goings generated by the market activity. A couple of Nes meh ghala only cost 160drs and the owners are very helpful. Above the *Kalafatis* are the 'remains' of the *Hotel Ipnoy*.

One of the best, value for money eateries is:-
**Taverna H Kambana** (*Tmr* 13B/C5) Diadhohou Konstantinou St
*Directions*: From the Esplanade, along the side-street of Metaxa past the National Bank (*Tmr* 15C4/5), paved Plateia Konstantinou and on the other side of Odhos Diadhohou Konstantinou. The taverna is in the shadow of a great clock tower to the right (*Sbo*), in the ground floor of which is a ceramic workshop.
Don't be put off by appearances. To the left of the dark interior, in a sort of shed, is the spit roasting gear. Apart from the more traditional taverna activities, Yianni, the owner, who is distinctly Cretan in appearance, does a roaring, local 'takeaway trade' in spit roasted chicken and stick souvlaki pita. A sort of 'Greek chippie'. An excellent sit down meal, for a couple, of two enormous plates of liver served with chips (227drs each), a fresh Greek salad complete with onions & olives (150drs), 2 bottles of local retsina (124drs a bottle) & bread (15drs each) cost 880drs. As it is a grill house, no vegetables are available but who cares? I exaggerate not when I state that the size of one of the liver helpings was about that of a large T bone steak.

## THE A TO Z OF USEFUL INFORMATION
**AIRLINE OFFICE** (*Tmr* 14C4) Between the Market and the Ferry-boat Quays, along the side-street of R Vergoti, off the Esplanade (behind the Ionian & Popular Bank and *Hotel Tourist*). The office is open Mon-Sat between 0800-1730hrs; Sundays & holidays 0930-1730hrs.

**Aircraft timetables** (Mid-season)
**Cephalonia to Athens** (& vice-versa)
Daily          1655hrs
*Return*
Daily          1530hrs
One-way fare 6000drs; duration 45mins.

**Cephalonia to Corfu**
Tues & Sun     1335hrs
*Return*
Tues & Sun     1110hrs
One-way fare 5100drs; duration 50mins.

**Cephalonia to Zakynthos**
Tues & Sun     1215hrs
*Return*
Tues & Sun     1255hrs
One-way fare 1750drs; duration 20mins.

**BANKS** The **Ionian & Popular Bank** (*Tmr* 17C3/4) is north of the Market, next to the *Hotel Tourist*, bordering the Esplanade. The **Bank of Greece** (*Tmr* 16C3) is (almost) flanked by a couple of vehicle hire firms, across broad Odhos Valianou from the massive Government offices (*Tmr* G Inset) and close by the *Restaurant Kefalos* (*Tmr* S Inset). The **National Bank** (*Tmr* 15C4/5) is between the two streets of Diadhohou Konstantinou and Siteborou, that parallel the Esplanade, east of *Taverna H Kambana* (*Tmr* 13B/C5).

**BEACHES** There is a microscopic, top pocket hint of a beach, created by a change of direction in the sea wall, beyond the Ferry-boat Quay.
For more spacious recreation, it is necessary to make the 3km journey along the airport road to the beaches of Makris Gialos or Platis Gialos. (*See* **Excursions to Argostoli Town Surrounds**). Leave town by turning up Odhos Vironos from the Esplanade, in the region of the Market, or catch a bus.

**BICYCLE, SCOOTER & CAR HIRE** Cephalonia does not lend itself to great bicycle rides, unless a reader is in strict training for mountain sections of the *Tour de France*. In the main, automotive hire is in the hands of professionals with the sort of smooth, smart offices more usually associated with advertising agencies and public relations firms – all glass, thick pile carpets and desks on which it would be possible to play table tennis. Odhos Valianou, which runs along the east side of the massive Government building from the Main Square, is one 'Hire alley'. These include a number of businesses either side of the Bank of Greece (*Tmr* 16C3). They include **Rent A Car Ford/A. Pefanis** and **CBR** who hire cars, Vespas and motorbikes. The other 'Renta' street is Odhos R Vergoti, which 'quarters' **Budget Rent A Car, Rent A Car** as well as **Motorbike Hire.**

For those who wish to search out a more homely outfit, there is the Esplanade sited **Rent Motor** (*Tmr* 24C/D5/6) at No 158 Akti I Metaxa, south of the Fina Petrol Station (*Tmr* 25C5), which also hires scooters.

I do have a rather revolutionary suggestion. Why don't prospective clients catch the ferry to Lixourion? There, at the friendly offices of **Orion Rent A Car** (*See* **Bicycle, Scooter & Car Hire, A To Z, Lixourion**), a (similar) car costs between 2000drs and 4500drs less for three days hire. Furthermore the deposit requested is 3000drs less for one day and 1900drs for three days, yes 1900drs. It is a thought. The 30 minute ferry fare for a passenger costs 110drs and about 650drs for a vehicle, if a hirer does not want to drive back round.

**BOOKSELLERS** None, but there is an overseas newspaper shop (*Tmr* 26C4) on Odhos Diadhohou Konstantinou.

**BREAD SHOPS** Opposite the north end of the Market, and across the road, between the side-streets of Sotoros and A. Choida, is the excellent Bakety (*sic*) Pastry shop & Zacharoplasteion (*Tmr* 27C4). There is another smarty bread & cake shop in the same block.

**BUSES** The Bus terminus and office (*Tmr* 1C/D4/5) shares the dusty, scrubbly Market building and its environs.

### Bus timetable (Mid-season)
**Argostoli Town to Athens\* via Poros, Killini & Patras**
Daily                0745, 1330hrs
*Return journey*
Daily                0630, 1215hrs
One-way fare 2400drs plus ferry fares; duration 8hrs.

**Argostoli Town to Athens\* via Killini**
Daily                0845hrs
*Return journey*
Daily                0800hrs
One-way fare 2550drs.

**Argostoli Town to Athens\* via Sami**
Daily                0745hrs
*Return journey*
Daily                0915hrs
One-way fare 2500drs.
\*100 Kifissou St, Tel 5129498

**Argostoli Town to Poros**
Daily                0930, 1000, 1330, 1845hrs
Sun & holidays 1000, 1845hrs
*Return journey*
Daily                0615, 0730, 1330, 1700, 1900hrs
Sun & holidays 0615, 1700, 1900hrs
One-way fare 2400drs.

**Argostoli Town to Nea Skala via Kato Katelios**
Daily                1030, 1400, 2000hrs
Sun & holidays 1030, 2000hrs
*Return journey*
Daily                0615, 0800, 1330, 1700hrs
Sun & holidays 0615, 1700hrs
One-way fare 210drs.

**Argostoli Town to Sami**
Daily                0745, 1200, 1300, 1500, 2000drs
Sun & holidays 0745, 1300, 1500hrs
*Return journey*
Daily                0730, 0830, 1730hrs
Sun & holidays 0830, 1730hrs
One-way fare 140drs.

**Argostoli Town to Valsamata & St Gerasimos Convent**
Daily              0830, 0930, 1200, 1400, 1930hrs
Sun & holidays 0830hrs
*Return journey*
Daily              1000, 1230, 1630hrs (I know...less buses returning than arrived!)
Sun & holidays 1030hrs
One-way fare 85drs.

**Argostoli Town to Hotel Irina (Ag Pelagia) via Kourkoumeleta**
Daily              0720, 1000, 1200, 1345, 1930hrs
Sun & holidays 0630, 1230, 1930hrs
*Return journey*
Daily              0630, 0730, 1015, 1215, 1400, 1615, 1945hrs
Sun & holidays 0645, 1615, 1945hrs
One-way fare 80drs.

**Argostoli Town to Platis Gialos via Makris Gialos**
Daily              0930, 1000, 1030, 1100, 1130, 1200, 1230, 1300, 1330,
                   1400, 1430, 1500, 1700, 1800hrs
*Return journey*
Daily              0945, 1015, 1045, 1115, 1145, 1215, 1245, 1315, 1345,
                   1415, 1445, 1530, 1645, 1730, 1830hrs
One-way fare 50drs.

**Argostoli Town to Hotel Irina (Ag Pelagia) via Kourkoumeleta**
Daily              0720, 1000, 1200, 1345, 1930hrs
Sun & holidays 0630, 1230, 1930hrs
*Return journey*
Daily              0630, 0730, 1015, 1215, 1400, 1615, 1945hrs
Sun & holidays 0645, 1615, 1945hrs
One-way fare 80drs.

**Argostoli Town to Platis Gialos via Makris Gialos**
Daily              0930, 1000, 1030, 1100, 1130, 1200, 1230, 1300, 1330,
                   1400, 1430, 1500, 1700, 1800hrs
*Return journey*
Daily              0945, 1015, 1045, 1115, 1145, 1215, 1245, 1315, 1345,
                   1415, 1445, 1530, 1645, 1730, 1830hrs
One-way fare 50drs.

**Argostoli Town to Ag Evfimia via Divarata**
Daily              0745, 1230hrs
*Return journey*
Daily              0730, 1730hrs
Note there aren't any Sunday or holiday buses.
One-way fare 195drs.

**Argostoli Town to Assos**
Daily              1400hrs
*Return journey*
Daily              0645hrs
Note there aren't any Sunday or holiday buses.
One-way fare 210drs.

**Argostoli Town to Fiscardon**
Daily              0930, 1400hrs
Sun & holidays 0930, 1500hrs (via Sami)
*Return journey*
Daily              0630, 1700hrs
sun & holidays  0630 (via Sami), 1700hrs

Note there isn't a Lixourion service. Travellers must catch the ferry
(*See* **Ferry-boats, A To Z**).

Interestingly the bus company also lays on a couple of excursions.

Excursion 1: Drogarati Cave, Melissani Lake, Fiscardon & Assos.
              Mon, Thurs & Sat depart at 0830hrs, return at 1830hrs at a cost of 1500drs.

Excursion 2: To Stavros & Frikes (Ithaca).
              Wed, Fri & Sun depart at 0730hrs, return at 1830hrs at a cost of 1900drs.

**COMMERCIAL SHOPPING AREA** The Market (*Tmr* 1C/D4/5) ranges along a rather messy, dirty series of buildings. These are laid out in the form of a flat 'W , mounted on a quay jutting into the sea. The forecourt is shared with the bus company, who use it as the terminus. The original structure has been extended and where these end, in the mornings, some 30/40m of stalls are erected south along the Esplanade. To give an idea of the all encompassing range of activities, apart from the rows of fruit and vegetable stands, from north to south, businesses include a 'Coffee Shop Bar'; plant hire; a fish shop; a general store; a kafeneion; a butcher; an 'International Tourist Office'; an electrical business; another smarter kafeneion; another fish shop; a zacharoplasteion; a couple of hardware shops; a kafeneion, which serves breakfast and toasted sandwiches; a builders merchant; a butcher; a flower shop and a drink shop selling Cephalonian wines. Additionally, two petrol stations are set into the complex.

Ranged opposite the Market, across the Esplanade, are, from south to north, the Athena Petrol Station; a builders merchant; *Restaurant Kalafatis* (*Tmr* 8C5); a butcher; the *Restaurant Diana*; Antonatos Supermarket (*Tmr* 9C5); a clothing shop; (the side-street Odhos Metaxa) a butcher; a carpentry business; a fruit & vegetable shop; (Odhos Drakopolo side-street) a zacharoplasteion; a dairy shop; (Odhos Vandorou); a supermarket; the 'Bakety' & zacharoplasteion; a hardware shop; mini-market; a smart store; another bread & cake shop and a butcher.

The other busy shopping area is the south end of Odhos Diadhohou Konstantinou in which are gift shops, chemists, clothes shops, photographic and jewellery shops. For instance, south of the Post Office is one of the only camera shops (*Tmr* 28C4) on any island which sells 36 frame 200ASA 35mm film.

**DISCO** Night life lovers will have to travel to the top of Lassi Peninsula, where is, for instance, Noufaro Music Hall, or the Makris and Platis Gialos Beach surrounds. For both *See* **Excursions to Argostoli Town Surrounds**.

**FERRY-BOATS** Whereas, in the past, Argostoli only served the Lixourion ferry, now there is a mainland service to Killini. Poros also has a Killini connection. Notwithstanding, the island's main port for inter-island travel remains Sami, although tiny, northern Fiscardon has a daily, if smaller, car ferry link with Sami, Frikes(Ithaca), Nidri(Lefkas), Vassiliki(Lefkas) and Meganissi island. Ag Evfimia hosts a daily car ferry link with Vathi(Ithaca) and mainland Astakos. Not to be forgotten is the Pesada summer months ferry to Korithi Port(Skinaria) on Zakynthos island.

### Ferry-boat timetable (Mid-season)
**Argostoli Town to Lixourion**

| | |
|---|---|
| Daily | 0730-1330 every hour on the half hour, 1500, 1630, 1830, 2040, 2230hrs. |
| Sunday | 0730, 0930, 1100, 1300, 1500, 1630, 1830, 2040, 2230hrs. |
| *Return* | |
| Daily | 0630, 0800-1300 every hour on the hour, 1430, 1600, 1800, 1900, 2000, 2200hrs. |
| Sunday | 0700, 0900, 1030, 1230, 1430, 1600, 1800, 2000, 2200hrs. |

One-way fare 110drs; duration ½hr.

**Argostoli town to Killini(M)**

| | |
|---|---|
| Daily | 0900hrs |
| Tues & Fri | 1700hrs |
| *Return* | |
| Daily | 1330hrs |
| Tues & Fri | 2115hrs |

One-way fare 875drs; duration 2¾hrs.

**FERRY-BOAT TICKET OFFICE** Tickets are purchased on board the Lixourion boat but one useful office is:-
**Seven Islands** (*Tmr* 32C4)                                                                                    Tel 22000
*Directions*: Edging the Esplanade.
   Apart from the tourist aspect of the office, the business owns the **CF Ionis** and **Ionian Glory**, the major ferries that ply the Ionian islands.

Another firm is:-
**Vartholomos Shipping Travel Agency** (*Tmr* P Inset)
*Directions*: On the right (*Sbo*) of Odhos 21st Maiou.
   Main office for the HML Line.

## MEDICAL CARE
**Chemists & Pharmacies** Plentiful, with a number grouped in the area of the Market (*Tmr* 1C/D4/5) including several across the street, others in the main streets west of the Esplanade as well as some in Odhos Diadhohou Konstantinou.
**Doctor** (*Tmr* 29C4) The surgery of Dr Andreas Michaelides is across the street from the Post Office.
**Hospital** (*Tmr* 20C6) South along the Esplanade, turning right on Odhos Devossetou, opposite the arched lagoon bridge, and off to the left, after some six or seven blocks.
**NTOG** Feast or famine. Argostoli Town possesses not one but two offices.
**Argostoli Town Tourist Office** (*Tmr* H Inset)
*Directions*: In the shadow of the massive Government office on the side of the broad pavement edging Odhos Valianou.
The full title is 'Argostoli Council Tourist Board Information Centre'. The pretty, helpful ladies hand out a town plan, in addition to the more usual information. Currency exchange is transacted and there is an international phone. Sensibly the office opens daily, weekdays between 0800-1430hrs & 1730-2100hrs, weekends between 0800-1300hrs & 1730-2100hrs.
**NTOG** (*Tmr* 18C/D3)
*Directions*: Located on the large 'Cruise Liner' Quay.
Mr Messaris speaks good English. He is very helpful, if rather overwhelmed with inconsequential queries by BPTs, many of which should be answered by the Tour office that sold this or that excursion. There are lists of accommodation but outside of August the office only opens weekdays between 0800-1500hrs.
**OTE** (*Tmr* 19B/C3/4) Across G Vergoti St from the curiously elongated and narrowing block that contains various municipal offices. (Incidentally, these include, from the Main Square end, the Town Hall, the Police administration and Archaeological museum). The OTE office opens daily between 0700-2400hrs.
**PETROL** There are two petrol stations in the Market complex (*Tmr* 1C/D4/5) and several edging the Esplanade, south of the Market.
## PLACES OF INTEREST
**British Cemetery** Over the causeway bridge and on the right.

### Museums
*Archaeological Museum* (*Tmr* 21C3/4) At the southern end of the spread of municipal buildings, at the junction of Valianou and R Vergoti streets.
*Cultural & Historical Museum* (*Tmr* 22C3/4) Situated in Odhos R Vergoti in the Public Library and much more interesting than the rather dull Archaeological Museum. The local interest exhibits embrace English memorabilia and photographs covering the last 100 years or so, including those of earthquake devastated Argostoli Town in 1953.

**Ruins of Ancient Walls of Krani** South from Argostoli Town and across the multiple arched bridge which spans the inlet of sea. This route leads past a minor road branching off to the right, which circumscribes the enclosed lagoon. Half-way around this latter road and a track ascends a hill to whence part of the terraced walls can be viewed. Fine, if you get pleasure from sometimes and nebulous lumps and bumps! The remains relate to the fourth century BC, and were part of a large defensive system for the ancient Kingdom of Krani.
Incidentally, the road circles around to rejoin the main Argostoli road, further south of the Town.

**Sea Mills** The repaired remains of the rather unique Sea Mills are about two kilometres north of the town, at the top end of the Lassi Peninsula (on which Argostoli Town stands). They were originally built in the nineteenth century, at the instigation of an Englishman, to exploit the phenomenon of an underground river of sea-water, coursing inland. A team of scientists recently established that the water reappears the other side of Cephalonia at Melissani, above Sami Port. The oft-referred to 1953 earthquake probably altered the levels as the flood has slowed to a trickle.
Half a kilometre further on advances to the pretty, Doric-styled lighthouse at the headland tip of the peninsula.
## POLICE
**Port** (*Tmr* 30C/D3) On the Cruise Liner Quay.
**Town** (*Tmr* 31C/D2/3) Bordering the Esplanade.

**POST OFFICE** (*Tmr* 23C4) On Odhos Diadhohou Konstantinou, between the side-streets of Vironos and A. Choida.

**TAXIS** Two main ranks, one on the Main Sq (*Tmr* 2C3), the other down by the Bus terminus (*Tmr* 1C/D4/5). They also line up to meet the Killini and Lixourion ferries.

**TELEPHONE NUMBERS & ADDRESSES**

| | |
|---|---|
| Doctor (*Tmr* 29C4) | Tel 23338 |
| Hospital (*Tmr* 20C6) | Tel 22434 |
| Olympic Airways (*Tmr* 14C4) | Tel 22808 |
| Police, port (*Tmr* 30C/D3) | Tel 22224 |
| town (*Tmr* 31C/D2/3 | Tel 22300 |
| Taxi Rank | Tel 28545 |
| Town Tour office (*Tmr* H Inset) | Tel 22847 |

**TOILETS** (*Tmr* R Inset) Across a narrow side-street from the *Hotel Kastello* and set down in a children's playground. Rather basic squatties.

**TRAVEL AGENTS & TOUR OFFICES** Apart from a number on R Vergoti and 21st Maiou Sts, there is an office (*Tmr* U Inset) edging the Main Sq, and distinguished by a parrot kept in the window. Also *See* **Ferry-boat Ticket Offices, A To Z**.

# EXCURSIONS TO ARGOSTOLI TOWN SURROUNDS
## Excursion to Makris & Platis Gialos Beaches via Lassi Peninsula & on to Ag Pelagia Beach, Kourkoumeleta, Metaxata, Spartia, Spartia Beach, Keramies, Pesada, Pesada Port & Ag Thomas Beach (Circa 30km)Proceeding
north along the Esplanade, the road passes a boatyard about where the main route jinks inland a mite, opposite which junction is the rather pretty looking *Rooms Marina*.

The northern end of the headland is a bit of a mishmash, being littered with diverse enterprises in various stages of disintegration, set in a flat prospect of haphazard, messy bamboo.

As detailed, the campsite is sited close to the head of the peninsula, next door to a grandiose, totally out of place building, housing the 'Noufaro Music Hall'. (No mother, not Henry Hall). Not much further on is the rotunda like structure, the Sea Mills (*See* **Places of Interest, A To Z, Argostoli Town**). Hereabouts the surprisingly narrow, poorly surfaced lane turns back in a southerly direction, along the west coast of the peninsula.

In this wasteland, the first tenuous signs of 'package tourist civilisation' evinces itself with the outcrop of one or two, extremely smart hotels. The coastline is still boulderous but in the neck of an outcrop is a pleasant, grey shingle, kelpy beach, accessed along a track, past a prettily outfitted pension, to the nearside of the shore. The remorseless acceleration of spaced out holiday apartments, tavernas, hotels and cafe-bars builds up into a full-blown villa hodgepodge, a 'moussaka pot mess' of breathtakingly crass development encircling:-

**Makris Gialos Beach (circa 5km from Argostoli Town round the peninsula)** The area is very reminiscent of the 1960s Spanish Costa Brava. Fortunately the barbarians responsible for this disarray have left standing many of the tall and slender trees. These groves, through which it is necessary to walk, supply welcome shade. This is a lovely sweep of sand which BPTs have 'Clactoned'. A beach bar and Cantina serve canned beer to the 'public bar crowd' throughout the day. Sun-beds and umbrellas are available, at a cost of 250drs each per day, as are pedaloes but I must report that there aren't any donkey rides, nor, more importantly, are there any showers. Being a lee shore, in any wind the foreshore is subject to breakers but the beach is very clean.

Further to the south, and separated only by a rock outcrop, is the 'saloon bar':-
**Platis Gialos Beach (Circa 6km from Argostoli Town)** A neat cobbled slip road descends the cliff-face to double back and terminate on a car park edged by a toilet block, complete with loo rolls – I've dreamt of...

Although smaller than Makris, it is equally sandy, clean and a superior location, with an ambience of structured refinement as evinced by the speckling of signs and permanent sunshades. Instead of canned beer at the Cantina, its gin and tonics in the cafe-bar patio let into the right-hand (*Fsw*) headland. This tiny complex, set down on a concrete platform laid over the rocks, includes changing huts, toilets, a line of beach showers and a diving board. Mind you, a snack for two of a couple of rolls (320drs), a Henninger beer (130drs) and a lemonade (65drs), plus tax, totalled 545drs – a sum which we would have purchased a full-blown evening meal a few years ago. (Maudlin old twit).

Set on the low cliffs overlooking the beach is the fenced in, discreet and modern *White Rocks Hotel & Bungalows* (Class A, tel 23167) where the en suite rooms kick off at 4750drs for a single room & 6500drs for a double, increasing to 6150drs & 8600drs. (Just thought I'd let you know). It has to be reported that the rooms facing the road are permanently in the gloom.

Further to the south of Platis is an attractive outcrop or isthmus of sand, stopped off by a large rock.

Both Makris and Platis Gialos are situated on the aircraft line up for the final runway approach.

The main road must have formed a firebreak hereabouts as the inland countryside is extensively fire damaged.

Another few kilometres further on is the Airport access avenue. Considering the amount of traffic generated by the Airport, the main thoroughfare really is very narrow and rural, no sweeping, sodium lit highway this. Beyond the Airport turning there is a 'Pick Your Own Sign' advertising wine tasting and *Rooms*, to the right, and some beautiful houses prior to:-

**Irina Hotel & Ag Pelagia Beach (circa 13km from Argostoli Town)** This enormous hotel, advertising 'Peace & Tranquillity, is set down on a rather bleak moorland headland, 'miles from anywhere'. That is, apart from the one kilometre trek along the wide, chalky track in a northerly direction to Ag Pelagia Beach. This is a small but very sandy shore entirely devoid of commercialism, in a rather wild setting. Buses journey out to the *Hotel Irina*, where en suite rooms start off at 1885drs for a single room & 2535drs for a double, rising to 2200drs & 3225drs (1st-15th June & 16th-30th Sept) and 3170drs & 5575drs (16th June-15th Sept).

**KALIGATA (circa 11km from Argostoli Town)** Those searching for the sea will have to be careful they don't finish up in the village wine factory. On the descent, the track passes one or two massive old olive trees on the way to pleasant:-

**Kaligata Beach** (circa 12km from Argostoli Town) This is a fairly narrow, very sandy, but shadeless shore, which serpentines along the foot of low cliffs. There is a Cantina caravan on the side of the ramp down from the car park, a few metres prior to the beach backshore. The Cantina prices are not unreasonable with a bottle of beer costing 90drs, a lemonade 70drs, a brandy with mezes 100drs and a Nes meh ghala 80drs. As elsewhere along this stretch of west facing coast, Kaligata Beach is subject to wind and breakers. This is a 'get away from it location' for those Argostoli Town breakouts who don't wish to continually socialise with fellow 'BPTs. But transport is necessary.

**KOURKOUMELETA (circa 12km from Argostoli Town)** The villages of Kaligata and Kourkoumeleta almost run into each other.

This is almost a 'Home Counties Suburb'. The large, affluent looking bungalows and houses have lawns and there are a number of big public buildings including a 'mega' stadium. This totally unexpected occurrence is due to the village being completely rebuilt by one Vergotis, a wealthy Greek shipowner, after the 1953 earthquake. It is an irony that the comparatively recent forest fires that swept this region very nearly destroyed the settlement. Nearly, but not quite.

The next village is:-

**METAXATA (circa 13km from Argostoli Town)** This also only just escaped the ravages of the fire. Lord Byron stayed here, in 1823, whilst awaiting news that would result in him proceeding to Messolongi to further the War of Independence, and where he would die.

A right-hand turning advances to:-

**SPARTIA (circa 15km from Argostoli Town)** An attractive village with *Rooms*, a small taverna, a small store alongside a church with a quite splendid campanile, and close by, two signs to 'The Beach'.

To the right advances past a supermarket, *Angelina's Rooms* and the scattered settlement of **Koriana**. As is often the case the initial burst of signposting quickly evaporates to leave travellers to their own devices on the mainly unsurfaced track.

**Spartia Beach (circa 17km from Argostoli Town)** There is a parking spot above the small cove from whence it is possible to look out to sea where is an offshore, chapel topped islet. The narrow sea entrance to the cove is almost blocked off by a rock. The track continues on down to a formally laid out area on which are set down with some small, framed and bamboo covered open-air taverna/beach bars. To one side is a sweet water well. For a change, this manifestation of beach activity is not tourist inspired but promoted by a local society, mainly supported by expatriates from the villages of Spartia and Koriana.

As the Cephalonian, now a New York resident, told us, until recent years it was necessary to ride donkeys as close as possible and then walk the rest of the distance. But over the years the society has invested in the necessary roadworks and the backshore area for festivities.

Another larger and more suitable beach from which to swim is **Agialos**, but it is only accessible on foot.

By continuing east from Spartia, the road ends up in a fishing hamlet, with a sea swept concrete pier, surrounded by rather messy countryside. There is a smidgin of beach and a solitary showerhead mounted on a small square. Despite the rural, unsophisticated, bucolic nature of this settlement, unbelievably there are some villa holiday apartments.

Voyagers in this area must bear in mind that the tracks and roads really are rather a maze.

From Spartia the route can be followed to:-

**KERAMIES (circa 16km from Argostoli Town)** Here are a number of surprisingly large, Victorian buildings, harking back to an age of much affluence.

To the east of Keramies, on the way to Karavados, a side turning is signposted to:-

**PESADA (circa 18km from Argostoli Town)** On the approaches, any number of signs highlight the direction of this Zakynthos ferry-boat port.

From the village, **Monastery Estavromenou** is indicated to the left and the ferry to the right. Following the ferry signs, almost immediately there is another fork. To the right is, in the direction of **Kountourata**, the *Sunset Inn* and to the left winds down the gentle hillsides on a gravel track to:-

**Pesada Port (circa 19km from Argostoli Town)** This really is out in the sticks and is more a small fishing boat harbour than a full-blown port.

**Ferry-boat timetable**
**Pesada to Korithi Harbour (Skinaria), Zakynthos**
Only operates between middle of May – end of August.
Middle of May – middle of June: Fri & Sun.
Middle of June – middle of July: Wed, Fri & Sun.
Middle of July – end of August: Daily.
Departure 0800, 1600hrs.

*Return*
Departure 0945, 1745hrs.
One-way fare 305drs.
Note, a bus links with the Korithi Harbour boat arrivals, connecting to Zakynthos Town.

Strangely there is no palpable evidence of accommodation in Pesada and I do not think Argostoli buses journey to Pesada.

Returning to the Keramies road, at **Karavados** a sign indicates 'Two km very nice beaches' which abruptly ends at:-
**Ag Thomas Beach (circa 20km from Argostoli Town)** The narrow, defile constricted road comes to a dead stop at the sea's edge. There are some changing huts, a taverna and beach showers. A tiny, sandy cove is to the left (*Fsw*), with a bigger sweep of rather kelpy beach round to the right. This is a 'height of summer months' only spot, 'dying' out of season.

## ROUTE TWO
**To Lixourion ($\frac{1}{2}$ hour by ferry, circa 30km by road)**The town is across the Gulf of Argostoli and is most easily and effortlessly reached by ferry-boat.

The road involves heading along the main causeway, turning north towards Assos, bearing left at **Kardakata** and round on to the peninsula of Paliki, more popularly known as Lixourion Peninsula. Where the road rejoins the top of Argostoli Gulf, at sea-level, the foreshore is covered in kelp and rubbish. Beyond the *Lotus Pizza House*, incongruously set down almost at the 'beginning of the beyond', the seaward vista is rather marshy. At about 21km a sign to the right indicates Athera (and thus Ag Spiridon – *See* **Excursions to Lixourion Town Surrounds**). The generally unattractive countryside can only be described as 'low-lying Aldershot'. The bay sea-shore continues to be marshy and tussocky, whilst the cultivated terrain is occasionally broken up by bands of cypress trees. Generally the road surface of this route is good.

The northern outskirts of Lixourion are scattered with valley homesteads.

## LIXOURION (Lixouri): town & port (Illustration 26) Tel prefix 0671. A
large, sleepy town with a simply massive but underused port. Lixourion is a pleasant alternative to the clamour of Argostoli but tends to open up late and close down early in the summer months.

**ARRIVAL BY FERRY** Turning right on leaving the Argostoli Ferry-boat Quay (*Tmr* 2B/C3/4) leads the traveller to the Main Square (*Tmr* 3B3/4). The Plateia is edged by a number of cafe-bars and a couple of banks. The main trading activity of the town takes place in or around the Main Square, its surrounding streets and those behind the 'Bus Square' church.

## THE ACCOMMODATION & EATING OUT
**The Accommodation** A major problem for aspiring visitors is the lack of accommodation. There are few if any *Rooms* and the sprinkling of hotels and pensions are, in the main, booked by package holiday firms.

**Aravantinos Rooms** *Tmr* 4A4) No 1                                          Tel 92681
*Directions*: Proceed south on the gently ascending High St, as far as the large church. Turn right (*Main Square behind one*) beyond the church and climb the side-street. This establishment is on the left, in a three storey, modern 'block of flats'.

Unfortunately block booked by two British tourist companies. Enquirers in the early months of the summer might succeed but as September draws to a close, will probably find that life has 'drained away'. Those fortunate to find a 'bed at the inn' will be charged about 2500drs for a double room.

Whilst in this street don't miss the little terrace of two or three, old, single storey, wooden houses across the street.

The best option, a most pleasant alternative is the:-
**'Taverna Apolafsis Rooms'**
*Directions*: Situated on the right of the Lepeda Beach road south of the town. From the Argostoli Ferry-boat Quay (*Tmr* 2B/C3/4), follow the quayside road along the Harbour, jinking right and then left round the Port police (*Tmr* 9B/C4/5). The downtown dock street parallels the seashore, past the Town police (*Tmr* 8B/C5), on the right, and (all on the left) a school; an abandoned Nissen shed factory, alongside which is the *Hotel Summery*; the *Hotel Poseidon*; holiday apartments; a few private homes and a reinforcing rod steel stockyard. From hereon is a wide, undeveloped, rather doo-hickey swathe of backshore, littered with caiques, fishing boats and the occasional abandoned motor car. For an idea of scale, the distance between the Town police and the *Hotel Summery* is about 100m. After about 1¼kms, the Apolafsis is on the right, standing in its own gardens.
   A pleasantly sited pension/restaurant (rather too smart to be a taverna) with an enormous dining room and pleasant patio overlooking the gulf. Part booked, in 1988, by *Thomsons* but has room for independents, with an en suite double room costing 2500drs. Spiros, the friendly owner, speaks English and accepts payment by *Visa*.

As indicated, the aforementioned street passes by two hotels, both modern and booked by package holiday companies. They are the:-
**Hotel Summery** (Class C)                                                                          Tel 91771
*Directions*: As above. Between the backshore and the hotel an attempt has been made to create formal gardens but they are rather overgrown.
   All rooms have en suite bathrooms, a single costing 1990drs & a double 2565drs, increasing to 2655drs & 3320drs (1st July-15th Sept).
and the:-
**Hotel Poseidon** (Class C)                                                                        Tel 92518
*Directions*: As above.
   More expensive, with the en suite rooms priced at 2400drs for a single & 3500drs for a double, rising to 3250drs & 4450drs (1st July-15th Sept).
   Both hotels look out over the gulf but the boulderous, fine shingle seashore is despoiled by piles of rocks and kelp and is smelly.
   The *Hotel Giardino* (*Tmr* 10A3), at the back of the town, is actually furnished apartments and block booked, in 1988, by *Thomsons*.

## The Eating Out
There are several cafes spaced out around the Main Square. At one of the traditional establishments (*Tmr* 11B3) two Nes meh ghala, nicely served with plenty of milk and a jug of boiling water, and a large ouzo cost 230drs.

Possibly one of the most reasonable and pleasant (Lixourion) eateries is:-
**Restaurant Antonis** (*Tmr* 5B/C4)
*Directions*: Bordering the Esplanade, to the south of Argostoli Ferry-boat Quay. Identification might be aided by the window notice 'We speak your language'. The restaurant is set in an uninspiring row of buildings with steel framed windows and lofty ceilings, but don't be put off by any adverse, initial impressions.
   Tony is a taciturn professional and watching him cook will convince diners of his competence. Proof, as they say, is in the eating... The meals are very tasty and served hot! A dinner for two of tzatziki (freshly made, 150drs), a Greek salad (small but good and lively, 120drs), a stuffed tomato & pepper (very nice, 250drs), a plate of chicken & chips (good & hot, 285drs), meatballs, in a sauce, & chips (tasty, 285drs), bread (fresh & inexpensive at 12drs each) and a small bottle of Demestica (265drs) cost a total of 1374drs. I must admit to being irritated at the lack of kortaki retsina but that is general throughout the town, if not the island. This phenomena is usually evident where an island produces wines of some quality. But I carp... One last detail is that it is nice to see the display cabinet fish and meat protected by a net.
   To the left (*Sbo*) of *Antonis* is a competitor which, in the evening, appears to serve a rehash of the lunchtime dishes...

There is a pizzeria, the *Canta Napoli*, where a large, 'two people' pizza costs between 650-750drs, on the left-hand (*Sbo*), Esplanade side of the Main Square.
   Alongside the Bus office (*Tmr* 13B3), in one single storey building is a kafeneion and a fast food snackbar. The Baker (*Tmr* 14B3), alongside the OTE/Post Office, sells pies but the shop tends to be absolutely chaotic with locals fighting for the bread.

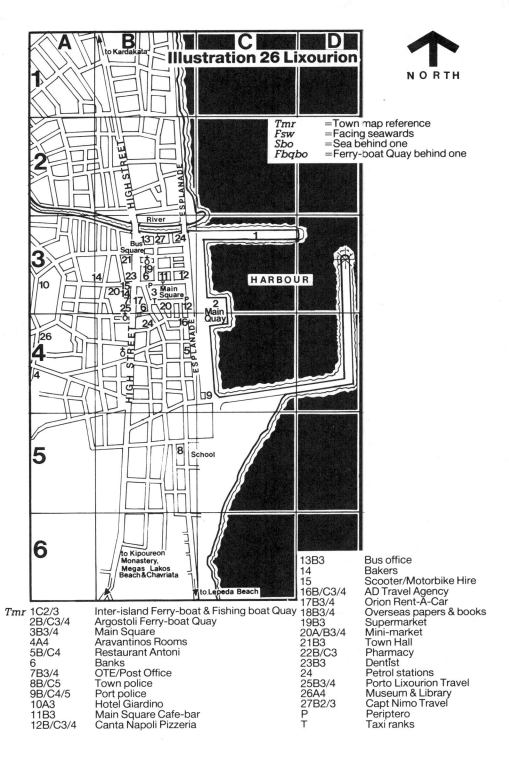

Illustration 26 Lixourion

NORTH

| | |
|---|---|
| *Tmr* | =Town map reference |
| *Fsw* | =Facing seawards |
| *Sbo* | =Sea behind one |
| *Fbqbo* | =Ferry-boat Quay behind one |

HARBOUR

Main Quay

Main Square

Bus Square

River

HIGH STREET

ESPLANADE

School

to Kardakata

to Kipoureon Monastery, Megas Lakos Beach & Chavriata

to Lepeda Beach

| *Tmr* | 1C2/3 | Inter-island Ferry-boat & Fishing boat Quay |
| | 2B/C3/4 | Argostoli Ferry-boat Quay |
| | 3B3/4 | Main Square |
| | 4A4 | Aravantinos Rooms |
| | 5B/C4 | Restaurant Antoni |
| | 6 | Banks |
| | 7B3/4 | OTE/Post Office |
| | 8B/C5 | Town police |
| | 9B/C4/5 | Port police |
| | 10A3 | Hotel Giardino |
| | 11B3 | Main Square Cafe-bar |
| | 12B/C3/4 | Canta Napoli Pizzeria |
| | 13B3 | Bus office |
| | 14 | Bakers |
| | 15 | Scooter/Motorbike Hire |
| | 16B/C3/4 | AD Travel Agency |
| | 17B3/4 | Orion Rent-A-Car |
| | 18B3/4 | Overseas papers & books |
| | 19B3 | Supermarket |
| | 20A/B3/4 | Mini-market |
| | 21B3 | Town Hall |
| | 22B/C3 | Pharmacy |
| | 23B3 | Dentist |
| | 24 | Petrol stations |
| | 25B3/4 | Porto Lixourion Travel |
| | 26A4 | Museum & Library |
| | 27B2/3 | Capt Nimo Travel |
| | P | Periptero |
| | T | Taxi ranks |

# THE A TO Z OF USEFUL INFORMATION

**BANKS** One (*Tmr* 6B3) borders the north side of the Main Square and the **National Bank** (*Tmr* 6B3/4) is to the south of the Main Square.

**BEACHES** None in the town itself but all is not lost. The coast road to the south of Lixourion Town passes *Taverna Apolafsis Rooms*, (See **The Accommodation**, beyond which the last section of the 2km road is rather similar to a country lane, prior to a very steep, ramp-like descent to:-

**Lepada Beach** An excellent, clean, broad sweep of orange coloured sand. To the left (*Fsw*), bounded by an outcrop of rock, is a tiny lagoon in which small children can safely paddle. The only hint of intrusive tourist commerce is a small beach bar, towards the far end of the beach. For other (magnificent) beaches See **Excursions to Lixourion Town Surrounds**.

Between Lixourion Town and Lepada Beach is a sign **Michalitsa**, but this track requires donkeys or a moon buggy.

**BICYCLE, SCOOTER & CAR HIRE** There are a number of scooter and motorbike hire firms including **Pelatos** (*Tmr* 15B3) on the corner of the High St and Main Sq crossroads 'We rent cars, motorcycles, sailing boats, colour TV, windsurfing'; another south of the National Bank (*Tmr* 6B3/4) as well as a tiny shop ('Info' and selling drink), which operates **Pedikis Rent Motor Cycles**, next door to AD Travel Agency (*Tmr* 16B/C3/4) edging the Esplanade. Incidentally, scooter hire is inexpensive with an average daily rate of 1100drs.

The town's, if not the island's, best car hire firm is:-

**Orion Rent A Car** (*Tmr* 17B3/4) 11 P. Basia St                                  Tel 91476
*Directions*: South of the High St 'crossroads', and on the left (*Crossroads behind one*).
   The office opens daily between 0800-1330hrs & 1730-2130hrs. John Zervos, the owner, is charming, urbane and most helpful. He was a merchant ship captain and speaks excellent English. His prices are (possibly) the lowest on the island, as is the deposit he requires. Rates for a Suzuki start off at 8500drs for a three day hire and he accepts payment by credit card. As I have pointed out it is worth travelling from Argostoli Town to hire a car here and lest readers should think we are related... we aren't, and I am not on the payroll.

**BOOKSELLERS** (*Tmr* 18B3/4) This Main Square edging business stocks a good range of English newspapers.

**BREAD SHOPS** The busiest Baker (*Tmr* 14B3) is situated on the south, right-hand (*Crossroads behind one*) side of the High St. It doubles up as a zacharoplasteion selling pies and milk. Customers may find it rather unruly whilst the locals scrap for the bread. There is another Baker (*Tmr* 14A/B3) in a side-street to the west of the High St crossroads.

**BUSES** The Bus office (*Tmr* 13B3) is on the north, right-hand (*Crossroads behind one*) side of the High St, close by the river-bed. The buses turn round where the High St widens out, in front of the adjacent church.

**Bus timetable** (Mid-season)
**Lixourion Town to Athens***
Daily          0730hrs
*Return journey*
Daily          0830hrs
NB See Bus timetable, Buses, A To Z, Argostoli town
One-way fare 2630drs (plus ferry fares), duration 8hrs
*100 Kifissou St, Tel 5129498

**COMMERCIAL SHOPPING AREA** Most of the shops are in the streets off, behind and around the Main Square (*Tmr* 3B3/4) and the High St crossroads. A fruit & vegetable street market operates in the small square and streets behind the 'Bus Sq' church.
   Particular businesses include a Supermarket (*Tmr* 19B3), in a side-street alongside the 'Bus Sq' church, just down from which is a Fish shop, and a Mini-market (*Tmr* 20A/B3/4).

**FERRY-BOATS** Apart from the Argostoli Town 'shuttle' service arriving and departing from a Quay (*Tmr* 2B/C3/4) within the Harbour wall, there is a larger, inter-island ferry-boat that docks (*Tmr* 1C2/3). I think this is the mainland Killini to Argostoli boat, but on what basis I do not know... I'm sorry I cannot be more exact (slapped hand Geoffrey).
   For details of the Argostoli connection See **Ferry-boat timetables, A To Z, Argostoli Town**.

Timetables and fare structures are stuck up on the Esplanade, in the area of the Main Quay. Tickets for the craft are purchased on the boat.

**MEDICAL CARE**
**Chemists & Pharmacies** A Pharmacy (*Tmr* 22B/C3) is located on the (north) corner of the Main Sq and Esplanade.
**Dentist** (*Tmr* 23B3) Above a High St gift shop.
**Hospital** To the north of the river-bed.

**OTE (& Post Office)** (*Tmr* 7B3/4) North and on the right (*Crossroads behind one*) of the High St. The OTE is open weekdays & Saturday between 0730-2200hrs.

**PETROL** Two petrol stations (*Tmr* 24B/C2/3 & 24B3/4) in the town as well as some on the northern approaches.

**PLACES OF INTEREST**
**Museum** (*Tmr* 26A4) The museum is combined with the public library in a pleasant, old building enclosed by a high wall. The museum opens weekdays between 0800-1330hrs, as well as between 1730-1930hrs on Mon, Tues & Thurs, Sat between 0930-1230hrs and is closed Sundays.

Incidentally, those who wander up to this area will be able to observe a number of old-fashioned, single storey, wooden houses still standing, usually in small terraces edging the side-streets.

**POLICE**
**Port** (*Tmr* 9B/C4/5) At the south end of the Harbour Quay.
**Town** (*Tmr* 8B/C5) In the southern outskirts of the town, on the right-hand side of the Lepeda Beach road.
**POST OFFICE** *See* **OTE, A To Z.**

**TAXIS** (*Tmr* T) Rank on the Main Square (*Tmr* 3B3/4) as well as lurking in the area of the 'Bus Sq' and the Ferry-boat Quays.

**TELEPHONE NUMBERS & ADDRESSES**

| | |
|---|---|
| Hospital | Tel 91233 |
| Police (*Tmr* 8B/C5) | Tel 91207 |
| Taxi rank (*Tmr* T) | Tel 91524 |

**TRAVEL AGENTS & TOUR OFFICES** There are quite a few, including:-
**Porto Lixourion Travel & Tourist Agency** (*Tmr* 25B3/4).
*Directions*: South and on the right-hand (*Crossroads behind one*) side of the High St, beyond the OTE/Post Office.

Agents for Olympic Airways as well as Seven Islands Shipping, owners of the **CF Ionis & Ionian Glory**, the ferry-boats which scurry up and down the length of the Ionian islands.

**AD Travel Agency** (*Tmr* 16B/C3/4)
*Directions*: Bordering the Esplanade, almost opposite the Argostoli Ferry-boat Quay.

Sells ferry-boat tickets, transacts money exchange, lets rooms and accommodation, as well as organising cruises.

Another agency is **Captain Nimo Tourism & Travel Bureau** (*Tmr* 27B2/3) located in a back street behind the Bus office.

**WATER** There is a pump fed, drinking water fountain on the Main Sq side of the High St crossroads.

## EXCURSIONS TO LIXOURION TOWN SURROUNDS
**Excursion to Kipoureon Monastery via Soularia, Megas Lakos Beach, Kounopetra, Chavriata & Chavdata (circa 32km)**The main road south of Lixourion passes a turning to the left to:-

**SOULARIA (2¼km from Lixourion Town)** In this village are community signs to Mega Lakos and Ag Georgios. Immediately beyond Soularia the unmade track, across 'quarried lunar landscape', forks at a handwritten sign. To the left advances on another very up and down, tank training panorama to **Ag Georgios Headland (5¼km from Lixourion Town)**.

Back at the fork, the right-hand track progresses past a kafeneion and a new chalet house development edging :-

**Megas Lakos Beach (5km from Lixourion Town)** A long, beautiful stretch of shadeless, reddy orange sand edged by a low, 3m high cliff of clay. This underlying clay has a consistency of soft butter.

Offshore is the islet of Vardiani which appears closer than pinpointed on the maps. It is a pity that the authorities have allowed the development, however small, on this once deserted stretch of coastline.

Returning to the main road, the next village is:-

**MANTZAVINATA (3½km from Lixourion Town)** The inhabitants brew a muscatel style wine. Towards the far end of the village is choice of routes. The left-hand, recently surfaced road sallies forth across a lunar landscape, which appears to have been extensively quarried (but hasn't been), towards:-

**KOUNOPETRA** This is more an area than even a hamlet. Close to Cape Akrotiri, on the left, is the *Hotel Ionian Sea* (Class B, tel 92280) where single rooms start off at 3000drs & doubles 3500drs, rising to 5000drs & 6000drs (1st July-31st Aug). The high prices certainly aren't due to it being a pretty setting.

Beyond the hotel, and to the left (*Fsw*), is a bay bordered by the 'white cliffs of Dover' and at the foot of which is another orangey red beach. But this bay, which is enclosed to the right by the Cape, is not ideal for bathing. In the crook of the headland is a natural harbour and a gapped reef of rocks runs away round the bay. Close by the hotel, the shore is rather rubbish strewn.

More promising is the track to the right, to the other, west side of Cape Akrotiri, signed to 'Remettzo Taverna Ouzerie & Akrotiri Beach'.

The square, two storey building of the taverna starkly stands on the high, semi-circular rim of a lovely, red coloured, sandy beach, edging a super, if shadeless, cove encircled by rocks and backed by flat featureless countryside. There are a few pebbles and some kelp bespattering the, otherwise perfectly textured beach. The cove is part of a larger bay and the track continues on to some changing huts set in a cliff face.

Returning to Mantzavinata and following the right-hand road progresses to:-

**CHAVRIATA (7km from Lixourion Town)** This village possesses a 'chatty', wedding cake of a church. From hereon the road's surface becomes indeterminate, going unmetalled here and there and or mauled by some primeval, tarmacadam eating rodent.

**CHAVDATA (9km from Lixourion Town)** At or about this settlement, the landscape loses its quarried appearance. Also, despite most maps detailing the matter differently, the unmade turning off for the monastery is in the village.

The steeply climbing, sometimes badly surfaced route passes a man-made quarry, complete with the usual complement of dead civil engineering vehicles spaced out around the workings. The scenery takes on a Dartmoor appearance and the views are magnificent, more especially where the road winds round to reveal a staggering prospect out along the west coast of Lixourion Peninsula.

The track gently descends to the unusually low sited:-

**Kipoureon Monastery (13km from Lixourion Town)** Constructed in 1744 and nicely up together, having been rebuilt in 1976. The entrance is beneath a campanile. Inside the exterior walls is a rather garishly, yellow and red painted chapel. I don't really think the journey to this monastery is really worth the effort.

A track continues northwards to another, ruined monastery, **Ag Paraskevis Tafion**.

Between the villages of Chavriata and Chavdata a track appears to descend to a small, sandy cove close by the lighthouse headland of Cape Gerogompos. In actuality, the 'beach' is nothing more than a concrete vehicle turn round point edging a pebbly cove.

A crude wooden ladder leads over the right-hand, boulderous rocks to yet another rocky little bay. Don't bother.

**Excursion to Ag Spiridon (16km)** To the left of the Lixourion to Kardakata road, a signpost (at circa 8km) indicates Athera. This metalled road crosses once fire ravaged, moorland hillsides to:-

**ATHERA (13km from Lixourion Town)** The road surface breaks down at the entrance to the rather grey, hill village, at the outskirts of which is a large drinking water well. There is a pretty yellow church, but little else apart from a sign indicating the artfully concealed *Restaurant To Fanari*. Well I could not locate it.

To proceed, carry straight on through Athera, ignorning the left and right-hand turnings beyond the well. The surfaced, pretty route, subject to potholes and unexpected unsurfaced sections, narrows and steeply winds down through spaced out olive trees towards an attractive, 'U' shaped bay backed by a flat, agricultural plain boxed in by hillsides. Offshore is a granite islet in the mouth of the bay of:-

**Ag Spiridon Beach (16km from Lixourion Town)** Close to the coast is a doo-hickey bar and a number of almost paranoiac 'Do Not Enter' signs. Beyond them the road spills on to a small turn round area at the left (*Fsw*) side of a long sweep of grey sand beach. Sadly, this shore is badly, very badly polluted with kelp and sea-blown rubbish and the rubbish bins are full to overflowing. On the edge of the turn round is a squat changing hut, resembling a wayside karzy. On the left-hand slopes of the bay are a number of buildings coated with a bright, but peeling blue paint. The owner is responsible for the 'shrieking' notices forbidding entrance, probably having experienced trespass by the great unwashed, at some time in the past. Ag Spiridon could be so attractive.

## ROUTE THREE
**To Sami Port (25km)**(*See* **Route One**) The journey between Argostoli Town and Sami is truly dramatic (as are most journeys on this mountainous island), the route climbing the central mountain range through the Pass of Agrapidies. The road surface is, on the whole, good but here and there rock-falls create potholes which can unseat the unwary.

**SAMI: main port (25km from Argostoli Town)** (Illustration 27) Tel Prefix 0674. Sami is set in a lovely bay, with the ferry-boat finger pier jutting into the deep blue sea, with the dark, mountainous bulk of Ithaca island lowering in the distance. The oversized development is spread out as if space didn't matter, resulting in a rather aimless feel to the place. Travellers landing at Sami might experience a similar atmosphere to that evoked in one of those endless Mexican towns, as portrayed in spaghetti westerns – anticipation. Here nothing appears to happen, ever, if the comings and goings of the ferry-boats are discounted. Maybe the bland, aimless appearance and ambience is due to the fact that Sami is amongst these Ionian towns that had to be rebuilt (with British help) after the devastating 1953 earthquake.

The general aspect of the Esplanade is greatly enhanced by the cafe-bars and tavernas now having awning covered terraces bordering the quay wall.

**ARRIVAL BY BUS** Comments as for Poros, but Sami connects to Athens via the mainland port of Patras.

**ARRIVAL BY FERRY** The ferry-boats dock at the far north end of the Esplanade (*Tmr* 1C1/2). Room owners meet disembarking passengers.

## THE ACCOMMODATION & EATING OUT
### The Accommodation
**The Hotel Melissani** (*Tmr* 2D2) (Class D)            Tel 22464
*Directions*: Almost due east from the Ferry-boat Quay and ascend the street.

A modern, two storey building. All rooms have en suite bathrooms with a single priced at 1700drs & a double at 2100drs, increasing to 2500drs & 3150drs (21st June-5th Sept).

Apart from **Rooms** (*Tmr* 15C/D2) above the smart *Riviera Pizzeria Cafeteria*, which borders the Esplanade, there are a couple of houses with accommodation (*Tmr* 6D2/3 & 6D3) in the lane two back and paralleling the waterfront.

**The Hotel Kyma** (*Tmr* 3C3/4) (Class D) Plateia Kyprou                    Tel 22064
*Directions*: Overlooking the port's Main Square.

An older hotel with single rooms, sharing the bathroom, costing 1180drs, double rooms sharing 1850drs & with an en suite bathroom 2450drs, increasing, respectively, to 1450drs & 2100/3100drs (1st July-31st Aug).

**Hotel Ionian** (*Tmr* 5A/B5/6) 5 Horofilakis                    Tel 22035
*Directions*:From the Main Square proceed along the 'Argostoli' road, leaving the Post Office (*Tmr* 14B/C4/5) on the right and the OTE (*Tmr* 10B/C5) on the left. Beyond the Cathedral, turn right down a short street and at the bottom turn left. The hotel is on the right.

A modern building in a dusty back street. Single rooms share the bathrooms at a cost of 1200drs, whilst a double room sharing costs 1700drs & en suite 2300drs, increasing, respectively, to 1500drs & 2500/3100drs (1st July-31st Aug).

Alongside the Argostoli road is the modern, swanky, if faceless *Hotel Remezzo* (*Tmr* 16B6). There is also accommodation close by both the old and new Argostoli road entrances to *Caravomilos Beach Camping*, as well as **Rooms** on the side of the quay wall path in the direction of the campsite. The 'old' entrance accommodation is *Rooms For Hire* (Tel 22076) in a fairly modern building. For other **Rooms** enquire at the *Waterfront Cafe-bar* (*Tmr* 4C/D2/3).

## Camping
**Caravolmilos Beach Camping** Tel 22480
*Directions*: Some 900m south-west around the bay and accessed along either the Argostoli road or the quay wall path.

A pleasant campsite, formally laid out, well sheltered by reasonably mature trees. Facilities include a self-service restaurant/cafeteria and a mini-market. The site is open between April-Oct and the office daily between 0800-1100hrs & 1700-2200hrs. Charges are as follows:- per person 350drs, children 180drs, a tent 280drs, large 350drs, tent hire 540drs, a car 180drs, a trailer 425drs and a camper-van 800drs. It is of note that the restaurant offerings are worth considering, even if not staying on the site. Incidentally, this is often the case.

## The Eating Out
**The 'Waterfront' Cafe-bar** (*Tmr* 4C/D2/3)
*Directions*: Bordering the Esplanade.

Caters for nearly everyone's requirements. Perhaps one of the most important considerations is that it is within 'eyeball' distance of both the bus marshalling point and the Ferry-boat Quay. The cafe is a source of widely differing opinions!

Other Esplanade establishments include a pair of side-by-side cafe-bars (*Tmr* 17C/D2), one of which serves 'Fast Souvlaki'; a Restaurant (*Tmr* 18C3) and *Captain Jimmy's Snackbar* (*Tmr* 19B/C3/4). Edging the Main Sq is an old-fashioned Kafeneion (*Tmr* 20B/C3/4).

## THE A TO Z OF USEFUL INFORMATION
**BANKS** A Bank (*Tmr* 21B4) edges the street which continues to 'shadow' the waterfront, south-west of the Main Sq.

**BEACHES** The main beach is to the left (*Fsw*) of the port. Access is along a formal waterfront quay path as well as a street which turns sharply away from the sea-shore, alongside a large water header tank. Beneath this are some shower heads, which do not work, and alongside are a row of changing huts. There is another pier and small, local fishing boat harbour. Unfortunately the beach is pebble and fine shingle with a fairly thick band of kelp and some backshore rubbish. The backshore is shaded by a row of pleasantly mature gum trees. There is a 50m smidgin of pebbly shore with a sandy sea-bed to the right (*Fsw*) of the Ferry-boat Quay (*Tmr* 1C1/2).

**BICYCLE, SCOOTER & CAR HIRE** An outfit (*Tmr* 22C3) in the Esplanade 'Back Lane' advertises 'We Rent Vespa Scooters, Motorbikes, Boats & Cars'.

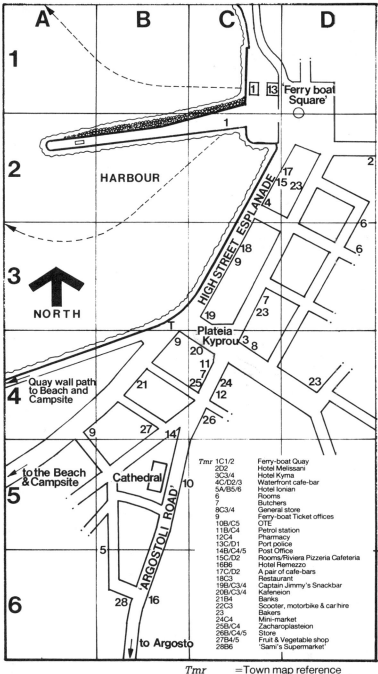

| Tmr | | |
|---|---|---|
| 1 | C1/2 | Ferry-boat Quay |
| 2 | D2 | Hotel Melissani |
| 3 | C3/4 | Hotel Kyma |
| 4 | C/D2/3 | Waterfront cafe-bar |
| 5 | A/B5/6 | Hotel Ionian |
| 6 | | Rooms |
| 7 | | Butchers |
| 8 | C3/4 | General store |
| 9 | | Ferry-boat Ticket offices |
| 10 | B/C5 | OTE |
| 11 | B/C4 | Petrol station |
| 12 | C4 | Pharmacy |
| 13 | C/D1 | Port police |
| 14 | B/C4/5 | Post Office |
| 15 | C/D2 | Rooms/Riviera Pizzeria Cafeteria |
| 16 | B6 | Hotel Remezzo |
| 17 | C/D2 | A pair of cafe-bars |
| 18 | C3 | Restaurant |
| 19 | B/C3/4 | Captain Jimmy's Snackbar |
| 20 | B/C3/4 | Kafeneion |
| 21 | B4 | Banks |
| 22 | C3 | Scooter, motorbike & car hire |
| 23 | | Bakers |
| 24 | C4 | Mini-market |
| 25 | B/C4 | Zacharoplasteion |
| 26 | B/C4/5 | Store |
| 27 | B4/5 | Fruit & Vegetable shop |
| 28 | B6 | 'Sami's Supermarket' |

**Illustration 27 Sami**

| | | |
|---|---|---|
| *Tmr* | = | Town map reference |
| *Fsw* | = | Facing seawards |
| *Sbo* | = | Sea behind one |
| *Fbqbo* | = | Ferry-boat Quay behind one |

**BREAD SHOPS** There are two bakers, one (*Tmr* 23D2) in the area of the Ferry-boat Quay and the other (*Tmr* 23D4) east of the Main Sq.

**BUSES** The buses 'terminus' on the Esplanade, between the *Waterfront Cafe-bar* (*Tmr* 4C/D2/3) and a Restaurant (*Tmr* 18C3). For schedule details *See* **Bus timetables, Buses, A To Z, Argostoli Town**.
   Some journeys are of a most interesting nature. The initial foray being in the manner of a false start, meandering from Sami into the foothills and back to Sami again, only to commence the 'proper' journey, in earnest, an hour later.

**COMMERCIAL SHOPPING AREA** None but there are a reasonable selection of shops including Butchers (*Tmr* 7C3 & 7B/C4); a General store (*Tmr* 8C3/4), that sells fruit and vegetables; a Mini-market (*Tmr* 24C4); a Zacharoplasteion (*Tmr* 25B/C4); a Store (*Tmr* 26B/C4/5); a Fruit & Vegetable shop (*Tmr* 27B4/5) and Sami's Supermarket (*Tmr* 28B6). This latter really is a 'proper' supermarket, which also sells fruit and vegetables and is open daily between 0730-1330hrs & 1615-2115hrs, Wed 0730-1400hrs and closed on Sundays.

**FERRY-BOATS** The craft berth at the Ferry-boat Quay (*Tmr* 1C1/2). Apart from the scheduled inter-island ferries, there is a very useful service connecting Sami to Fiscardon and Vassiliki(Lefkas).

**Ferry-boat timetable** (Mid-season)

| Day | Departure time | Ferry-boat | Ports/Islands of Call |
|---|---|---|---|
| Daily | 0130hrs | Ionis/Ionian Glory | Vathis(Ithaca),Gaios(Paxos), Igoumenitsa(M),Corfu. |
| | 0830hrs | Aphrodite | Fiscardon(Cephalonia),Vassiliki(Lefkas). |
| | 0900hrs | | Patras(M). |
| | 1230hrs | Ionia/Ionian Glory | Patras(M). |
| | 1700hrs | Kefalinia | vathi(Ithaca). |
| | 1800hrs | | Vathi(Ithaca). |

One-way fare: Sami to Vathi 365drs; duration 1hr.

**FERRY-BOAT TICKET OFFICES** There are at least three offices (*Tmr* 9C3, 9B/C3/4 & 9A/B4/5) spaced out along the Esplanade.

**MEDICAL CARE**
**Chemists & Pharmacies** (*Tmr* 12C4) On the left of the Argostoli road, beyond the Main Square.

**OTE** (*Tmr* 10B/C5) Now in a very smart building, across the Argostoli road from the Cathedral. Open weekdays between 0730-2200hrs.

**PETROL** Apart from petrol filling stations along the Argostoli road, there is one on the right (*Tmr* 11B/C4) (*Sbo*), close to the Main Square.

**PLACES OF INTEREST** Not a lot! Well, not quite...
   Behind the town are the remains of a Roman building and its mosaic.
   The surrounding hills have sections of ancient walls that were once part of the defences of a much older city (Sami), but they are best seen outlined against the skyline from approaching ferry-boats.
   Two nearby caves are worthy of a visit (*See* **Excursion to Ag Evfimia**).

**POLICE**
**Port** (*Tmr* 13C/D1) Borders the 'Ferry-boat Square'.
**Town** Close to the OTE (*Tmr* 10B/C5) on the Argostoli road, about 200m from the Main Square.

**POST OFFICE** (*Tmr* 14B/C4/5)

**TAXIS** Rank (*Tmr* T) on the Esplanade .

**TELEPHONE NUMBERS & ADDRESSES**

| | |
|---|---|
| Clinic | Tel 22040 |
| Police | Tel 22008 |

**TRAVEL AGENTS & TOUR OFFICES** *See* **Ferry-boat Ticket Offices**.

# EXCURSIONS TO SAMI PORT SURROUNDS
**Excursion To Ag Evfimia (10km)**Initially take the Argostoli road and then the Ag Evfimia turning. This road follows, at some distance, the curve of large, elongated Sami Bay, passing through:-

**KARAVOMILOS (2½km from Sami Port)** A rather straggly village increasingly picking up some of Sami's business. At the north end of the settlement a short lane to the right leads to a pool fed from the Melissani cave and lake. A taverna minds the needs of the inner man and woman.

Beyond Karavomilos, at about 3km, a turning to the left climbs the 200 or so metres to:-
**Melissani Cave & Lake** The large, dark, turquoise water-filled, stalactite dotted caves are approached via a small lake in a small boat accompanied by a guide. It is here that the sea-waters that used to power the Argostoli Sea Mills emerge after the long underground journey across the island's width. The entrance fee, including the rowing boat, costs 120drs.
  It is possible to walk along the sea's edge from Sami Port swinging inland by the aforementioned seaside pool.

The main route continues to pleasantly corniche along the coastline, passing three attractive, white pebble beaches set in olive groves, and, close to Ag Evfimia, a lovely, small, silver sand beach, edged by an almost horizontal rock strata. There is a petrol station immediately prior to:-

**AG EVFIMIA (10km from Sami Port)** A lovely fishing port, complete with a small harbour, prettily folded around the waters edge. Prior to the 1953 earthquake, Ag Evfimia was the main east coast port and the harbour is reasonably popular with yachtsmen.

**ARRIVAL BY FERRY** In recent years a permanent, year round ferry-boat link has been established between Ag Evfimia, Vathi(Ithaca) and mainland Astakos.

**Ferry-boat timetable**

| Day | Departure time | Ferry-boat | Ports/Islands of Call |
|---|---|---|---|
| Daily | 0915hrs | Thiaki | Vathi(Ithaca),Astakos(M). |

One-way fares: Ag Evfimia to Vathi ; duration 1½hrs
                            to Astakos 590drs; 3½hrs

Note, in July & August the **Cephalonia Express** comes on stream to supplement the route.
  The Ferry-boat docking point is at the far, top, left-hand (*Fsw*) horn of the short, 'U' shaped bay. Much of the development of the village flows along the wide main quay, connecting the Ferry-boat dock with the main road which borders the bottom of the bay. From the Ferry-boat pier along the Harbour quay wall to the main road advances past a ferry-boat ticket office, which represents the **Thiaki** and also hires scooters; *Rooms To Let* at No 7, a low house with a bougainvillea covered front wall fence; a fast food snackbar; a kafeneion, where a beer and lemonade costs 140drs, and with a ladies hairdresser hung on the side; a baker; an old-fashioned Post Office; a general store with a metered telephone; a periptero and a local kafeneion).

At the junction with the main road, to the right (*Sbo*) is towards Assos and Fiscardon, straight ahead is a local street and left leads to Sami Port.
  The *Hotel Logara* (Class C, tel 61202), located on the Assos road, is more furnished apartments, with suites costing 2905drs & 3950drs, increasing to 3430drs & 5420drs (1st July-31st Aug).
  Various side-streets branch off the 'High St' Sami road. On the corner of the first side-street is a butcher and down which is a photo & gift shop and the port authority.
  Returning to the 'High St', there is the *Hotel Pilaros* (Class C, tel 61210). At this inn a single room, with en suite bathroom, costs 1500drs, a double room sharing 2000drs & a double en suite 2300drs, increasing, respectively, to 2100drs & 2600/2950drs. It is

rumoured that non-residents can make use of the hotel's showers. Opposite the hotel, across the 'High St' edging the bay, is a fairly large quay probably used as an alternative ferry-boat berthing point in particular weather conditions. The hotel is followed by a gift shop and three more side-streets. Along the last, an unmetalled track, is signed 'To Mantri... fresh meats, local cheese, frozen foods, yoghurts, all milks (*sic*), eggs 25m'.

Quite a lot of the old, pre-earthquake village lurks on the bay's surrounds.

From Ag Evfimia the road progresses over a narrow neck of the island to Divarata (*See* **Route Four**). There is a petrol filling station at **Potamianata**.

**Excursion to Spileon Drogarati (4km)** Take the Argostoli road. The cave is signposted off to the right, some ½km distant.

**Spileon Drogarati** A very large cave hung with stalactites. Admission during daylight hours, costs 70drs.

# ROUTE FOUR
**To Fiscardon via Divarata & Assos (50km)**From Argostoli Town head south along the Esplanade and across the causeway, from whence the road starts to climb. The road to Sami Port bears off to the right, whilst the Fiscardon road swings northwards, hugging the mountainside. At each bend, the views of the Gulf of Argostoli and Livadi Bay become more and more dramatic – truly a magnificent drive.

The road, for the most part, is excellent – wide and well metalled. Here and there, on some of the bends, small rock-falls cause the occasional obstruction and the surface has been broken up by the passage of heavy traffic over the fallen stones. The route passes through the pretty village of **Farsa** (11km from Argostoli Town) and **Kontogrourata** (14km from Argostoli Town), before reaching:-

**KARDAKATA (16km from Argostoli Town)** To the left is the road round and down the peninsula to Lixourion Town, to the north is a road through **Nifi**, indicated on the maps as being the main route but actually unsurfaced. On the other hand, the Agkonas road, despite being drawn in as a minor road, is surfaced.

Those selecting the **Agkonas** choice can make the diversion down the unmade track to:-
**AG KYRIAKIS (22km from Argostoli Town)** A doo-hickey, 'shacky', homely little place, with a track spreading along the dirty, in places, boulderous, seashore to the right. There is a stretch of fine shingly sand and the settlement spreads along to the left (*Fsw*). Almost immediately to the left is a taverna with accommodation. The taverna garden appears to double up as an informal campsite. Further along is the *Trattoria Dipeskas* (the what..?), beyond which is the harbour encircled by a rocky mole.

A steep, surfaced, rather gnawed and narrow lane climbs the side of the mountain, past *Homes & Rooms To Let, 500m*, to:-
**ZOLA (23km from Argostoli Town)** At the junction with the main Zola road is the nicely signed *Alexander Cafe.*

From Zola, instead of retreating over the approach route, it is possible to select the main road out of the village. After 3km this makes a junction with the Kardakata/Lixourion highway, from whence it is but 2km back to the main route.

Returning to the main route, the Kardakata/Agkonas/Divarata road is a mountainside hugger. Where bridges and viaducts have been utilised to span difficult sections, the locals have used the underside as the roof of various shacks and shelters. There is a dramatic, exposed white cliff-face and glimpses of Mirtos Beach, shortly after which the route swings inland and joins the Sami Port to Fiscardon road at Siniori (29km from Argostoli Town). Both here and at the pretty, neighbouring village of **Divarata**, there are a taverna or two, some shops and *Rooms*. Although disappointment may well accompany a stay on Cephalonia, travellers should cross the north-south divide. Once across this imaginary line, drawn between Divarata and Ag Evfimia, then a completely different island is revealed.

Beyond Divarata the route rejoins the coast to reveal one of the most beautiful views in the Ionian islands:-

**Mirtos Bay & Beach (34km from Argostoli Town)** This is a wide, dazzling white crescent of shingle, flanked by towering cliffs and a sea of the deepest blue, patchworked with aquamarine – breathtaking and idyllic. Until recently, the bay was heavily polluted but not any more. The rather hair-raising descent, from opposite the signpost indicating **Karousata**, is a steep, sharply hairpinned, loose surfaced track (1 in 3 in places). The drive is amply rewarding since, if anything, the rugged scenery is even more dramatic when viewed from the shore. The sea's edge is fine shingle, there is some kelp and the sea-bed shelves quickly into deep murky waters. One drawback is the lack of shade, despite which a few erect tents and one or two camper-vans make the difficult drive down.

Returning to the main route, the mountain scenery becomes even more sensational. The rock wall on the right seems awfully close, as does the enormous drop on the left. The sight of goats perched on rocky cliff-niches at eye-level is a little disconcerting, at first, especially when they suddenly leap off, seemingly into the wild blue yonder, only to land and nimbly perch on impossible pinnacles of rock.

**ASSOS (38km from Argostoli Town)** Tel prefix 0674. Viewed from high above the panorama is dramatically beautiful. The tear droplet of land, a Venetian fortressed peninsula, appears to float on the blue shimmering Ionian sea.

Buses do not descend to the hamlet but stop alongside a footpath that tumbles down from the main road. Either side of the narrow neck of land are anchorages and tiny white shingle beaches.

The winding vehicle thoroughfare descends along the south side of the peninsula, is about 3km long and the surface becomes rather indeterminate close to the upper buildings of the settlement. To the right is signposted the first accommodation, the *Pension Gerania* along a pebbly track. Seemingly only a few metres further on down the road is the *Kavos Snackbar Rooms* (Tel 51376). This modern, very smart accommodation is owned by Vasilis and Vaso Skiadaresis. The location is stunning, being perched on the edge of the peninsula, looking out along the cliffs to the south. An en suite double room starts off at 3000drs. On the other side of the street, on the right, is more private accommodation.

Where the road bottoms out, about 100m further down and still on the south side of the neck of the peninsula, there is an inordinately large, if 'dead' restaurant/rooms building on the left. There is even formal, covered car parking. Most strange.

The road now swings round into the heart of the village, towards the port, past a very small, rubbish and kelp covered cove. The main beach is large pebble with some fine shingle at the sea's edge but once again is polluted with rubbish and kelp. The village centre is unexpectedly dominated by a long, flower and shrub planted rectangular square, shaded by lovely trees, some flowering. This is edged on three sides by a number of old, sad, once grand but earthquake ruined houses. The tottering facades of the devastated mansions, some with the upper storey balconies, front doors and window shutters still miraculously in position, irresistibly remind one of a film set. A few gun barrels are neatly positioned pointing out over the harbour bay. In amongst these are sprinkled the (one and only) taverna, a small general store and the *Snackbar Assos*, beyond which is the harbour quay. At this far end of the plateia, a side street climbs back up the peninsula, leaving a church on the right. After about 75m there is **Rooms** on the left (*Harbour behind one*) as well as more derelict, once large dwellings. Further on the street becomes unmetalled, with olive groves to the right and yet more derelict houses to the left. A tablet on the edge of the square commemorates the generosity of Paris City in donating money to help reconstruct Assos after the devastation of the 1953 earthquake.

A double room in the recommended *Snackbar Assos* costs 3000drs. They serve breakfast and snacks during the day, and don't close the bar until the last local 'falls' over. The single storey taverna opens at 2000hrs, serving simple but good food at an average cost, for two, of between 1600-2000drs.

For the energetic there are splendid walks up and around the large tree clad, Venetian fort and prison topped headland.

Rosemary summed up the place rather nicely as 'crumbly, with lots of shrubs, flowers and trees'.

Regretfully returning to the main route, the road passes through a number of wayside hill villages including:-

**MAGGANOS (47km from Argostoli Town)** Here is fuel, a store (with bus seats on the verandah) and a kafeneion/taverna, where a bottle of beer cost 75drs and a lemonade 50drs (*See* my bleating vis-a-vis Fiscardon prices). Across the 'High St' from the kafeneion, alongside the store, is a turning variously signposted Ventourata (2km), Katsarata (3km), Matsoukata (2km) and Seletata (3km). These are simply small hamlets on an anticlockwise, circular, part unmade track round to Fiscardon (*See* **The Accommodation, Fiscardon**).

Beyond Magganos, to the left are the extensive remains of an abandoned settlement (a deserted medieval village?). **Antipata (Erisou)** has a rather unusual Russian style church. The wooded hillsides beyond are particularly lovely with a very variegated mix of trees. The outset of the chalky track down to Emblisi Beach (*See* **Beaches, A To Z, Fiscardon**) is distinguished by the presence of a panoramic taverna, from whence the road descends quite steeply to:-

**FISCARDON (50km from Argostoli Town)** (Illustration 28) Tel prefix 0674. This Cornish 'look alike' is a captivating, busy, small boat fishing village, set at the end of a very pretty, angled inlet. The arm of the sea ends in a bay, around the south side of which the houses of the village are laid out, in a haphazard fashion. The devastating earthquake of 1953 did not damage Fiscardon, leaving the village in its original, delightful form, some say not unlike St Tropez of forty years ago. The port is extensively used by flotilla yachts and at the height of season becomes rather crowded on the days they put into harbour. Moreover, as elsewhere throughout the islands, the presence of organised fleets of yachties pushes up the prices of food and drink.

Unfortunately, the village's infrastructure is experiencing ever increasing pressure, now not only from the various scheduled ferry-boats but also tour coaches. The human and vehicular traffic has resulted in far-reaching plans to bypass Fiscardon (sounds familiar doesn't it). These involve swinging one road round the back of the settlement and another on to the castle headland, as well as pushing the Ferry-boat Quay (*Tmr* 21B1/2) round the bay towards the Music Bar Dionyssis (*Tmr* 22D1). The proposals are approved but await finance...

It is pleasing to note that some of the buildings are being restored. A fine example is No 83 (*Tmr* C5/6), at the foot of the steps up to the church. Not only is this a settlement of beauty but of characters. Two of the most helpful village men you could wish and probably will meet are wildly disparate personalities. Gerry, who owns the small, whitewashed village general store (*Tmr* 1B4/5), is a rather introverted, shy man but very patient and solicitous, despite possessing little English. On the other hand, Tassou, mine host at the *Captains Cabin*, is a shrewd extrovert. He not only speaks excellent English but used to take the *Sunday Times* to keep abreast of world events. One other personality that should not be ignored is Irena's daughter-in-law, Vlacha (I hope I have it correct). In her mid-thirties she is a smiley, pleasant, ample lass usually dressed in black, who now runs *Kafeneion Irena* (*Tmr* 3C4/5).

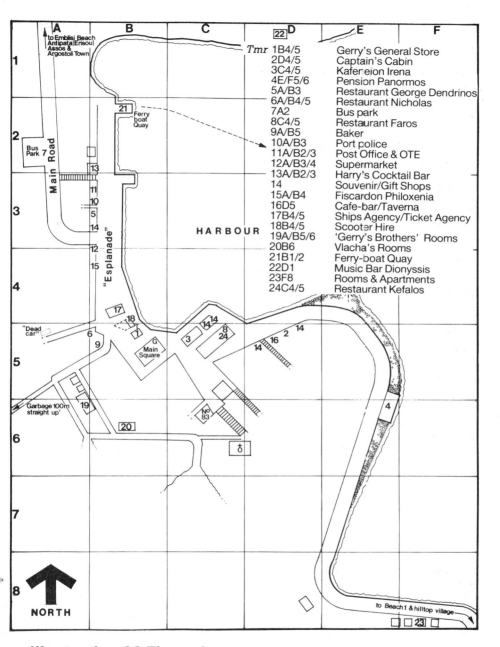

| | | |
|---|---|---|
| Tmr | 1B4/5 | Gerry's General Store |
| | 2D4/5 | Captain's Cabin |
| | 3C4/5 | Kafereion Irena |
| | 4E/F5/6 | Pension Panormos |
| | 5A/B3 | Restaurant George Dendrinos |
| | 6A/B4/5 | Restaurant Nicholas |
| | 7A2 | Bus park |
| | 8C4/5 | Restaurant Faros |
| | 9A/B5 | Baker |
| | 10A/B3 | Port police |
| | 11A/B2/3 | Post Office & OTE |
| | 12A/B3/4 | Supermarket |
| | 13A/B2/3 | Harry's Cocktail Bar |
| | 14 | Souvenir/Gift Shops |
| | 15A/B4 | Fiscardon Philoxenia |
| | 16D5 | Cafe-bar/Taverna |
| | 17B4/5 | Ships Agency/Ticket Agency |
| | 18B4/5 | Scooter Hire |
| | 19A/B5/6 | 'Gerry's Brothers' Rooms |
| | 20B6 | Vlacha's Rooms |
| | 21B1/2 | Ferry-boat Quay |
| | 22D1 | Music Bar Dionyssis |
| | 23F8 | Rooms & Apartments |
| | 24C4/5 | Restaurant Kefalos |

# Illustration 28 Fiscardon

| | |
|---|---|
| *Tmr* | =Town map reference |
| *Fsw* | =Facing seawards |
| *Sbo* | =Sea behind one |
| *Fbqbo* | =Ferry-boat Quay behind one |

**ARRIVAL BY BUS** The buses park on a lay-by (*Tmr* 7A2), a short walk up the main road.

**ARRIVAL BY FERRY** Daily 'landing craft' style car ferries connect to Sami Port, Frikes(Ithaca), Nidri(Lefkas), Vassiliki(Lefkas) and Spartochori (Meganissi).

## THE ACCOMMODATION & EATING OUT

**The Accommodation** When enquiring about accommodation it is essential to ascertain how far away any offers may be. Much of that available is situated in the village of Antipata or the Old Chora hamlet of Seletata, both a couple of kilometres distant.

**'Gerry's Brothers' Rooms** (*Tmr* 19A/B5/6)
*Directions*: From Gerry's General Store (*Tmr* 1B4/5) turn up 'Bakery Lane', follow the sign 'Garbage 100m straight up' and take the first left street. The two storey and basement house on the right is the largest in the row. Apart from the 'Rent Rooms' notice, white steps lead up to the first floor of the pale green house with wooden shutters and dull terracotta tile roof.
    The 'going' rate, mid-season, is 2500drs but negotiation may help reduce the initially quoted figure. This splendid house is owned by Gerry's brother so why not enquire at his store.

Gerry has a house with a couple of apartments in Antipata (Erisou) village. When we last met he hadn't finalised the prices, nor the name of the building. He is sure it will be titled after his daughter, Eleftheria. The telephone number of his store is 51478 and that of his house 51438.

**Vlacha's Rooms** (*Tmr* 20B6)
*Directions*: As for *'Gerry's Brothers' Rooms* and keep on to the end of the street where turn left. The pleasant, very nice house is on the left. Here again, why not make enquiries at *Kafeneion Irena* (*Tmr* 3C4/5), where Vlacha now stands in for Irena, her mother-in-law.
    Rates as for 'Gerry's Brother's Rooms'.

**Tassou's Rooms**                                                                Tel 51474
*Directions*: As they are in a splendidly located house, high up in The Chora hamlet of Seletata, why not proceed direct to *Captain's Cabin* (*Tmr* 2D4/5) where Tassou presides as mine host.
    The house certainly is in a very lovely, if somewhat isolated position, with magnificent sea glimpses. The inquisitive cannot miss the place as there is a 'border customs post' style barrier. Tassou has purchased a mini bus and intends to run a daily shuttle service to and from the accommodation and HQ (Captain's Cabin).

**Fiscardon Philoxenia** (*Tmr* 15A/B4)                                            Tel 51487
*Directions*: Bordering a broad section of the Esplanade, quite close to the main road junction.
    A wall mounted sign advises 'Information in the blue door', which is on the left (*Sbo*) This imaginative but staggeringly expensive accommodation was new in 1988 and is owned by Makis Kavadias. The sturdy property has been excellently executed but at these prices... Low season double rooms cost 3500drs & a traditional apartment 9000drs, increasing to 4500drs & 10000drs (mid-season) and 5500drs & 11000drs (high season). Incidentally, Makis also offers 'Offshore Trolling Game Fishing on a Special Boat'.

**Pension Panormos** (*Tmr* 4E/F5/6)                                              Tel 51340
*Directions*: Around the corner from the *Captain's Cabin* beyond the harbour light. The position is admirable and the views magnificent, looking down the sound between Cephalonia and Ithaca but...
    A reliable source advises that apart from being seedy and run down, the tour company holiday-makers often thoughtlessly disturb other guests with uncontrolled, early morning revelry. Despite this, the management has to be persuaded to let rooms to independents, especially out of the height of season months. I shouldn't bother. Accommodation sharing a bathroom or en suite costs 2500drs for a single & 3000drs for a double, increasing to 3000drs & 3500drs (1st July-30th Sept).

Further on along this road (to Beach 1 and the hilltop villages), on a sharp bend, is a steep track to a terrace of some rather unattractive looking, cabin like buildings (*Tmr* 23F8, tel 51578) squashed together in the gouged out hillside.

In the other direction, close to the Emblisi Beach track, is a sign 'Rooms To Let. G Dendrinos Tel 51495'. This house is owned by the Dendrinos of *Restaurant George Dendrinos* fame (*Tmr* 5A/B3).
    One other source of accommodation is the Ticket Agency (*Tmr* 17B4/5). The window sign, in several languages, advises '1 or 2 Rooms, House for Rent including bathroom and kitchen. Accommodation for 2, 3, 4 and 5 people'. It has to be pointed out this may well only be *Vlacha's Rooms*.

**Camping** There is a camping ground on the 'Lighthouse' headland, across the harbour from the village.

**The Eating Out** Fiscardon is an exemplar of the guide book writer's ultimate dilemma. No, let's personalise the matter and cease to hide behind third person generalities. Fiscardon presents me with the supreme predicament (What is he on about?). The necessity to criticise the unacceptable when I am as fond as I am of the perpetrators. The complaint? Prices. The cost of kafeneion, taverna and restaurant drink and food is quite unnecessarily high. Despite Tassou's vigorous protestations that the recently imposed VAT and the country's endemic inflation justify the charges, I am of the opinion that, as elsewhere in the world, they are consumer driven. The various patrons' standard of living expectations are pleasantly matched by the glut of steady pickings, sorry tourists.

The worst offenders must be the 'grotty yachties' and in case they imagine I have it in for them, I must point out I am one myself! Not in Greece, yet, but the south coast, yes. Rather than relate every twist and turn of Tassou's argument, simply refer to Magganos village on the main road close to Fiscardon, and mentioned in the Route description, or one or two other Cephalonia/Ithacan seaside resorts. On the other hand, I simply love the location and the inhabitants. Furthermore, on our last visit we could not have received a kinder, more generous reception. As I pointed out, it is a double bind.

Now down to the facts, rather than capricious drivelling. Whilst writing about the unacceptable, lets discourse about one of the least creditable, namely:-

**Restaurant George Dendrinos** (*Tmr* 5A/B3)
*Directions*: Bordering the north end of the 'Esplanade'.

The 'colourful' owner is reputed to have lost his hand whilst fishing with dynamite. Sounds a dangerous sport to me. Nowadays George is more often than not assisted by his 'masterful' daughter and less authoritative, not so evident son. A generally unenjoyable meal, for a couple, of tiropites, (nice), a Greek salad (plentiful but tired), giant beans (good), kalamares (tasteless), bread (little of it) and an Amstel beer cost 2070drs. The tiropites were priced at 250drs each helping, which accounted for 500drs of the bill, but over 2000drs... No kortaki retsina is available, only the larger bottles of retsina and the more expensive wines. The menu includes Cephalonia pie and fried aubergines. I must point out that a legal beaver couple we met happily passed over some 2600drs for a slap-up dinner and were very happy... but perhaps lawyers are less drachmae pinching than us ordinary folk!

**Nicholas Restaurant/Taverna** (*Tmr* 6A/B4/5)                                        Tel 28084
*Directions*: Turn right down the cul-de-sac, beyond *Fiscardon Philoxenia* and prior to the Main Square, and at the top end of which a 1930s motor car may be parked.

Nicholas Donados, the neat, friendly, attentive owner, with good English, runs a very clean, tight ship. No sloppy, slow service here. I have actually observed him break into a trot at least three times in one evening. Apart from that of all the Fiscardon restaurants this is quite possibly the best. After that panygeric it must be pointed out there aren't any kortaki retsinas available, only the large bottles, in addition to the more expensive, general wines, as well as Cephalonian offerings. The restaurant is a high-ceilinged building with a large walled, courtyard garden to the side. The excellent offerings include pizzas, barbecued dishes as well as tzatziki, Greek salad, briam and Cephalonian fish pie. An average meal for two costs about 1800drs and a full-blown extravaganza, with a sweet dish and coffees, some 2500/2700drs. The evening's attractions now include a tasteful display of Greek dancing.

**Kafeneion Irena** (*Tmr* 3C4/5)
*Directions*: Edging the quay road beyond the Main Square, across from where the harbour wall sharply changes direction. The external walls of the kafeneion are plastered with various signs including one in respect of the Romantica excursion boat, a 'Rent Rooms', crudely painted in faded blue, and one advertising a brand of ice creams.

The Kafeneion is now run by Vlacha, Irena's capable daughter-in-law. A couple of admittedly good Nes meh ghala cost an expensive 200drs.

Further along the quay road are the side-by-side: *Restaurant Faros* (*Tmr* 8C4/5) and *Restaurant Kefalos* (*Tmr* 24C4/5), both serving average meals at average prices.

Another twenty or thirty metres on is:-
**Captain's Cabin** (*Tmr* 2D4/5)
*Directions*: As above. The bar-cum-restaurant looks out over the full expanse of the harbour.

Tassou serves an excellent breakfast of scrambled eggs, toast and butter and fruit juice, at one of the pavement tables under the giant awning. Seated here, his clientele can idly watch the sea sparkle and the shimmering water reflect the outlines of the gently bobbing fishing boats... and the scrambled eggs are good too!

Tassou, when not ensuring his customers are being adequately succoured, is splendid company, a man who is larger than life, despite rather incongruously, being a resident of once sleepy Fiscardon. He personifies that elusive character which newspaper editors occasionally demand a travel reporter to go and search out. You know... 'Go find a Zorba, it'll make good copy'. His Rhodesian born Greek wife Rowena is more English than the English. Apart from breakfasts as well as drinks and ice-creams, Tassou offers snacks and absolutely splendid home-made pizzas. The standard menu fare is supplemented by various dishes of the day, which might include vegetable soup and tzatziki. In an effort to encourage relations with other European countries, he would like his menu labelled 'Common Market Cuisine'! A sample of prices include Nes meh ghala 90drs, a Coke 75drs, a fried eggs & bacon breakfast 280drs , yoghurt & honey 170drs, (various) omelettes & chips 350drs, Greek salad 200drs, a baked spaghetti 400drs, chicken chasseur 500drs, a magnificent pizza 650drs (enough for two), an Amstel 120drs, a 3 star Metaxa 150drs and an ouzo 100drs. Little niggles include the naff habit of serving ouzos with the water already added and a wine list which does not include a kortaki retsina, prices starting off at 400drs a bottle.

# THE A TO Z OF USEFUL INFORMATION

**BANKS** None, but the 'Ships Agency' (*Tmr* 17B4/5) effects exchange.

**BEACHES** In the environs of Fiscardon are two small beaches in beautiful settings.
**Beach 1:** Beyond the *Captain's Cabin* (*Tmr* 2D4/5), and about a fifteen minute amble to a small, fjord like bay with olive trees growing down to the clear blue water's edge. The trek is enlivened by the various villas scattered along the walk; the beautiful view of the sea-channel between Cephalonia and Ithaca and wonderment that, in such a magnificent setting, a philistine could have constructed the now abandoned, stone crushing plant on the tree covered hillside. The inland side of the road adjacent to the bay sports a snackbar and a monstrous, American owned caravan. Concrete steps descend to the rather rubbish littered olive grove backing the shore of the 'U' shaped cove. A few boats are drawn up on the medium sized pebble beach which extends into the sea. After about 3m the sea-bed supports the ubiquitous grass-like weed and the shore has a kelp line.

**Beach 2 or Emblisi Beach:** Climb out of the village on the main road for about 10 minutes. The wide, chalky track, which zig-zags down to the turn-round behind the backshore, sets out alongside a *Panoramic Taverna*. Unfortunately, the land backing the shore has been crudely excavated in a large, saucer shaped depression, on the edge of which an electricity sub station hums away. The tiny bay has been scoured out of the rocky coastline by the sea. The tree fringed shore consists of large rounded pebbles with a simdgin of sand at the sea's edge, on the right (*Fsw*). The pebble sea-bed becomes weedy after three or four metres. The large, almost horizontal slabs edging the cove are ideal on which to sunbathe after a swim in the azure sea.

**BICYCLE, SCOOTER & CAR HIRE** A row of scooters for hire are lined up in front of a roofless building (*Tmr* 18B4/5). This business is operated by Nikos, Gerry's brother. Thus, if no one is to be found, pop in to see Gerry at his General store (*Tmr* 1B4/5). It is only next door.

**BREAD SHOP** (*Tmr* 9A/B5) The bakery is on the right (*Sbo*) of 'Garbage' lane and is difficult to spot. Over the low door frame is an indistinct sign, APTOMOIEION. Once inside, the building is much larger than would appear from the outside. Apart from bread they sell tiropites for 70drs.

**BUSES** 'Terminus' on a lay-by (*Tmr* 7A2) adjacent to the main road. *See* **Bus timetable, Buses, A To Z, Argostoli Town** for the itinerary.

**COMMERCIAL SHOPPING AREA** Apart from the one and only Supermarket (*Tmr* 12A/B3/4), which also sells fruit and vegetables, there are a number of Souvenir/Gift shops (*Tmr* 14) It is a pity that a number of these are located in buildings where were previously stores.

**DISCOS** Rock music lovers will have to make do with Music Bar Dionyssis (*Tmr* 22D1). More a cocktail bar, owned by a man from Patras, where most drinks cost 300drs.

**FERRY-BOATS** To progress or not? Nowadays a widespread scheduled daily ferry-boat service makes the independent's life a lot easier, but I can't help missing the nail-biting uncertainty of the arrangements of yesteryear. Then the scheduled Sami Port ferry-boats used to 'pull up' in the mouth of Fiscardon's sea inlet. But on what basis, I never knew. Similarly an informal trip boat connection could be arranged with Polis Bay (Ithaca).

In addition to the scheduled car ferries, the **Romantica** makes daily cruises to 'the port of Odysseus' (Ithaca) at 1000hrs, returning at 1800hrs.

**Ferry-boat timetable** (Mid-season)

| Day | Departure time | Ferry-boat | Ports/Islands of Call |
|---|---|---|---|
| Daily | 1000hrs | Aphrodite | Vassiliki(Lefkas). |
| | 1030hrs | Meganisi | Frikes(Ithaca),Nidri(Lefkas),Meganissi. |
| | 1630hrs | Aphrodite | Vassiliki(Lefkas). |
| | 1915hrs | Aphrodite | Sami Port(Cephalonia). |

Sample one-way fare: Fiscardon to Nidri 400drs;duration to Frikes 40mins.
to Nidri 2hrs.
to Vassiliki 350drs;  to Meganissis 2hrs 20mins.
to Vassiliki 1hr.

**FERRY-BOAT TICKET OFFICES**
**Ships Agency** (*Tmr* 17B3/5) Also quadruples up as a ticket office, money changer and kafeneion. Tickets for the **Romantica** are certainly available here. I omitted to establish the link between this office and *Kafeneion Irena*, but it must be family – probably Irena's son.

**OTE** *See* **Post Office, A To Z.**

**PLACES OF INTEREST** On the headland opposite the village are the ruins of a possibly Norman church and a very pretty lighthouse. It is postulated that the name Fiscardon derives from a Norman knight, one Robert Guiscard, who died on his ship in the harbour, whilst capturing the settlement from the Turks.

**POST OFFICE (& OTE)** (*Tmr* 11A/B2/3) Bordering the 'Esplanade', towards the Ferry-boat Quay. Apart from opening the usual weekday Post Office hours, the OTE section opens evenings for a time from 1930hrs.

**POLICE**
**Port** (*Tmr* 10A/B3).

**WATER** The drinking water is of an interesting, soupy, nature, often holding some plant life in suspension.

# EXCURSION TO FISCARDON SURROUNDS

A clockwise, circular route to Magganos & back round to Fiscardon (10km). Proceed as to Beach 1. From this olive grove backshore, the road climbs steeply, winding through massed, stately cypress trees into a 'humbly-bumbly' village. The ascent continues on a concrete surfaced lane, through olive trees, to the next, spaced out village of **Seletata** at the outset of which is a circular threshing floor. There are a number of quite large private houses as well as Tassou's accommodation, on the left.

Beyond Seletata, the route becomes a chalky track, the white dust from which covers the surrounding trees and bushes to such an extent that the countryside resembles a winter scene. The route becomes metalled again, after which the road joins the main road at Magganos.

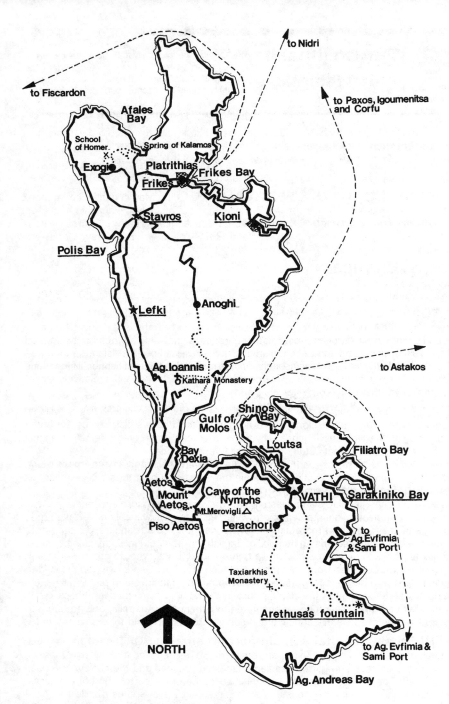

to Fiscardon

to Nidri

to Paxos, Igoumenitsa and Corfu

Afales Bay

School of Homer

Spring of Kalamos

Exogi

Platrithias

Frikes Bay

Frikes

Kioni

Stavros

Polis Bay

Lefki

Anoghi

Ag. Ioannis

Kathara Monastery

to Astakos

Shinos Bay

Gulf of Molos

Loutsa

Filiatro Bay

Bay Dexia

Aetos

Mount Aetos

Cave of the Nymphs

VATHI

Sarakiniko Bay

Mt. Merovigli

Piso Aetos

Perachori

to Ag. Evfimia & Sami Port

Taxiarkhis Monastery

Arethusa's fountain

to Ag. Evfimia & Sami Port

NORTH

Ag. Andreas Bay

**Illustration 29 Ithaca Island**

# 16 ITHACA (Ithaki)
## Ionian Islands

★★★★★

---

**FIRST IMPRESSIONS** Mellifluous sheep bells; Martello towers; fjord-like indents; Homer; desperately drinking water short; a domestic rubbish problem in Vathi.

**SPECIALITIES** Homer; ravani (sweet cake made up of honey, sugar & semolina); baklava (a pastry filled with honey & nuts); a lamb dish, casserole cooked; local wine.

**RELIGIOUS HOLIDAYS & FESTIVALS** include: 1st May – Festival Taxiarchon, Perachori; 24th June – Festival of Ag Yiannis, Kioni; 20th July – Panaghia, Ag Elias Church, Kioni; August – Wine Festival, Perachori; 5-6th August – Festival, Sotiros Church, Stavros; Mid-summer – Theatre Festival, Vathi; 8th September – Feast day, Monastery of Kathara; 14th September – Folk Festival, Anoghi.

**VITAL STATISTICS** Tel prefix 0674. The island is 29km long, up to 6¼km wide with a total area of 92½sqkm. The population numbers between 3500-6,000 (depending on which authority you believe), of which the capital, Vathi, houses some 2,000-3400.

**HISTORY** The island's past is dominated by the 'Homer connection'. This link was fostered by British archaeologists who remained convinced of the island's true heritage. This dedication was in strict contrast to other Europeans, including a Dutchman, a German and a Greek, who dashed about the Ionian declaring on behalf of other islands as the true home of Ulysses (Odysseus). The association has resulted in the prolification of locations associated with this or that reference in Homer's Odyssey. Otherwise the relatively recent history followed that of the other Ionian islands.

**GENERAL** Ithaca, one of the smallest islands in the Ionian chain, has a 'village' ambience, with fewer concessions to the holiday-maker. Ithaca's claim to be the home of the hero of the Homeric legends, Ulysses (Odysseus) has given rise to an annual summer seminar that attracts students from all over the world.

Prior to the blasting of the road system into a coherent, if limited, layout, much island travel was by caique. Some vestiges remain in the occasional boat trips between various fishing villages and Vathi, the capital.

Ithaca is a rather singular island. Despite the 'drawbacks', or more accurately the lack of concessions to the twentieth century traveller, visitors will invariably be left with fond memories of their visit, and more especially the warmth of the islanders. To the north, the few villages have a surprising number of English, or rather colonial, speaking natives. (Colonial will be well understood by those right-minded 'Brits' who do not consider that the US of A ever departed from the Empire's glorious fold). They are only too pleased to engage in long and detailed conversation, answering any enquiries and regaling listeners with details of their overseas travels. It is surprising just how many men left Ithaca, when they were young, to go seafaring, or emigrated to America or Australia, only to return to take up the reins of the family agricultural holding or retire and build their dream home.

**VATHI (Ithaki): capital & main port** (Illustration 30) The town is set in a beautiful, deeply indented bay. This opens out in front of the ferry-boat's onward progress, once the mountainous and barren headland has been rounded and the narrow approach channel cleft. The setting is romantic. Vathi is built around the bottom end of the horse-shoe shaped bay, on a narrow coastal plain hemmed in by a low range of hills.

In appearance the town is not unlike Dartmouth in Devon, the houses clinging to the hillside and linked with shallow steps, more steps and even more steps.

Two items of immediate note are the rather pleasant, pedal-operated litter bins and, lo and behold, a public toilet block, to one side of the Customs House. Despite these facilities, rubbish disposal is a monumental problem and the toilets are mind boggling, added to which, the drinking water is in very, very short supply. Vathi is one of those locations where an alarm clock is almost superfluous for, being essentially a rural community, roosters abound and commence their clamorous dawn chorus at around 0400hrs. Vathi 'dies' on Sunday. For that matter, there is not much activity any afternoon between 1500-1800hrs.

**ARRIVAL BY FERRY** Nowadays the island is well serviced, by not only the larger, inter-island ferries but a Vathi, Astakos(M) and Ag Evfimia (Cephalonia) craft as well as a Frikes link to Fiscardon (Cephalonia), Nidri (Lefkas) and Meganissi.

From the Ferry-boat Quay (*Tmr* 1B/C3), the main Town is to the left (*Sbo*), spread along the bottom of the bay. Generally the ferries are not met by swarms of room-offering islanders. The few owners of accommodation who do attend a ferry-boat's arrival, loiter quietly in the background, close by the adjacent ticket office, thoroughly vetting possible clients, prior to making an approach.

The reverberations of a ferry's siren echoing around the sound, as it enters the bay, is guaranteed to send a shiver of anticipation down the back-bone of even the most blasé traveller.

## THE ACCOMMODATION & EATING OUT

**The Accommodation** What is available, is quickly taken as Vathi lacks an abundance of hotels, pensions and *Rooms*.

The two, 'proper' hotels are at opposite ends of the town. They are the:-

**Hotel Odysseus** (*Tmr* 2A1) (Class B)      Tel 32381
*Directions*: To the right (*Sbo*) of the Ferry-boat Quay (*Tmr* 1B/C3). This rather uncompromising 'neo Greek municipal' building is on the left, bordering the Stavros road.

Actually classified as a Pension. Single rooms sharing the bathrooms are priced at 1355drs, single rooms with en suite bathroom 2385drs, whilst double rooms sharing cost 2800drs & en suite 3615drs, increasing, respectively, to 1810/2710drs & 2980/4020drs (1st July-31st Aug).

**Hotel Mendor** (*Tmr* 3E/F5) (Class B) Akti Dracouli/Paralia St      Tel 32433
*Directions*: Quite a long haul from the Ferry-boat Quay (*Tmr* 1B/C3). Turn left (*Sbo*) off the boat, follow the Esplanade around past the Town Hall and the Customs House, cut across the Main Square (keeping to the sea wall), on along the Esplanade to where it bears left again. The hotel is on the right.

A rather up-market, pleasant hotel but it is largely booked by tour companies. Rooms, when available, are comparatively expensive. Single rooms with en suite bathroom cost 2350drs, double rooms sharing the bathrooms 3000drs & en suite 4070drs, increasing to 2950drs & 3800/4650drs (1st May-31st Oct).

Other accommodation includes:-

**Rooms** (*Tmr* 6B3)      Tel 32606
*Directions*: Conveniently situated along the broad side street to one side of the Taverna (*Tmr* 12B3) and Ticket office (*Tmr* 13B3), across the Esplanade from the Ferry-boat Quay, and the far side of Odysseos St, up a flight of steps.

Average prices for rooms sharing the bathroom.

**Pension Aktaeon** (*Tmr* 4B/C3) (Class E) Akti Gratsou      Tel 32387
*Directions*: Conveniently situated, almost adjacent to the Ferry-boat Quay, bordering the Esplanade road.

The lady owner, whose only other language is French, prefers Greeks. The rooms are very clean and pleasant.

**Pension Enoikiazomena** (*Tmr* 5A/B3/4) ΝΟΣΤΟΥ (Alleyway), off Odysseos St
*Directions*: From the Ferry-boat Quay, turn left along the Esplanade and right along the narrow lane between the Wool shop (*Tmr* 10B/C3/4) and the Town Hall (*Tmr* 11B/C3/4). This spills on to Odysseos St, which runs parallel to the Esplanade. Turn right and almost immediately left up the narrow, stepped alley. The pension is half-way up, on the right.

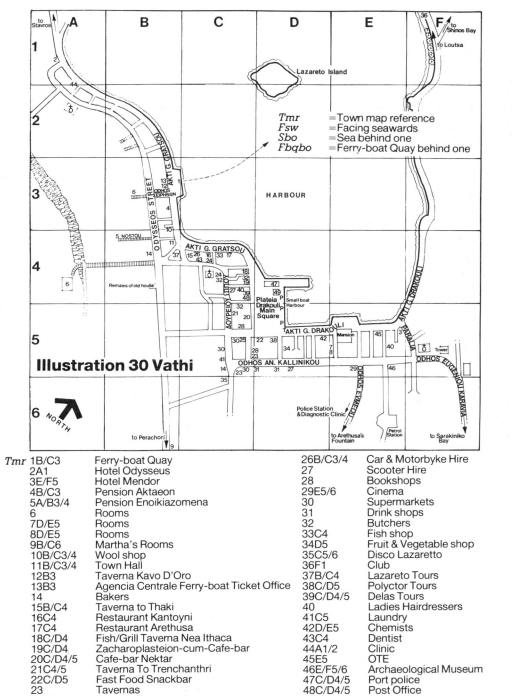

**Illustration 30 Vathi**

| Tmr | | |
|---|---|---|
| 1B/C3 | Ferry-boat Quay | |
| 2A1 | Hotel Odysseus | |
| 3E/F5 | Hotel Mendor | |
| 4B/C3 | Pension Aktaeon | |
| 5A/B3/4 | Pension Enoikiazomena | |
| 6 | Rooms | |
| 7D/E5 | Rooms | |
| 8D/E5 | Rooms | |
| 9B/C6 | Martha's Rooms | |
| 10B/C3/4 | Wool shop | |
| 11B/C3/4 | Town Hall | |
| 12B3 | Taverna Kavo D'Oro | |
| 13B3 | Agencia Centrale Ferry-boat Ticket Office | |
| 14 | Bakers | |
| 15B/C4 | Taverna to Thaki | |
| 16C4 | Restaurant Kantoyni | |
| 17C4 | Restaurant Arethusa | |
| 18C/D4 | Fish/Grill Taverna Nea Ithaca | |
| 19C/D4 | Zacharoplasteion-cum-Cafe-bar | |
| 20C/D4/5 | Cafe-bar Nektar | |
| 21C4/5 | Taverna To Trenchanthri | |
| 22C/D5 | Fast Food Snackbar | |
| 23 | Tavernas | |
| 24C4 | Pizzeria Restaurant | |
| 25C5 | National Bank | |

| 26B/C3/4 | Car & Motorbyke Hire |
|---|---|
| 27 | Scooter Hire |
| 28 | Bookshops |
| 29E5/6 | Cinema |
| 30 | Supermarkets |
| 31 | Drink shops |
| 32 | Butchers |
| 33C4 | Fish shop |
| 34D5 | Fruit & Vegetable shop |
| 35C5/6 | Disco Lazaretto |
| 36F1 | Club |
| 37B/C4 | Lazareto Tours |
| 38C/D5 | Polyctor Tours |
| 39C/D4/5 | Delas Tours |
| 40 | Ladies Hairdressers |
| 41C5 | Laundry |
| 42D/E5 | Chemists |
| 43C4 | Dentist |
| 44A1/2 | Clinic |
| 45E5 | OTE |
| 46E/F5/6 | Archaeological Museum |
| 47C/D4/5 | Port police |
| 48C/D4/5 | Post Office |
| 49C/D4/5 | Public toilets |
| P | Periptero |
| T | Taxi rank |

Papa George's wife meets the ferries. The rooms and furnishings of this ethnic accommodation are aged, colonial Victorian in character and rather messy. Access to some bedrooms is via an ante-room, wherein a local may be asleep on the sofa (at any time of the day or night). The garden is a tip, Granny lives in the basement and the shared bathroom shower delivers very hot water. The per person charge is 500drs.

**Rooms** (*Tmr* 6A4)                                                                    Tel 32119
*Directions*: As for *Pension Enoikiazomena* (*Tmr* 5A/B3/4) but left on Odysseos St (not right), past a Bakery (*Tmr* 14B4) and up the long, steep flight of steps to the right.
Island ethnic, in a series of spaced out, single storey shacks about which gourds are spread about. Room rates are 500drs per person per night.

The Esplanade Wool shop (*Tmr* 10B/C3/4) has a sign 'Rooms To Let' with the telephone numbers 32104, 32128 & 32145.

Without doubt, the best rooms in the port are side-by-side in the narrow street to the nearside of Mansion (*Tmr* D/E5) bordering the Esplanade. This unusual building is the more noticeable due to the pond to the front of the house. The houses are on the right (*Sbo*), about half-way down.

**Rooms To Let** (*Tmr* 7D/E5)                                                          Tel 32819
*Directions*: As above, and the first building.
Very nice ground floor double rooms, complete with en suite bathroom and (I think) a kitchen fitted with cooker and fridge. Damned good news, with a mid-season charge of 2000drs.

**Furnished Rooms** (*Tmr* 8D/E5)                                                       Tel 32267
*Directions*: Next door to the last mentioned accommodation. A board advises 'Information opposite house'.
As above but definitely with a fitted kitchen.

Another good choice, if a little distant from the centre of town, is:-
**Martha's Rooms** (*Tmr* 9B/C6)                                                        Tel 32352
*Directions*: On the left of the Perachori road out of Vathi.
Martha Manya is a smiley lady with little English. Admittedly her double rooms share the bathroom but enjoy the advantage of the use of (also shared) kitchen facilities. Mid-season rates of 1500drs increase, at the height of the summer, to 2500drs.

Both the Main Square Travel offices, Polyctor Tours (*Tmr* 38C/D5) and Delas Tours (*Tmr* 39C/D4/5), can assist with locating (expensive) accommodation. (*See* **Travel Agents & Tour offices, A To Z**). Their offers tend to be more apartments than rooms. For instance, Captain Kostas, he of Polyctor Tours, will offer one of his palatial suites, with its own entrance door, at a mid-season price of some 2500drs per night. Certainly those independents who consider comfort before cost will be well advised to proceed directly to these portals.

**The Eating Out** Nowadays there are any number of establishments open at night, including Sundays. Opposite the Ferry-boat Quay (*Tmr* 1B/C3) is the:-
**Taverna Kavo D'oro** (*Tmr* 12B3)
*Directions*: As above.
An unpretentious but rather expensive establishment. The only outside seating is along the pavement but the rendezvous is popular with those waiting on the ferry-boats. The slim, roguish, extrovert owner, who is aged about 50, speaks American. A bottle of beer costs 100drs.

Bordering the Esplanade, on the way to the Main Sq, are a number of 'average' establishments, including *Taverna To Thaki* (*Tmr* 15B/C4) and the *Restaurant Kantoyni* (*Tmr* 16C4), which is rather doo-hickey and more a small taverna than a restaurant. The *Cafeteria Arethousa* (ΑΡΕΕΙΟΤΣΑ) (*Tmr* 17C4) is a pleasant, reasonable value establishment, with an awning covered pavement quayside strip across the street. The friendly, attentive patron has his work cut out as he serves a good English breakfast of (pita bread, 2 eggs, bacon & sausage) and a large cup of coffee (70drs) for 320drs. Continuing along the Esplanade progresses past a cafe-bar; the *Fish/Grill Taverna Nea Ithaca* (*Tmr* 18C/D4), a popular, local joint serving souvlaki, and a Zacharoplasteion-cum-Cafe-bar (*Tmr* 19C/D4).
The Main Square is bordered by a zacharoplasteion/cafeteria; the rather tourist trap *Nektar Cafe Bar* (*Tmr* 20C/D4/5), Athenian owned and only serving small tins of Amstel, alongside which is the *Kafeneion Odysseus*, a more local set-up, which sensibly offers bottles of beer. Both the latter have a pleasant spread of awning covered chairs and tables ranged along the front of their establishments.

In Odhos Doreou Ippou, the street one back from the Main Sq, is:-
**Taverna To Trenchanthri** (*Tmr* 21C4/5)
*Directions*: As above, and almost across the road from a scooter repair business, which appears to carry out most of its business in the gutter – most diverting.

Despite one correspondent dismissing the establishment with a '...good food but in Greek fashion, cold, and priority given to Greeks', it does merit much consideration. Menu choice includes pistachio, moussaka, chicken, liver, pork, stuffed tomatoes, beef with rice, giants, fassolakia freska, potatoes, Greek salad, tzatziki, a local wine from the barrel and kortaki retsina. It has to be admitted that the meals are often served no more than a cool warm(!) but the helpings are enormous. For instance, should a couple both wish to eat green beans, only order one helping – it will be quite enough. The per person helping of bread is almost two-thirds of a loaf. A meal for two of 'moussaka, chicken & chips, 2 plates of fassolakia freska, a plate of beans, bread and ½ litre of local red wine cost 1175drs. Incidentally, do not arrive late in the evening as the taverna fills quickly and the menu options rapidly diminish.

**Fast Food Snackbar** (*Tmr* 22C/D5).
*Directions*: On the south-east side of the Main Sq, in the same block as Polyctor Tours.

This establishment, which is owned by a nice, smiley lady and her husband, serves 'fast Greek food', as distinct from fast American food. It is very popular with locals and tourists alike. There is room to sit down inside, despite the frontage being rather narrow, as well as a garden at the rear. The bill of fare includes a variety of sandwiches and individual plates of mezes selected by the client from the large range of vegetable and meat goodies on display. A bottle of Amstel costs 78drs and a kortaki retsina 100drs. A meal for two (greedy) people of single dishes of cold gigantes, meatballs, sausages, (Greek) hamburger, aubergines, potato croquets, chips, bread and 2 bottles of Amstel cost 980drs. Not at all expensive considering the number of plates of meat. Also available is giro souvlaki.

Just around the corner are two good, tourist taverna stand-bys, the *Taverna O Nikos* (*Tmr* 23C/D5) and *Taverna Athenai Ki Gonia* (*Tmr* 23C5/6). Another possibility is an establishment specialising in pizzas, the *Pizzeria Restaurant* (*Tmr* 24C4) edging Odhos Doureou Ippou. It has a garden, *Panos Corner*, around the bend and across from a church, in the angle of an alleyway. A small, 'local affair' taverna, opposite the Odysseos St Baker (*Tmr* 14B4), is worthy of consideration. But only by the intrepid who should ensure the contents of the pots and pans are freshly prepared.

Those prepared to walk should proceed round the bay along the far, Loutsa road for some ten to fifteen minutes. On the inland side of the bay hugging road is the esteemed, pleasantly situated, if more expensive, *Gregory's Restaurant*, specialising in lamb and fish dishes. Beyond *Gregory's* are a couple more restaurants.

# THE A TO Z OF USEFUL INFORMATION

**BANKS** The **National Bank** (*Tmr* 25C5) is off the south corner of the Main Square.

**BEACHES** Apart from the long, out-of-town hikes, the Loutsa side of the bay is edged by a narrow, tree-shaded, not very satisfactory, rather dirty shingle beach which stretches from just beyond the yacht fuel station as far as the Shinos turning off the Loutsa road. Edging the bay opposite the Loutsa road restaurants, are one or two concrete platforms from which it is possible to swim.

At Loutsa, which is just below some Venetian fort gun emplacements (a historic **Guns of Navarone?**), is a small bay with an even smaller, mostly sandy beach.
For other beaches *See* **Excursions to Vathi Town Surrounds**.

**BICYCLE, BOAT, SCOOTER & CAR HIRE** There is an Esplanade motorbike and car hire firm (*Tmr* 26B/C3/4) on the way round to the centre of the town from the Ferry-boat Quay (*Tmr* 1B/C3). There are at least two other scooter hire businesses, one (*Tmr* 27C4) in the maze behind the Main Sq, which advertises 'scuters' *sic*), and another (*Tmr* 27D5/6) on Odhos An Kallinikou. Machines are generally in good condition and a Honda automatic/Vespa costs 900/1000drs a day. It is debatable if it is worth hiring wheels, due to the comparatively small size of the island, the few roads, the mountainous terrain and the excellent and reasonably priced taxi service. Scooter hirers must be cautious as the surface on some of the sharper bends of the main roads have suffered as a result of rock falls. Great care should also be taken when negotiating the section between Aetos and Lefki in high winds, since sudden gusts can push a machine and rider perilously close to the unguarded edge and precipitous drop! You have been warned!

On the Loutsa Esplanade side of the bay is an outfit hiring small, outboard powered dinghies.

**BOOKSELLER** (*Tmr* 28C5) There are two off the south corner of the Main Square. One (*Tmr* 28B5) is almost opposite the National Bank, and the other (*Tmr* 28C/D5), which also sells overseas papers, is in an adjacent side street.

**BREAD SHOP** The main Baker (*Tmr* 14C5/6), which is to the right (*Main Square behind one*) of the same street as the Disco Lazaretto, also opens on Saturday evenings, in the summer months. The other Baker (*Tmr* 14B4) on Odhos Odysseos keeps unreliable opening hours... or days... or weeks.

**BUSES** The buses 'terminus' on the Main Square. The simple route service has, over the years, remained consistently inconsistent. The day, nay, week long service disruptions are due to the unreliability of the 'transport modules'. One 'machine's misfortune' results in the taxi drivers being exultant and busy.

**Bus timetable** (Mid-season)
**Vathi Town to Kroni via Stavros, Platrithias & Frikes**
Daily          0600, 1100, 1600, 1900hrs
*Return journey*
Daily          0700, 1400, 1700, 2000hrs
One-way fare 200drs; duration 1hr.

**CINEMA** (*Tmr* 29E5/6) Next door to the Library.

**COMMERCIAL SHOPPING AREA** There is no specific market area but most of the shops are in and around the Main Square. Apart from a clutch of Supermarkets (*Tmr* 30C5, 30C/D5 & 30C/D5/6), of which the one in 'Disco Lazaretto' St is possibly the best, there are two Drink shops (*Tmr* 31C/D5/6 & 31D5/6) on Odhos An Kallinikou; a number of Butchers (*Tmr* 32C/D4, 32C4 & 32C4/5); a Fish shop (*Tmr* 33C4); a Fruit & Vegetable shop (*Tmr* 34D5); a few small stores scattered about the suburbs and plenty of gift & souvenir shops. Apart from the Peripteros (*Tmr* P), there is a Drink & Tobacco shop, close by the *Fish/Grill Taverna Nea Ithaca* (*Tmr* 18C/D4). Ithaca is one of those islands where closing times are adhered to, strictly, and shops cannot be expected to be open 'out of hours' or on Sunday.

**DISCOS** The Disco Lazaretto (*Tmr* 35C5/6) is, or was, owned by a German woman, one of the founder members of the Sarakiniko Bay commune. Another 'entry' is the music bar/club (*Tmr* 36F1) alongside the Loutsa Bay road.

**FERRY-BOATS** The Ionian sea now positively bristles with ferry-boat routes to not only the ports of other islands, but mainland connections.

**Ferry-boat timetable** (Mid-season)

| Day | Departure time | Ferry-boat | Ports/Islands of Call |
|---|---|---|---|
| Daily | 0230hrs | Ionis/Ionian Glory | Gaios(Paxos),Igoumenitsa(M),Corfu. |
| | 0700hrs | | Sami(Cephalonia),Patras(M). |
| | 1100hrs | Thiaki | Astakos(M). |
| | 1230hrs | Ionis/Ionian Glory | Sami(Cephalonia),Patras(M). |
| | 1600hrs | Thiaki | Ag Evfimia(Cephalonia). |
| | 1800hrs | | Sami(Cephalonia). |

One-way fare: Vathi to Sami     365drs;duration  1hr
                    to Patras  1054drs;          4½hrs
                    to Astakos  436drs;          1¾

**FERRY-BOAT TICKET OFFICES**
Agenzia Centrale, (*Tmr* 13B3) Akti Gratsou
*Directions*: Across the Esplanade from the Ferry-boat Quay.
   The office is run by a Greek 'character' with good English, the staff are very helpful and the office 'opens up' for ferry-boat arrivals. They sell tickets for the main Corfu-Patras inter-island ferries.

**Lazareto Tours** (*Tmr* 37B/C4) Akti Gratsou                                    Tel 32587
*Directions*: Bordering the Esplanade, close by the Town Hall.
   A very friendly office, a joy to patronise, with a pleasant, smiling young lady in attendance. Agents for the **Thiaki**, the office possesses a metered telephone.

**HAIRDRESSERS** One Ladies Hairdresser (*Tmr* 40C4) hides away in a narrow side-street off the Main Sq, and another (*Tmr* 40E5) on a side-street off the Esplanade, to the nearside of the *Hotel Mendor*.

**LAUNDRY** More a Dry Cleaners (*Tmr* 41C5).

**MEDICAL CARE**
**Chemists & Pharmacies** There is a Chemist, alongside Delas Tours (*Tmr* 29C/D4/5), and another (*Tmr* 42D/E5) bordering the bottom, flattened part of the 'U' of the horse-shoe bay.
**Clinic** (*Tmr* 44A1/2) Towards the far, west end of the Esplanade.
**Dentist** The clinic of Julia Varvarigou (*Tmr* 43C4) is in a street one back and parallel to the Esplanade.
**Diagnostic Clinic** On Evmeou St, which curves south, from Odhos An. Kallinikou, from behind the Esplanade Bay Mansion (*Tmr* D/E5).

**OTE** (*Tmr* 45E5) Edging the east end of the Esplanade, towards the *Hotel Mendor* (*Tmr* 3E/F5). Only open weekdays between 0730-2200hrs.

**PETROL** There is a Petrol filling station (*Tmr* E6) along a lane south-east of the Esplanade, in the area of the *Hotel Mendor.*

**PLACE OF INTEREST**
**Archaeological Museum** (*Tmr* 46E/F5/6) Odhos An Kallinikou.

**The Cathedral Ag Georgios** (*Tmr* F5) Possesses an icon, possibly executed by El Greco.

**N Lazareto Island** (*Tmr* C/D1/2) A rather incongruous, tiny islet, set down in the Harbour. Once a prison and quarantine stop, it is floodlit at night. I have an 'itch' that Byron is reputed to have taken a daily constitutional swim to the islet and back, whilst staying at Ithaca.

**POLICE**
**Port** (*Tmr* 47C/D4/5) Beside the Customs House, in a building close by the jetty that juts out into the Harbour.
**Town** On Evmeou St, south-east of the Esplanade Mansion (*Tmr* D/E5).

**POST OFFICE** (*Tmr* 48C/D4/5) Bordering the Main Square.

**TELEPHONE NUMBERS & ADDRESSES**
| | |
|---|---|
| Clinic (*Tmr* 44A1/2) | Tel 32282 |
| Police, town | Tel 32205 |
| Taxi Rank (*Tmr* TD5) | Tel 33030 |

**TAXIS** An excellent service, with sharing cabs as 'order of the day'. There are several ranks (*Tmr* T), including one adjacent to the Agencia Centrale (*Tmr* 13B3), close by the Ferry-boat Quay, and another by the Main Square.

**TOILETS** The Main Sq public lavatories (*Tmr* 49C/D4/5) are pretty disgusting with little or no running water. Certainly the 'chaps' bit is 'mind boggling'.

**TRAVEL AGENTS & TOUR OFFICES** The two, Main Sq firms are **Polyctor Tours** (*Tmr* 38C/D5, tel 33120) and **Delas Tours** (*Tmr* 39C/D4/5, tel 32145). Both owners manifest serious signs of Grecociliousness. They become rather disinterested, indifferent, even easily bored by all or any detailed and persistent enquiries.

**WATER** The original British installed drinking water supply systems were, unfortunately, destroyed by earthquakes. 'Aqua pura' is now a very great problem and the locals do not trust the 'line supply'. This difficulty may not be unassociated with the almost comic opera fate, of Wagnerian proportions, that befell the island's desalination plant. It is suggested in a wild, unsubstantiated rumour that a Swiss firm gave two to Ithaca, in an effort to promote the sale to the Greek government, of a large number of water plants. Thus the island's water supply was ensured. Ah, no. The firm omitted to inform the Government, and the beneficiaries, that the systems required two skilled bio-chemist technicians and 4 million drs a year to be operated efficiently. Needless to say they now 'lay a-rotting'. Hence the water shortage.

# EXCURSIONS TO VATHI TOWN SURROUNDS
**Excursion to Sarakiniko & Filiatro Bays (about 3km)**For this 30-40 minute hike, leave Vathi by turning right beyond the *Hotel Mendor* (*Tmr* 3E/F5), past the Cathedral and along Odhos Eugeniou Karavia. This route climbs a winding lane, lined with pretty cottages. Beyond a Church, fork left and keep left at the chapel. At the summit of the hill, immediately after the chapel, are views out over pretty:-

**Sarakiniko Bay (circa 2km from Vathi Town)** The bay is made up of two coves. Bear left (not on up the mountain) and start down the unmade road past a goat track to the nearside cove, which is a quite clean, pebble shore. This is reached by scrambling over the rocks on the foreshore or cutting down the referred to path, half-way down the unmade road.

The far, left (*Fsw*) hand cove, is approached down a steep, unsurfaced track which loops round to the rear of the valley gully behind the beach. This has been occupied by a self-supporting community of Germans who cultivate some of the land. The commune, which has been here for at least the last ten years, was reported to have been disbanded but... it was very much in evidence in 1988. It would be nice to report the site was a model of Green aspirations but the place is a squalid, rather filthy shambles. The ravine is scattered with animal pens, enclosures, tents and some shacks. One of the sheds is signed as a cafe and there is a karzy hut on the left-hand (*Fsw*) hillside. Some couples sleep out on the rubbish strewn backshore of this pebble beach. The 'great unwashed' are welcome, but should take their own goat.

From the approaches to the second cove, a very rough track crosses over to:-
**Filiatro Bay (3km from Vathi Town)** At the crest of the hill is yet another collective, a 'bivouac' of stone-hut dwellers. In amongst the olive groves that range up the old terraces are a number of tents and some 75m back from the pebble beach is a quite large, two storey, ruined farmhouse. All in all, a once very lovely location now blighted by the presence of the 'undesirables'.

**Excursion to Arethusa's Fountain & Ravens Crag (5km)** Both have strong Homeric connection. They are reached from the south-east of Vathi Town by advancing past the Diagnostic Clinic and forking left. The two hour plus walk is signposted, but the unsurfaced road quickly deteriorates, becoming nothing more than a path. Disappointing, if it were not for the views.

**Excursion to Perachori Village (2km), Paleochora and Taxiarkhis Monastiri (Monastery) (4½km)** The steep climb to Perachori is a continuation of Odysseos St.

**PERACHORI (2km from Vathi Town)** A very spread out village that winds up the mountainside with few concessions to tourism. There are some embryonic *Rooms* at the foot of the castle walls.

Half-way through the village a signed track on to the right-hand mountainside is labelled 'Old City 1500AC'. This was the fortified, Middle Ages settlement of **Paleochora**, but since abandoned. I'm not quite sure how one determines the difference between an old, deserted village and an old, currently inhabited community.

Two-thirds of the way up Perachori is a taverna-cum-restaurant, embellished with a window mounted horn gramophone, followed by a kafeneion, beyond which the route forks. To the left is another restaurant (closed for all but the height of season months), from whence marvellous views out over the southern end of the island. The right-hand choice is the walk to **Taxiarkhis Monastery** (4km from Vathi Town). Built in 1645, the monastery is part ruined.

**Excursion to Shinos Bay (2km)** From the Loutsa bay road, immediately prior to the Club (*Tmr* 36F1), an appalling track crosses to Shinos Bay, past one or two large, fenced private houses. Here is a large pebble, small beach favoured by nudists. Any amount of rubbish might well be stacked in neat, if unremoved piles. Hardly worth the trip.

## ONE & ONLY ROUTE
**To Kioni via Stavros (circa 24km) with detours to Piso Aetos, Kathara Monastery, Polis Bay, Exogi & Afales Bay**The main road to the north of the island sets off, leaving Vathi Bay to the right and ascending the hillside. Hardly one kilometre on is the signposted turning to the:-

**Cave of Nymphs** The steep ascent through various hillbilly backyard farmsteads is on an intermittently concrete surfaced track. The final ascent is a paved footpath.

The metalled grill entrance to the cave may well be left open. From the first chamber, a flight of shaky steps gives access to the bowl of a cave. Despite a shaft of light that penetrates somewhere high up in the ceiling, it is imperative to bring a torch. Unless a committed, 'hands on' Homeric explorer, I shouldn't bother. And watch out for those steps.

To the left of the cave's entrance is indicated 'Kasinaki, Sculptured Grave with bas-relief, representation of animals'.

Returning to the main route, the road descends steeply to the stone and pebble shore of Molos Gulf. To the right (*Fsw*) stretches a pleasant, olive tree shaded crescent of pebble beach.

Hereabouts is the initially wide, steep ascent and descent over to attractive:-
**Piso Aetos (5km from Vathi Town)** Two-thirds of the way up the mountainside is an inexplicable stretch of unsurfaced road. Once over the col, the massive bulk of Cephalonia island forms an impressive backdrop to the tiny little harbour on the left (*Fsw*), and white pebble beach to the right. From where the road runs out at sea-level, to reach the beach it is necessary to scramble over some quite large boulders. The large pebble sea-bed is rather weedy. No beach 'support facilities'.

Aetos is the Greek word for eagle and this magnificent bird of prey nests on Ithaca. On the side of Mount Aetos are the remains of an ancient city.

The main road hereabouts thrusts through very dramatic and breathtakingly beautiful panoramas. Initially the route runs along the sea's edge of the Gulf of Molos, which almost separates the north from the south of the island by its bold intrusion. To the far west of the gulf is the small horseshoe Bay of Dexia, which is believed to be that of **Phorkys**, where Ulysses (Odysseus) was landed by the Phoenicians. Whatever, the shoreline is very pretty with olive trees edging the road, which is about 6m above sea-level. At the far end of this crescent is a small sweep of stony beach, part covered in kelp and polluted by some tar and seaborne rubbish. There is rumoured to be a sandy shore and sea-bed. Certainly the sea of the bay is beautifully clear. It is a 20-30 minute walk or a 5 minute taxi ride to this area from Vathi Town.

The road climbs on to a spine and for a short length of the isthmus seems to 'tightrope' between the sea, on both left and right. The Gulf of Molos sometimes hosts two or three laid up tankers, floating at anchor in the startingly clear water. From here the main route clings to the western flank of the mountainside, all the way to Stavros. But that is rather leaping ahead.

Prior to the Kathara Monastery turning, a dirt track descends the precipitous hillside to a pebble shore with a kelpy waterline.

At about 6km, to the right, is an initially metalled, abruptly ascending detour in the direction of:-

**KATHARA MONASTERY & ANOGHI (circa 14km)** About half-way up the mountainside, the surface disappears, only to become metalled again. There is evidence that plans might be afoot to complete the road making, but at present, the route can be frightening because the appallingly rough track is also narrow and the precipitous edges extremely close. Where the road both switches sides of the island and dips, there are wonderful views over the sound or Bay of Vathi. Almost at the top of the climb is a sign along a stony track to the left to:-

**Kathara Monastery (circa 10km from Vathi Town)** On the left of the rocky approaches is a dead van, with a well to the right and then the gates. The location is outstanding for the far ranging vistas but the Monastery and its scrubbly surroundings are rather disappointing. The simple buildings are centred on a chapel, built in 1696. The site is alleged to have been chosen when some farmers, who were clearing the area of scrub, discovered an icon of the Virgin Mother, supposedly executed by St Luke! Icons must have been a regular menace in the Middle Ages. If they weren't floating about the Mediterranean in boats, they were appearing on impossible cliff-faces or in burning bushes. I digress. There is a modern looking tower to the left, alongside which is a radio mast.

Beyond the monastery turning, after a particularly rough section, the road's surface becomes acceptable, even if still unmetalled. The hillsides hereabouts are generally painfully inhospitable, being gorse clad, that is until a band of cypress trees heralds:-

**ANOGHI (circa 14km from Vathi Town)** Quite a large settlement with little of anything for the tourist. At the centre of the village is a kafeneion, a 'sort of' campanile and a palm tree. For Stavros, turn right past the kafeneion, beyond which is a little sign 'WC' pointing to the right. Perhaps it is the site of the worlds largest open-air toilet?

From Anoghi the road to Stavros is metalled, despite which travellers should be extremely careful when negotiating the serpentine bends. Here the surface is often very loose. The countryside is much softer, more verdant and, to the right, are some noticeable Martello towers. There are splendid views of the mountain range opposite, on the very top of which, some demented fellows, in times of yore, built an ancient structure.

Returning to the main, west coast road at the Kathara Monastery/Anoghi detour, the northern advance passes through **Ag Ioannis** (circa 8km from Vathi Town), from whence a short ramble descends to a series of shingly beaches. A further track proceeds, in a loop, back to the main road at the sprawling and extensively rebuilt village of **Lefki** (13km from Vathi Town). The next major settlement is:-

**STAVROS (17km from Vathi Town)** The inhabitants emanate a welcoming and good humoured ambience, but the village cannot be termed pretty. Some of the once earthquake-shattered dwellings have been rebuilt as ugly, concrete boxes. The village has a wide main street with a tree shaded Main Square close by the junction of the Vathi Town, Anoghi and Polis Bay roads. At the outset of the Anoghi road is a baker and a mini-market, which opens on Sunday morning. The Vathi road is edged by a butcher as well as a sign to a telephone. In between the two is a track alongside which is a small (garden) shed – perhaps it is Stavros' first and only public toilet? On the corner of the steep descent to Polis Bay, or the 'Ancient City', is the *Kafeneion To Kentron*. The building may be rather unattractive and the surrounds sprawling, but the reception is extremely friendly. The tables and chairs are strewn around the forecourt beneath a canopy, which is an 'interesting' mix of bamboo and old canvasses. I'm fairly certain that some of the 'old hand' customers were the same ones I last saw about ten years ago. So long as clients have a drink or two, bags and backpacks may be left in the owner's care, which saves lugging baggage about all day. Incidentally, drinks here are inexpensive with a Nes meh ghala, 2 brandies and a lemonade costing 250drs.

On the right (*Vathi Town behind one*) is a quite magnificent Church painted in pastel brown, picked out in white. It is reassuring to observe that the hands of the various clock tower faces on one of the cupola's all show different times.

On the left, across the way from the church, is a small park, wherein a drinking water tap. Beyond the park is the inordinately large *Taverna Petisoras*, itself opposite a rather garishly painted building, alongside a restaurant specialising in souvlakia, followed by a zacharoplasteion/kafeneion, facing, on the left, a pizzeria with accommodation. This reminds me to point out that quite a few of the Stavros eating places have **Rooms**, but don't shout about it. For steeped in the retsina Grecophiles, who are not sand and sea crazed, this village would be an ideal location at which to tarry awhile.

There are a couple of mini-markets and, goodness me, a scooter hire business. Gathered around the junction of the Frikes and Platrithias roads, at the north end of the village, are a butcher, a souvenir/gift shop, a store, the *Cafe-bar Valentino*, a local newspaper shop and, on the right a large post box and Post Office, which carries out exchange transactions.

When the bus is not functioning, an excellent taxi service makes a 'scheduled' run to Vathi Town, at least once a day.

As detailed, alongside the *Kafeneion To Kentron* is the twisting, turning down to:-

**POLIS BAY (18¼km from Vathi Town)** Apart from the interest of its inevitable Homeric connections, a supposedly sunken city and to the north of the bay, the Cave of the Nymphs, the present-day quay and finger pier to the left (*Fsw*) are used by a small fleet of fishing benzinas and caiques. At the far left-hand side of the quay is a smidgin of sand. Beneath the spreading branches of a prominent tree, close to where the road runs out on the waterfront, is the office of a Rent A Boat business which hires outboard powered fibreglass dinghies. To the right is a pebbly sweep of the rather scrubbly, shadeless beach. A Cantina might burst into life in the busiest summer months.

From Stavros there is a choice of route to Frikes Port. The 'high road' branches off from Platrithias village, whilst the 'low road', a very pretty lane, gently descends past some surprisingly substantial villas set in a cultivated and tree filled valley. The reason for the sizeable dwellings becomes apparent if the journey is enlivened by conversing with almost any one of the elderly Greek gentleman passed on the road. One chat (carried out in perfect Australian), was with a man who had left Ithaca when he was twelve years of age. He lived in the southern hemisphere for 62 years, only returning home on the death of his parents. His was one of the large homes under construction. (Incidentally, the property settlement with that particular man's four brothers was made on the 'short straw' method. I imagine many a Greek family would prefer this sudden death, but simple method of settling an inheritance, compared to the more usual, tortuous state of affairs which results from the present antiquated laws. The all too evident, once solid but crumbling ruins of 'property in dispute', often located in prime positions, substantiates the enormous complexities of Greek property law).

**FRIKES (19½km from Vathi Town)** The outskirts of the pretty village are marked by a number of old houses, which spread up the valley. A large, corrugated iron building is prominent, as is the *Hotel Nostros*, on the left, a Martello tower still watching over the now narrow defile and the Pub Remetzio. The road then spills out on to the waterfront on an irregular, small square, with the slender sea entrance attractively framed by the encircling hillsides. To the right (*Fsw*) is a building simply named the 'White House'. I don't think this manifests delusions of grandeur, simply the building is, in the main, white. Alongside is the *Taverna Andreas*, the tables and chairs of which spread along the edge of the tree lined water's edge. The harbour backshore, which accommodates a number of benzinas and caiques, curls round to the left, as does most of the settlement. The first building houses the *Cafe-Restaurant Frikes*, owned by large, smiling, helpful, bespectacled, laid back Georgio, who speaks English well. Next door is the small office of Polyctor Tours, followed by Kikki Travel, who represent *Greek Islands Club* and rent mopeds. Alongside is a souvenir shop proclaiming 'I rent out my own rooms, newly built, modern with bathroom en suite. Unbeatable prices'. The *Penelope Taverna*, which has a patio up against the backshore, is followed by *Frikes Sailing Studios*.

Towards the far, left-hand side of the cove, beyond a small, embryonic, public garden, is a summer-dry river-bed, edged by the Platrithias road out of the valley. A supermarket, at the outset of this latter route, opens weekdays and Saturdays, between 0830-1300hrs and 1630-2100hrs. A path edges along the foot of the left-hand (*Fsw*) cliff-face, for some 250m, to a small pebble cove whereon wind surfers and pedaloes.

The pretty harbour is an attractive port of call for flotilla yachts as well as an important ferry-boat link for the independent traveller, allowing a daily connection with Lefkas and Meganissi islands.

**Ferry-boat timetable** (Mid-seaon)

| Day | Departure time | Ferry-boat | Ports/Islands of Call |
|---|---|---|---|
| Daily | 1100hrs | Meganisi | Nidri(Lefkas),Meganissi. |

**Hotels include:-** *Hotel Nostros* (Class C, tel 31644). All rooms have en suite bathrooms. A single room costs 2100drs & a double 3000drs, increasing to 3150drs & 4200drs (16th June-20th Sept).

The coast road south-east from Frikes curves past a substantial port quay and around a bluff to the right. Once beyond the headland, the snake-like, hill-hugging route borders the clean sea with steps down to a number of little, white pebble coves. After rounding a truncated Martello tower, a large bay hoves into view, as does that part of Kioni village which drapes over the distant hillside saddle. The cypress tree supporting hillsides are well vegetated.

Prior to the outskirts of Kioni is another pebble beach, with some boulders on the sea-bed, attractively backed by terraces of vines. The pine and olive tree lined road winds past a ruined windmill across a gulch to the left, a desalination plant and some dwellings.

**KIONI (24km from Vathi Town)** The oldest part of the village is on the hilltop, shared with the now defunct windmills, and overlooking the 'U' shaped harbour set in the bay. On the left of this col is *Rooms*. The right-hand horn of land enclosing the bay is capped by three ruined windmills.

From 'Upper Kioni' the road descends through olive groves, unattractively littered with building materials, to a confusion of road signs including 'No Entry' and 'This Way', on the same post! On the way down are passed a surgery, a mini-market, a supermarket, which transacts money exchange, and Kioni Travel. The road then spills on to the waterfront alongside the *Taverna* Αυρα. Once a simple kafeneion, the establishment is now equally popular with both Greeks and tourists. The family owners are friendly, the assistants casual and the service pleasantly chaotic. A lunchtime snack of stuffed tomatoes, a Greek salad, a bottle of Amstel and plenty of bread cost a rather expensive 630drs. It has to be pointed out that the presence of both flotilla yachties and a well groomed, English package holiday set can only result in pricey eating out.

As a consequence of the concentration of villa lets, there are a number of purpose built, if discreet apartments, tucked into the harbour dwellings which spread around to the left (*Fsw*). In amongst these are the *Cafe-bar Haygia*, the *Hotel Kioni Cafe-bar*, more holiday accommodation, then a hotel, a souvenir shop, with a sign babbling on about the turquoise eye of the Cyclops, and the rustic *Taverna Teralamani*. This straddles the Esplanade which runs out on the quay against which the flotilla yachts moor. Opposite the main pier is a lovely old house.

The harbour beach is nothing more than a pebble foreshore at the bottom of the bay. Beach loving holiday-makers have to travel further afield, along the cliff-top lane to the right of Kioni Harbour. Initially, this byway curves up from sea-level advancing past, after about 250m, *Rooms*, below which is a small, rocky swimming cove. This ½km long lane continues out along the right-hand horn of the bay, prior to narrowing down and rapidly descending past a backshore cemetery to the beach of an exposed, large pebble and stony cove. The sea-bed is rather boulderous. One small problem is that the locals regard the cemetery end of the path as a rubbish dump.

Returning to Frikes, the Platrithias road ascends from sea-level past some doo-hickey farmsteads to the settlement of **Ag Seranta**. Here is 'Rooms with en suite shower', on the left, followed by one-eyed **Platrithias**, beyond which is a rough track to the right, bumping down to **Afales**. This divides. The right choice descends along a gulch to the rocky sea-shore of a wild bay, where a chunk of concrete bears the crossly scrawled diminishments 'Private This Is Property'. The left fork doubles back to a mainly boulderous, rubbish strewn, but fine shingle beach edged by some rather outlandish boat sheds.

Back at the main route, close by a road junction, is an eye-catching square house, the upper storey of which appears to be all window. The building bears a skew-whiff sign 'North Queensland Bungalow'. At the junction is the *Cafe-bar Leventi* and confusion. One sign indicates 'Ag Athanios, Homers School'. Hereabouts is the famous, if incongruous memorial to the toiling peasants of Ithaca, followed by signs along an overgrown track to one or two ruined hamlets. A road, initially concreted and then tarmacadamed, climbs the pleasantly vegetated, cypress and fir tree clad, old terraced mountainside to the large, well kept, orderly hill village of:-

**EXOGI (21km from Vathi Town)** Most guidebooks extol the hard-working, industrious virtues of the inhabitants who are kind to animals, make handicrafts, till the fields, breed farm animals. Yes, well I imagine all this toil tires the chaps out because they seem to me to closely resemble many other kafeneion loving Greeks I've met. Exogi does possess a quite magnificent church for a place its size and from the village heights are marvellous views out over Afales Bay.

From Exogi the surfaced road loops back round to less well behaved Stavros.

*'Local sailing club dinghy storage....'.*

*Afales Bay, Ithaca.*

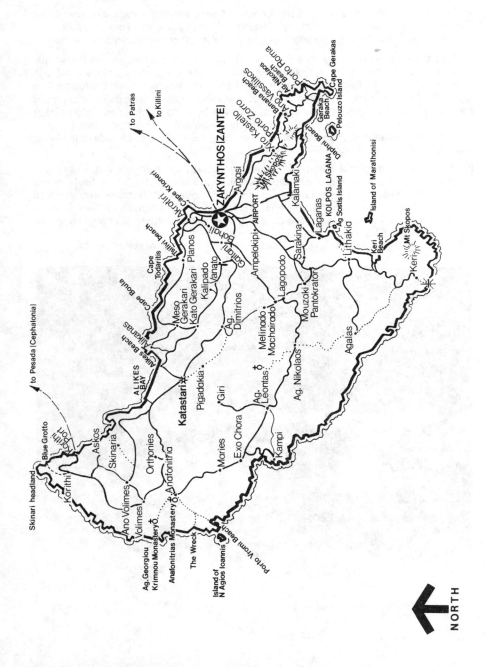

**Illustration 31 Zakynthos (Zante) Island**

# 17 ZAKYNTHOS (Zante, Zakinthos) ★★
## Ionian Islands

**FIRST IMPRESSIONS** English county lanes & fertile plains; primitive agriculture; snakes; motorbikes; friendly people; dramatic views; beautiful beaches; tourist raddled; excursions to almost every (moving) rock.

**SPECIALITIES** Mandolato nougat; pastelli – a sesame and honey biscuit; perfumes; sea turtles; raisins.

**RELIGIOUS HOLIDAYS & FESTIVALS** include: (The whole) Easter weekend, Zakynthos Town; 24th August & 17th December – Feast of St Dionysios, Zakynthos Town.

**VITAL STATISTICS** Tel prefix 0695. The island is about 36km wide, & 28km long with an area of 435sqkm. Of the 30,000 residents, about 10,000 live in Zakynthos Town.

**HISTORY** The island's name dates back to Homer, the Venetians coining the alternative Zante. Unusually, Zakynthos was not occupied by the Turks, the Venetians almost hanging on until the British assumed overall responsibility, between 1809-1864. The island's great artistic traditions were reinforced by Cretans fleeing the Turkish invasion of their island, in 1669.

**GENERAL** Once one of the most attractive of the Ionian islands, with a splendid mix of countryside, beaches and sympathetic rebuilding after the earthquake of 1953. But the full-scale, tour-operator exploitation has put paid to these erstwhile delights.

The island is unequally divided by a mountain range which runs from the north-west to the south-east. The narrow, diagonal west coast strip parallels the spine of the hills, descending very steeply into the sea. Almost all the rest of the island is a large fertile plain. The countryside of Zakynthos remains lovely and rather reminiscent of England with hedgerowed fields, orchards of trees (even if they are olives, cypresses, orange and pines), tree-topped hills, green-clad slopes and winding lanes.

My mention of snakes under First Impressions should be quantified, more especially as a lady reader contacted me, some years ago, to expand on the subject. Certainly, in the remote countryside, they are more noticeable than on the other Ioanian islands, but I can assure readers that any snakes encountered are more interested in getting out of the way than hanging around. Care should be taken when (and if) sitting down or leaning up against country lane stone walls.

On an island where the outward signs of wealth and glitz include combine harvesters rusting in the fields, Mercedes Benz motor cars and A Class hotels, it never ceases to amaze me that the Greece of old continues to shine through, here and there. This strip, close to Tsilivi Beach, I observed a farmer baling his hay by allowing the overnight dew to wet out the sythe cut grass. In the morning he stuffed it into a box resembling a trunk, but without a top or bottom. When he had piled as much grass in as he could, the farmer jumped up and down on the contents to squash it flat, and pushed out the contents. Hey presto, a crude bale of hay.

In the short space of some ten years, tourism has 'transformed' this quiet, lazy, undiscovered, green and pleasant land. Now package tourists rule and their support facilities prosper. The once deserted country lanes, remote beaches and laid back hamlets buzz with tourists hauled from here to there on air conditioned tour coaches or under their own steam, on a stream of hired scooters, motorbikes or cars. In the remorseless quest to revive jaded palates, to alleviate boredom and ennui, no unturned stone or quiet niche is left undisturbed. Even the major turtle nesting site of Gerakas Beach is exposed and exploited by sun loving hedonists and the locals money-mad enough to exploit their demands for sun umbrellas and beds. Hey ho.

## ZAKYNTHOS (Zante): capital & main port (Illustration 32) The town
was extensively damaged by the 1953 earthquake. Fortunately the citizens preferred reconstruction to take place along the lines of the previous layout, rather than have a grid imposed on them. To realise how sympathetically much of this has been carried out, it is only necessary to compare the rebuilt capitals of Zakynthos and Argostoli (Cephalonia). Certainly the town has an air of vigorous commerce and prosperity.

Much of the old back street ambience has been maintained by the retention of attractive, colonnaded walkways and first floor covered pavements. In contrast the harbour Esplanade, Plateia Solomou, Vassileos Georgiou B and Plateia Ag Markou have benefited from a spacious, imaginative, if rather disconnected redevelopment.

Some of the town maps are inaccurate, showing various areas as open spaces. These were built on a long time ago, and very little of the harbour promenade is not developed.

**ARRIVAL BY AIR** The airport is located close by Ampelokipi, some 7km from Zakynthos Town. Over the years the facility has been extended to take the larger jumbo jets. The old days of two or three internal flights a week have been overtaken by progress(!). Now the daily connection with Athens and twice weekly flights to both Corfu and Cephalonia are augmented by round the clock, international charter flights.

**ARRIVAL BY BUS** The Athens bus arrives via the mainland port of Killini (*See* **Chapter Ten**).

**ARRIVAL BY FERRY** Despite the mass tourist exploitation, the island is not the easiest to reach by ferry-boat, unlike say Corfu or Cephalonia. In fact the only links are with the fly-blown, scruffy Killini, on the Peloponnese mainland and Patras. Between the middle of May and the end of August there operates a Korithi port to Pasada (Cephalonia) car ferry.

The Killini ferries moor stern to the harbour's south pier (*Tmr* 1D5) and the Patras ferries utilise the main Esplanade quay (*Tmr* 1B/C3/4).

## THE ACCOMMODATION & EATING OUT
**The Accommodation** Apart from rooms in private houses 'offered' on arrival, there are a number of hotels. Radiating out from the centre of the town are the:-

**Strada Marina Hotel** (*Tmr* 3B/C3/4) (Class B) 14 Lombardou      Tel 22761
*Directions*: Towards the north end of the Esplanade.
All rooms have en suite bathrooms with a single room priced at 2440drs & a double 3150drs, increasing to 3430drs & 4830drs (6th-13th April & 1st July-15th Sept).

**Hotel Aegli** (*Tmr* 3B/C3/4) (Class C) 1 Anast. Loutzi/12 Lombardou      Tel 28317
*Directions*: On the corner of the Esplanade and the side-street, at the far end of the block in which the *Hotel Strada* is located.
All rooms have en suite bathrooms with a single costed at 1900drs & a double 2500drs, rising to 2400drs & 3100drs (1st July-15th Sept).

**Xenia Hotel** (*Tmr* 4B/C2/3) (Class B) 60 Dionissiou Roma      Tel 22232
*Directions*: North of Plateia Solomou, past the large Government building and small church, and on the left.
Only double rooms, with en suite bathrooms, at a cost of 2600drs, increasing to 3600drs (7th-11th April & 1st July-31st Aug).

**Hotel Vria** (*Tmr* 23B/C2/3) (Class B) 4 Kapodistriou      Tel 24682
*Directions*: The second side-street off Akti Dionissiou Roma, to the north of the *Hotel Xenia*.

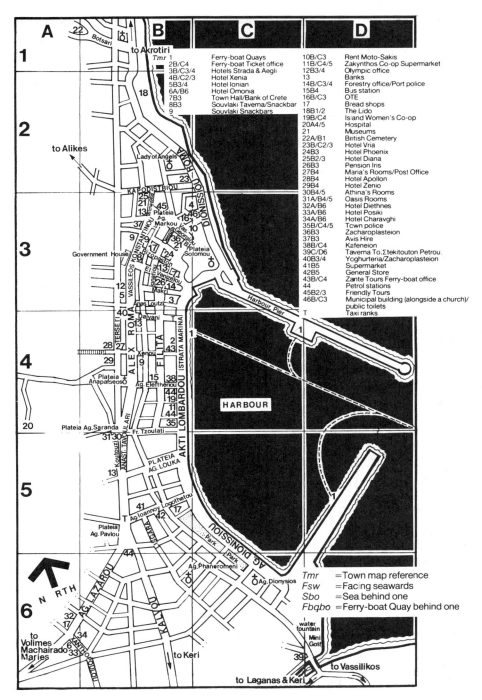

**Illustration 32 Zakynthos (Zante) Town**

Actually a pension with all rooms en suite. A single room costs 2000drs & a double 3000drs, increasing to 3000drs & 4500drs (7th-13th April & 1st July-15th Sept).

Those travellers prepared to proceed along the coast road some 2km north of Zakynthos Town, towards Akrotiri, will find at least a dozen *Rooms*, once the road commences to wind up the headland hill.

Back at Plateia Solomou, to the west of the square is:-
**Hotel Phoenix** (*Tmr* 24B3) (Class C) 2 Plateia D. Solomou                     Tel 22419
*Directions*: As above.
   Bedrooms have en suite bathrooms with a single room charged at 2450drs & a double 3100drs, rising to 3000drs & 4100drs (3rd-17th April & 15th June-15th Sept).

**Hotel Diana** (*Tmr* 25B2/3) (Class C) 11 Kapodistriou/Mitropoleos            Tel 28547
*Directions*: From Plateia Solomou make for Plateia Ag Markou and along Odhos Mitropoleos. The hotel is on the left.
   Priced as for the *Phoenix*.

One black back from the Esplanade, behind the Forestry office/Port police building is the *Pension Iris* (*Tmr* 26B3).

From the Esplanade, along the side-streets of either Odhos Makri or Anas. Loutzi progresses to the High St of Alex. Roma, on the other side of which is the:-
**Hotel Ionian** (*Tmr* 5B3/4) (Class D) 18 Odhos Alex. Roma                    Tel 22511
*Directions*: As above.
   The owners would appear to own the art and craft shop below this small hotel. A singe room, sharing a bathroom, costs 2500drs & en suite 3500drs, whilst a double room sharing costs 3500drs and en suite 4000drs.

Further south on Odhos Alex. Roma, and on the right (*Sea to the left*), are *Rooms*, behind which is the Post Office on Odhos Tertseti.

**Maria's Rooms** (*Tmr* 27B4)
*Directions*: As above, with an entrance in the side-street connecting Odhos Alex. Roma and Odhos Tertseti, beyond the first shop on the corner.
   Rather a noisy area. Maria does not speak any English. Rooms with en suite bathrooms ('showers are hot') cost 1000drs per person.

Across Tertseti street from the Post Office is the:-
**Hotel Apollon** (*Tmr* 28B4) (Class C) 30 Tertseti                             Tel 22838
*Directions*: As above.
   All rooms have en suite bathrooms with a single room costing 1840drs & a double room 2200drs, rising to 2145drs & 2580drs (16th March-31st Oct).

**Hotel Zenio (Zenith)** (*Tmr* 29B4) (Class C) 44 Tertseti/Martinegou           Tel 22134
*Directions*: Further south on Odhos Tertseti and on the right.
   Over the years this hotel has not been very forthcoming in respect of its pricing policy.

Continuing south along Odhos Tertseti, or Alex. Roma, and on the far side of Plateia Ag Saranda (also named Ag Tessarakonta) are:-
**Athina's Rooms** (*Tmr* 30B4/5) Plateia Ag Saranda                            Tel 25794
*Directions*: This accommodation is above a dress shop, in a noisy location.
   Athina's rooms are very clean and share the bathrooms, with a mid-season double costing 1400drs. and
**Oasis Rooms** (*Tmr* 31A/B4/5) Odhos Koutouzi                                 Tel 22287
*Directions*: Just around the corner from *Athina's* on the west side of Koutouzi St.
   As for *Athina's*.

Proceeding in the same direction south down Alex. Roma St (which becomes Odhos Anast. Tavoulari) to the fork at Plateia Ag Pavlou, select the right-hand Ag Lazarou St.
**Hotel Diethnes** (*Tmr* 32A/B6) 102 Ag Lazarou                               Tel 22286
*Directions*: From Plateia Ag Pavlou, on the right beyond the fourth side-street.
   Only double rooms, both sharing and with en suite bathrooms, costing 2530drs.

From the *Diethnes*, the next side street to the right from Odhos Ag Lazarou is Xanthopoulou St. This accommodates (oh dear) three, neat, fairly new or refurbished hotels, the:-

**Hotel Omonia** (*Tmr* 6A/B6) (Class D) 4 Xanthopoulou                    Tel22113
*Directions*: As above and on the right (*Odhos Ag Lazarou behind one*).
I stayed in Christina and her husband's old pension, many years ago. It has now been refurbished. Double rooms sharing or with en suite bathrooms cost 2530drs.
Next door is the *Hotel Posiki* (*Tmr* 33A/B6, tel 28361) and across the narrow street is the:-
**Hotel Charavghi** (*Tmr* 34A/B6) (Class D) 3 Xanthopoulou                    Tel 22778
*Directions*: As above.
Single rooms sharing a bathroom cost 2000drs & en suite 2110drs, with a double room sharing a bathroom priced at 2530drs.
The Town police offices (*Tmr* 35B/C4/5) house a Tourist officer. He 'performs' between 0830-1300hrs & 1500-1700hrs and can advise of accommodation, as well as lending a hand in other directions.

**The Eating Out** Instead of retsina, it is necessary to search out local wine 'apo vareli' (from the barrel) which costs about 150-200drs a litre. The paved, almost Venetian style Plateia Ag Markou (*Tmr* B3), on all but the west side, is lined with 'so-so' cafe-restaurants and restaurants, some with neon-lit display cabinets (enough said).

In the area of Plateia Ag Markou, south-east along Leoforos Vas. Georgiou and on the right is a:-
**Zacharoplasteion** (*Tmr* 36B3)
*Directions*: As above, and a small outfit with a few chairs and tables outside on the broad pavement. Informal and convenient to the hub of the town.
Specialises in 'Special Tiropites' as well as serving a range of small, saucer sized pizzas and pies. A Nes meh ghala cost a rather expensive 100drs and a pizza 140drs.
Of the Vassileos Konstantinou/Plateia Ag Markou eateries, the *Clock Restaurant*, across the wide street from Avis Hire (*Tmr* 37B3), is popular but expensive.
The best of the town's bustling, sit down or take-away souvlaki pita snack-bars are spread along the High St, Odhos Vass. Konstantinou, with two (*Tmr* 9B3) almost opposite each other, not far from Plateia Ag Markou, and another (*Tmr* 9B4) towards Plateia Anapafseos. These three only open evenings, and never on a Sunday, having written which one or all of them will... open, that is. Of the first two, the one on the right (*Plateia Ag Markou behind one*) serves Amstel beer and the one on the left Heineken. The last establishment (*Tmr* 9B4) only offers stick souvlaki but has spit roasted chicken and serves chips – yes chips, just like the 'Brit chippies'.
Another souvlaki pita snackbar/taverna (*Tmr* 8B3) spreads along the left-hand (*Government House behind one*), broad pavement of El Venizelou St. The excellent souvlaki pita are charged at 65drs and 110drs for those who sit down, the latter helpings still only being served 'in the wrap', and not on a plate. Diners can also order a (more than satisfactory) Greek salad, a plate of chips, bottled beer and bread. The service is excellent and a meal for two, including 3 souvlaki, a Greek salad, chips, 2 bottles of beer and bread, cost 770drs.
On either side of Odhos Dessila, north-east from Odhos Rizospaston (*Corner Baker* (*Tmr* 17B3) *behind one*) are two tavernas. The right-hand one looks as if it is a private house. A below average meal, for two, costs 970drs. This included veal in tomato sauce (380drs), a chicken & chips (pretty badly beaten up, 220drs), a Greek salad (tired and too oily – even for me, 140drs), bread (10drs each) and ½kilo of local wine (110drs). I realise the sum of the parts does not add up to the total... The left-hand taverna is rather smarter and more expensive but my comments were that the food looked pretty appalling.
Bordering the Esplanade, beyond Zante Gold, is a 'genuine budding, ethnic, sleazo Kafeneion (*Tmr* 38B/C4). Inside the unbelievably chaotic building is a shed, yes a shed, from which they serve a range of stick souvlaki, Greek salad, chips and bread. All very reasonably priced but I'm not sure I'd eat here. Two ('acorn') Nes meh ghala and an ouzo cost 210drs. This is the place for potential clients who wish to experience a fascinating, wide ranging mix of local life, in most of its facets. Those who prefer a more genteel ambience should stick to the top end of town.
As will have been observed, Zakynthos Town would appear to be a wasteland for taverna gourmets, but all is not lost for at the far, south end of town, almost beyond the city bounds, is:-
**Taverna To Στεκι ton Petrou** (*Tmr* 39C/D6)
*Directions*: As above and on the right (*Town behind one*), immediately prior to the river-bed.

The list of merits include popularity with the locals, so much so that it is necessary to arrive early in the evening; a lack of any precooked and or cabinet displayed dishes as well as a fairly priced, imaginative menu. Diners will note that the service is attentive; orders take that time necessary to finalise preparation and cook, confirming their freshness; meals are served in a semblance of order, salads and *hors d'oeuvres* type dishes being presented with time to devour them, prior to the main course arriving at the table and the vast servings are piping hot. Where am I? A meal for two of a plate of gigantes (235drs), a helping of tzatziki (tasty and sharp, 120drs), a Greek salad ('crunchious' 156drs), fried herrings (312drs), a plate of chips (tasty, 63drs), a plate of beef in lemon sauce (tender and not a gob of fat, 450drs), a kilo of local white wine from the barrel (200drs), bread ('moreish') and tax (12drs each) cost 1560drs. As there is only one waiter and one chef, orders take their time, which is as it should be, allowing sufficient pause to 'appreciate' the wine, and bills take longer.

To the more mundane... the Main Square handcarts of the nut vendors have simulated chimneys from which belches smoke, yes smoke. The gentleman who wheels his lantern lit, three wheeled cart out for the evening trade has been in business for as long as I can remember. The old-fashioned Yoghurteria/Zacharoplasteion (*Tmr* 40B3/4) located on the High St purveys home-made yoghurt for 50drs. The bimbling husband and wife couple (he thin and plaintive, she aggressive and large) also sell 3 Star Metaxa brandy, which is very difficult to find elsewhere in town. Most drink shops only sell 5 and 7 star brandies, displaying open disbelief that 'capitalista's' should stoop to such a lowly rated request. It is no use trying to explain that it's not the money, I prefer it.

The garden *Restaurant Ellas* which straddles Ag Ioannoy Logothetou (*Tmr* B5) is forgettable. Sited on the corner of the latter street and the Esplanade is the *Ship Inn*. Its appeal (!) will hinge on whether or not a customer enjoys clamorous beat music and half litres of draught Heineken (costing 200drs) in a mock English pub where bar service is the order of the day! The young man is married to an English girl and the Ship is clean, but not my scene. Another establishment that should be mentioned, if only to highlight its lack of Greekness, is 'Patrick's Midas Bar'. This is in a side-street off Plateia Ag Markou. This cocktail bar is heralded with a sign 'Just don't read this, stop and have a drink please, we need the 'money'. The owner sounds Irish as well.

## THE A TO Z OF USEFUL INFORMATION

**AIRLINE OFFICE & TERMINUS** (*Tmr* 12B3/4) The Olympic office is on Odhos Vassileos Konstantinou, alongside the *Hotel Ionian*. The usual airport bus costs 50drs.

**Aircraft timetable** (Mid-season)
**Zakynthos to Athens** (& vice-versa)
Daily          1110hrs
*Return*
Daily          0945hrs
One-way fare 5900drs; duration 45mins.

**Zakynthos to Cephalonia**
Tues & Sun    1255hrs
*Return*
Tues & Sun    1215hrs
One-way fare 1750drs; duration 20mins.

**Zakynthos to Corfu**
Tues & Sun    1255hrs
*Return*
Tues & Sun    1110hrs
One-way fare 6650drs; duration 1½hrs.

**BANKS** In the main, they are gathered together in the 'Municipal' area (*Tmr* B3), flanked by Plateia Solomou, Odhos El Venizelou, Vassileos Konstantinou and Plateia Ag Markou. The *Bank of Crete* (*Tmr* 7B3) is to the rear of the Town Hall, there is a Bank (*Tmr* 13B3) one block back and another (*Tmr* 13A/B2/3) bordering Plateia Ag Markou. A Bank (*Tmr* 13B3/4) borders Odhos Alex. Roma and another (*Tmr* 13B5) Odhos Koutouzi.

**BEACHES** The town's drab, and stony foreshore stretches away to the north and south but it is, at the southern end, signposted *Zante Beach & Bungalows*, which appears promising. Forget it! The referred to site is a few kilometres away and is reached by passing through a dusty, 'Soweto' of stone bungalows which border a boulderous sea-shore.

All is not lost. To the side of Akti Dionissiou Roma, a continuation of the Esplanade, is:-
**The Lido** (*Tmr* 18B1/2). A very pleasant, orderly, clean, well run facility with changing rooms and showers, in a setting of lawns and flower beds. Entrance costs 100drs. The sea-bed is pebbly.

**BICYCLE, SCOOTER & CAR HIRE** Most of the hire firms are centred in the Municipal area. There is an **Avis** office (*Tmr* 37B3) on Odhos Vassileos Konstantinou, close to Plateia Ag Markou. For scooter and motorbike hire, it is difficult to beat the old firm of:-
**Rent Moto-Sakes** (*Tmr* 10B/C3) 3 Democracy                                        Tel 23928
*Directions*: On the left (*Sbo*) of the main avenue from Akti Dionissou Roma, in the direction of Plateia Ag Markou.

No fly-by-night outfit this, having been in business for 10 years. Still enthusiastically run with extremely reasonably priced machines. A two seater scooter costs 1000drs for one day, which price falls to 800drs a day for a three day hire.

Although there are more petrol stations throughout the island than a few years ago, it is still prudent for hirers of two wheeled conveyances to fill up as soon as possible, especially those venturing to the northern extremities of the island.

**BOOKSELLERS** No specialist shop, only the usual scattering of tourist postcards and guide books. A useful publication is a fortnightly English language newspaper, which costs 100drs. Articles may cover topics as varied as nudist beaches, possible island trips, the plight of the turtles and Aids. Unfortunately useful general information is sparse.

**BREAD SHOPS** Here, as is often the case elsewhere, they are rather hidden away. The 'best buy' is the corner shop (*Tmr* 17B3) on Rizospaston St whilst others lurk on Odhos Ag Ioannoy Logothetou (*Tmr* 17B/C5) and Odhos Ag Lazarou (*Tmr* 17A/B6).

**BUSES** A rather sparse service which goes to great lengths to deny prospective clients any knowledge, the schedules being very difficult to ascertain. The Bus station (*Tmr* 15B4) is on the junction of Filita and Ag Eleftheriou Sts. The mishmash of a waiting room must vie for a premier award and the clerks are particularly unhelpful.

**Bus timetable** (Mid-season)
**Zakynthos Town to Athens* via Patras**
Daily          0800, 1200, 1500hrs
*Return journey*
Daily          from Athens 0930, 1230hrs
              from Patras 1245, 1600, 1930hrs
One-way fares: Zakynthos Town    to Patras  425drs+ferry fare; duration 2½hrs.
                              to Athens 1485drs+ferry fare; duration 7hrs.
*100 Kifissou St, Tel 5129432.
**Zakynthos town to Laganas**
Daily          0715, 0915, 0930, 1000, 1100, 1200, 1300, 1400,
              1530, 1700, 1800, 1900, 2000hrs.
*Return journey*
Daily          0730, 0940, 1000, 1030, 1130, 1230, 1330, 1415,
              1545, 1715, 1830, 1930, 2000hrs.
One-way fare 70drs.
**Zakynthos Town to Alikes**
Daily          0730, 1000, 1200, 1630hrs.
*Return journey*
Daily          0630, 0820, 1030, 1300, 1600, 1900hrs.
One-way fare 100drs.
NOTE: I accept there are one or two anomolies but...

**CAMPING** *See* **Tsilivi Beach, Excursions to Zakynthos Town Surrounds**.

**CINEMA** Just prior to and across Akti Dionissou Roma from The Lido (*Tmr* 18B1/2).

**COMMERCIAL SHOPPING AREA** There is no central market, more scattered clusterings of fish as well as fruit & vegetable shops and stalls. The upper, Vass. Konstantinou, end of Odhos El Venizelou and associated side-streets (*Tmr* B3) have plenty of shops and small stores; there is a splendid fruit & vegetable shop on Plateia Ag Saranda (*Tmr* B4/5) and a massive Esplanade supermarket, Zakynthos Island Co-operative (*Tmr* 11B/C4/5), alongside a BP Petrol Station. One block further to the north, along the Esplanade, is an island Women's Co-operative (*Tmr* 19B/C4), adjacent to another (Fina)

Petrol Station. Edging Odhos Ag Ioannoy Logothetou is a Supermarket (*Tmr* 41B5) and a small General store (*Tmr* 42B5). Gift & Souvenir shops are plentiful, especially along the Esplanade, and Drink shops need no pinpointing.

**DISCOS** One or two on the town's outskirts.

**FERRY-BOATS** Zakynthos Town is now serviced by Killini and Patras ferry-boat links. Independent travellers should bear in mind the height of season service between Korithi Port (*See* **Route Three**) and Pesada(Cephalonia). This latter craft saves having to make time consuming mainland connections.

**Ferry-boat timetable** (Mid-season)

| Day | Departure time | Ports/Islands of Call |
|-----|----------------|------------------------|
| Daily | 0800hrs | Killini(M). |
| | 0815hrs | Patras(M). |
| | 1200hrs | Killini(M). |
| | 1245hrs | Patras(M). |
| | 1500hrs | Killini(M). |
| | 1515hrs | Patras(M). |
| | 1830hrs | Killini(M). |

**FERRY-BOAT TICKET OFFICES** An office (*Tmr* 2B/C4) borders the Esplanade and is open daily between 0800-1300hrs & 1530-1900hrs. Next door is Zante Tours Ferry-boat Office (*Tmr* 43B/C4), which represents a large, round the island excursion boat.

**HAIRDRESSERS** Ladies hairdressers are plentiful.

**MEDICAL CARE**
**Chemists & Pharmacies** Plentiful.
**Dentist** There is a clinic over a Camera shop edging Odhos Alex. Roma, opposite a Souvlaki snackbar (*Tmr* 9B4), close to Plateia Anapafseos. A dental Surgeon, B. Kolios, is on the right (*Plateia Ag Margou behind one*) of Odhos Alex. Roma, just beyond the side-street turning of Odhos Dalvani.
**Hospital** (*Tmr* 20A4/5) Proceed west from Plateia Anapafseos to the large facility behind the town, on the white scarred hillside.
   Incidentally, the town is encircled by a hill range, pitted with great chalky scars, possibly a result of landslips caused by the fifteenth century earthquake.
**Specialists** There is an Ear, Nose & Throat man opposite the Bus station (*Tmr* 15B4)

**MONIPOS** A few are ranked in the area of Plateia Solomou.

**OTE** (*Tmr* 16B/C3) On the right (*Sbo*) of Leoforos Democracy and open daily between 0700-2400hrs.

**PETROL** There are several petrol filling stations (*Tmr* 44) edging the Esplanade and another at the junction of Odhos Kalvou and Ag Lazarou, on Plateia Ag Pavlou.

**PLACES OF INTEREST**
**British Cemetery** (*Tmr* 22A/B1) As with other Ionian islands, there is a British cemetery, dumb witness to the years of Great Britain's administration. It is situated adjacent to the ruins of the Church of Ag Ioannis, beyond The Lido (*Tmr* 18B1/2), and along Botsari St.

**The Castle** More accurately, the remains of an old Venetian fortress, reached through the village of Bohali (Bokhali). Allows magnificent views of the town, much of the island, the Zante channel and the Peloponnese.

**Churches and Cathedrals** A number of the town's churches are noteworthy. These include:-
*Ag Dionysios* (*Tmr* C6) Easily identified by its distinctive tower. The church is dedicated to the patron saint of the island – whose embalmed remains can be viewed by request to the priest. It is claimed that the saint's slippers have to be changed several times a year. This is because he is alleged to rise from his coffin, at night, and walk about the island doing good works (well, yes).

Nearby, and to the west is the:-
*Church of Phaneromeni* (*Tmr* B/C5/6) This was the island's finest religious building prior to the 1953 catastrophe, after which it was sympathetically rebuilt.
*Krias ton Angelon (Lady of Angels)* (*Tmr* B2) This very pretty church is located to the west of Akti Dionissiou Roma turning up Odhos Archiepiskopou Kokkini.

**Museums** One (*Tmr* 21B/C3) edges Plateia Solomou, at the junction with Vassileos Georgiou B. and displays Ionian art as well as some splendid icons from various island churches.

The other Museum (*Tmr* 21B2/3) is on Odhos Mitropoleos, off Plateia Ag Markou. This is dedicated to and named after the famous Zakynthos poet, one Dionysos Solomos. Also exhibited are the works of two other famous island poets, Andreas Kalvos and Ugo Foskolo, as well as the legacies of some noble Zantiot families.

### POLICE
**Port** (*Tmr* 14B/C3/4) At the rear of the Forestry offices, alongside Odhos El Venizelou.
**Tourist** Now ensconced with the Town Police.
**Town** (*Tmr* 35B/C4/5) Housed in a splendid, colonnaded building, bordering the Esplanade, and noticeable by the massed police cars and motorbikes parked outside.

**POST OFFICE** (*Tmr* 27B4) On Odhos Tertseti, to the right (*Sbo*) of Plateia Anapafseos.

**TAXIS** A number of main ranks, including one (*Tmr* T B/C3/4) close to the junction of Odhos Dalvani and the Esplanade and another (*Tmr* T B5) on Plateia Ag Pavlou.

### TELEPHONE NUMBERS & ADDRESSES
| | |
|---|---|
| Hospital (*Tmr* 20A4/5) | Tel 22514 |
| Olympic office (*Tmr* 12B3/4)16 Vass. Konstantinou | Tel 28611 |
| Police, port (*Tmr* 14B/C3/4) | Tel 22417 |
| tourist | Tel 22550 |
| Taxi rank (Plateia Ag Pavlou) | Tel 28261 |

**TOILETS** (*Tmr* 46B/C3) The attendant operated public toilets are on the rear, north side of a large Municipal building that faces south.

**TRAVEL AGENTS & TOUR OFFICES** Apart from **Zante Tours** ferry-boat office (*Tmr* 43B/C4), edging the Esplanade, there is **Friendly Tours** (*Tmr* 45B2/3). They are indeed friendly and represent Greek Islands Club. Tours include excursion boat trips to the 'Blue Grotto', adjacent to the Skinari headland, at the north-western tip of the island.

**WATER** There is a drinking water fountain on Plateia Anapafseos (*Tmr* B4) and another (*Tmr* C/D6) close to the weighbridge south of the Harbour south pier, alongside the main road. Both require the taps on the reverse side to be switched on.

## EXCURSIONS TO ZAKYNTHOS TOWN SURROUNDS
**Excursion to Tsilivi Beach (5km)**The coastal road north of Zakynthos Town runs parallel to the rocky shoreline. There is a wide swathe of scrubbly land between the two and the inland side is edged by a tall cliff face. Towards Cape Krioneri the road winds up the headland past dozens of *Rooms*. At the top the route becomes a country lane edged by olive groves in which are scattered homesteads and backyard farms. The road gently descends past more *Rooms* to the west side of the long bluff. Here is a large taverna/restaurant specialising in a Greek musical night out, which appears to drag in the package tourist punters from miles around. This establishment looks out over a large, flat bay enfolded by the nearside Vodi islet and the far Cape Todaritis and edged by a long sweep of sandy beach. The road is some 150m back from the water's edge and on the inland side is sprinkled by an incompletely developed Shrangri-la of *Rooms*, apartments, villas and other tourist accommodation, as well as Rent A Motorbikes and a couple of mini-markets. These buildings are interspaced by fields, some of which are cropped whilst others are grazed by flocks of sheep, accompanied by their shepherds.

**Tsilivi Beach (5km from Zakynthos Town)** A wide, unsurfaced track arrows across the very wide, untidy swathe of marshy, sand duney land that separates the beach from the road. Naturally, the powers that be have designated a part of this wasteland as a reclamation rubbish dump! Where the track runs out on the backshore, there is an untidy Cantina with an awning covered patio of uneven paving slabs.

This really is a delightfully sandy beach. Away to the right (*Fsw*) is a taverna and beyond that the blob of rock that is Vodi islet. At the distant, left-hand end is the main development of Planos (*See* **Route Three**).

## ROUTE ONE

### To Vassilikos & the south-east bays (circa 16km)

From the south of Zakynthos Town, the route towards Argasi crosses the river bridge and sallies past the 'old' suburbs development, once a slum of bungalows. These are now masked by holiday hotels and pensions.

At the Kalamaki junction (1km from Zakynthos Town) is a petrol filling station, beyond which the coastal road edges a rubbish and demolition rubble bestrewn backshore all the way to:-

**ARGASI (4km from Zakynthos Town)** A 60s style 'Sunset Strip' of a High Street, with the pebble foreshore edged by a seemingly endless row of massive hotels. I have not applied the adjective 'Kosta'd', as years ago there was nothing here to despoil, that is, apart from a huddle of shanty dwellings and the remains of an 1805 bridge. This stands proudly isolated and lapped by the sea. Prior to some earthquake originated coastal erosion, this must have been the old road line.

The long stretch of main street/highway parallels the shore and is bordered, not only by hotels, but *Rooms*, scooter and car hire, fast food, cocktail bars, the Disco Argasi and other typical auguries of early Greek holiday civilisation!

Hotels, all of which have en suite bathrooms, include the:- *Akti Zakantha* (Class A, tel 25375) where a single room costs 5000drs & a double 6000drs, increasing to 6500drs & 7500drs (16th June-15th Sept); the Class B *Chryssi Akti* (Tel 28679), *Levante* (a B Class pension, tel 23608) & *Lockanda* (Tel 25563) with average single room charges of 2500drs & doubles 3500drs, increasing to 3400drs & 4000drs; *Yliessa* (Class B, tel 25346) with a single room rate of 5000drs & a double room price of 6800drs; the Class C *Argassi Beach* (Tel 28554), *Captain S* (Tel 22779) & Family Inn (Tel 25359), where average single room rates are 2500drs & double rooms 3500drs, and the *Charavgi* (Class E, tel 22054).

A side turning off the High St advances to the small beach. This is a 50m long by 10m wide strip of hard-packed, dark sand with bits of kelp at the sea's edge and a shallow, gently shelving sea-bed. There is another very small, triangular beach at the far, east end of the waterfront.

The hill beyond Argasi allows a revealing backward view and the poorly surfaced road is under some reconstruction. The inland backdrop of Mt Skopos makes for a lovely drive as the thoroughfare skirts the lower slopes. The approaches to the hillside village of **Xirokastello** (circa 7km from Zakynthos Town) are heralded by *Rooms* and some apartments, as well as the *Blue Horizon Pension*. Incidentally, the 1988 'in colour' was ochre and the area's rubbish is dumped in a handy ravine, which no doubt, leads to the sea...

At the far end of Xirokastello a stony, rough, and, in places, extremely steep track sallies forth to the right, over to the south coast, signed 'Welcome Daphne Beach Bar'. This bumps and crashes all the way to:-

**DAPHNI BEACH (circa 10½km from Zakynthos Town)** Travellers must bear in mind this is an extremely hazardous detour. To add to the fun there is an unposted tri-way choice of routes. I am pleased to advise that the left one (*Fsw*) curves back round to the **Monastery Skopiotissas**, the centre one descends to Daphni Beach and the right-hand option to an unnamed beach.

Selecting the centre route, the very rocky track plunges towards the coastline. The journey ends on an informal turn-round, shielded from the shore by a stand of trees. A number of shacks, in various states of disrepair, are scattered about, as are piles of rubbish. The location has the air of a spot selected for great things and since abandoned. A discarded signboard boasts 'Canoeing, wind surfing, sailing, skiing, diving. Excursion to Keri Cave'. The long stretch of beach has a pebbly back and middle shore, subject to some kelp and seaborne rubbish, and a very sandy, few metres strip of foreshore.

Back at the tri-way, the right-hand option is an appallingly steep, rough and, in sections, sandy autocross course, edging a deep ravine. I would not advise any hirers of two wheeled conveyances to tackle this terrain, which would not disgrace a scrambling circuit.

The rather wild, not over-pretty, but certainly isolated, small bay is encircled by two horns of low rock which enclose the sandy beach. There is some kelp on the middle shore. As this is a turtle nesting location, it is commendable that there are no signs of any commercialism.

Offshore is Pelouzon islet, which possesses some small, sandy coves which also host the turtles. Both these beaches are worthwhile locations as they are unattainable by the excursion coaches and tour buses that infest much of Zakynthos island.

Returning to the main road, it is only a hop, skip and a jump to the first, well signposted turning down to:-
**PORTO ZORRO (11km from Zakynthos Town)** Sounds rather as if it should feature in a Spaghetti Western. The short but rough, steep descent passes a quarry on the way down to run out on a wide backshore, across which vehicles drive. The bay is hemmed in by hillside cliffs clad with fairly substantial bushes. The right-hand horn of the bay is very prettily edged by a cluster of rocks that have tumbled down into the sea. Beyond them is a tiny cove. There is another road down from the main road to the beach at that end.

The main body of the extremely pleasant, sandy beach is about 100m from side to side and 50m deep. The sea's edge is fine pebble and the sea-bed gritty sand. About mid-way are the remains of a part collapsed, multi-sided, bamboo covered beach bar. The shore continues to sweep along to the left (*Fsw*), past a rather doo-hickey beach taverna and quite modern pension, becoming scrubbly and kelpy towards the far side.

The *Beach Taverna* and *Pension Porto Zoro* are separated by a tract of hard-packed land, but are owned by the same family. As there is no other development, even bordering the main road, for Zakynthos, this is an ideal 'away from it all' night time location. A double room mid-season in the pension costs 2500drs.

The beach sun-beds are laid out in serried ranks and cost 100drs a day, as do the umbrellas. The per hour charge for a canoe is 200drs and for a pedalo 500drs.

The main road advances across pleasant countryside supporting olive trees pleasingly offset by the cypress and deciduous tree clad inland hills.

**ANO VASSILIKOS (12km from Zakynthos Town)** The approaches to this once one-eyed, scattered hamlet are blazoned by **Rooms**, set in an olive grove, more **Rooms**, a bar, an exchange bureau, some houses, Harry's Place Snackbar (Ugh!) – souvlaki with pita, Motorbike Rentals, **Rooms**, two more Motorbike Rentals, **Rooms**, *Camping Mavranatsis* and Logos Dancing Bar. In an unexpectedly thickly tree'd wood is the chalky track off to:-

**Vassilikos or Banana Beach (13km from Zakynthos Town)** Prior to discussing the location, I would like to muse about the descriptive adjective 'Banana'. This is occasionally found describing a particular beach, throughout the Greek islands. I can never make up my mind if it refers to the outline of the shore or men's genitals. Perhaps a reader will elucidate. Back to the matter in hand.

The approach terminates on an almost circular car park. This is separated from the enormous sweep of exposed golden sand by some 200m of untouched sand dunes. It is an almost unbelievable sight.

The truly enormous swathe of shadeless dunes are absolutely undeveloped and the wide tract of beach, as well as the sea-bed, is beautiful, hard sand. There are a number of permanent grass/bamboo cone roofed sun umbrellas, a couple of 'deadish' Cantinas and white plastic rubbish bins. It even appears that the beach is swept every day. The snag, the drawback? There must be one. Oh yes. It appears that most of the island's tourists assemble here, every day. There is chat of a nudist section away to the right.

Before departing, it is unbelievable that the despoilers have not been allowed to throw up the usual rash of hotels and garish fast food joints, but time is on their side.

The Vassilikos Beach turning is followed, quite soon, by one to:-
**St Nikolaos Beach (16km from Zakynthos Town)** The metalled road passes through olive groves and by the occasional homestead farm. Close to the shore is a reasonably pleasant cluster of development including *Rooms Villa Virginia*, *Maison de Christina*, *Snackbar Bellino*, and *Hotel Vassilikos Beach*. Pressing on, beyond some rubbish bins and, on the left, a tidy beach bar belting out beat music, is a fairly broad, sandy beach, set in a small, tightly pincered headland bay. The beach, subject to some sea's edge kelp, is split up by a small outcrop of rock, on which is mounted an octagonal, 'bamboo bandstand' cafe-bar. A twin row of bamboo roofed sun-shelters 'march' along the shore. Water sport enthusiasts are well catered for with water skiing, para skiing, ski-bikes, windsurfing, pedaloes, canoes and boat trips. Yes, the beach is quite busy.

Despite the aforementioned, the location does not quite feel right. I think this is due to the very low, shelterless, unattractive headlands, which hem in the bay. The one to the right (*Fsw*) is vegetated whilst the chapel topped, left-hand one is arid, dry and rocky.

On the far side of the referred to beach bar is a single shower head – one of the only one's on Zakynthos, and it works. In recognition of the 'BPTs', the beach bar possesses a darts board and offers a range of toasted sandwiches and filled rolls at 180drs, with a friendly service. It irresistibly reminds me of a sunny, fun, British Rail Waiting Room.

I would suggest there is a lot of development growth left in this site – there is far too much space left between the last hotel and the beach area for some speculator to leave well alone.

From the Ag Nikolaos Beach turning, the main road countryside reverts to one of olive groves. Set down in a particularly backyard farm setting is the doo-hickey *Stavlos Bar*, which advertises 'Rooms for Rent, telefono and cold drinks'. This 'arresting' establishment is followed by *Rooms* and Mavratis Beach Bar, surrounded by olive groves and the outskirts of widespread:-

**VASSILIKOS (16km from Zakynthos Town)** There isn't a core settlement, more widely scattered clumps of houses. This nebulous centre is more an unsatisfactorily signposted, rural countryside crossroads. To the right is a 'No Way Out' track to **Kato Vassilikos**, straight ahead is the road to Gerakas Beach and to the left is the surfaced turning which gently snakes down to:-

**PORTO ROMA (18km from Zakynthos Town)** The gradual descent is across an agricultural setting. About two-thirds of the way down are several, low-key, backyard surrounded *Rooms*, on the left. The usual incongruity is present, of farmyard animals wandering in and out of the new construction work in hand. The now, olive grove spanned road, passes a small mini-market, telephone, a fish taverna, some holiday apartments and then decants on to the hard-packed earth square of a very Greek harbour hamlet. The plateia is some metres above the seashore and is hemmed in, on the right-hand side (*Fsw*), by a new accommodation block and a pleasantly located, rural taverna. On the left is a particularly ethnic block of public toilets, and a couple of changing rooms. A note on the door of the taverna refers to these facilities as follows, 'The toilet is in the new building, half-built, over the road there are two toilets on the right'. Whatever, this new building now has a distinctly vintage, if picturesque ambience.

The taverna's balcony, where service is very much 'self', overlooks the particularly lovely, if rather enclosed, bay which is backed by low, vegetated cliffs. To the right is a rock mole, enclosed harbour and a prominent headland. The not very wide, sandy beach, with some pebble and a distinct belt of kelp, sweeps round to the left. Beyond a rocky outcrop, and a steeper cliff, is a pretty, small cove with a large, hut-like beach bar and hosting wind surfers and pedaloes.

Back at the crossroads, straight ahead passes through a gap in the hedge, on a now tarmacadamed surface, towards:-

**Gerakas Beach (18km from Zakynthos Town)** The short road sweeps across farming land, past a restaurant and a grill bar, to swing sharp right to where a customs style barrier bars further vehicle movement. During the daylight hours the *ad hoc* car park is packed with motorbikes, scooters and cars, most of them rented vehicles.

Prior to the flight of steps down to the beautiful stretch of broad, sandy beach, there is a sign which advises 'Note this is a protected sea turtle nesting beach. Sea turtles use this beach as a nesting area. It is strictly prohibited to camp or remain on the beach after sunset as any noise or light prevents nesting'. With this admonishment to hand, it is even more difficult to understand the fog of reasoning that has actually allowed this prime, turtle nesting beach to be commercialised. The mind numbing duality of the Greek mind(!) is underlined by the fact that some bloody cowboy is allowed to 'plant' serried ranks of spiked sun umbrellas and sun-beds on the selfsame beach. Admittedly the nesting areas are staked out, but as these lovely, dinosaur like creatures only lay their eggs in September and October, it is totally incomprehensible that all tourist traffic is not prohibited during these months. Rumour has it that the dichotomy is money related, a conflict of interest between conservation and the financial rewards that the landowners regard as their rightful due. That would explain everything.

The gently shelving beach is bounded by the long, curving headland of Cape Gerakas to the left and a higher, less prominent bluff to the right. Almost round the corner of this latter peeks the offshore islet of Pelouzou. In the far distance, way across the Gulf of Lagana, is Marathonissi islet and the looming headland of Mt Skopos, at the south-west of the island. The backshore is bordered by medium height, vegetation covered cliffs, the soil of which has a quarried or lunar like appearance.

To the right of the top of the steps down to the beach is the smart hut of the 'Sea Turtle Protection Society of Greece'. I suggest they shoot the beach boy, then the landowner, followed by whichever Government Official allows this mindless desecration of a harmless animal's fast dwindling Mediterranean nesting grounds.

## ROUTE TWO
**To Keri (21km) with detours to the Airport, Laganas & Kalamaki** The main Laganas/Keri road takes off from the south of Zakynthos Town over the bridge and immediately right to parallel the murky river. In order to keep the banks of the river as attractive as possible, the rubbish bins are piled up and excavation plant is parked. The road passes the town's fire engine centre and a couple of petrol filling stations. The outer suburbs of Zakynthos Town are rather squalid.

**The Airport (5km from Zakynthos Town)** The first branch road to the left of the main route passes through very unattractive countryside, part farming, part industrial, part ruins, part rubbish dumps on the way to the Airport. When the runway was originally constructed there were about three flights a week. Now there are something like eight or nine a day.

Just beyond the Airport turning there is a petrol filling station and **Rooms**. The countryside sprawl is dominated by small homesteads, with a cow or some goats tethered in the front gardens. There are two turnings off the main route, to the left. One cuts the corner but the next, primary road (8km from Zakynthos Town), around about where signs appear for Pantokrator, is almost straight all the way to:-

**LAGANAS (10km from Zakynthos Town)** The farming land has been increasingly encroached by tourist development. 'From the top', the blemishes include dozens of **Rooms**, the *Levant Hotel, Village Motel*, a new style bar (which in 1988 was new style closed), *Hotel Olympia*, 'Passer By We Serve Breakfast', *Pension Manos, Hotel Hellinis*, Studio Ceramic, restaurant bar, cocktail bars, taverna this, taverna that, *Zante Beach Bungalows*, Rent A Bicycle, Car, *Bonanza Taverna*, Relaxing Greece Bar, happy hour, Welcome To Kostas, supermarkets, *Hotel Australia, Hotel Galaxy, Hotel Sireni, Restaurant Albatross, Pension Pelouzou*, Rent A Bike, a supermarket, Rent A Bike, *Taverna Tassos*, fast food, quick food and a baker on the left *(Fsw),* quite close to the 'frying pan turnaround' on which the approach road terminates. This once quiet, rather lovely location, has been horrendously, wantonly 'Kosta'd'. A correspondent succinctly put it that he would prefer to spend his time at Southend-on-Sea than at Laganas.

One thing that doesn't change is the beach, which unfolds for kilometres to the left, in fact all the way to Kalamaki. In that direction the shore widens out, but the ever increasing tourist build up augers ill for the turtles, who are losing their one-sided fight for egg nesting space on this front. Years ago it was possible, in fact necessary, to drive along the beach shore if access was required to any location other than the immediate waterfront. Nowadays, due to the almost unbelievable hordes of people, as well as the serried, packed ranks of sun umbrellas and beach beds, it would require a large tank. Additionally, a concrete crash barrier bars vehicles' progress (spoil sports). To ensure that nobody gets bored, there is a frenzy of water sports, including water skiing, para gliding, windsurfing and pedaloes. The immediate backshore is bordered by hotels and restaurants; the rest by a thoughtful planting of young trees. The hard sand of the beach continues on, gently shelving under water making it possible to walk some 70m out to sea. The sea-water is rather murky but that is probably due to the sheer number of people.

To the immediate left of the 'frying pan' is the original *Restaurant/Snackbar Mouria* and on the right *Restaurant Kalofonos*. Incidentally, the menu at the latter establishment includes an English breakfast at 350drs, compared to a French one for 200drs. A Nes meh ghala costs 67drs, an omelette 180drs, English soups 200drs, a Greek salad 160drs, stuffed tomatoes & macaroni pie 250drs, chicken 285drs, meat dishes 450drs, soft drinks 50drs and a bottle of beer 95drs. Lovers of saganaki should bear in mind this restaurant's offering is more a 'fried cheese with a tomato on top'.

To the right, the bay curves quickly around to a small headland, at the end of which is the islet of Ag Sostis.

Hotels, the rooms of which all have en suite bathrooms, with a very few exceptions, include:- the Class B *Esperia* (Tel 51505) with a single room costing 2700drs & a double 3600drs, rising to 3600drs & 5000drs (1st July-31st Aug); *Galaxy* (Tel 51171) where a single room is priced at 4300drs & a double 5800drs, increasing to 5500drs & 8600drs (16th June-15th Sept); *Laganas* (Tel 51793); *Megas Alexandros* (Tel 51580) where a single room costs 3850drs & a double 4900drs; *Zante Beach* (Tel 51130) with a single room costing 2800drs & a double 2980drs, rising to 4200drs & 4515drs (1st July-31st Aug); the Class C *Alkyonis* (Tel 51194) with a single room charged at 3000drs & a double 4000drs; *Asteria* (Tel 51191); *Atlantis* (Tel 51142) with a double room costed at 2500drs; *Australia* where a double room is charged at 3500drs, increasing to 5500drs (11th June-31st Aug); *Blue Coast* (Tel 22287) & *Eugenia* (Tel 51149) where double rooms cost about 2500drs; *Hellinis* (Tel 51164); *Ilios* (Tel 51119); *Ionis* (Tel 51141) where a single room is priced at 2000drs & a double 3300drs, increasing to 3300drs & 4500drs (1st July-15th Sept); *Margarita* (Tel 51534) with double rooms costing 4400drs; *Medikas* (Tel 51129) with a double room charged at 2300drs; *Olympia* (Tel 51644) where a single room costs 4500drs & a double 5400drs, increasing to 5800drs & 6900drs (1st June-31st Aug); *Panorama* (Tel 51144) with 2700drs doubles; *Selini* (Tel 51154) where a double room costs 2270drs; *Sirene* (Tel 51188); *Vezal* (Tel 51155) with single rooms sharing a bathroom at a cost of 1200drs. A double room sharing costs 1700drs & with en suite bathroom 2270drs; *Victoria* (Tel 72265); *Vyzantion* (Tel 51136) with doubles costing 3000drs; *Zefyros* (Tel 72292) with 2800drs double rooms; the Class D *Anatoli* (Tel 51663) where a double room, sharing a bathroom, costs 1700drs & a double en suite 1900drs; *Galazia Thalassa* (Tel 51123) with double rooms only priced at 2200drs; *Hermes* (Tel 51117) and the *Thalassia Avra* (Tel 51110) with a single room costing 1600drs & a double room 3060drs.

From Laganas there is, in an eastwards direction, a fairly substantial, straight road that approximately parallels the coastline across an absolutely flat plain. There are, to date, only sporadic outbreaks of development alongside this thoroughfare but I am prepared to bet a bucket of retsina that it won't be many years before it is fully exploited. Why, well this is the major highway from Laganas to:-

**KALAMAKI (7½km from Zakynthos Town)** In actual fact the most direct route is to select the Argasi road from Zakynthos Town (*See* **Route One**) and take the branch road to the right. This is not signed Kalamaki but for a Kalamaki hotel. This latter approach passes through a steady build up of hotels; tavernas; olive groves; a small taverna on the left, quaintly labelled 'Mikaglo Playboys Shop and Love'; more olive groves; 'Rooms For Rent' in a small, new looking apartment with a (green) lawn to the front; *Rooms* (Tel 22774) and, close to the Laganas turning, a spaced out mishmash, a jumble of the few remaining farmsteads dotted about and in amongst which are spread gift shops, a supermarket and apartments.

The road, which continues on towards the shore, has to divert round the smart *Hotel Chrystal Beach* (Class C, tel 22917) to run out on a low cliff top overlooking a short length of sandy, gently shelving beach. This is fairly chock-a-block with beach umbrellas, sun-beds and wind surfers. As it is, or was, a turtle nesting beach, these obstacles must make the beach head the equivalent, to the beleaguered beasts, of a Normandy D-Day landing. To the left (*Fsw*) is the *Chrystal Hotel*, the foundations of which I peered at some ten years ago. There was a campaign, even then, to halt construction in order to preserve this turtle beach. Money must have talked! To the right is a crumbly headland, the other side of which is the outset of the sweep of beach all the way to Laganas.

Back on the main route, the thoroughfare continues on across a most fertile plain, with some lovely olive groves, on which a sprinkling of building work is in hand, in addition to scattered farmsteads and repair shops. Old Greece is cheek by jowl with new Greece. Signs for Pantokrator are, rather confusingly, all over the place, as are signs to an old, ruined mansion at **Sarakina**. Following the latter leads to a full-blown taverna promoting 'Greek Dancing Every Night'. The 18th century mansion, which was damaged beyond repair in the 1953 earthquake, is roped off during the day and sports a *Son et Lumiere* at night, to which tourists are coached.

Finally the one-eyed, extended village of **Pantokrator** is attained, beyond which is the village of:-

**LITHAKIA (13km from Zakynthos Town)** Here is a petrol filling station and a choice of routes. To the left is a sign for *Camping Lithakia*, to the right is the road to Agalas and straight on is the route continuing on to Keri. The right-hand selection allows a:-

**Detour to Agalas** This is a steep ascent, initially through an enormous mountainside quarry. Beyond this, the road surface becomes rather poor and the hill sides bear witness to extensive fire damage.

**AGALAS (17km from Zakynthos Town)** The village has a number of old roofed houses, a pretty church, a modern restaurant and some *Rooms*. The settlement's roads are rather rough.

As Agalas is an inland village, miles from the sea, and does not possess a ruined mansion, trembling rocks or old wrecks, it may well remain a pleasant location. But with the ingenuity of the excursion makers in mind there is no guarantee.

By keeping to the right (*Lithakia behind one*), an unsurfaced road, in places nothing more than a wide donkey track, but a donkey track that meanders through lovely countryside, progresses to:-

**AG NIKOLAOS (Kiliomeno) (circa 21km from Zakynthos Town)** Here the main Lagopoda/Ag Leontas road (*See* **Route Three**) runs through the village and petrol is available.

Returning to Agalas, the way to left is an unmade road. This passes through more fire damaged hillsides, to descend across conifer covered slopes. Even this road is 'thick' with hired motorbikes. Close to the junction with the main Keri route, in the triangle of land enclosed by the two roads, is the pleasant looking *Pension/Restaurant Keri*. A problem in staying here would be the need for transport.

Returning to Lithakia, to the main route to Keri, there is **Rooms** in a large, elongated building followed by a signpost to the left, indicating the site of *Camping Tatarouga* and self-service restaurant, 300m along an unmade track. As the road descends the flanks of the mountainside, the lush countryside supports well tended olive groves and sturdy vines.

At about 19km there are two turnings to the left. The first is metalled and branches off alongside a restaurant taverna and **Rooms**. The second is a rough, unsurfaced track.

Both lead to:-
**Keri Beach & Bay (circa 20km from Zakynthos Town)** The latter choice of approach passes between two of the possibly largest olive trees I have ever seen. Lining the track are at least five 'Rent Rooms' (one with the telephone number 33229), and, prior to joining the extensive backshore track, on the right, 'Parking Kavori we speak English. Fish Taverna fresh food'. The 'Esplanade' extends to the right (*Fsw*) some 100m and to the left some 200m, edging the fairly flat shoreline of the bay.

Straight ahead is a small jetty between which and the large, long, rocky harbour quay to the right, is a small cove of sand, as there is another, on the far side of the harbour quay. This second one has some kelp at the sea's edge. A sign indicates the presence of Flats for Rent. This side of the bay is shut off by a vegetated headland slope. Prominent to seawards is Marathonissi islet, another turtle nesting location. Various signs advertise the delights of a trip to Marathonissi (500drs), as well as the Keri Caves (1000drs) and an inducement to fish in a local stream (God give me strength!).

To the left is an extended, not over-wide stretch of pebble beach which has a firm, sandy sea's edge and sea-bed. Trees have been planted along the backshore but they are, at the moment, rather too small to give shade. The inland side of the gravelly 'Esplanade' is, in the main, given over to a large tract of marshland through which meanders the previously referred to fishing stream. There is a taverna close to hand and, on the far left headland, some development which includes a **Rooms**. The track that rises up into the hillsides at this end simply runs out up against the boulderous sea's edge. From hereabouts is a clear view along the low, sparse run of cliffs which stretch away towards Laganas.

Since time immemorial, a natural phenomenon resulted in a number of springs giving forth pitch. For many centuries fishermen caulked their craft, using this petroleum by-product, but I'm not sure the process still continues.

Back on the main road, three kilometres on is the village of:-
**KERI (22km from Zakynthos Town)** Situated on the most southerly headland of Zakynthos, nestling on the slopes of the 413m Mt Skopos, at the end of the range of hills which runs down and edges the western coastline of Zakynthos. This pretty and, in many parts, old village, has some **Rooms** to let, and a splendid church dating back to the seventeenth century. There is a bakery and a distinctly doo-hickey mini-market, the type where many of the goods are piled upon the floor.

A rough track continues on for another 2km to a lighthouse. Some maps indicate a

ZAKYNTHOS 323

beach here, but unless travellers list abseiling amongst their pursuits, they will be out of luck, as it is only accessible by boat, as are the cape's caves.

## ROUTE THREE
**To Korithi Port via Planos, Alikes Beach, Volimes & back via Anafonitria, Maries, Ag Leontas, Ag Nikolaos & Machairado (circa 95km).**For the first section of the route follow the **Excursion to Tsilivi Beach.**

**PLANOS (6km from Zakynthos Town)** This widespread holiday development, at the far west end of Tsilivi Beach, irresistibly reminds one of the Costa Brava, in the 1960s. There is all the necessary infrastructure in position. Some glitz set down in olive trees, surrounded by piles of rubbish amongst which chickens and roosters scratch and peck. Down at the strip of beach, a flagpole, bereft of a flag, declares 'Our beach was awarded the blue flag of Europe for its high standard of cleanliness'. It certa nly does not refer to the dirty, scrubbly land edging the beach. The beach is very narrow to the right (*Fsw*) and almost entirely covered with sun-beds, lined up like soldiers 'on parade'.

Apart from the extremely smart *Hotel Jupiter* there are a number of **Rooms** as well as far too many Parking signs.

Hotels, which mostly have en suite bathrooms, include: the Class C *Anetis* (Tel 24590) with a single room costing 1900drs & a double 2000drs, increasing to 2000drs & 2200drs (1st May-30th June & 1st-30th Sept) and 2200drs & 3000drs (1st July-31st Aug); *Cosmopolite* (Tel 28752) with single rooms sharing a bathroom priced at 1600drs, a double sharing 2200drs & en suite 2700drs; *Orea Heleni* (Tel 28788) where a double room is priced at 2530drs, rising to 3050drs (16th June-15th Sept) and the *Tsilivi* (Tel 23109) with singles costing 2000drs & doubles 3000drs, increasing to 3000drs & 4500drs (1st July-15th Sept).

To the west of Planos is a petrol filling station and, at the head of a small gorge, the nicely located *Camping Zante* and 'Rooms To Let'.

To counteract the excesses of Tsilivi and Planos, continue on beyond Cape Todaritis as far as Cape Boula. This road passes through a lovely area of countryside, much of it supporting olive groves. Admittedly the road surface is very poor. if present at all in places. Along this stretch are one or two **Rooms**, a petrol station, a 'Grosery' (*sic*) and a number of cul-de-sac tracks which detour down to local fishing communities spattered along the coastline. In places these have been expanded by quite a lot of holiday development, which is not apparent from the parallel but distant main road. A typical example is down the road signposted to *Fish Tavern O Andreos*.

**ANO & MESO GERAKARI (circa 12km from Zakynthos Town)** A widespread pot-mess of two farming hamlets. On the outskirts of the first (from the direction of Planos) is a posh, modern-day example of the old Zante sheds on stilts, this one being supported by metal uprights. There is **Rooms** and a mini-market. At Ano Gerakari there are **Rooms**, the large Ag Nikolaos Church, an old kafeneion and a store. The roads are narrow.

**KATO GERAKARI (directly, 10km from Zakynthos Town)** This large, agricultural village straddles the main road. There are one or two rather grand gateways here and there, the sole standing reminders of the earthquake devastated mansions that once ruled the land. Apart from a functioning water well, there is a restaurant, a shop, two petrol stations, a ruined church, with a tree or three growing out of the roof, and, on the Alikes side, several **Rooms**. With the sea in sight, and prior to the Alikanas turning, there are more **Rooms**, opposite an ancient farmhouse.

Branching off from the descent to the sea-level plain behind Alikes, is the gently hillside climbing road up to:-
**ALIKANAS (16km from Zakynthos Town)** This is hardly even a hamlet but alongside the cliff hugging track, to the headland of Cape Xechoriati, are 'Wrent (*sic*) Rooms', Rent

Bikes, a number of bars, a couple of restaurants, as well as some paths down to the narrow shore. Here are a few small coves of narrow, sandy beach. Set on the slopes are a number of the traditional, stilt mounted, thatch roofed huts (Kalives). It is incongruous to note that Zantiots quite often replicate these ancient structures by topping off their modern apartments with a bamboo shelter.

Continuing past Alikanas, on an unmade, chalky track to the east, is another beach.

Certainly Alikanas, which is more closely allied to Greece of yesteryear, is an excellent prospect for independents compared to the almost adjacent:-

**ALIKES (18km from Zakynthos Town)** This seaside resort encompasses the pleasant, long curve of Alikes Bay, which is bordered by a 15m wide sweep of sandy beach. At the near, east end is a track from the main road to the shore, along which trudge the 'happy' holiday-makers based hereabouts. Tucked into the conical shaped headland on the right (*Fsw*), is a medium sized fishing boat harbour. There are no beach tavernas, only several (hut) Cantinas. About 300m to the left is 'Jet Ski Hire', the activities of which include the rental of dinghy sailers, wind surfers, sun-beds and umbrellas, as well as pedaloes. Bordering the track down is the *Hotel Valais*.

The tract of land between the backshore and the road is scrubbly, rubbish strewn sand dunes, to date undeveloped.

As the main road advances towards the far end of the beach and the village of Alikes, so the build up of tourist related development increases with a straggle of **Rooms**, snackbars, villas, apartments and restaurant/tavernas.

A fairly large river flows across the beach. It is even spanned by a low, English style bridge. The river mouth is about 6m wide and effectively splits the shore. The west end of the bay is a wide, shadeless stretch of unattractively coloured grey sand in which is some pebble. It is edged by the usual buildings and hosts, as would be expected, sun umbrellas and beds. The messy village is rather squeezed in by the still worked salt flats, and,once over the river bridge, really gets 'under way'. Sundry delights include a skating club, books exchange, Rent A Bike, Rent A Scooter, Rent A Car, International Cuisine, Celebrity Saturday nights, 'Real Greek Home Cooking' and 'Speedy Pick Ups'! I must point out that the last item related to a rental outfit, not a massage parlour. Naturally there are excursions to almost each and every rock and drop of wet sea.

Almost out the other end is *Camping Alikes*.

It is best to ignore the siren call of the coast hugging track and stick to the main road. This climbs and winds into the range of mountains that spreads along the length of the island. There are not only splendid views back over the Plain and Bay of Alikes but along the more rugged northern coastline. The countryside is moorland in nature but lacks any heather. On the right of the road is a countryside cafe taverna possessing a loom and thus selling crochet items (spelt with a P) and rugs (spelt with an E). Two coffees and a 'slug' of brandy costs a very reasonable 180drs. The Korithi-Pesada ferry-boat link is signposted as far away as the turning off to Othonies.

**VOLIMES (33km by direct route from Zakynthos Town)** This village is set in harsh, bare, arid countryside. The villagers now specialise in flogging tourists crochet work, carpets and rugs. More usefully, a petrol filling station has been constructed, although it is nearly obscured by the 'overwhelm' of doilies.

From Volimes the indeterminately surfaced road ascends steeply to the part fire damaged heights above the village. Thence the route hard-workingly snakes past the **Askos** branch road, close by the scattered remains of a ruined village. There are wonderful views along the north-east coastline, as well as tantalising glimpses of the little harbour of Korithi and the tiny islet of Ag Nikolaos – the Ag Nikolaos ever present on signposts in the area.

**KORITHI (38km from Zakynthos Town)** In this village there is a colourful sign directing 'good road' traffic to the right for the 'Ferry, Ag Nikolaos & the Blue Cave'. Another sign indicates the 'Blue Caves' to the left.

**Blue Caves or Grotto** The second choice aforementioned is along a rough, boulderous track which descends on to the lighthouse headland past a barrack room taverna, popular with the locals for a lunchtime sup. Beneath the lighthouse, the track peters out but a handwritten board indicates the path to a jetty from which the trip boats pluck passengers for the Blue Grotto excursion. Strangely enough, the cost from here is 1000drs, for the 15 minute boat ride, compared to 350drs from Korithi Port, for the 'round hour' journey.

The two beautiful, sea eroded caves, which can hold four or five boats, well repay a visit. In the caves there is about 20m deep of iridescent blue, blue water and the sea is so clean that it is possible to see the coral and rock shelves of the sea-bed. A 'doorway' in the rocks allows access into other, smaller caves.

Back at Korithi village, the main route descends past a restaurant, which advertises 'we dispose a boat for the Blue Cave' and *Rooms*, followed by the 'Women's Co-op Tourist Office', offering 'Rent Rooms'.

**KORITHI PORT (39½km from Zakynthos Town)** Not much of a harbour/port, yet... The location is hemmed in by the parched lower foothills of a mountain, with Ag Nikolaos islet prettily positioned offshore. There is some chatter that the islet still belongs to the Vatican. This anomaly being due to an administrative bog-up perpetrated when the various official papers were drawn up, on handing the Ionian islands over to the Greek Government. Mmh!

The waterfront edging road is bordered by the *Remettzo Restaurant*, which offers an 'Italian Range' and has accommodation, and the *La Grotta Hotel* (yes, well). The latter has two side-by-side restaurants, separated by a narrow alley, and has bagged the canoes/pedaloes concession. The Class C *La Grotta* (Tel 31224) charges 3000drs for a single room, with an en suite bathroom, & 3800drs for a double, increasing to 4000drs & 4800drs (1st July-15th Sept).

A simple lunchtime meal for two at *Remettzo* of 2 Amstels, spaghetti bolognese, stuffed tomatoes and bread cost 770drs.

The obsession with Free Parking signs appears misplaced, seeing as there is room to park a cavalry detachment of tanks. It has to be admitted that tour buses arrive in droves as, incidentally, do excursion trip boats from Zakynthos Town. The Blue Grotto tickets are sold from the harbour quay.

For Ferry-boat details *See* **Pesada Port, Cephalonia Island**

Close by touristy Volimes is the settlement of Ano Volimes, which certainly is not a postcard location, mercifully remaining a committed agricultural village. A Cycladean style chapel is in the distance and a windmill has its roof extant, which means the main shaft is still in position.

Despite crudely hand painted signs, in Volimes, indicating a cross-country route to Anafonitria and the Monasteries, ignore them. The tracks are not only difficult to find, but close to impassable. Select the right-hand turning off the main road to:-

**ANAFONITRIA (30km from Zakynthos Town)** Apart from the village and its Monastery, there are indications for, amongst other delights, the Smugglers Wreck, Porto Vromi Beach and some Moving Rocks (!). The approach to Anafonitria is heralded by the cafe-bars and restaurants necessary to cater for the excursion trippers that deem it necessary to view these island phenomena. The initially very steep, appallingly rough track to them is to the left, alongside a taverna, a stall selling souvenirs and a table piled high with local produce. Even the Greek civil engineers have not been able to complete the route with a road, however rough, and it is necessary to scramble the last section of the 6km journey, on foot. Forget it, the sight of a rusting tanker stuck fast in the sands and a pleasant bay with two sandy coves is simply not worth the sweat.

Across the informal village square from this branch road, and on the right, is the ruined, night-time floodlit **Monastery of Anafonitria**. The roofless keep, or square tower, dates back to the fifteenth century. The monastery possesses a miraculous icon and at the rear is a cemetery, despite which there is a singular grave within the walls of the building.

From Anafonitria a reasonable swathe of a track has been bulldozed along to:-
**Ag Georgiou Krimnou Monastery (32km from Zakynthos Town)** The high, wall enclosed buildings are in a perilous state of disrepair. In 1988 there may still have been a solitary monk, as someone had left a bottle of wine hanging from the handle of the closely locked main door. Beyond the monastery are splendid views along the north-west coastline.

From Anafonitria, along the west coast, advances through **Maries**, a large, old, agricultural village set in very pleasant surroundings with the mountain range to the left and a fertile plain to the right. The next village is the smaller **Exo Chora**, more a hamlet with a magnificent building in the centre.

To the right of the main route is a now surfaced road down to the dusty village of:-
**KAMPI (circa 30km from Zakynthos Town)** Set at the foot of the reverse side of the coastal cliffs, the very top of which are dominated by an impossibly positioned, giant concrete cross, incongruously topped off by a lightning conductor.

The doo-hickey, way-station atmosphere has been replaced by a more sophisticated, tourist orientated approach. One sign advises 'Archaelogical area the best sunset, the mystery cave, it works'. The original, rustic taverna has been smartened up and now has competition. The path from the village to the heights remains unmade and the simple, small, hut-bar, bordering this, has been tidied up, somewhat.

**AG LEONTAS (27km from Zakynthos Town)** Gives an impression of being a rather newer village in comparison to Exo Chora and Maries. A small store-cum-kafeneion is supplemented by a mini-market, a couple of kafeneion/snackbars and a petrol station.

**AG NIKOLAOS (Kiliomeno) (17km from Zakynthos Town)** The village possesses a mansion-like church with a most attractive tower, as well as old buildings with old roofs. Perhaps it wasn't so badly affected by the 1953 earthquake. In the centre is the track to Agalas (*See* **Route Two**). On the outskirts is a traditional Ionian campanile and quite attractive, square church. Petrol is available.

Beyond Ag Nikolaos, the road tumbles down the Pennine-like mountainsides towards:-
**MACHAIRADO/MELINADO (10km from Zakynthos Town)** Apart from a monastery and a large church, there is, incongruously, a Post Office.

From Machairado there is a choice of routes. To the east crosses the widest part of the large plain that takes up most of this end of the island. This is where the most intensive raisin production is concentrated which has resulted in some large farm estates. In the autumn the grapes are placed on specially prepared, plastic covered ground or on concrete strips, both shaped in the form of a very shallow pitched roof. The configuration is to facilitate the grape liquid draining away.

To the south of Machairado, in the direction of Pantokrator (*See* **Route Two**), is the hamlet of **Mouzaki**, close to which can be seen fleeting glimpses of another ruined stately home.

*'Perhaps the tide's coming in'.*

*The old bridge at Argasi, Zakynthos.*

*'In need of some renovation....but lovely location'.*

*Ag Georgiou Krimnou Monastery, Zakynthos.*

# INDEX

# INDEX 329

# INDEX 329

Animals,See Greece....
Ano & Meso Gerakari,323
 (Zakynthos),
Ano Lefkimmi(Corfu),197
Ano Messonghi(Corfu),194
Ano Pavliana(Corfu),193
Ano Vassilikos(Zakynthos),317
Ano Volimes(Zakynthos),325
Anoghi(Ithaca),302
Anthoussa(M),118
Antipata(Erisou,Cephalonia),286
Antipaxoi,See Antipaxos
**Antipaxos island,221-222**
Acheron River(M),123,124
Arethusa's Fountain,300
 & Ravens Crag(Ithaca)
Argasi(Zakynthos),316
Argirades(Corfu),195
Argostoli capital & minor port,260-270
 (Cephalonia)
Arila,See Arilia
Arilia(M),116
Arilias(Corfu),184
Arilias Beach(Corfu),184
Arkadades(Corfu),182,185
Arkoudilas Beach(Corfu),198
Armenades(Corfu),185
Aronatika(Paxos),213
Arrilia,See Arilia
Arrival by Air,See Airline flights
 & Airports
Arrival by Ferry-boat,
 See Ferry-boats
Arrival by Train,See Trains
Arta(M),124
Arvanatatika(Paxos),213
Askos(Zakynthos).324
Aspiotados(Corfu),185
Aspirin,See Medical matters & medicines
Assos(Cephalonia),285-286
**Astakos(M),132-133**
Asteroskopeion(Athens),80
Astrakeri(Corfu),181
Athanasios(Corfu),182
Athani(Lefkas),247
**Athens City,75-107**
 airports,14,33,75-76
 camping,See Camping
Athera(Cephalonia),279
Atherinou Bay(Lefkas),251
Atokos island,131
Atsoupades(Cephalonia),258
Australia,13
Avlaki Beach(Corfu),179
Avliotes(Corfu),183

**B**
Backpacks,3
Bad buys,63
Bakers,64
Banana Beach,
 See Vassilikos(Zakynthos)
Banks,See Shopping & Services
Bank cards,5
Barbati(Corfu),177
Bari,25
 (Italy)
Bastatika(Corfu),197
Bathrooms,40-41
Beaches,41,45-46
Bedroll,3
Bedrooms,See Accommodation
Beer,See Drink
Belgrade,16,21
 (Yugoslavia)

Benitses(Corfu),200
Best buys,63
Beverages,non-alcoholic,4,53-54
Bicycles,47-48
Bin liners,4
Blue Caves or Grotto(Zakynthos),325
Bogdanatika,212
 (Paxos),
Bonaparte,Napoleon,146
Books,5
Bottle-opener,3
Bouka Beach(Corfu),198-199
Boukari Point(Corfu),195
Brandy,See Drinks
Bread shops,See Shopping
Brindisi,17-19,26
 (Italy)
British Cemetery,The,171
 (Corfu),
British summertime,6
Broadcasts,See Radio
**Buses**
 Athens,76,94-97
 domestic,46-47
 international,20-22
Butchers,See Shopping
Byron,Lord,125

**C**
Cafe-bars,See Drinking places
Calamine lotion,See Lotions
Cameras,
 See Photography
Camping,41
 Athens,88-89
Canada,13
Cape Akrotiri(Cephalonia),278
Cape Arilias(Corfu),184
Cape Boula(Zakynthos),323
Cape Drastis(Corfu),183
Cape Gerogompos(Cephalonia),278
Cape Kastri(Lefkas),241
Cape Lefkatas(Lefkas),247
Cape Todaritis(Zakynthos),323
**Car**
 Hire,48
 travel by,22-26
Cards,playing,5
Cave of Nymphs(Ithaca),301
**Cephalonia island,255-289**
Cefalonia,See Cephalonia
Charakti(Cephalonia),258
Charter flights,See Airline flights
Chavdata(Cephalonia),278
Chavriata(Cephalonia),278
Chemists,4
Chionata(Cephalonia),258
Cigarettes,See Smokers
Cigars,See Smokers
Climate,See Weather
Clocks alarm,5
Clothes pegs,3
Clothing,3
Coaches,See Buses
Coffee,See Beverages
Compass,5
Condiments,3
Containers,3
conversion tables,6
Cooking equipment,3
Corfou,See Corfu
Corfu Festival,172
**Corfu island,151-201**
Corfu capital & port,152-173

# The Candid Guides
## unique
# 'GROC's Greek Island Hotline'

Available to readers of the guides, this service enables a respondent to receive a bang up-to-the-minute update, to supplement the extensive information contained in a particular Candid Guide.

To obtain this paraphrased computer print-out, covering the Introductory Chapters, Athens, Piraeus & the Mainland Ports as well as any named islands, up to twenty five in number, all that is necessary is to:-

Complete the form below, enclosing a payment of £1.50 (to include postage), and send to:-

Willowbridge Publishing, Bridge House, Southwick Village,
Nr.Fareham, Hants. PO17 6DZ

**Note: The information will be of no use to anyone who does not possess the relevant, most up to date GROC's Candid Greek Island Guide. We are unable to dispatch the Hotline without details of the guide AND which edition.**

Planned departure dates ...................................................

.......................................................

Mr/Mrs/Miss ...........................................................................

of...........................................................................................

...........................................................................................

| I possess: | | I require: |
|---|---|---|
| **GROC's Greek Island Guides** | Edition | **GROC's Greek Island Hotline** |
| to: .................................... | .................... | to:............................................. |
| ........................................... | .................... | ............................................. |
| ........................................... | .................... | ............................................. |
| ........................................... | .................... | ............................................. |
| ........................................... | .................... | ............................................. |

and enclose a fee of £1.50. Signature........................................Date .......................
I appreciate that the 'Hotline' may not be dispatched for up to 7-10 days from receipt of this application.

# TRAVEL
# BOOKS
# FROM
# ASHFORD

AVAILABLE FROM
BOOKSHOPS
OR DIRECT FROM
ASHFORD, 1 CHURCH ROAD, SHEDFIELD, HANTS
Credit Card orders by phone  Tel: 0329 - 834265

# UNDER MOUNT IDA

## Reflections of Crete

## Oliver Burch

A refreshing and original look at this most popular and historic of Mediterranean islands. Oliver Burch skilfully evokes the full character of both people and place, from the bleached hillside villages to the sun-drenched tourist beaches.

Tales from Crete's turbulent past combine with sometimes hilarious, sometimes sad encounters with the less-noble present to produce a fascinating portrait of this beautiful island under siege.

Hardback 288 pages   1 85253 202 5   £13.95

# GROC's Candid Guides to
# THE GREEK ISLANDS

## Other titles in this series.

published by Ashford
1 Church Road, Shedfield, Hampshire, England. SO3 2HW

# GROC'S Candid Guides to THE GREEK ISLANDS

This highly acclaimed series has been continually refined to ensure that readers, be they armchair voyagers, annual holidaymakers or independent travellers, will be able to plunder a wealth of individualistic information, set out as a travelogue. The text is liberally interspersed with detailed maps and plans. As usual the guides praise the praiseworthy and damn the second rate.

## The Cyclades Islands, Athens and Piraeus

2nd Edition
Geoffrey O'Connell
Fully updated including Syros, Mykonos, Paros, Naxos, Ios, Santorini, Amorgos, Astipalaia, Tinos Andros, Sikinos, Folegandros, Milos, Siphnos, Serifos, Kithnos and Kea with excursion details to Delos, Antiparos, Anafi, Donoussa, Koufonissi, Shinoussa, Iraklia, Kimolos and Athens City, Piraeus and the mainland ports of Rafina and Lavrio.
Paperback 392 pages 56 maps and photographs        85253 174 6        £9.95

## Crete, Athens and Piraeus

2nd Edition
Geoffrey O'Connell
Crete is not so much an island as a land in its own right. The guide has been divided into a number of regions based on individual cities and towns. The island and town maps are interspersed with pen and ink illustrations. The various routes are described in detail to facilitate holiday-makers' and travellers' exploration of this unique island.
Paperback 226 pages 19 maps and photographs        1 85253 090 1        £7.95

## The Greek Mainland Islands

Geoffrey O'Connell
Including the Sporades and Argo-Saronic. Argo-Saronic include - Salaminas, Aegina, Angistri, Poros, Hydra, Spetses and Kithira. Sporades include - Skyros, Alonissos, Skopelos, Skiathos and Evia.
Paperback 280 pages 30 maps and diagrams        1 85253 083 9        £8.95

## Rhodes, The Dodecanese, Athens and Piraeus

Geoffrey O'Connell
Including Rhodes, Kos, Karpathos, Kasos, Simi, Tilos, Nisiros, Kalimnos. Leros, Patmos with excursion details to Chalki, Astipalaia, Kastellorizo, Pserimos, Yialos, Angathonisi, Arki and Lipsos.
Paperback 272 pages 31 maps and illustrations        1 85253 066 9        £8.95

## Samos and the N.E. Aegean Islands, Athens and Piraeus

Geoffrey O'Connell
Including Samos, Ikaria, Fournoi, Thimena, Chios, Psara, Oinoussai, Lesbos, Limnos, Ag. Estratios, Thassos, and Samothraki as well as Athens City, Piraeus and the mainland ports of Kavala and Alexandroupoli.
Paperback 298 pages 36 maps and photographs        1 85253 898 9        £7.95

Please add 10 % p & p for orders by post

# Enjoy a **real** holiday to the full!

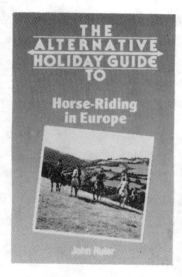

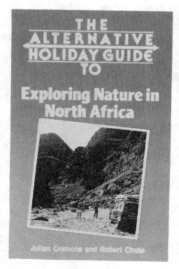

The Alternative Holiday Guides provide all the relevant information and expert guidance required for your chosen holiday pursuit. The Guides look at specific activities rather than holiday centres and contain useful ideas for travel, tours, equipment, dos and don'ts and local information.

# The Alternative Holiday Guides

## Exploring Nature in North Africa
Julian Cremona and Robert Chote
An essential companion for anyone venturing into the fascinating and varied landscapes of Morocco, Tunisia and Algeria, countries so far unspoiled by package tourism. Julian Cremona and Robert Chote have amassed a wealth of information on what to see and how to get there, in the process identifying an exotic new destination for the more adventurous holiday-maker. Their recommended routes encompass many of the region's greatest natural and cultural phenomena, from the high peaks of the Atlas mountains and the desolate beauty of the Sahara, to the teeming kasbahs of Fez and Marrakech.
Paperback                                                    1 85253 161 4

## Golfing in Europe                                          £9.95
Eric Humphreys
Distinguished golfer and travel writer Eric Humphreys has selected and appraised both the Championship and 'middle-handicap' courses of Europe, producing a guide that can be used either by the serious golfer planning a holiday or tour devoted entirely to golf, or by the enthusiast simply wanting a few hours play on an otherwise 'conventional' holiday.
Paperback                                                    1 85253 1C6 1

## Horse-Riding in Europe                                     £9.95
John Ruler
The traditional popularity of horse-riding means that it is possible to find a place to ride almost anywhere in the United Kingdom and Europe. John Ruler has selected the very best stables and touring centres, around which a wide variety of horse-riding holidays can be planned, including pony trekking, trail riding, hacking, instructional and special interest holidays. No-one need be exc uded by age, inexperience or disability - in horse-riding there's a holiday for everyone. The author's intimate knowledge of this specialised holiday field will help you to choose the safest and most enjoyable vacation for you or your children.
Paperback                                                    1 85253 092 8

## Deep Sea Fishing Around Europe                             £9.95
Graeme Pullen
Specific information on venues carefully selected by the author to be easy to reach, pleasant to stay at, and which have versatile and productive fishing, making a sporting trip both exciting and enjoyable. *"Overflowing with practical information and advice on everything from taxis to tackle, this book will prove invaluable to anyone planning to fish in foreign waters."* **Sea Fishing Magazine** *"The angler's travelling companion - pack it with your passport."* **Sea Angler**
Paperback 200 pages  40 B/W illustrations 6 maps            1 85253 072 3

## Exploring Nature in the Wilds of Europe                    £8.95
Julian Cremona and Robert Chote
Full of valuable advice on planning and enjoying nature exploration - from a family holiday to a field trip or major expedition. The authors are highly-experienced and well-travelled, offering detailed information on camping, accommodation, vehicles and transport, clothing, food and cooking, health, money, insurance and photography.
Locations include the Hebrides, Norway, Iceland and Spain. *"The authors have succeeded in making you want to go to see for yourself .. the routes and areas within the grasp of us all."* **Off Road and 4 Wheel Drive**
Paperback 200 pages 60 B/W illustrations 15 maps            1 85253 059 6

                                                             £8.95

Please add 10% p & p for orders by post